Introduction to Political Theory

Visit the *Introduction to Political Theory* Companion Website at **www.pearsoned.co.uk/Hoffman** to find valuable **student** learning material including:

- Additional case studies
- Extended essays on topics such as rights, property, and political obligation
- Guide to studying political theory
- Multiple choice tests
- Links to web resources
- Short introductions to key thinkers and texts

Introduction to Political Theory

Second Edition

John Hoffman
University of Leicester

Paul Graham
Glasgow University

PEARSON

Longman

Harlow, England • London • New York • Boston • San Francisco • Toronto • Sydney • Singapore • Hong Kong
Tokyo • Seoul • Taipei • New Delhi • Cape Town • Madrid • Mexico City • Amsterdam • Munich • Paris • Milan

Pearson Education Limited
Edinburgh Gate
Harlow
Essex CM20 2JE
England

and Associated Companies throughout the world

Visit us on the World Wide Web at:
www.pearsoned.co.uk

First published 2006
Second edition published 2009

ISBN: 978-1-4058-9988-8

British Library Cataloguing-in-Publication Data
A catalogue record for this book is available from the British Library

Library of Congress Cataloging-in-Publication Data

Hoffman, John, 1944-
    Introduction to political theory / John Hoffman, Paul Graham. -- 2nd ed.
      p. cm.
    ISBN 978-1-4058-9988-8 (pbk.)
    1. Political science. I. Graham, Paul. II. Title.
  JA71.H6133 2009
  320.01--dc22
                                2008054699

10 9 8 7 6 5 4 3 2
13 12 11 10

Typeset in Sabon 10/12.5 by 73

Printed by Ashford Colour Press Ltd., Gosport

The publisher's policy is to use paper manufactured from sustainable forests.

Brief Contents

Part 4   Contemporary Ideas

Contents

Part 2   Classical Ideologies

Supporting resources

Visit **www.pearsoned.co.uk/hoffman** to find valuable online resources

Companion Website for students

- Additional case studies
- Extended essays on topics such as rights, property, and political obligation
- Guide to studying political theory
- Multiple choice tests
- Links to web resources
- Short introductions to key thinkers and texts

Also: The Companion Website provides the following features:

- Search tool to help locate specific items of content
- E-mail results and profile tools to send results of quizzes to instructors
- Online help and support to assist with website usage and troubleshooting

For more information please contact your local Pearson Education sales representative or visit **www.pearsoned.co.uk/hoffman**

Publisher's Acknowledgements

The publisher would like to thank the following for their kind permission to reproduce their photographs:

12 Corbis: Bettmann. 37 Corbis: Fabrizio Bensch. 59 Corbis: Imageplus. 81 Corbis: Milk Photographie. 102 Corbis: Kim Ludbrook / epa. 121 Rex Features: Rex Features. 145 Getty Images: Zed Nelson. 175 Corbis: Michael Czajkowski / PAP. 196 Getty Images: Anwar Hussein. 217 Corbis: Bettmann. 243 Corbis: Anja Niedringhaurs / epa. 265 Corbis: Andres Kudacki. 286 Corbis: Michael St. Maur Sheil. 316 Corbis: Serge Kozak / zefa. 341 Corbis: Jerome Sessini / In Visu. 363 Corbis: Lloyd Cluff. 386 Corbis: David H. Wells. 409 Corbis: Daniel Laine. 430 Corbis: Bettmann. 452 Corbis: Paul Colangelo. 474 Corbis: Chris Rainier.

We are grateful to the following for permission to reproduce copyright material:

Figures 3.2 and 3.3 reprinted by permission of Sage Publications Ltd. from Laver, M. (1997) *Private Desires, Political Actions,* Copyright © Sage, 1997.

Every effort has been made to trace the copyright holders and we apologise in advance for any unintentional omissions. We would be pleased to insert the appropriate acknowledgement in any subsequent edition of this publication.

Authors' Acknowledgements

We are very grateful for the help received from Morten Fuglevand and David Cox of Pearson Education. David Cox read and commented on drafts with great enthusiasm and acumen and was an endless source of lively and interesting ideas. Morten and David's commitment to the book was inspiring and sustaining. In addition, the anonymous referees made invaluable, if at times painful, observations and have played an important part in improving the quality of the book. We are also grateful to Elizabeth Rix for all her help.

We found working together on this book a stimulating and enjoyable experience. Both of us are committed to making political theory more accessible and lively and have tried to write a book that is stimulating, provocative and interesting.

John Hoffman

I would like to thank the publishers of the *Cambridge Dictionary of Sociology*, Cambridge University Press, for permission to draw upon entries submitted to this project. I am also very grateful to Edinburgh University Press for permission to use material that has also been submitted to a *Political Glossary* dealing with political theory, and to Sage Publications Ltd. who have kindly allowed me to draw upon *Citizenship Beyond the State* that appeared last year.

I have been supported by my partner, Rowan Roenisch, and my son, Fred and daughter, Frieda. All three have encouraged me in the project.

Paul Graham

Edinburgh University Press kindly granted permission to draw upon an essay from *Political Concepts: a Reader and Guide* (edited by Iain Mackenzie), as did OneWorld Books for use of material from *Rawls* (forthcoming).

I would like to express my gratitude to my parents, Douglas and Heather Graham, for their support and encouragement, and to my colleagues in the Department of Politics at Glasgow University, for providing a stimulating intellectual environment in which to work.

About the Authors

John Hoffman has taught in the Department of Politics, University of Leicester since 1970. He is currently Emeritus Professor of Political Theory, having retired at the end of September 2005. He has written widely on Marxism, feminism and Political Theory, with his most recent book being *Citizenship beyond the State,* published by Sage in 2004. He is currently working on John Gray and the problem of utopia.

Paul Graham is a Lecturer in Political Theory at Glasgow University. He teaches and researches in German and Anglo-American political thought, with a special focus on multiculturalism, human autonomy and rationality, freedom, and distributive justice.

Introduction

What is Political Theory?

By political theory we do not mean simply mean the study of the state, for politics is far wider than the state. It takes account of activity that focuses on the state – like parties, for example, which in liberal democracies are not part of the state, but seek through elections to become the government. Nor is politics simply about activities that focus on the state. It is about conflict, and conflict occurs at every level of society – between nations and states, within trade unions, businesses, families, churches. There can even be conflict within an individual – whether to go swimming or fishing – and this too is politics although not a particularly profound example of it. However, the overall point is important. Politics is about conflict and its resolution, and resolving conflicts of interest occurs in all societies, at all levels.

Students of politics often believe that politics can be studied without theory. They take the view that we can focus upon the facts without worrying about general ideas, but we should never underestimate just how important theories and theorists are to politicians. For example, Ben Barber tells us in his website (http://www.benjaminbarber.com/bio2.html) that he was an informal advisor to President Bill Clinton between 1994 and 1999 because of his 'ability to bridge the worlds of theory and practice', which was reflected in his role as informal outside advisor to President Bill Clinton from 1994 to 1999. Tony Blair relied heavily upon Anthony Giddens, and Mrs Thatcher was great influenced by Frederick Hayek whom she later knighted. David Cameron, currently leader of the British Conservative party, gave his members of parliament advice on what they should read over the summer, and the novels of Kingsley Amis and Ian McEwan were turned to by the press after the atrocities of the attack on the twin towers in New York known generally as 9/11. Theorists are not only important to politicians: our notions of common sense and human nature are heavily infused with the views of thinkers we may never have actually heard of. Students of politics often identify with the concept of a chaotic state of nature – a world before the state – of the seventeenth-century political theorist Thomas Hobbes (see the website for his biography) because his somewhat gloomy realism strikes them as profound and meaningful.

Theory and Action

The truth is that in everyday life we are guided by notions of right and wrong, justice and injustice, so that everything we do is informed by concepts. Politicians are similarly guided. It is not a question of *whether* political animals follow theory, but a question of *which* theory or concept is supported when they present policies and undertake actions. We can argue as to whether the British prime minister or the United States president acts according to the right political concepts, but it is undeniable that their actions are linked to theory. Humans in general cannot act without ideas: indeed, it is a defining property of human activity that we can only act when we have ideas in our head as to what we should do.

In discussing ideas about the state or democracy or freedom in this book, we are talking about ideas or concepts or theories – we use the terms interchangeably – that guide and inform political action. Some courses are presented as courses in political *philosophy* and we feel that philosophical questions such as the nature of truth, will, determinism, etc. play a crucial role in our argumentation, but we prefer the term 'theory' because it seems less daunting to many students, and it seems less abstract. However, we don't see any substantive difference between theory, on the one hand, and philosophy, on the other.

As for theory and ideology, here the difference is more tangible. Ideologies seek to persuade, theories to expound and explain, and in a way that encourages the reader to think for themselves. Of course, there is overlap as well: ideologies are arguably more persuasive if the theory they draw upon is rigorous and accurate, but the two have different roles to play. It is vital that readers should feel encouraged and stimulated to form their own views, using logic, evidence and rigour to present their case. A student may feel, for example, that the invasion of Iraq was justified as a way of removing an evil and oppressive dictator: what is vital is that this view is not simply expressed as an opinion, but is backed up with evidence and thoughtful argument. It is important that views are not put forward simply because it is felt that they will please peers or tutors.

In the concepts presented here, the state is particularly important in Part 1 and readers should tackle this topic at an early stage. It is a great pity that theory is sometimes presented as though it inhabits a world of its own: as though it can be discussed and analysed in ways that are not explicitly linked to practical questions and political activity. This is, indeed, something this book seeks to address.

Theory as Abstraction

We accept that all theory by definition involves **abstraction**. The very words we use involve a 'standing back' from specific things so that we can *abstract* from them something that they have in common. To identify a chair, to use a rather corny example, one needs to abstract the quality of 'chairness' from a whole range of objects, all of which differ in some detail from every other. Take another example. The word 'dog' refers both to particular dogs and dogs in general. If we define a dog as a mammal with four legs, it could be said that a dog is the same as an elephant. So our definition is too abstract. We need to make it more particularistic. A dog is a four-legged mammal with fur. But does this mean that all dogs are poodles? Such a view is too particularistic: we need to argue that 'dogness' is more abstract than just being a poodle.

The point is that we are abstracting all the time, whether we like it or not! This is the only way to understand. Thus, in an analysis of the recent war in Iraq, we might use a whole host of abstractions to make sense of what we see: 'war', 'violence', 'law', 'armies', the elusive 'weapons of mass destruction', etc. Particular things are injected with a conceptual dimension, so that references to 'democracy' or 'terrorism' (for example) reflect interpretations as well as physical events.

Political theory, however, seems rather more abstract than say an analysis of the Iraq War, because it considers the notion, for example, of 'violence' beyond any particular instance, asking what violence is in every circumstance that we can imagine. This apparent remoteness from specific instances creates a trap and gives rise to a pejorative use of the term abstract. For thousands of years, theorists have believed that the abstraction is somehow independent of reality, or even worse, that it creates reality. Because we cannot act without ideas, the illusion arises that ideas are more important than, and are even independent of, objects. We can, therefore, talk about democracy or the state, for example, without worrying about particular states or specific kinds of democracies. Understandably students may find it bewildering to be asked 'what is power?' or 'what is democracy?', without this being related to, for example, the power which Mao Zedong exerted over the Chinese people before he died in 1976 or the question of whether the inequalities of wealth in contemporary Britain have a negative impact upon the democratic quality of its political institutions.

We believe that this link between theory and recognisable political realities is essential to an understanding and appreciation of the subject. What gives concepts and theories a bad name is that they are all too often presented abstractly (in the pejorative sense). Thinkers may forget that our thoughts come from our experience with objects in the world around us, and they assume that political thought can be discussed as though it is independent of political realities. It is true that a person who is destitute and asking for money in the street is not necessarily conscious of whether they are acting with freedom and what this concept means; but it is equally true that a theorist talking about the question of freedom may not feel the need to relate the concept of freedom to the question of social destitution. It is this act of abstraction that makes many students feel that theory is a waste of time and is unrelated to the world of realities. What we are trying to do in this book is to show that general ideas can help rather than hinder us in getting to grips with particular political events.

The Distinction between Facts and Values

One of the common arguments that aggravates theory's abstractness (unless otherwise stated, we will use the term abstraction in its pejorative sense), arises when people say that theory is *either* empirical *or* it is normative. In fact, it is always both. Facts and values interpenetrate, so that it is impossible to have one without the other.

Are facts the same as values? To answer this, we turn to a concrete example. It is a fact that in Western liberal societies, fewer and fewer people are bothering to vote. George Bush was elected in 2000 in a situation in which only about half of the electorate turned out to vote. This fact has an implicit evaluative significance, because historically, **democracy** has implied participation, and this fact suggests either that Western liberal societies are minimally democratic, or that the notion of democracy has to be revised. The implicitly evaluative dimension of this fact is evidenced in the way it is challenged, or at least approached. It might be said that low voter participation is only true of *some* Western liberal societies (the USA in particular), and it might be said that voting is not the only form of political participation that counts – people can participate by joining single-issue organisations such as Greenpeace or Amnesty International.

The point about facts is that they are generally agreed upon, and can be verified in ways that are not particularly controversial. They are accepted much more widely than explicit value judgements. Evaluation, on the other hand, refers to the relationships that are only implicit in the fact. Thus, the interpretation of the fact that fewer and fewer people in Western liberal societies vote, raises the question of why. Does the reason for this arise from a relationship with poverty, lack of self-esteem, education, disillusionment or is it the product of a relationship to satisfaction? The explanation embodies the evaluative content of the fact much more explicitly, since the explanation offered has obvious policy implications. If the reason for apathy is poverty, etc., then this has very different implications for action than an argument that people don't vote because they are basically satisfied with what politicians are doing in their name.

Therefore, we would argue that although facts and values are not the same, they are inherently linked. In our view, it is relationships which create values, so that the more explicit and far-reaching these relationships, the more obviously evaluative is the factual judgement. The fact that the earth goes round the sun is not really controversial in today's world, but it was explosively controversial in the medieval world, because the notion that the earth was the centre of the universe was crucial to a statically hierarchical world outlook.

The idea that facts and even ideas can be value-free ignores the linkage between the two. Not only is this empiricist view (as it is usually called) logically unsustainable, but it is another reason why students may find theory boring. The more you relate political ideas to political realities (in the sense of everyday controversies), the more lively and interesting they become. David Hume (1711–76) argued famously that it would be quite rational to prefer the destruction of the whole world to the scratching of my finger (1972: 157), but we would contest this scepticism. Reason implies the development of humans, and this is why political theory matters. Of course, what constitutes the well-being of people is complex and controversial but a well-argued case for why the world should be preserved and its inhabitants flourish, is crucial for raising the level of everyday politics.

The Contestability Thesis

As we see it, all theories and concepts are contestable. By contestable, we mean controversial so that we note that all theories are either challenged or at least open to challenge. Even the notion of **freedom** that we might think everyone subscribes to, can be contested by a religious fundamentalist on the grounds that it involves disrespect for God. To take another example, democracy is contestable because some identify democracy with liberal parliamentary systems that already exist such the British or French or Indian systems, while others argue that democracy implies a high level of participation so that a society is not democratic if large numbers are not involved in the process of government.

There is a more specialist use of the notion of '**contestability**', associated in particular with a famous essay by Gallie (1955: 188–93). Gallie argued, first, that only some political concepts are contestable (democracy was his favoured example) and that when concepts are essentially contestable, we have no way of resolving the respective methods of competing arguments. We can note the rival justifications offered (they are mere emotional outpourings), but we cannot evaluate them in terms of a principle that commands general agreement.

This implies that evaluation is only possible on matters about which we all agree. Such an argument stems from a misunderstanding of the nature of politics, for politics arises from the fact that we all have different interests and ideas, and the more explicit the difference between us is, the more explicit the politics. It therefore follows that a political concept is always controversial and it cannot command general agreement. Where an issue ceases to be controversial, it is not political. In this case differences are so slight that conflict is not really generated. Let us assume that chattel slavery – the owning of people as property – is a state of affairs which is so widely deplored that no one will defend it. Slavery as such ceases to be a political issue, and what becomes controversial is whether patriarchal attitudes towards women involve a condoning of slavery, or the power of employers to hire and fire labour gives them powers akin to a slave-owner. We think that it is too optimistic to assume that outright slavery is a thing of the past, but it is used here merely as an example to make a point.

All political concepts are inherently contestable since disagreement over the meaning of a concept is what makes it political, but does it follow that because there is disagreement, we have no way of knowing what is true and what is false? It is crucial not to imagine that the truth has to be timeless and above historical circumstance, but this rejection of ahistorical, timeless truth does not mean that the truth is purely relative. A relativist, for example, might argue that one person's terrorist is another person's freedom fighter. This would make an 'objective' definition of terrorism (to pursue our example) impossible.

To argue that something is true is not to banish all doubt. If something is true, this does not mean that it is not also false. It simply means that *on balance* one proposition is more true or less false than another. To argue otherwise is to assume that a phenomenon has to be one thing or another. Philosophers call this a 'dualistic' approach. By dualism is meant an unbridgeable chasm, so that in our example, a dualist would assume that unless a statement is timelessly true, it is absolutely false. In fact, to say that the statement 'George W. Bush is a good president' is *both* true and false. Even his most fervent admirers would admit (we hope!) that he is deficient in some regards, and even his fiercest critics ought to concede that he has some positive qualities.

Take the question of freedom, as another example. What is freedom for Plato (427–347 BC) differs from what freedom is for Rousseau (1712–78), and freedom for Rousseau differs from what we in the twenty-first century normally mean by freedom. So there is an element of relativity: historical circumstances certainly affect the character of the argument. Still we can only compare and contrast different concepts of freedom if we have an absolute idea as to what freedom is. The absolute notion of freedom refers to some kind of absence of **constraint,** but this absolute idea can only be expressed in one historical context rather than another, and it is this context which gives an absolute idea its relativity. As a consequence, there is *both* continuity (the absolute) *and* change (the relative).

There is a distinction between the absolute and the relative, but not a **dualism,** for we cannot have one without the other. The same is true of the distinction between the general and the particular, and the subjective and the objective. In our arguments in this book we strive to make our ideas as true as possible – i.e. we seek to make them objective, accurate reflections of the external world – but because they are moulded by *us,* and we live in a particular historical context, an element of subjectivity necessarily comes in.

What we think of freedom today will necessarily be refined by the events of tomorrow. We are only now becoming aware of how, for example, sexual orientation affects the question of freedom, and there is understandable concern about increasing freedom for people with disabilities. Health, physical and mental, also affects freedom, and all we can say is that our conception of freedom will inevitably alter in the future, but the change that will take place is not without its continuity with past concepts. Freedom is still an absolute concept, although it can only be identified in relative form.

The contestability thesis must, in our view, be able to address not merely the controversial character of political concepts, but how and why we can prefer some definitions in relation to others. Otherwise the thesis becomes bogged down in a relativism that merely notes disagreements, but has no way to defend preferences. A belief that post-war elections in Iraq will advance democracy is not an arbitrary assertion: it is the argument that can be defended (or challenged) with evidence and information to establish how much truth it contains.

The Structure of the Book

In our view, a work on political theory should address itself to the kind of issues that politicians and the media themselves raise, and which are part and parcel of public debate. In the first part of this work we seek to investigate the classical concepts. We start with these because these are the ones that readers are likely to be more familiar with, if they have already read some political thought, and they represent the 'staple diet' of courses on political theory. Hence we deal with these concepts first. We aim to explain even the older ideas as clearly as possible so that those who have had no contact with political theory at all will not feel disadvantaged.

Of course, the fact that these concepts are traditional does not mean that our treatment of them will be traditional. We seek to make them as interesting and contentious as possible, so that readers will be stimulated to think about the ideas in a new and more refreshing way. We aim to combine both exposition and argument to enable readers to get a reasonable idea of the terrain covered by the concept, and to develop a position on the concept, often in opposition to the one we adopt. The fact that this work is written by two people means that differences will manifest themselves in the way that ideas and ideologies are analysed. We think that this will benefit the reader since they will see, at first hand, how it is impossible for two individuals to agree about everything, and some readers might be able to note that certain chapters were drafted by one of us and differ from the others.

The ideas that we deal with are interlinked so that, for example, the argument about the **state** (and its problematic character) has a direct bearing on democracy. It is impossible to discuss the issue of citizenship without, for example, understanding the argument about **justice**. Of course, it is always possible to choose to present ideas differently. In some texts, for example, **sovereignty** is dealt with as a separate topic. In making sense of ideas and ideologies, it is crucial to say something about the key thinkers and the key texts. Our biography boxes in the website seek to show the background and wider interests of key thinkers and the exercises will try to emphasise why the ideas in the chapter are so relevant to understanding significant events. We have tried to make political theory challenging and enjoyable, and to deal with more detailed issues in special sections entitled 'Focus'. The use of arrows is intended to cross-reference both thinkers and ideas so as to emphasise linkages between them.

Although Part 1 is the same as it was in the first edition, in this second edition there has been some rearrangement. In Part 4, the concepts of difference and victimhood have been shifted to the website and the concepts of punishment and global justice have been added. What was called 'Terrorism' in the first edition is now called 'Political Violence'. So the contemporary concepts we look at are global justice, punishment, human rights and political violence. Punishment and global justice have been added because these are concepts which have been given a new urgency by contemporary events. People are concerned about the effect that globalisation is having on equality and there is concern about how to tackle violence and crime.

Thus:

Part 1 – classical ideas (state, freedom, equality, justice, democracy, citizenship, punishment)

Part 2 – classical ideologies (liberalism, conservatism, socialism, anarchism, nationalism, fascism)

Part 3 – contemporary ideologies (feminism, multiculturalism, ecologism, fundamentalism)

Part 4 – contemporary ideas (human rights, civil disobedience, political violence, global justice)

In what order should the concepts be read? This is a difficult question to answer in general terms because the reader may want to read the concepts in the order in which they are presented in the lectures they are attending. Another way of reading the book might be to select concepts in couples so that the chapter on the state is read with the chapter on punishment, and the chapter on justice is read with the chapter on global justice, and so on. It might be thought that the newer ideas relate more specifically to political controversies, and of course it is true that recent debates have raised these questions acutely, but the classical ideas have not lost their relevance. Think of the argument about smoking, for example. Arguments about the ban on smoking in public places revolves around contradictory interpretations of freedom.

All the ideas, whether contemporary or classical, are treated in ways that relate them to ongoing controversies, and show why an understanding of theory is crucial to an understanding of political issues. We hope that you find the chapters both helpful and entertaining. Political theory is hard work, but it can also be fun.

The Companion Website

It is also crucial to consult the website accompanying this book. Not only have the questions been completely reworked for this second edition, but the website contains material that focuses on additional concepts and ideologies relevant to this book. We have already mentioned that chapters on difference and victimhood have been shifted to the website. In the website we also look at questions of alienation, rights and the free market economy. We have chosen these questions because they deal with concepts that are often implicit in the material in the book and that help to sharpen the focus and linkage of the concepts and ideologies dealt with.

The website also contains biography boxes and sections on 'how to read' texts which were included in the text in the first edition. These biography boxes try to bring to life the thinkers who are mentioned in the text: not only is additional information provided about them, but they are shown to be real-life humans who lived in particular places at particular times. The 'how to read' sections provide advice of what to leave out and what to include so that lengthy texts become less daunting.

The website contains extracts from particular theorists so that the reader has a sense of reading some of the original work and making up their own mind what they think. The self-assessment questions have been added to see whether details were absorbed or simply ignored.

Beyond the Book

We have tried to make political theory relevant and interesting. We acknowledge that it is not easy since it necessarily deals with concepts rather than events, although much can be done to link ideas with the events and controversies of everyday life. There is also a very important point to remember and on which we will conclude this introduction.

The objective is not simply to acquaint you with a variety of ideas that you need to become familiar and comfortable with. It is ultimately to get you to think for yourself: not be afraid to have ideas of your own which you can defend and expound. Having your own views on the world is central to your identity, and if we have helped you to do this, then – whatever we may think of your own ideas – we would judge the book a success.

Questions

1. Is it possible to devise political concepts that have no normative implications, and are thus value-free in character?
2. Can one make a statement about politics without theorising at the same time?
3. Should political theory embrace or seek to avoid controversy?
4. Do teachers of political theory make practical political judgements?
5. Is the use of logic and the resort to factual evidence ethically neutral?

References

Gallie, W. (1955) 'Essentially Contested Concepts', *Proceedings of the Aristotelian Society*, 56, 167–98.

Hoffman, J. (1988) *State, Power and Democracy* Brighton: Harvester Wheatsheaf.

Hume, D. (1972) *A Treatise of Human Nature* Books 2 & 3, London: Fontana/Collins.

Part 1   Classical Ideas

What is Power?

As indicated in the *Introduction* the structure of the book is as follows:

Part 1	classical ideas (Ch. 1 state, Ch. 2 freedom, Ch. 3 equality, Ch. 4 justice, Ch. 5 democracy, Ch. 6 citizenship, Ch. 7 punishment)
Part 2	classical ideologies (Ch. 8 liberalism, Ch. 9 conservatism, Ch. 10 socialism, Ch. 11 anarchism, Ch. 12 nationalism, Ch. 13 fascism)
Part 3	contemporary ideologies (Ch. 14 feminism, Ch. 15 multiculturalism, Ch. 16 ecologism, Ch. 17 fundamentalism)
Part 4	contemporary ideas (Ch. 18 human rights, Ch. 19 civil disobedience, Ch. 20 political violence, Ch. 21 global justice)

In introducing the concepts of the state, liberty, equality, justice, democracy and citizenship here, we need to find an idea that underpins them all, and indeed, politics in general. In our view, this is *power*.

We are always talking about power. Do ordinary people have any? Do Prime Ministers and Presidents have too much? Do people decline to vote because they feel that they have no power? The question of power inevitably merges into the question of authority. Is might right? Are those who have power entitled to exercise it? When we raise questions like these, we are in fact asking whether power is the same as, or is different from, authority. No one can really dispute the fact that after Operation Iraqi Freedom in Iraq, the US has power, or considerable power in Iraq, but does that mean that it is entitled to exercise this power? The critics of US policy would argue that it lacks authority. Does this mean that it will be frustrated in its exercise of power?

It is not difficult to see that when we talk about power and its relation to authority, we are also implicitly raising issues that have a direct bearing on the classical concepts of Part 1.

The Link with Other Concepts

The definition of the state that we will adopt is that of the famous German sociologist, Max Weber (1864–1920), who defined the state as an institution claiming a monopoly of legitimate force. How does the notion of 'legitimate force' connect to the notion of power? Is the use of force the same as power? We will try to argue that while the two ideas sound similar, in fact power requires compliance, whereas force does not. Of course, it is easy to think of examples where the two come very close to one another. In the proverbial case of the person with a gun who demands your money or life, you have a 'choice' in a technical sense, but the 'power' exercised involves a threat of credible force, so that in reality your choice is illusory. In this case we would prefer to speak of coercion rather than power.

One of the most frequently debated topics is the question of whether force can be legitimate and by legitimacy, we mean force that has been authorised and limited. Clearly a soldier or a member of the police can use force, and usually this force has been authorised by parliament and, therefore, ultimately by those who can vote and hold parliament accountable. Does this make the force legitimate and thus, an act blessed by authority? And if the act of state force is authoritative, in whose eyes does it have authority? Those who are subject to this force (let us say protesters in a demonstration that is deemed to get out of hand), or those who are not part of the demonstration and approve of the action of the police? These are difficult questions, and we introduce them here in order to show why in a discussion of the state, it is important to involve questions of power and its relation to authority.

Consider the question of freedom or liberty. We usually think of a person being free if she can exercise power, thus changing herself and her surroundings. But if freedom is defined 'negatively', it may simply mean that you are free when no one deliberately interferes with you. Being free in this case is merely being left alone, not actually exercising power. On the other hand, if freedom is defined 'positively', it relates to a person's capacity to do something, so that, for example, freedom of speech is concerned with the power of a person to speak his mind, not the restrictions that may be placed on someone's right to do so. When does a person's freedom become an act of power that should be accepted or tolerated, and when should it be curbed? Clearly, a person who had no power at all, could not (say) smoke, but should smoking be banned from public places on the grounds that it is a form of power that is harmful? It is impossible to discuss these issues and the famous argument raised by the British liberal thinker, John Stuart Mill (1806–73), without having some kind of idea about power and authority and that is what Chapter 2 of this book sets out to do.

Equality and justice rest upon ideas of 'rightness'. Some people see a conflict between equality and freedom on the grounds that redistributing wealth through high taxation prevents individuals from being rewarded according to their merits. The state has too much power and the individual too little. This, it is argued, undermines the authority of the state: people pay their taxes because they have to, not because they want to. Egalitarians, on the other hand, link equality with justice, and argue that everyone should be treated equally. We should aim to spread power so that one person or group cannot tell another individual or group what to do, and governments should implement policies that move in this direction. People have the same rights, and therefore exercise similar power. Bill Gates, the billionaire owner of Microsoft, has rather more power than Josephine Bloggs who cleans his office or Willhelm Peter who removes some of the four million emails that Bill Gates receives every day. Is this just? Equality and justice rely, as we have already commented, upon the question of rightness, and can it be right that some individuals have so much more power than others?

Indeed, one definition of democracy is the 'power of the people'. Historically, the objection to democracy was precisely that the wrong kind of person would exercise power, and nineteenth-century liberals like Lord Macaulay feared that democracy would enable the poor to plunder the rich. On the other hand, left-wing critics of liberal democracy complain that the right of vote does not in itself give a person power to influence the course of events and that material resources must be available to people if they are to exercise power. The authority of liberal democracy rests upon equal rights rather than equal power so that the notion of power is indissolubly tied to debates about democracy.

The same is true with the concept of citizenship. Being a citizen gives you power. But does it give you enough? Is the housewife a citizen? She may have the right to vote and stand for parliament, but at the same time she may feel compelled to do what her husband tells her, and have limited power over her own life. Nancy Hartsock, an American academic, wrote a book entitled *Money, Sex and Power* (1985). Yet one of the most central questions in the debate about citizenship is whether the unequal distribution of resources distorts the power that people exercise. Are we already citizens or can we only become citizens if resources are more evenly spread both within and between societies? It is not difficult to see why the question of power, how we define it, identify it and analyse it is central to this (as to other) classical political ideas.

Power and Authority: an Indissoluble Link?

Power, as defined here, is a social concept. By this we mean that power is concerned with human relations and not with the mere movement of inanimate objects.

Power and authority are often contrasted. The police have power (power comes from the barrel of a gun, the former Chinese leader Mao Zedong is supposed to have said) whereas the late Queen Mother in Britain had authority (she inspired love and warmth – at least among some). A simple definition to start with would be to argue that power involves dominating someone or some group, telling them what to do, whereas authority is concerned with the rightness of an action. A person has to be pressured into complying with power, whereas they will obey authority in a voluntary way.

Alas, things are not so simple, because power and authority always seem to go together. This problem particularly bothers Jean-Jacques Rousseau, the great French eighteenth-century thinker (1712–78). On the one hand, might can never be transformed into right, since 'force is a physical power; I do not see how its effects could produce morality' (1968: 52). On the other hand, Rousseau famously insists that people must obey the law. The social contract would be worthless unless it could ensure that those who refuse to abide by the general will must be constrained to do so. Dissenters must, in that most celebrated of phrases, be 'forced to be free' (1968: 64).

Power and authority contradict each other, and yet there is an indissoluble link between them.

Our problem can be presented in a diagram as follows:

Power implies	Authority implies
constraint	consent
force	morality
subordination	will
dependence	autonomy

This is the problem of the 'two levels'. Power and authority appear to exclude one another, but they are never found apart.

Does a Broad View of Politics Help?

It might be argued that the problem of power and its relationship to authority is not a serious one. All we need to do is to point to a state that rests purely on power, and one that rests solely upon authority, and the problem is solved!

But April Carter in her *Authority and Democracy* concedes that in the political sphere, 'authority rarely exists in its pure form', and she says that even a constitutional government acting with great liberalism, would still lack 'pure authority' since, as she puts it, such a government 'relies ultimately upon coercion' (1979: 41, 33). Political authority (defined in statist terms) is paradoxical – a contradiction in terms – since no state, however benevolent, can wholly abstain from the use of force. Pure authority turns out to be a pure abstraction, at least as far as politics is concerned, and Carter demonstrates that rigorous definition and common sense cannot avoid the problem of paradox. Power and authority may be mutually exclusive, but it seems impossible to effect a clean divorce.

This is why Barbara Goodwin in her *Using Political Ideas* (1997) argues that the attempt to distinguish rigorously between power and authority is 'doomed to failure. In any normal political situation, and in every state institution, they co-exist and support each other' (1997: 314). It might be objected that politics is far broader than the state, and involves social relations between individuals. Surely here, at least, we can find a sharp separation between power and authority.

Taylor, who is interested in anthropological material on stateless societies, argues that a society without any form of coercion, is 'conceivable' (1982: 25), and the New Left theorist, C.B. Macpherson (1911–87), takes the view that in a simple market model in which every household has *enough* either to produce goods and services for itself or to exchange with others, then we have an example of cooperation without coercion – or in our terminology, authority without power. But it could be objected that the market mechanism constrains and Marx argues under capitalism, 'the dull compulsion of economic relations' subordinates the labourer to the capitalist (1970: 737). Even the independent producers of commodities suffer what Marx calls 'the coercion exerted by the presence of their mutual interests' (1970: 356).

But what about social examples that not only avoid the state, but do not involve the market either? What of the relationship between parent and child, teacher and student, doctor and patient? Are these not spheres in which we *can* (although do not always) witness the kind of respect that is essential for authority but which excludes power? However, J.S. Mill raises a problem that calls this analysis into question. In *On Liberty* Mill champions the right of the individual to think and act freely. In his argument he contrasts the physical force of the state to what he calls 'the moral coercion of public opinion' (1974: 68). Morality itself is seen as constraining, and we would contend that the very notion of a relationship subverts the idea that power and authority can be spliced apart. If all relationships are governed by norms (i.e. morality) of some kind, how then can any relationships be free from pressures of a constraining kind?

Negative and Positive Power

We have assumed that power and authority are contrasting concepts. But a distinction is often made between power as a negative and power as a positive concept. This, as we will see, has important implications for the concept of authority.

Power is negative in the sense that it relates to my ability to get you to do things that you otherwise would not do. The negative view of power is associated with the liberal tradition, and centres around the capacity of the individual to act freely and take responsibility for their actions. It is a notion deeply rooted in our culture, and, in our view, forms a necessary part of any analysis of power. People who exercise power, can and should be punished (or helped) when they exercise this power in ways which harm others or, indeed, irreversibly harm themselves. By this latter point, we mean a situation in which people can't change their minds because, as with serious self-abuse, or taking addictive drugs, it is too late! This notion emphasises the differences between people and their conflict of interests. Each individual is separate, and we are all capable of exercising negative power.

In contrast, power is deemed *positive* when it is expressed as empowerment. Empowerment occurs when one person helps ('empowers') themselves or another, or when a group or community enables people to develop. Contrary to what people may think, the notion of power as negative is a modern one while the ancients took the view that power was always expressed positively within communities. The idea of power being exercised to strengthen our relations with others, is a very old one.

Positive power is seen as the ability to do things by the discovery of our own strength – a capacity – a power *to* – as opposed to negative power which is seen as a power *over* – a domination. The conventional view sees power in negative terms, linked to the state, and force or the threat of force. Elshtain distinguishes between *potestas* – which relates to control, supremacy, domination, and *potential* – which relates to ability, efficacy and potency, especially that which is 'unofficial and sinister' (Elshtain, 1992: 117).

However we distinguish them, it is impossible to separate negative and positive power in an empirical sense. It is clear from Lukes's commentary, that positive power broadly corresponds to what has sometimes been called authority, and negative power expresses the conventional view of power. Defining power in a way which separates out logically the negative from the positive, does not resolve the power/authority problem, and like power and authority, negative and positive power always go together. It is impossible to think of a relationship in which one exists without the other.

Negative and Positive Power as a Relationship

The reason why negative and positive power cannot be divorced is that all relationships contain both. It is true that earlier notions of power were predominantly positive in character, but the problem, historically, is that this power has in practice been repressively hierarchical: the power of fathers, of lords, of priests, of kings. Positive power has been exercised in the past by people who claim (somewhat implausibly) to be acting on behalf of everyone else – men acting on behalf of women and children, lords for their serfs, priests for parishioners, sovereigns for subjects.

As liberals rightly object, 'negative power' is smuggled in through the back door. The holders of positive power see themselves as chastising others for their own good. The master may imagine that he is acting in the slave's interests – but when the slave is thought of as an individual, then things seem rather different! Power must be both positive and negative. It is important that we do not reject the individual focus of negative power, but seek to build upon it. We must come up with the proposition that if I am to exercise power as an individual, then I must allow you to exercise power as an individual. In other words, to sustain negative power, it must be exercised in terms of a *relationship* – or positively – so that I exercise power in a way that enables you to exercise power.

Power implies mutuality – but it can only be mutual if it is both positive and negative. If it is positive 'on its own', as it were, it stresses unity at the expense of separation, the community at the expense of the individual, so that (as liberals suspect), it becomes oppressive and hypocritical. Positive power exercised 'on its own' is as one sided as negative power when the latter is conceived in an abstract manner, because when negative power is exercised on its own, separation is expressed at the expense of unity. One individual exercises power in a way that prevents another from doing the same.

If the notion of 'negative' power is crucial for a person's freedom and individuality, it is not enough. 'On its own', it presents power in what is sometimes called a 'zero sum game' i.e. I have power because you don't. I exercise power *over* you – if I win, you lose. I am separate from you, and therefore my power differentiates me from you. Normally when people think of power, they think of power in negative terms.

Why is this notion a problem? It assumes – as its classical liberal roots reveal – that individuals can exist in complete isolation from other individuals, whereas in fact as any parent can tell you, we only acquire our sense of individuality (and thus separateness) in conjunction with others. Logically, if each person is to exercise power, then this negative power must take account of the right of each individual to be the same as everyone else. In other words, power can only be consistently 'negative' if it also has a social, positive and what we want to call a 'relational' attribute.

Three-dimensional Power and the Problem of Power and Authority

Lukes argues that power can be divided into three dimensions. The one-dimensional view identifies power as decision-making, the two-dimensional view argues that power can be exercised beyond the decision-making forum as in a situation where certain issues are excluded from an agenda and people feel that their interests are not being met. Three-dimensional power arises when people express preferences that are at variance with their interests: they support a system through a consciousness that is 'false'.

Lukes's argument is that the first dimension is highly superficial. He is sharply critical of Dahl's defence of power as decision-making in *Who Governs* (1961) on the grounds that those taking decisions, may not exercise decisive power at all. The second dimension is an improvement but still confines itself to observable activity: we have to be able to show that groups outside the decision-making forum are consciously exercising power, while three-dimensional power is deemed the most subtle of all. People do not protest precisely because they are victims of a power system that creates a phoney consensus, and those exercising power (like the media or educational system) may do so unintentionally. An example of three-dimensional power could be taken to be the Great Leap Forward in China that was supported by many who believed that through their heroic will-power the arrival of a communist society would be hastened. They certainly did not want the famine that followed.

But how can Lukes prove the existence of a 'latent' conflict, a potential event and a non-existing decision? How can he demonstrate an exercise of power when nothing takes place? The gulf between interests and preferences can, it seems, be demonstrated if it can be shown that with more information, people's preferences would have changed, and that interests only come into line with preferences when no further unit of information would cause any further change. Lukes has indicated that at least under some circumstances (for example where partial information leads to people in the town of Gary, Indiana not campaigning for an air pollution ordinance), power can be exercised which *appears* authoritative. Power and authority seem to go together but in fact the authority is an illusion. Power is being exercised all along.

But has this really resolved the power/authority problem? It certainly points to the way in which unintended circumstances pressure people to do things they otherwise would not have done. But the fact is that the separation remains because when power is expressed in a situation without observable conflict, the authority is simply a propagandist illusion – an idealised mystification of the reality of power. Indeed, Lukes seems to be saying that where people are fully informed, there is authority; where information is blocked even unintentionally, there is power. The problem is still not resolved.

Accounting for the 'Indissoluble Link'

Long after liberals rejected the notion of a state of nature in which individuals live in splendid isolation from one another, they continue to write as though individuals can be conceived in the absence of relationships through which they in fact discover their identity.

Constraint is unavoidable since no agent can exist except through a structure: these structures are both natural and social. You have to obey the laws of gravity and you have relationships with your family and friends whether you like it or not. Constraint should not be confused with force, although classical liberals and anarchists use the terms as though they were synonyms. Although we know of many societies that were or (in the case of international society) are, stateless in character, we know of no society in which there is an absence of constraint. Consensus arises when people can 'change places' and show empathy with one another's point of view, and this necessarily involves constraining pressures. Force, on the other hand, disrupts consensus and relationships, since when force is used, the other party ceases to be a person, and becomes a 'thing'.

To see how this translates into the argument about power and authority, the following chart can be drawn up:

Power	Authority
Necessity	Freedom
Circumstances	Rational consciousness
Negative power	Positive power
Pressure	Will
Constraint	Autonomy

All relationships involve constraints (power) and entitlements (authority). Remove one side of the power/authority equation, and the other crumbles. Take two diametrically opposed examples by way of illustration. In a master/slave relationship, power is obvious and manifest. Not only are there constraints, but there is also a threat of credible force. But at the same time unless slaves (however reluctantly or under whatever duress) 'acknowledge' or 'accept' their slavery, then the relationship between them and their masters is impossible, and they will die or escape. Relationships are mutual: being a slave obviously limits your freedom, but so too does *having* one even if in one case, the constraint causes pain and in the other, pleasure. To put the point *in extremis:* slave owners who simply kill their slaves or fail to keep them in service, destroy the basis of their own power. Even the slave, in other words, makes some input in this most repressive of relationships, and it is this input that gives the relationship its (minimally) authoritative character. In this case, we would want to say that slave owners exercise 'much' power and 'little' authority.

Let us turn to a relationship at the other end of the political spectrum, that between doctor and patient (or if you prefer, between teacher/pupil; priest/

parishioner, etc.). In this case, it seems that only authority exists, and there is no power. People normally go to the doctor because they want to, and if they accept the advice offered, it is because there is a communication of a persuasive or potentially persuasive kind. Authority predominates, but power also exists. Doctors communicate with their patients by pointing to constraints. If the advice they offer is not taken, highly unpleasant circumstances will follow! In these circumstances a person may have as much or as little freedom to choose as in a situation where they are threatened with force, since what choice does a chronically ill person have when told of the need for a dangerous operation, if the alternative is a swift and certain death? In this case, we have a relationship in which there is 'much' authority, but there is by no means a complete absence of power.

What has to be excluded from power and authority is the use of force itself, since this makes compliance impossible and is therefore a violation not merely of authority, but of power as well. Obviously the more authority predominates, the better, but even a purely consensual relationship involves some element of constraint.

Let us conclude by giving an example of a member of the police seeking to persuade football supporters who have been unable to obtain tickets, to go home. Initially, mild pressures would be invoked: 'it would be a good idea not to hang around but go home'. If this does not work, something stronger might be tried like: 'I would like you to go home – it would be silly not to'. If this does not work, a command follows: 'I am ordering you to go home'. Then – a threat: 'if you don't go home, I will arrest you' and black marias around the corner are indicated. If the police authority has to actually seize the protester, then force is used and both power and authority have failed! But the point is that even in the most authoritative statement, power is also implied, and in the sternest expression of power, authority is also present. The two always go together, and unless they are linked, no relationship is possible.

There is therefore a difference between what are conventionally called democratic and authoritarian states. The latter rely far more upon power and the former have much more authority. But the two concepts always go together, even though they are different, and it is a sobering thought that for those subject to force, neither power nor authority can be said to exist.

Power is not merely a crucial but the central concept of politics. It underpins, as we have tried to show, the other ideas that are elaborated in Part 1 and hence it deserves a separate (and fairly extended) treatment of its own by way of prefacing this section of the book.

References

Bachrach, P. and Baratz, M. (1969) 'Decisions and Non-Decisions: an Analytical Framework' in R. Bell *et al.* (eds) *Political Power* New York and London: The Free Press and Collier-Macmillan, 100–9.

Carter, A. (1979) *Authority and Democracy* London: Routledge and Kegan Paul.

Dahl, R. (1961) *Who Governs?* New Haven: Yale University.

Elshtain, J. (1992) 'The Power and Powerlessness of Women' in G. Bock and S. James (eds), *Beyond Equality and Difference* London and New York: Routledge, 110–25.

Goodwin, B. (1997) *Using Political Ideas* 4th edn Chichester, New York, Toronto: John Wiley and Sons.

Hobbes, T. (1968) *The Leviathan* Harmondsworth: Penguin.

Hoffman, J. (1988) *State, Power and Democracy* Brighton: Wheatsheaf.

Lukes, S. (2005) *Power: A Radical View* 2nd edn Basingstoke: Palgrave.

Macpherson, C.B. (1973) *Democratic Theory* Oxford: Clarendon.

Marx, K. (1970) *Capital*, vol. 1 London: Lawrence and Wishart.

Mill, J.S. (1974) *On Liberty,* Harmondsworth: Penguin.

Plato (1955) *The Republic* Harmondsworth: Penguin.

Rousseau, J.-J. (1968) *The Social Contract* Harmondsworth: Penguin.

Taylor, M. (1982) *Community, Anarchy and Liberty* Cambridge: Cambridge University Press.

Chapter 1

The State

Introduction

If you asked the average person to identify the state, they may look at you in astonishment, and say that they were not aware of living under a state, unless by that you meant the 'government'. Indeed, some writers have spoken of Britain and the USA as stateless societies, although this is to confuse what people think about the state, and what the state really is. In tackling this question, we shall also try to deal with the problem: does the state really exist?

Chapter Map

- The history of the concept of the state so as to decide whether the state is purely modern.

- Various definitions of the state, and our own definition.

- The link between the state and conventional notions of sovereignty.

- The argument that holds that it is possible to look beyond the state, provided certain conceptual distinctions are put in place.

Margaret Thatcher and the State

Margaret Thatcher, British Prime Minister, 1979-90

Source: © Bettmann/CORBIS

Thatcher was British Prime Minister between 1979 and 1990 and during her period of office, she introduced dramatic changes to the British political landscape.

She sold off council houses, introduced 'reforms' into the trade union movement (particularly with regard to the election of leaders), reduced welfare benefits and preferred private to public transport, championing the interests of what she called the individual against the interests of what she saw as established institutions, included among which was the civil service. All this was presented in a famous phrase that was invoked during her period of office, 'getting the state off the backs of the people'.

Thatcher was seen by her critics as an old-fashioned liberal. She expressed scepticism about the existence of society as a force that stands above the individual, she was a passionate free marketeer and she knighted Frederick Hayek who challenged the consensus support for the economist, John Maynard Keynes, in the 1950s and 60s.

The aspect of the state that she opposed was the 'welfare state'. Her policies certainly weakened welfare provisions, and she argued passionately that welfare state 'handouts' undermined the independence of the individual. But what of the coercive dimensions of the state? She strengthened the police (increasing their pay), built more prisons and the military victory over Argentina in the Falklands War boosted the prestige of the armed forces and led to a strong revival of patriotism. Her suspicious attitude towards 'aliens' and multiculturalism took the form of a potent English nationalism and lack of enthusiasm for the European Union. If she was a liberal, she was a conservative liberal who appointed hereditary peers to the House of Lords and opposed the African National Congress of South Africa.

Her period of office raises sharply the question of the nature of the state. If the state is defined in terms of its welfare aspects, then she was certainly anti-statist, but if we stress the link between the state and force, then she strengthened rather than weakened the state. Moreover, critics saw her as a great centraliser, establishing rule through appointed committees (called quangos) and using the state's interventionist power to engineer denationalisation on favourable terms to private investors. Thomas Hobbes, a seventeenth-century champion of state sovereignty, was reputedly her favourite philosopher.

1. Do you see Thatcher as a Tory or a liberal?
2. Is the state an institution that is more concerned with providing welfare for citizens than resorting to force?
3. It is sometimes said that Thatcher sought to establish a strong state and free economy. Do you agree?
4. How would you interpret the slogan of 'getting the state off the backs of the people'?

How Modern is the Concept of the State?

The question of what the state is is linked to the question of when the state emerges historically. T.H. Green (a nineteenth-century British political philosopher) believed that states have always existed. Families and tribes require an ideal of what is right, and this ethical system is the basis of the state (1941). Hegel (who was a nineteenth-century German philosopher) took the view that tribal societies had neither states nor history. Lacking reason, these stateless societies cannot even be understood (1956: 61).

More common, however, is the argument that the **state** is a modern institution since its 'forms' are as important as its 'content'. The state, in one account, is defined in terms of five attributes (Dunleavy and O'Leary, 1987: 2).

1. *A public institution separated from the private activities of society*. In ancient Greek society, the polis (wrongly called, Dunleavy and O'Leary argue, the city state) did not separate the individual from the state, and in a feudal society kings and their vassals were bound by oaths of loyalty that were both public and private. Certain sections of society, like the clergy, had special immunities and privileges, so that there was no sharp separation between members of society, on the one hand, and the polity on the other.

2. *The existence of sovereignty in unitary form*. In a feudal society, for example, the clergy, the nobility, the particular 'estates' and 'guilds' (merchants, craftsmen, artisans, etc.) had their particular courts and rules, so that the only loyalty which went beyond local attachments, was to the Universal Church, and in Europe this was divided between Pope and Emperor. **Laws** confirmed customs and social values – they were not made by a particular body that represented citizens and expressed a united '**will**'.

3. *The application of laws to all who live in a particular society*. In the ancient Greek polis, protection was only extended to citizens, not slaves, and even a stranger required patronage from a citizen to claim this protection. Under feudalism, protection required loyalty to a particular lord. It did not arise from living in a territory, and the ruling political system could not administer all the inhabitants.

4. *The recruitment of personnel according to bureaucratic as opposed to patrimonial criteria*. Whereas the state selects people for an office according to impersonal attributes (are they well qualified etc.?), earlier polities identified the office-holder with the job, so that offices belonged to particular individuals and could be handed to relatives or friends at the discretion of the office holder. Imagine the vice-chancellor of a university deciding to name their own successor!

5. *The capacity to extract revenue (tax) from a subject population*. In pre-modern polities, problems of transport and communication meant that tax-raising power was limited, and rural communities in particular were left to their own devices.

The argument is that only the state is sovereign, separate from society, can protect all who dwell within its clearly demarcated boundaries, recruits personnel according to bureaucratic criteria and can tax effectively. These are seen not merely as the features of a modern state, but of the state itself. We will later challenge this argument but it is very widely held.

Defining the State

The Force Argument

Definitions of the state vary depending upon whether the question of **force** or **morality** is stressed, or a combination of both. The definition that commands a good deal of support is that of the German sociologist, Max Weber (see his biography on the website) – that the state is an institution that claims a **monopoly** of legitimate violence for a particular territory.

Robert Dahl, a US political scientist who taught at Yale, defines **Government** (with a capital 'G' – a term which he uses synonymously with the state) in terms explicitly taken from Weber. David Easton, on the other hand, criticises an anthropologist for focusing on organised force as the distinguishing quality of political systems, and identifies this emphasis upon force with the position laid down by Thomas Hobbes (see his biography on the website) and reinforced by Weber (Hoffman, 1995: 34). Marx highly appraised Hobbes as a theorist who saw 'might' rather than will as the basis of right or the state (1976: 329) and force has been seen as the most important of the factors that accounts for the state. It is true that it is not the only one, and supporters of the force definition of the state acknowledge that other factors come into play. Marx called these 'symptoms' (1976: 329), and Weber himself specifically stated that force is not the only attribute of the state. Indeed his definition makes it clear that the force of the state has to be 'legitimate', monopolised and focused on a particular territory. Nevertheless, as Weber himself says, force is a 'means specific to the state' (Gerth and Wright Mills, 1991: 78, 134).

The other factors are important but secondary. Force is central to the state, its most essential attribute.

The Centrality of Will

Those who see morality or right as the heart of the state, are often called 'idealists' because they consider 'ideas' rather than material entities to be central to reality. Hegel, perhaps the most famous of the idealist thinkers, described the state as the realisation of morality – the 'Divine Idea as it exists on Earth' (Hegel, 1956: 34).

T.H. Green argued that singling out what he called 'supreme coercive power' as the essential attribute of the state, undermines the important role which morality plays in securing a community's interests (1941: 121). Green supports the argument of Jean-Jacques Rousseau, an eighteenth-century French writer. Rousseau took the view that morality, **rights** and duty form the basis of the state. Green does not deny that what he calls 'supreme coercive power' is involved in the state, but he insists that central to the state are the moral ends for which this power is exercised. This led Green's editor to sum up his argument with the dictum that 'will, not force, is the basis of the state' (Hoffman, 1995: 218–19).

More recently, writers like Hamlin and Petit have argued that the state is best defined in terms of a system of rules which embody a system of rights – this is crucial to what they call a 'normative analysis of the state' (1989: 2).

The State as a Mixture of Will and Force

Others argue that the state does not have a 'basis' or central attribute, but is a mixture of both force and morality. It is wrong to regard one of these as more important than the other.

Antonio Gramsci, an Italian Marxist, traced this view of the state back to Machiavelli's *The Prince*. Machiavelli, writing in the sixteenth century, declared that there are two means of fighting: 'one according to the laws, the other with force; the first way is proper to man, the second to beasts'. Machiavelli argued that the first is often not sufficient to maintain power, so that 'it becomes necessary to have recourse to the second' (1998: 58). The state was seen as analogous to the mythical creature, the centaur, which was half-human and half-beast. Gramsci embraced this argument. The state is linked to force, he said, but equally important is law, morality and right (Gramsci, 1971: 170). The state in this argument has a dual character, and although Gramsci subscribed to the Marxist argument that the state would wither away, he argues that what disappears is force, and an 'ethical state' remains (Hoffman, 1996: 72).

It has become very common to contend that theories that argue that the essential property of the state is either morality or force are 'essentialist' or 'reductionist'. By this is meant an approach that highlights one factor as being crucially relevant. Just as it is wrong to ignore the part of the state which imposes force upon those who will not voluntarily comply with the law, so it is wrong to downgrade the 'civilising' aspects of the state – the aspects of the state which regulate peoples' lives in ways which make them healthier and happier. The notion of a welfare state captures this amalgam, since it is argued that the state acts in a way that is both negative and positive – a mixture of force and will. Your local hospital is part of the National Health Service and funded from taxes that people have to pay, but the staff there are trained to help you with healthcare. The hospital is part of a state that is both negative and positive in its role.

Force and the Modernity Argument

Those who stress the centrality of force argue that the state is far older than the 'modernists' assume. It is true that earlier states are different from modern ones and lack the features described by Dunleavy and O'Leary. Force is regarded as the defining attribute of the state. Feudal and ancient polities may have been more partisan and less effective than the modern state, but they were states nevertheless. They sought to impose supreme power over their subjects. We come back to Weber's definition of the state as an institution that claims a monopoly of legitimate force for a particular territory. Does this mean that only the modern state is really a state, or do all post-tribal polities act in this way (albeit less efficiently and more chaotically), and therefore deserve to be called states as well?

Proponents of the force argument contend that differences in form should not be allowed to exclude similarities. Once we argue that only modern states can be

Exercise

List the features that make the state modern.

Are these features enough to bolster the argument that the modern state is the state, and that earlier polities should not be called states at all?

T.H. Green called the Tsarist state a state by courtesy (1941: 137). What would you call the following states?

- Iraq under Saddam Hussein
- (Contemporary) Yugoslavia
- Apartheid South Africa
- USA
- Afghanistan.

Make two columns, one headed 'Difference in Degree', the other 'Difference in Kind'. Now list the features that differentiate modern states from pre-modern states, or the state from earlier (but post-tribal) polities under what you see as the appropriate column.

called states, we ignore the problem of defining totalitarian states (like Iraq under Saddam Hussein). Are they not states because they are corrupt and violate in all sorts of ways bureaucratic criteria for recruiting functionaries and the **public/private** distinction, as elaborated above?

The danger with the 'modernist argument' (as we call it) is twofold. It assumes that states have to be liberal in character, and that modern states live up to the forms which are prescribed for them. Yet even liberal states that consider themselves democratic do not always practise what they preach. They are also are plagued with corruption (think of the role played by money in the election process in the USA) so that criteria for appointments are violated and the rule of law is breached. Is the Italian state not a 'real' state, for example, because it fails to live up to the 'ideals' of the state? If it is not a state, then what is it? It would be much better to identify states in terms of the supreme force that they exercise (albeit in different ways) over subjects. Weber's definition applies to all (post-tribal) polities for roughly the last 5,000 years.

The Argument Against the Concept of the State

Three bodies of argument contend that the state is not a suitable concept for political theory, since it is impossible to define it. The state has been described as one of the most problematic concepts in **politics** (Vincent, 1987: 3) and it has been seen as so problematic as to defy definition at all.

The Behaviouralist Argument

The first group to subscribe to what might be called the 'indefinability thesis' was developed by political scientists who worked in the United States in the 1960s but whose influence was not confined to the USA. It extended throughout Europe. This group is generally known as the *behaviouralists*.

The founding father of behaviouralism is considered to be Arthur Bentley, who argued that the state was afflicted with what he called in 1908 'soul stuff' – an abstract and mystical belief that the state somehow represents the 'whole' of a community. Much better, Bentley argued, to adopt a process view of politics that contends that the state is no more than one government among many (1967: 263).

The term 'behaviour' was intended to capture the fact that humans, like animals, behave: hence the approach denied that human society is different in kind from animal society or the activity of other elements in nature. This led to a view that the study of politics was like a natural science, and behaviouralists argued that as a science, it must not make value judgements. Just as biologists would not describe a queen bee as 'reactionary' or 'autocratic' so the political scientist must abstain from judgements in analysing the material they study. Behaviouralists believe that a science of politics should not defend particular values, and should instead draw up testable hypotheses by objectively studying political behaviour.

The Argument of David Easton

David Easton was a leading figure of the behavioural political scientists who examined the theoretical credentials of the state in his book *The Political System* (1953). He argues that the state is a hopelessly ambiguous term. Political scientists cannot agree on what the state is or when it arose. Some define the state in terms of its morality, others see it as an instrument of exploitation. Some regard it as an aspect of society, others as a synonym for government, while still others identify it as a unique and separate association that stands apart from social institutions like churches and trade unions. Some point to its sovereignty, others to its limited power.

What makes the state so contentious, Easton argues, is that the term is imbued with strong mythical qualities, serving as an ideological vehicle for propagating national sovereignty against cosmopolitan and local powers. Given this degree of contention and controversy, there is no point, Easton argues, in adding a 'definition of my own' (1971: 106–15). If political theory is to be scientific, then it must be clear, and clarity requires that we abstain from using the concept of the state altogether.

For around three decades after the Second World War the state, conceptually at any rate, appeared in the words of one writer to have 'withered away' (Mann, 1980: 296). Yet in 1981 Easton commented that a concept which 'many of us thought had been polished off a quarter of a century ago, has now risen from the grave to haunt us once again' (1981: 303). What had brought the state back into political science? Easton noted:

- the revival of interest in **Marxism**, which places the state at the heart of politics;

- a conservative yearning for stability and authority; a rediscovery of the importance of the **market** so that the state is important as an institution to be avoided (see case study);
- a study of policy which found the state to be a convenient tool of analysis.

Easton is however still convinced that the state is not a viable concept in political science. He recalls the numerous definitions that he had noted in 1953, and argues that 'irresolvable ambiguities' have continued to proliferate since then. To make his point, he engages in a hard-hitting and witty analysis of the work of a Greek Marxist, Nicos Poulantzas (who was much influenced by the French theorist, Louis Althusser). Poulantzas, Easton tell us, concludes after much detailed and almost impenetrable analysis, that the state is an 'indecipherable mystery'. The state is 'the eternally elusive Pimpernel of Poulantzas's theory' – an 'undefined and undefinable essence' (Easton, 1981: 308). All this confirms Easton's view that the concept of the state is obscure, empty and hopelessly ambiguous. It should be abandoned by political science.

David Easton's Concept of the Political System

If the concept of the state should be pushed to one side by political theorists, what do we put in its place? Easton argues that at the heart of our study of politics lies not the idea of the state, but rather the concept of the political system. This Easton defines as 'the authoritative allocation of values for society as a whole' (1971: 134). Politics, he contends, is far better defined in this way. Such a definition avoids the ambiguity of the state-concept, but at the same time, it is not so broad that it considers all social activity to be political. After all, a political system refers to the allocation of values for society as a whole. It, therefore, confines the term 'political' to public matters, so that, as far as Easton is concerned, the pursuit of power that may take place in trade unions, churches, families and the like is not part of politics itself.

The notion of a political system makes it possible to sharply differentiate the political from the social. It also resolves historical problems that afflict the concept of the state. Whereas the state only arose in the seventeenth century (in Easton's 'modernist' view), the concept of the political system can embrace politics as a process existing not only in medieval and ancient times, but in tribal societies which had no significant concentrations of power at all. Once we free politics from the state, we can also talk about a political system existing at the international level, authoritatively allocating values for the global community.

In his later work, Easton contends that a political system can persist through change so that one could argue that a system continues to allocate values authoritatively while its structures change dramatically. Thus it could be said, for example, that a political system persisted in Germany while the imperial order fell to the Weimar Republic, which yielded to the Nazi regime that was replaced by a very different order after the Second World War (Easton, 1965: 83).

Easton's concept of the political system is, he claims, superior to the concept of the state. The latter is ambiguous, limited and ideological. Even though Robert Dahl is critical (as we will see) of Easton's particular definition, he too prefers to speak of a 'political system' which can exist at many levels, and which he defines as any persistent pattern of human relationships involving to a significant extent, control, influence, power or authority (1976: 3).

The Linguistic and Radical Argument

The **linguistic analysts** were a philosophical school fashionable in the 1950s and 1960s in Britain and the USA. Their doyen, T.D. Weldon, wrote an extremely influential book, *The Vocabulary of Politics*, in 1953 in which he argued that analysts are only competent to tackle what linguistic analysts called 'second order' problems. This referred to the words politicians use, and not the realities to which these words are supposed to refer. The concept of the state is (Weldon argued) a hopelessly muddled term, frequently invested with dangerously misleading mystical overtones. Practical political activists use it but it is an unphilosophical 'first order' term that has imported into political theory its confusions from the world of practice. Whereas we all know (as citizens) that the USA and Switzerland are states whereas Surrey and the United Nations are not, the term has no interest for political philosophers (1953: 47–9).

We refer to the radical argument as one that is in favour of radical democracy and sees the concept of the state as a barrier to this end. Why conceive of politics in statist terms when we want people at all levels of society to participate in running their own affairs? Radicals come in many forms. Some see the term guilty of a kind of monopolisation of politics, so that political activity outside the state is downgraded. Others argue that the term is so complex that it is fruitless to try and define it. Richard Ashley, a postmodernist or poststructuralist in international relations, takes the view that it is impossible to 'decide what the state is' (1988: 249), while Pringle and Watson quote the words of the French postmodernist,

Focus

Behaviouralism

Not to be confused with behaviourism – a psychological theory – behaviouralism developed in the USA after the Second World War as an intellectual concept that stressed precision, systems theory and pure science. The idea is that all living things behave in regular ways and it is possible to see them as adjusting to their environment as a result of the inputs they receive and the outputs they produce. Generalisations can be made that can be verified through methods that have no ethical implications. Theory must be scientific in the sense that no values are involved, and the social sciences do not involve any special approaches that are not relevant to the natural sciences. Indeed, the notion of behaviour makes it possible to examine all living things since humans express themselves through regularities which can be scientifically investigated. The behavioural 'revolution' (as its supporters called it) reached its height in the 1960s, but was accused of taking the politics out of politics by its critics who felt that the methods of natural science were not appropriate to the social sciences, and that the notion anyway that science could be value-free, is naive and superficial.

Michel Foucault, that 'to place the state above or outside society is to focus on a homogeneity which is not there' (1992: 55). The state, says Foucault, is 'a mythical abstraction whose importance is a lot more limited than many of us think' (Hoffman, 1995: 162). Pringle and Watson, for their part, find the state too erratic and disconnected to evoke as an entity (1992: 63), while a feminist, Judith Allen, takes the view that the state is too abstract, unitary and unspecific to be of use in addressing the disaggregated, diverse, specific or local sites which require feminist attention (Allen, 1990: 22).

The radicals agree with the linguistic analysts and the behaviouralists that the concept of the state should be abandoned. Their particular argument is that the notion discourages participation and involvement at local levels and in social institutions, and is therefore an unhelpful term.

Problems with the Argument Against the State

Many of the points that the critics of the concept of the state make are useful. It is certainly odd to identify politics with the state and, therefore, to take the view that families, tribes, voluntary organisations from cricket clubs to churches and universities, and international institutions are not political because the state is either not involved at all or at least directly at any rate, in running their affairs.

However, it does not follow from this that we cannot define the state, or that the state is not an important concept and institution for political scientists to study. Indeed, we will argue that it is impossible to ignore the state, and that unless one can contend that the state no longer exists, it can and must be defined.

The Argument of David Easton

At no point does Easton suggest that the state does not exist, and Dahl, his fellow behaviouralist, speaks explicitly of the state as 'the Government' (1976: 10). In a more recent book, Easton identifies with those who argue that the state has never really been left out (1990: 299n).

Nevertheless, we must consider Easton's argument that the concept of the political system is a much clearer and more flexible idea than the concept of the state. Easton's notion might seem ingenious but in fact it has serious difficulties of its own. Easton's argument is that when we define a political system as the authoritative allocation of values for society as a whole, we can say that the conflict within a tribe which leads to secession of one of its clans is 'exactly similar' to conflicts between states in international institutions (1971: 111). But what is the meaning of 'society as a whole'?

Easton defines society as a 'special kind of human grouping' in which people develop 'a sense of belonging together' (1971: 135). When secession occurs within a tribe or war between states takes place, there would seem to be the absence, not the presence, of that sense of belonging together which Easton defines as a society. To say that tribes and international orders which involved warring states, are 'genuine societies' (1971: 141) seems to empty the term society of any content. The same problem afflicts his argument that a political system can persist through change even though (in the case of Germany, for example) the authorities and the regimes not only change drastically, but are divided until 1991 into two warring halves! The political system appears to be a shadowy abstraction that could only perish if all popular participants were physically obliterated. It could be argued that Easton's 'political system' seems no less mysterious than (the target of his 1971 article) Poulantzas's elusive state.

In later definitions, Easton speaks of the political system not as a 'something' that authoritatively allocates values for society as a whole, but as that which takes decisions 'considered binding by most members of society, most of the time' (1990: 3). But this does not solve his problem. Indeed, in an early review of *The Political System*, Dahl raises the problem of Easton's definition, by asking how many have to obey before an 'allocation' is deemed binding. Criminals, as Dahl points out, do not believe that criminal statutes must be obeyed (Hoffman, 1995: 28). The point is a good one, and it is not answered by saying that most of the members of society, most of the time have to consider allocations binding. What happens if the order is an authoritarian one in which relatively few people support the regime? Moreover, what counts as genuine support as opposed to compliance based upon fear? Think of 'popular support' in Nazi Germany, Stalinist Russia or in Saddam Hussein's Iraq. How useful is it to say that people considered the allocations binding? This is a real problem, and what it shows is that Easton has not done away with the ambiguities and elusiveness that characterise the state.

Indeed, it has been argued that Easton can only bring his political system down to earth by making it synonymous with the state, so that we can give some kind of empirical purchase to the notion of society as a whole. Once we return to the state, the problems of ambiguity and abstractness remain. The substitution of the political system for the state has not solved any of the problems that led Easton to reject the concept of the state in the first place.

The Question of Existence

Moreover, Easton's argument suffers from the same difficulty that confronts all who argue that the state cannot be defined. We have to ask: does the state exist? None of the critics of the concept of the state suggest that the state as a real-life institution has disappeared. Easton tries to adopt a sceptical position to the effect that political life has no 'natural' coherence so that we could, for argument's sake, construct a political system out of the relationship between a duck-billed platypus and the ace of spades. But he does insist that a conceptually 'interesting' idea must have 'empirical status' (1965: 33, 44), and this seems to suggest that there must be something in the world out there which corresponds to the political system as he defines it. Such an institution is the state.

Neither behaviouralists, nor linguistic theorists nor radicals argue that the state does not exist. If states do exist, then the challenge is surely to define them. Weber's notion of the state as an institution that claims a monopoly of legitimate force for a particular territory is a useful definition: as we see it, it is rather silly to talk about the state and then deny that it can be defined.

Force and Statelessness

The value of highlighting force as the central attribute of the state is that it focuses upon a practice that is extraordinary: the use of force to tackle conflicts of interest. It is true that states defined in a Weberian way have been around for some 5,000 years, but humans have been in existence for much longer, and therefore an extremely interesting question arises. How did people secure order and resolve disputes before they had an institution claiming a monopoly of legitimate force?

Most anthropologists would dispute Green's argument that states have always existed. They argue that in tribal societies, political leaders rely upon moral pressures – ancestor cults, supernatural sanctions, the threat of exclusion – to maintain social cohesion and discipline. Although many of these sanctions would strike us today as being archaic and unworkable, the point about them is that they demonstrate that people can live without a state.

International relations writers have also become aware of how international society regulates the activities of states themselves, without a super or world state to secure order. Moral and economic pressures have to be used to enforce international law, and as the recent conflict in Iraq has demonstrated, there is nothing to prevent states from interpreting international law in conflicting ways.

The Distinction between Force and Constraint, State and Government

When we define the state in terms of force, we naturally are curious about the political mechanisms in societies without a state. But to understand how order is maintained in societies without institutions claiming a monopoly of legitimate force, we need to make two distinctions that are not usually made in political theory.

The first is the distinction between force, on the one hand, and **constraint**, on the other, and the second (which we will come to later) is the distinction between state and government. If stateless societies exert discipline without having an apparatus that can impose force, how do we characterise this discipline? In our view, it is necessary to distinguish between force and constraint. The two are invariably lumped together, particularly by classical liberal writers who often use the terms force and constraint synonymously. Yet the two are very different.

Force imposes physical **harm**, and it should be remembered that mental illnesses like depression create physical pain so that causing depression counts as force. **Coercion** we take to be a credible threat of force: a two-year-old with a plastic gun cannot be said to coerce because the force 'threatened' is not credible. Thus, in the standard example of 'your money or your life' demand, what causes you to comply is the knowledge that force will be used against you if you do not.

It is true that coercion can be defined in a much broader way. Here coercion is seen not as the threat of force, but as moral and social pressures that compel a person to do something that they otherwise would not have done. It is better, however, to describe these pressures as 'constraints': constraints certainly cause you to do something you would not have otherwise done, but these pressures do not involve force or the credible threat of force. Constraint may involve pressures that are unintentional and informal.

Take the following example. You become religious and your agnostic and atheist friends no longer want to have coffee with you. You are cycling on a windy day and find that you have to pedal considerably harder! Constraints can be natural or social, and when moral judgements are made about a person's behaviour, these constraints are 'concentrated' in ways that are often unpleasant. The point about these constraints, whatever form they take, is that they are impossible to avoid in a society. They do not undermine our capacity for choice. On the contrary, they are conditions that make choice both possible and necessary.

This distinction between force and constraint translates into the second distinction we want to discuss, that between state and government. The latter two are not the same, even though in state-centred societies, it may be very difficult to disentangle them. The term 'governance' is often used but the argument is better expressed if we stick to the older term. Government, it could be argued, involves resolving conflicts of interest through sanctions which may be unpleasant but do not involve force. Families, schools, clubs and voluntary societies govern themselves with rules that pressure people into compliance but they do not use force. States on the other hand, do use force. It is true that states do not always act as states. In other words, they may in particular areas act 'governmentally', as we have defined it: in these areas they can be said to constrain, rather than resort to force. Of course in real life institutions in state-centred societies, these two dimensions are invariably mixed up. The NHS in Britain is a good example of an institution that is mostly governmental in that its rules do not have force attached to them, but rely upon social pressures – naming and shaming, embarrassing and using verbal sanctions – to enforce them. On the other hand, it cannot be said that the state (strictly defined) does not play a role as well. After all, the NHS is tax-funded, and if people refuse to pay taxes, they are likely to be subject to more than moral pressures to pay up!

The Argument So Far ...

- We have argued that the state is not just a modern institution, even though the 'modern state' does have features that distinguish it from more traditional states.

- We have defended Max Weber's 'force argument'. Although force is not the only attribute of the state, it is the central attribute so that the state is distinguished from other social institutions because it uses 'legitimate force' to address conflicts of interest. The police, the army and the prisons are the distinctive attributes of the state.

- We have assumed that the state is an important concept in political theory, but there are those who argue that the state is too vague, elusive, divisive and ambiguous to merit attention. We have identified these critics as behaviouralists,

linguistic analysts and radicals. Their arguments are rejected on the grounds that since states clearly exist in the real world, it is important to try and define them, however difficult this task might be.

- States have not always existed. In fact throughout most of human history, people have resolved conflicts without relying upon a special institution that claims a monopoly of legitimate force. Even today states are (usually) bound by international law and treaties even though there is no world state to maintain order. These facts make it important that we distinguish between constraints of a diplomatic kind (relying upon economic pressures, self-interest, ostracism etc.) and force as such, just as we need to distinguish between the state and government.

State, Politics and Government

Is there a case for distinguishing between politics and the state? List all the things in your life that you would call 'political' and see whether it can be said that the state is directly involved.

It is sometimes argued that:

• the family is political

• the church is political

• sport is political

• relations between people are political.

Do you agree, and if so, what makes these institutions political? How would you counter the argument that if 'everything is political, then nothing is political'?

Do you see government as a synonym for politics; is there a distinction between government and the state? List the institutions that have governments, starting with yourself (do you govern your own life?).

Consider the following institutions: are they inherently statist in character, or could they be run without the state?

• the National Health Service

• the prisons

• the post office

• the army and police.

The distinction between state and government is important, first because it explains how stateless societies have rules and regulations which make order possible, and why people conform or dissent through pressures which most of the time are non-statist in character. You may try to get to the doctor's on time – not because you are fearful of being arrested and put in prison – but because it seems discourteous and improper not to do so. The distinction separates force (or violence) – the terms seem to boil down to the same thing in this context – from human nature, pointing to the fact that force comes into play only in situations in which moral and economic pressures do not work.

State and Sovereignty

It is impossible to talk about the state without saying something about sovereignty. This is the aspect of the state that relates to its supreme and unchecked power. Hence sovereignty is commonly regarded as an attribute of states but here agreement ends, since some argue that only modern states are sovereign, while others that all states are sovereign. Does claiming a monopoly of legitimate force mean that this monopoly endows the state with sovereignty?

Sovereignty as a Modern Concept

It is argued by Justin Rosenberg, for example, that sovereignty only arises when the state is sharply separated from society. His argument is that only under capitalism, do we have a sharp divide between the public and the private, and this divide is necessary before we can speak of the sovereign state (1994: 87).

Rosenberg takes the view that sovereignty is a modern idea just as the state is a modern institution. F. H. Hinsley, on the other hand, argues that while the state can be broadly defined as a modern as well as an archaic institution, sovereignty cannot, since sovereignty requires a belief that absolute and illimitable power resides in the 'body politic' which constitutes a 'single personality' composed of rulers and ruled alike (1986: 125). This means effectively that rulers and ruled must be deemed 'citizens' – a modern concept. Even the celebrated theory of Jean Bodin's (1529/30–1596), that sovereignty is unconditional and unrestrained power is, for Hinsley, undermined by the assumption that the holder of sovereignty is limited by divine and natural law. With Hobbes, however, law in all its forms is the creation of the sovereign, so that there is no distinction to be made between sovereign and subject. The sovereign is simply the individual writ large.

In Hinsley's view therefore, the state can take a pre-modern form but sovereignty cannot. This is also the position taken by Murray Forsyth in his entry on the state in *The Blackwell Encyclopaedia of Political Thought* (Forsyth, 1987).

Sovereignty as a Broad Concept

It is perfectly true that the concept of sovereignty was not known 'in its fullness' before the fifteenth and sixteenth centuries (Vincent, 1987: 32). Like the state, it was only explicitly formulated in the modern period, but that does not mean that it did not exist in earlier times. The Roman formulation – 'whatever pleases the prince has the force of law' – demonstrates not only that the notion of sovereignty existed in pre-modern periods, but that formulations like these clearly influenced the modern conception. The idea that God exercised sovereignty rather than secular rulers still expressed the notion of absolute and illimitable power, and although sovereignty was more chaotic in pre-modern times, it clearly existed. One writer has spoken of 'the parcellized sovereignty' of the medieval period (Hoffman, 1998: 35–6) so that those who define the state broadly, often define sovereignty broadly as well.

Alan James argues that states have always been sovereign, and that sovereignty is best defined as constitutional independence: a sovereign state is a state that is legally in control of its own destiny (1986: 53). Although he is preoccupied with states in the modern world, the notion of sovereignty applies to all states, whether ancient, medieval or modern.

Problems with the Theories of State Sovereignty

Those who assume that sovereignty is about the power of the state are mistaken. They take the view that the state is capable of exercising absolute power whereas it has been argued that in fact the state only claims this sovereign power, because others – terrorists, criminals, etc. – challenge it. In other words, the state claims something that it does not and cannot have, so that the notion of the state as sovereign imports into the notion of sovereignty the problem of the state itself.

Difficulties with the Modernist Conception

The idea that sovereignty is purely modern confuses formulation with institution. It is true that sovereignty is only explicitly formulated by modern writers, but the notion of supreme power is inherent in the state.

The modernist notion misses the ironic part of Weber's definition: that a monopoly can be claimed, not because it exists, but precisely because it does not. The sovereign state claims an absolute power that it does not and cannot have. Unless criminals and terrorists also exercise some of this 'supremacy', it cannot be claimed. In other words, the notion of sovereignty merely brings into the open the problem that has existed all along. Like the state itself, the idea of state sovereignty has severe logical difficulties associated with it.

On the one hand, sovereignty is unitary in its scope. It is absolute and unlimited. In modern formulations, rulers and ruled are bonded together as citizens. On the other hand, there has to be a sharp **division** between the public and the private, the state and society, before modern sovereignty can be said to exist. There is a clear contradiction here since we can well ask, how can an institution have absolute power, and yet be clearly limited to a public sphere? Sovereignty allows the state to have a hand in everything – and yet we are told that it is confined to the public sphere and must not interfere in private matters! The formulation of **state sovereignty** in the modern period serves only to highlight its absurd and contradictory character.

It is true that in 'normal' times the sovereign character of the state is not obvious to the members of a liberal society but if there is crisis or emergency – as when war breaks out between states – the capacity of the state to penetrate into all aspects of life, becomes plain. During the Second World War, the British state told its citizens what they must plant in their back gardens, and today, for example, the state tells us through advertising about safe sex, that we should conduct the most private of activities with adequate protection. The British Cabinet even had a discussion in the early 1980s about the importance of parents teaching children how to manage their pocket money (*The Guardian*, 17 February 1983).

We are told that state sovereignty needs to be limited and restricted. Yet it is clear from the practice of state even in 'normal' times, that sovereignty is seen as a power that can penetrate into the most private spheres of life.

The Broad View of State Sovereignty

Realists in international relations define sovereignty in terms of states, whether these states are ancient or modern, but it is not difficult to see that state sovereignty is a problematic concept, however the state is defined.

James's theory of state sovereignty is a case in point. James (1986) regards sovereignty as an attribute of any state, ancient or modern, and defines it as a state's legal claim to constitutional independence. Sovereignty, James argues, is a formal attribute: a state is sovereign no matter how much it may in practice be beholden to the will of other states. However, his argument comes to grief over the question of identifying sovereignty in situations when it is explicitly contested.

James contends that sovereignty expresses a legal, not a physical reality. Yet this position is contradicted by the position he takes on Rhodesia (today, Zimbabwe). In 1965 Ian Smith, a right wing white Rhodesian leader, declared a 'unilateral declaration of independence' to prevent Britain from pushing the country into some kind of majority rule. However, James argues that the Smith regime was a sovereign state, even though it came about in what he concedes was an unlawful manner. What is the basis for arguing that the Smith rebel regime was sovereign? Because, James tells us, it was able to keep its enemies at bay – to defend itself through force of arms.

This implies that it is not legality that ultimately counts but physical effectiveness. In another of James's examples, he argues that the country Biafra (which broke away from Federal Nigeria in the late 1960s) did not become a sovereign state because it was defeated by the superior strength of the federal state of Nigeria (after a long and bloody civil war). James makes it clear that sovereignty is ultimately the capacity of a state to impose its will through force. But if this is what sovereignty is, then it suffers from the same problem that afflicts states in general: the problem of asserting a monopoly that it does not have. James speaks of sovereignty as a statist effectiveness that rests upon 'a significant congruence between the decisions of those who purport to rule and the actual behaviour of their alleged subjects' (Hoffman, 1998: 27–9). But this congruence, in the case of Smith's Rhodesia – a state that only lasted 14 years – was met with massive resistance from those who challenged this sovereignty and sought to achieve a sovereignty of their own.

In other words, the supposedly absolute and illimitable will is shared with wills that have a power of their own. State sovereignty is as illogical and problematic as the state itself.

Rescuing the Idea of Sovereignty

The idea of sovereignty is too important to be chewed to pieces by those who embrace the concept of the state uncritically. We will suggest a way in which the notion can be reinstated without the problems that inhere in the state.

The classical liberals saw individuals as sovereign, and they were right to do so. The problem with classical liberals is that they assumed that individuals could enjoy their supreme power in complete isolation from one another, and indeed, for this reason, depicted individuals as living initially in a 'natural' condition outside of society. This assumption runs contrary to everything we know about individuals. The individual who has not been 'socialised' cannot speak or think, and certainly cannot identify themselves as an individual! Individuals acquire their identity through their relations with others – they are social beings. Our life develops through an infinity of relationships – with parents, friends, teachers, and more abstractly, with people we read about or see and hear on the media.

Sovereignty is an attribute which individuals enjoy, and which enables us to govern our own lives. This definition frees sovereignty from the problems that blight it when it is linked to the state. Not only is the search for self-government developed in our relations with others, but it involves an infinite capacity to order our own lives. We aspire to sovereignty, but we never reach a situation in which we can say that no further progress towards sovereignty is possible. The fact that sovereignty is individual does not mean that it is not organisational, for individuals work in multiple associations at every level – the local, regional, national and global. Each of these helps us to develop our sovereignty – our capacity to govern our lives.

Ironically, therefore, the idea of state sovereignty gets in the way of individual sovereignty as we see from the way in which states often resist demands for the implementation of human rights on the grounds that they, states, should be entitled to treat their inhabitants as they see fit. The Chinese authorities object when their policies are criticised, and the American administration considers that it is entitled to continue incarcerating prisoners in Guantanamo Bay. When we define sovereignty as self-government, we place the rights of humans above the power of the state, and argue that only by locating sovereignty in the individual can it become consistent and defensible as a concept.

Moving to a Stateless World

Why are most people so sceptical about the possibility of a world without the state? Part of the reason, it could be argued, is that people think of government as the same as the state, but if we make a sharp distinction (as we have above) between government and the state, then it can be seen that a stateless society is not a society without government, but rather a society in which an institution claiming a monopoly of legitimate force becomes redundant. What prevents this from happening?

People, it seems to us, can settle their conflicts of interest through moral and social pressures where they have a common interest with their opponents: when they can, in other words, imagine what it is like to be 'the other'. This does not mean that people have to be the same in every regard. On the contrary, people are all different, and these **differences** are the source of conflict. Still it does not follow that because people are different and have conflicting interests, they cannot negotiate and compromise in settling these conflicts. It is only when they cannot do this that force becomes inevitable, and even if this force begins outside the state, the state will soon be involved, since the state claims a monopoly of legitimate force, and is concerned (quite rightly) about the force of private individuals. We are not, therefore, suggesting that we should not have a state in situations where people resort to force to tackle their conflicts.

However, instead of taking this force for granted, as though it was part and parcel of 'human nature' (as Hobbes does), it could be argued that force arises where people lack what we have called common interests. Policies that cement and reinforce common interests help to make government work. There is a case for resorting to force where this is the only way of implementing policies that will strengthen common interests. The debate around the war in Iraq revolved around the question as to whether the use of force, in the form of a war, was the only way to defeat Saddam Hussein's regime, and whether the use of force could lead to a democratic reconstruction of the country.

It is true that force can never really be legitimate since it necessarily deprives those whom it targets of their freedom, but it can be justifiably used if it is the only way to provide a breathing space for policies that will cement common interests. For example, it could prove impossible to involve residents in running their own lives on a rundown housing estate, until force has been used to stop gangs from intimidating ordinary people.

In early tribal societies, conflicts of interest were settled through moral and social pressures. This historical reality is a huge resource for pursuing the argument that it is possible to find ways of bringing about order that dispense altogether with the use of the state. Max Weber's definition has implications that he himself did not see. When he read that Leon Trotsky had said that 'every state is founded on force', he commented 'That indeed is right' (Gerth and Wright Mills, 1991: 78). But in making this endorsement, Weber had not committed himself to Trotsky's Marxist analysis of politics. In the same way, we find Weber's definition immensely useful, even though we see implications in the definition of which Weber himself would not have approved.

Moreover, it is not only tribal societies in the dim and distant past that were stateless. It is now over two decades since Hedley Bull (1977) noted the 'awkward facts' confronting a state-centric view of the world. These awkward facts embrace:

- the increasing importance of international law as a body of rules which has no wider monopoly of legitimate force to impose it;
- the globalisation of the economy which makes the notion of autonomous state sovereignty peculiarly archaic; and
- a growing number of issues – Bull mentioned the environment in particular – which can only be settled through acknowledging the common interests of contending parties.

This is why Bull characterised the international order as an 'anarchical society', and it is clear that developments of the kind noted above mean that statist solutions are becoming ever more dangerous as a mode of resolving conflicts. The increasing degree of interdependence that characterises both domestic and international society makes the resort to force (the chosen and distinctive instrument of the state) increasingly counterproductive. The fact that criminal individuals like criminal states are also the beneficiaries of a technology of violence (whose sophistication escalates all the time) means that if we want a secure future, it is vital that we learn how to settle differences without the use of force, i.e. in a stateless manner.

As we will demonstrate in a later chapter, anarchists also wish to do away with the state, but they seek to abolish it rather than see it wither away, and they usually reject the kind of distinctions that appear in this chapter – the distinction between state and government, force and constraint.

The State

The state is often identified with civilisation, and it is easy to see why the state has such a profound impact upon our thought. Conventional religion depicts God as a sovereign overlord, and classical political thinkers like Hobbes and Rousseau assumed that without a conception of God, no state would be possible. It is also very tempting to translate contemporary concerns into a frozen notion of human nature as though how people behave in, for example, Britain today, represents the nature of humankind. Moreover, where people do resort to force to tackle their conflicts, a world without the state makes a bad situation even worse, and it would hardly be an advantage to do away with the state, if the alternative was rule by warlords or the Mafia. Yet it is ultimately an illusion to think that we can do away with force by resorting to the state, for what could be called a 'statist' mentality assumes that violent people are inexplicably evil. We cannot understand them; we can only crush them. The statist mentality never asks the question 'why'. Why are people so brutalised that they resort to force? Of course, it is no help to merely invert the idea that people are evil so that we consider them to be naturally 'good' instead. Pacifists naively suppose that brutalised people or states will respond to moral pressures in a purely moral way, and anarchists fail to see that in conditions where force can be dispensed with, we still need government to regulate social affairs. Firmness and rules are actually undermined by the use of force, since force encourages us to ignore complexities and not try and imagine what it is like to be in the shoes of another. The fact that the state remains hugely influential in our lives does not mean that we should not start thinking about ways and means of living without it.

Globalisation and the State

Hyper-globalists are those who argue that the notion of the nation-state disappears under the cut and thrust of the free market. They are called hyper-globalists (by their critics) because it is felt that they take a naive and extreme view of the growing internationalisation of the economy and society.

Take the arguments of Kenneth Ohmae, for example. Ohmae argues that the nation-state has become 'a nostalgic fiction' (1995: 12) in the face of the global market. Ohmae rests his case on what he calls the 'Californisation' of taste and preference. There is a ladder of economic development, he contends, upon which more and more societies climb, reaching the US$5,000 threshold of per capita development. The spread of information-related technology is infectious and Adam Smith's invisible hand now works in a global context.

This is a neoliberal or free-market argument which is starkly inegalitarian and is hostile to democracy. Ohmae argues that the rules of electoral logic and popular expectations lead to general, indirect long-term benefits being sacrificed in favour of immediate, tangible and focused pay-offs (1995: 42). The tyranny of modern democracy, as he calls it, seeks an **equality** of results, not of contributions (1995: 53). What he refers to as the 'civil minimum' is like a drug and takes the form of broad-based social programmes, welfare, unemployment compensation, public education, old-age pensions and health insurance. Established political systems have become the creature of special interests and the poorer districts. Whereas the nation-state solution assumes a zero-sum game for limited resources, the region state model, he argues, open to the global economy, is a 'plus sum' as prosperity is brought in from without (Ohmae, 1995: 55, 57, 62).

Yet Ohmae notes that huge disparities have opened up – disparities measured by a factor of 20 or more – between inland and coastal regions in countries like China. He concedes that the gap between the developed and developing world has substantially widened. Despite his defence of the 'trickle-down' effect – that the poor ultimately benefit from the prosperity of the rich – he is not only hostile to democracy, but his argument is basically state-centric throughout. States are seen as having an unproblematic sovereignty, the European Union is described as a 'supernation state', and those worried about the most economically backward areas of the world are regarded as defending 'vested interests' that get in the way of global logic. Besides, regional states are seen as states that constitute 'natural economic zones' (1995: 80).

It is clear that if so-called **globalisation** aggravates and deepens inequalities in the world, then this will generate wars, fundamentalism and, of course, the need for states. John Gray takes the view that economic liberalisation and religious fundamentalism go together (1998: 103). Globalisation can only weaken the state if it cements common interests and allows conflicts of interest to be subject to governmental sanctions.

The Case for Global Government

If globalisation is to be positively conceived – as an opportunity rather than as a source of violence and division – then it is crucial that we see free market fundamentalism and the abstract similarity that it seeks to impose as a distortion of globalisation. If by globalisation we mean a sense of interconnectedness between the peoples of the world, then we must distinguish between this and 'Americanisation' which inevitably creates a fundamentalist reaction.

Globalisation is a cultural and political as well as an economic phenomenon. It is not simply that states are losing economic power: their claim to impose a monopolistic outlook is being more and more openly challenged both within and between societies. We need to be clear that the case for global government is not a case for a global state. If we are moving, as Barry Jones supposes, to a world of 'complex, multi-layered' public governance (2000: 270), then it is crucial that we challenge the view that diversity is the same as fragmentation. States will remain for the foreseeable future, and the case for global government is one in which states become less important and increasingly devote their energies to governmental activities, thus gradually transcending themselves. The problem with Kant's argument for perpetual peace is that it rests upon a liberal republican notion of a federation of states – whereas what is required is the development of global identities that go beyond the state.

It is important not only to democratise the United Nations (UN), but in so doing to challenge the arguments of those who see the UN Charter as bestowing a kind of state sovereignty on the Security Council and the General Council. International law is already a stateless law, and it is vital to strengthen the common interest that makes it enforceable. The problem is that the UN is an organisation with two souls. The one is certainly globalist in scope since the Preamble to the Charter refers to the existence of universal human rights and Article 1 speaks of the universal peace for the peoples of the world based on self-determination. Article 2, however, speaks of sovereign equality for member states with Article 2(7) declaring that no intervention is allowed in the domestic jurisdiction of any state. Many have sought unsuccessfully to tackle the unrepresentative character of the Security Council. Pressure needs to grow on the UN to boost its peacekeeping role and its post-statal activities where the plight of children, the spread of disease and problems of development are tackled imaginatively and effectively.

In the same way, the European Union has two souls – the market and democracy. The one can be particularist and short-termist, but the other is empowering and has tremendous potential – as in the concept of European citizenship that offers a wider identity, not in competition with but as a supplement to, state identity. A global civil society is also developing around non-governmental organisations (NGOs), which could be better called non-statist organisations, given the fact that NGOs within and between countries act in ways that help to cement common interests. NGOs like the World Wildlife Fund, Amnesty International, Oxfam, Human Rights Watch and Christian Aid support a concept of order that stresses resource provision rather than military action. Organisations like Amnesty International confront national governments with transgressions of the UN Charter. It is true that some of the 29,000 NGOs suffer from problems of bureaucracy and authoritarianism, but they are becoming increasingly influential and they do represent proof that organisations can tackle problems without claiming to exercise a monopoly of legitimate force. They are no substitute for coordinated, collective global action to tackle the problem of global inequality but they do make a significant practical and theoretical contribution to the question of global government.

Globalisation has demonstrated that humans face problems of a global kind and that global institutions have to be forged which, in conjunction with local, regional and national governments, are able to contribute positively to a world that recognises difference, but works against division.

Summary

The state is seen by some theorists as a modern institution that has, as its identifying features, a sharp separation of the public from the private; a capacity to exercise sovereignty throughout its domain and protect all who live in its territory; an ability to organise its offices along bureaucratic rather than patrimonial lines, and to extract tax revenues from its population.

The state can be defined in a way that sees its central attribute as the exercise of legitimate force; is based upon morality, or a mixture of the two. When it is defined in a way that stresses the importance of force, then it can be argued that modern states are crucially different from pre-modern states, but like all states, they claim to exercise a monopoly of legitimate force.

Three bodies of argument contend that politics is best identified without using the concept of the state. Behaviouralists argue that the state as a concept is too ambiguous and ideological to be useful, and the notion of a political system is preferable; linguistic analysts see the idea of the state as a practical institution rather than a coherent philosophical concept, while radicals argue that the notion of the state gets in the way of a pluralist and participatory politics.

The problem, however, is that the state does not simply disappear simply because it is not defined. The contradictory nature of the institution can only be exposed if we define it, and the definition of the state as an institution claiming a monopoly of legitimate force makes it possible to underline the state's problematic character.

The contradictory character of the state also undermines the notion of state sovereignty. Sovereignty can only be coherently defined as the capacity of individuals to govern their own lives. Globalisation is only positive if it recognises differences between countries, and works to reduce disparities so that the development of a global government becomes a realistic possibility.

Questions

1. Do you agree with the argument that the state is essentially a modern institution?
2. What is the best way of defining the state?
3. Is it possible to differentiate government from the state, and if so, how?
4. Do you see the notion of state sovereignty as irrelevant in the contemporary world?
5. Why do people physically harm one another?

References

Allen, J. (1990) 'Does Feminism Need a Theory of the State?' in S. Watson (ed.), *Playing the State* London: Verso, 21–37.

Ashley, R. (1988) 'Untying the Sovereign State: a Double Reading of the Anarchy Problematique', *Millennium* 17(2), 227–62.

Barry Jones, R. (2000) *The World Turned Upside Down* Manchester and New York: Manchester University Press.

Bentley, A. (1967) *The Process of Government* Cambridge, MA: Belknap, Harvard University Press.

Bull, H. (1977) *The Anarchical Society* Basingstoke: Macmillan.

Dahl, R. (1976) *Modern Political Analysis* 3rd edn Englewood Cliffs, NJ: Prentice-Hall.

Dunleavy, P. and O'Leary, B. (1987) *Theories of the State* London and Basingstoke: Macmillan.

Easton, D. (1965) *A Framework for Political Analysis* Englewood Cliffs, NJ: Prentice-Hall.

Easton, D. (1971) *The Political System* 2nd edn New York: Alfred Knopf.

Easton D. (1981) 'The Political System Besieged by the State' *Political Theory* 9, 203–25.

Easton, D. (1990) *An Analysis of Political Structure* New York and London: Routledge.

Forsyth, M. (1987) 'The State' in D. Miller (ed.), *The Blackwell Encyclopaedia of Political Thought* Oxford: Basil Blackwell, 503–6.

Gerth, H. and Wright Mills, C. (1991) *From Max Weber* London: Routledge.

Gramsci, A. (1971) *Selections from the Prison Notebooks* London: Lawrence and Wishart.

Gray J. (1998) *False Dawn* London: Granta.

Green, T.H. (1941) *The Principles of Political Obligation* London, New York and Toronto: Longmans, Green & Co.

Hamlin, A. and Pettit, P. (1989) 'The Normative Analysis of the State: Some Preliminaries' in A. Hamlin and P. Pettit (eds), *The Good Polity* Oxford: Basil Blackwell, 1–13.

Hegel, G. (1956) *The Philosophy of History* New York: Dover.

Hinsley, F.H. (1986) *Sovereignty* Cambridge: Cambridge University Press.

Hoffman, J. (1995) *Beyond the State* Cambridge: Polity Press.

Hoffman, J. (1996) 'Antonio Gramsci: The Prison Notebooks' in M. Forsyth and M. Keens-Soper (eds), *The Political Classics: Green to Dworkin* Oxford: Oxford University Press, 58–77.

Hoffman, J. (1998) *Sovereignty* Buckingham: Open University Press.

James, A. (1986) *Sovereign Statehood* London: Allen and Unwin.

Machiavelli, N. (1998) *The Prince* Oxford: Oxford University Press.

Mann, M. (1980) 'The Pre-industrial State', *Political Studies* 28, 297–304.

Marx K. and Engels, F. (1976) *Collected Works* vol. 5, London: Lawrence and Wishart.

Ohmae, K. (1995) *The End of the Nation-State* New York: Free Press

Pringle, R. and Watson, S. (1992) 'Women's Interests and the Post-Structural State' in M. Barrett and A. Phillips (eds), *Destabilizing Theory* Cambridge: Polity Press, 53–73.

Rosenberg, J. (1994) *The Empire of Civil Society* London: Verso.

Vincent, A. (1987) *Theories of the State* Oxford: Blackwell.

Weldon, T. (1953) *The Vocabulary of Politics* Harmondsworth: Penguin.

Further Reading

- Bhikhu Parekh's essay *When will the State Wither Away* is a thoughtful and accessible presentation on the state as a modern institution.

- John Hoffman's *Beyond the State* (referenced above) deals with the way in which different traditions have approached the state, and makes the case for the kind of conceptual distinctions need to provide an effective critique.

- Alan James *Sovereign Statehood* (referenced above) provides a clear defence of a traditional view of sovereignty with an attempt to sort out the confusions that the concept generates.

- David Easton's *The Political System* (referenced above) makes the classic case against the state and the need to conceptualise politics as a system rather than a set of institutions.

- Hedley Bull's *The Anarchical Society* (referenced above) seeks to argue that international society is a stateless order and yet there is order. An ingenious and extremely interesting text.

- Bernard Crick's *In Defence of Politics* (Harmondsworth: Penguin, 1964) (and subsequent editions) offers a very interesting first chapter on the nature of political rule, and what he sees as distinctive about the political process.

- Adrian Leftwich's edited volume, *What is Politics?* (Cambridge: Polity, 2004) (2nd edn) contains a very useful and thought-provoking Chapter 3 on the question of 'Politics and Force' by Peter Nicholson.

- Colin Hay, Michael Lister and David Marsh have edited a most useful volume, *The State* Basingstoke: Palgrave, (2006) Chapter 9 by David Marsh, Nicola Smith and Nicola Hothi is entitled 'Globalization and the State'.

Weblinks

http://www.keele.ac.uk/depts/po/prs.htm
http://www.york.ac.uk/services/library/subjects/politint.htm

Chapter 2

Freedom

Introduction

Freedom is regarded by many as the pre-eminent political value, but what does it mean to be free? Do we have to justify freedom, or do it we take it as axiomatic that we should be free, and that it is *restrictions* on freedom which require justification? And what are those justifications? If we go into the street and survey people's attitudes to freedom, we might find that they favour the freedom to do things of which they approve, but would like the state to use its power to restrict freedom to do things of which they disapprove. Is there then a *principled* way to establish what we should be free to do? At the core of freedom is the idea of 'choice', but can we choose to do anything we want?

Chapter Map

In this chapter we will:

- Provide a working definition of freedom.

- Outline one of the most important contributions to the debate over freedom – that advanced by John Stuart Mill in his book *On Liberty* – and use Mill's argument as a framework for discussing other perspectives on freedom.

- More specifically, we will consider the distinction between action and expression; harm-to-self and harm-to-others; and offensive (the offence principle) and legal moralism.

- Illustrate arguments over freedom through the use of case studies, and, in particular, the ban on smoking in enclosed public spaces.

Smoking in the Last Chance Saloon?

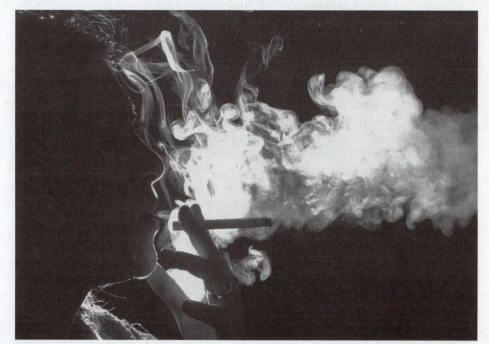

More and more cities, provinces and countries are adopting restrictions, and complete bans, on smoking in enclosed public places. Most attention has focused on bars and restaurants, but the prohibitions extend much further. In March 2004 the Republic of Ireland became the first to institute a nationwide ban, although state and city bans had already been introduced in the United States. Since 2004 there has been an astonishing acceleration in the rate at which such bans have been introduced. As of 2008 legal restrictions on smoking in public places in some form exist in (among others) Albania, Argentina (Buenos Aires), most Australian states, Belgium, Bosnia-Herzegovina, Brazil, Britain, most Canadian provinces, Chile, China (Guangzhou and Jiangmen), Cuba, Denmark, Estonia, France, Germany, Iceland, India, Italy, Kazakhstan, Lithuania, Malta, Montenegro, Netherlands, New Zealand, Norway, Portugal, Singapore, Slovenia, and Turkey. Some jurisdictions have opted to allow smoking in self-contained smoking areas of bars. Most countries permit smoking in prison cells and hotel rooms, so long as non-smokers can choose not to use them, and manufacturers of outdoor heaters have benefitted hugely as most countries permit smoking in designated outdoor areas. There are some oddities: Belgium permits smoking in bars that serve 'light meals' and derive no more than 30 per cent of their sales from food, whereas England toyed with – but ultimately rejected – the possibility of permitting smoking in bars that did not serve food.

At the end of this chapter we will apply the arguments advanced through the course of the chapter to the smoking ban, but before tackling the rest of the chapter it would useful to consider your own reactions to the ban: are such bans justified? Can you think of arguments against a smoking ban? Is it possible to develop a position midway between no significant regulation of smoking in enclosed public places and a complete ban? Alternatively, should the prohibition on smoking be extended to all public places, and even to private homes – in short, should the sale and use of tobacco be made illegal?

Berlin's Two Concepts

The starting point for many, although not all, political theorists is what can be termed *the presumption in favour of freedom*. That is, we assume people ought to be free unless there are compelling reasons for restricting their freedom. This argument is not uncontroversial, for it presupposes there is a conception of freedom that is pre-political – that is, exists prior to the formation of the state, even if we rely on the state to *protect* our freedom. However, we will – for the purposes of the discussion – assume it makes sense to talk of a pre-political freedom. The discussion then focuses on the legitimate limits to freedom. Here we face a conceptual problem: can we agree on a single concept of freedom (even if we disagree about which freedoms matter or more generally about the value of freedom)? The most influential contribution to this debate was provided by Isaiah Berlin in his famous essay 'Two Concepts of Liberty'.

Acknowledging that in the history of political thought there have been more than two concepts of freedom, Berlin maintains that 'negative liberty' and 'positive liberty' have had the greatest influence, and the contrast between them throws into relief fundamental differences about the role of the state:

- *Negative liberty* is involved in the answer to the question: 'what is the area within which the subject – a person or group of persons – is or should be left to do or be what he is able to do or be, without interference by other persons?' (Berlin, 1991: 121–2)
- *Positive liberty* is involved in the answer to the question: 'what, or who, is the source of control or interference that can determine someone to do, or be, this rather than that?' (1991: 122).

So, negative liberty is about being left alone, whereas positive liberty is about being in control of one's life. For example, a person may be unfree to leave her home because she is under 'house arrest'; alternatively, she may be unfree to leave because she has a phobia that makes her fearful of leaving. In the first case, she is negatively unfree to leave, whereas in the second she is positively unfree. Of course, elements of both types of 'unfreedom' may be evident: she may be fearful about leaving her home because she suspects she is under surveillance and that she is at greater harm away from home. Perhaps she is slightly paranoid, but if that paranoia has been caused by actual past experience, then the source of the unfreedom, or 'control', is not straightforwardly internal or external. Even if we cannot determine the source of unfreedom we can still make an analytical distinction between such sources, and therefore also between positive and negative freedom.

Berlin was hostile to the concept of positive liberty. He thought it implied a belief in psychological sources of unfreedom concealed from the person who is deemed unfree – this belief forms the basis of a political theory in which people are 'forced to be free'. Although he identifies the presence of the concept in the work of a long line of thinkers we can take the work of one as representative of positive liberty: Immanuel Kant. Kant defines freedom as self-government or self-direction: to be free is to act from laws (or reasons) that one gives oneself. The self is split in two – or bifurcated – meaning that each of us possesses a lower self driven by desires, and a higher self that is motivated by reasons that transcend desire. A 'reason' is something categorical: one can have a reason to do something that one has no desire to do. For example, if you plan to spend six months in Italy one year from now and at present speak no Italian you have have *reason* to enrol now in an Italian class even if you have no *desire* to do so (Nagel, 1970: 58–9). Of course, a rational person will desire to enrol in that class but the point is that the reason is not explained by the desire, but rather the desire follows from the reason. For Kant, the rational is not something political, but Berlin sees in Kant's conception of freedom the danger that the 'rational' will become identified with the state, for if your desires are not a guide to what you should do then perhaps another agency – the state – can help you achieve 'true freedom'.

Some political theorists have sought to dispense with Berlin's two concepts and argue for one. Gerald MacCallum suggests that 'freedom is . . . always *of* something (an agent or agents), *from* something, *to* do, not do, become, or not become something' (MacCallum, 1991: 102). Freedom is therefore a 'triadic' relationship – meaning, there are three parts to it: (a) the agent, or person, who is free (or 'unfree'); (b) the constraints, restrictions, interferences and barriers that make the agent free or unfree, and (c) what it is that the person is free to do, or not do. It is important that (c) means a person is free to do *or* not do something – that is, they have a *choice*: an inmate of a jail is not prevented from residing in that jail, but has no choice whether or not they reside there. MacCallum's definition is useful, but it leaves open a couple of important issues. First, what is the source of (b)? Must it be another person (or persons) who constrains or restricts your action? Could the source of your unfreedom be yourself – that is, your own weaknesses and irrationality? Second, some things are trivial – is your freedom to watch inane daytime television as valuable as your freedom to study challenging poetry? The difficulty with MacCallum's concept is not so much that it is wrong, but that it is uninformative, or even banal. Even if the triadic framework can be applied to all instances of freedom the most interesting political questions are about the nature of the agent who is free or unfree, the source of that agent's (un)freedom, and what it is that the agent is free or not free to do. For this reason, despite MacCallum's attempt to transcend the distinction, Berlin's two concepts of liberty remain important.

Unfreedom versus Inability

Human physiology combined with the laws of gravity make it impossible for human beings to fly unaided. Does that mean that human beings are not free – as distinct from unable – to fly? This is an important political question because some social conditions are attributed to inability rather than unfreedom. David Miller provides a useful scheme for distinguishing unfreedom and inability. He asks us to imagine a room the door to which can only be opened from the outside and to consider six ways in which you might be trapped in the room (Miller, 1983: 70–1):

1. Person Y, knowing you are in the room, pushes the door shut. For Miller this is an unproblematic case of unfreedom, as you are prevented from leaving by the deliberate act of another agent.

2. Person Y, not knowing you are inside, pushes the door shut. This case is more problematic, but still a case of unfreedom – Y does not intend to imprison you, but he is negligent, and so you are unfree.

3. The wind blows the door shut. Y is supposed to check the room at 7 p.m. each evening, but fails to do so on this evening. You are unfree to leave *from 7 p.m.*

4. The wind blows the door shut. At 6.30 p.m. you call to a passer-by X to unlock the door, but X, who knows Y's duties, is busy and pays no attention. In this case X is causally, but not morally, responsible for your confinement from 6.30 p.m. to 7 p.m.

5. Y, whose job it is to check rooms, comes to your room, and looks around it. You have concealed yourself in a cupboard and Y closes the door without having seen you. In contrast to the second scenario Y here took all reasonable precautions and so this cannot be described is a situation in which you are unfree, even though you are unable to leave.

6. The wind blows the door shut. There is no one assigned to check rooms, and no passer-by within earshot. This situation is, for Miller, unproblematic – the cause of your imprisonment is entirely the result of natural causes, thus you are unable to leave but not unfree to leave.

It is clear that for Miller – and for many other political theorists – freedom is interpersonal: not only must unfreedom be attributed to the actions of other agents, but personal responsibility also plays a role. If you are simply unable to do something then this cannot be described as a case of unfreedom unless that inability can be sourced to other people. When we move away from the highly artificial example used above and consider social and economic phenomena such as wealth distribution or unemployment it can be difficult directly to attribute a person's situation – being rich or poor, in or out of work – to the actions of others. This is a problem to which we return in Chapters 3 (Equality) and 4 (Justice).

Mill on Freedom

Mill's essay *On Liberty* has been hugely influential in discussions of political freedom. As well as being important in its own right it also provides the framework for a broader discussion of freedom: it is through that framework that we can explore alternatives to Mill.

On Liberty has to be located in Mill's broader philosophical project: grounding political principles in a utilitarian moral theory. Utilitarianism is a form of consequentialism, meaning that we assess the validity of political principles or institutions by the extent to which they bring about good consequences. In Mill's words:

> Utility, or the Greatest Happiness Principle, holds that actions are right in proportion as they tend to promote happiness, wrong as they tend to produce the reverse of happiness.

> By happiness is intended pleasure, and the absence of pain; by unhappiness, pain, and the privation of pleasure (Mill, 1991: 137).

Mill's definition of 'utility' is ambiguous, for pleasure and happiness are not identical. Elsewhere he contrasts satisfaction and happiness: 'better to be a human dissatisfied than a pig satisfied; better to be Socrates dissatisfied than a fool satisfied' (Mill, 1991: 140). Underlying this distinction is a concern with quality as well as quantity. The quality/quantity distinction and the idea of maximisation generates problems for Mill's defence of freedom. The deep, underlying justification for freedom is that it is the means by which the Greatest Happiness Principle is most effectively advanced, but this is an empirical claim: what if freedom were shown to make people unhappy? Would that not justify restricting freedom? Furthermore, if it is a certain kind of pleasure that matters – the 'higher pleasures' – then why not force people to cultivate those pleasures? These problems become more acute if we interpret Mill as primarily a theorist of negative liberty – although as we will see there is also a positive conception of liberty present in his work. His statement of negative liberty is encapsulated in his famous 'harm principle':

> the sole end for which mankind are warranted, individually or collectively, in interfering with the liberty of action of any of their number, is self-protection. [. . .] The only purpose for which power can be rightfully exercised over any member of a civilized community, against his will, is to prevent harm to others. His own good, either physical or moral, is not a sufficient warrant (Mill, 1991: 14).

Mill goes on to clarify to whom the harm principle applies. A number of points of clarification can be made about the harm principle (we will address criticisms later):

1. Mill's aim is to establish what rights people should have by determining when it is legitimate to interfere with their actions – the harm principle amounts to this: only *non-consensual* harm to others is a ground for limiting a person's liberty.
2. Mill rejects paternalism – people should not be protected against themselves (note the last sentence of the quotation).
3. A standard criticism of the harm principle is that all actions affect other people and there are very few purely 'self-regarding actions' – even knowing that things are going on of which you disapprove could count as 'harmful'. To counter this objection Mill must clarify what is meant by harm, and he does so by arguing that it is harm to a person's fundamental interests.
4. To say that only non-consensual harm to others is a ground for limiting a person's freedom does not entail saying that every non-consensual harm should be outlawed. The person you kill in self-defence is certainly harmed and has not consented, but you are justified in taking his life.
5. The harm principle does not apply to children – nor to 'uncivilized peoples' – clearly, we do need an account of children's rights, but it may require a much more complex theory.

Underpinning the harm principle is a certain conception of what it means to live a properly human life, as distinct from a merely animal existence. To be human is to enjoy a sphere in which one is able to think, express ideas, and lead a lifestyle of one's own choosing.

Freedom of Thought and Expression

Even if a person finds himself alone in expressing an opinion he should, according to Mill, be free to express it: 'if all mankind, minus one, were of one opinion, and only one person were of the contrary opinion, mankind would no more be justified in silencing that one person, than he, if he had the power, would be justified in silencing mankind' (Mill, 1991: 21). Mill has a neat defence of this claim. First, if the opinion is true then by suppressing it humanity is deprived of the truth and will not progress. Second, if the opinion is false then humanity again loses, because if the opinion is false it will be shown to be so, but its expression is useful, for it forces us to restate the reasons for our beliefs. A competition of ideas is healthy (1991: 21). Third, the truth is often 'eclectic' (1991: 52). This argument is frequently misunderstood. It can mean: (a) an opinion can be broken down into a number of discrete claims, some of which are true and some false; (b) the conclusion of an argument might be correct and the premises sound, but the conclusion does not follow from the premises; (c) two conflicting arguments may require a third argument to resolve the conflict between them. What Mill did *not* mean by eclecticism was that the truth is subjective. Such a claim would undermine the fundamental basis of his defence of freedom of expression, which is that it is the means by which truth is advanced.

People who seek to suppress an opinion assume their own beliefs are infallible; they confuse *their* certainty with *absolute* certainty. Mill accepts that people must make decisions and act on them, and those decisions are based on beliefs. It would, for example, be irrational for you to jump off the edge of a cliff if that action were motivated by a belief that you could fly unaided; a rational person is guided by a belief in the law of gravity. However, Mill distinguishes holding a belief to be certain, and not permitting others to refute it – people should be free to question the law of gravity, and this is consistent with the rest of us acting as if the law were true.

Mill's defence of freedom of expression is paradoxical. While it is a good thing for people to express different and conflicting opinions, the basic justification is that truth is advanced in the competition of ideas. This assumes that there is a truth (or set of truths), and the pursuit of that truth establishes an end for humankind. The implication is that as we progress false beliefs lose their power over us, and we increasingly come to hold the same true beliefs. What Mill fears is that as a result of this process the beneficial aspects of the expression of false beliefs will be lost: 'both teachers and learners go to sleep at their post, as soon as there is no enemy in the field' (1991: 48). This suggests a distinction between the prevalence of true beliefs, and how human beings hold those beliefs; it is essential that we understand the reasons for our beliefs, otherwise the belief becomes 'dead dogma'.

Finally, although there is a distinction between freedom of action and freedom of expression, the line between them is fuzzy: some forms of expression are very close to action. A person 'must not make himself a nuisance to other people' (1991: 55). And Mill goes on to argue that:

> an opinion that corn dealers* are starvers of the poor, or that private property is robbery, ought to be unmolested when simply circulated through the press, but

---

*One of the major debates of the nineteenth century was over free trade versus protectionism, especially in foodstuffs; corn dealers controlled the price of corn and kept it high, relative to its free trade price, and so were deeply unpopular people.

may justly incur punishment when delivered orally to an excited mob assembled before the house of a corn dealer, or when handed about among the same mob in the form of a placard (1991: 55).

There is a close causal relationship here between speech and action. It might be argued against Mill that incitement should be defined more widely: for example, in 2000 the British newspaper *News of the World* published the names and photographs of a number of sexual offenders – that is, those who had criminal records for sexual offences – with a view to naming all sexual offenders, and even publishing addresses. It would be difficult not to deem the newspaper's campaign to be one of incitement to violence. More problematic is the notion used in English law of incitement to *hatred*, as distinct from violence: libertarians argue that to prohibit incitement to hatred amounts to censuring an attitude rather than an action (see Hurd, 2001).

Freedom of Action

In Chapter 3 of *On Liberty* Mill discusses freedom of action and lifestyle. While acknowledging that 'no one pretends that actions should be as free as opinions' (1991: 62) Mill claims the same reasons which show an opinion should be free demonstrate that an individual should be free to put his opinions into practice, even if the action is foolish. The only constraint is that the agent should not harm others. Some doubts can be raised as to whether freedom of expression and freedom of action really do rest on the same arguments, but for the moment we will follow the course of Mill's argument.

In discussing freedom of action, Mill introduces a concept not used in the discussion of expression: *individuality*. He regards individuality as 'one of the principal ingredients of human happiness' (1991: 63), and so it is linked to the well-being of society. The development of individuality requires two things: freedom and a 'variety of situations' (1991: 64). Although children need to be guided by those who have had experience of life, adults must be free to develop their own lifestyle and values, and not be subject to *custom*. The word custom can be defined as accumulated, shared and often taken-for-granted experiences. Mill criticises custom. First, experience may be too narrow, and wrongly interpreted. Second, other people's experiences may not be relevant to you, given *your* character and *your* experiences. Third, the custom may be 'good', but to conform to it as custom 'does not educate or develop . . . any of the qualities which are the distinctive endowment of the human being' (1991: 65). People need to make choices, and following custom is an evasion of choice. Following custom is analogous to holding beliefs without understanding the reasons for those beliefs.

At the heart of the notion of individuality is *originality*. To be original is to bring something into the world; this need not be a creation out of nothing, and it is quite possible that other people have thought the same thoughts and performed the same actions. Nor indeed must an action be uninfluenced by others; what makes an action original is that a person consciously sets themself against custom and thinks for themself. Originality is most likely to take a 'synthetic' form, that is, originality is demonstrated in the ability to produce something new through the synthesis of diverse experiences and reflections. It serves a social function, for it provides role models for those who, by character or inclination, may be more timid about thinking or acting in ways not supported by custom. Those who are original are providing what Mill calls *experiments in living*, some of which may have bad, even disastrous, consequences, but taken together experiments are over time beneficial. The link between freedom of expression and freedom of action is clear: the original person is the 'one in a hundred' prepared to advance a heterodox belief, and the failed experiment parallels the false belief.

Mill rejects paternalism – that is, stopping people harming themselves. If a person starts to cross a footbridge, unaware that it is insecure and liable to collapse into the ravine below, if we cannot communicate with them – perhaps we do not share a language – then we can intervene (Mill, 1991: 106–7). If, however, they know the risk then we are *not* entitled to stop them (paternalism is discussed in greater detail in the section on Criticisms and Developments).

It should be stressed that we do not have to approve of other people's behaviour. If a person manifests a 'lowness or depravation of taste' we are, Mill argues, justified in making them a 'subject of distaste, or . . . even of contempt' (Mill, 1991: 85). What we are not justified in doing is interfering in their actions. There is a tension here between encouraging diversity of lifestyle as if it were an intrinsically good thing, but being free to disapprove of it. If diversity is to be *promoted* rather than merely *tolerated* then the state should not just protect people's freedom, but actually encourage a change in attitudes among the majority.

Criticisms and Developments

Mill's argument provides a useful framework for discussing the nature and limits of freedom. As we suggested at the beginning of this chapter many political theorists concerned with freedom presume freedom to be a good thing, and search for legitimate reasons for limiting it. Mill claims that only non-consensual harm to others can constitute a legitimate ground for limiting another person's freedom. But he may be wrong, and in the box below we present for consideration a number of additional 'freedom-limiting principles' alongside the non-consensual harm to others one.

Liberty-limiting principle:		Mill's view (YES: reason for restricting freedom; NO: not a reason)
Harm to others	Non-consensual	YES – only ground for restriction
	Consensual	NO
Harm to self (paternalism)		NO (argument is closely tied to the consent-to-be-harmed argument)
Offensiveness		NO (but Mill is not consistent)
Harmless wrongdoing *or* badness (these two are not the same)		NO: harmless wrongdoing is a contradiction in terms.

Using these four or (arguably five) principles we can both criticise Mill and consider alternative perspectives on freedom.

Harm to Others

We start with some general comments about Mill's harm principle, ignoring for the moment the distinction between consensual and non-consensual harm to others. The first, and rather obvious, objection to the harm principle is: what, in fact, constitutes harm? Surely every action has some effect – good or bad – on others?

Mill concedes that no person is an 'entirely isolated being' (Mill, 1991: 88) and almost all actions have remote consequences. If by harm we mean any bad effect another person's action may have then few actions would be purely self-regarding and it would be difficult to use harm as a criterion for restricting freedom at the same time as guaranteeing a significant sphere of freedom for the individual. Mill operates with a 'physicalist' rather than a 'psychological' definition of harm; if we were to expand the concept of harm beyond physical harm to the person (and his property) to include psychological harm then the private sphere in which a person would be free to act would be severely contracted.

Another kind of harm might be caused when a person sets a bad example: if Mill is going to appeal to the *good* consequences of 'experiments in living', he must surely accept that some experiments may also have *bad* consequences for other people. Part of Mill's response to this problem is to argue that you cannot have the benefits of freedom without also suffering the negative consequences. To try to determine what are good experiments in living and what are bad, and seek to restrict the latter is to prejudge what is good and bad, and it is precisely only in the competition of lifestyles that such a judgement can be made. The consequences of an action are always in the future, and so we cannot know those consequences *now* such that we can predict them.

The appeal to competing lifestyles is an important argument but it is quite different to a defence of freedom based on the possibility that many important actions are self-regarding and do not therefore harm others. To save the harm principle Mill must clarify what can count as harm. One option is to redefine harm as: having one's fundamental interests damaged such that one's life goes (significantly) less well than it would otherwise have gone. It could be added that in most circumstances the individual who is harmed should judge what is, or is not, in her interests – this raises the issue of consent, which is discussed in the next section. Obviously, this needs to be elaborated, but the point is that the threshold for deeming an action harmful is high; it cannot simply be an action which has negative effects on another person. This would rule out temporary discomfort caused by someone else's action. We might still want to attach some importance to temporary discomfort, but rather than call it harmful we call it offensive. If we do this then we need a different principle for judging something offensive – this principle is discussed in the section on Offensiveness.

Consent

Mill argues that people can consent to be harmed. Activities such as boxing or duelling, even though they carry the risk of considerable harm, and even death, must be free so long as the people concerned consented, and were capable of consent, where being 'capable' means being an adult. It might be objected that there is no necessary connection between harm and consent: if something is harmful to other people then we should be prevented from engaging in it. But if the state were justified in interfering in consensual, albeit harmful, activities between consenting adults then the space in which people could associate would be severely restricted. A legal case in England from the early 1990s is interesting. In 1990 a number of men were charged with 'assault occasioning actual bodily harm' (*R. v. Brown and Others* (1993); the arrest was codenamed 'Operation Spanner'). The men had engaged in a rather protracted session of sadomasochistic sexual activity, which, foolishly, they had filmed. Their defence – that they all consented – was dismissed by the court. The parallel of boxing was used as part of the defence: if two men can beat each other up, then why can they not get sexual pleasure from inflicting pain on each other? The judge argued that consent was a ground for harm but it had to be backed up by a justification of the activity itself, and the following were legitimate: surgery; a 'properly conducted game or sport'; tattooing and ear-piercing. On sport, Foster's *Crown Law* (1792) was cited: boxing and wrestling are 'manly diversions, they intend to give strength, skill and activity, and may fit people for defence, public as well as personal, in time of need'. The court deemed that consent was a necessary *but insufficient* ground for the action, and that the intrinsic qualities of the action could justify a restriction on the action. We return to this argument in the section on Harmless Wrongdoing.

Harm to Self – Paternalism

Consenting to be harmed amounts to harming oneself and raises the issue of whether the state ought to protect people against themselves – that is, whether the state should act *paternalistically*. For example, having an age of consent for various activities amounts to a judgement that a person – or group of people, such as children – are incapable of giving consent, or, at least, *informed* consent. Richard Arneson defines paternalism in this way:

> Paternalistic policies are restrictions on a person's liberty which are justified *exclusively by consideration of that person's own good or welfare*, and which are carried out either *against his present will* (when his present will is not explicitly overridden by his own prior commitment) or *against his prior commitment* (when his present will is explicitly overridden by his own prior commitment) (Arneson, 1980: 471, emphasis added).

Present will is straightforward: it means what you want to do now. Prior commitment is a decision made at time *t* to be prevented from doing x at *t+1* (or, alternatively, made to do y at *t+1*). To take a trivial example: you *now* empower someone to force you to get up *tomorrow morning*. Arneson thinks that forcing someone to do something for which they granted prior authorisation does not amount to paternalism. But what if we were to extend the idea of authorisation (or consent)? We might say that a six-year-old child sent to school in floods of tears really consented to go to school because the twenty-year-old she will become would be glad that she – as a six-year-old – was forced to go to school. Because the six-year-old and the twenty-year-old are the same person then it is possible to argue that the child *hypothetically* consents to go to school.

However, the implications of such an argument for paternalism towards adults should also be acknowledged. This can be illustrated by an extreme case. In 2001 computer technician Armin Meiwes killed and partially ate IT professional Bernd Brandes at the former's home in Eastern Germany. Meiwes had advertised on the web for a man willing to be killed and eaten, and eventually he met up with Brandes, who (it appears) consented to be killed. In 2004 Meiwes was convicted of manslaughter but not murder and sentenced to eight-and-a-half years in prison, although in 2006, as a result of a prosecution appeal Meiwes was sentenced to life imprisonment for murder. In both trials Brandes' consent was taken as relevant to the case. In 2004 the prosecution struggled to prove that Brandes had not consented. In 2006 the prosecution succeeded in convincing the court that in the final stages of life Brandes could not have consented, and Meiwes' failure to get medical help constituted non-consensual killing. Putting to one side issues about German law, we can pose a political-philosophical question: was it right to punish Meiwes? Why should a person not be allowed to consent to be killed and eaten? If we apply the idea of hypothetical consent, then we might conclude that Brandes would not have consented had he been fully rational. A rational person sees his life as lived over time – Brandes, who was 43 and in good health, should want to live a full life. Of course, few people (if any) give equal weight to all parts of their life: for example, at 18 you tend not to be obsessed with pensions; likewise, people frequently engage in risky activities and risk and excitement must have some value. If paternalism is premised on the importance of prudential concern – that is, equal concern for all times in your life – then the potential for state interference is very great.

If you want to test your own reactions to paternalistic policies, consider this example (taken, with some modifications, from Richard Arneson; see Arneson, 1980: 477–8). Imagine there is a microchip which, if inserted in your brain, can give you the 'motivation' to avoid doing stupid things (and enables you to do things which, without the chip, you would lack the will to do):

- You *choose* to have the chip implanted.
- *You* control it and you can 'time limit' it.
- You can select from a software menu which actions you would like to be prevented or 'willed': getting up in the morning, not drinking too much, doing exercise and so on.
- Because it can be fun you can randomise for risk – for example, you can programme it to stop you drinking too much three times out of four.

If you find the chip attractive, then what is the *fundamental* difference between implanting the chip and asking the state to stop you doing certain things? Of course, we might trust the chip, but not politicians – this is, however, a *non-fundamental* difference. That said, the fact that you can decide which actions you would like to be prevented from doing – or given the will to do – suggests a level of autonomy not characteristic of those subject to the paternalistic controls outlined in the box overleaf (go down the list of laws and ask yourself how likely it is that the individuals who are subject to paternalistic action would actually consent to those laws).

Expression and Harm

We turn now from action to expression. It is sometimes thought that, in the words of the children's nursery rhyme, 'sticks and stones will break my bones, but words

Paternalistic Laws

There are many laws in force that rely on paternalistic reasons for their justification – although some might also be defended on non-paternalistic grounds:

1. Laws requiring motorcyclists to wear helmets.
2. Laws requiring the wearing of car seat-belts.
3. Laws prohibiting self-medication.
4. Laws prohibiting possession of recreational drugs.
5. Laws requiring the testing of drugs before sale.
6. Laws prohibiting the sale of pornography to minors.
7. Laws prohibiting certain kinds of child labour.
8. Curfews on children.
9. Prohibition of (or controls on) gambling.
10. Prohibition on duelling.
11. Compulsory education of the young.
12. Prohibition on assistance in cases of requested suicide.
13. Compulsory vaccination.
14. Compulsory participation in social security schemes.
15. Prohibition on voluntary self-enslavement.
16. 'Sectioning' (civil commitment of the mentally ill).
17. Distribution of welfare in kind rather than cash.
18. Fluoridation of water.
19. Compulsory folic acid fortification of bread.
20. Prohibition on purchase of fireworks.
21. Waiting periods for divorce.
22. Smoking bans.

Most of these cases are taken from Donald Van de Veer, *Paternalistic Intervention: The Moral Bounds of Benevolence* (1986: 13–15). He lists 40 examples: however, some of them do not refer to legal paternalism (state coercion), but rather to medical paternalism (for example, not informing a patient of the seriousness of his condition for fear that anxiety will worsen it).

will never hurt me'. However, as Thomas Scanlon suggests, expression can cause harm (Scanlon, 1972: 210). His examples include: (a) direct physical harm, as when your voice causes an avalanche; (b) a situation when one person intentionally places another in apprehension of imminent bodily harm as a result of a threat ('assault' as distinct from 'battery'); (c) public ridicule to the point where a person's reputation and livelihood are destroyed; (d) shouting fire in a crowded theatre; (e) issuing an order to another; (f) advertising the means to cause destruction (Scanlon, 1972: 210–12). Scanlon argues that some of these 'expressive acts' should be prohibited but expression should not be prohibited simply because it is harmful. Expression, he argues, has a special status.

Scanlon distinguishes two types of argument for freedom of expression – appeal to a social good and appeal to individual rights. Put simply, a person can justify their freedom of expression by saying (a) society benefits from my expression, or

(b) I have a right to express myself. These are not mutually exclusive positions, but despite his emphasis on individual freedom Mill's defence of free expression is primarily derived from (a). Scanlon argues (basically) for type (b), but maintains there are social benefits to freedom of expression. Scanlon's argument has to be located in a broader theory of political obligation (Chapter 19 Civil Disobedience pp. 432–36). He maintains that state power has to be justified, and that means citizens must retain a degree of moral autonomy – that is, the capacity to make independent moral judgements, and thus be able to *criticise those laws which they have a moral obligation to obey*. Citizens can accept that their actions may be coerced – they can be prevented from doing something – but they will not be prepared to give up their right to criticise the state's interference in their action. For example, most, if not all, states prohibit the private sale and (most) use of heroin.* A citizen, for Scanlon, is under a moral obligation to obey the state and thus accept the state can legitimately interfere in their freedom to sell (or possess, or use) heroin, but they should be free to *criticise* the law.

This may seem very obvious, for few people would argue that a person should be prevented from (a) campaigning for the legalisation of heroin. And there seems to be a clear distinction here between expression and action. But consider these expressive acts: (b) valorising the use of heroin in novels or films; (c) setting up a website giving information on how to produce heroin; (d) giving information about sources of supply of heroin. Scanlon would certainly defend (a) and (b), and under most circumstances (c), but not (d).

It is the case that even campaigns for legalisation might serve to 'legitimise' heroin use and thus cause – albeit very indirectly – harm. Likewise, artistic representations can contribute to a social environment in which something appears good. Scanlon, however, takes a permissive attitude, arguing for personal responsibility: 'a person who acts on reasons he has acquired from another's act of expression acts on what *he* has come to believe and has judged to be a sufficient basis for action' (Scanlon, 1972: 212). In other words, if Mary tells John how to produce heroin and John uses this information to produce heroin John must have gone through a process of reasoning which makes John responsible for any harm produced; Mary may well have *caused* him to act but she is not *responsible* for his actions. A society that values autonomy will tolerate the harm caused by expressive acts. Obviously, this assumes that the person being addressed is a responsible agent, and we might want to restrict expression when the addressee is immature or in some way particularly susceptible to influence. However, if we treat everybody as immature or susceptible then the possibility of a vibrant society is lost.

Offensiveness

Although Mill does not directly address the problem of offensiveness, implicit in his argument is the view that to say 'I find x offensive' is equivalent to saying 'I don't agree with x', and he rejects disagreement as a ground for limiting a person's freedom. The alternative is to say that the action is not offensive but harmful – perhaps 'psychologically harmful'. This would, however, severely restrict the sphere

*This is our example, not Scanlon's.

in which a person is free to act (a point made earlier). Mill does, nonetheless, appeal to the notion of 'public decency' to forbid certain non-harmful (that is, non-harmful to others) acts:

> There are many acts which, being directly injurious only to the agents themselves, ought not to be legally interdicted, but which, if done publicly, are a violation of good manners, and coming thus within the category of offences against others, may rightfully be prohibited. Of this kind are offences against decency; on which it is unnecessary to dwell . . . (Mill, 1991: 109).

It would, in fact, have been interesting had Mill dwelt a while on these activities. Sex in public is not (normally) injurious to the participants, but most people, even if they themselves are not offended, would probably accept that it should be prohibited. Mill's argument does not follow from his harm principle. Joel Feinberg argues that there should be an 'offence principle'; this would be in addition to the harm principle, for offence cannot be assimilated to harm (Feinberg, 1985: 1).

Feinberg distinguishes immediate and mediated offence. *Immediate offence* is offence to the senses. Imagine the neighbours from hell: they party and play loud music all night; they have a rusting car in their front garden and pile up household refuse – which stinks – in the back garden. These things hit the senses – sight, sound, smell. *Mediated offence* is when a norm or value is violated: the swastika is only offensive if you associate it with Nazi Germany, and with the implication that the person wearing the armband sympathises with Nazism (it is not offensive when, for example, found decorating buildings predating the 1930s). The offence is here *mediated* by a set of beliefs and values. Immediate offence is less problematic because in most cases we can agree on what should be prohibited – such prohibition is value-neutral. In a society marked by a pluralism of beliefs and values a prohibition on expressive acts based on mediated offence is more problematic.

Take the case of Steve Gough (the 'Naked Rambler'). In 2003–4 Gough took seven months to walk naked – except for boots and a hat – the length of Britain (Land's End to John O'Groats). He was arrested seventeen times and spent two brief terms in prison. Unless you object to Gough's walk on grounds that you find him physically repulsive his is an example of mediated rather than immediate offence, and his actions are quite explicitly grounded in his beliefs and values: he has a website on which he says he is engaged in a 'celebration of the human body and a campaign to enlighten the public, as well as the authorities that govern us, that the freedom to go naked in public is a basic human right'.

Feinberg sets out his offence principle:

1. The offence felt must be a reaction that a person chosen at random would have (excepting, offence to specific subgroups – in this case we choose a person at random from that group).
2. The offensive behaviour cannot reasonably be avoided.
3. The offence must not be the result of abnormal susceptibility.
4. The person who is restrained must be granted an allowable alternative outlet or mode of expression.

Feinberg seeks to distinguish the offence principle from the harm principle, but avoid making judgements regarding the intrinsic goodness or badness of particular actions – in other words, he wants to avoid legal moralism (discussed in the next section). Anthony Ellis (1984) argues that Feinberg fails. Ellis lists various dictionary definitions of 'offence': 1. Annoyance; 2. Quasi-physical disgust; 3. Transgression; 4. Moral outrage (Ellis, 1984: 7). The first would be too weak for the offence principle: we cannot prohibit everything we find annoying. The second is unproblematic: immediate offence hits the senses – smell, sight, and sound – and is normally viewpoint-neutral. The third is just a synonym for violation of rules and does not tell us anything about the rules. The fourth is the problematic one, because it could lead to legal moralism. Take the case of someone forced to watch a pornographic film. The person says he found the film 'disgusting': this could mean that it made him feel sick (an example of 2: quasi-physical disgust), or that it offended him in a moral sense (an example of 4). If it is 4 then the knowledge that such films exist and other people are watching them could be grounds for prohibition. And indeed this is what legal moralists maintain: *all* should be prevented from watching such a film.*

In an attempt to distinguish prohibition on grounds of offensiveness from prohibition on grounds of moral disapproval Feinberg introduces the concept of a charientic judgement (the 'Charites' are the Greek goddesses of grace: they are often represented as the Three Graces). If we wish to judge an act or expression *uncharientic* we might say it is vulgar or uncouth or boorish or tasteless. If we were to judge something *immoral* we would say it is wrong or bad or evil or selfish. Moral disapproval may entail resentment, whereas charientic disapproval entails contempt. Crucially, there is no charientic equivalent to guilt, although we can feel shame if we realise we have inadvertently committed a charientic *faux pas*.

Harmless Wrongdoing

This is the most difficult principle to grasp. In part, the difficulty lies in its formulation: if 'wrongness' is defined as 'that which is harmful' then harmless wrongdoing is a contradiction in terms. It may however be that a distinction is being made between, on the one hand, right/wrong, and, on the other, good/bad. In everyday speech, we use these pairs interchangeably, so right equals good, and wrong equals bad. But philosophers do make a distinction between (a) rightness, or that which is obligatory, and (b) goodness, or an end that we should pursue. For example, if we obey the law we are doing right – we are fulfilling our obligations – but 'doing right' tells us nothing about *why* we do right. We might obey the law from purely self-interested reasons, or we might obey it because we recognise that other people matter – they have interests just as we have interests. Goodness is a quality of character, whereas rightness is a quality of behaviour. For this reason, it would be better to use a different label to that of 'harmless wrongdoing'.

---

*The liberal position is to permit the sale and viewing of (some forms of) pornography but restrict who can buy or view it. A phrase used in English Law is 'the tendency to corrupt and deprave'. It is implied that those consumers who could not be further harmed by such consumption should be free to consume, so long as they do not 'corrupt and deprave' other people. Put (rather too) crudely, they are already sufficiently depraved, such that exposure to potentially depraving materials has no additional effect! This is one of the arguments underlying film and video classification as well as the 'blanking out' of the fronts of sex shops.

In Mill's lifetime a view was articulated – by James Fitzjames Stephen (Stephen, 1993, originally published 1873) – that to permit an 'immoral' act is equivalent to allowing an act of treason to go unpunished: the good of society was at risk. This view was rearticulated in the 1960s by Patrick (Lord) Devlin (Devlin, 1965) in response to the recommendation of a commission (Wolfenden Commission, 1957) that laws on homosexuality should be liberalised. Devlin argued that there was a 'shared morality' and that permitting 'immoral acts' in private threatened that morality (Devlin, 1965: 13–14). There was a danger of social disintegration. At first sight, Devlin's argument appears simply to be the claim that no action is completely self-regarding, and, of course, we have discussed a revised Millian response, which is to suggest that fundamental interests must be at stake for an action to be deemed harmful. Devlin's argument is however a little more sophisticated: actions may not have discernible harmful effects, but cumulatively they erode social norms, and that erosion is *seriously* harmful. However, this still seems to be concerned with harm. A number of objections have been raised to Devlin's argument (what has become termed the 'social cohesion thesis'): (a) He was wrong about homosexuality; (b) Is there really a shared morality? Don't people disagree about morality? (c) Even if there is a shared morality does permitting 'private immorality' undermine it?

What is worth reflecting on is whether there is something in Devlin's argument that cannot be captured in a debate dominated by the concept of harm. The problem with the concept of harm is that it always requires identifying harms to *particular* individuals or groups, whereas there may be a good which cannot be reduced to identifiable individuals or groups; this might be an image of society which guides people to behave in a certain way. We can call this a *free-floating good* because although it is the product of human experience it cannot be reduced to the interests of individuals, or even groups. It could be argued that no society will survive unless it pursues some goods and the protection and promotion of these goods provide the justification for restricting human freedom. (One could also argue that we have an obligation to future generations to reproduce these goods, that is, reproduce a particular kind of culture.) If certain things are objectively valuable then any rational mind, contrary to Mill's fallibility argument, will recognise them to be so. John Finnis, in his book *Natural Law and Natural Rights*, observes that almost all cultures, despite apparent differences between them, exhibit a commitment to certain goods. He cites anthropological research (although, unfortunately, fails to give any reference for that research), suggesting that almost all cultures value the following: human life and procreation; permanence in sexual relations; truth and its transmission; cooperation; obligation between individuals; justice between groups; friendship; property; play; respect for the dead (Finnis, 1980: 83–4).

Stephen, Devlin and Finnis would not reject the idea that people should have a sphere of freedom ('private sphere'), but would maintain that it is a function of the state to change human behaviour, and that law should reflect morality. This position is termed legal moralism. For example, Finnis has been a vocal critic of laws which treat homosexuals and heterosexuals equally, arguing that equal treatment implies that they are equally valid: a position he rejects, maintaining that homosexuality is contrary to natural law. There is a parallel between legal moralism and the judgment made in the Operation Spanner case. Recall that the judgment maintained that consent was a necessary *but not a sufficient* condition for permitting another person to harm you, for the activity in which you are engaged must have some intrinsic value. This suggests that the men involved in sadomasochism have to justify the practice of sadomasochism. Legal moralists would argue that such an activity cannot be justified: it is a sexual perversion – that is, a misdirection of the libido on to an inappropriate object.

The difficulty with legal moralism is that it assumes more than just a shared morality – it assumes a shared conception of what is *ultimately valuable*. Many defenders of freedom would agree that we need a shared morality – respecting other people, and not harming them without their consent, is a moral position. But such a morality leaves open many questions of what is truly valuable in life – individuals, it is argued, must find their own way to what is valuable. This does not mean that there are no objectively valuable ends, but simply that coercion, by definition, will not help us to get there: the state can stop people harming one another, but it cannot make people good.

The Smoking Ban Reconsidered

We can now apply the framework discussed above to the case of the smoking ban. It should be stressed that this is a case study and that we could have selected many other examples – it is important that political theory raises *general* arguments applicable across *different* cases. In popular debate a common attitude to the smoking ban is: 'I'm not a smoker, so it doesn't bother me.' This is an inadequate basis for supporting the ban. Any ban must be supported by reasons that could be advanced by smokers and non-smokers alike – this is what we mean by a general argument.

To be fair to those engaged in popular debate, there is often an implicit recognition that reasons and principles are at stake that extend further than the smoking ban itself – when people get beyond the simple statement made above and actually engage in debate they use analogies. An opponent of a ban might say 'if you ban smoking, then why not ban the consumption of fatty foods'; a proponent of a ban might respond by pointing out that the analogy is false because there is no direct harm to others involved in the consumption of fatty foods. The point is that both proponent and opponent are attempting to apply general arguments to specific cases. Without necessarily realising it, they are engaging in political theory. So in the spirit of seeking general arguments that can be applied to the ban, let us apply the freedom-limiting principles discussed in Criticisms and Developments to the smoking ban (the last – harmless wrongdoing – is not really applicable to this case).

Harm to Others

We argued that Mill's harm principle needs to be revised so that harm is defined as serious harm, and suggested that the temporary discomfort of being in a smoky environment cannot constitute harm – although if you follow the popular discussion around the smoking ban the immediate discomfort from smoking is a common theme. If we do revise Mill's harm principle along the lines just suggested – that is, damage to a person's long-term interests – we still have a problem: your action in itself may not harm another person. If you go to a particular bar just once, and sit by the bar chain-smoking for a couple of hours, then your action will not kill the barman. Accepting for the purposes of the argument that passive smoking can kill, and that working long shifts in a bar puts a person in harm's way, then the barman will still contract cancer without your two-hour period of chain-smoking. The paradox is that if the barman comes into contact with thousands of people during his career *no single one of them* will be responsible for his death. This is Sorites paradox: millions of grains of sand make a heap of sand, subtract a grain and you still have a pile, keep subtracting and you will end up without a pile, but no single grain makes the difference between a pile and no pile. So we have to make a second revision to the harm principle: your action (smoking in a bar) belongs to a set of actions (thousands of people smoking in that bar) which together cause harm.

Consent

This brings us to the second part of the harm to others principle: harm to others does not, for Mill, in itself constitute grounds for restricting freedom. Rather, it must be *non-consensual* harm to others that triggers a restriction. This is where debates about the effects of passive smoking slightly miss the point: we could agree that passive smoking is harmful, or, if we are not sure, we could adopt the 'precautionary principle' – we assume, until we have the evidence, that if smoking is harmful to the smoker, then sustained contact with cigarette smoke in an enclosed environment will be harmful to non-smokers. So let us just accept that passive smoking is harmful. That in itself does not justify a ban on smoking bars because non-smokers might consent to be harmed. That then shifts the debate to the meaning of consent: do low-paid bar staff consent? Maybe they have no meaningful alternative to working in a bar or club. If so, an alternative to a complete ban would be a licensing scheme.

A further objection to the consent argument is that it assumes that by entering a bar a non-smoker *intends* to be among smokers, rather than entering a building in which they know they will have to *tolerate* smokers. If you go into a boxing ring you intend to participate in an activity in which harm is intrinsic to the activity – you do not intend to get brain damage, but such damage is part and parcel of boxing. To make the equivalent case for consent to go into a smoking pub, you would have to say that smoking is an intrinsic part of pub life, but actually it is not – or at least not in the same way that harm is a risk intrinsic to boxing.

Harm to Self

Much of the argument in favour of banning smoking is not just to prevent harm to others, but is a public health measure intended to reduce the number of smokers. For some anti-smoking campaigners this seems to be the main objective of a ban. If it were not an objective then licensing rather than banning would be the obvious policy to adopt. Is the aim of reducing the amount of smoking justified? It has been argued that smokers welcome the ban because it will help them to give up. British journalist (and ex-smoker) Simon Hoggart argued:

> Smoking is not like drinking. Booze has its drawbacks, as a visit to any British town centre on a Friday night will demonstrate. But we drink wine and beer because we like it. People do not like smoking. They smoke because smoking is the only relief from the pain of not having a cigarette. It is a wholly negative pleasure. That is why there has been so little fuss over the ban. Most smokers are privately relieved that it might help them give up (Hoggart, 2007).

Evidence from smoking cessation services would seem to provide empirical support for this claim: in many countries there has been a surge in smokers seeking medical help to give up after the introduction of a smoking ban. However, just because something is addictive that does not make it unpleasurable or lacking in value.

Offensiveness

Some people find smoking offensive – could this be a ground for banning it? Most likely it is the immediate 'offensiveness' of smoking that would create the basis for banning it. If you look at comments made by 'ordinary people' some of them describe smoking as a disgusting habit. One advocate of a complete smoking ban, commenting on the inadequacy of having demarcated smoking areas, likened bars with segregated smoking areas to a swimming pool in which one lane is reserved for people to urinate in. Presumably this analogy was intended to convey the problems of restricting the harmful effects of smoking to one area of a bar, but perhaps it also reveals his disgust at smoking.

Summary

We have explored both freedom of expression and action, using Mill's harm principle as the starting point. That principle is not as simple as Mill suggests, and to address the complexities of freedom we have discussed further liberty-limiting principles: harm to self, offensiveness, harmless wrongdoing. It is for the reader to assess the validity of these different principles, but it is clear that a discussion of freedom must at least address the charge that the harm principle is inadequate as an explanation of the limits of freedom. Freedom is certainly regarded as a positive word and this may reflect an underlying belief not just of political theorists, but also ordinary people, that although freedom must on occasion be limited we assume freedom to be a good thing – there is a 'presumption in favour of freedom'.

Questions

1. If the protection of a person's interests is so important should the state permit a person to harm him- or herself?
2. If the protection of a person's interests is so important should the state permit a person to consent to be harmed by somebody else?

3. Should the fact that someone finds an expression or action offensive be a reason for banning that expression or action?

4. Are some activities 'intrinsically bad' and therefore can they justifiably be banned?

References

Arneson, R. (1980) 'Mill versus Paternalism', *Ethics* 90(4), 470–89.

Berlin, I. (1991) 'Two Concepts of Liberty' in D. Miller (ed.), *Liberty* Oxford: Oxford University Press, 33–57.

Devlin, P. (1965) *The Enforcement of Morals* London: Oxford University Press.

Ellis, A. (1984) 'Offense and the Liberal Conception of Law' *Philosophy and Public Affairs* 13(1), 3–23.

Feinberg, J. (1985) *The Moral Limits of the Criminal Law, Vol. 2: Offense to Others* New York: Oxford University Press.

Finnis, J. (1980) *Natural Law and Natural Rights* Oxford: Clarendon Press.

Foster, M. (1792) *A Report on Crown Cases and Discourses on the Crown Law*, 3rd edn London: M. Dodson.

Hoggart, S. (2007) 'Is the Smoking Ban a Good Idea?', *The Guardian* 14 May 2007: http://www.guardian.co.uk/society/2007/may/14/health.smoking

Hurd, H. (2001) 'Why Liberals Should Hate "Hate Crime Legislation"', *Law and Philosophy,* 20(2), 215–32.

MacCallum, G. (1991) 'Negative and Positive Freedom' in D. Miller (ed.), *Liberty* Oxford: Oxford University Press, 100–122.

Mill, J.S. (1991) *On Liberty and Other Essays* (ed. John Gray) Oxford: Oxford University Press.

Miller, D. (1983) 'Constraints on Freedom', *Ethics* 94, 66–86.

Nagel, T. (1970) *The Possibility of Altruism* Princeton, NJ: Princeton University Press.

Scanlon, T. (1972) 'A Theory of Freedom of Expression' *Philosophy and Public Affairs* 1(2), 204–26.

Stephen, J.F. (1873, 1993) *Liberty, Equality, Fraternity* Indianapolis: Liberty Fund.

Van de Veer D. (1986) *Paternalistic Intervention: The Moral Bounds of Benevolence* Princeton, NJ: Princeton University Press.

Wolfenden, J. (1957) *Report of the Committee on Homosexual Offences and Prostitution* London: HMSO.

Further Reading

Apart from Mill's *On Liberty*, the best starting points for a further exploration of freedom are Tim Gray, *Freedom* (London: Macmillan, 1991), George Brenkert, *Political Freedom* (London: Routledge, 1991), David Miller (ed.), *Liberty* (Oxford: Oxford University Press, 1991), which is a collection of important essays on freedom, and Alan Ryan (ed.), *The Idea of Freedom* (Oxford: Oxford University Press, 1979), again a collection of essays. Also useful, but arguing a line, is Richard Flathman, *The Philosophy and Politics of Freedom* (Chicago and London: University of Chicago Press, 1987). Matthew Kramer, *The Quality of Freedom* (Oxford: Oxford University Press, 2003), is far from introductory, but is interesting, especially as he stresses the measurability of freedom. Two books that explore 'autonomy', which is a concept cognate to freedom, are: Richard Lindley, *Autonomy*

(Basingstoke: Macmillan, 1986) and Robert Young, *Personal Autonomy: Beyond Negative and Positive Liberty* (London: Croom Helm, 1985). Specifically on Mill, the following works are useful: John Gray, *Mill on Liberty: A Defence* (London: Routledge, 1996); Gerald Dworkin (ed.), *Mill's On Liberty: Critical Essays* (Lenham: Rowman & Littlefield, 1997); C. L. Ten, *Mill on Liberty* (Oxford: Clarendon Press, 1980); Nigel Warburton, *Freedom: An Introduction with Readings* (London and New York: Routledge, 2001). See also John Skorupski, *John Stuart Mill* (London: Routledge, 1989), and relevant essays in John Skorupski (ed.), *The Cambridge Companion to Mill* (Cambridge: Cambridge University Press, 1998).

Weblinks

- There are some interesting sites that attempt to 'measure' freedom in different countries. Obviously there are philosophical issues here, such as whether we can say one society is more free than another without making judgements about the value of different freedoms. The best-known site is http://www.freedomhouse.org/

- There are a couple of good websites on John Stuart Mill: http://www.utilitarian.net/jsmill/ and http://www.utilitarianism.com/jsmill.htm

Chapter 3

Equality

Introduction

Equality is a fundamental political concept, but also a very complex one. While the core idea of equality is that people should be treated in the same way, there are many different principles of equality. To provide a coherent defence of equality requires separating out the various principles, and explaining what it is that is being equalised: is it income, or well-being, the capacity to acquire certain goods, or something else? Equality, or particular principles of equality, must then be reconciled with other political values, or principles, such as freedom and efficiency. For that reason, this chapter is primarily conceptual, in that it aims to set out a number of principles of equality, and explain the relationships between them. The discussion will necessarily refer back to Chapter 2 (Freedom), and forward to Chapter 4 (Justice).

Chapter Map

In this chapter we will:

- Set out various principles of equality: formal equality, moral equality, equality before the law, equal liberty and equal access, material equality (equality of opportunity, equality of outcome and affirmative action).

- Discuss, in more detail, those principles.

- Consider a radical anti-egalitarian perspective.

- Consider the relationship between freedom and equality.

- Discuss Dworkin's distinction between 'welfarist' and 'resourcist' theories of equality.

Does Inequality Make you Ill?

There is some evidence that inequality makes people ill. The link between poverty and ill-health is not surprising, but research has revealed that as incomes rise across society there is no corresponding decline in ill-health (see Wilkinson, 2005). This implies that it is not simply poverty that explains ill-health but the very fact of being unequal: put simply, inequality reduces self-esteem and lowered self-esteem makes people ill.

This debate suggests two ways of viewing the value of equality. We could simply view inequality as a reflection of the fact that some people are not having their needs satisfied, consequently we seek to raise people in *absolute* terms – for example, ensuring they have decent housing and their children receive a proper education – but we are not concerned with their *relative* status. The fact that some people are

'stinking rich' is irrelevant. Alternatively, we can view inequality as *intrinsically* bad for the reason outlined above: greater inequality undermines self-esteem.

Let us assume – *for the sake of argument* – that there is evidence for a link between inequality and illness. What would be the political-philosophical significance of this finding? Should the state be responsible for a person's happiness or self-esteem? Is happiness the only value? Maybe there is a cultural value to inequality and unhappiness: it makes us strive to be better. If people are unhappy because others have more is this not just jealousy? And do we want to live in a society that is more concerned with what the rich get than what the poor get? What do you think: is inequality intrinsically bad?

Principles of Equality

The term 'equality' is widely used in political debate, and frequently misunderstood. On the political left, equality is a central value, with socialists and social democrats aiming to bring about if not an equal society, then a more equal society. On the political right, the attempt to create a more equal society is criticised as a drive to uniformity, or a squeezing out of individual initiative. However, closer reflection on the nature of equality reveals a number of things. First, there is no one concept of equality, but a range of different forms. Second, all the main ideological positions discussed in this book endorse at least one form of equality – formal equality – and most also endorse one or more substantive conceptions of equality. Third, principles of equality are often elliptical, meaning that there is an implicit claim that must be made explicit if we are to assess whether the claim is valid. To explain, since human beings possess more than one attribute or good, it is possible that equality in the possession of one will lead to, or imply, inequality in another. For example, Anne may be able-bodied and John disabled. Each could be given equal amounts of resources, such as health care, and so with regard to health care they are treated equally, but John's needs are greater, so the equality of health care has unequal *effects*. If Anne and John were given resources commensurate with their needs, then they would be being treated equally in one sphere (needs) but unequally in another (resources). The recognition of this plurality of goods, and therefore spheres within which people can be treated equally or unequally, is essential to grasping the complexity of the debate around equality and inequality. What is being distributed – and, therefore, what we are equal or unequal in our possession of – is termed a 'metric'. As the argument of this chapter progresses we will develop a framework within which we can come to some conclusions on the value we should attach to equality. We start with some principles of equality. Each principle is discussed in more detail in the course of the chapter, but an initial outline of each will help elucidate the connections between them:

- *Formal equality* To say we should treat like cases alike states nothing more than a tautological truth. If two people are alike in all respects then we would have no reason for discriminating between them; of course, no two people are alike, and the principle is indeed 'formal' – it does not tell us how to treat dissimilar people. Racists do not violate the principle of formal equality, because they argue that racial groups are not 'similar' and so need not, or should not, be treated in the same way.

- *Moral equality* The concept of moral equality is sometimes presented in negative form as a rejection of natural hierarchy, or natural inequality. In many societies it is taken for granted that people are, in important respects, deserving of equal consideration. Much discussion in political theory – especially in the dominant liberal stream of the discipline – is about the characterisation of moral equality, which, paradoxically, can take the form of *justifying inequality*: that is, if people are morally equal, how do we explain their unequal treatment in terms of the distribution of social goods, such as income? The very idea that such inequality must be justified assumes that people are morally equal – in a society where there is an overwhelming belief in natural inequality, such as, say, a caste society, it would simply not occur to those in a higher stratum that they must justify their advantaged position, or that those in a lower stratum should question their subordinate position.

- *Equality before the law* That laws apply equally to those who are subject to them is widely accepted as a foundational belief of many, if not most, societies. It could be argued that this applied even in Hitler's Germany. After the 1935 Nuremburg Laws were passed Jews (as defined by the state) were denied many rights, but consistent with 'treating like cases alike' it could be argued that legal equality was respected insofar as all members of the class defined by the state as Jews were treated alike: all were equally subject to the laws, despite the laws themselves being discriminatory. However, we argue in the section on Legal Equality that equality before the law is a stronger idea, which implies that there must be compelling reasons for unequal treatment.

- *Equal liberty* A common assumption, especially on the right, is that equality and liberty (freedom) conflict. Certainly, if we were in Hobbes's state of nature, and enjoyed 'pure' liberty, that is, we were under no duties to refrain from behaving as we choose, then the exercise of liberty would reflect natural inequalities, including any bad luck that might befall us. But under a state, while our liberty is restricted, the possibility exists for a degree of protection (through 'rights'), such that a space is provided in which we are free to act without the danger of other people interfering in our actions. Once we move from pure liberty to protected liberty an issue of distribution – and, therefore, a trade-off between equality and liberty – arises. Although the state cannot distribute the *exercise of choice*, it can distribute *rights* to do certain things. Of course, even though liberty-protecting rights can be distributed this does not mean that equality and liberty never conflict (we discuss possible conflicts in the section on Equal Liberties).

- *Material equality* The most significant disputes in many societies are connected with the distribution of income, and other tangible material goods, such as education and health care. To understand this debate requires a discussion of class, because the capacity to acquire material goods is to some extent, and perhaps a very great extent, conditioned by structures that individuals do not control. From birth – and even before birth – a person is set on a course, at each stage of which they have some power to gain or lose material goods, but, arguably, the choices are restricted. Put simply, a person born into a wealthy family has more opportunities than someone with a poor background.

- *Equal access* If a society places barriers in the way of certain groups acquiring material goods, such as jobs and services, as happened with regard to blacks in the Southern States of the United States until the 1960s, then equal access is denied. On the face of it, guaranteeing equal access may appear closely connected with material equality, but, in fact, it has more to do with equal civic and political rights, or, *liberty*: the liberty to compete for jobs, and buy goods.

- *Equality of opportunity* Unlike equal access this *is* a principle of material equality, and although it commands rhetorical support across the political spectrum, in any reasonably strong version it has significant implications for the role of the state in individual and family life. If a society attempts to guarantee the equal opportunity to acquire, for example, a particular job, then it is going much further than simply removing legal obstacles to getting the job. Realising equal opportunity would require, among other things, substantial spending on education. Indeed, given the huge influence that the family has on a child's prospects, to achieve equal opportunity may entail considerable intervention in family life.

- *Equality of outcome* Critics of equality frequently argue that egalitarians – that is, those who regard equality as a central political principle – want to create a society in which everybody is treated equally irrespective of personal differences, or individual choice. This is a caricature, for it is possible to argue for equality of outcome as a prima facie principle, meaning that we should seek as far as possible to ensure an equal outcome consistent with other political principles. Equality of outcome may also function as a proxy for equality of opportunity: if there are significantly unequal outcomes, then this indicates that there is not an adequate equality of opportunity. This last point leads us into a consideration of affirmative action.

- *Affirmative action* This term originated in the United States and is an umbrella term covering a range of policies intended to address the material deprivations suffered by (especially) black Americans, but also gender inequalities. Although it embraces a wider range of policies, it is often used as a synonym for 'reverse discrimination', or 'positive discrimination'. Examples of reverse discrimination include the operation of quotas for jobs, or a reduction in entry requirements for college places. Reverse discrimination is best understood as operating somewhere between equality of opportunity and equality of outcome: the principle acts directly on outcomes, but is intended to guarantee equality of opportunity.

Moral Equality

Moral Autonomy and Moral Equality

That people are morally equal is a central belief – often implicit rather than explicit – of societies influenced by the Enlightenment (post-Enlightenment societies). Sometimes people talk of 'natural equality', but this has connotations of natural law – the belief that moral principles have a real existence, transcending time and place. Moral equality can, minimally, be understood as a negative: people should be treated equally because there is no reason to believe in natural inequality. In Chapter 2 it was suggested that in post-Enlightenment societies there was a presumption in favour of liberty, meaning that people should be free to act as they wish unless there was a good reason for limiting that freedom. Parallel to the presumption in favour of liberty, there is also a presumption in favour of equality – people should be treated equally unless there is a strong reason for treating them unequally. But the negative argument does not adequately capture the importance of moral equality: to be morally equal, that is, worthy of equal consideration, implies that you are a certain kind of being – a being to whom reasons, or justifications, can be given. This reflects the roots of the concept of moral equality in the Enlightenment, which challenges authority, and assumes that the human mind is capable of understanding the world. Among the political implications of this philosophical position are, first, that the social world is not 'natural' – inequality must be justified and not dismissed as if it were simply the way of the world. Second, the Enlightenment stresses that human beings are *rational* – they are capable of advancing and understanding arguments, such that justifications for equality, or inequality, are always given to *individual* human beings.

It is a standard, but not necessary, starting point of liberalism – but also of other ideologies such as socialism, anarchism, feminism, and multiculturalism – that coercively enforced institutions must be justified to those who are subject to them (although anarchists conclude that coercion cannot be justified); that is, subjects should in some sense consent to those institutions. Since it is unrealistic to think we can reach unanimity on how society should be organised, we must assume a moral standpoint distinct from the standpoints of 'real people'. The most famous recent elaboration of this idea can be found in the work of John Rawls. Rawls asks us to imagine choosing a set of political principles without knowing our identities – that is, we do not know our natural abilities, class, gender, religious and other beliefs, and so on. This denial of knowledge constitutes what Rawls calls the 'veil of ignorance': because individuals do not know their identities they must, as a matter of reason, put themselves in the shoes of each other person and people are necessarily equal. The idea of equality in Rawls's theory is highly abstract, and the use of the veil itself tells us little about how people should be treated. To generate more concrete principles of equality Rawls makes certain claims not implied by the veil of ignorance, and in that sense he goes beyond moral equality; nonetheless, the starting point for Rawls is a situation of moral equality.

Ch. 4:
Justice
pp. 82–89

While Rawls draws strongly egalitarian conclusions from the idea of moral equality, other political theorists, while endorsing the idea of moral equality, derive rather different conclusions. Robert Nozick, in his book *Anarchy, State, and Utopia* (1974) argues that individuals have strong rights to self-ownership, and they enjoy these rights equally, and for that reason there are certain things we cannot do to people, including taxing their legitimate earnings, where legitimacy is established by certain principles of justice. We discuss Nozick's theory in more detail in Chapter 4 (pp. 89–93), but the point is that a commitment to moral equality can lead in different directions in terms of whether or not we accept further principles of equality. Although Nozick's theory can only very loosely be described as Kantian, both Rawls and Nozick make explicit appeal to Kant's notion of respect for persons: treating people as ends in themselves and never merely as ends for others. In Rawls's case this idea is expressed in the equality of the original position, whereas for Nozick it is implicit in the notion of (equal) property rights as constraints (or 'side constraints') on what others can do to us.

Nietzsche contra Moral Equality

Although it has been open to significantly divergent interpretations Friedrich Nietzsche's work has been the source of the most important critique of moral equality in modern Western political thought. Rawls identifies him as a radical perfectionist, where 'perfectionism' is understood to be a theory whereby society is organised with the aim of advancing certain values or ways of life. In Nietzsche's case, this means that 'mankind must continually strive to produce great individuals . . . we give value to our lives by working for the good of the highest specimens' (Rawls, 1972: 325). Other theorists have argued for a more liberal-democratic interpretation: what Nietzsche terms the 'will to power' ('Wille zur Macht') denotes an internal struggle: each individual should strive to overcome his weaknesses and pursue a higher good (Cavell, 1990: 50–1). Willing to power does not necessarily entail domination over others. It follows that on *this* interpretation Nietzsche (implicitly) endorsed moral equality.

Nonetheless there are many passages in Nietzsche's work which support an elitist and fundamentally anti-egalitarian position (Detwiler, 1990: 8). Even if we cannot decide finally on the interpretation of his work it is clear that Nietzsche has inspired anti-egalitarian streams of thought and drawing on various concepts – in addition to the will to power – we will reconstruct the Nietzschean case against moral equality. Nietzsche's style is aphoristic rather than systematic, but among the more systematic works is *On the Genealogy of Morality* (published 1887). Divided into three Treatises, in the first Treatise Nietzsche distinguishes the valuations good/bad and good/evil (Nietzsche, 1998: 14–17). Since 'good' can only be understood relative to its opposite it follows that the 'good' in each pair does not mean the same thing. The good of the first pair denotes something powerful and life-affirming, whereas the good in the second pair corresponds to the Judaic-Christian notion of self-denial or meekness. Nietzsche traces the historical origins of goodness as self-denial to the slave revolt of the Jews against the Romans, and through Judaism to Christianity. The slave does not take revenge against the master through physical action but through an imaginary – we might say metaphysical – act (Nietzsche, 1998: 18–21). The slaves convince themselves that the meek will inherit the earth and they define the strong as 'evil'.

The struggle between slave and master is internalised with the construction of the 'soul'. Corresponding to this internalisation is the development of social forms, such as the state. The basic drive of human beings – the will to power – is turned inwards as human beings move from being nomadic 'birds of prey' to socially constricted citizens. Since the will to power cannot be extinguished it is turned inwards and takes the form of 'guilt', as distinct from 'shame'. Protestant Christianity is the clearest expression of a culture of guilt. Kant's moral philosophy is often described as secularised Protestantism: that the highest good for Kant is a pure will means that all those things that make us human – that, for Nietzsche, constitute 'life' – are devalued in favour of a characterless self. We are all morally equal but at the price of lacking any character. Morality requires that we will a law that all rational agents could will – we 'put ourselves in the shoes of each other person' – and we should feel guilt when we fail to do so. For Nietzsche the internalisation of guilt entails forgetting the historical origins of this 'slave morality': the resentment (*ressentiment*) of the weak against the strong (Nietzsche, 1998: 45–6).

Ch. 8:
Liberation
pp. 187–89

In a culture of shame – as distinct from guilt – we judge ourselves to have failed insofar as we fall short of a basically non-moral ideal. The soldier who shows cowardice in the face of the enemy feels ashamed without necessarily feeling guilt. Shame is outward-looking whereas guilt is introspective. There is, for Nietzsche, no 'inwardness' in the Christian sense and therefore the idea of moral equality makes no sense. Value is extrinsic. Rawls may be right to argue that Nietzsche is committed to a strong perfectionist ideal of creating and serving great men, but such a perfectionism might also take a softer but still elitist form: what is of greatest value is the sustenance, or transmission from one generation to the next, of cultural goods. This might well require a class-based society in which elites transmit values to the masses.

Legal Equality

We need now to move from moral equality to more specific principles of equality, although the concept of moral equality must always be in the background. A starting point for building up a more substantial political theory would be to distinguish the core legal–political institutions from broader socio-economic institutions. In most societies, but especially liberal–democratic ones, the core institutions of the state are divided into legislature, executive and judiciary. Put simply, the legislature creates laws, the executive administers powers created through law, and the judiciary interprets and enforces the law. But a social institution is any large-scale, rule-governed activity, and can include the economic organisation of society, such as the basic rules of property ownership, and various services provided by the state that extend beyond simply the creation and implementation of law. We will deal with the wider concept of a social institution later, but in this section we will concentrate on the narrower concept.

Ch. 13: Fascism pp. 293–95

We need to distinguish 'equality before the law' and 'equal civil liberties'. To be equal before the law is to be equally subject to the law, whereas to possess civil liberties is to be in a position to do certain things, such as vote or express an opinion, and obviously we are equal when we possess the same liberties. There is, however, a close relationship between equality before the law and equality of civil liberties, and a historical example will help to illustrate this point. On 15 September 1935 the German Parliament (Reichstag) adopted the so-called 'Nuremberg Laws' governing German citizenship, one of which defined German citizenship (citizenship law, or Reichsbürgergesetz). The law made a distinction between a subject of the state (Staatsangehöriger) and a citizen (Reichsbürger). Article 1 stated that 'a subject of the state is one who belongs to the protective union of the German Reich', while Article 2 stated that 'a citizen of the Reich may be only one who is of German or kindred blood, and who, through his behaviour, shows that he is both desirous and personally fit to serve loyally the German people and the Reich'. Only citizens were to enjoy full, and equal, political rights. The First Supplementary Decree (14 November 1935) classified subjects by blood, and denied citizenship to Jews, where Jewishness was defined by the state.

It could be argued that these citizenship laws are compatible with equality before the law, since all subjects are equally subject to the law, despite the fact that the laws are themselves discriminatory (and much the same argument could be applied to the laws of Apartheid South Africa). While on the face of it this argument appears valid, and seems to show how weak both the idea of moral equality and equality before the law are, there are grounds for arguing that Nazi Germany could not maintain that all subjects were equal before the law. US legal theorist Lon Fuller, writing in the early post-war period, observed that Nazi law was not really law at all because it violated certain requirements for any legal system. For Fuller, the essential function of law is to 'achieve order through subjecting people's conduct to the guidance of general rules by which they may themselves orient their behaviour' (Fuller 1965: 657). To fulfil this function law (or rules) must satisfy eight conditions:

1. The rules must be expressed in general terms.
2. The rules must be publicly promulgated.
3. The rules must be prospective in effect.
4. The rules must be expressed in understandable terms.
5. The rules must be consistent with one another.
6. The rules must not require conduct beyond the powers of the affected parties.
7. The rules must not be changed so frequently that the subject cannot rely on them.
8. The rules must be administered in a manner consistent with their wording.

Fuller's argument is not uncontroversial, and many legal theorists will reject these rules, but it is plausible to maintain that a condition of a law (so-called) being a law is that is not arbitrary. Since the first article of the penal code of Nazi Germany asserted that the will of the Führer was the source of all law, it was impossible for subjects to determine what was required of them. Once it is accepted that law cannot be arbitrary then certain conditions follow, including at least a minimal idea of equal basic civil liberties. Chief among the civil, or political, liberties are the right to vote and to hold office; significantly, both these rights were explicitly denied to non-citizens in the Nuremberg Laws (Article 3, First Supplement).

There are other theories of law that do not rest on what Fuller terms an 'internal morality', and which presuppose neither moral equality nor equal liberties. Legal theorist John Austin characterised a 'law' as a general command issued by a 'sovereign' (or its agents). The sovereign is that person, or group of people, who receives 'habitual obedience' from the great majority of the population of a particular territory. So whereas Fuller would argue that (most) Nazi laws were not really laws at all, Austin would have identified Hitler as the sovereign, who, insofar as he commands obedience, issues valid law. This does not mean that his laws were moral: Austin made a sharp distinction between legality and morality. The relationship between morality and legality will be discussed in later chapters, and especially when we turn to the topic of human rights.

Equal Liberties

As suggested above, the state cannot directly distribute choice, but it can distribute the conditions for choice by granting individuals rights, or civil liberties. In liberal democratic societies the most important rights, or liberties, are freedom of expression, association, movement, and rights to a private life, career choice, a fair trial, vote, and to hold office if qualified. A couple of points are worth noting. First, it is difficult to distribute liberty per se; rather, what is distributed are specific rights-protected liberties. Second, you can have freedom without that freedom being recognised by the state, for no state can exercise complete control. However, when we talk about the distribution of liberty, it is not so much the freedom itself which is being distributed, but rather the *protection* of that liberty – if Sam is guaranteed that he will not be thrown in jail for expressing views critical of the state, but Jane is not given that guarantee, then clearly Sam and Jane are not being treated equally. It is the guarantee – the right to free expression – rather than the expression itself which is up for distribution. The separation between the guarantee (protection of the capacity to choose; right to choose) and the action that is guaranteed does not hold for all liberties. For example, voting – a 'participatory' rather than a 'private' or 'personal' right – is something which is clearly susceptible to *direct* distribution in a way that the freedom to marry whoever you wish (a private right), or not get married, is not (you can, of course, still choose not to vote). Some people can be awarded extra votes than others, or whole groups, such as workers or women, can be denied the vote.

Do Freedom and Equality Conflict?

Freedom (or liberty) necessarily entails choice, and individuals must make choices for themselves. It would follow that the state cannot – and indeed should not – attempt to control individual choice. At best, it can affect opportunities to make choices through the distribution of rights. Does this mean that freedom and equality necessarily conflict? In addressing this question we need to make a further distinction to the one already made between choice and the capacity, or opportunity, to make choices, so that we have a threefold distinction:

1. Choice, which must be under the control of the individual, and for which the individual can be held responsible.
2. Capacity, or opportunity for choice, which is not under the control of the individual, and for which the individual should not be held responsible.
3. Outcome of the choices of individuals, where outcomes are determined to a large degree by the interactive nature of choice.

Voting illustrates these points. You have a right to vote (2), which you may or may not exercise (1), but even if you exercise that right and vote for a party or a candidate, that choice may be less effective than another person's choice (3). It is less effective if your chosen party or candidate loses, but it might also be less effective in a more subtle way. Imagine that there is just one issue dimension, say the distribution of wealth, with the left supporting high tax and a high degree of redistribution of wealth, and the right supporting low taxes and a low degree of redistribution. These represent the two extremes and there are various positions in between. Voters are ranged along this axis from left to right. Consider the voter distributions shown in Figures 3.1 and 3.2.

If there are just two parties then to maximise its vote a party has an incentive to adopt a policy position as close to the median voter as possible. This is the case even under Figure 3.2 where the median voter is in a tiny minority. The point is that where you locate yourself relative to other voters will determine how effective your vote is. Equality (or inequality) of outcome is therefore the result of an interaction between the choices of many individuals, and it is impossible to protect freedom of choice and at the same time guarantee equality of outcome.

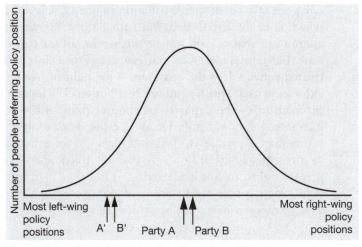

Figure 3.1 One-dimensional policy competition between two parties with voter preferences concentrated in the centre of the policy spectrum. From Laver 1997.

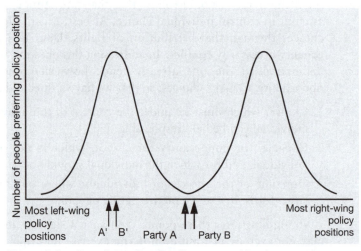

Figure 3.2 One-dimensional policy competition between two parties with voter preferences in the two concentrations, on the left and on the right. From Laver 1997.

The relationship of freedom to equality will be discussed in greater detail in Chapter 4, where the focus is on theories of justice – the aim here is simply to introduce the problem and encourage some reflection on it. At this stage it would be useful to consider two thought experiments (see the Exercise opposite), the first of which is taken from the work of Robert Nozick, and the second from G. A. Cohen (the work of both theorists is discussed in greater detail in Chapter 4).

Let us consider Nozick's example. If we measure equality by the number of marriage partners available then there is an unequal distribution: A and A′ have the greatest number of options, and Z and Z′ the fewest options. And if freedom is understood as choice, then arguably Z and Z′ have no freedom, because they have no choice but to marry each other. But, perhaps, the relevant liberty is determined by the relationship of each person to the *state*: in relation to the state Z and Z′

Exercise

Nozick: Marriage Partners

Imagine 26 men and 26 women, one for each letter of the alphabet. Each person wants to marry, and each of the 26 men has the same preference ordering of the women as the others, and likewise each of the 26 women has exactly the same preference ordering of the men. So if we name each person by a letter of the alphabet A, B, C, etc. for the men, and A′, B′, C′, etc. for the women, each man prefers A′ to B′ and B′ to C′ and so on, down to the last preference Z′. Likewise, each of the women prefers A to B and B to C, etc., down to Z. That means that all the women want to marry A, and so A has plenty of choice! Likewise, with regard to the men A′ has a full range of options. B and B′ have one less option, but still a lot of choice, and so on, down to Z and Z′ who have no choice but to marry one another (Nozick, 1974: 263–4).

Question
Are Z and Z′ denied (a) freedom, and (b) equality?

Cohen: The Locked Room

There are ten of us in a locked room. There is one exit at which there is a huge and heavily locked door. At roughly equal distances from each of us there is a single heavy key (each of us is equally distant from the door). Whoever picks up the key (each is physically able to do so) and with very considerable effort opens the door can leave. But there is a sensor that will register when one person has left, and as soon as they leave the door will slam shut and locked and nobody else will be able to leave – *forever* (Cohen, 1979: 22).

Question
Are we free to leave?

have as many options as A and A′. It is the conjoint choices of individuals that creates an inequality of outcome. Nozick can legitimately maintain that Z and Z′ are as free as A and A′ because his starting point is the concept of a natural right (to self-ownership); that right will always be held equally regardless of how individuals exercise the right. Nozick's example shows rather more dramatically what we suggested earlier about the differential consequences of voting – each person has a vote, but the effects of exercising that vote vary.

We turn now to Cohen's locked room. If, prior to anyone leaving, a voice heard from outside asked each in turn 'are you free to leave?' then we would be forced to say 'yes'. If we – plural – were asked whether we were free, the question is more difficult. Collectively, we are not free to leave: *each* is free to leave but *we* are not free to leave. Once again, conditionality is at work, but Cohen draws a different conclusion to that of Nozick from this conditionality. Working with certain Marxist assumptions, Cohen argues that a collectivist political order – one in which there is a much more equal distribution of income – would, in effect, enable more people to leave the room. In real-world terms, that means workers losing their subordinate class position. Unlike Nozick, Cohen is concerned with the choices people actually make, rather than their legal position vis-à-vis the state.

Material Equality

The example of inequality in the outcome of voting preferences illustrated problems of distributing political power, and certainly political power is a major good, but the most involved debates, both in everyday politics and in political theory, are focused on the distribution of material goods, such as income, or education, or health care. In liberal societies respect for equality before the law and equality of liberties is fairly well embedded in the political culture – while there is controversy over *particular* liberties, the majority of the population expresses support at least for the *principles*. The same cannot be said for principles of material equality. As was suggested in the section on Principles of Equality, while lip-service is paid to equality of opportunity, that term encompasses a great many possible principles of resource allocation, some of which entail radical state intervention in individuals' lives. More often than not, what is being advocated is equal access to jobs and services rather than equality of opportunity.

Equal Access

Equal access is sometimes referred to as 'formal equality of opportunity'. Equal access requires that positions which confer advantages on their holders should be open to all, and that the criteria for award of those positions is qualification(s). The qualifications required must be publicly acknowledged and intrinsically related to the position. The list of illegitimate grounds for denial of access to a position has gradually expanded, but in, for example, European Union countries, it would include: gender, race, ethnic or national origin, creed, disability, family circumstance, sexual orientation, political belief, and social or economic class. This list, which is not comprehensive, provides prima facie guidance on equal access.

It may be that certain of those characteristics are relevant to a job. For example, the priesthood in the Catholic Church is restricted to men, and normally unmarried, celibate, men. Employment in a women's refuge would normally be restricted to women. Legislation outlawing gender discrimination will contain clauses that permit what appears, at first glance, to be discrimination, but which may, in fact, be consistent with gender equality. We argued at the beginning of the chapter that there was a presumption in favour of equal treatment – people should be treated equally unless there were compelling grounds for unequal treatment. The nature of work in a women's refuge obviously provides compelling grounds, consistent with gender equality: since the client group in a refuge is seriously disadvantaged, women employed in the refuge are working towards a more gender-equal society. However, the restriction of the priesthood to men is more problematic and reveals the limits to equal access; this may not be a criticism, for we can say that because equality conflicts with other values, or principles, it necessarily has limits.

The compelling reason for setting aside gender equality in the case of the priesthood is derived from the importance of the equal liberties (or freedoms), among which is freedom of religion. Since freedom of religion requires that adherence to a church is voluntary, the church could be said to constitute a private sphere in which consenting adults should be free to act, and that includes being free to discriminate. However, this argument, if extended to other spheres of life, would corrode equal access: if churches can discriminate, then why not other employers? It is to block off the claim that firms, universities, shops, sports centres and so on are private spaces in which people should be free to discriminate, that anti-gender-discrimination legislation defines the public sphere widely. Churches are given a special exemption because of the interconnectedness of theological belief with employment: the very nature of the institution requires an all-male priesthood. This contrasts with, say, a restaurant where the customers may have a simple gut preference for eating with people of their 'own kind', and so seek to deny access to ethnic minorities. Nonetheless, it is reasonable to debate the correct limits between the public and private spheres: if you are renting out your house for a year while you go abroad, should you not be free to choose who occupies the house, where that choice might take the religion or ethnicity or marital status or sexual orientation of putative tenants into account? Other people may justifiably condemn your selection criteria, but taking liberty seriously may entail the recognition of a private sphere in which a person is free 'to do wrong'. On the other hand, it might be legitimate to prevent a landlord with a string of properties from applying discriminatory criteria in selecting potential tenants. We are not arguing for a particular line between public and private, but simply identifying a potential limit to the application of the equal access principle.

Equality of Opportunity

Equal opportunity is a much stronger principle of equality than equal access: as the name suggests, it requires that opportunities for acquiring favourable positions are equalised. This principle is attractive across the political spectrum because it seems to assume a meritocracy. For example, in Britain there is much popular debate about the social composition of the student bodies in the highest-rated universities. Students educated at fee-paying schools, or at state schools with relatively wealthy catchment areas, make up a disproportionately large part of the student intake of these universities. Even on the political right this situation is condemned: the brightest students, rather than the wealthiest students, should get, it is felt, the most desirable university places.

Although politicians disagree about the causes and the solutions to this situation, there is agreement that equal access alone does not ensure a meritocratic outcome. The difficulty is that an 18-year-old student has 18 years of education and socialisation behind them – every day they have been presented with 'opportunities' that a peer may have been denied. Those opportunities will include the emotional support necessary to achieve self-confidence and a sense of self-worth, stimulating conversation that enables them to develop a range of linguistic skills, interesting foreign holidays and activities, the presence of books in the family home, the imposition of a degree of parental discipline sufficient to encourage self-discipline, family networks and contacts, a good diet, and the provision of an adequate workspace. This list could go on, and none of these items relate to formal educational provision. Even parents who do not send their children to fee-paying schools may pay for such things as ballet classes or piano lessons. In short, every day of their life for the previous 18 years they have been given opportunities. To equalise such opportunities would require a very high degree of intervention in family life.

This description of a privileged child may overstate the requirement for an equalisation of opportunity. Perhaps it is not necessary that children have strictly equal opportunities, but rather that each child has a sufficient degree of opportunity to acquire advantageous positions. The idea is that there is a threshold level of opportunity below which a child should not fall. (Although it is not a serious objection to the threshold theory of equal opportunity, there would inevitably be dispute over the correct threshold.)

Another point about equality of opportunity is that the principle presupposes that inequality can be justified, so long as any inequalities are the result of desert. We can distinguish social advantage, native ability (intelligence) and effort. It is a commonly held view that 'IQ + effort' is an appropriate ground for discrimination, and that equal opportunity policies should endeavour to eliminate social advantage as a cause of inequality. Rawls argues that people no more deserve their native abilities, including their propensity to hard work, than they do those advantages gained from their family and social background (Rawls, 1972: 104). Other theorists, such as Ronald Dworkin and David Miller, argue that Rawls's rejection of desert is inconsistent with other important aspects of his theory, which stress the importance of choice and responsibility (Dworkin, 2000: 287–91; Miller, 1999: 131–55). Nonetheless Dworkin (especially) seeks to eliminate *natural ability* as a justification for inequality, while retaining responsibility for choices made. In this respect both Rawls's and Dworkin's arguments are significantly at variance with popular attitudes. This is an observation rather than a criticism – in Chapter 4 we discuss Rawls's argument in more detail.

Not all liberal theorists defend equality of opportunity. Friedrich Hayek argues that the free market is an example of a 'spontaneous social order' that cannot be recreated by human minds, and that has no central direction. Some redistribution of wealth is justified, but the attempt to overcome inequality of opportunity is doomed to failure. Regardless of whether they deserve their wealth the rich are the vanguard of socially useful change (Hayek, 1973: 88). Consider the high prices in today's values of cars in the 1920s, air travel in the 1930s, colour televisions in the 1960s, videotape machines in the 1970s, or personal computers in the 1980s. Innovative companies had to make a profit in order to spur development and a class had to exist capable of buying these things. What we call today the 'web' was not simply the product of one man's leap of imagination – Tim Berners-Lee's hypertext idea – but of a series of discrete technological developments, each requiring privileged consumers to make them commercially viable. Too much equality – including the attempt to achieve an elusive equality of opportunity – undermines the social conditions for innovation and progress.

Equality of Outcome

Equalisation of outcome seems, on the face of it, neither desirable nor coherent. It is not desirable because it would deny individual choice, and responsibility: if one person chooses a life of leisure and another person chooses a life of hard work why should the state seek to equalise the outcome of those choices? The outcome may not, in fact, be susceptible to equalisation. If income level is the metric subject to distribution, then the outcome can be equalised *for that metric*; but welfare (or well-being) is also a relevant metric, and the person living a life of leisure has presumably enjoyed greater well-being than the hard worker, such that the only way the two can enjoy an equal level of well-being is if they had not lived their respective lives of leisure and hard work. The point is that equality is always equality *of something*, and the attempt to equalise along one metric, say income, may result in inequality along another metric. Another difficulty with attempting to achieve equality of outcome is that some goods are 'positional': a positional good is one the enjoyment of which depends on the exclusion of others. For example, the slogan 'elite education for all' is a contradiction in terms. Likewise, eating at the best restaurant or driving the fastest car depends on that restaurant indeed being better than all the others and the car faster than all other cars. It follows that it is impossible to equalise positional goods. It could, of course, be argued that we can have *good* education, restaurants, or cars for all and that the desire to be better has in fact nothing to do with the intrinsic qualities of the good, but simply the *perceived* qualities of the good in question. The more common slogan 'excellence for all' still seems oxymoronic, but if we define excellence relative to a baseline of mediocre then it does make sense to talk of excellence for all.

Ch. 14:
Justice,
pp. 86–88

Despite these objections, equality of outcome can play a role in political debate even if it cannot be made to work as a principle. Rawls justifies inequality by use of the difference principle, but that principle rests on recognising that any inequalities must be to the benefit of the worst off. This argument takes equality of outcome as the baseline against which alternative distributions are to be measured; in effect, Rawls maintains that moral equality generates equality of outcome, but may also generate inequality of outcome if the worst off consent to that inequality. Equality of outcome has, therefore, a special moral status in Rawls's theory. It should be noted that if Rawls recognised desert as a legitimate source of inequality this tight connection between moral equality and equality of outcome would not hold.

Rawls does not, in fact, defend equality of outcome as a substantive principle. Anne Phillips, however, does defend this principle of equality. Much of Phillips's work has been concerned with political representation, and especially the under-representation of women and ethnic minorities in political institutions, and she takes the case of women in parliament as an example of the need for a principle of equal outcome. The under-representation of women in the British Parliament cannot, she argues, be attributed to lack of ability, or the conscious choice not to enter politics, but must be a consequence of the failure of equal opportunity (Phillips, 2004: 8). Women are not denied equal access to parliamentary represen-tation, and many political parties now have dedicated support for female candidates, which include women's officers, training days, support networks, and the requirement to have at least one woman on every shortlist for candidate selection in a particular constituency. Despite this the only political party that has been successful in increasing female representation in the House of Commons (the elected chamber) has been the British Labour Party, and that success can be attributed to 'all-women' shortlists imposed on local constituencies by the central party. The point being that all-women shortlists guarantee an increase in the number of candidates in Labour-held or winnable seats – the policy acts on outcomes and not on opportunities. The inequality of outcome in the other political parties is an indication that, despite various efforts, equality of opportunity has failed.

Affirmative Action

Affirmative action policies involve an explicit departure from the normal 'equal access' and 'equal opportunity' criteria for awarding a person a favoured position. The normal criteria include: (a) the position is open to all, and (b) selection is by competence, which is measured by qualifications. There are various types of affirmative action policies:

- *Encouragement* The job is advertised in newspapers read by particular communities, such as ethnic minorities.
- *Tie-breaking* If two people are 'equally qualified' then you choose the person from the 'disadvantaged group'. This is the weakest form of affirmative action.
- *Handicapping* An example of this would be requiring higher entry points, or grades, for applicants to university from wealthy backgrounds.
- *Quota system* A certain percentage of jobs must be filled by a particular group – this is usually subject to a requirement of minimum competence.

All-women shortlists are a version of the quota system and involve a setting aside of (a), and some critics would argue that it also entails setting aside (b). Affirmative action could, however, be defended on grounds that the evidence of qualification for a position cannot be taken as an accurate indication of a person's competence. To illustrate this point, let us imagine that entry to a good university normally requires 20 points in a school-leaving exam. Person A, from a poor background, scores 17 points, and person B, from a wealthy background, scores 21 points. However, evidence from the performance of previous cohorts of students suggests that (economically) poor students with lower entry points achieve a better final result on graduation than wealthy students with higher entry points, and so person A is predicted to do better than B, and therefore objectively is better qualified. Interestingly, this argument is meritocratic, and indeed is a technical, rather than a philosophical, objection to other principles of equality: existing evidence of competence is not reliable, so we have to broaden selection criteria to include prospective performance based not on the individual applicant's past behaviour but on the statistical behaviour of students from their background. However, distribution is still tied to the actions of individuals.

There are other ways of understanding affirmative action: it may be intended to provide role models; compensate a *group* for past injustices; increase the level of welfare of a disadvantaged group. Some defences are backward-looking, in that they seek to redress something that happened in the past; other defences, such as the one discussed above – prospective student performance – are forward-looking. A common, everyday objection to affirmative action is that it undermines respect and creates resentment: if a person achieves a position through positive discrimination then others may not respect that person, while the apparently better-qualified person passed over for the position will resent what seems an unfair selection procedure. This objection, whether or not valid, does identify an important aspect of equality (and inequality): there is an intersubjective dimension to human relationships, such that inequality can result in a lack of respect. Where that inequality seems unconnected to a person's actions – that is, when you end up in an unfavourable position regardless of what you have done – there is a feeling of *resentment* rather than simply disappointment. This suggests that equality should not be understood merely as a mathematical question of who gets what, but is intimately connected to other concepts, such as autonomy, responsibility, and well-being.

Equality of Welfare versus Equality of Resources

At the start of the chapter we posed the question: is inequality intrinsically bad? This question is best tackled through consideration of a distinction between equality of welfare and equality of resources. Ronald Dworkin argues against equalising welfare and for equalising resources, so long as resource inequality cannot be traced to decisions for which a person can be held responsible. By welfare Dworkin means well-being, which is a subjective state (it should not be confused with a belief in the welfare state: both welfarists and resourcists could defend the idea of an extensive welfare state).

Dworkin asks us to imagine a man who has five children, each with a dominant characteristic: (a) one is blind; (b) a playboy, (c) an ambitious politician; (d) a poet with humble needs: (e) a sculptor who works with expensive material. What would be a fair will for this man? A welfarist would say that the man should divide his estate according to the needs and preferences of each. A resourcist, on the face of things, would argue for an equal division. Welfarism looks like a strong theory of equality, for it weighs what is intrinsically valuable rather than what is of merely instrumental value: it is what we want to do, rather than what we have, that is valuable. It also addresses the problem of disability: surely the blind son's needs are greater than those of the playboy? The difficulty is that a welfarist cannot distinguish the preferences of each. If we extend the example and imagine the huge range of preferences that people have, should we compensate the racist for his disappointment in living in a society that has strong laws against racism? Should we compensate a person because she has wildly unrealistic expectations? Or a person who has expensive tastes? Or not compensate a person who is happy with her lowly – and, arguably, oppressed – position in society? If welfarism is to make sense we need a standard of what it is reasonable to want and, therefore, of when it is reasonable to feel resentment or unhappiness about not getting or achieving something, but once we impose a reasonableness standard we are moving away from pure 'welfare'. This is the problem with making the equalisation of happiness the aim of public policy.

To develop an alternative – resourcist – theory of distribution Dworkin works with two linked ideas: the hypothetical auction and the hypothetical insurance system. We start with the hypothetical auction. We imagine a group of shipwrecked people (immigrants) washed up on a desert island with abundant resources and no native population. The immigrants have equal personal resources (circumstances), but differing tastes. They endorse the principle that no one is antecedently entitled to any of the resources, and instead they shall be divided equally between them. They also accept what Dworkin calls the 'envy test': 'no division of resources is an equal division if, once the division is complete, any immigrant would prefer someone else's bundle of resources to his own bundle' (Dworkin, 2000: 67). A problem, however, emerges which evades the envy test: the bundles might not be equally valuable to each person given differing tastes. In other words, each person gets an identical bundle of goods, but because tastes differ they may not attach equal value to them – they do not envy other people's bundles, but nonetheless they would rather have a different bundle.

To deal with this problem the immigrants set up an auction. Each immigrant is given an equal set of clamshells, to be used as currency. We assume the goods have been created, but it is open to any immigrant to propose new goods. The auction proceeds, with prices set and bids made, until all markets have been cleared – all goods are sold – and the envy test passed. Of course, individuals might be lucky or unlucky in their tastes. If there is high demand for goods which are in short supply then the price of those goods will be high. Dworkin argues that taking responsibility for our lives means accepting our tastes, or if necessary adjusting them, and not expecting that resources will be redistributed to satisfy those tastes (Dworkin, 2000: 69–70). It should be added that the products we bid for can include leisure – if one person chooses to work twelve hours a day, and another opts for a leisurely four hours, then the income difference is the price paid by the latter person for eight hours of leisure. If he were to look simply at the income of the hard worker then he might feel envy, but the envy test requires a 'whole life' comparison: the hard worker has lost something by being a workaholic.

A crucial assumption of the auction is that the participants enter on equal terms – they differ only in their tastes. Resources are equal, meaning we all start with the same number of clamshells, but our personal resources are also equal: nobody is, for example, severely disabled. It does not take much reflection to see that people are not born equal in personal resources, and on the desert island itself it would not be long before there was an inequality of resources, and the possibility that the envy test will not be satisfied. Luck will play a part, but Dworkin makes a distinction between calculated gambles and brute bad luck. You might, for example, take all reasonable precautions but still contract lung cancer. Alternatively, you may be a heavy smoker and as a result contract cancer: the smoker took a calculated gamble and lost (Dworkin, 2000: 74–5).

Since the immigrants on the desert island know luck will play a significant role in their lives and they are rational in the sense of being prudential – adopting a 'whole life' perspective – they will insure themselves against misfortune, such that among the products for which they bid will be insurance policies. Of course, individuals are free to buy different policies, but because we assume that risk is random – let us say the chances of a coconut falling on your head from a great height is pretty much equal for all individuals – the premiums will be the same for each person, and so the insurance market will reflect the choices people make. The problem comes when we introduce identifiable brute luck – that is, we know from the day someone is born, and in fact even before they are conceived, that they will have a poor natural endowment.

To deal with this problem we agree to randomise risk. Although Dworkin does not use the term, in effect he argues for a veil of ignorance, albeit one much thinner than Rawls's: an individual knows their talents but does not know the price those talents command in the market (Dworkin, 2000: 94). Dworkin wants the agent to know enough about their talents and preferences to make judgements about the appropriate level of insurance cover to buy. The difficulty is that even when we are denied knowledge of the price our talents can command, the insurance premiums can never match the income a talented person will acquire through the exploitation of his or her talents. Not everyone can earn as much as J. K. Rowling earns and although buying an insurance policy which will pay out the millions that she has earned may at first sight seem the rational approach, further reflection shows it to be irrational. Let us assume that Rowling is in the 99th income percentile, but at the time she selects an insurance policy she does not know she will earn $X million per year – imagine she is returned to the state of being a struggling writer trying to get her first book published. We also assume that once the veil is lifted the actual payout will equate to what the market can bear and that she will be obliged to pay whatever premium she has agreed. If the market can bear coverage to the 30th percentile and Rowling has taken out a policy which covers her to the 90th percentile, and she remains a struggling writer on, let us say, the 35th percentile, then she will be far worse off than if she had opted for a cheaper policy. Importantly, the wealthy Rowling (on the 99th percentile) is also worse off, as she has to keep writing the Harry Potter books just so as to cover her premiums (Dworkin, 2000: 98). The aim of Dworkin's argument is to calculate how much income should be transferred across classes and he does not suggest that poor people have to pay the premiums, but in order to work out how much wealth should be transferred agents behind his veil we must assume they will be obliged to pay up. No insurance system will fully compensate a person for lacking talent, or, more accurately, lacking *marketable* talents.

Summary

We have surveyed a number of principles of equality, and sought to put them into some kind of order. A coherent defence of equality requires a number of things: (a) clear distinctions between different kinds of equality; (b) recognition that any principle of equality must explain what is being equalised, because equality in one sphere (along one metric) can result in inequality in another; (c) a scheme for connecting different principles of equality together; (d) an explanation of how equality fits with other political principles, such as freedom and efficiency. One of the tasks of a theory of justice is to connect and order different political values and principles, so the discussion in the next chapter follows directly from this one.

Questions

1. Must freedom and equality conflict?
2. Are there any valid positional goods?
3. Is equality of opportunity desirable?
4. Should we seek to equalise happiness?

References

Cavell, S. (1990) *Conditions Handsome and Unhandsome: The Constitution of Emersonian Perfectionism* Chicago, IL: University of Chicago Press.

Cohen, G. (1979) 'Capitalism, Freedom, and the Proletariat' in A. Ryan (ed.), *The Idea of Freedom* Oxford: Oxford University Press, 9–25

Detwiler, B. (1990) *Nietzsche and the Politics of Aristocratic Radicalism* Chicago, IL: University of Chicago Press.

Dworkin, R. (2000) *Sovereign Virtue: The Theory and Practice of Equality* London and Cambridge, MA: Harvard University Press.

Fuller, L. (1965) 'A Reply to Professors Cohen and Dworkin' *Villanova Law Review*, 655–66.

Hayek, F.A. (1973) *Law, Legislation and Liberty* London: Routledge.

Laver, M. (1997) *Private Desires, Political Actions: An Invitation to the Politics of Rational Choice* London: Sage.

Miller, D. (1999) *Principles of Social Justice* Cambridge, MA: Harvard University Press.

Nietzsche, F. (1998) *On the Genealogy of Morality*, translated by Maudemarie Clark and Alan J. Swenson, Indianapolis, IN: Hackett.

Nozick, R. (1974) *Anarchy, State, and Utopia* Oxford: Blackwell.

Phillips, A. (2004) 'Defending Equality of Outcome' *Journal of Political Philosophy*, 12(1), 1–19.

Rawls, J. (1972) *A Theory of Justice* Oxford: Clarendon Press.

Wilkinson, R. (2005) *The Impact of Inequality* London: Routledge.

Further Reading

J. Roland Pennock and John Chapman (eds), *Equality* (New York: Atherton Press, 1967), is a useful collection of essays. Single-authored general works include: Alex Callinicos, *Equality* (Cambridge: Polity Press, 2000); John Rees, *Equality* (New York and London: Praeger, 1971). A longer, and more advanced, work is Larry Temkin, *Inequality* (New York and Oxford: Oxford University Press, 1993). Other interesting single-authored works include Anne Phillips, *Which Equalities Matter?* (Oxford: Polity, 1999) and Matt Cavanagh, *Against Equality of Opportunity* (Oxford: Clarendon, 2002), who challenges traditional assumptions about the nature of meritocracy. Amartya Sen, *Inequality Reexamined* (Oxford: Clarendon, 1992) stresses the importance of the 'equality of what?' question (the importance of identifying metrics). James Fishkin, *Justice, Equal Opportunity, and the Family* (New Haven and London: Yale University Press, 1983) explores the family as a problem for equality. The most important contributions to the equality debate are gathered together in a couple of edited collections: Louis Pojman and Robert Westmoreland (eds), *Equality: Selected Readings* (New York and London: Oxford University Press, 1997) and Matthew Clayton and Andrew Williams, *The Ideal of Equality* (Basingstoke: Palgrave, 2000).

Weblinks

A large number of 'equality' sites are maintained by pressure and interest groups, or formal government bodies dedicated to increasing equality. It is interesting to see how the concept is used by these organisations; do not, however, expect sophisticated philosophical discussions. The best sites are those maintained by universities, which provide further links:

- Equality Studies Centre at University College, Dublin (Ireland): http://www.ucd.ie/esc/

- Cardiff University (Wales): http://www.cardiff.ac.uk/learn/try/equality/

- Human Rights and Equality Centre, University of Ulster (Northern Ireland): http://www.ulst.ac.uk/hrec/hrec_otherlinks.phtml

Chapter 4

Justice

Introduction

Should people who are intelligent, or good-looking, or naturally charming, be allowed to keep whatever they gain from their exploitation of those natural attributes? Should people be free to pass on their material gains to whoever they choose? If it is a good thing for parents to care about their children, then why should they not be allowed to benefit them? These questions go to the heart of debates about distributive – or 'social' – justice. Distributive justice is concerned with the fair – or 'just' – distribution of resources. In the early modern period, the focus was on property rights as the moral basis for the distribution of resources, and justifications for the state – that is, individuals' obligations to obey the state – were often grounded in the role the state played in protecting those rights. In this chapter we concentrate on contemporary theories of justice, in which private property rights are often regarded as problematic – although one of the three theories discussed is a contemporary restatement and defence of strong private property rights.

Chapter Map

In this chapter we will:

- Discuss an important *liberal egalitarian* theory of justice – that of John Rawls.

- Contrast Rawls's theory with a *libertarian* alternative, advanced by Robert Nozick.

- Consider a major challenge to both theories – that of Gerald Cohen, who argues from a *Marxist* perspective.

- Apply these theories to real-world examples of distributive justice.

Just Deserts? What do People Deserve?

Source: © Milk Photographie/Corbis

The chances are that anybody reading this book will either be on above-average income or be in the process of acquiring the skills that will generate such an income. Studies have shown that in Britain graduates earn, over a lifetime, 20–25 per cent more than people with only school-leaving qualifications (A levels and equivalent). A study by PricewaterhouseCoopers estimated that the average graduate earned an extra £160,000 over a lifetime (for medics it was £340,000). Precise percentages will vary, but studies from other European countries, and North America, reveal a similar picture. Do graduates *deserve* this advantage? If we go back a stage we could also ask whether those graduates deserved their university places. A common response to this question might be: it depends on what family advantages they had. Two students may have the same entry qualifications, but if one has a relatively disadvantaged family background, while the other is relatively advantaged, the former might be thought more deserving than the latter. The difference in attitude rests on a distinction between naturally derived and socially derived advantages: natural ability, such as intelligence, is

widely considered a legitimate basis for distribution, and any inequality that results from the exercise of intelligence is justified, whereas benefiting from socially inherited advantages, such as an expensive schooling, is regarded as illegitimate. In addition, what a person does with their natural abilities is thought morally relevant: people deserve to keep what they have acquired through their own efforts. Of course, this belief in 'meritocracy' – IQ + effort – need not be absolute; most people would support an *unconditional* minimum set of resources.

Before moving on, ask yourself the following questions:

1. Should university places be distributed simply on the basis of performance in public examinations, or should other factors, such as socio-economic background, be taken into account?

2. How far should the state go in trying to create equality of opportunity?

3. Should people with fewer natural abilities get extra state-funded educational resources?

Theories of Just Distribution

Distributive justice is, as the name suggests, concerned with the just distribution of resources. It must be distinguished from *retributive* justice, which is concerned with how a punishment fits a crime. What might be the basis for the distribution of wealth? Here are some possibilities:

- *Threat advantage* The amount a person earns is the result of that person's relative bargaining power.
- *Need* Everyone should have their needs satisfied – there should be a guaranteed minimum set of resources equivalent to that required to satisfy those needs.
- *Desert* If you work hard and as a consequence increase your earnings relative to others you deserve to keep those additional earnings.
- *Freedom* The pattern of distribution is the result of the choices people make – if you have a product that others *choose* to buy, in buying the product other people have *consented* to the income you gain from selling it, and therefore also to any resulting inequality.
- *Labour* The profit made from the sale of commodities should reflect the contribution that the producer (labourer) makes to the commodity.
- *Maximise utility* We should aim to maximise the overall level of utility in society; 'utility' may be defined as happiness or pleasure or welfare or preference satisfaction.
- *Equality* Resources should be distributed equally.
- *Priority to the worst off* The worst off should be as well off as possible.

Rather than run through all these options we will focus on the work of three thinkers – John Rawls, Robert Nozick and Gerald Cohen. In the course of the discussion comments will be made on all the above options. Although the focus on social justice, as distinct from justice as an individual virtue, is a very recent development, there is a history to these contemporary debates, as will be particularly evident in the discussion of Nozick. Furthermore, the debate over social justice set out in this chapter connects to an even more recent development: the concern with global justice, which we discuss in Chapter 21.

Rawls: an Egalitarian Liberal Theory of Justice

Rawls's book *A Theory of Justice* (published 1972) had a huge impact on political philosophy. In it he advances a method for making moral decisions about the distribution of resources – not just material resources, but also freedom and political power – and argues that the operation of that method would result in a particular conception of justice, one which is significantly 'redistributivist' (or egalitarian).

Rawls locates his work in the social contract tradition of Locke, Rousseau and Kant, and indeed he is credited with reviving this tradition, which had gone into abeyance after about 1800. The classical idea of the contract was that it was the device by which power was legitimated: it is rational from the standpoint of the individual to hand over some (most, all) of the 'rights' they enjoy in the 'state of nature' to a coercive authority. Rawls differs from the classical theorists by taking it for granted that social cooperation under a state is normally a good thing, and so the focus of his theory is not the justification of the state but the distribution of the 'benefits' and 'burdens' of cooperation under a state. The *benefits* are material goods, personal freedom and political power. The *burdens* include not only any inequality which may arise, but the fact that principles will be coercively enforced – we are required to obey the state. Rawls developed his theory of justice in opposition to the then dominant utilitarian one, and we will have more to say about utilitarianism in our discussion of Rawls.

Before we set out Rawls's method for choosing 'principles of justice' and discuss what principles would be chosen, two very important points must be made:

1. A theory of justice applies to what Rawls calls the 'basic structure' of society. There is some ambiguity about this concept, but for the purposes of the present discussion we can say the basic structure consists of those institutions that fundamentally affect a person's life chances. Included would be the structure of the economy – the rules of ownership and exchange – and the provision of services such as health and education, as well as constitutional rights that define how much freedom a person enjoys.

2. While Rawls has been influential on the left of politics, he is a philosopher rather than a politician. What is at issue is the basic structure of society, and not the detailed policy decisions that may be made *within* that basic structure. Furthermore, Rawls is not aiming to persuade merely a majority of people to endorse his theory – he is not fighting an election – but rather offering arguments that no reasonable person could reject: he is aiming for *unanimity*.

The Original Position

Rawls's theory has two parts: an explanation of how we decide what is just, and a discussion of what he believes we would decide is just. We start with the first part. Rawls employs what he terms the original position. The original position is a thought experiment – you are asking a 'what if?' question: what if such-and-such were the case? It is not a 'place' – you only 'go into' the original position in a figurative sense. The most important feature of the original position is the veil of ignorance: you do not know your class and social position, natural assets and abilities, strength and intelligence, particular psychological characteristics, gender, to which generation you belong, who your family and friends are, and perhaps most controversially of all, your conception of the good – that is, your ideas about what makes life valuable or worth living, such as your religious and philosophical beliefs, but which are not necessarily shared by other people (Rawls, 1972: 12). You do know certain general things about your circumstances. You know you live in a society characterised by moderate scarcity: there are enough resources to satisfy basic needs and leave a significant surplus to be distributed, but that surplus is not sufficient to overcome conflict between people over its distribution. Rawls assumes that people want more rather than less of the benefits generated by cooperation. As well as knowing your society is marked by moderate scarcity you also have a general knowledge of psychology and economics.

Motivation in the Original Position

Rawls attributes to people in the original position a certain psychology, or set of motivations. It is important to stress that Rawls makes these assumptions *for the purposes of his theory*; he does not claim that 'real people' – that is, people who know their identities – have this psychology. In the original position the following holds:

- We *all* value certain things – what Rawls terms the (social) primary goods. The primary goods are rights, liberties, powers and opportunities, income and wealth, and the 'bases of self-respect'. The primary goods are valuable to many different ends, so if you choose a career trading in stocks and shares, or, alternatively, living in a self-sufficient community on a remote island, you will value these things (Rawls, 1972: 93).
- You seek to *maximise* your share of the primary social goods (Rawls, 1972: 142).
- You are not a gambler. Rawls tries to avoid assuming a particular attitude to risk; nonetheless, the way the original position is set up would suggest that we would be 'risk-averse' (Rawls, 2001: 106–7).
- You are not envious of other people (Rawls, 1972: 143).
- We are mutually disinterested: that is, we are not interested in one another's welfare. You do know, however, that once the veil has been lifted you will have family and friends who you do care about (Rawls, 1972: 144–5).
- We live in a 'closed society' – entered at birth and exited at death. Again, this point can easily be misunderstood. We do not know what principles of justice will be chosen – we have not got to that point yet – but it is highly likely that among the principles will be a right to emigrate. The reason Rawls assumes we live our whole lives in one society is that it makes the choice of principles very serious; John Locke is often interpreted – perhaps wrongly – as arguing that remaining in a society and using the state's resources – riding along the King's highway – constituted 'tacit consent' to the state. Rawls rejects that argument: for an individual to leave a society and seek asylum elsewhere (or migrate for economic reasons) is such a major step that deciding not to seek asylum (or migrate) cannot be taken to constitute consent to the existing regime. This generates two motivational points: because the choice of principles is a serious one, we would (a) not gamble our interests (a point already made), and (b) we accept the chosen principles will be binding on us once the veil has been lifted – Rawls terms the acceptance of the principles the strains of commitment (Rawls, 1972: 145).

It has probably struck you that there is something odd about the motivation of people in the original position. On the one hand, they are purely self-interested – they seek to maximise their individual shares of the primary goods. On the other hand, because they do not know their identities they are *forced* to be impartial, that is, each individual can only advance their interests by viewing the choice of principles from the standpoint of each individual. Expressed metaphorically, we have to put ourselves in each other's shoes.

Exercise

Imagine you do not know your age, gender, social class, what you look like, how intelligent you are, your beliefs (religious and philosophical views), who your family and friends are, and so on. The task is to get the best deal for yourself – the biggest income possible. Below is a table setting out a number of income distributions (A, B1, B2, C1, C2, D). These distributions represent average annual earnings for a whole lifetime. What you have to do is choose one. In making your choice, bear in mind the following:

- Because you don't know your identity you could end up in the top quarter of earners, or the bottom quarter, or somewhere in between.

- You care only about your own level of income – you are not envious of other people.

- You have got one shot – whatever you choose is binding on you for the rest of your life.

- Once you have chosen you will be told your identity.

Table 4.1

	A	B1	B2	C1	C2	D
Wealthy	3	70	50	120	97	250
	3	25	28	30	29	10
	3	20	23	25	24	7
Poor	3	15	15	7	10	4
Average:	3	32.5	29	45.5	40	67.75

What would be Chosen in the Original Position?

Now we come to the second part of Rawls's theory: the choice of principles. Agents in the original position are completely free to choose whatever they wish, but Rawls does discuss some possible candidates (Rawls, 1972: 124). It should be noted that these are expressed in philosophical language – Rawls does not talk about choosing state socialism or a free-market economy:

1. Everyone serves my interests – I get what I want (first-person dictatorship).
2. Everyone acts fairly except me (free rider).
3. Everyone is allowed to advance their interests as they wish (general egoism).
4. We maximise the aggregate level of goods (classical utilitarianism).
5. Option 4 but with a minimum level of goods for each individual.
6. We maximise the average (per capita) level of goods (average utilitarianism).
7. Option 6 but with a minimum level of goods for each individual.
8. Certain ways of life are to be privileged because they have greater intrinsic value (perfectionism).
9. We balance a list of prima facie valid principles, that is, we make an intuitive judgement about the correct trade-off between freedom and equality should they conflict (intuitionism).
10. The two principles of justice (democratic conception).

Rawls argues that we would choose option 10: the democratic conception. Options 1–3 are incoherent. Because you can only have one dictator we would never agree to dictatorship. Option 2 contradicts the strains of commitment, and 3 is unstable. Options 4–7 represent utilitarianism. Utilitarians hold that what we ought to do is maximise the overall *level* of well-being (or 'utility'). They are not concerned with the *distribution* of utility (although options 5 and 7 do give some weight to individuals – they create a 'floor' below which nobody should fall). Classical utilitarianism measures the level of welfare without reference to the number of utility-generating beings (we say 'beings' because non-human animals might generate utility), whereas average utilitarianism divides the level of welfare by the number of utility-generating beings. Compare the following two situations:

(a) 2,000 units of welfare divided by 500 beings;

(b) 1,000 units of welfare divided by 20 beings.

Ch. 2:
Freedom
pp. 51–53

Ch. 3:
Equality
pp. 63–65

For a classical utilitarian (a) is superior to (b), whereas for an average utilitarian (b) is superior to (a): 50 units versus 4 units. Perfectionists (option 8) hold that there are certain ways of life worthy of pursuit and the state should aim to bring these ways of life about ('to perfect' means to complete, or bring to fruition). This argument does not have great significance for the distribution of income, but it certainly affects what amount of freedom we should have (it relates back to Chapter 2: John Finnis is one kind of perfectionist, as – arguably – is Nietzsche, whose work we discussed in Chapter 3). Rawls argues that because we are denied knowledge of our particular conceptions of the good we would not opt for perfectionism; we would not, for example, choose to give a particular religion special status. Intuitionism (option 9) entails 'resolving' conflicts of values and interests on an ad hoc, case-by-case basis – we have no method for resolving them. The aim of Rawls's theory is to provide just such a method.

The Democratic Conception: the Two Principles of Justice

Rawls argues that agents in the original position would choose the democratic conception. He distinguishes between a special and a general conception, which are versions of the democratic conception. The general conception is: 'all social primary goods . . . are to be distributed equally unless an unequal distribution of any or all of these goods is to the advantage of the least favoured' (Rawls, 1972: 303). Rawls hopes that he can persuade the reader that the general conception would be endorsed even if the special conception, as one version of it, is rejected. The special conception consists of the two principles of justice. As Rawls's original presentation of the two principles was slightly confusing, we will use, in abbreviated form, his revised version from *Justice as Fairness: A Restatement* (Rawls, 2001: 42–3):

1. Equal liberty: each person is guaranteed a set of basic liberties.

2a. Equal opportunity: there must be equal access to jobs and services under fair equality of opportunity.

2b. Difference principle: inequalities are only justified if they benefit the least-advantaged members of society. (In addition to the two principles – 1 and 2a/2b – there is also the just savings principle, which is intended to determine how much should be saved for future generations.)

The first principle is a familiar one – each person has an equal right to free speech, association, conscience, thought, property, a fair trial, to vote, hold political office if qualified and so on. Principle 2a is also familiar – jobs and services should be open to all (equal access), but furthermore society should be so arranged that as far as possible people have an equal *opportunity* to get jobs and gain access to services. 2b – the difference principle – is the novel one, and it is the one we shall focus on in the next section.

Rawls maintains that there is a lexical priority of 1 over 2a and 2a over 2b. That means that you cannot sacrifice liberty for economic justice – you must satisfy fully the equal liberty principle before applying the difference principle (Rawls, 1972: 42–3). For example, the greatest source of unequal opportunity is the family – parents favouring their children – but Rawls argues that even though people in the original position are 'mutually disinterested' they do value personal freedom, which includes the freedom to form personal relationships, marry, have a family, and enjoy a 'private sphere' of life. They would, therefore, opt to protect this private sphere even if it resulted in unequal opportunity. Although Rawls's theory does not operate at the detailed level of public policy, he would probably have argued that, for example, outlawing private education contravenes the first principle of justice. On the other hand, he does support high inheritance tax, and that tax not only works directly against privilege but generates resources which can be used to fund an extensive state education system. Lexicality also entails that equal opportunity takes priority over the difference principle. Discrimination in access to jobs might improve the position of the worst off, but it would violate the equal opportunity principle.

Would we really Choose the Difference Principle?

If you consider the exercise on p. 85, we asked you to choose one of six distributions. Rawls argues that the rational strategy is to choose distribution B2.

Rational agents in the original position, recognising the seriousness of the choice, will, Rawls maintains, ensure that should they end up in the bottom quarter of society they will be as well off as possible. The reasoning behind this is termed 'maximin': *maximum minimorum*, or the *maxi*mization of the *min*imum position (Rawls, 1972: 154). Although Rawls avoids committing himself to any particular view on agents' attitude to risk, only highly risk-averse agents would select B over the most credible alternative, principle C2.* To be fair, the table fails to capture the dynamic nature of income distribution, for

---

*Rawls claims to eschew any view on risk, arguing that agents in the original position face *uncertainty* rather than *risk* (Rawls, 2001: 106). This seems at first sight a meaningless distinction, for uncertainty is at the heart of gambling. But developing the distinction Rawls maintains that gamblers have some knowledge of probabilities, knowledge denied to agents in the original position. This, however, would amount to denying agents *general* knowledge of society. Whilst Rawls seeks to avoid attributing a 'special psychology' to agents – that is, a controversial set of motivations – his argument does seem to amount to the claim that as 'trustees' (or representatives) agents would not risk the fundamental interests of those they represent. Agents are indeed risk-averse.

what is presented is a one-off 'time slice' of income, whereas in the original position agents are not choosing a *particular* distribution but a *principle* of distribution, and the principles underlying B and C2 are quite different: C2 says 'maximise average expected utility (subject to a floor)' whereas B says 'maximise the position of the worst off'. There is a shifting sands quality to C2: it does not concern itself with any particular group in society, but takes only average income to be morally significant. It is possible that over time distributions could move quite dramatically and compared to B the worst-off class under C2 could become a lot worse off. B, on the other hand, always gives priority to the worst off. Nonetheless, the floor – which is defined as a fraction of the average, but could be a fraction of the income of the best-off – provides some reassurance to agents that their economic position will not be dire even if they end up among the worst-off.

Let us look at the other two distributions, and the reasoning which might lead to them. Maximax – maximise the maximum – is the reasoning leading to distribution D. This is highly risky. One thing you might have noticed is that per capita income is higher in A than C, and thus one might think the average utilitarian would opt for A over C. However, we talk of *expected utility*: a maximiser wants to get the highest income possible – everybody, and not just a risk-taker, wants to earn 250. Each person knows they have under distribution D only a one in four chance of earning that amount of money. They have a one in four chance they will end up with 4 units of income. Does their *desire* for 250 units outweigh their *aversion* to earning only 4 units? Given certain facts about human psychology – for example, that the utility from an extra amount of income diminishes the more income you have – they will reason that greater weight should be attached to the avoidance of lower incomes than the enjoyment of higher incomes. We come now to distribution A. It is *relativities* which concern someone who opts for A. Rawls argues we are not envious, and therefore we are not concerned with what other people earn, so relativities are unimportant. It might, however, be argued that if one of the primary social goods is self-respect any inequality will undermine it: there is no easy answer to this, and it does seem that for 'real people' – as distinct from people in the original position – self-worth is (to some extent) attached to income or social status.

Finally, we need to consider the distinction between distributions B1 and B2. Two concepts are relevant here: close-knitness and chain-connection. The distribution table does not capture the first concept, which is empirical in character: if we maximise the position of the worst-off the likely consequence is that the prospects of the next-poorest class will be improved. Chain-connection, on the other hand, pertains to the principle that the prospects of each class should be improved so long as the position of the worst-off is maximised and each succeeding class is as well off as possible consistent with maximising the income of the worst-off. This argument is intended to address the criticism that a small gain for, say, unskilled workers is achieved at a significant cost to semi-skilled workers. Since agents in the original position have knowledge of economic theory, including empirical studies of economic behaviour, they will choose the difference principle in the knowledge that income redistributions are close-knit and chain-connection is, therefore, possible.

Nozick: a Libertarian Theory of Justice

Robert Nozick advanced an alternative to Rawls's egalitarian theory of justice; one that lays stress on the importance of private property rights. In his book *Anarchy, State, and Utopia* Nozick seeks to defend the notion of the state against philosophical anarchists, who argue the state can never be justified: but what he defends is a minimal state. A minimal state is a monopoly provider of security services. A more extensive state – one that intervenes in the economy and supplies welfare benefits – cannot be justified. 'Utopia' would be a world in which diverse lifestyles and communities would flourish under the protection of the minimal state.

Nozick's Starting Point: Private Property Rights

The very first line of *Anarchy, State, and Utopia* reads: 'individuals have rights, and there are things no person or group may do to them (without violating their rights)' (Nozick, 1974: ix). Jonathan Wolff argues that Nozick is a 'one-value' political philosopher (Wolff, 1991: 3–4). Other philosophers accept that there is more than one value; for example, they might maintain freedom is important, but so is equality, and since freedom and equality often conflict we need a method for 'resolving' that conflict. Rawls's *two* principles of justice express this idea. Wolff maintains that Nozick's one value is private property, or, more precisely, the *right* to private property. When we use the term property in everyday speech we tend to think of real estate. Everyday usage is not wrong, but political philosophers have a wider conception of private property: it is the legally sanctioned (or morally legitimate) appropriation of things. A *right* is an advantage held against another person – if you have a right, then another person has a duty to do something (or *not* do something: that is, not interfere), so a right is a relationship between people. Bringing together the two concepts – private property and rights – we can say that a right to private property entails the exclusion of other people from the use of something. Nozick's 'entitlement theory' of justice is based on the inviolability of private property rights. There are three parts to the theory:

Part 1: Just acquisition

Part 2: Just transfer

Part 3: Rectification.

Just Acquisition – Locke and Nozick

Ch. 8:
Liberalism
pp. 186–87

The first question to ask is: how did anybody acquire the right to exclude other people from something? Nozick draws on the work of John Locke (1632–1704), specifically, his defence of private property, especially his argument for 'first acquisition'. We have to imagine a historical situation in which nobody owns anything, and then explain (justify) the parcelling up of that which has hitherto been held in common. The standard interpretation of Locke is that he was attempting to reconcile Christianity and capitalism at a time – the seventeenth century – when capitalism was beginning to replace feudalism as the dominant form of economic organisation. Locke began with three Christian premises:

1. God had entrusted the material world to human beings, who were its 'stewards' and thus had a duty to respect it.
2. The implication of 1 is that the world is owned in common by humanity.
3. God as creator had rights to what he created. As God's creatures human beings have a duty to God to preserve themselves.

Capitalism poses a challenge because it was wasteful of natural resources, which violates stewardship; capitalism implied private ownership and not common ownership, and it threatened to push large numbers of people into poverty and starvation, thus undermining their capacity to fulfil their duty to God to preserve themselves. For example, in seventeenth-century England we begin to see the movement from smallholdings to large estates, with smallholders (serfs) forced to hire out their labour for a daily wage, thus becoming wage labourers. The creation of a class of rural wage labourers presaged the development of an urban working class with the industrialisation of the eighteenth and (especially) the nineteenth centuries. The risks of starvation were significantly greater for the wage labourers than for their earlier counterparts, the serfs.

Christian theology, Locke argued, did not strictly require common ownership, but rather the promotion of the common good, and capitalism, through its capacity to generate wealth, did indeed promote it (Locke, 1988: 291). Locke's starting point for a defence of capitalism is his account of how we go from common ownership to private ownership: if a person mixes his labour with something external to himself then he acquires rights in that thing. Mixing one's labour is sufficient to establish ownership so long as two 'provisos' are satisfied:

- *Sufficiency proviso* There must be 'enough and as good left for others' (Locke, 1988: 288).
- *Spoilage proviso* There must be no wasting away of the product (Locke, 1988: 290).

In practice these two provisos are easily met because of the development of wage labour and money (Locke, 1988: 293). Wage labour is premised upon the notion of having property rights in your own body – rights which you cannot alienate, that is, you cannot sell your body – but the product of the use (labour) of your body can be sold, such that your labour becomes a commodity which is hired out.

Wage labour is important for Locke because it enables the buyer of labour to say to the potential seller of labour (wage labourer) that you can acquire sufficient goods to preserve yourself if you sell your labour to me. If you do not, *you* (not me) are violating your duty to God to preserve yourself. Crucially – and of great significance for Marx – that labour does not create rights for the labourer in the product, since the labour which the labourer sells to the buyer is an extension of the buyer's body; Locke argued that 'the turfs my servant has cut are *my* turfs' (Locke, 1988: 289). Wage labour, therefore, satisfies the sufficiency proviso. Money deals with the spoilage proviso – a person's property can be held in this abstract form and thus will not 'spoil', unlike, say, crops, which rot, or animals, who die.

Ch. 10:
Socialism
pp. 223–24

Exercise

Imagine a basketball match watched by 3,000 people, each of whom pay $20 to see Chamberlain play, and $8 of that $20 goes directly to Chamberlain (the $8 can be taken to be Chamberlain's marginal value: if he was not playing the organisers would have to sell the tickets at $12). Let us assume that each of the 3,000 spectators and Chamberlain earn $40,000. This is, of course, unrealistic, but it is intended to make a point. We can compare earnings – what Nozick calls 'holdings' – before and after the tickets were bought:

	Spectators' holdings	Chamberlain's holdings
Before purchase	$40,000 × 3,000	$40,000
After purchase	$39,980 × 3,000	$64,000

Is there any reason why Chamberlain should not keep the $24,000 he has gained as a result of the ticket purchases?

Nozick draws heavily on Locke's acquisition argument, but drops its theological basis. He begins with the assumption of 'self-ownership', that is, you own your body, and all that is associated with it – brain states, genetic make-up and so on, but this is no longer grounded in God's rights as creator. He then adopts Locke's mixed labour device, but he alters the provisos:

- *Sufficiency proviso* Locke was worried that there would come a point in the development of capitalism where some people really did not have enough to survive on, even with the possibility of wage labour. Nozick is not so concerned: so long as everyone is *better off* after appropriation then that appropriation is just (Nozick, 1974: 175–6).
- *Spoilage proviso* Nozick is not worried about 'spoilage', but he does insist that a person cannot acquire a monopoly control over certain goods, such as a water supply (Nozick, 1974: 180–1).

Just Transfer

Just transfer is dependent upon just acquisition, for you cannot justly transfer what you have not justly acquired. Furthermore, acquisition is a very strong idea – it entails full control over the thing that is acquired, including the power to transfer it to another person. Nozick takes the example of Wilt Chamberlain (1936–99), considered by many to be the greatest basketball player of all time. Consider the exercise above.

Nozick argues that so long as Chamberlain did not use threats or fraud to acquire each $8 then his additional earning is legitimately his by a simple transfer (Nozick, 1974: 161–3). The fact that such transfers will over time create significant inequalities – in the example we went from equality to inequality – is irrelevant, for what matters is that individuals have consented to the transfer. Those who object to such transfers want, in Nozick's words, 'to forbid capitalist acts between consenting adults' (Nozick, 1974: 163). To evaluate the force of Nozick's argument we need to compare his theory of justice with the alternatives.

Types of Theory

Nozick divides theories of justice up into two groups – end state and historical (Nozick, 1974: 153–5) – with a subdivision of the second into patterned and unpatterned theories (Nozick, 1974: 155–60).

End-state theories These theories are not concerned with what people *do*, but only with the *end result*. Utilitarian theories fall into this category – the aim is to maximise total, or alternatively, average utility. Who gets what under this arrangement is irrelevant: person A may get 25 units and person B 10, and the total is 35 (and average 17.5), but if A got 10 and B 25 the end result would be the same.

Historical theories What people have done (note the past tense) is relevant to the distribution of resources. For example, distribution according to desert, that is, hard work, is a historical principle (actually, 'historical' is a bad label – it would have been better, though less elegant, to talk of *person-regarding* theories, because it is not necessarily what a person has *done* that is relevant – need would be person-regarding). Historical theories are further divided into:

- *Patterned* Any principle that involves the phrase 'to each according to _____' (fill in the blank: desert, need, labour and so on) is going to create a pattern (Nozick, 1974: 159–60). Nozick includes Rawls's theory as patterned: priority to the worst off (maximin) generates a pattern.
- *Unpatterned* Nozick calls his own theory unpatterned, because whatever distribution exists should be the result of choice. You could argue that this is patterned with the blank filled in as 'choice', but 'choice' is not really the same as desert or need – the latter two provide objective criteria that can be used by a redistributive agency (the state) whereas you choose to do whatever you like.

Individuals may, under Nozick's utopian framework, aim to bring about an end-state or patterned distribution, but what may not happen is that the state *coerces* people into creating that end state or pattern. To appropriate some of Chamberlain's $24,000 is tantamount to forcing him to labour (Nozick, 1974: 172).

Rectification

Nozick's comments on the third part of his theory are brief and underdeveloped. If something was acquired or transferred as the result of fraud or theft or force then some mechanism is required for rectifying the situation (Nozick, 1974: 152–3). All that Nozick offers in the way of a theory is the suggestion that counterfactual reasoning be applied: what would be the pattern of holdings if the unjust acquisition/transfer had not taken place? This raises the problem of increased value: if you steal a dollar and make a million dollars as a result, what should you pay back – the dollar or the million dollars? This is a live issue, for unlike Locke, who argued that the United States was 'unowned' prior to European colonisation

(Locke, 1988: 299–301), Nozick argues that native Americans had rights to their land and these were violated and thus rectification is required. But Manhattan – whose only trace of native ownership is its name – has increased vastly in value since it was 'acquired' by Europeans: how do we rectify that injustice? Nozick provides no answer.

Left Libertarianism

A distinction is made between right libertarianism and left libertarianism. Self-ownership is the starting point for all libertarians, but right and left libertarians divide over the implications for the ownership of external things from the self-ownership premise. One of the most influential left libertarians – Hillel Steiner – argues, contra Nozick, that the natural right to self-ownership does not 'ground' a right to ownership of the external world:

(a) a set of rights must be 'co-possible', meaning that it is logically impossible for one individual's exercise of rights to constitute an interference in another person's exercise of their rights (within the same set);

(b) for a right to be natural it cannot be the result of a contract;

(c) all actions consist in some kind of motion (material and special components of an action are its *physical components*);

(d) one individual's actions cannot interfere with another's if none of their physical components is identical (Steiner, 1974: 42–4).

Two points follow from these claims. First, self-ownership can be a natural right, but Nozickian ownership of the external world cannot be. Second, if you impose any constraint, such as Locke's 'enough and as good left for others' or Nozick's 'no monopolies' requirements, on acquisition, then the 'first owner' must be capable of predicting the effect of his action on all future people – first ownership is only retroactively legitimate – but this is impossible to do. Self-ownership does not suffer from these problems. Although Steiner does not endorse his argument many left libertarians follow Henry George's idea of a site (or land) value tax as a means by which a person's acquisition of external things can be made compatible with the idea that nobody has a natural right to the world.

Henry George (1839–97) was an American self-taught economist remembered primarily for his proposal that there should be just one tax – on land. George noted that the poor of New York were considerably poorer than those of California, and concluded that exploitation had its roots in monopolistic control of land rents, which was determined by supply and demand. Land is in limited supply, whereas the value humans can add to land is indeterminate, and so we distinguish: (a) the site value – which is determined by externalities, and (b) the value added to the land by the owner. We should tax only (a). Many things affect the site value, including location, natural beauty, and deposits, and we calculate site value by using a similar but 'empty' or undeveloped plot – the site value of such a plot should (ideally) account for its full value and so we can use market prices. Site value tax revenues should be used to compensate those who are not in a position to acquire land because of the history of acquisition and transfer. The idea is that the value we add is 'ours' because it is an extension of ourselves, whereas the land itself can never be ours.

Cohen: a Marxist Perspective on Distributive Justice

Marx's critique of private property has to be located in his theory of history: human beings have a drive to increase productivity, and this generates two struggles. The first is a struggle against nature, and the second a struggle between human beings. The two are related, for how we organise production will determine how effective we are at using nature to our advantage. Over time the particular structure of organisation – 'mode of production' – changes, but what characterises all modes is a class relationship in which one class exploits another. Exploitation is made possible by the unequal ownership of the two things that enable an increase in production: the means of production, and labour power. The former includes such things as factories and tools, while the latter consists of the skills of labour, both physical and mental. At the time at which Marx was writing – the mid- to late-nineteenth century – capitalism had emerged as the dominant mode of production. For Marx, the key features of capitalism are as follows.

- *Ownership* Under capitalism, in contrast to previous modes of production, every person owns their own labour power. However, a minority class – the capitalists, or bourgeoisie – own a monopoly of the means of production, with the consequence that the majority class – the working class, or proletariat – can survive only by selling their labour power to the capitalists.
- *Capital* which can be defined as an 'expanding source of value', is unequally owned: one class (capitalists, or the bourgeoisie) are in a position to benefit from this expansion of value by virtue of their ownership of the means of production.
- *Exploitation* The true value of labour is not the price it commands in the market (the wage) but the amount of time that goes into the production of the commodity (labour value). The worker does not receive the full value of his product – the difference between the wage and labour value is the amount creamed off by the capitalist. This is what Marx means by exploitation.
- *Use value and exchange value* A distinction is drawn between the value we get from a commodity (use value) and its price (exchange value). Every commodity has a use value, but not everything that has a use value is a commodity. For example, air has a use value but it is not a commodity and hence does not have an exchange value. If pollution became very bad, and everybody had to carry a supply of clean air, and somebody started bottling and selling it, then it would acquire an exchange value in addition to its use value.
- *Markets* Interaction between individuals takes place through the laws of supply and demand. These laws fulfil two functions: (a) to provide information on how much of a particular product should be produced and at what price, and (b) to provide incentives to produce, and these incentives derive from self-interested motivations. Marx argues that the market is not in long-term equilibrium, and is

subject to increasingly severe depressions. He further argues that capitalism assumes people are *by nature* selfish; this Marx rejects as an 'ontologisation' of historical experience – that is, turning something transitory into an ahistorical fact.

Marxists have tended not to engage in debate with liberals (or libertarians), rejecting as they do certain fundamental claims about the nature of human motivation and political epistemology. On human motivation, for example, Rawls maintains that the principles of justice apply to a society characterised by moderate scarcity in which people are in conflict over the distribution of those (moderately) scarce resources. A Marxist would maintain that when production levels reach a certain point – and capitalism is historically useful because it massively increases productivity – we will be in a position to say that there is no longer scarcity and the causes of social conflict will be removed. Regarding political *epistemology* – that is, how we *know* what is just – Marxists maintain that it is only in a post-scarcity situation that we will be able to determine the correct distribution of resources. Gerald Cohen is unusual amongst Marxists in his engagement with liberal (libertarian) thinkers such as Rawls and Nozick. What makes his argument interesting is that he attacks liberals on what they believe to be their strongest ground: freedom.

Cohen contra Nozick

Cohen does not deny that capitalism gives people freedom to buy and sell labour, but he argues that defenders of capitalism make the illegitimate claim that their society is comprehensively free: they falsely equate 'capitalism' with the 'free society'. Cohen maintains that liberals – both left-wing (egalitarian) and right-wing (libertarian) – are wrong. Capitalism does not guarantee the maximum amount of freedom possible. He argues that a moralised definition of freedom is used – the validity of private property rights is taken for granted, such that freedom comes to be defined in terms of private property, and any infringement of it is a reduction of freedom. Cohen provides an example to illustrate his point: Mr Morgan owns a yacht. You want to sail it for one day, returning it without any damage done to it. If you take it you will be violating Mr Morgan's rights, but which situation creates more *freedom*, Mr Morgan's exclusive use of the boat, or your one-day use combined with his 364-days-a-year use (Cohen, 1979: 11–12)?

Cohen argues that for *one day* Mr Morgan is prevented from using his yacht and is forced not to use it – his freedom has indeed been restricted. But Mr Morgan's private property rights prevent you from using the yacht for *365 days* in the year, and force you not to use it (Cohen, 1979: 12). Capitalism – the exercise of private property rights – is a complex system of freedom and unfreedom. One could, of course, maintain that the difference between Mr Morgan's use of the yacht and your use of the yacht is precisely that it is *his* yacht; but then we need to justify Mr Morgan's acquisition of the yacht – to say Mr Morgan ought to own the yacht because he does own the yacht is a circular argument.

A more restricted defence of capitalism is then discussed by Cohen: capitalists do not maintain that their preferred economic system promotes freedom in general, but merely economic freedom. So Mr Morgan's property rights do not restrict your economic freedom, and a capitalist society is better able than any alternative to maximise *economic* freedom (Cohen, 1979: 14). To grasp Cohen's response we need to refer back to the important distinction made earlier between use value and exchange value:

(a) If economic freedom is defined as the freedom to *use* goods and services then it restricts freedom whenever it grants it – Mr Morgan's freedom to use his yacht correlates directly to your unfreedom to use it.

(b) If economic freedom is the freedom to buy and sell – that is, exchange products – then this looks better for capitalists, but it is an extremely restricted definition of economic freedom.

Is there then an alternative to capitalism and – crucially – one that increases freedom? Cohen gives a 'homespun' example. Persons A and B are neighbours and each owns a set of household implements, such as a lawnmower, saws, paintbrushes and so on. Each owns what the other lacks. We now imagine a rule is imposed, whereby when A is not using something he owns, B has the right to use it, just so long as he returns it when A needs it. This 'communising rule' will, Cohen maintains, increase 'implement-using' freedom (Cohen, 1979: 16–17).

A capitalist response to this example would be that A and B could increase their implement-using freedom by entering a contract, either a kind of barter, or a money-based relationship. Cohen's response to this move is to argue that in the example A and B are roughly equal and, therefore, capable of entering a freedom-enhancing contract, but if you generalise across society then that equality does not exist. In fact, there is another response to Cohen, which appeals to efficiency and *indirectly* to freedom: while Cohen's argument is in many ways sound – capitalism entails unfreedom as well as freedom – one has to look at the empirical consequences of different economic systems. Cohen's 'homespun' example does not help because it is a very simple situation in which there are no communication problems. One argument for capitalism is that it avoids an excessively powerful state; it might even be argued that liberalism is the unintended gift of capitalism. The history of socialism has been characterised by an attempt to acquire the advantages of coordination associated with the market, while avoiding the inequalities generated by it.

Cohen contra Rawls

We now turn to Cohen's response to Rawls. As we have seen Rawls does not defend unregulated capitalism, and advances a theory of justice that would entail a significant redistribution of income to the worst-off. What then is wrong with Rawls? There are three main Marxist objections:

1. Rawls has an incoherent model of human psychology (motivation).

2. Rawls restricts the principles of justice to the basic structure of society, and that conceals exploitation.

3. Rawls rejects self-ownership as morally irrelevant to the distribution of resources. Curiously enough, on this point Cohen sides with the 'right-wing' libertarian Nozick against Rawls.

The first two objections are closely related to one another. If you recall, people in the original position are motivated to maximise their share of the primary goods, but from behind a 'veil of ignorance', meaning that although they are self-interested, they are forced by the way the original position is set up to be impartial. Rational people will, Rawls argues, select the two principles of justice, including the 'difference principle', which entails maximising the position of the worst-off (maximin). The original position is intended to 'model' how real people *could* behave. The difficulty is that the theory itself pulls in two different directions: on the one hand Rawls assumes that we – that is, 'we' in the real world, and not in the original position – can develop a commitment to giving priority to the worst-off in society, and the difference principle is the structural device by which this is achieved. But how much the worst-off *actually receive* will depend on everyday human behaviour. Consider the exercise on p. 85: under maximin the richest quarter get 50 units and the poorest quarter get 15 units. Imagine you are in the top quarter. What motivations will you have in the 'real world', assuming you endorse Rawls's theory?

(a) You will be committed to giving priority to the worst-off and so will regard redistributive income tax as legitimate.

(b) You will be motivated to maximise your income.

These two motivations do not necessarily conflict if we assume – as Rawls does – that inequality generates incentives to produce and thus help the worst-off, but if you are really committed to helping the worst-off do you not have a moral duty to:

(a) give *directly* – not just through tax – to the poor; and

(b) work to bring about a society in which the poorest earn more than 15 units?

Cohen borrows a slogan from the feminist movement: the 'personal is political' (Cohen, 2000: 122–3). How you behave in your personal life is a political issue. Rawls, along with most liberals, rejects this claim, arguing that the distinction between public and private is essential to a pluralistic society, and that not all aspects of morality should be enforced by the state: while it is right to require people to pay taxes to help the worst-off, it is for individuals to decide what they do with their post-tax income. This may not resolve the tension that Cohen identifies between, crudely expressed, public generosity and private avarice, but the onus is on Cohen to explain the role of the state in 'encouraging' private generosity.

This brings us to the second criticism, which relates to the basic structure argument. The rich fulfil their duties to the poor by accepting the legitimacy of taxation, and that taxation is used to fund certain institutions, such as the pre-university education system, money transfers (social security, pensions, etc.) and health care. Outside the scope of the original position is a 'private sphere' that includes the family. Rawls accepts that the family is a major source of inequality – the transmission from parent to child of privilege undermines equality of opportunity – but because liberty (the first principle of justice) takes priority over equality (the second principle) there has to be a legally protected private sphere. Not only is the private sphere a source of inequality, it also produces within itself inequality. Here Cohen joins forces with feminist critics of Rawls: families are based on a division of labour, and one loaded against women, but because the recipient of redistribution is the household, and not the individual, there is a class of people – mostly women – who are worse off than that class which Rawls identifies as the 'worst-off'.

Cohen argues that what Rawls includes in the basic structure is arbitrary – Rawls cannot give clear criteria for what should or should not be included. He cannot say that the basic structure consists of those institutions which are coercively enforced, that is, we are forced to fund through taxation, because the basic structure is defined *before* we choose the principles of justice, whereas what is coercively enforced is a decision to be made in the original position (Cohen, 2000: 136–7). The basic Marxist point is this: Rawls assumes that human motivations are relatively constant – certainly, people can develop a moral consciousness, but they will remain self-interested. Motivations will always be a mix of self-interest and morality. Marxists reject this, and maintain that social structures determine how people behave.

We come, finally, to the third criticism. Marx argued that the workers do not get the full value of their labour. This argument assumes that there is something a person owns, which generates a moral right to other things: in effect, as a Marxist, Cohen, along with Nozick (who is not a Marxist!), endorses Locke's 'mixed labour' formula. What Cohen rejects is the idea that mixing your labour establishes merely 'first acquisition'. For Locke and Nozick, once the world is divided up into private property the mixed labour formula ceases to be of any use. Cohen argues that a worker *constantly* mixes their labour, such that there is a continuous claim on the product. Locke's argument that 'the turfs my servant has cut are *my* turfs' is rejected by Cohen; insofar as the servant (worker) does not get the full value of their labour they are exploited, and the resulting distribution is unjust. Rawls implicitly rejects the notion of self-ownership; that does not mean we do not have rights over our bodies, but rather we have no pre-social rights. The rights we have are the result of a choice made in the original position. This becomes clearer if we look at the concept of desert.

Desert is tied to effort: we get something if we do something. Rawls argues that because we are not responsible for our 'natural endowments' – strength, looks, intelligence, even good character – we cannot claim the product generated by those natural endowments. Under the difference principle one person may earn 50 units and another 15 units, but not a single unit of that 35 unit difference is *justified* by reference to desert. Of course, in *causal terms*, the difference may be attributed, at least in part, to native ability, but that does not *justify* the difference. Rawls goes as far as to say that natural endowments are a social resource to be used for the benefit of the worst-off (Rawls, 1972: 179). It is strange that on desert Rawls is the radical, whereas Cohen sides with Nozick. It is true that Nozick does not believe that the rich are rich because they deserve to be rich – Wilt Chamberlain was rich because *other people chose to give him money* to play basketball – but the idea of self-ownership (private property rights) does imply a right to keep the fruit of your labour.

Whether you accept Cohen's argument against Rawls depends to some extent on whether you endorse Marx's labour theory of value. Many people would, however, follow Thomas Nagel in arguing that the value of a product is not the result of the amount of labour which went into it, but rather the other way round: the value of labour is the result of the contribution that labour makes to the product (Nagel,

1991: 99). Ask yourself this: if you have a firm making 'next generation' mobile phones, which group of workers do you *least* want to lose: the canteen staff? Cleaners? Assembly line workers? Phone designers? Venture capitalists? It could be argued that the last two groups are the most important. The conclusion to be drawn is that if we want to justify an egalitarian distribution of wealth we need what Rawls attempts to offer, which is a moral justification that assumes that many of the poorest will get *more* than that to which their labour 'entitles' them.

Summary

Human beings need to decide how resources are to be distributed, and unless we endorse the anarchist position then the state, which is a coercive entity, will play a role in their distribution. Political theorists disagree about the extent of state involvement in the distribution of resources – Nozick argues for a minimal role, while Rawls – and, implicitly, Cohen – argue for a more extensive role. Underlying the three theories discussed are different conceptions of what it means to be an agent, and of human motivation. Rawls assumes that human beings have mixed motives: they are self-interested but also 'reasonable'. Nozick avoids a discussion of motivation by arguing for a strong conception of human agency – property rights are an extension of self-ownership: so long as we do not violate others' rights, what we do with our rights is for us to decide. Cohen endorses the emphasis on self-ownership, but uses it against Nozick's initial acquisition argument; he also rejects Rawls's motivational assumptions, arguing that we need to change our attitudes and become less acquisitive.

Questions

1. Do people *deserve* to keep the fruits of their labour?
2. If you are as well off as you could possibly be, can you have any grounds for objecting that other people are better off than you?
3. Is taxation 'forced labour'?
4. Should there be an unconditional minimum income for each person?
5. Should the state reward men and women for bringing up children, and doing housework?

References

Cohen, G.A. (1979) 'Capitalism, Freedom, and the Proletariat' in A. Ryan (ed.), *The Idea of Freedom* Oxford: Oxford University Press.

Cohen, G.A. (2000) *If You're An Egalitarian, How Come You're So Rich?* Cambridge, MA: Harvard University Press.

Locke, J. (1988) *Two Treatises of Government* (ed. P. Laslett), student edn, Cambridge: Cambridge University Press.

Nagel, T. (1991) *Equality and Partiality* New York: Oxford University Press.

Nozick, R. (1974) *Anarchy, State, and Utopia* New York: Basic Books.

Rawls, J. (1972) *A Theory of Justice* Oxford: Oxford University Press.

Rawls, J. (2001) *Justice as Fairness: A Restatement* Cambridge, MA: Harvard University Press.

Steiner, H. (1974) 'The Natural Right to Equal Freedom' *Mind* 83(330), 41–9.

Wolff, J. (1991) *Robert Nozick: Property, Justice and the Minimal State* Oxford: Polity Press.

Further Reading

The primary texts are Rawls (1972), Part One; Nozick (1974), Chapter 7; Cohen (1979); Cohen (2000). There are several commentaries on Rawls, the first of which was Brian Barry, *The Liberal Theory of Justice* (Oxford: Clarendon, 1973), but more recent ones are: Samuel Freeman, *Rawls* (Routledge, 2007); Thomas Pogge, *Rawls* (OUP, 2007); Catherine Audard, *John Rawls* (McGill Queen's University Press, 2007), Paul Graham, *Rawls* (Oxford: Oneworld, 2007). A collection of early essays on Rawls can be found in Norman Daniels (ed.), *Reading Rawls: Critical Studies on Rawls's A Theory of Justice* (Stanford, Calif.: Stanford University Press, 1989, first published 1973); slightly more recent works on Rawls are Chandran Kukathas and Philip Pettit, *Rawls: A Theory of Justice and its Critics* (Cambridge: Polity Press, 1990) and Thomas Pogge, *Realizing Rawls* (Ithica, NY: Cornell University Press, 1989). There are fewer works on Nozick. The best is Wolff (1991). Others – both collections of essays – are Jeffrey Paul (ed.), *Reading Nozick: Essays on Anarchy, State and Utopia* (Totowa, NJ: Rowman & Littlefield, 1981) and David Schmidtz (ed.), *Robert Nozick* (Cambridge: Cambridge University Press, 2002).

Weblinks

- The following are useful websites on Rawls:
  http://www.epistemelinks.com/Main/Philosophers.aspx?PhilCode=Rawl
  http://plato.stanford.edu/entries/rawls/

- The following are useful websites on Nozick:
  http://www.epistemelinks.com/Main/Philosophers.aspx?PhilCode=Nozi
  http://dmoz.org/Society/Philosophy/Philosophers/N/Nozick,_Robert/

Chapter 5

Democracy

Introduction

It is very difficult to find anyone who disagrees with democracy these days. Politicians from the extreme left to the extreme right insist that the politics which they support is democratic in character, so it is no wonder that the term is so confusing. Although fundamentalists may reject the notion of democracy, nobody else does, and whether the ruler is a military dictator, a nationalist demagogue or a liberal, the concept of democracy will be piously invoked in support of an argument.

So in asking what democracy is, we also have to address the question as to why it has become almost obligatory for politicians to claim adherence to the concept.

Chapter Map

- Democracy has been more and more widely acclaimed from almost all sections of the political spectrum, so that it has become increasingly confusing as a concept.

- Liberals traditionally opposed democracy, even if the universal assumptions of their theory led their opponents to argue that liberalism was democratic in character.

- Liberals only reluctantly converted to democracy in the nineteenth century, and then only on the assumption that extending the franchise would not undermine the rights of property.

- After the Second World War politics was seen as the business of a decision-making elite, and participation by the masses was discouraged.

- Democracy involves both direct participation and representation, and representation needs to be based on a sense that the representative can empathise with the problems of their constituents.

- There is a tension between democracy and the concept of the state, and this creates problems for Held's case for a 'cosmopolitan democracy'.

- The question of the state helps to account for the confusions about the polity in Ancient Greece, and among conservative critics of liberalism.

- A **relational** view of democracy enables us to tackle the 'tyranny thesis', and to defend the rational kernel of political correctness.

Zimbabwean Elections June 2000

Zimbabweans protesting against the 'stolen election' of 2008, eight years on from the 2000 election

On 24 and 25 June 2000, parliamentary elections took place in Zimbabwe. The ruling party, the Zimbabwean African National Union – Patriotic Front (ZANU-PF) had been badly shaken by a referendum on a new constitution that they had held in February and which they lost. There was substantial violence and intimidation before the June elections (most of it by the supporters of ZANU-PF) and none of the international observers thought that the election was 'fair and free'.

Four voters are waiting to vote in a constituency in the capital city, Harare. The first calls himself a war veteran (though he was too young to have fought in the independence war), and is grateful to the ruling party for providing him with income. He has just come from a farm outside Harare where he has been involved in burning down the house of a white farmer and helping to take over the land. He will certainly vote for the ruling party and feels that the whites and the main opposition party, the Movement for Democratic Change (MDC), are trying to return Zimbabwe to its former colonial past and are basically in the pay of the British government.

The second voter is an elderly white woman. Unlike some of her friends who cannot vote because they hold British passports, she is a Zimbabwean citizen who was born in the country. She is alarmed at the high inflation and the land seizures that she believes to be unconstitutional, and will vote for the MDC.

The third voter is a resident in one of the townships in Harare. He is angered by the decline in his living standard and the fact that he recently lost his job. He is worried about the future of his family and is thinking of going to South Africa. Although he initially supported ZANU-PF, he will now vote for the MDC.

The fourth voter is a domestic worker in Harare. She was initially hostile to the dwindling minority of whites since her white employer is somewhat arrogant and paternalistic. But she has heard from relatives in the rural areas of the massive intimidation of voters, and can buy less and less with her meagre income. Although she would like to see more blacks own land, she feels that the land seizure programme is basically benefiting wealthy ministers in the government and will not help ordinary people. She will vote MDC.

Democracy and Confusion

The term democracy means rule of the people, but such a concept has created real problems for those who believe that political theory should be value-free in character. It is revealing that Dahl in the 1960s preferred to speak of 'polyarchies' rather than democracies, in the hope that the substitute term could appear more 'scientific' in character. For whether democracy in the past has been a good thing or a bad thing, it is difficult to say what democracy is, without 'taking sides' in some ongoing debate.

As democracy has become more and more widely praised, it has become more and more difficult to pin it down. John Dunn has noted that 'all states today profess to be democracies because a democracy is what it is virtuous for a state to be' (1979: 11). A term can only be confusing if it is taken to mean contradictory things: majority rule or individual rights; limited government or popular sovereignty; private property as against social ownership. Consider the following: participation versus representation; the collective versus the individual; socialism versus capitalism. All have been defended as being essential to democracy!

It has been argued that the term should be abandoned, and Crick has taken the view that politics needs to be defended against democracy not because he is opposed (at least not under all circumstances) to the idea, but because he is in favour of clarity and precision against vagueness and ambiguity. Democracy, he comments, is perhaps 'the most promiscuous word in the world of public affairs' (1982: 56). Bernard Shaw once devoted an entire play to the problem. His play, *The Apple Cart*, tackled the ambiguities of democracy with such flair that the play was banned by a nervous Weimar Republic in the 1920s, and in a witty preface, Shaw complains that democracy seems to be everywhere and nowhere. It is a long word that we are expected to accept reverently without asking any questions. It seems quite impossible, Shaw protests, for politicians to make speeches about democracy or for journalists to report them, without obscuring the concept 'in a cloud of humbug' (Hoffman, 1988: 132).

What makes democracy so confusing is that it is a concept subject to almost universal acclaim: but this was not always the position. In the seventeenth century nobody who was anybody would have called themselves a democrat. As far as landowners, merchants, lawyers and clergymen were concerned – people of 'substance' – democracy was a term of abuse: a bad thing. Even in the nineteenth century, social liberals like J.S. Mill felt it necessary to defend liberty against democracy. It is only after the First World War that democracy becomes a respectable term. It is true that Hitler condemned democracy as the political counterpart to economic communism, but Mussolini, the Italian fascist, could declare in a speech in Berlin in 1936 that 'the greatest and most genuine democracies in the world today, are the German and the Italian' (Hoffman, 1988: 133).

The left have generally approved of democracy, but it is possible to find the Russian revolutionary, Trotsky, for example, declaring democracy to be irretrievably bourgeois and counter-revolutionary. A Communist Party secretary declared in Hamburg in 1926 that he would rather burn in 'the fire of revolution than perish in the dung-heap of democracy' (Hoffman, 1988: 133). By the twentieth century attacks on the idea of democracy have become the exception rather than the rule, and with this growing acclaim, the concept has become increasingly confusing.

Crick complains that the term has become a bland synonym for 'All Things Bright and Beautiful', a hurrah word without any specific content (1982: 56). The glow of approval has made it an idea very difficult to pin down.

Democracy and Liberalism

Weldon, the linguistic analyst, has argued that 'democracy', 'capitalism' and 'liberalism' are all alternative names for the same thing (1953: 86). Yet this view has been challenged by a number of theorists. They note that historically liberals were not democrats, even if they were attacked as democrats by conservative critics of liberalism. John Locke (see his biography box on the website), for example, took it for granted that those who could vote were men, merchants and landowners, and the question of universal suffrage (even for men only) is not even raised in his *Two Treatises of Government*. The fact that liberals declared that men were free and equal was taken by conservatives to denote support for democracy, but this was not true!

A hapless King Charles (1600–49) reproached English parliamentarians (who had taken him prisoner) for 'labouring to bring about democracy' (Dunn, 1979: 3). Yet it is clear that Oliver Cromwell (1599–1658) and his puritan gentry did not believe in democracy, and even the left wing of the movement – the Levellers – wished to exclude 'servants' and 'paupers' from the franchise. Cromwellians were alarmed that the egalitarian premises of liberal theory might extend the freedom to smaller property owners to rule (Hoffman, 1988: 154–5). It is true that Tocqueville (1805–59) writing in the 1840s, could describe the America of his day as a democracy, but in fact until the 1860s, Americans themselves identified democracy at best with one element (the legislature) of the constitution – an element to be checked and balanced by others.

Madison, one of the founders of the US Constitution, had spoken in the *Federalist Papers* of democracies as 'incompatible with personal security or the rights of property', and John Jay, one of the authors of the famous Papers, declared that the 'people who own the country should govern it' (Hoffman, 1988: 135). Tocqueville might describe Jefferson, author of the Declaration of Independence (1787) as 'the greatest democrat ever to spring from American democracy' (1966: 249), but in fact Jefferson was a liberal who took the view that voters should be male farmers who owned property. The American political scientist Hofstadter has commented on how modern American folklore has anachronistically assumed that liberalism and democracy are identical (Hoffman, 1988: 136), and it has missed the point which Crick makes, that there is 'tension as well as harmony' between the two bodies of thought.

Tension – because liberals did not intend the invocation of universal rights to apply to all adults – and harmony – because their critics from the right assumed that they did, and their critics from the left felt that if rights were universal in theory, then they should be universal in practice. It is important not to assume that liberal theorists were necessarily democratic in orientation. Rousseau, the eighteenth-century French theorist, felt that democracy was unworkable. It assumed a perfectionism that human nature belied, and was a form of government ever liable to 'civil war and internecine strife' (Rousseau, 1968: 113).

Tocqueville's portrait of America is that of a society of radical liberalism, not of democracy: he himself notes the enslavement of blacks and the appropriation of the lands of native Americans. A government publication in the USA could describe democracy even in the 1920s as 'a government of the masses . . . Attitude towards property is communistic – negating property rights . . . Results in demagogism, license, agitation, discontent, anarchy' (Hoffman, 1988: 141). Thus spoke the voice of traditional liberalism!

The Problem of Exclusion

Conservative critics could speak of democracy as turning 'natural' hierarchies upside down. In an historic passage, the ancient Greek theorist Plato complains that in a democracy, fathers and sons 'change places' and 'there is no distinction between citizen and alien and foreigner'. Slaves come to enjoy the same freedom as their owners, 'not to mention the complete equality and liberty in the relations between the sexes generally'. In the end, Plato adds with a flourish, even 'the domestic animals are infected with anarchy' (1955: 336).

It is true that during the fourth and fifth centuries BC, an astonishing model of popular rule came to exist in ancient Athens. A popular assembly met some 40 times a year. All citizens were actually paid to attend. All had the right to be heard in debate before decisions were taken, and this assembly had supreme powers of war, peace, making treaties, creating public works, etc. Judges, administrators and members of a 500-strong executive council were chosen, and since they only held office for one or two years, this meant that a considerable portion of Athenian citizens had experience of government.

Despite the fact that some have referred to Athenian democracy as 'pure' and 'genuine', it was rooted in **slavery**, patriarchy and chauvinism. Slaves, women and resident aliens had no political rights so that, as has been said, the people in Athens were really 'an exceptionally large and diversified ruling class' (Hoffman, 1988: 145). Not only was Athenian society divided internally, but the payment for jury service, public office and the membership of the executive council, the expensive land settlement programme and the distribution of public funds would not have been possible without the Athenian empire. Democracy was an exclusive idea: the demos – the people with the right to participate in decision-making, were certainly not all the adults who lived in the society.

Surely all this changed when liberals became converted to the notion of democracy? It is true that after the French Revolution, British liberals began to accept the case for universal suffrage, at least among men, but they did so very cautiously and reluctantly, with Macpherson arguing that liberals like Jeremy Bentham (1748–1832) would have preferred to restrict the vote to those who owned their own houses, but this was no longer acceptable (Macpherson, 1977: 35). James Mill (1773–1836) asserts that all men should have the vote to protect their interests, and then argues that logically these interests could be secured if all women, all men under 40 and the poorest third of the male population over 40 were excluded from the vote. In Macpherson's view, James Mill and Bentham were less than wholehearted democrats (1977: 39).

The argument between the liberals and the liberals-turned-democrats was over whether the male poor would use their rights to strip the rich of their wealth, or whether they would leave decision-making to the middle rank – whom James Mill described as the class in society which gives to science, art and legislation their most 'distinguished ornaments' and is the chief source of all that is 'refined and exalted in human nature'. Both sides of the argument agreed that the business of government is the business of the rich (Hoffman, 1988: 167).

The question of exclusion becomes more subtle as liberals become more enthusiastic about the idea of democracy. T.H. Green and Leonard Hobhouse, two British social liberals, both supported the idea that women as well as the men should have the vote, and by 1928, women were enfranchised. But Green could still take it for granted that men were the head of the family, and Hobhouse argued that women should stay at home and mind the children (Hoffman, 1988: 180). It could be argued that even when women had political and legal equality with men, social equality eluded them, and therefore their democratic rights were thereby impaired. This would be vigorously argued by feminists later (see Chapter on Feminism p. 315). Socialists, for their part, continued to contend that even when workers have the vote, they do not have the resources to exercise their political rights as effectively as those who have wealth, social connections, the 'right' education, etc.

What about international exclusions? Hobhouse argues that 'a democrat cannot be a democrat for his country alone'. Does democracy require support for political rights throughout the world? Hobhouse cannot make up his mind whether to support home rule for the Irish, and he argues that as far as the Crown colonies are concerned, a semi-despotic system is the best that can be devised (Hoffman, 1988: 181). The problem is still relevant. Is US support for democracy compromised by the fact that the government supports regimes like Kuwait and Saudi Arabia that are not democratic?

The 'Tyranny of the Majority' Thesis

Both J.S. Mill and Tocqueville raised the problem of democracy as a 'tyranny of the majority'. What is there to prevent a government representing the majority, from crushing a minority? Crick endorses what has been called a 'paradox of freedom' – a situation in which an elected leader acts tyrannically towards particular individuals or groups. Crick gives the example of the German elections of 1933 that saw Hitler being appointed Chancellor. A more recent example – which Barbara Goodwin raises (1997: 289) – is of the Islamic Salvation Front in Algeria winning an election, but prevented from governing by the army, on the grounds that the intention of the Front was to install a non-democratic Islamic theocracy (see the Chapter on Fundamentalism, p. 385).

This resurrects the ancient Greek argument that democracy as the rule of the poor, could take the form of a popular despotism. Crick cites the French revolutionary, Robespierre, who speaks of a democratic defence of terror, and Crick comments, in a rather startling passage, that the problem with (totalitarian) communists is that they do not merely pretend to be democratic: they 'are democratic' (1982: 60–1, 56).

This leads most commentators to say that democracy must be linked to liberalism so that the term liberal qualifies democracy. A democratic society must respect the rights of minorities as well as majorities. Otherwise, democracy can become dictatorial and oppress individuals by imposing majority tastes and preferences on society as a whole. Built into the American tradition is what one writer has described as a 'neurotic terror of the majority', and new liberals like Hobhouse argued that checks should be placed upon the British House of Commons to restrain 'a large and headstrong majority' (Hoffman, 1988: 136; 181). Ian Paisley's conception of a 'Protestant state of the Protestant people' may appear democratic, but it certainly did not facilitate participation by the Catholic minority.

The Problem of Participation

Towards the end of the Second World War, the concept of democracy was redefined, in order to bring it into line, so it was argued, with practical realities. Joseph Schumpeter, an Austrian economist and socialist, led the way, contending that the notion of democracy must be stripped of its moral qualities. There is nothing about democracy that makes it desirable. It may be that in authoritarian systems – Schumpeter gives the example of the religious settlement under the military dictatorship of Napoleon I – the wishes of the people are more fully realised than under a democracy (Schumpeter, 1947: 256).

In Schumpeter's view, democracy is simply a 'political method'. It is an arrangement for reaching political decisions: it is not an end in itself. Since all governments 'discriminate' against some section of the population (in no political system are children allowed to vote, for example), discrimination as such is not undemocratic. It all depends upon how you define the demos, the people. Schumpeter accepts that in contemporary liberal societies, all adults should have the right to vote, but this does not mean that they will use this right or participate more directly in the political process. In fact, he argues that it is a good idea if the mass of the population do not participate, since the masses are too irrational, emotional, parochial and 'primitive' to make good decisions.

The typical citizen, he argues, yields to prejudice, impulse and what Schumpeter calls 'dark urges' (1947: 262). It is the politicians who raise the issues which determine peoples' lives, and who decide these issues. A democracy is more realistically defined as 'a political method' by which politicians are elected by means of a competitive vote. The people do not rule: their role is to elect those who do. Democracy is a system of elected and competing elites.

The 1950s saw a number of studies which argued that politics is a remote, alien and unrewarding activity best left to a relatively small number of professional activists. Elected leadership should be given a free hand, since 'where the rational citizen seems to abdicate, nevertheless angels seem to tread' (Macpherson, 1977: 92). The model of elitist democracy, as it has sometimes been called, argued the case for a democracy with low participation.

Solutions to the Problem of Low Participation

It could be argued, however, that low participation undermines democracy. How democratic are liberal political systems if, in the USA, for example, the President can be elected with hardly more than half the population exercising their vote? (Although in the recent presidential election, the percentage of those voting rose to close on 60 per cent.) This means that whatever his majority, he is supported by a minority of the electorate.

In his *Life and Times of Liberal Democracy* Macpherson sets about constructing a participatory model, arguing that somehow participatory democrats have to break the vicious circle between an apathy which leads to inequality (as the poor and vulnerable lose out), and inequality which generates apathy (as the poor and vulnerable feel impotent and irrelevant). Macpherson's argument is an interesting one, because he takes the view that one needs to start with people as they are. Let us assume that the individual is simply a market-oriented consumer who does not feel motivated to vote, or if they vote, do so in order to further their own immediate interests. There are three issues which Macpherson feels work to break this vicious circle.

To consume comfortably and confidently, one needs a relatively decent environment. Going fishing assumes that there are fish to catch and they are safe to eat; swimming can only take place if the sea is not so polluted as to be positively dangerous. A concern about the environment leads the most politically apathetic consumer to contemplate joining an ecological organisation. That is the first loophole.

From a concern with the physical environment, the consumer moves onto the social environment. Inner urban decay; ill-planned housing estates, the ravages of property developers: all these and related issues, compel people to become concerned with politics, while insecurity and boredom at the workplace makes it inevitable that there will be involvement in trade union and professional association campaigns for job protection, better pensions, etc.

One can add numerous other issues that are forcing people to take a greater concern in the political process. It is crucial not to define politics too narrowly since people participate in all kinds of different ways, and even the person who does not vote, may join say Amnesty International or Greenpeace in Britain. There is an argument (that we will consider in a moment) for increasing the number of people who vote in parliamentary elections, but it is important to see that democracy requires participation at different levels, and in different ways. The large numbers of people who turned out to protest against the war with Iraq in London, showed that a lack of concern with politics can be exaggerated, and the rise of what are usually called the New Social Movements – single-issue organisations concerned with peace, the environment, rights of women, etc. – indicate that there is increasing participation, even if some of this participation seems unconventional in character.

There is a growing feeling that 'normal' political processes – in local government, in electing people to parliament – must change in the sense that these institutions need to become more accessible and intelligible to people on the street. In Britain, for example, there is growing interest in schemes to assist voting and voter registration; in reforming legislative chambers; making local government more exciting; introducing devolved and regional government, and other schemes to increase levels of interest and involvement in conventional political processes.

Even if voting is not the only form of democratic participation, it is important and there is, we think, a strong argument for compulsory voting in the UK. The argument that the citizen has a right not to vote, ignores the fact that rights are indissolubly linked to responsibilities, and the act of non-voting harms the interests of society at large. It is true that some may feel that voting is a farce, but the defensible part of this objection – that the voter does not feel that existing parties offer real choice – can easily be met by allowing voters to put their cross on a box which states 'none of the above'. This would signal to politicians the extent to which people were voting negatively through protest.

It is true that the case for compulsory voting would not, taken simply on its own, create a more effective participation. It has to be accompanied by policies that address the inequalities underlying the problem of apathy. A lack of jobs, housing, adequate health care, physical and material security remain critical causes of despair and low self-esteem. There is plenty of evidence that mandatory voting raises participation levels, and as Faulks point out, when the Netherlands dropped compulsory voting in 1970, voting turnout fell by 10 per cent (2001: 24). Italy, Belgium and Australia still compel their citizens to vote. Compulsory voting would encourage people to take an interest in political affairs – become more literate and confident – and it could reduce the time and resources parties use to try and capture the public interest in trivial and sensational ways.

While fines could be imposed upon defaulters, the real sanctions for non-compliance would be moral. Compulsory voting could play an invaluable role in altering our political culture in a socially responsible direction. Faulks quotes Lijphart who comments that compulsory voting is an extension of universal suffrage (2001: 25). A simple and comprehensive system of voter registration in Britain would also assist people in taking responsibility for governing their own lives, and one can think of numerous devices to facilitate voting. The greater use of postal votes, the extension of time for voting, and a more proportional system would do much to overcome the cynicism that is often expressed at election times. Additionally, we would point to the use of referenda on important issues, and the employment of citizens' juries. In this latter case, a number of citizens, statistically representative of the wider population, discuss particular issues in an intense and deliberative way, and make recommendations based upon questions to relevant experts.

A number of writers have argued that the use of information technology could radically enhance the possibility for direct democracy since as a result of email, the Internet, video conferencing, the digitisation of data, two-way computer and television links through cable technology, citizens could remain at home and shape policies rather than rely upon representatives to do so. Clearly such a technology has tremendous potential to empower citizens, and Faulks gives the example of how a citizens' action group used the communications network to raise $150,000 in Santa Monica in the USA for the local homeless (Faulks, 1999: 157). Television shows in Britain like *Pop Idol, Big Brother* and *Strictly Come Dancing* already have vast numbers of viewers voting for their chosen 'star': does this indicate the potential for using TV as a medium for giving people greater choice on policies and personalities? Already TV programmes invite viewers to express their views on current controversies of the day.

Representational and Direct Democracy

Do we need to make a choice between representational democracy and direct democracy: between situations in which people elect representatives to govern them, or they directly take decisions themselves?

Rousseau, in a famous passage in *The Social Contract*, argues the case for direct involvement, passionately insisting that to be represented is to give up – to alienate – powers that individuals alone can rightfully exercise. Deputies are acceptable since they are merely the agents of the people. Representation, on the other hand, an odious modern idea, involves a form of slavery – a negation of 'will', one's capacity to exert influence (Rousseau, 1968: 141). Rousseau's position is generally regarded as untenable. The very notion of representation as a re-presenting of the individual, arises from the classical liberal view that citizens are individuals. This is an important and positive idea but to be democratic, representatives can only act on behalf of those they represent if they understand their problems and way of life.

We do not, therefore, have to make a choice between representational or direct democracy. It is revealing that the argument associated with Edmund Burke (1729–97) – one of the great liberal conservatives – that representatives simply act in what they see (in their infinite wisdom) is the real interest of their constituents, inverts the Rousseauan view that representation is necessarily alienation. Those who have neither the time nor resources to make laws directly, need to authorise others to do so on their behalf. Only through a combination of the direct and the indirect – hands-on participation and representation – can democratic autonomy be maximised. Of course, there are dangers that representatives will act in an elitist manner: but this is also true of what Rousseau called 'deputies' as well. Democracy requires accountability, so that people can get decisions made which help them to govern their own lives.

Representation, it should be said, involves empathy – the capacity to put yourself in the position of another – and while it is impossible to actually be another person, it is necessary to imagine what it is like to be another. Hence, as noted above, accountability is 'the other side' of representation: one without the other descends into either impracticality or elitism. The notion of empathy points to the need for a link between representatives and constituents. Unless representatives are in some sense a reflection of the population at large, it is difficult to see how empathy can take place. Women who have experienced oppression by men (or partners) at first hand, are more likely to have insight into the problems women face than men who – however sympathetic they may be – may have never been the recipients of that particular form of discrimination. The same is true with members of ethnic and sexual minorities, etc. To have experienced humiliation directly as a disabled person, makes one far more sensitive to questions of disability. We need a form of representation that is sensitive to the particular identities and problems of those they represent.

Democracy requires participation, but it would be wrong to assume that this is only possible through direct involvement in political processes. Direct involvement needs to be linked to representation, and it is worth noting that in the ancient Greek polis – often held up as an example of direct democracy – the assembly elected an executive council.

The Argument So Far . . .

- Democracy is a particularly confusing concept because nearly everyone claims to subscribe to it.

- In fact this is a relatively recent development. Liberals historically disagreed with democracy, but because liberal theory seemed to apply to everyone, this makes it difficult to see who was being excluded. Conservatives accused liberals of wanting to be universally inclusive, just as Plato in ancient Greece accused democrats of wanting to abolish the distinction between citizen and slave.

- Liberals in the nineteenth century reluctantly accepted the need for universal suffrage, although they continued to fear that democracy might express itself as a 'tyranny of the majority'. This fear helps to explain the post-war argument that a realistic view of democracy requires that the people only minimally participate.

- In fact, low participation is something that undermines democracy, and suggestions are offered as to how participation could be increased. It is important in arguing for more participation that we see democracy as both representative and 'direct'.

Focus

The 'Mirror' Theory of Representation

It is sometimes argued that representation can only be fair if exact percentages of groups within the population at large are 'reflected' in the composition of representatives. If the population of a particular city (like Leicester in Britain) contains, say, 40 per cent of people with black faces, then a mirror theory of representation demands that there should be 40 per cent of representatives who are black. The same is argued about poor people, gays, etc. It is not difficult to see the problem with this notion. Ethnic minorities, like people in general, are not all the same. Black people in Leicester are divided ethnically, regionally, along class and gender lines, etc. and it would be wrong, therefore, to assume that one black person is the same as another. A black businessman may not identify with a black trade unionist. It does not follow, therefore, that black representatives will necessarily represent the interests of black constituents, any more than we can assume that women representatives will necessarily represent the interests of women. It is one thing to argue that representatives must have knowledge of (and experience of) the people they represent; quite another that they must represent them in precise numbers.

The mirror theory has a grain of truth in it: representatives should be sensitive to the problems of their constituents, and it helps if a predominantly black constituency, for example, has a black representative. But it has only a grain of truth: it is not the whole story. There are an infinity of other factors to consider – gender, class, sexual orientation, etc. We need to distinguish between politically relevant differences (see the website piece on Difference) and those 'differences' (like wearing spectacles) that are not normally relevant.

Democracy and the State

The problem with much of the analysis of democracy is that it assumes that democracy is a form of the state. Yet it could well be argued that there is a contradiction between the idea of the 'rule of the people' and an institution claiming a monopoly of legitimate force for a particular territory.

This is not to deny that the more liberal the state the better, or that states which have the rule of law, regular elections and universal suffrage are preferable to states which do not. A liberal society has to be the basis for democracy: it is necessary, although not sufficient. Thus to the extent that, for example, Singapore does not allow its citizens to freely express themselves, it is undemocratic.

We want to argue that what makes a liberal society 'insufficient', is that it still needs a state, and the state, it could be suggested, is a repressively hierarchical institution that excludes outsiders and uses force to tackle conflicts of interest. Conservatives who complained that democracy is incompatible with the state are right. You cannot be said to govern your own life within the state. When the supreme ruler of the moon was told, as H.G. Wells recalls, that states existed on earth in which everybody rules, he immediately ordered that cooling sprays should be applied to his brows (Hoffman, 1995: 210).

Dahl, in fact, has argued that when individuals are forced to comply with laws, democracy is to that extent compromised (1989: 37). If you vote for a particular party through fear of what might happen to you if you do not, then such a system cannot be called democratic. Liberals have argued that a person cannot be said to act freely if they are threatened with force: yet the logic here points to a position that Dahl does not accept. If force is incompatible with self-rule, then it follows that the state cannot be reconciled with democracy. The use of force against a small number of people – something that no state can avoid – makes the idea of self-government problematic. This is why the notion of democracy as a form of the state is not self-evident, and it could be argued that this assumption weakens David Held's otherwise persuasive case for a 'cosmopolitan democracy'. Held acknowledges that the concept of democracy has changed its geographical and institutional focus over time. Like Dahl (1989: 194), he accepts that the notion of democracy was once confined to the city-state. It then expanded to embrace the nation-state, and it has now become a concept that stands or falls through an acknowledgement of its global character.

Since local, national, regional and global structures and processes all overlap, democracy must take a cosmopolitan form (Held, 1995: 21). Held argues (as, indeed, Dahl does) that people in states are radically affected by activities that occur outside their borders. Whether we think of the movement of interest rates, the profits that accrue to stocks and shares, the spread of AIDS, the movements of refugees and asylum seekers, or the damage to the environment, government is clearly stretching beyond the state.

What obstructs the notion of international democracy, Held argues, is the assumption that states are sovereign, and that international institutions detract from this sovereignty. The position of the USA under the Bush leadership (alarmingly reinforced rather than undermined by the reaction to the appalling

Ch. 1:
The State

events of 11 September 2001) is rooted in the archaic belief that institutions that look beyond the nation-state are a threat to, rather than a necessity for, democratic realities.

The post-war period has seen the development of what Held calls the UN Charter Model (1995: 86). However, although this has made inroads into the concept of state sovereignty (hence the US hostility to the UN), it coexists uneasily with what Held calls the 'the model of Westphalia' – the notion that states recognise no superior authority and tackle conflicts by force (1995: 78). A first step forward would involve enhancing the UN model by making a consensus vote in the General Assembly a source of international law, and providing a means of redress of human rights violations in an international court. The Security Council would be more representative if the veto arrangement was modified, and the problem of double standards addressed – a problem that undermines the UN's prestige in the south (Held, 1995: 269). Welcome as these measures would be, they still represent, Held contends, a very thin and partial move towards an international democracy.

Held's full-blown model of cosmopolitan democracy would involve the formation of regional parliaments whose decisions become part of international law. There would be referenda cutting across nations and nation-states, and the establishment of an independent assembly of democratic nations (1995: 279). The logic of this argument implies the explicit erosion of state sovereignty and the use of international legal principles as a way of delimiting the scope and action of private and public organisations. These principles are egalitarian in character and would apply to all civic and political associations.

How would they be enforced? It is here that Held's commitment to the state as a permanent actor on the international scene bedevils his argument. The idea of the state remains but it must, Held contends, be adapted to 'stretch across borders' (1995: 233). While he argues that the principle of 'non-coercive relations' should prevail in the settlement of disputes, the use of force as a weapon of last resort should be employed in the face of attacks to eradicate cosmopolitan law.

Held's assumption is that the existence of this force would be permanent. Yet these statist assumptions are in conflict with the aim of seconding this force, that is 'the demilitarisation and transcendence of the war system' (1995: 279). For this is only possible if institutions claiming a monopoly of legitimate force give way to what we have called governments, and the logic of government is, it has been argued above, profoundly different from that of the state. Held contends that we must overcome the dualisms between (for example) globalism and cultural diversity; global governance from above and the extension of grass roots organisations from below, constitutionalism and politics. These polarities make it impossible to embed utopia in what Held calls 'the existing pattern of political relations and processes' (1995: 286).

As challenging as this model is, its incoherence is manifest in Held's continuing belief in the permanence of the state. In an analysis of democracy and autonomy, he argues that the demos must include all adults with the exception of those temporarily visiting a political community, and those who 'beyond a shadow of a doubt' are legitimately disqualified from participation 'due to severe mental incapacity and/or serious records of crime' (Held, 1995: 208). Temporary visitors would, it is true, be citizens of other communities, but excluding the mentally incapacitated from citizenship is far from self-evident, and while there may be a tactical argument for excluding serious criminals from voting (although the position on this is changing), the very existence of such a category of intransigent outsiders indicates how far we are from having a democracy.

Held argues that the nation-state would 'wither away' but by this he does not mean that the nation-state would disappear. What he suggests is that states would no longer be regarded as the 'sole centres of legitimate power' within their own borders but would be 'relocated' to and articulated within, an overarching global democratic law (1995: 233). Democracy would, it seems, be simultaneously statist, supra-statist and sub-statist, but although this is an attractive argument, there remains a problem. States, after all, are institutions that claim a monopoly of legitimate force in 'their' particular territory. They are jealous of this asserted monopoly (which lies at the heart of the notion of state sovereignty) and, therefore, cannot coexist equally with other bodies that do not and cannot even claim to exercise a monopoly of legitimate force.

Held seeks to transform the world environment in the interests of self-government and emancipation, but he remains prisoner of the liberal view that the state is permanent. As far as Held is concerned, the state merely remains as one of many organisations. Yet the state is incompatible with democracy, and as it gives up its claim to a monopoly of legitimate force, it ceases to be a state.

The Ancient Greek Polity and the Problem with Liberalism

The ancient Greek polity was, as noted above, exclusive and Athenian democracy rested, among other things, upon imperialism. It is revealing that Rousseau, as an admirer of the ancient system, is uncertain as to how to respond to its reliance on slavery. On the one hand, he argues fiercely against slavery and takes great exception to Aristotle's comment that there are slaves 'by nature'. On the other hand, he concedes that without slavery, democracy in ancient Greece would not have been possible (1968: 52, 142; Hoffman, 1988: 146).

The fact is that ancient Greek democrats took democracy to be a form of the state, although their concept of democracy was mystified by its apparent linkages with the old clan system of tribal times. When Kleisthenes overthrew the oligarchs and forged a new constitution at the end of fifth century BC, the external features of the old system were faithfully reproduced in the arrangements of the new. 'Restoring' the popular assembly, the festivals and the electoral system made it appear as though the people were simply recovering the ancient rights of their old tribal system.

The continuity was deceptive. The new units of the constitution, though tribal in form, were geographical in reality, so that in practice the new democratic constitution actually worked to accelerate the disintegration of the clan system. The development of commerce and industry helped to dissolve away the residues of the old kinship bonds, and introduce a system based on slavery. Morgan, a nineteenth-century American anthropologist, complained that a 'pure democracy' was marred by atrocious slavery (Hoffman, 1988: 147–8), but once we understand that this was a statist form of democracy, then the paradox of popular rule and slavery ceases to be a problem.

Conservatives failed to understand this when they feared that democracy would undermine 'natural' hierarchies. John Cotton, a seventeenth-century divine in New England, spoke of democracy as the meanest and most illogical form of government, since he asked: when the people govern, over whom do they rule? Many conservatives overlooked the statist character of classical liberalism. After all, the whole point of the classical liberal concept of the state of nature was to establish the impossibility of life without the state. It is true that classical liberals assumed that humans were 'naturally' free and equal, but they construed these qualities as market-based abstractions, so that inevitably as 'inconveniences' (as Locke politely terms them) set in, the state was required to maintain order. Rousseau could speak of people leaving the state of nature in order to rush headlong into the chains of the state, but he takes it for granted that the legitimate rule, which forces people to be free, is of course a state.

When King Charles upbraided English liberals for labouring to bring in democracy, and told them that a subject and a sovereign 'are clear different things' (Dunn, 1979: 3), he need not have bothered. Liberals were clearly aware of this distinction! This is why Tocqueville could describe the USA as a democracy – democracy could be many things, but Tocqueville never imagined it doing away with the state. Dunn describes democracy as 'the name for what we cannot have' – people ruling their own state (1979: 27) – but this is because he views the world from the standpoint of a liberal, and he takes it for granted that people cannot govern without an institution claiming a monopoly of legitimate force for a particular territory. One of the delegates of the South German People's Party declared at a conference in 1868 that 'democracy wants to become social democracy, if it honestly wants to become democracy' (Bauman, 1976: 43). It could be argued that the same thing should be said about democracy and the state. Only an institution that looks beyond the claim to exercise a monopoly of legitimate force can call itself a democracy!

Democracy and the Relational Argument

Once we challenge the idea that democracy can be a form of the state, then the argument that the will of the majority may favour arbitrary and repressive rule ceases to be persuasive.

For the point is that majorities cannot repress minorities unless their rule expresses itself in the form of the state. The examples that Crick gives are clearly statist in character, so that the problem is not really with majority rule: it is with the state. For how can we reconcile democracy with an institution claiming a monopoly of legitimate force?

The idea that democracy can express itself as a tyranny of the majority is not only empirically invalid, it is also logically problematic as well. For it assumes that individuals are completely separate from one another, so that it is possible for one section of the population (the majority) to be free while their opponents (the minority) are oppressed. However, this argument is only defensible if we draw a sharp (and non-relational) line between the self and the other. If we embrace a relational approach, then the freedom of each individual depends upon the freedom of the other. As the Zimbabwean greeting puts it, I have slept well, if you have slept well: we may be separate people, but we are also related. It is impossible for a majority to oppress a minority, without oppressing itself.

Let me illustrate this logical point with an empirical example. Take the idea that was noted above of Ian Paisley's 'Protestant State for the Protestant People'. Up until 1972, it can be said that in Northern Ireland, the Catholic minority were oppressed, and the Protestant majority ascendant. But how free was the majority? What happened if an individual Protestant wished to marry a Catholic, or became sympathetic to their point of view? What happened to Protestants who decided to revere the anti-colonial heritage of Protestants like Wolfe Tone? How open could loyalist-minded Protestants be about the partisan character of police or the electoral malpractices designed to devalue Catholic votes? The point is that in a society in which there is a 'tyranny of the majority', no one is free and thus able to govern their own lives.

Chantal Mouffe, a radical post-structuralist theorist, has argued that democracy leads to the dictatorial rule of the popular will. It embodies the logic of what she calls identity or equivalence, whereas liberalism (which she prefers to democracy) respects difference, diversity and individual self-determination (1996: 25). But is this liberal polity a form of the state? On this crucial matter, Mouffe is silent, and it is not surprising that her admiration for the pre-war conservative Carl Schmitt, places her argument in still more difficulty. While she praises Schmitt for identifying politics with conflict, she is embarrassed by the avowedly statist way in which he interprets conflict (Hoffman, 1988: 60).

For Schmitt, the other is an enemy to be physically eliminated. While Mouffe identifies politics with conflict and difference, she is reluctant to see differences 'settled' in a statist manner through force. She seeks to distinguish between a social agent and the multiplicity of social positions that agents may precariously and temporarily adopt. The pluralism of multiple identities is 'constitutive of modern democracy' and 'precludes any dream of final reconciliation' (Mouffe, 1996: 25). But if democracy is a form of the state, then it will, indeed, rest upon an oppressive logic of equivalence that suppresses, rather than celebrates, difference.

The argument that democracy can be tyrannical makes the assumption that individuals and groups can be totally separated from each other. Democracy is conceived of as a Hobbesian Leviathan in majoritarian form (Hoffman, 1995: 202), by which is meant that democracy is analysed in terms of the kind of unrelated individuals that lie at the heart of Hobbes's argument for the state. Once we argue that the mechanisms of government must replace those of the state, then the notion of democracy becomes a means of resolving conflict in a way that acknowledges the identity of the parties to a dispute. It goes beyond the need for an institution claiming a monopoly of legitimate force – the state.

Focus

Democracy and Political Correctness

Political correctness (PC) swept across American universities in the 1990s and occasioned much controversy. Although it has not made the same impact in British universities, it is often used in conservative discourse as a response to feminist and multiculturalist arguments. The law passed in the British parliament to outlaw fox-hunting – to take a recent example – has been condemned as PC by its opponents.

Political correctness is considered by its critics to be a negation of democracy. There is no doubt that what has given PC its unsavoury reputation is the problem of dogmatism. Feminist and multicultural arguments have been advanced on occasion in an anti-liberal manner that has enabled conservative-minded publicists and thinkers to identify emancipatory causes as being inherently illiberal in character. However, it could be argued that it is counterproductive (and indeed contradictory) to try and advance good causes through intolerance (and even worse harassment and the threat of violence). Emancipation should be liberating – to make it dreary and painful is to crush it and distort it.

The cause of anti-racism or the cause of feminism, for example, is not advanced by pushing people into positions for which they are not qualified. The policy of affirmative action – promoting people because they are black or women or belong to a disadvantaged minority – is a risky one which only works at the margins and can easily backfire. The question is always: what is the best and quickest way of making our public and private institutions more representative of the population at large? Given the regrettable fact that elitism and prejudice have existed for so long that some even think that they are 'natural' and 'normal', there are no quick and easy solutions – no shortcuts. Would that there were!

The insistence that the right kind of language is used is helpful in so far as it changes peoples' attitudes and behaviour. But what if it does not? What if people use their 'correct' language but still continue to behave in the old way? Democracy, alas, requires more than a change of language if it is to advance.

Democratic causes are those that empower people. If this is done in a way that commands wide support, we all benefit. Democracy can only advance if it tackles those who are hostile to democracy. PC needs defending both against those who advocate racism, sexism or homophobia etc. and against those who ruin good causes by acting in an illiberal and unemancipatory manner. The best argument against those who promote good causes in an intemperate and divisive way, is to tell them that they are not PC!

Summary

What makes democracy such a confusing concept is that it has been acclaimed from almost every part of the political spectrum – and is held to stand for contradictory ideals. Contrary to the notion of 'liberal democracy', it is important to remember that before the twentieth century, liberals generally opposed democracy even though they were often accused by their conservative opponents of being democratic in character. Although liberalism presented its ideals in universal terms, there were all manner of exclusion clauses in practice. Liberals only reluctantly converted to democracy in the nineteenth century when they felt that extending the franchise would not undermine the rights of property.

The argument has been advanced even after the Second World War that democracy could mean a 'tyranny of the majority' and that democracy should be 'redefined' to involve a vote for competing elites to make decisions. In fact, increasing political participation is necessary for democracy and the argument for compulsory voting in elections should be taken seriously. It is misleading to argue that democracy involves either direct participation or representation. It involves both. Although representation does not require that those elected 'mirror' the precise proportions of the population, empathy between representative and elector is crucial.

If democracy is to involve self-government, there is a conflict between democracy, on the one hand, and the state, on the other. This is why Held's concept of a 'cosmopolitan democracy' can only be coherently sustained if the international community ceases to be composed of states. The question of the contradiction between democracy and the state has direct relevance for understanding the character and quality of the democracy in Ancient Greece. Only by analysing democracy in relation to the state can we develop a relational view that makes it possible to tackle the 'tyranny of the majority' argument effectively.

Questions

1. How democratic are 'liberal democracies'?
2. Is a society more democratic if more people participate in decision-making?
3. Can a system be called democratic if it is illiberal in character?
4. Does democracy lead to the 'tyranny of the majority'?
5. Why is democracy such a confusing concept?

References

Bauman, Z. (1976) *Socialism as Utopia* London: George Allen and Unwin.

Crick, B. (1982) *In Defence of Politics*, 2nd edn Harmondsworth: Penguin.

Dahl, R. (1989) *Democracy and its Critics* New Haven, CT: Yale University Press.

Dunn, J. (1979) *Western Political Theory in the Face of the Future* London: Cambridge University Press.

Faulks, K. (1999) *Political Sociology* Edinburgh: Edinburgh University Press.

Faulks, K. (2001) 'Should Voting be Compulsory?' *Politics Review* 10(3), 24–5.

Goodwin, B. (1997) *Using Political Ideas* 4th edn Chichester, New York, Toronto: John Wiley and Sons.

Held, D. (1995) *Democracy and the Global Order* Cambridge: Polity Press.

Hoffman, J. (1988) *State, Power and Democracy* Brighton: Wheatsheaf Books.

Hoffman, J. (1995) *Beyond the State* Cambridge: Polity.

Macpherson, C. (1977) *The Life and Times of Liberal Democracy* London, Oxford and New York: Oxford University Press.

Mouffe, C. (1996) 'Radical Democracy or Liberal Democracy' in D. Trend (ed.) *Radical Democracy* New York and London: Routledge, 19–26.

Plato (1955) *The Republic* Harmondsworth: Penguin.

Rousseau, J-J. (1968) *The Social Contract* Harmondsworth: Penguin.

Schumpeter, J. (1947) *Capitalism, Socialism and Democracy* 2nd edn New York and London: Harper.

Tocqueville, A. de (1966) *Democracy in America* London and Glasgow: Fontana.

Weldon, T. (1953) *The Vocabulary of Politics* Harmondsworth: Penguin.

Further Reading

- Crick's chapter 3, 'A Defence of Politics Against Democracy' in his *In Defence of Politics* (referenced above) is an absolute must for all interested in the question.
- C.B. Macpherson's *The Life and Times of Liberal Democracy* (referenced above) contains a very useful assessment of different 'models'.
- Dahl's *Democracy and its Critics* (referenced above) is clear and comprehensive, and particularly memorable for its critique of majoritarian rule.
- John Dunn has a very thought-provoking chapter on democracy in his *Western Political Theory in the Face of the Future* (referenced above).
- M. Finley, *Democracy Ancient and Modern* (London: Chatto and Windus, 1973) has an excellent description of ancient Greek democracy.
- David Held's *Democracy and the Global Order* (referenced above) is very useful for those particularly interested in reworking the concept in the light of international trends.
- Fareed Zakaria in *The Future of Freedom* (New York: Norton, 2003) deals knowledgeably with the problem of liberalism and democracy.

Weblinks

For the treatment of democracy in political theory, see
http://www.keele.ac.uk/depts/po/prs.htm or
http://www.york.ac.uk/services/library/subjects/politint.htm

For those interested in the direct democracy debate, see
http://www.homeusers.prestel.co.uk/rodmell/quest.htm

David Held's arguments can be seen at
http://www.mpi-fg-koeln.mpg.de/pu/workpap/wp97-5/wp97-5.html

Chapter 6

Citizenship

Introduction

Is the term 'citizenship' legal, philosophical, political, social or economic? Or is it a combination of all these dimensions? Does this flexibility make the term so elastic that it is effectively unusable?

The literature on citizenship has burgeoned massively over the past decade with a journal devoted to the concept; reports on the teaching of the idea to school students; ministerial pronouncements on the subject, and articles and books galore in scholarly and popular publications. There is even a ceremony that has been devised for new citizens! Although the classical concepts of citizenship go back to the ancient Greeks (as we shall see in a moment) and were reworked in classical liberalism, contemporary commentators have sought to develop a concept of citizenship which is much more inclusive than earlier views.

Chapter Map

- The limitations of the ancient Greek concept of citizenship, and the exclusiveness of the liberal view. The abstract character of the liberal view of citizenship, its universal claims to freedom and equality and the inequalities of class.

- Marshall's argument that citizenship, in its modern form, requires social as well as political and legal rights. The rise of the New Right in Britain and the USA and its challenge to the concept of citizenship in the welfare state.

- The barriers that women face to a meaningful citizenship. How and why these barriers prevent women from running their own lives and impoverish their citizenship.

- The case for a basic income as a way of enhancing citizenship.

- Global citizenship as a status that does not contradict citizenship as member of a state. Citizenship as an identity at local, regional and national levels as well. The development of citizenship in the European Union.

- The tension between the state and citizenship, the question of class and citizenship, the case for transforming the market, and the presentation of citizenship as a relational concept.

'Being British': Pride, Passports and Princes

Prince Charles presenting certificates of British Citizenship

Source: Rex Features

In February 2004, 19 immigrants received British passports in a ceremony in which they took an oath of allegiance to the Queen as head of state. The Prince of Wales handed out certificates, congratulating those receiving them. 'Being British', declared the Prince, 'is something of a blessing and a privilege for us all.' He hoped that the ceremony added something to the significance of acquiring British citizenship, and 'that it's reinforced your belief, if indeed any reinforcement is required, that you belong here and are very welcome'. He added that 'being a British citizen becomes a great source of pride and comfort for the rest of your life'. *Guardian* journalists in September 2003 found that when they questioned nine British citizens about key aspects of British life, the average score was just 37 per cent. Only a third of the sample could name the Home Secretary and knew what NHS Direct was, about 10 per cent knew what the national minimum wage was, and none knew what the basic rate of income tax was.

- Everyone agrees that British citizens should be able to speak English, but what other duties should someone fulfil in order to become a British citizen? Should they have a basic knowledge about British history, its political institutions and its society?

- Should would-be British citizens have to take an oath of allegiance to the Queen? What if they are republican-minded, or feel as Jews, Catholics, Muslims, atheists, Hindus, Sikhs etc. that the head of the state as an Anglican cannot be said to represent them?

- Should citizens have to vote in elections? Should they be expected to do community service at some stage? Should they receive as citizens a basic income from the government?

- Does citizenship require people to be involved in their locality and region? Should they also be concerned with developments in the European Union? Should they regard themselves as citizens of the world?

Citizenship and Liberalism

Ch. 1:
The state

The notion of citizenship arises with ancient Greek thinkers (much of the argument here follows Hoffman [2004]). The citizen is traditionally and classically defined as one who has the ability and chance to participate in government (by which is meant the state), but in Aristotle's aristocratic view, citizenship should not only exclude slaves, foreigners and women, but should be restricted to those who are relieved of menial tasks (Aristotle, 1962: 111).

We must always bear this in mind when the argument is put for a 'revitalisation' and extension of the Aristotelian ideal of citizenship as the alternation of ruling and being ruled (Voet, 1998: 137). For the positive attributes of ancient Greek theory are undermined by the fact that they express themselves through gender, ethnic, and (it should not be forgotten) imperial hierarchies, and we need to challenge the elitist notion of citizenship that the ancient Greeks took for granted.

Even when slavery was apparently rejected by a liberal view of humanity, the concept of citizenship has remained limited and exclusionary. It is revealing that Rousseau insists that the 'real meaning' of citizenship is only respected when the word is used selectively and exclusively (1968: 61). Citizens have property, are national (in their political orientation), and are public and male. Even the classical liberal opposition between citizenship and slavery is weakened by Rousseau's astonishing comment that in unfortunate situations (as in ancient Greece) 'the citizen can be perfectly free only if the slave is absolutely a slave' (1968: 143).

Classical liberalism injects a potential **universalism** into the concept of citizenship by arguing that all individuals are free and equal. Yet the universalism of this concept is undermined by support for **patriarch**y, elitism, colonialism – and as Yeatman has recently reminded us in the case of Locke (see the Chapter on Liberalism) – by an acceptance of outright slavery (Yeatman, 1994: 62; Hoffman, 1988: 162). Locke not only justifies slavery in his *Two Treatises*, he was a shareholder in a slave-owning company in Virginia. These rather startling facts coexist with the liberal notion of free and equal individuals.

Medieval thinkers, like the ancient Greeks, have no universal concept of citizenship, because although medieval Christians, for example, had a notion of equality before the Fall, once humans are corrupted by sin ('the mother of servitude'), people divide into citizens and slaves, men and women, etc. in the time-honoured way.

Citizenship and Class

The recent literature on citizenship challenges the liberal concept of citizenship on the grounds that this concept leaves out many categories of people in society. The argument for a broader franchise was essentially an argument for broadening the concept of citizenship so that male workers could enjoy political rights.

Classical liberalism assumed that the individual had property, and as we have seen in the chapter on socialism, some socialists like Eduard Bernstein saw the notion of citizenship as something that workers could and should aspire to. Marx, on the other hand, appears to be bleakly negative towards the concept of citizenship, arguing that it seems to ignore the realities of a class-divided society. The rights of the citizen, he comments in an oft-cited passage, are simply the rights of the egoistic man (i.e. the property owner) of 'men separated from other men and the community' (Marx and Engels, 1975: 162). Marx's language is not only sexist, but he seems to be saying that citizenship is simply the right to exploit others through the ownership of private property. The possession of citizenship is seen as an anti-social activity.

His argument is not quite as negative as it sounds. Marx comments that in the possessive individualist society, it is not 'man as citoyen but man as bourgeois who is considered to be the essential and true man' (Marx and Engels, 1975: 164). Marx's argument is that classical citizenship is abstract in so far as it implies an equality of an ideal kind, for this equality is contradicted by the concrete inequalities that exist in the real world. Even if the male worker can vote, how much power does he have over his life if his employer can have him summarily dismissed from this work?

It is important to stress that for Marx, the notion of abstraction does not imply unreality, in the sense that the abstract citizen does not exist. What makes the liberal notion of citizenship abstract is that it *conceals* beneath its benevolent-sounding principles the reality of class. While the *Communist Manifesto* sees the establishment of the 'modern representative State' (Marx and Engels, 1967: 82) as a crucial historical achievement, this state cannot be said to be representative of the community but acts on behalf of the capitalists. The celebrated description of communism as 'an association in which free development of each is the condition for the free development of all' (Marx and Engels, 1967: 105) could be taken, in our view, as a description of citizenship in a classless society.

Marx's concept of abstraction makes it possible to explain why Locke and the classical liberals of the seventeenth and eighteenth centuries could imagine that individuals existed in splendid isolation from one another in a state of nature, while continuing to trade as market partners. The market involves an exchange between individuals that conceals their differing social positions.

Marx's analysis can still be used as a critique of the liberal concept of the citizen, even though the notion of labour as the source of value is contentious. It is clear that how we evaluate goods depends upon the activities of numerous people – managers, workers, supervisors, consumers, entrepreneurs, etc. – and that it would be wrong to suggest that certain categories of people do not contribute to the labour process, and therefore perhaps, should be 'second class' citizens. This type of argument simply turns liberalism inside out: it discriminates against the haves in favour of the have-nots, whereas it could be argued that the point is to eliminate the distinction altogether.

Citizenship, Marshall and Social Rights

Liberalism establishes the formal freedom and equality of all members of society itself. Those who have no independent property cannot rest content with legal and political equality but must press on for social equality as well. The Chartists, although campaigners in the nineteenth century for political rights, were fond of saying that the vote is a knife and fork question: the demand for citizenship must be a demand for resources which make individuality not simply a condition to be protected, but a reality to be attained. J.S. Mill presents a developmental view of human nature when he argues that women and workers could become 'individuals'. T.H. Green and Hobhouse, as social liberals, argue the case for more security for workers (see their biographies on the website).

Marshall (1893–1981), a British sociologist, wrote a much-cited essay on *Citizenship and Social Class* in 1950. He presents a classic argument that civil and political rights do not, on their own, create a meaningful citizenship. Social rights are also crucial. For Marshall, 'taming market forces was an essential precondition for a just society' (Marshall and Bottomore, 1992: vi). Marshall is concerned, despite the inadequacies of an argument which have been extensively commented upon, to try and give white male workers a human rather than a purely market identity. He cites with approval the nineteenth century economist Alfred Marshall's notion of a 'gentleman' in contrast to a mere 'producing machine' (1992: 5) and he uses the terms civilisation and citizenship to denote people who are, he argues, 'full members of society' (1992: 6). As T.H. (not Alfred!) Marshall sees things, the right to property, like the right of free speech, is undermined for the poor by a lack of social rights (1992: 21).

It is true that Marshall does not see himself as a critic of capitalism. His concern is to make a case for a basic human equality that is not inconsistent with the inequalities that distinguish the various economic levels in a capitalist society, and he even argues that citizenship has become the architect of legitimate social inequality (1992: 6–7). But the point is that he does perceive citizenship in tension with capitalism. In a famous passage he sees capitalism and citizenship at war, although (as Bottomore tartly comments), Marshall does not develop this argument (1992: 18, 56). It is important not to overlook the extent to which his new liberal reformism unwittingly challenges a class-divided society.

As a social liberal, Marshall believes that a pragmatic compromise between capitalism and citizenship is possible, even though he can argue that the attitude of mind which inspired reforms like legal aid grew out of a conception of equality which oversteps the narrow limits of a competitive market economy. Underlying the concept of social welfare is the conception of equal social worth and not merely equal natural rights (1992: 24). He notes – as part of his critique – early liberal arguments against universal male suffrage. The political rights of citizenship, unlike civil rights, are a potential danger to the capitalist system, although those cautiously extending them did not realise how great the danger was (1992: 25) (see Chapter on Democracy, p. 101).

Citizenship has imposed modifications upon the capitalist class system on the grounds that the obligations of contract are brushed aside by an appeal to the rights of citizenship (1992: 40–2). In place of the incentive to personal gain is the incentive of public duty – an incentive that corresponds to social rights. Marshall believes that both incentives can be served – capitalism can be reconciled to citizenship since these paradoxes are inherent in our contemporary social system (1992: 43).

The preservation of economic inequalities has been made more difficult, Marshall concedes, by the expansion of the status of citizenship. To concede that individuals are citizens is to invite them to challenge the need for class divisions. The great strength of Marshall's argument is that he depicts the drive for social equality as a process that has been taking place for some 250 years (1992: 7). He opens up the prospect of the need to continue progress, given the fact that he later concedes that at the end of the 1970s, the welfare state is now in a precarious and battered condition (1992: 71).

It is certainly true that Marshall ignores the position of women and ethnic minorities; the sectarianism in Northern Ireland, and the peculiar conditions in the immediate post-war period that made a new liberal compromise seem plausible – to conservatives as well to many social democrats. There were, as Bottomore has noted (1992: 58), exceptionally high rates of economic growth, and the deterrent example of the Communist Party states, the self styled 'real socialism'. Marshall treats capitalism in terms of the income of the rich, rather than the property they own. Our point is that Marshall demonstrates that a concern with the social rights of the citizen challenges the class structure of a capitalist society.

Citizenship and the New Right

The expansion of social rights, it has been frequently noted, was checked in the mid-1970s, as the capitalist market economy became dominant over the welfare state (Marshall and Bottomore, 1992: 73). New Right or neo-liberal thought seeks to defend individualism and the market against what it sees as menacing inroads created by a post-war consensus around reform. The New Right project, which lasts until the 1990s, is indirectly related to the image of a citizen as a successful entrepreneur who benefits from 'free' market forces.

The argument is that the concept of society is a dangerous abstraction – there are only individuals – but although neo-liberals appear to return to the classical liberal position, gone is the assumption that humans are free and equal individuals. Free, yes, but equal no! Individuals radically differ according to ability, effort and incentives and, therefore, it is a myth to imagine that they are in any sense equal. New Rightists argue that any attempt to implement distributive or social justice can only undermine the unfettered choices of the free market. 'Nothing', Hayek argues, 'is more damaging to the demand for equal treatment than to base it on so obviously untrue an assumption as that of the factual equality of all men' (1960: 86; see also Heater, 1999: 27). Equality before the law and material equality are seen to be in conflict, and Hayek is in the curious philosophical position of arguing for an 'ideal' or 'moral' equality while denying that any basis for this equality exists in reality.

Ch. 4:
Justice

Both Hayek and Nozick, despite their differences in many theoretical respects, agree that intervention in the market in the name of social justice is anathema. Both link citizenship to inequality. New Right thinkers in trying to 'roll back the state', seek to confine it to its so-called negative activities – the protection of contracts. Not surprisingly, New Right policies under Thatcher in Britain radically increased the role of the state (in its traditional law and order functions), since weakening the trade unions, cutting welfare benefits and utilising high unemployment as a way of punishing the poor and the protesters, involves a radical concentration of state power. Both Thatcher and Hayek share an admiration for General Pinochet, who demonstrated in Chile that enhancing the power of the market may be bad for democracy!

Gray speaks of Hayek 'purifying' classical liberalism of its errors of abstract individualism and rationalism (Faulks, 1998: 61). It could be argued that the New Right supports the weaknesses of classical liberalism without its conceptual strengths. Faulks challenges the argument that the pressure against social rights takes the form of a reassertion of civil rights, since in practice, Faulks argues that civil rights without social rights are hollow and extremely partial. What is the point of allowing freedom of speech without the provision of education that develops linguistic capacity, or freedom under the law in a system that denies most of the population the resources to secure legal representation?

The notion of freedom as power or capacity is seen by Hayek as 'ominous' and dangerous (1960: 16–17). Hayek supports what he sees as purely negative freedom, but the truth is that negative without positive freedom is an impossible abstraction and a distinction that is alien to the classical liberal tradition. Classical liberal thinkers assumed that (certain) individuals had the capacity to act: what they needed was the right to do so. Hayek divorces freedom from capacity, and contends that since to be free can involve freedom to be miserable, to be free may mean freedom to starve (1960: 18). No wonder traditional conservatives like Ian Gilmour see these views as doctrinaire and utopian (1978: 117), and it is revealing that in *The Downing Street Years* (1993) Thatcher discusses socialism and 'High Toryism' in the same breath (Faulks, 1998: 79).

The New Right unwittingly demonstrates the indivisibility of rights. Hayek is far from enthusiastic about the exercise of political rights since the mass of the population might be tempted to use their political rights to secure the kind of capacities and power that the free market denies them. In practice, Hayek is an elitist and, as Faulks comments, his version of liberalism is difficult to distinguish from authoritarian conservatism. Conflict of a violent kind is simply increased by the creation of vast inequalities, and insofar as modern America approximates to the neo-liberal view of citizenship, it is not surprising that this is a society that marginalises its inner city areas and is afflicted by high rates of drug abuse and organised crime (Faulks, 1998: 71–2). A Hobbesian Leviathan state, aggravated by the hysteria that has followed the dreadful events of 11 September 2001, reveals the free market as a Hobbesian state of nature without the equality!

Thatcher argues, as Faulks has recalled, that many people fail in society because they are unworthy. 'With such a view, Thatcherism carried to its logical conclusion the abstract and elitist logic of the individualism in neo-liberal political theory' (1998: 86). She makes a distinction between active and passive citizens, and although the coexistence of the free market and strong state seems paradoxical, in fact, as Gilmour has commented, the establishment of a free market state is a 'dictatorial venture' which demands the submission of dissenting institutions and individuals (Faulks, 1998: 89; Gray, 1999: 26).

It would be wrong, however, to see the New Right in purely negative terms. Those who subscribed to New Right ideas sought to free 'individuals' from dependency upon others and often employed sophisticated theories to demonstrate their arguments. The New Right emphasised what is surely an essential ingredient in citizenship: the need to be independent and think critically for oneself. The challenge is to extend this notion to all inhabitants in society so that the skills of enterprise can be enjoyed widely.

Citizenship and the Case for a Basic Income

As long as social rights are seen as special entitlements for those who have 'failed' they will always be divisive, and reaffirm rather than undermine, class differences.

In her assessment of the welfare state, Pateman makes the case for a guaranteed income for everyone (Hoffman, 1995: 205), and the value of this proposal as a citizens' or basic income is that it would be universal. This proposal is also made by New Rightists who speak of the need for a 'negative income tax'. All would receive this income, regardless of employment status. As Faulks points out (2000: 120), it could decommodify social rights (i.e. take them away from the market), and break with the argument that those who lack capital must work for others. A guaranteed basic income would give people a real choice as to how and in what way they wanted to work, and empower citizens as a whole.

It would enable people to think much more about the 'quality of life' and the ecological consequences of material production. It would enhance a sense of community and individual autonomy, and underpin the social and communal character of wealth creation (Faulks, 2000: 120). It is not difficult to see how a basic income would also dramatically improve the position of women whose precarious economic position makes them particularly dependent upon men or patriarchal-minded partners. It is true that were this idea taken in abstraction from other policies concerned with reducing inequality (as in the development of a democratic policy for ethnic minorities and movements towards genuinely universal education), then it could be divisive, tying women to domestic duties, and leaving the capitalist labour contract unreformed, but as Faulks comments, 'no one policy can address all possible inequalities' (2000: 120).

People seek to work outside the home for social reasons (and not simply economic ones), and a guaranteed income would give people time and resources to be more involved in community enhancing activities such as life-long learning, voluntary work and political participation. The argument that universal benefits undermine personal responsibility (Saunders, 1995: 92) seems to us precisely wrong since the assumption that people will only act sensibly if they are threatened with destitution and poverty reflects an elitist disregard for how people actually think.

What of the cost? Surely a citizens' income is not economically feasible, given the argument that the rich will not tolerate paying higher levels of taxation. The idea of a guaranteed income appears to be a non-starter. There are a number of counter-arguments that should be put.

- A guaranteed income would markedly simplify the difficult and complex tax and benefits system: significant savings could be made here.
- People will pay for universal benefits if they are convinced of the need for them. The widespread support for, say, the British National Health Service as a

provider of universal benefits shows that increasing taxation is much more palatable if people are convinced that it is linked to changes which will really improve their lives. Adair Turner lists some of the collective goods – subsidised public transport, traffic calming measures, noise abatement baffles and tree screens to make our motorways less intrusive – which he would prefer to (for example) a bigger and more stylish car. 'I would rather pay more tax to get those benefits than have the extra, personal income available to buy more market goods' (2002: 125).

- A guaranteed income is in the interests of all. A basic income would (along with many other egalitarian measures) help to reduce crime and the consumption of drugs, and make society as a whole a more secure and safer place. Would not the rich benefit from such a measure? Capitalism's beneficiaries, Adair Turner argues, should support investment in measures that promote social cohesion, out of their own self-interest (2002: 244). Gray argues that British public opinion wishes to see some goods – basic medical care, schooling, protection from crime – provided to all as a mark of citizenship (1999: 34). Is it not possible that given the right leadership and explanation, this could extend to the kind of economic security provided by a citizens' income?

Of course, it could be argued that a basic income will destroy incentives, just as it was said that a minimum wage would create unemployment, and in the nineteenth century, it was contended that a 10-hour day would undermine the labour process. But a government committed to such a dramatic victory of 'the political economy of the working class' (in Marx's celebrated phrase) could find ways of presenting the case for a guaranteed income that would isolate die-hard reactionaries.

It is important to stress that while a basic income would do much to increase the quality of citizenship, it would still leave open the question of including people from other countries in a global citizenship. Such an innovation would initially be limited to people of a particular community (Faulks, 2000: 123). It would only really succeed if it was part and parcel of policies that addressed the problem of inequalities between societies.

Citizenship and Women

Are women citizens in modern liberal states? Although women have been citizens in a formal sense in Britain, for example, since 1928 (when they received the vote), there are important senses in which women have yet to obtain real citizenship as opposed to a more conventional, classically defined citizenship.

Women, even in developed liberal societies like Britain, are significantly under-represented in decision-making, and this occurs because of structural and attitudinal factors. The exclusion of women from political processes has been justified by a liberal conception of a public/private divide.

It is true that with Wollstonecraft's *Vindication of the Rights of Woman* (1792) (→ Chapter on Feminism), the Enlightenment concepts of freedom and autonomy are extended to women. At the same time Wollstonecraft does not (explicitly at any rate) challenge the division of labour between the sexes or the argument for a male-only franchise. Women, she contends, if they are recognised as rational and autonomous beings, become better wives, mothers and domestic workers as a result – 'in a word, better citizens' (Bryson, 1992: 22–7). Here the term does not imply someone with voting rights, although it does suggest that the citizen is an individual whose activity is both public and private in character. Of course, when Wollstonecraft was writing most men could not vote, and there is some evidence to suggest that Wollstonecraft was in favour of female suffrage, but felt that it was not a demand worth raising at the time she wrote.

Bryson has noted that women find it more difficult to have their voices heard, their priorities acknowledged and their interests met (1994: 16). A recent report documents in detail the under-representation of women in all major sectors of decision-making in Britain, from parliament, the civil service, the judiciary, the legal profession, the police, local government, health, higher education, the media, public appointments and the corporate sector. For example, the UK is the fourth lowest in terms of the representation of women in the European Parliament at 24 per cent in 2000; it does better in a relative sense (in 1997) in terms of representation in national parliaments where it has 18 compared to Denmark's 33 per cent. Only 4.3 per cent of life peers in the House of Lords were women in 2000, while in the most senior grades of the civil service, 17.2 per cent were women in 1999. Nine per cent of the High Court Judges in 1999 were women, although this is three times as many as women who were Lord Justices! There were 6.4 per cent of Chief Constables who were women in 2000; 10 years previously there were none (Ross, 2000).

It is true that the representation of women is complex, and it does not follow that women representatives automatically and necessarily represent the interests of women in general. But there is clearly something wrong, as Voet acknowledges, with political institutions that dramatically under-represent women (1998: 106–8). Citizenship requires both the right and the capacity to participate in political decision-making. The real difficulty of women's citizenship is 'the low level of female participation in social and political decision-making' (Voet, 1998: 124, 132).

The public/private divide, as formulated in liberal theory, prevents women from becoming meaningful citizens. It undermines the confidence of women; prejudices men (and some women) against them; puts pressures on leisure time; trivialises and demonises those women who enter public life; and through a host of discriminatory practices which range from the crudely explicit to the subtly implicit, prevents women from taking leadership roles. Women members of the British Parliament still complain that their dress or physical appearance is commented upon in the media, although it would be unthinkable to do the same for men.

It is true that the public/private divide as it operates as a barrier to citizenship, is only implicit in liberal societies today. Whereas ancient (by which we mean slave-owning) societies and medieval societies explicitly divided the activities between men and women, under liberalism the public/private divide focuses on the relationship between individuals and the state.

Yuval-Davis has argued that we should abandon the public/private distinction altogether – a position which Voet challenges (1998: 141). It is both possible and necessary to reconstruct the concept of the public and the private so that it ceases to be patriarchal in character. Liberal theory sees freedom, in Crick's words, as 'the privacy of private men from public action' (1982: 18). As Crick's comment (and his revealing use of language) suggests, this is a freedom that extends only to males, since (as MacKinnon puts it) 'men's realm of private freedom is women's realm of collective subordination' (1989: 168). Citizenship requires participation in public arenas. Domestic arrangements are crucial which allow women to be both child-bearers (should they wish to), and workers outside the home, representatives at local, national and international level, and leaders in bodies that are outside the domestic sphere. This is not to say that women (like people in general) should not cherish privacy, but the public/private concept needs to be reconstructed (as we have suggested above), so that it empowers rather than degrades and diminishes women.

Women cannot be citizens unless they are treated as equal to men, and by equality we mean not merely sameness but an acknowledgement (indeed a celebration) of difference, not only between women and men but among women themselves.

The involvement of women in contemporary liberal societies as members of the armed and police forces is a necessary condition for women's citizenship because it helps to demystify the argument that only men can bear arms and fight for their country. Deeply embedded in traditionalist notions of citizenship, is the idea that only those who go to war for their country can be citizens. It is worth noting, however, that armies in liberal societies will increasingly be used for peacekeeping and even development purposes, so that the notion of soldiers bearing arms is likely to become more and more redundant anyway. But being conscious of the link between patriarchy and war involves rather more than 'opening' up armies to women. It involves a recognition of the link between male domination and violence. Citizenship requires security – not simply in the sense of protection against violence – but in the sense of having the confidence, the capacity and the skills to participate in decision-making. What Tickner calls a people-centred notion of security (1995: 192) identifies security as a concept that transcends state boundaries so that people feel at home in their locality, their nation and in the world at large.

It can be argued that the traditional caring role of many women brings an important dimension to citizenship itself. The notion that feminist conceptions of citizenship should be 'thick' (i.e. local and domestic) rather than 'thin' (i.e. public and universalist) rests upon a dichotomy which needs to be overcome. This is why the debate between 'liberals' and 'republicans' is, in our view, an unhelpful one for women (as it is for people in general). Both liberalism and republicanism presuppose that politics is a 'public' activity that rises above social life. Liberals argue for a negative view of the individual who is encouraged to leave public life to the politicians, while republicans stress the need to participate, but both premise their positions on a public/private divide that is patriarchal in essence.

Bubeck (1995: 6) instances Conservative proposals in Britain to extend the notion of good citizenship to participation in voluntary care, protection schemes, or neighbourhood policing. These are useful ways of enriching citizen practices for both women and men, but what is problematic is a notion of political participation that ignores the social constraints that traditionally have favoured men and disadvantaged women. The fact that the obligation to care for children and the elderly have fallen upon women as a domestic duty, does not make it non-political and private. Bubeck speaks of the existence of 'a general citizen's duty to care' (1995: 29) and, as she puts it later, the performance of this care needs to be seen as part of what it means, or it implies, to be a member of a political community (1995: 31).

Care should be transformed from what Bubeck calls a 'handicap' of women to a general requirement for all (1995: 34). Providing care should be seen as much of an obligation as fighting in a war (1995: 35), but whereas fighting in a war implies a sharp and lethal division between friends and enemies, the provision of care seeks to heal such divisions. The notion of 'conscription' into service that could either exist alongside or be an alternative to the army, is an attractive one. A caring service of some kind has an important role to play in developing a citizenship that combats patriarchy and recognises the position of women.

However, we cannot accept Pateman's argument that citizenship itself is a patriarchal category, although it is perfectly true that citizenship traditionally has been constructed in a masculinist image (Mouffe, 1992: 374). Men are different from women, and some women are different from others. Respecting difference is an important part of extending citizenship, so that Mouffe puts the matter in a misleading way when she argues that sexual difference is not a 'pertinent distinction' to a theory of citizenship (1992: 377) (→ website entry on Difference). Biological differences remain 'relevant' to citizenship even if these biological differences should not be used as a justification for discrimination. Differences between men and women no more exclude the latter from citizenship than differences between men can justify exclusion. But it does not follow that these differences cease to be 'pertinent'. We should not, in other words, throw the baby out with the bathwater. One-sided points need to be incorporated – not simply cast aside. Differences between men and women remain relevant but they do not justify restricting citizenship – with all this implies – to either gender.

Global Citizenship

Is citizenship limited to the membership of a particular nation? Writers like Aron (cited by Heater, 1999: 150) have declared that 'there are no such animals as "European citizens". There are only French, German or Italian citizens'. In this view, citizenship involves the membership of a national or domestic state.

Cosmopolitans argue, however, that the assertion of rights and responsibilities at the global level in no way contradicts loyalties at a regional, national and local level. People in whatever area of government they are involved, must be respected and empowered, whether they are neighbours in the same block, people of their own nation and region, or members of the other countries in distant parts of the world. One of the most positive features of globalisation is that people meet others of different ethnic and cultural origin and outlook, not only when they travel abroad, but even at the local level. The media (at its best) presents people suffering and developing in other parts of the world as though they were neighbours, so that it becomes increasingly possible to imagine what it is like to be the other. Modern conditions have contributed much to realise Kant's argument that 'a violation of rights in one part of the world is felt everywhere' (cited by Heater, 1999: 140).

Lister links the notion of 'global citizenship' with a 'multi-layered conception' of citizenship itself (1997: 196), with states acknowledging the importance of human rights and international law. Each layer, if it is democratically constructed, strengthens the other. Global citizenship – a respect for others, a concern for their well-being and a belief that the security of each person depends upon the security of every one else – does not operate in contradiction with regional, national and local identities. People can see themselves as Glaswegian, Scottish, British and European. Why do they have to make a choice? As Lister puts it, either/or choices lead us into a theoretical and political cul-de-sac (1997: 197). Heater argues that the 'singular concept' of citizenship has burst its bounds (1999: 117) and it is true that dual citizenship (which already exists in some states) represents a much more relaxed view of the question so that a person can exercise state-centred citizenship rights in more than one country. Heater presses the case for a fluid and flexible notion of citizenship, stating that membership of a voluntary association in civil society can qualify a person for citizenship, so that we can legitimately speak of a person as the citizen of a church, a trade union, a club, an environmental group, etc. (1999: 121). Heater insists that civil society offers a useful and even superior option to traditional state membership (1999: 121).

It goes without saying that the notion of a world or global citizen cannot prescribe rights and responsibilities with the precision that citizenships set out in written (or indeed unwritten) constitutions can and do. Nor, as Heater shows at some length, is the notion of a world citizen a new one. He gives examples of cosmopolitanism in ancient Greek thought, and quotes the words of the ancient Roman, Marcus Aurelius, that 'where-ever a man lives, he lives as a citizen of the World-City' (1999: 139).

The Argument so Far . . .

- Citizenship has traditionally been seen as membership of the state.

- This has linked citizenship to *exclusion* whether of slaves, women or the propertyless.

- The problem of exclusion has been addressed by developing a concept of citizenship that embraces not merely political and legal, but social rights as well. The latter have proved controversial and the New Right has argued that the welfare state creates a 'dependency' that undermines the autonomy of the citizen. The idea of giving all citizens a basic income as of right could, it has been argued, enhance citizenship.

- Even in liberal societies where women have acquired political rights, it is arguable that they have been confronted with a number of barriers preventing them from exercising their rights.

- Cosmopolitans argue that citizenship should extend to the world as a whole, so that people are not merely citizens of a particular country, but citizens of the globe.

The celebrated Kantian argument for world government is for a loose confederation of states. Heater is sympathetic to the notion of a global citizen, writing that 'a fully-fledged modern world state' might well require 'a transfer of civil allegiance from the state to the universal polity' (1999: 151). He argues that 'political citizenship, so intimately reliant on the possession of the means of force by the state, must remain absorbed in the state as the necessary catalyst for its vitality' (1999: 152). The ideal of cosmopolitan citizenship is the condition in which all human beings have equal recognition as co-legislators within a 'global kingdom of ends' (Linklater, 1999: 56). Soysal even insists that the identity of personhood stressed in human rights discourse, takes us beyond both citizenship and the state. National and citizenship identities are, in her view, unthinkable without the state (1994: 165).

Citizenship within the European Union

The European Union (EU) is concerned about equalisation and redistributive social policies. Richard Bellamy and Alex Warleigh's edited *Citizenship and Governance in the European Union* (2001) sees the EU and its concept of citizenship as a paradox and a puzzle. Is the Union seeking to establish a new kind of political entity or is it simply another (and larger) version of a state? The EU, this volume argues, has two aspects: one is the market, the other is democracy. Neo-liberals may think of the two as synonymous, but that view is not shared by the contributors to this volume, who point out that citizenship is a political issue which necessarily transcends a market identity.

The argument advanced is that while the current rights of the EU citizen may at present seem somewhat limited, we should be concerned with unanticipated outcomes. Under the provisions of the Maastricht Treaty, European citizens have the right to stand and vote in local and European parliamentary elections even if they are not nationals in the states where they reside; they can petition the Ombudsman as well as the European Parliament, and they are entitled to diplomatic protection in third states where one's 'own' state is not represented (Bellamy and Warleigh, 2001: 23).

To be sure, the EU was initially conceived as a transnational capitalist society, an economic union that was a free trade area. It could, however, be argued that people like Jean Monnet had explicitly political objectives right from the start. There is a logic to the EU that extends beyond the purely economic. It may well have been (for example) the *intention* of EU founders to confine sexual equality to the notion of a level playing field constituted by the cost of factors of production, but economic rights require a political and social context to be meaningful. It is the potential of EU citizenship that is important. It is this which links a rather passive, state-centred notion to a much more 'active, democratic citizenship' (Bellamy and Warleigh, 2001: 117), a move from a politics of identity – which implies a rather repressive homogeneity – to a politics of affinity which recognises and respects difference.

Citizenship is a 'surprisingly elusive concept' (Bellamy and Warleigh, 2001: 143), and the concept is an excellent example of an idea which compels us to think the unthinkable. Indeed, the very notion of citizenship was introduced as an attempt to overcome the 'democratic deficit' – to combat the view that the EU is an alien body and that only nation-states really matter. Undoubtedly there is a 'dualism' at the heart of concept of EU citizenship. On the one hand, the term is tied to states and markets. On the other hand, the European Court of Justice has interpreted the question of freedom of movement in broad social terms, as a quasi-constitutional entitlement, and not simply as a direct economic imperative. Thus, to take an example, the right to freedom of movement is linked to the right not to be discriminated against by comparison with host-state nationals (Bellamy and Warleigh, 2001: 96).

Bellamy and Warleigh (and those who contribute to their volume) acknowledge that current rights of EU citizens are limited, but their point is that once the notion of citizenship is established, the anomaly of confining political rights to those who are already citizens of member states, becomes plain. Already, limited rights – like the right to petition the Parliament and refer matters to the Ombudsman – are bestowed on individuals even if they are not members of one of the constituent nation-states, and are therefore not 'citizens'. In Heater's view, the EU is a sophisticated example of a new kind of citizenship: but 'at the moment, to be honest, it is a mere shadow of that potential' (1999: 129).

The European Ombudsman was introduced in 1992 as a result of Spanish enthusiasm for EU citizenship and Danish concern for administrative efficiency. The Ombudsman can deal with a wide range of issues including matters relating to the environment and human rights. Questions of administrative transparency and the use of age limits in employment have been pursued vigorously, and the Ombudsman should not be seen as a 'stand-alone' institution, but one which coexists with courts, tribunals, parliaments and other intermediaries at European, national, regional and local levels.

It is clearly wrong to think that greater rights for European citizens will happen automatically. Those who favour this development will need to struggle for it, arguing that a European identity does not exist in competition with other identities. On the contrary, European institutions have the potential to add to and reinforce national and subnational governance, although conflict and dialogue exist between these levels.

This requires a movement both upwards and downwards – involving more and more people at every level. The crucial question facing the EU at the moment seems to us to be the status of residents who are currently excluded from EU citizenship. Here, as the Bellamy and Warleigh volume argues, a statist 'nationality' model currently prevails, with ethnic migrants being seen as vulnerable 'subjects' rather than as active and entitled members of the EU. Yet, as is pointed out, Article 25, for example, of the draft Charter of Fundamental Rights does allow residents who are non-citizens to vote and stand for EU elections (Bellamy and Warleigh, 2001: 198).

Enlargement of the EU poses another set of challenges. The accession of a state like Turkey can only broaden the cultural horizons of Europeans, and the problem with Turkey's admission arises around the question of human rights, not because the country is predominantly Muslim in its culture. European citizenship, it could be argued, demonstrates that a citizenship beyond the state is a real possibility.

Does the State Undermine Citizenship?

Citizenship has been conceived classically as membership of the state. Lister comments that 'at its lowest common denominator' we are talking about the relationship 'between individuals and the state' (1997: 3). Voet likewise takes it for granted that citizenship is tied to the state (1998: 9). Oommen argues that the term is meaningless unless it is anchored to the state, so that notions of 'global' or 'world' citizenship cannot be authentic until we have a world or global state. Thus European Union citizenship, he insists, will only become a possibility when the union becomes a multinational federal state (Oommen, 1997: 224). Although Carter is critical of those who reject cosmopolitanism, she takes it for granted that global citizenship requires a global state (2001: 168). Marcus Aurelius is cited by Heater as saying that we are all members of a 'common State' and presenting the 'Universe' as if 'it were a State' (1999: 135).

Yet the case for assuming that being a citizen is only possible if one is a member of a state is contestable. There is, for example, considerable unease among feminist scholars about presenting citizenship as membership of the state. Virginia Held argues that the notion that the state has a monopoly on the legitimate use of force is incompatible with a feminist view as to how society should be organised (1993: 221). Jones sees the nation-state 'as an out-moded political form' (1990: 789) and speaks of the need for a women-friendly polity.

But the question of the state needs to be addressed explicitly. It is not enough to speak, as David Held does, of limiting drastically the influence of the state and market (1993: 224). There has to be a plausible way of looking beyond both institutions, so that an emancipated society becomes possible. It could be argued that the state is actually a barrier to the notion of citizenship, defined here as a set of entitlements which include everyone.

Rowan Williams, the Archbishop of Canterbury, delivered a Dimbleby lecture on 19 December 2002, in which he argues – and this was the aspect of his lecture headlined in *The Times* (27 December 2002) – that 'we are witnessing the end of the nation state' (Williams, 2002: 1). He takes the view that we need to do some hard thinking about what these changes mean for being a citizen. These changes are, he argues, 'irreversible' (2002: 2). Williams' contention is that the nation-state is in decline and is giving way to something he calls the 'market state'. Although he is critical of the latter, he shies away from the argument that the state itself – in all its forms – is the problem.

The notion of citizenship needs to be separated from the state. As we have pointed out in Chapter 1, the state is an institution which claims a monopoly of legitimate force for a particular territory: it is a contradictory institution which claims a monopoly which it does not and cannot have. This is true both of its claim to have a monopoly of force and a monopoly of legitimacy. This critique of the state challenges the standard view of citizenship as denoting membership of a state. For how can one be a citizen when laws are passed and functionaries exist to manage an institution that is underpinned by, and claims to exercise a monopoly of legitimate force? Even when force is authorised, it still prevents the recipient of this force from exercising rights and duties that are crucial to citizenship, and it means that those against whom such force is not directly exercised, live in its shadow. They know that the

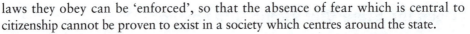

laws they obey can be 'enforced', so that the absence of fear which is central to citizenship cannot be proven to exist in a society which centres around the state.

It is the role of the state to impose solutions by force when faced with divisions and conflicts of interest that cannot be tackled through arbitration and negotiation. A person who is not free, is not a citizen. It may be objected that the state does not simply use force, but claims – in the celebrated definition that is central to our analysis – a monopoly of legitimate force. But this is not a convincing argument since legitimacy implies limits, whereas force cannot be limited (however hard authorities might try). Legitimate force is thus a contradiction in terms, and the state, therefore, is an institution that seeks to achieve the impossible. Williams argues that the state can no longer protect citizens, given the existence of intercontinental missile technology (2002: 2), but the state's mechanism for protecting 'its' subjects has always been contradictory and paradoxical.

The Problem of Class

Williams argues that the 'market state' is 'here to stay' (2002: 5), but the nation-state itself has been a market state as long as capitalism and the market have been around. For these systems create divisions of interests that make the interventions of the state necessary.

Hence an inclusive citizenship has to chart a path beyond both the state and capitalism. Class divisions are, however, more complex than classical Marxism has assumed, even though inequality is crucial to the existence of the state since the challenge to the monopoly of the state comes from those who either have too much or too little. Because interests conflict radically, force is necessary to try and sort them out. This is the link between class and the state, and both act as barriers to an inclusive citizenship. Although Marx argues that people are not simply 'individuals' but members of a class, workers also have a gender and national identity, etc., and this materially affects how they relate to others. It is not that the class identity is unimportant: it is merely that it fuses with other identities since these other identities are also a crucial part of the process that organises individuals into a **class**. If blacks or Catholic Irish in Northern Ireland or northerners in Britain are more likely to be unemployed, their negatively perceived social identity is an integral part of their class status.

It could be argued that membership of a class is a barrier to citizenship. Working-class people often feel that they should not stand for parliament or take part in politics because they lack the confidence, linguistic skills and education to make decisions. Upper-class people may take it for granted that they and their offspring are 'natural' rulers, and in this way display an insensitivity and understanding of the less well off. Whether class expresses itself in gender or national terms, regional or sexual terms, etc., a society that does not recognise difference in a positive way, is a society with a restricted citizenship. By difference, we do not mean division. Divisions prevent people from 'changing places' and having common interests. Common interests make it possible to resolve conflicts in a way that relies upon arbitration, negotiation and compromise, and avoids violence. But how is it possible to overcome class division and capitalism? Marx argues that every historically developed social form is 'in fluid movement' – it has a transient nature (1970: 20). In the third volume of *Capital*, Marx refers to capitalism as a 'self-dissolving contradiction' (1966: 437) in which each step forward is also a step beyond.

The struggle by women to achieve respect and autonomy; the demands by blacks that they should be treated as people and not as a despised racial category; and the insistence by gays that they should be recognised as a legitimate group in society, etc. is as much a blow against the 'free market' as traditional trade union demands for a fairer share of profits. For each time a challenge is successful, the concrete human identities of supposedly abstract individuals is affirmed, and with this challenge, the propensity of the market to deal with real people as abstractions is overcome.

Marx, as has been argued in the chapter on socialism, is torn between a view of revolution simply as change, and a notion, derived from the model of the French Revolution, of revolution as a dramatic single event. Reforms have a revolutionary significance, and underpin the character of capitalism as 'a self-dissolving contradiction'. Yet it is both central to the dialectical logic of Marx's analysis and to some of his explicit statements, that capitalism can be gradually transformed so that, increasingly, a society develops in which freedom and individuality become more and more meaningful.

Citizenship can only develop at the expense of capitalism. Bryan Turner argues that while capitalism promotes early notions of citizenship, it also generates massive inequalities that prevent the achievement of citizenship. He sees a conflict between the redistributive character of citizenship rights and the profit motive of the free market (1986: 38; 24). It is true that he assumes that citizenship should be defined as membership of a state, and he takes a rather abstract view of class which means, as noted above, that he juxtaposes class to gender, ethnicity, etc. in a somewhat mechanistic fashion. Nevertheless, he regards the welfare state as a site of struggle, and he stresses over and over again the contradictory character of capitalism and its fraught relationship with citizenship.

Citizenship, he says, develops as a series of circles or waves (Turner, 1986: 93). It is radical and socially disruptive, moving through a number of expanding processes, so that social membership becomes increasingly universalistic and open-ended. Citizenship exists (as he puts it pithily) despite rather than because of capitalist growth (1986: 135, 141). The point is that the argument that citizenship requires a transformation of capitalism can be posed without having to make the case for a dramatic one-off revolution.

A number of 'issues papers' put out by the British Department for International Development point to the fact that the private sector can and must change. Indeed, the argument implies that to speak of capitalist companies simply as 'private' is itself problematic: the largest of these companies can – and need to – be pressurised further along a public road so that they operate according to social and ethical criteria. The reputation and image of companies with prominent interests abroad are tarnished by adverse publicity around issues like the pollution of the environment; the use of child labour; and the support for regimes that have poor human rights records. Companies should join organisations like the Ethical Training

Initiative (Department for International Development, 2002: 6). It is revealing that some companies speak of a corporate citizenship that shows awareness that production and sales are social processes with political implications. The link between profit and support for ethically acceptable social practices demonstrates that capitalism can be transformed by a whole series of 'victories for the political economy of the working class' – an ongoing process which, arguably, is still in its relatively early stages.

There are no short cuts to the transformation of capitalism (→ website on Alternatives to the Free Market Economy). Where the market cannot provide universal service 'autonomously', as it were, it needs to be regulated – and it is through regulation that capitalism is transformed. Adair Turner establishes this interventionist logic when he argues that where market liberalisation (i.e. making people conform to capitalist norms) conflicts with desirable social objectives, 'we should not be afraid to make exceptions' (2002: 174). If citizens desire an efficient and integrated transport service, then this is an objective that must be govern-mentally provided if the market cannot deliver. Perhaps the exceptions are rather more prolific than Adair Turner – an advocate of socially responsible capitalism – imagines, but it is only through demonstrating that the market cannot deliver, that it is possible to transcend the market. Adair Turner is right to argue that the demand for a cleaner environment, safer workplaces, safe food, and the right to be treated with respect in the workplace whatever one's personal characteristics, are just as much 'consumer demands' as the desire for more washing machines, Internet usage, or more restaurant meals (2002: 187).

Where the market cannot meet these kind of consumer demands, regulation is necessary. The need for public interventions is, Turner argues, increasing as well as changing. This intervention is more explicit in the provision of services that deliver equality of citizenship (2002: 238). Who can disagree with Turner's proposition that we cannot intervene too strongly against inequality in the labour market (2002: 240)? Indeed, for Turner, the key message of 11 September 2001 is the primacy of politics – the need to offset the insecurities and inequalities which capitalism undoubtedly creates (Turner, 2002: 383). Here in a nutshell, is the case for transformation.

Transcending the market means that the objectives of the market – freedom of choice, efficiency in delivery – can only be met through regulation and controls. It is not a question of suppressing or rejecting the market but seeking to realise its objectives through invoking standards 'foreign to commodity production'. Adair Turner argues that demands for public intervention are going to rise as our markets become freer (2002: 191). Freedom of the market can only be justified when it meets human need: this is the radical difference between suppressing the market and going beyond it.

We are arguing that because markets abstract from differences, at some point they will need to be transcended – but only at the point at which it is clear that they cannot deliver the objectives which a society of citizens requires. Turner takes the view that the market economy has the potential to 'serve the full range of human aspirations' (2002: 290), but he himself acknowledges market failures (as he calls them) in transport policies where there is a bias in favour of mobility and combating environmental degradation (Turner, 2002: 300). It is these failures that make the case for transformation.

Exercise

Imagine that there are five people in a room. One is a well-to-do male financier, the second a female academic, the third a female cleaner, the fourth a male Albanian asylum seeker, and an unemployed Somalian woman who is an 'illegal' refugee.

The first obviously regards himself as a citizen: he not only votes but dines frequently with cabinet ministers and the permanent secretaries of the civil service. The second has useful contacts with the legislature where she is researching into the question of women MPs. The third only occasionally votes but has a passport and travels to Spain for her holidays. The fourth is currently in receipt of modest benefits while his application for asylum is being looked into, while the fifth lives in constant fear that her status will be uncovered and she will be deported.

They are all human beings:

- In what sense can they all be regarded as citizens?

- What kind of programmes can be introduced to help persons four and five?

- What kind of policies will 'encourage' the first person to use his influence to help others?

- Can the second person do more to help? Is the third person really a citizen if she ignores the plight of the less fortunate?

Citizenship as a Relational Concept

Why can't some be citizens while others are subject to force? This argument can only be met if we adopt a 'relational' approach that means that we can only know who we are, when we know the position of others. When these others are deprived of their freedom, we have no freedom either. Although force particularly harms those who are targeted, the perpetrators of force also lose their autonomy, so that unless everyone is a citizen, then no one is a citizen.

It could be argued that the 'market state', as Williams describes it (2002: 7), promotes an atomistic attitude, by which we mean an attitude that denies that individuals must be seen in relationship to one another. For example, the critique of patriarchy can be called relational because it argues that men cannot be free while women are subordinated. It is true that in a patriarchal society, men enjoy privileges that make them 'victors', but patriarchy oppresses everyone (albeit in different ways). Men have begun to realise that patriarchy not only strips them of involvement in child-rearing, but subjects them in particular to the violence of war. The idea that our 'right' to exploit or be violent has to be curbed is a problematic use of the term right, since ultimately being exploitative or violent not only harms others, but it also ultimately harms the perpetrator himself. No one, it could be argued, can have a right to harm themselves.

A dramatically unequal world is a world in which large numbers of people will move out of poorer countries in search of a 'better' life. It is in the interest of the 'haves' that they pay attention and work to rectify the deprivations of the 'have nots'. This is what is meant by a relational view of citizenship. Unless everyone is a citizen, then no one is a citizen. It could be argued that if we want to work towards a more inclusive view of citizenship, we need to isolate those who are staunchly opposed to extending citizenship whether on misogynist (i.e. anti-female), racist, nationalist grounds or because they are so privileged that they cannot identify with others. The well-being of each depends upon the well-being of all.

It is important that we evaluate all differences positively (→ website on Difference). Although it is likely that the struggle for an inclusive citizenship will be pursued by those who are the victims rather than the beneficiaries of the market and state, people with education and status have a vital part to play in the struggle for emancipation. They may be less subject to prejudice based upon ignorance. In the same way 'outsiders' are more likely to see the need to integrate with the host community in a way that enables people to contribute to (rather than passively accept) dominant norms. The need for self-government affects everyone, for even the well-to-do are vulnerable to problems in the social and natural environment.

Focus

Citizenship as a Momentum Concept

Momentum concepts are those that are infinitely progressive and egalitarian: they have no stopping point and cannot be 'realised'. **Static concepts**, by way of contrast, are repressively hierarchical and divisive. The latter must be discarded whereas the former have an historical dynamic which means they must be built upon and continuously transcended. The state, patriarchy and violence are examples of static concepts; freedom, autonomy, individuality, citizenship and **emancipation** are examples of momentum concepts. Tocqueville famously formulated democracy as a momentum concept – a concept that has no stopping point. However, his account is marred by static features, like a traditional notion of God and a fatalist view of 'destiny'. Momentum concepts, as we formulate them, seek to avoid this inconsistency by being infinite in their egalitarian scope. It is crucial to avoid the kind of scepticism and relativism that makes it impossible to identify progress at all.

Citizenship is a momentum concept in three ways.

1. First, the struggle for citizenship can be developed even by those who seek only limited steps forward and are oblivious of a more wide-ranging agenda.
2. Second, citizenship involves a process of change that is both revolutionary and evolutionary – it is important that we do not privilege one over the other.
3. Third, citizenship is an ongoing struggle with no stopping point.

It is not that the ends of an inclusive citizenship are not important: it is rather that achieving one element of inclusion (for example, the enfranchisement of women) enables us to move to the next – for example, the unfair allocation of tasks in the home. People do need to have the right to vote, speak freely and stand for election: but they also need to think about those whose conduct makes it necessary to put them in prison. This is why the case for an inclusive citizenship makes it essential that we look beyond the state.

Summary

Ancient Greek notions of citizenship are linked to notions of slavery and imperialism, and liberalism historically has regarded citizenship in an exclusive way. The liberal view of citizenship suffers from being abstract, which means that while in theory it offers freedom and equality to all, beneath the abstractions is to be found inequality.

Marshall argues that citizens require social rights as well as political and legal ones, since the latter are seriously weakened if access to material resources is denied. The New Right in Britain and the USA rejected as 'socialistic' the argument for social rights, preferring to define citizenship in marketing rather than in welfare terms. Women are subject to informal pressures in liberal democracies that prevent them from exercising an effective citizenship. It could be argued that individuals would become more independent and involved as citizens if they were in receipt of what has justifiably been called a 'citizens' income'.

Cosmopolitans take the view that it would be wrong to juxtapose involvement at local, regional and national levels with a concern with the world. The European Union has pioneered a concept of citizenship that, although undeveloped, offers a tantalising glimpse of what is possible in future.

Despite the tendency to define citizenship as membership of the state, it could be argued that the state is actually a barrier to citizenship. As an institution claiming a monopoly of legitimate force, its interventions undermine rather than enhance citizenship. Like the state, the existence of class divisions restricts meaningful citizenship. This point can be underlined when we develop the idea of citizenship as a relational and momentum concept.

Questions

1. Is the notion of global citizenship simply a dream?
2. Is the use of force a barrier to citizenship?
3. Should we extend citizenship to children and animals?
4. Is the liberal view of citizenship satisfactory?
5. Is the view of Marshall as a pioneer of the modern concept of citizenship justified?
6. Does a relational view of citizenship help to assess citizenship in relation to either class or the state?

References

Aristotle (1962), *The Politics* Harmondsworth: Penguin.

Bellamy, R. and Warleigh, A. (eds) (2001) *Citizenship and Governance in the European Union* London and New York: Continuum.

Bryson, V. (1992) *Feminism and Political Theory* Basingstoke: Macmillan.

Bryson, V. (1994) *Women in British Politics* Huddersfield: Pamphlets in History and Politics, University of Huddersfield.

Bubeck, D. (1995) *A Feminist Aproach to Citizenship* Florence: European University Institute.

Carter, A. (2001) *The Political Theory of Global Citizenship* London and New York: Routledge.

Crick, B. (1982) *In Defence of Politics*, 2nd edn Harmondsworth: Penguin.

Department for International Development (2002) *Issues Paper 3* Kingston upon Thames: DFID Development Policy Forums.

Faulks, K. (1998) *Citizenship in Modern Britain* Edinburgh: Edinburgh University Press.

Faulks, K. (2000) *Citizenship* London and New York: Routledge.

Gilmour, I. (1978) *Inside Right* London, Melbourne, New York: Quartet.

Gray, J. (1999) *False Dawn* London: Granta Books.

Hayek, F. (1960) *The Constitution of Liberty* London and Henley: Routledge and Kegan Paul.

Heater, D. (1999) *What is Citizenship?* Cambridge: Polity Press.

Held, D. (1995) *Democracy and the Global Order* Cambridge: Polity Press.

Held, V. (1993) *Feminist Morality* University of Chicago Press: Chicago and London.

Hoffman, J. (1988) *State, Power and Democracy* Brighton: Wheatsheaf Books.

Hoffman, J. (1995) *Beyond the State* Cambridge: Polity Press.

Hoffman, J. (2004) *Citizenship Beyond the State* London: Sage.

Jones, K. (1990) 'Citizenship in a Women-Friendly Polity', *Signs* 15(4), 781–812.

Linklater, A. (1999) 'Cosmopolitan Citizenship' in K. Hutchings and R. Dannreuther (eds), *Cosmopolitan Citizenship* Basingstoke: Macmillan, 35–59.

Lister, R. (1997), *Citizenship: Feminist Perspectives* Basingstoke: Macmillan.

MacKinnon, C. (1989) *Toward a Feminist Theory of the State* Cambridge MA: Harvard University Press.

Marshall, T. and Bottomore, T. (1992) *Citizenship and Social Class* London: Pluto Press.

Marx, K. (1966) *Capital*, vol. 3 Moscow: Progress Publishers.

Marx, K. and Engels, F. (1967) *The Communist Manifesto* Harmondsworth: Penguin.

Marx, K. (1970) *Capital*, vol. 1 London: Lawrence and Wishart.

Marx, K. and Engels, F. (1975) *Collected Works*, vol. 3 London: Lawrence and Wishart.

Mouffe, C. (1992) 'Feminism, Citizenship and Radical Democratic Politics' in J. Butler and J. Scott (eds), *Feminists Theorize the Political* New York and London: Routledge, 369–84.

Oomen, T. (1997) *Citizenship, Nationality and Ethnicity* Cambridge: Polity.

Ross, K. (2000) *Woman at the Top* London: Hansard Society.

Rousseau, J-J. (1968) *The Social Contract* Harmondsworth: Penguin.

Saunders, P. (1995) *Capitalism: A Social Audit* Buckingham: Open University Press.

Soysal, Y. (1994) *The Limits of Citizenship* Chicago and London: University of Chicago.

Thatcher, M. (1993) *The Downing Street Years* London: HarperCollins.

Tickner, J. (1995) 'Re-visioning Security' in K. Booth and S. Smith (eds), *International Relations Theory Today* Cambridge: Polity Press, 175–97.

Turner, A. (2002) *Just Capital* London: Pan Books.

Turner, B. (1986) *Citizenship and Capitalism* London: Allen and Unwin.

Voet, R. (1998) *Feminism and Citizenship* London, Thousand Oaks, New Delhi: Sage.

Williams, R. (2002) Full text of Dimbleby lecture delivered by the Archbishop of Canterbury, http://www.Guardian.co.uk/religion.

Yeatman, A. (1994) *Postmodern Revisionings of the Political* London: Routledge.

Yuval-Davis, N. (1997) 'Women, Citizenship and Difference', *Feminist Review* 57, 4–27.

Further Reading

- Faulks's book on *Citizenship* (2000) (referenced above) is a very useful overview.

- Lister (referenced above) surveys the feminist and citizenship literature with commendable thoroughness.

- Linklater's *Cosmopolitan Citizenship* (referenced above) is a collection of essays that is worth reading for those concerned about the idea of a global citizen.

- A very interesting critique of the Crick Report on Citizenship Education and much else besides can be found in Osler, A. and Starkey, H. (2001) 'Citizenship Education and National Identities in France and England: inclusive or exclusive?' *Oxford Review of Education* 27(2), 288–305.

- Turner's *Citizenship and Capitalism* (referenced above) provides a very useful view of the strengths and weaknesses of the Marxist analysis of citizenship.

- Heater's work on citizenship (1999 – referenced above) is very comprehensive.

Weblinks

For a very useful overview:
http://www.citizen21.org.uk/citizenship/index.html

For material explicitly on being a British citizen:
http://www.historylearningsite.co.uk/citizenship.htm

For material on European citizenship, see:
http://www.whsmith.co.uk/whs/go.asp?breakcontext=y&pagedef=/yso/about.htm

Chapter 7

Punishment

Introduction

In no activity – except perhaps in waging war – does the state express its coercive nature so clearly as in the practice of punishment. For this reason it is central to the legitimacy of the state that punishment can be distinguished from arbitrary violence. We explore whether this is possible: can the state justify the practice of punishment? And what exactly is punishment? As we will see the definition and justification of punishment are intertwined, such that it is not possible to define punishment in a way that does not presuppose a particular justification of it. Two theories dominate the debate over punishment – retributivism and consequentialism – and critics of consequentialism argue that under certain, admittedly very unusual circumstances, it is right to punish an innocent person. Retributivism, on the other hand, requires that only the guilty are punished.

Chapter Map

In this chapter we will:

- Begin by providing a working – but necessarily not final – definition of punishment.

- Outline the retributivist argument for punishment.

- Outline the consequentialist argument for punishment.

- Discuss theories that seek to incorporate the strengths and avoid the weaknesses of retributivism and consequentialism.

- Consider two theories that purport to be alternatives to the dominant theory: the communicative theory of punishment and restorative justice.

- Engage in an extended discussion of capital punishment.

The Ultimate Punishment?

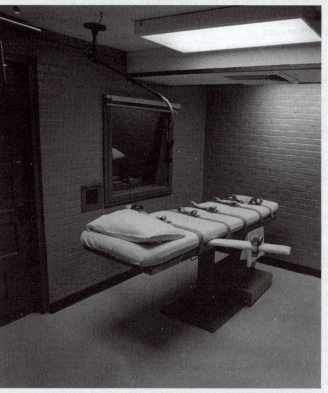

Death Chamber in Huntsville, Texas, USA

Source: Zed Nelson/Getty

The United States is certainly not the only country to practise the death penalty, but it is the country with the most transparent appeal and review procedure, and a country in which there has been a long and complex debate over its continued use. Europe, on the other hand, has emphatically rejected the death penalty: Protocols 6 and 13 of the European Convention on Human Rights (ECHR) prohibit member states of the Council of Europe from reintroducing the death penalty under any circumstances, and ratification of the ECHR is a condition for membership of the European Union. To an extent the European position reflects a desire to define Europe as different to – we might say more 'civilised' than – the United States. However, that the debate in the United States has been so complex and involved suggests that capital punishment cannot be dismissed as an atavistic activity incapable of any justification. Before reading the chapter consider your own attitudes to the death penalty: what arguments can you think of in its favour, and which against? How much weight would you attach to each argument? Are your arguments for the death penalty consistent with one another? Likewise, are the arguments against consistent? (Although popular debate focuses to a great extent on whether capital punishment deters it is important to recognise that deterrence is only one consideration.)

What is Punishment?

In Chapter 1 we argued that the state is a coercive entity. In Max Weber's words, the state is that entity that successfully commands a monopoly on the legitimate use of violence in a given territory. The state is most obviously coercive when it punishes its citizens, and although most people do not possess a criminal record, the threat of punishment conditions the behaviour of everybody. However, the state also claims the *right* to punish, which means that punishment cannot simply be the application of arbitrary force or violence, but must be *reasoned*. It is the reasons for punishment that concern us in this chapter: why punish? What justifies punishment? The case study focused on one specific type of punishment – what some people call the 'ultimate punishment': the death penalty (or capital punishment). Capital punishment illustrates in a compelling way competing justifications for punishment and connects back to the fundamental question about the nature of the state: one argument advanced against the death penalty is that it is an act of pure revenge, or violence, and incompatible with the reasoned use of force supposedly characteristic of the state. Defenders of the practice have to demonstrate that this is not the case.

Unlike some other concepts employed by political theorists, punishment is one widely used in everyday discussion. The person in the street would probably not offer an abstract definition but rather equate punishment with imprisonment, or being fined, or required to do community service. And although most people would no doubt 'accept' that sometimes the innocent get punished it is considered outrageous *deliberately* to punish an innocent person. The difficulty is that the most popular justification for punishment is that it deters crime. Yet, as we will see later, if we punish to deter then there are circumstances in which punishing an innocent person might be justified (of course, we – or, at least, most of us – have to *believe* the person is guilty, but belief is distinct from fact). Therefore, we cannot start by defining punishment as the infliction of suffering by the state on a *guilty* person. More broadly, how we define punishment is bound up with why we punish – we cannot operate with a morally neutral definition of punishment and then simply move on to its justification. That said, we will provide a very rough, working definition (which will then have to be refined depending on how we justify it): *punishment is the infliction of 'hard treatment' by an authorised authority (that is, the state) where the suffering is* in some way *connected to the actual or potential violation of a law* (the phrase 'in some way' leaves open the possibility that an innocent person could justifiably be punished).

With that definition in mind we can now consider what justifies the infliction of hard treatment, and, in the process, clarify the phrase 'in some way'. Traditionally, two theories dominate the debate over the justification of punishment: retributivism and consequentialism. Both have significant weaknesses and so in response a third kind of theory has developed which seeks to avoid the weaknesses and incorporate the strengths of both, although this third type is basically consequentialist. We will start with retributivism, move on to consequentialism, and finally discuss 'compromise theories'.

Retributivism

Retributivism – the Crude Version

Most people equate retributivism with the slogan 'an eye for an eye, and a tooth for a tooth'. Punishment is 'payback', or, in more philosophical language, 'restitution', a word which has its roots in the idea of repaying a debt. Before discussing various objections to this version of retributivism it is worth pointing out the historical origins of the 'eye for an eye' doctrine – a doctrine that can be found in the teachings of the great monotheistic religions, Judaism, Christianity and Islam. What it meant was that there should be *no more than* an eye for an eye, or a tooth for a tooth. In close-knit communities a slight committed by one person (or family) against another could lead to a process of blood-letting. The 'eye for an eye' rule meant that punishment could only be meted out by a properly constituted authority – punishment was not a private matter – and had to be proportional and intended to break, not continue, a cycle of violence. From retributivism we derive the concept of *lex talionis* – equivalence between the crime and the punishment. In more sophisticated versions of retributivism this does not entail a qualitative identity of the two: punishment need not literally require taking an eye for an eye.

Even with this clarification it does seem that retribution is little more than revenge, albeit carried out by a proper authority and not by private individuals. Furthermore, it does not seem coherent, and for two reasons. First, there cannot be restitution: executing a murderer does not bring the murdered victim back to life. Second, often there is no direct match between the crime and the punishment: how, for example, do you punish treason, or sedition, or the violation of a contract? There are no equivalents between the criminal act and the punishment. If retributivism were nothing but an eye for an eye there would be little to be said for it. However, in the history of legal and political philosophy there have been advanced much more sophisticated retributivist theories of punishment.

Retributivism – the Sophisticated Versions

The two great figures in the development of retributivism are Immanuel Kant (1724–1804) and G.W.F. Hegel (1770–1831). Their contributions to retributivist theory are extensively cited, criticised, and developed in contemporary discussions of punishment. What we offer here is a composite version of the theory, but drawing mainly on Hegel.

The easiest way to present this version of retributivism is in a series of steps, but we need first to make a couple of distinctions: (a) between egoism and morality; (b) between public power and private action:

(a) *Egoism versus morality:* people can act from purely self-interested – that is, egoistic – reasons, or from a 'moral law'. For example, why should you not steal? One answer: because you will be punished if you are caught. This is an egoistic motivation. An alternative answer to the question might be: you reason that if everyone stole then property would become insecure – you want your property to be secure but that commits you to respecting other people's property. You are acting from a law you give yourself. This may appear to be enlightened self-interest but it is not, for self-interest would lead you to steal *if you could get away with it*. The purely self-interested person acts capriciously – they are incapable of 'universalising' their action – whereas the morally motivated person is truly rational, because rationality equates with the ability to universalise.

(b) *Public power versus private action:* if somebody breaks into your house and steals your things then your most likely reaction is to feel that this is an attack on *you* (your property being an extension of yourself). But it is also an attack on the collective. Although the police might give you the discretion to press charges (or not), the decision to pursue and prosecute the perpetrator is not yours. In Anglo-Saxon political thought – especially in the contract tradition of Hobbes and Locke – we give up the private right to pursue criminals; in contracting into the state we pool our private rights to pursue violence against those who harm us in order to win the benefits of collective action. The remnants of justifiable private action can be observed in the right to self-defence: this is stronger in the United States, where the Second Amendment to the Constitution guarantees the right to bear arms. The public power/private action distinction is connected to, but does not directly mirror, the division between criminal law and civil law.

Ch. 8:
Liberalism
pp. 181–85

With these distinctions now in place we can set out the steps in a retributivist theory of punishment:

1. Crime entails the assertion of egoism (pure self-interest) over morality – this may appear simply as a conflict between the individual (ego) and society (morality), but crucially it is also a conflict within the criminal between their egoistic and moral self. Furthermore, what seems to be a purely egoistic act implies a moral judgement. *Crime is the first act of coercion.* It is the coercion of other citizens by the criminal.

2. Punishment is the annulment (or negation) of the criminal's egoistic act – *punishment is the second act of coercion.* It is the coercion of the criminal by the state.

3. However, step 2 is not a straightforward negation of step 1 (it is not simply an eye for an eye). The second act of coercion is not an egoistic act, meaning that unlike the crime it is not a random act of violence, but rather it is the universalisation of the criminal's will: the criminal does not consciously will their own punishment, but it is implicit in their actions.

4. The negation of the crime must address the will of the criminal and not just the external aspect of their act. There are two important subpoints: (a) the criminal's intention – what is called *mens rea* – is important; (b) restitution is inadequate – indeed, in many cases it is impossible.

5. A crime is a false universalisation of will: in killing another person you will that there should be a law permitting killing. Your punishment, which for Kant must be death, is not simply an act of restitution – of course, it is not even that, for your victim cannot be brought back to life – but the expression of your will: you will your own execution. As a moral agent – acting from a truly rational will – you recognise the validity of the punishment. Furthermore, you have a *right* to

be punished – the state's failure to punish you is a denial of your status as a moral agent.

Two further points should be made (these are not further steps in the argument, but important elaborations of what has been set out above):

1. The punishment need not be strictly analogous to the crime: its nature is determined by the 'generalised' will of the criminal. The *lex talionis* requires not strict equivalence but 'proportionality': we do not fine mass murderers and execute speeding drivers! Furthermore, we are not barbaric: because a murderer tortured his victims to death it does not follow that we should do likewise – as we will see later this opens up the possibility that a retributivist might be opposed to the death penalty.

2. Punishment must have certain characteristics: it must be the result of a due process; appropriate; carried out by an authorised authority; and coolly implemented.

Consequentialism

As the label suggests a consequentialist judges the rightness of an action by its consequences. So applied to punishment and, put simply, we punish in order to bring about good consequences, or avoid (or reduce) bad ones. The term 'consequentialism' covers a broad family of moral and political theories, the best known of which is utilitarianism, which is a maximising form of consequentialism. Consequentialism is discussed in more detail in Chapter 8 (Liberalism), but in summary its main features are:

- In its utilitarian version consequentialism requires that legal and political institutions should function to maximise the overall level of welfare – or utility – of a society. Utilitarians differ over the definition of utility, but all must agree that:

- Instances of utility are commensurable – that is, you can compare different things by their capacity to increase or reduce utility. For example, you can compare the pain inflicted on a criminal when they are punished with the pain a victim suffers when the criminal goes unpunished. You cannot maximise something unless you can compare instances of utility. However, not all consequentialists are maximisers – we might say, for example, that punishment should (a) deter; (b) satisfy the victim; (c) reform the criminal, but not believe that you can measure all these things, or put them all onto one scale.

There are a set of standard criticisms of utilitarianism: (a) What makes people happy, gives them pleasure, or what they prefer is completely open: if torturing another person gives you pleasure, then it must be counted into the 'maximand' (that which is to be maximised); (b) We cannot respect the law if breaking it will increase utility; (c) Utilitarians cannot respect individual rights – John Stuart Mill's attempt to establish a 'sphere of non-interference' (rights) on the basis of 'human interests in the widest sense' (utility) is incoherent; (d) One person could be made to suffer excruciating pain in order to give a million people each a minuscule amount of pleasure. A less extravagant criticism is that utilitarians cannot be concerned about the distribution of welfare, but merely its overall level; (e) You are as much responsible for what you allow to happen as what you do in a more direct sense of doing. For example, given the choice between killing 1 person and 'allowing' 19 to live, or 'standing by' while all 20 are killed, utilitarianism requires you to kill that 1 person. There are answers to these criticisms and they form the basis of the 'compromise' theories of punishment, but we will focus on one very common objection to utilitarianism: it justifies the punishment of the innocent.

Imagine the following scenario. A child has been murdered and somebody who has a criminal record of sexual offences against children has been arrested (we will call him A). Some very high-ranking police officers have evidence which proves that he could not have murdered the child, but they believe that the chances of apprehending the real killer (call him B) are remote. Although they know that A is innocent they are confident that they can construct a case against A such that lower-ranking police officers, the courts, and the general population will be convinced that A is guilty. In the absence of any conviction society will be faced with a series of negative consequences (or disutilities):

1. There will be considerable public disorder – for example, riots.
2. There will be attacks on anyone who 'looks' like a paedophile.
3. Parents will be afraid to let their children out of their sight and they will communicate that fear to their children.
4. There will be a loss of respect for authority.
5. Knee-jerk, illiberal legislation might be passed.
6. There will be a loss of deterrence as the murder is seen by other potential offenders to have gone unpunished.

Although there is a risk that B will strike again the police calculate that it is better that A is arrested, tried and convicted, than that no arrest is made. Obviously, if the truth were to emerge then there would be massive negative consequences, but the police can calculate probabilities – the less likely that the truth will emerge the more they will discount the negative consequences of revelation. Clearly, there are some conditions attached to the consequentialist 'success' of punishing A: (a) most people must believe that A really is guilty, and (b) that requires a very high level of deception and conspiracy. But, in principle, a utilitarian cannot explain how on utilitarian grounds it is wrong to punish A. Indeed, utilitarianism is a moral theory, such that the police and judiciary have a *moral duty* to pursue and convict A in order to avoid or reduce the negative consequences of non-conviction outlined above.

There are several other problems with the consequentialist theory of punishment. First, if deterrence is justified then so is prevention. This opens up the *Minority Report* scenario whereby the state seeks to identify crimes ('precrimes') before they have been committed. That film was a bit far-fetched – and complicated rather than complex – in that it presupposed the existence of 'pre-cognitions', but a less fanciful version of precrime would be the identification of social or behavioural characteristics that suggest an increased likelihood of commiting crime. We would not be punishing to *deter*, but rather to *prevent* crime. Second, consequentialists need not believe in *mens rea* (intentionality). In fact, in many legal systems there is the idea of strict liability, meaning that for certain offences courts do not need to establish intentionality. There may be justifications* for strict liability but the rejection of intentionality appears incompatible with respect for human freedom and responsibility. Third, consequentialists have problems with equity. For example, one person might receive a six-year prison sentence and another a one-year sentence for what is essentially the same crime on grounds that the six-year sentence is intended to 'send out a message' – and thus deter others. This is incompatible with equal treatment. Fourth, consequentialists have only a very weak sense of *lex talionis*. Some crimes may be more sensitive to deterrence than others: speeding offences may be more susceptible to reduction as a result of harsher punishment, whereas murder may not be. In this case we should have draconian anti-speeding measures but relatively light sentences for murder.

Retributivism versus Consequentialism: the Argument so Far

Before discussing theories of punishment that seek to avoid the weaknesses of both retributivism and consequentialism it is worth outlining in summary form the key differences between them:

Retributivism	Consequentialism
Backward-looking to the crime committed. However, punishment does address the implications of crime: if you steal you assert (or will) that 'anybody can take property' – therefore, being deprived of something, such as your liberty, is simply the expression of your will: in *this* sense punishment is forward-looking.	Forward-looking to the consequences of punishment. For a utilitarian, punishment must serve the global goal of maximising utility. For a non-utilitarian consequentialist, punishment can serve a plurality of goals, without necessarily seeking to maximise something.
Intentionality is central – only the guilty should be punished. Punishment is concerned with the *will* of the criminal. Certainly, there can be miscarriages of justice, but you can never *justify* punishing an innocent person.	Intentionality is important but not central – punishment should deter, so it does act on a person's intentions: deterrence gives you a reason not to commit a crime. However, a utilitarian is obliged to punish an innocent person if by so doing utility is maximised.
Punishment must be strictly distinguished from treatment and prevention. Retributivists can support treatment and reform, but these are secondary aims of punishment. They can also recognise the value of deterrence, but they cannot 'pre-emptively' punish.	Punishment is not fundamentally different from treatment and prevention – deterrence, treatment, and prevention are all different ways to increase utility. This opens up the possibility of the *Minority Report* (precrime) scenario.
Punishment must be proportional to the crime. Unlike crude retributivism, more sophisticated versions do not see punishment as restitution – the victim is actually not that important. There must, however, be some notion of equivalence: we do not give someone a fine for murder and execute another for a parking offence.	The character of the punishment is calculated by its consequences, for example, it must be sufficient to deter. This disconnects the gravity of the punishment from the seriousness of the crime – if most people are disinclined to murder this suggests that its punishment need not be that severe.
There must be equity – you cannot give one person a six-year prison sentence and another a one-year sentence for what is essentially the same crime, committed with the same degree of intentionality.	Sentences for the 'same' offence can vary depending on the likely deterrent impact. There is an equity problem with consequentialism.

*Strict liability often applies in hazardous occupations. The justifications of strict liability include: (a) consequentialist – it is proven to be effective; (b) it simplifies litigation because the courts do not have to prove intentionality; (c) used selectively it can capture the 'real villains'.

Compromise Theories (Indirect Utilitarianism)

What we call 'compromise theories' are essentially consequentialist theories that seek to avoid the problem of perceived injustice – the punishment of the innocent and inequity. Some theorists argue that it is, by definition, impossible to punish an innocent person – if you look up 'punishment' in the *Chambers Dictionary* then you will find this definition: 'to cause (someone) to suffer for an offence', with the implication that the preposition 'for' states a causal relationship. This argument is very weak. First, dictionaries – indeed, everyday usage of words – do not settle philosophical arguments, and, second, we could just invent another word to denote something like punishment.

A better starting point for dealing with the problems thrown up by consequentialism is to distinguish acts and rules (and so act-utilitarianism from rule-utilitarianism). Act-utilitarianism requires: (a) that utility be maximised; (b) that each person should on each occasion act to maximise utility. If we then apply this to punishment, state officials (police, judiciary) should always have in mind the maximisation of utility. Rule-utilitarianism endorses (a) – we have a duty to maximise utility – but we should not always act as if we are utilitarians. So long as a person's (police officer's, judge's) actions contribute to the maximisation of utility it is not necessary to *think* (be *motivated*) like a utilitarian. State officials could think like retributivists. At the core of rule-utilitarianism is the idea that by respecting rules – for example, the rule that only the guilty should be punished – we maximise utility. It should be made clear that this is an empirical argument: we have to show that it is in fact the case that respecting rules does indeed maximise utility. Some critics of utilitarianism are not convinced. So in response a further refinement of the theory has been made – we do not just follow rules, but we separate out roles: this theory has been termed 'institutional utilitarianism' and has been advanced by H.L.A. Hart and by John Rawls.*

In his essay 'Prolegomena to the Principles of Punishment', Hart argued that three questions are central to the philosophical debate over punishment:

1. What is the 'general justifying aim' of punishment?
2. Who may properly be punished?
3. How should the appropriate amount of punishment be determined? (Hart, 1959–60: 3)

What is at issue is whether 1–3 can all be adequately answered by reference to a single principle such as the moral requirement to maximise utility, or whether they require separate treatment. Compromise theories maintain that different principles must be applied to address each of these questions. However, as the title of his essay suggests, Hart is not offering a fully fledged theory of punishment (a 'prolegomena' is a preface or programmatic statement). Other theorists have offered more substantial contributions to the development of a compromise theory.

*As suggested in Chapter 4 Rawls was opposed to utilitarianism – his book *A Theory of Justice* (1971) attempts to offer an alternative political theory to the then-dominant utilitarian one. However, the essay discussed here – 'Two Concepts of Rules' – was an early piece (2001, published 1955) and at that stage Rawls was still operating within a utilitarian framework, although we can see signs in the essay of his later rejection of it.

In his essay 'Two Concepts of Rules', Rawls seeks to reconcile two moral intuitions: (a) only the guilty should be punished (a retributivist intuition), and (b) punishment should serve a purpose (a consequentialist intuition) (Rawls, 1999: 22). Rawls also makes the distinction between rules and actions mentioned above, and from that distinction emerge two correspondingly roles: the 'legislator' (who determines the rules) and the 'judge' (who applies the rules to particular cases without considering the wider purpose of punishment). The rules require that only a person who has committed the crime be punished. The argument is a form of institutional utilitarianism rather than rule-utilitarianism, because the latter would collapse into act-utilitarianism if we had perfect knowledge. Central to Rawls's argument is the idea that given *imperfect knowledge* it is better to have a moral division of labour between legislator and judge.

Rawls then tackles the problem of how a consequentialist can avoid punishing an innocent person. In response to the linguistic (or dictionary) objection Rawls coins a word 'telishment': telishment allows for the imposition of hard treatment on an innocent person whenever the officials empowered by that institution judge that by deterring crime it will maximise utility. Rawls argues that such an institution would require a very high level of deception, and so the legislator would never empower the judge to 'telish' somebody (Rawls, 1999: 27).

There is, however, a fundamental problem with Rawls's argument. We can distinguish the offices of legislator and judge, but legal and political philosophy aims to provide a comprehensive justification for political principles and institutions. There must, therefore, be a standpoint from which we can understand the reasons why we punish people, and that standpoint must incorporate the reasoning of both legislator and judge. In other words, these two officers are metaphors for a division within the moral psychology of the citizen and not descriptions of real people within political institutions. For citizens to *believe* that punishment is fundamentally connected to personal responsibility, such that only the guilty ought to be punished, they must be denied knowledge of the utilitarian justification for the institution. In short, citizens can only think like judges and not legislators. This restriction is arguably incompatible with one of the conditions of a liberal-democratic society – some would say, of any legal system – namely, that law and its purposes be public, and resembles what Bernard Williams dubbed 'Government House Utilitarianism', where an elite understand the purpose of the institution, but for reasons of stability must deny the masses access to that understanding (Williams, 1973: 108–10).

Beyond Retributivism and Consequentialism? Censure and Restoration

We round off our discussion of different theories by briefly considering two that appear to be distinct from the dominant theories (treating the compromise theories discussed above as essentially consequentialist). One aim of punishment could be to censure. A theory based primarily on the idea of censure might be termed 'educative' or 'communicative'. Despite a claim to distinctiveness, such a theory can be given a consequentialist cast if the aim is to strengthen respect for laws, or tend towards retributivism if the communication is directed at the punished person.

It is claimed that censure is morally superior to deterrence because it treats the punished person as a responsible agent rather than a Pavlovian dog. We want the punished person to understand why she is being punished and in future be *morally motivated* to respect the law, rather than conform out of fear of punishment. The problem is that it might not work – punishment would have no motivational effect on psychopaths. The theory does, however, raise other interesting issues. First, is there a difference between censure and reform? If censure is (re-)education, then why punish at all? Second, is it the correct role of the state to *motivate* people to behave in certain ways? Certainly, the state can coerce behaviour but can, or should it coerce thought? Deterrence motivates but leaves open the reasons why people respect the law, whereas censure implies obedience for the right reasons. Third, what kind of punishment is appropriate? It may be that 'naming and shaming' is more effective than incarceration. Fourth, is censure too subjective? Left to the 'court of public opinion', people guilty of relatively minor sexual offences might be lynched while the popular British train robber Ronnie Biggs would be given a knighthood by the Queen.

Another idea is 'restoration', or restorative justice. In fact, we can distinguish two quite distinct ideas – restitution and restoration. Restitution entails an *individualist* relationship of law-breaker to victim, whereby the former must make restitution to the latter, whilst restoration is more concerned with repairing a social relationship, with implications beyond the immediate law-breaker/victim one. The two theories are justified from very different philosophical premises: libertarian (restitution) and communitarian (restoration). But they do share certain character-istics: (a) a strong focus on the victim of crime (the 'forgotten person' of traditional theories of punishment); (b) an emphasis on 'making good' the original action (this is slightly different to retributivism); (b) a challenge to the distinction between civil and criminal law (but there is a basis for bridging the distinction in tort law – for example, careless driving causing personal injury).

Randy Barnett defends the idea of restitution and challenges the existing 'paradigm' of punishment, which he argues is based on an outdated 'sovereignty' model of the state. Crime, he maintains, entails harming an *individual*, not the state or community (Barnett, 1977: 287–8). He notes that restitution plays a minor role in existing law, taking the form of relatively small cash payments to victims. This is inadequate, because it comes mostly out of tax; is discretionary rather than a right; is needs-assessed; is limited to certain crimes; and, finally, is assumed to be compatible with traditional theories of punishment. Barnett wants a complete 'paradigm-shift' to restitution: 'the idea of restitution is actually quite simple . . . it views crime as an offense by one individual against the rights of another' (Barnett, 1977: 287). The robber did not rob society, he robbed the victim.

Restoration, on the other hand, tends to be a grounded in a communitarian, rather than an individualist, theory of society. Communitarianism encompasses philosophical theories that stress the communal nature of the self and more sociological theories that emphasise the importance of social ties (social capital; social ecology) in legitimating the political order. The Restorative Justice Consortium (RJC) – a British organisation – claims research shows that: (a) 90 per cent of victims want to tell the offender the impact the crime had on them; (b) 73 per cent wanted an apology; (c) 65 per cent wanted to negotiate restitution (http://www.homeoffice.gov.uk/documents/rj-local-needs-guidance?view=Binary). The RJC argues that traditional penal policy sees crime as an offence against the state, whereas advocates of restorative justice see it as an offence against the individual and community, meaning not an abstract but a concrete community, such as one's neighbourhood. Traditional theories of punishment take conflicts out of the hands of individuals and communities and 'professionalise' them. Restorative justice policies and projects usually involve an independent mediator, who need not be a judicial figure. As with retributivism, emphasis is placed on personal responsibility but hard treatment for its own sake is rejected. Along with consequentialists an emphasis is placed on good outcomes, although recognition of the past is important. The main features of restorative justice can be summarised: (a) there must be a deep exchange between offender and victim – and it must be mutual; (b) the offender must acknowledge the harm – especially psychological harm – which they have caused: there is an element of 'shaming' involved; (c) there must be a tangible 'redemption' – this part comes closest to the 'sentence' handed out in traditional punishment.

There are problems with the theory. First, the 'mutuality' of the exchange implies that the victim – or, perhaps, the 'community' – carries some responsibility: 'I (the criminal) have hurt you, but there are reasons . . .'. Second, saying sorry may come easily to an offender – the test of the effectiveness of restorative justice is the recidivism rate after punishment. Third, the victim may not achieve closure. Fourth, allowing victims to determine punishments can lead to inequitable outcomes – and if victims do not determine the outcome, then what is the point of restorative justice? Finally, the shaming element of restorative justice conflicts with the idea of building up the self-respect of the offender which is implied in the idea of mutuality.

Capital Punishment

Because capital punishment is extreme it illustrates in a stark way the different theories of punishment discussed above. Although our primary concern is with the moral arguments for and against capital punishment, there is an interesting political dimension to the debate. Protocols 6 and 13 of the European Convention on Human Rights (ECHR) prohibit member states of the Council of Europe from reintroducing the death penalty under any circumstances, and ratification of the ECHR is a condition for membership of the European Union. Prohibition on capital punishment in Europe has – at least for the political elites – become part of European consciousness and a way of defining America as 'other'. Europe has, in effect, declared an absolutist position on capital punishment. This raises the question whether it is possible to be a non-absolutist opponent of the death penalty: there might be strong arguments against the death penalty but no single argument leads to the conclusion that it is *always* wrong. To address this issue requires structuring the debate around retributivist and consequentialist theories of punishment.

In Britain, as in most European countries, the history of the practice of capital punishment over the past two hundred years has been one of increasing restriction in its use, eventual abolition, and, through ECHR commitments, absolute prohibition on its reintroduction. The United States has followed a different course. Since there is a huge focus on the USA in debates over capital punishment it is useful to outline the salient features of its present use:

- Capital punishment exists in 37 of the 50 states. In addition, Federal and military execution is permitted. Execution of a minor (someone under 18) is not allowed.

- Conviction rates vary considerably between states. Since clemency is possible the conviction-to-execution rate – that is, percentage of death sentences actually carried out – also varies significantly.

- Capital punishment was suspended between 1972 and 1976. In the consolidated case *Furman v. Georgia* the Supreme Court found the death penalty to be in violation of the Eighth Amendment of the US Constitution, on grounds of it being 'cruel and unusual'. The 'unitary trial' procedure practised in Georgia, whereby the jury simultaneously determined guilt and whether the death penalty should be imposed, made sentencing arbitrary. This is one interpretation of the word 'unusual'.

- In 1977 (*Coker v. Georgia*) the death penalty was (effectively) restricted to murder, although the Federal State retains the death penalty for treason, espionage and some military offences.

- After various legal changes, such as the introduction of bifurcated jury trials, the death penalty was restored (the term 'post-*Furman*' is used in the literature to denote post-1976 executions).

- There is a lengthy review and appeal procedure (hence the long time spent on death row). After step 1 – sentencing at the original trial, there is: (a) Step 2 – direct review by an appeal court to check for errors in the initial trial. Possible judgments that can be made at step 2 include: affirming the original death sentence; reversing that sentence, which means there has to be a new capital sentence hearing; acquittal of the crime, which could mean downgrading the judgment from, say, first degree murder to second degree murder (there is a 40 per cent 'success rate' – reversal or acquittal – at this stage). (b) Step 3 – State Collateral Review, for example, on grounds of incompetent legal representation at steps 1 and 2 (6 per cent success rate); (c) Step 4 – Federal Habeas Corpus, meaning that it must be determined that a prisoner's federal rights have not been violated (until some restrictions were introduced in 1996 there was a 40 per cent+ success rate at this stage); (d) Step 5 – Section 1983: this has now become used as a way of attacking not the death sentence (step 4) but the mode of execution (see next point).

- The current controversy over the death penalty has focused on what is now the standard method – lethal injection (previously, methods included hanging, the electric chair, the gas chamber, and shooting). Again, we are back to the Eighth Amendment and the judgment that execution (by lethal injection) is 'cruel and unusual'.

- Another controversy is the make-up of the death row population, which is composed disproportionately of black Americans.

Retributivism and the Death Penalty

Kant argued that

even if civil society [i.e., the state] were to be dissolved by consent of all its members, the last murderer remaining in prison would first have to be executed, so that each has done to him what his deeds deserve and blood guilt does not cling to the people for not having insisted upon this punishment; for otherwise the people can be regarded as collaborators in this public violation of justice (Kant, 1996: 474).

This is a very pure statement of retribution: (a) since society (or the state) is going to be dissolved it carries no practical consequences (primarily, deterrence) if the murderer is not executed; (b) the people have no choice but to execute the murderer: if they do not execute him they are complicit in his act.

Recall the earlier discussion of retributivism: the act of murder is a universalisation by the murderer of the killing of an innocent person, such that the murderer wills his own death. The murderer's will cannot be allowed to stand, so the state must reassert its will by forcing the murderer to accept the consequences of his willing 'that innocent people be killed'. On the face of it, this argument seems odd: if we execute him then we are legitimating the principle 'that innocent people be killed'. We surely do not think the murderer is innocent, so in executing him we are not acting out the principle of killing innocent people. Moreover, why should the murderer dictate to us what we should do? If the state is superior to the murderer then surely it could choose not to execute him. This second point is extremely important and allows for a retributivist rejection of capital punishment, but some clarification of Kant's position is required. What the murderer wants to do is to kill and get away with it. In executing him we are forcing him to accept the logic of his action – it is not an eye for an eye, but an attempt to recognise the murderer as a responsible agent and force him to accept that responsibility.

However, even allowing for this clarification, Kant's position does seem crude, and Hegel's theory of punishment, which is still retributivist, can be seen as an attempt to offer something more sophisticated. Hegel did support the death penalty, although he welcomed the reduction in its use, but more significantly for contemporary retributivists he offered a way out of *requiring* the death penalty on retributivist grounds. Alan Brudner contrasts Kant's and Hegel's positions (Brudner, 1980: 345–8). For Kant we are required by justice to execute murderers, for to fail to do so is unjust to the victims. Hegel allows for clemency: 'pardon is the remission of punishment, but it does not annul the law. On the contrary, the law stands and the pardoned man remains a criminal as before' (Hegel cited in Brudner, 1980: 352). To pardon is an expression of the power of the state: to be able to apprehend, justly convict, and execute a person is enough. The state need not choose to execute the person. Justice does not require it. The authority of the state rests for Kant on a contractual relationship between the individual and the state, such that the state cannot disregard the rights of the victim. For Hegel, the legitimacy of the state is more complex: the individual realises themselves in the state, such that their interests are bound up with the state. To decide not to execute murderers is not a violation of the victim's rights.

Consequentialism and the Death Penalty

Consequentialist arguments for and against the death penalty come down – unsurprisingly – to an assessment of the consequences of the practice. Popular debate is dominated by one particular issue: whether or not capital punishment deters murder. However, there are other possible consequences, starting with some possible positives:

- The feeling of satisfaction of the victim's family when the murderer is executed.
- The popular sense of satisfaction at the death of a murderer.
- Reinforcement of a sense of legitimacy of the legal system (especially if there is majority support for the death penalty).

But some negative consequences must also be weighed in the balance:

- The sense of injustice if it is found that an innocent person has been executed.
- The loss to the executed person, both the immediate pain and the loss of his future (it is, in fact, incredibly hard to 'compute' the costs of death for the dead person).
- The loss to the murderer's family.
- The brutalising effects of capital punishment on state officials and the population in general.

These are not exhaustive lists, but hopefully it is sufficient for you to get the point. In assessing consequentialist arguments for and against the death penalty it is important not to concentrate entirely on the issue of deterrence. However, given the centrality of deterrence to the consequentialist debate over capital punishment it is useful to make a few points about the *interpretation* of the evidence for and against deterrence. Steven Goldberg, who supports capital punishment on grounds of deterrence, makes the following points (see Goldberg, 1974):

1. Capital punishment quite obviously does not deter the murderer – if it did, he would not be a murderer – but it might deter *potential* murderers. A similar point can be made about imprisonment – even if there were a 100 per cent recidivism rate this would not prove that prison does not work to deter people, because it is the people who do not commit crimes, but in the absence of lengthy prison sentences, might commit crime, who matter.

2. Comparing different countries can be misleading. Many European countries have a lower murder rate than the USA, and some of the 13 non-retentionist American states have a lower rate than some retentionist states. This does not in itself disprove the deterrence argument, because Texas, for example, might have an even higher murder rate in the absence of the death penalty. Much depends on the cultural characteristics of a society.

3. Comparing countries over time can be misleading. Until the end of the Second World War most European countries retained the death penalty, and some (Western) European countries have practised it until quite recently (France carried out its last execution in 1977 and abolished the death penalty in 1981). These societies may still carry the socialised effects of marking out a particular offence – premeditated murder – with a very particular kind of punishment (death). We might have to wait generations to see the effects of abolition on European countries.

Ernest van den Haag – another defender of the death penalty – cites as evidence of the deterrence effect the fact that very few prisoners on death row accept death over life imprisonment: this is why the overwhelming majority seek to exhaust all channels of appeal against their sentences (van den Haag, 1986: 1665). It follows that even murderers – who admittedly were not deterred from murder (see point 1 above) – recognise that death is worse than life imprisonment. Both Goldberg and van den Haag admit that the statistical evidence for deterrence is inconclusive but we can, they suggest, surmise that death does deter.

There is, however, some confusion here, which is picked up by Jeffrey Reiman (Reiman, 1985: 144). To be fearful of something is not equivalent to saying that the feared thing is a deterrent. Most normal people will be terrified at the thought of execution, but they do not under normal circumstances need the existence of the death penalty to deter them, because there are other reasons why they would not commit murder.

Respecting Persons versus Using Them

We will deal with some broader objections to the death penalty in the next section, but an illustration is useful in drawing out the distinction between a retributivist and a consequentialist attitude to the death penalty. Consider these two questions:

1. Is capital punishment ever justified?
2. Even if your answer to question 1 is 'no', consider two scenarios: (a) a person is 'straightforwardly' executed with a bullet through the heart: death is instantaneous; (b) that person is executed with a bullet through the head (death is instantaneous) but then his or her organs are 'harvested' for transplant operations. Are (a) and (b) equally bad, or is (b) worse/better than (a)? (Assume that in both scenarios the condemned person has not given consent for the use of his or her body parts.)

Obviously, in the United States most defenders of capital punishment do not support this policy. But if we are concerned with good consequences then why not? If a person is going to die then why not use their body parts? One consequentialist argument against this practice is that people might feel distaste towards it: it just seems unpleasant and for that reason is disutilitarian. Another consequentialist argument against it would be that it might encourage the state to kill people for their body parts.

A retributivist would have a very clear answer: in executing a person we respect them. We do not use them as a means to an end, but simply give them what they deserve: they brought their execution on themself. Killing a person is not, morally speaking, a violation of that person's integrity – strange as this may sound: after all it is their physical destruction – but using their body parts *is* a violation. There is an interesting moment in the British film *Pierrepoint* (2005) when the state executioner Albert Pierrepoint is washing down and preparing for burial the woman he has just hanged, when his assistant asks why they should be doing this – why cannot it be left to the people at the morgue? Pierrepoint responds that they would not show sufficient respect: *she is innocent now because she has paid the price*. Whether the real Albert Pierrepoint actually said this, or the scriptwriter put the words in his mouth, is irrelevant: it encapsulates the retributivist view of the executed person.

Arguments against Capital Punishment

We can now draw together arguments against capital punishment and consider how much force they have. It is important when considering these arguments to keep in mind the two main theories of punishment: retributivism and consequentialism. One of our aims in discussing capital punishment is to draw out the distinctions between the two theories. Also, it is worth considering the implications of the various arguments for other forms of punishment, such as imprisonment.

Killing is wrong

We kill in self-defence, both individual self-defence and collective self-defence, so it is not a widely held assumption that killing is *always* wrong. Perhaps the argument is that capital punishment is *murder*, but then we need a definition of murder that renders the killing by an individual of another person without the authorisation of the state equivalent to state-sanctioned killing. There are plenty of reasons why we should resist this equivalence: state execution is not arbitrary but based on principles set out in (public) law and the decision to execute is the result of a deliberative process in which evidence is produced and tested. Then again, perhaps the objection is not to killing as such but to the *deliberate* killing of a person. But self-defence can also involve deliberate killing.

There is a risk of killing an innocent person

This is a very common objection to capital punishment, and it is weighty. However, can we live in a risk-free world? What would such a world be like? At best, we have to calculate risks and determine an acceptable level of risk. If you are persuaded either that the guilty deserve to die (retributivism), or that capital punishment deters (consequentialism), then the risks of killing an innocent person must be weighed in the calculation. The danger of killing an innocent person may be a strong consideration against capital punishment but it is only decisive if you place an *absolute* value on avoiding such an act – the requirement to avoid killing an innocent person must be upheld regardless of the consequences. If, for example, you are convinced that capital punishment saves 100 lives per year through its deterrent effect but at the cost of 1 innocent person being executed then if you place absolute value on avoiding executing an innocent person you must be prepared to allow 100 people to die. To be clear, this is a perfectly respectable moral position: for the state to kill one person (commit an act) is not the same as the state omitting to act in such a way that 100 lives are lost. Normally, consequentialists are much more prepared to treat omission and commission as equivalent and so seek to avoid the hundred deaths (or 99 if you subtract the executed person). Retributivists, on the other hand, would quite concerned about the danger of killing an innocent person because they necessarily treat commission as far more serious than omission. However, even a retributivist would only elevate this argument to an absolutist objection to capital punishment if the avoidance of committing an act – that is, executing an innocent person – *always* took priority over saving lives.

Capital punishment assumes a person is beyond redemption

The physical destruction of a person implies that offenders are incapable of change. This idea is behind the film *Dead Man Walking* (1995). The film was based on an autobiographical novel by Sister Helen Prejean and has a strong message of Christian redemption behind it. The murderer, played by Sean Penn, finally comes to realise what he has done and through Prejean achieves redemption. The film is intended to send out a strong abolitionist message but it is to the credit of the film that it does not entirely succeed in this aim: we see a person redeemed and ready to meet his maker (if we choose to follow the Christian message of the film). If you are a consequentialist then the film might be a challenge – should we execute a reformed person? Would it not communicate a stronger message to society (potential murderers) that there is a better way? On the other hand, it might be argued that only by being faced with the reality of death could the murderer recognise his crimes and seek redemption (and you do not have to believe in heaven and hell to maintain this view). A retributivist would have less problem in supporting execution because retributivism, unlike consequentialism, maintains respect for the executed person: the murderer is paying the price for his actions, but we do not assume he is evil. Furthermore, although a consequentialist can maintain that a person survives his physical death in a legal sense – this must hold if we are to make sense of a person's Last Will and Testament – retributivists have a stronger idea of survival. This may have theological roots, but a secular retributivist would recognise that a dead person has a moral integrity that survives death.

We are using people

If we argue that punishment is intended to deter then are we not using people as a means to an end – the end being to deter murder – rather than as ends in themselves? Is this not a violation of their integrity? In itself this is an objection entirely directed at consequentialists, because a retributivist would argue that a person wills their own execution and is therefore acting autonomously. Certainly, if you deliberately execute an innocent person – something which might be justified on a very crude consequentialist theory (recall the example of child murder) – then it is hard to resist the objection that we are using someone. However, on a more sophisticated consequentialist theory – one which incorporates the retributivist intuition that only the guilty should be punished – a person would not be executed unless we believed him to be guilty: in choosing to commit murder a person in effect authorises his own execution. It should be noted that this objection to capital punishment applies to all forms of punishment, unlike the first three, which were objections specifically to the death penalty.

Capital punishment is arbitrary

This was at the core of Furman and although attention has now shifted to the mode of execution (see below), it remains a concern that sentencing and execution is racially biased: in the United States 80 per cent of death sentences are for the murder of white people although 50 per cent of murder victims are white.

The ethnicity of the murder victim is the biggest predictor of whether someone will be executed. Does arbitrariness matter? Van den Haag argues not: that some people (literally) 'get away with murder' is not an argument for refusing to execute any murderers (Van den Haag, 1986: 1665). However, we need to make a few distinctions and a relatively trivial example will help: there are speed cameras at various points along a road and these are public cameras. Furthermore, drivers know that only every tenth person will be fined (although the light flashes every time a speeding car passes so no driver knows whether or not he or she is the tenth). We assume that the 'every tenth driver rule' is based on consequentialist reasoning: it is enough to deter without overwhelming the police and courts. Is this arbitrary? No, for two reasons, only one of which is analogous to capital punishment: (a) the 'every tenth driver rule' does not discriminate on the basis of racial, gender or other such characteristics; (b) the chances are that speeders will eventually get caught (and the sanction is relatively light). Capital punishment will always fall foul of (b) – you can only be executed once! To avoid (b) you either abolish capital punishment or try to ensure that it is consistently practised – but that is extremely difficult because every case is different. On the other hand (a) can, in principle, hold but does not do so in practice: sentencing is racially (and class) biased (Nathanson, 1985: 153–4).

There are problems in selecting juries

Support for the death penalty is strong in the United States but there is still a significant minority opposed to capital punishment. In addition, the USA has a strict requirement to do jury service. This creates a problem: a person who has a profound moral objection to the death penalty must either be forced to participate in a practice they find repugnant, or else be excused service on this occasion, but with the result that the jury is not representative of society. In a democratic society there must be not merely a majority in favour of such a controversial policy but an overwhelming one (as there is for jailing people: only a very small minority has a *principled* objection to imprisonment). This is indeed a problem and it illustrates the danger of moving from the premise that 'murderers deserve the death sentence' to the conclusion '*therefore*, they should be executed'. This is a non sequitur: there are considerations of legal process – of trying to operationalise the death penalty – that make it undesirable to execute people.

Most murderers are not really responsible for their actions

Even if capital punishment were not arbitrarily imposed, it is a fact that murderers are drawn disproportionately from the most disadvantaged sections of society. Behind many murders there is a very sad story of neglect and abuse. Of course, this objection to capital punishment applies to punishment in general – it applies, for example, to the prison population. However, it could be argued that at least prisons can be reformed and education provided (literacy classes, anger management and so on). Capital punishment, on the other hand, is final. This objection to capital punishment derives from a more fundamental concern with personal responsibility: are we responsible for our actions? Perhaps the most that can be said in answer to this question is that (a) people are capable of formulating reasons for their actions, even if they are bad reasons, which suggests that we do not just act on instinct; (b) people learn from their mistakes, so that human beings – uniquely – are self-correcting beings; (c) people want to be held responsible for their actions: the test of responsibility is not whether a person could have done other than they did – the obsession in the free will–determinism debate – but whether that person accepts responsibility for his actions (Dennett, 2003: 220–2). A person who really does not want to accept responsibility is most likely a person who is not, in fact, responsible for their actions and we judge them to be suffering from 'diminished responsibility' and make them a subject of treatment rather than punishment.

Capital punishment is cruel

The recent debate over the death penalty in the United States has focused on whether a person suffers a very high level of pain when they are executed by lethal injection. Lethal injection involves a cocktail of drugs, administered in three stages, with the first intended to induce unconsciousness, the second muscle paralysis, and the third cardiac arrest. It was introduced as a more humane method than the electric chair, which itself was thought at one time to be painless (it was inspired by domestic accidents involving electrical appliances). A defender of capital punishment might well argue that many forms of punishment involve pain, whether it be physical or psychological: so why single out capital punishment? It may be wrong *deliberately* to inflict pain, and this might require the state to explore more humane ways of killing, but it does not undermine the case for capital punishment. Indeed, opponents of capital punishment are charged with bad faith: they are simply using 'cruelty' as a way of ending the death penalty. They ought to be honest about their intentions. On the other hand, people should be permitted to use any arguments they think have force or are persuasive and we should concentrate on the arguments and not on *ad hominem* observations.

Capital punishment is brutalising and barbaric for society

Death is an industry. It requires juries and judges, a prison administration, manufacturers of execution equipment, doctors to oversee lethal injections, and clergy to provide religious guidance. Is it possible to participate in this 'industry' and remain decent people? Surely people become sadists? Does it not coarsen people? You get people outside Departments of Correction (execution centres) waving frying pans on execution day (the use of euphemisms, such as 'Departments of Correction' could also be taken as evidence of the costs to civilisation of capital punishment). A defender of capital punishment might argue: (a) it is important that the process is carried out in a disciplined and respectful way; (b) that people are bound to find execution revolting but that does not make it wrong. We can develop these two points: normal human beings ought to be appalled by killing – that is what makes us good people – but murderers deserve to die: it is right that they die. For that reason to do the *right* thing we need temporarily to suppress our *good* instincts. Rightness and goodness are distinct: we can do bad things for the right reasons (kill a person) but also the wrong thing for good reasons (spare a murderer). To avoid becoming bad people it is essential that we organise executions in such a way that we retain our humanity. But perhaps the opponent of capital punishment is making a wider point about society, and here we come to the issue of European identity touched upon earlier. Protocols 6 and 13 of the European Convention on Human Rights are not merely legal statements but moral statements: the death penalty is absolutely prohibited. Europe – with its history of war and genocide – has collectively made the decision to abjure violence to human beings. Jeremy Waldron argues that what we call the 'law' is not just a pile of individual rules and judgments but forms a structure (Waldron: 41–3). Within that structure some rules or prohibitions act as 'archetypes': they are not just rules among other rules but actually define the legal system as a whole. They also form moral images in the minds of citizens. The British 1807 Abolition of Slavery Act was not just another Act of Parliament, although *technically* given the sovereignty of Parliament – or the Queen-in-Parliament – it is, but rather it defines what 'we' are. Waldron develops this point in relation to torture, arguing for its absolute prohibition, but some might argue that the abolition of the death penalty functions in the same way.

Conclusion

We have presented the two dominant justifications for punishment – retributivism and consequentialism – and a number of 'compromise' and alternative theories. No single theory seems to capture all our everyday intuitions about punishment – that only the guilty should be punished, that punishment should be equitable, and that the practice should serve a purpose. What is clear is that punishment must be firmly distinguished from arbitrary violence. This is one of the reasons why many people feel discomfort towards 'crude' retributivism (but we have sought to show that there are also sophisticated versions of retributivism). The debate over the death penalty throws into relief many of our attitudes towards punishment – including the issue of arbitrary violence – which is one of the reasons why it has so often been the subject of literature and films. In criticising capital punishment we need to ask whether our objections have implications for the wider practice of punishment.

Questions

1. Is capital punishment justified?
2. 'Murderers should be executed and their organs harvested for transplant operations'. Do you agree?
3. 'The logic of consequentialism is the identification of potential criminals and, if necessary, their incarceration'. Do you agree?
4. Should punishment take the form of compensation of the victim by the criminal?

References

Barnett, R. (1977) 'Restitution: A New Paradigm of Criminal Justice' *Ethics* 87(4), 279–301.

Brudner, A. (1980) 'Retributivism and the Death Penalty' *University of Toronto Law Journal* 30(4), 337–55.

Dennett, D. (2003) *Freedom Evolves* London: Penguin Books.

Goldberg, S. (1974) 'On Capital Punishment' *Ethics* 85(1), 67–74.

Hart, H.L.A. (1959–60) 'The Presidential Address: Prolegomenon to the Principles of Punishment', *Proceedings of the Aristotelian Society*, New Series, 60, 1–26.

Kant, I. (1996) 'The Metaphysics of Morals', in M. Gregor (ed.), *Practical Philosophy* Cambridge: Cambridge University Press.

Nathanson S. (1985) 'Does it Matter if the Death Penalty is Arbitrarily Administered?' *Philosophy and Public Affairs* 14(2), 149–64.

Rawls, J. (1999) 'Two Concepts of Rules', in S. Freeman (ed.), *Collected Papers* Cambridge MA and London: Harvard University Press, 20–46.

Reiman, J. (1985) 'Justice, Civilization, and the Death Penalty: Answering van den Haag' *Philosophy and Public Affairs* 14(2), 115–48.

Restorative Justice Consortium: http://www.restorativejustice.org.uk/.

Van den Haag E. (1986) 'The Ultimate Punishment: A Defense' *Harvard Law Review* 99(7), 1662–9.

Waldron, J. Torture and Positive Law: Jurisprudence for the White House, unpublished manuscript, available at: http://www.columbia.edu/cu/law/fed-soc/otherfiles/waldron.pdf

Williams, B. (1973) *Utilitarianism: For and Against*, with J.J.C. Smart, Cambridge: Cambridge University Press.

Further Reading

Useful general works on punishment (collections, readers and overviews) include R.A. Duff and David Garland (eds), *A Reader on Punishment* (Oxford University Press, 1994); R.A. Duff, *Punishment* (Dartmouth, 1993); Gertrude Ezorsky (ed.), *Philosophical Perspectives on Punishment* (SUNY Press, 1972) (this includes important 'classic' pieces by Bentham, Kant, Hegel, Rawls and Hart); Matt Matravers (ed.), *Punishment and Political Theory* (Hart, 1999); A. John Simmons *et al.* (eds), *Punishment: a Philosophy and Public Affairs Reader* (Princeton University Press, 1994); Ellen Frankel Paul, Fred Miller and Jeffrey Paul (eds), *Crime, Culpability, and Remedy* (Basil Blackwell, 1990). Explorations of retributivist theory include Jeffrie Murphy and Jean Hampton, *Forgiveness and Mercy* (Cambridge University Press, 1988); Jeffrie Murphy, *Retribution Reconsidered: More Essays in the Philosophy of Law* (Kluwer, 1992); C.L. Ten, *Crime, Guilt and Punishment: a Philosophical Introduction* (Clarendon, 1987). On consequentialist and indirect consequentialist theories see: H.L.A. Hart, 'Prolegomenon to the Principles of Punishment, in *Proceedings of the Aristotelian Society,* 1959–60 (this is also in H.L.A. Hart, *Punishment and Responsibility: Essays in the Philosophy of Law* (Clarendon, 1968)); John Rawls, 'Two Concepts of Rules', *The Philosophical Review*, 64(1), 1955 (this is also in John Rawls, *Collected Papers*, ed. by Samuel Freeman, Harvard University Press, 1999, and in various other collections). Discussions of 'communicative theories' of punishment can be found in R.A. Duff, *Trials and Punishment* (Cambridge University Press, 1986); R.A. Duff,

Punishment, Communication, and Community (Oxford University Press, 2001); Nicola Lacey, *State Punishment: Political Principles and Community Values* (Routledge, 1988); Matt Matravers, *Justice and Punishment: the Rationale of Coercion* (Oxford University Press, 2000); Andrew von Hirsch, *Censure and Sanctions* (Oxford University Press, 1993). On restorative justice: Wesley Cragg, *The Practice of Punishment: towards a Theory of Restorative Justice* (Routledge, 1992); Declan Roche (ed.), *Restorative Justice* (Ashgate, 2004); Andrew von Hirsch *et al.* (eds), *Restorative Justice or Criminal Justice: Competing or Reconcilable Paradigms?* (Hart, 2003). Finally, works on capital punishment include: Adam Bedau (ed.), *The Death Penalty in America: Current Controversies* (Oxford University Press, 1997); Roger Hood, *The Death Penalty: a Worldwide Perspective* (Oxford University Press, 2008); Tom Sorell, *Moral Theory and Capital Punishment* (Basil Blackwell, 1987).

Weblinks

The following are academic and legal websites on punishment in general and/or capital punishment in particular:
http://ethics.sandiego.edu/Applied/deathpenalty/
http://www.pro-capital-punishment.com/links.html
http://www.wmin.ac.uk/law/page-144

Part 2   Classical Ideologies

What is Ideology?

The term '**ideology**' has acquired a fairly unsavoury meaning. Politicians regularly condemn policies they disagree with as 'ideological', meaning that such policies are dogmatic, prejudiced and blinkered. Ideologies are seen as closed systems, beliefs that are intolerant and exclusive, so that socialists, conservatives, liberals and anarchists are often anxious to deny the ideological character of their thought.

We are sceptical about this narrow use of the term ideology. An ideology is a system of ideas, organised around either an attempt to win state power or to maintain it. To call a set of beliefs ideological is merely to argue that ideas are organised for a particular statist purpose: they form the basis of a political movement (focused around the state) whether this is a movement we approve of or not. The term is generally used to denote a belief system: in our view, it is more than this. Ideologies are belief systems focused around the state. 'Moderate' movements are as ideological as extremist ones although some movements may embrace many ideologies, and in the case of nationalism, for example, ideologies that contradict one another. Tony Blair spoke of the 1997 election as the last election in Britain based on ideology, although he certainly identified New Labour as embracing a set of ideas.

The 'negative' connotation of the term can only be preserved by linking ideologies to the state; a post-ideological world is a world without the state.

Origins and Development of the Term

The reality of ideology goes back to the birth of the state, so that it is impossible to agree with Habermas' argument that 'there are no pre-bourgeois ideologies' (McLellan, 1995: 2). We would see no problem in describing Aristotle's theory or St Thomas Aquinas' position as ideological since these were ideas that impacted upon society and moved people into action in relation to the state. However, the term itself was coined in the aftermath of the French Revolution by Antoine Destutt de Tracey who used the idea positively to denote a science of ideas. The term referred to ideas that were progressive, rational, based upon sensation, and free from metaphysical and overtly religious content. De Tracey was placed in charge of the *Institut de France* and regarded the spreading of ideology as the spreading of the ideas of the French and European Enlightenment.

However, the term soon became pejorative: Napoleon denounced ideology as an idea that was radical, sinister, doctrinaire and abstract – a 'cloudy metaphysics' that ignores history and reality (McLellan, 1995: 5). This seems to have been the view that Marx and Engels put forward in *The German Ideology* (1845), but they inject into the term two new connotations. First, ideologies are seen as infused with idealism – ideas held by individuals are substituted for reality: the belief that people drown because they subscribe to the notion that gravity exists is supremely ideological, as it blithely ignores the harsh facts of material reality. Second, ideologies appear to be ideas that mask material interests. Bourgeois ideologies may support the proposition that it is natural for people to exchange products and for the thrifty to accumulate wealth, but these beliefs merely reflect the interests of the capitalist class. Unmasking such an ideology requires placing such ideas in their historical and social context.

Does that mean that Marxism itself cannot be ideological? Lenin and his Bolshevik supporters used the term ideology positively, so that Marxism was described as a scientific ideology that reflected the class interests of the proletariat. Because the proletariat was the class whose historical mission is to lead the struggle to convert capitalism into communism, its outlook (as interpreted by Marxists) is deemed scientific *and* ideological. Leninist Marxists would have no problem in describing their views as both ideological and true. Having nothing to fear from history and reality, the outlook of the proletariat is free from the 'cloudy metaphysics' that characterises the thought of classes that are in decline.

Is it possible to reconcile the views of Marx and Lenin on this matter? It could be argued that when Marx and Engels speak negatively of ideology, they are referring to idealist ideology. There is an analogy here with their use of the term 'philosophy'. Marx refers dismissively to philosophers, not because he rejects philosophy, but because he challenges those who substituted philosophy for a study of historical realities. In other words, the term ideology is used negatively when it refers to idealists like the Young Hegelians but Marx and Engels' own theories are themselves ideological in the sense that they seek to transform society and the state through a political movement.

In the post-war world, many academic political theorists argued that ideology was dead – by which they meant that ideas like Marxism that sought to transform society from top to bottom, were now archaic and dated. However, this was itself the product of a political consensus as Partridge (1967) pointed out at the time, and it was a view held not only by academics, but by politicians as well. The argument was that all sensible people agreed on the foundations of society – liberal, welfare state capitalism – so that disagreements were over details and not the overall direction of society. Bernard Crick wrote a lively book *In Defence of Politics,* in which he argues that politics is a flexible, adaptive and conciliatory activity. As such, it needs defending, he argues, against ideology. Ideological thinking is totalitarian in character: it reduces activity to a 'set of fixed goals'. It is rigid and extremist, and should be rejected by conservatives, liberals and socialists who believe in debate, toleration and the resolution of conflict through negotiation (Crick, 1982: 55). However, Crick also identifies politics with the state, and, in our view, this makes his own definition of politics ideological.

Isms as Ideologies

Liberals often argue that their values are too coherent and rational to be called ideological. Here is a belief system (liberals contend) that has a plausible view of human nature, links this with a wide view of freedom and has become the dominant set of values in modern democratic societies: how can such views be called ideological? Certainly **liberalism** is a very successful ideology, and that has rendered acute the problem of the variety of liberalisms that confront the student of politics. This problem afflicts all ideologies, it is true, but liberalism seems particularly heterogeneous and divided. Old liberalism expresses the belief in a free market, limited state and an individual free from external interference. New liberalism, on the other hand, champions an interventionist state, a socialised and regulated market and social policies that are concerned with redistributing wealth and supporting collectivist institutions like trade unions and cooperatives. Indeed, in the USA, old liberalism is confusingly called **conservatism** and new liberalism identified as a form of **socialism**. The 'L' word is highly pejorative, and it is a brave politician in the United States who calls themselves a liberal.

Nevertheless, two points can be made about liberalism that bear upon the question of ideology. The first is that all forms of liberalism have a belief in the priority of the individual over society even though old and new liberals differ significantly in how they interpret the freedom of this individual. Second, and perhaps more importantly, what makes liberalism an ideology is that it is a movement focused on the state. All liberals feel that the state is necessary to the well-being of society even though they differ in the kind of state they would support, and they may champion different movements to achieve their political ends. The fact that liberalism is a movement that has rationality, toleration and universality as its key virtues does not make it less ideological than movements that challenge these values. Liberalism is a belief system concerned with building a particular kind of society through a particular kind of state – that is enough to make it ideological.

For the same reason, conservatism is an ideology, although some conservatives strenuously deny this. Ideologies, they argue, ignore realities and existing institutions, and seek to impose abstract values upon historical facts. Ideologies seek to perfect the world whereas the truth is that humans are imperfect, and it cannot be said that people are rational beings who seek to govern their own lives. The fact that conservatives may even disapprove of explicit political ideas on the grounds that it is an ill-governed country that resorts to political theory does not make their 'ism' non-ideological. Ideals might be identified as abstractions imposed upon a complex reality, and tradition exalted as a source of wisdom and stability. However, this does not make conservatism less of an ideology than say liberalism or socialism. The point about ideologies is they differ – not only from other ideologies – but internally as well. The relationship of the New Right and Mrs Thatcher's ideas and policies to conservatism (to take a British example) is quite complicated: there is a break from traditional conservatism in some areas that is sharp enough to allow her critics to accuse her of liberalism or, a peculiarly British term, Whiggism, i.e. seventeenth- and eighteenth-century liberalism. But conservatives see the state as essential even though they are more inclined (than old liberals) to view it as a 'natural' institution that is necessary to keep 'fallen' men and women in order. This makes conservatism ideological. It is true that where conservatism denotes an attitude, as in the argument, for example, that Stalinist communists are conservative in the sense that they idealise the past, it is not ideologically specific, but this is not a politically informed use of the term.

What of socialism? Social democrats have long regarded themselves as pragmatic and flexible and regarded their opponents – whether on the left or the right – as being rigid and ideological. Giddens has written a work entitled *Beyond Left and Right* (1984) in which he seeks to defend a non-ideological politics, and the New Labour hostility to ideology is linked to a belief in a 'third way' that tries to avoid the choice between traditional socialism and traditional capitalism. Whatever social democracy is (and it is a divided movement), it is certainly ideological in the sense that its policies and beliefs focus on the state. However, what are we to say of Marxism? This is a strand within socialism that explicitly rejects what it calls 'utopias' – beliefs that do not arise from the historical movement going on before our eyes – and sees its objective as the attainment of a society that is both classless and stateless in character. Marxism raises an important point about ideologies. Although it seeks to usher in a stateless society, it is ideological for two reasons. First, because it seeks to organise its supporters around a set of ideas that are concerned with the seizure of state power, and second, because although its long-term objective is the disappearance of the state, it could be argued that it makes assumptions that ensure that it will fail to achieve this end. It is therefore a statist doctrine, and that makes it as ideological as any other political movement (See p. 223).

The one exception to this argument appears to be **anarchism**. After all, anarchists argue that political movements as they conventionally operate, concentrate power in unaccountable leaderships, and seek either to control an old state or build a new one. Anarchism seeks to do neither. Surely, therefore, it is not an ideology. Here we must sharpen up a distinction that is implicit in our earlier analysis. Just as conservatives (or socialists and liberals) may *think* that they are not being ideological, but are, so is this true of anarchists as well. In practice, anarchists have to organise, and if they were ever successful, they would, we think, have to establish a state in the short term, and what we call government in the long term – contrary to their own principles. A state tackles conflicts of interest through force; government, as we define it, addresses conflicts through social pressures of a negotiating and arbitrational kind. Both ideas are rejected by anarchists, but it is impossible to envisage a society without conflicts of interest, and therefore it is impossible to envisage any society without a government to resolve these. Whether ideology will dissolve with the dissolution of the state, is a matter we will tackle later, but it is clear that anarchism in practice would have to organise in relation to the state, and that makes it (in the particular view of ideology we have adopted here) ideological.

Ch. 11:
Anarchism

What about **nationalism**? Nationalism has the opposite problem to anarchism. Nationalists are clearly ideological because they seek to organise 'their' people to win or to maintain the power of the state, but they attach themselves to different ideologies in doing so. Nationalists may be conservative or socialist, liberal and (in practice) anarchist, so that to call someone a nationalist, is to leave open which particular social, economic and state policies they advocate. Nationalism, in our view, is ideological in a general sense: all nationalists use beliefs to galvanise their followers into action around a state but the particular values that they adopt differ significantly, and invariably one finds one nationalism in collision with another. The African National Congress sees South Africa as a country that is mostly inhabited by blacks but in which there is a significant white minority within it: the old National Party (now dissolved) saw South Africa as a white country and sought through apartheid to give black Africans homelands in separate states. Both are or were nationalist: but their nationalism had a very different political content.

All political movements that seek to run the state are ideological in character, since we define ideologies as belief systems that focus on the state. Even movements that claim to reject ideology are ideological nevertheless, if this is what they do.

Mannheim's Paradox: Are we Stuck?

Karl Mannheim wrote a classic book in 1929 entitled *Ideology and Utopia* (Mannheim, 1936). In this work, he raised an intriguing problem. Can we talk about ideology without being ideological ourselves? After all, if ideologies arise because of a person's social context, then is not the critique of ideology also situationally influenced, so that the critic of ideology is himself ideological? Mannheim was conscious that the term ideology was often regarded as a pejorative one, so that he sometimes substituted the word 'perspective' when he talked about the way in which a person's social position influences the ideas they adopt (McLellan, 1995: 39).

Mannheim's argument raises very sharply the question as to whether we should define ideologies negatively or positively. If, as is common, we identify ideologies as negative bodies of thought, then we identify them as dogmas, authoritarian thought constructs that distort the real world, threats to the open-minded and tolerant approach that is crucial to democracy. Yet the negative definition seems naive, because it implies of course that while our opponents are ideological, we are not. The dogma expelled through the front door comes slithering in through the back, since the implication of a negative view of ideology might be that while ideologists distort reality, we have the truth! This seems not only naive, but also uncritical and absolutist.

On the other hand, a purely positive or non-judgemental view of ideology raises problems of its own. Supposing we insist that all ideas and movements are equally ideological, how do we avoid what philosophers call the problem of relativism? This is the idea that all ideas are of equal merit. There are a number of dictums – 'beauty lies in the eye of the beholder', 'one man's meat is another man's poison', etc. – that suggest that it is impossible to declare that one's own views are right and another's wrong. If all belief systems are ideological, does this imply that all are equally valid? After all, which of us can jump out of our skin, our time and place, and escape the social conditions that cause us to think one way rather than another? A relativist view of ideology has at least two problematic consequences.

The first is that it prevents us from 'taking sides'. Supposing we are confronted by a Nazi stormtrooper dragging a Jewish child to be gassed in a concentration camp. Each has their own set of values. A purely positive view of ideology might lead us to the position in which we note the ideology of the Nazi and the (rather different) ideology of his victim, and lamely conclude that each are valid for their respective holders. Mannheim sought to resist this argument by contending that his theory was one of 'relationism' and not relativism, and a relational position seeks to prefer a view that is more comprehensive and shows 'the greatest fruitfulness in dealing with empirical materials' (McLellan, 1995: 40). But are not 'comprehensiveness' and 'fruitfulness' other words for the truth? The question still remains: what enables some observers to find a true ideology, while others have ideologies that are false?

Mannheim's solution to the paradox was to focus on the particular social position of intellectuals, arguing that they constitute a relatively classless stratum that is 'not too firmly situated in the social order' (McLellan, 1995: 42). It is true that intellectuals do have positions that may allow for greater flexibility and a capacity to empathise with the views of others. Reading widely and travelling to other countries 'broadens the mind', but does it follow from this that intellectuals can cease to be ideological? John Gray cites the words of a Nazi intellectual who speaks the need to exterminate gipsies and Jews, enthusing that 'we have embarked upon something – something grandiose and gigantic beyond imagination' (2002: 93). Expansive ideas need not be progressive. It could be argued that intellectuals are particularly prone to impractical ideas that are especially ideological in the sense that they take seriously values and schemes that 'ordinary' people would reject. The attempt to transcend ideology by being a supposedly classless intellectual has been unkindly likened to Baron Munchausen in the German fairy story trying to get out of a bog by pulling on his own pigtail. It can't be done!

We need a view of ideology that is both positive and negative. On the one hand, ideology is problematic and distorting, but it is inescapable in our current world. On the other hand, the notion of ideology as a belief system focused on the state does, we will argue, combine both the negative and the positive. While it is impossible not to be ideological in state-centred societies, in the struggle to move beyond the state itself, we also move beyond ideas and values that are ideological in character.

Facts, Values and the State

We have argued in the introduction to our book on political concepts that it is impossible to separate facts and values, since all statements imply that a relationship exists, and relationships suggest that values exist within facts. Thus, behaviouralists – a school of empiricial theorists who claim to be scientific and value-free – argue that when people don't vote, this enables experts to make decisions for society. The link between apathy and democracy is deemed 'functional', but this contention necessarily implies that apathy is a good thing. When apparently value-free linguistic philosophers define the word democracy in parliamentary terms, they are taking a stand on the debate between representative and participatory democracy that is certainly evaluative or normative in character. One meaning of the term ideology is thought that is normative, but this, we would suggest, is unsatisfactory for at least two reasons. First, it naively assumes that ideas can be non-evaluative or purely factual in character; second, it fails to see that ideology can be transcended, not by avoiding morality in politics, but by moving beyond the state.

Why should the state be linked to ideology? In our view, the state is best defined as an institution claiming a monopoly of legitimate force – a claim that is contradictory and implausible. In claiming a monopoly of legitimacy, supporters have to denigrate those who challenge this monopoly, presenting their own values as an exclusive system. Inevitably, a statist focus distorts realities. This problem is exacerbated by the fact that the state not only claims a monopoly of legitimacy, but a monopoly of force, and the use of force to tackle conflicts of interest acts to polarise society into friends and enemies, those who are respectable and those (an inexplicably violent minority) who are beyond the pale. This gives ideas an absolutist twist that is characteristic of ideologies, and explains why ideologies are problematic in character. This is unavoidable where the objective of a movement is to win (or retain) state power. The Movement for Democratic Freedom seeks to unite conservatives, liberals and socialists against the tyrannical rule of Robert Mugabe and his ZANU-PF party, and it cannot avoid an ideological character. In the same way, gay rights activists who organise to protect their interests and call upon the state to implement appropriate policies are acting ideologically.

However, movements are not purely ideological, where they seek not only to transform the state, but to move beyond it altogether. Take feminists for example. Feminists do not normally believe that punishing aggressive men through the courts will solve the problem of male domination, although they may support it as a short-term expedient. In the longer term, they would argue that we need to change our culture so that **force** is seen as an unacceptable way of tackling conflicts of interest, and that we must resolve conflicts in what we have called a governmental way – i.e. through negotiation and arbitration and not through force. This longer-term aim is non-ideological because it rests upon trying to understand why **violence** arises and how we can move beyond it. It involves a politics beyond the state, and in seeking to face reality in all its complexities, it is moving beyond ideology as well. The notion of monopoly and the use of force that are inevitable when the state is involved, limit the realism of ideas and make them ideological.

References

Crick, B. (1982) *In Defence of Politics,* 2nd edn Harmondsworth: Penguin.

Giddens, A. (1994) *Beyond Left and Right* Cambridge: Polity Press.

Gray, J. (2002) *Straw Dogs* London: Granta.

McLellan, D. (1995) *Ideology,* 2nd edn Buckingham: Open University.

Mannheim, K. (1936) *Ideology and Utopia,* English translation London: Routledge & Kegan Paul.

Partridge, P. (1967) 'Politics, Philosophy and Ideology' in A. Quinton (ed.) *Political Philosophy* Oxford: Oxford University Press, 32–52.

Chapter 8

Liberalism

Introduction

Liberalism has emerged as the world's dominant ideology, and much of the political debate of 'liberal democratic' societies takes place within liberalism. Because of its dominance liberalism can be a difficult ideology to pin down, and there are several quite distinct streams of thought within it. Liberals take individual freedom – or liberty – as a fundamental value, and although an individual's freedom can be limited – because it clashes with the freedom of others or with other values – what defines liberalism is the *presumption* that freedom is a good thing, meaning that limitations on freedom must be justified. A less obvious aspect of liberalism is its emphasis on equality, and again the presumption is that people are equal. Although this appears to generate a major contradiction at the heart of liberalism – after all, the exercise of freedom will often lead to inequality – the two can be reconciled if we assume people are *naturally* equal. Natural, or 'moral', equality may be compatible with material, or social, inequality. To say people are naturally equal amounts to the claim that political institutions must be justified to each individual, and each individual counts equally.

Chapter Map

In this chapter we will:

- Explore the historical roots of liberalism.

- Identify the fundamental philosophical core of liberal thought.

- Recognise the distinct streams of liberal thought, and the tensions between them.

- Analyse political practice in liberal democracies and apply the insights gained to that practice.

Prostitution Laws in Sweden

Source: © Michael Czajkowski/PAP/Corbis

In 1998 the Swedish Parliament passed the Prohibition of the Purchase of Sexual Services Act. The Act does what its title suggests: it prohibits the sale of sexual services. Most countries have legal controls on prostitution, which often include banning brothels, pimping, kerb-crawling and advertising. The Swedish Act tightened up on these aspects, but it achieved international attention because it went much further than other European countries: it made it illegal to purchase, or attempt to purchase 'casual sexual services'. The prohibition applied not only to street prostitution, brothels and massage parlours, but also to escort services or 'any other circumstances' in which sexual services are sold. Obviously existing laws covered many of these cases, but the new law was a 'catch-all', and in that sense quite radical. One important point was that the buyer rather than the seller was criminalised.

In contrast, the Netherlands has adopted a quite different approach: there prostitution is defined as a profession, at least for those from European Union (EU) countries. Prostitutes have access to welfare services and pay taxes on their earnings. Whereas in Sweden prostitution is viewed primarily as violence against women, in the Netherlands so long as coercion is not used – and that means that the participants must be of the age that they are deemed capable of giving consent – it is a voluntary exchange.

Both Sweden and the Netherlands have long histories as liberal democracies and in defending their respective policies they draw on liberal arguments, yet they come to quite different conclusions on the regulation of prostitution. How might these differences be explained and which policy do you prefer? (See the weblinks at the end of this chapter for further material on the Swedish and Dutch Prostitution laws.)

The Meaning of Liberalism

Liberalism has emerged as the world's dominant ideology. Europe provides a good example of the spread of liberal-democratic values and institutions: the 1970s saw the transition from right-wing, military regimes in Greece, Spain and Portugal, and in 1989–91 the process of democratisation spread to Eastern Europe in the dramatic overthrow of state socialism from the Baltic states to Romania. While the depth of commitment at elite and popular levels to liberal-democratic values in the 'emergent democracies' of Eastern Europe is a matter of much debate among political scientists, all these states subscribe to a liberal ideology. The accession in 2004 of nine Eastern European states, plus Malta, and of Romania and Bulgaria in 2007 to the European Union, bringing the total from the original 6 in the 1950s to 27 today, is indicative of this commitment.

The very dominance of liberalism can make it a difficult ideology to grasp. In the history of political thought quite different bodies of thought are identified as liberal and in popular political discourse confusion can be caused when the term is applied to particular parties, movements or strands of thought *within* a liberal democracy. For example, many political parties have the word 'liberal' in their name; in Canada the Liberal Party is towards the left of the political spectrum, while in Australia the Liberal Party is on the right. In many European countries liberalism is associated with a strong commitment to the free market, whereas in the United States the term denotes a belief in central – that is, federal – state intervention in society and the economy, and so to be 'liberal' is to be on the left. Clarification is sometimes provided by a qualifying adjective: *economic* liberalism or *social* liberalism. Occasionally the term *classical* liberalism is employed to denote support for free trade and the free market.

Some distinctions will help to cut through the confusions of popular usage:

- *Justification* Political institutions can be described as 'liberal', but so can the method by which they are justified. Hobbes's defence of the state is a good example of this distinction. The institutions he defends appear highly illiberal but his method of justifying those institutions – contractarianism – is liberal. State authority is justified because we, as rational individuals, would calculate that it is in our interests to submit to it. Most of our attention in this chapter will be on the justification of institutions.

- *Constitution and policy* Turning to institutions, we can distinguish between the constitution and policy (or law making). The constitution determines the procedure by which laws are passed, while to a large extent leaving open the content of those laws. Although there may be debate about the constitution, most people are implicitly 'liberal' on the essentials of the constitution: the division of powers and the basic rights of individuals. They may not, however, support parties that describe themselves as liberal. The struggle between political parties normally operates *within* the constitution, rather than being a battle over the constitution. In short, at the constitutional level most of us are liberals, but at the policy level this may not be the case.

- *Attitudes* There is a distinction between how political theorists have defended – justified – liberal principles and institutions, and popular attitudes to those institutions. Understanding such attitudes is primarily the focus of empirical political science, using quantitative methods such as surveys. Although we do not discuss it here, the work of political scientists provides a useful perspective on liberalism – if people find it difficult to endorse liberal values then it should force liberals to reconsider how they defend liberal institutions.

Keeping these distinctions in mind, we can now attempt a rough definition of liberalism. As the etymology of the word implies, liberals emphasise liberty (freedom). As we will argue, a less obvious aspect of liberal thought is its emphasis on equality – not necessarily material equality, but a basic moral equality. A more precise definition of liberalism carries the risk of excluding from the liberal tradition important strands of thought. The best approach then is to look at a number of liberalisms. Although there may be more, four important ones can be identified: liberalism as toleration (or modus vivendi liberalism), contractarianism, rights-based liberalism (and, relatedly, libertarianism) and utilitarianism. If we look at ideas in their social context we will find these strands coexist. Much of the debate *within* liberalism is generated by the tensions between these different forms of liberalism, such that separating them out and clarifying each one is essential to understanding the values that underlie liberal democratic society.

Liberalism as Toleration

The Reformation and Wars of Religion

Many historians of political thought locate the origins of liberal discourse in the struggle for religious toleration generated by the Reformation and subsequent Wars of Religion. Although the term 'Wars of Religion' is sometimes reserved for a series of civil wars fought in France between 1562 and 1598, the term can be used more widely to include the struggle of the Protestant Netherlands (United Provinces) to free themselves from Catholic Spain, and the Thirty Years War (1618–48) in Germany. That the motivations of the protagonists was not necessarily theological in character does not detract from the fact that these wars produced a *philosophical discourse* in which toleration of difference became a central concern. It is this discourse, rather than the details of the wars, that concerns us.

To understand the development of the concept of toleration we need a basic understanding of the theological core of the Reformation. The causes of the Reformation are many and varied, and as suggested a moment ago it is possible to explain it in social and economic, rather than theological, terms. However, we will take seriously the Reformation as a theological dispute. It is important to recognise that what is termed the Reformation had a number of distinct streams.

The two theological issues central to the Reformation were how doctrine is established and how human beings achieve salvation. Let us consider doctrine. Christianity is a bibliocentric religion – its teachings, or doctrine, are determined by a body of scripture. However, there has always been a debate over the correct interpretation of scripture and, relatedly, whether the Bible is a sufficient source of truth – the Catholic Church (Church of Rome) maintained not only that the priesthood played a special part in interpreting scripture, but that the Church, because it was founded by Christ, had the authority to augment Christian doctrine.

1. *Catholic – tradition 1 plus 2* Doctrine is determined by scripture as interpreted by the Church (tradition 1) and developed by the Church's leaders (tradition 2).
2. *Magisterial reformers – tradition 1* Human beings still require a body – the Church – which provides authoritative interpretation (tradition 1), but Christianity should rid itself of post-Biblical accretions, so no tradition 2. In addition, the Bible should be translated into vernacular languages so that believers – or at least the literate among them – can read it.
3. *Radical reformers – tradition 0* When you read the Bible you have direct experience of the word of God, unmediated by any tradition (McGrath, 1988: 144).

The second major theological issue was the nature of salvation. The common medieval view was that God had established a covenant with humanity, whereby he was obliged to justify – that is, allow into a relationship with himself, or 'save' – anybody who satisfied a minimum standard, which was defined as recognising one's sin. In practical terms it meant remaining 'in communion' with the Church. Luther challenged this, arguing that human beings were so damaged by sin that there was nothing they could do by their own – or the Church's – efforts to save themselves. Rather, God freely gives – gratis, by grace – to those who have *faith* in him the means of salvation. The Catholic view came to be known, somewhat misleadingly, as salvation by works, in contrast to the Reformed position of salvation by faith alone.

Taken together these two theological disputes generated significantly different views of the role of the Church. For the mainstream reformers the Church's task is to teach doctrine rather than create it, and it has no direct role in human salvation – the Church cannot guarantee salvation. As the label suggests, the radical reformers went further: it was for individuals to determine correct doctrine. We can summarise the three positions on the nature of the Church:

1. *Catholic position* The Church was a visible, historical institution, grounded in the authority of Christ through his Apostles.
2. *Magisterial position* The visible Church is constituted by the preaching of the word of God – legitimacy is grounded in theological, not historical, continuity. The Church will contain both the saved and the unsaved.
3. *Radical position* The true Church was in heaven and no institution on earth can claim the right to be the community of Christ.

These two theological disputes, and the consequent re-evaluation of the role of the Church, had important immediate and long-term political implications. The immediate impact was on the relationship of the secular and spiritual powers. In the longer term the theological ideas generated by Reformed Christianity, and also, importantly, by Reformed Catholicism, gave rise to secular equivalents. For example, the theological individualism of Protestantism was 'translated' into a secular, philosophical individualism, which stressed individual responsibility. As we shall see, some theorists attribute the rise of national consciousness to the translation of the Bible into the vernacular languages of Europe. We shall focus here on the immediate political impact of the Reformation.

Simplifying a great deal: political power in medieval Europe was characterised by a dual structure. On the one side there was the spiritual authority of the pontiff, and on the other his secular equivalent, the Holy Roman Emperor. The latter was relatively weak, and most secular power resided in the national and city-state powers. Nonetheless, the loyalties of individual citizens were split between pontiff and the national (or local) secular powers. Throughout the fourteenth century there were continual pressures on the Church to reform itself, and this was expressed as a demand for a general council (a council of lay people) to discuss reform. Although the Church of Rome was relatively tolerant of doctrinal difference – it only became authoritarian after the Reformation – there was a refusal to call a council. Had such a council been called it is a matter of conjecture whether the schism between Rome and the various streams of the Reformation would have taken place; but the fact is that a council was not called, and an *institutional* break became inevitable.

The religious intolerance that eventually hardened into war cannot be attributed to the Church of Rome's attempt to suppress dissent. Rather, the institutional break created a legitimation crisis for the secular authorities. In states where the prince (or elector) had embraced Lutheranism or Calvinism, the continuing allegiance of some of their citizens to Rome was a threat to the prince's authority. Conversely, where the prince had remained loyal to Rome but some of his subjects had embraced Reformed religion there was a loss of spiritual authority – an authority that had underwritten secular authority in the pre-Reformation period. In addition, the medieval division of spiritual and secular power had resulted in a dual structure of law, with much domestic law – for example, marriage – the responsibility of church courts rather than secular courts. In Reformed states, the legitimacy of that domestic law was now in question.

The first Europe-wide attempt to address, rather than simply suppress, this conflict of loyalties was the Treaty of Augsburg (1555), which produced the formula: *cujus regio, eius religio* – roughly translated as 'the ruler determines the religion'. Two points can be made about this formula. First, it tolerated rulers and not individual citizens. Second, it was a mere modus vivendi – that is, a way of living together, but without any underlying respect for the other person's beliefs or way of life. It was a recognition of the reality of power: neither could destroy the other, and it was in neither's interest for there to be continual war, so they 'agreed to disagree'. However, once the balance of power shifted, the newly dominant side had no reason not to suppress the other. Not surprisingly, the Augsburg settlement proved unstable, and it took a century more of conflict before the so-called Peace of Westphalia (1648) created a new, and relatively stable, European order. The Peace of Westphalia is the name given to a series of treaties that ended the last of the great wars of religion – the Thirty Years War (1618–48). It reaffirmed the formula of *cujus regio, eius religio*, but made some concession to toleration of individuals by respecting the beliefs of those resident in a particular territory prior to 1618. In addition, there was an implication that private belief and public practice should be separated – there were to be 'no windows into men's souls', to use Elizabeth I of England's expression. So long as there was outward conformity, there could be inner dissent.

Toleration

The settlement of the Wars of Religion is credited with making toleration a central concept of political life, and in the process generating a body of political reflection and writing that can be described as liberal. The term 'toleration' has, to twenty-first-century ears, a slightly negative connotation. It suggests grudging acceptance rather than respect. However, toleration remains an important concept for liberals and it is important to be clear about its structure.

Toleration appears to require approving and disapproving of something at the same time. For example, person A:

1. believes that salvation is mediated by the Church (of Rome), so that outside the Church there can be no salvation;
2. accepts that person B has the right to express their religious (or other) beliefs – person B is justified in not seeking salvation through the Church (of Rome).

The apparent tension between 1 and 2 is resolved if we recognise they refer to different actions: 2 is not direct approval of person B's choices, because that would contradict 1. The 'approval' in 2 might be of B's capacity to make a choice (we say 'might' because other reasons are possible). Nonetheless, there is still a tension between 1 and 2; what is required is a 'bridge' between them.

One bridge might be the acceptance of the sheer fact of religious difference. This is the Augsburg modus vivendi argument applied to toleration of individuals: terrible torture and other deprivations will not force (some) people to abandon their religious beliefs and practices, so it is both useless and politically destabilising to oppress them. Toleration grows out of recognition of this reality. This is not really a justification for toleration – it does not provide reasons for toleration. To go beyond a modus vivendi person A would have to find something in their own religious beliefs that enables them to accept B's dissent from those beliefs. In the history of the development of religious toleration in the sixteenth and seventeenth centuries a range of such arguments were advanced. They included the following:

- *Latitudinarianism:* the belief in a minimal set of Christian doctrines, and the acceptance of dissent beyond that minimum.
- *Catholicism:* (in the generic sense) the importance of Christian unity over uniformity.
- *Christian choice:* God gives us a choice, and so we are not entitled to deny people choice.

The list is far from exhaustive. What is striking, however, is that there is assumed an underlying commitment to Christianity, however Christianity might be understood. Insofar as there was toleration in the sixteenth and seventeenth centuries it tended to be limited to Catholicism and the two major branches of the magisterial Reformation – Lutheranism and Calvinism. It was rarely extended to radical Reformers, Jews and atheists. Only in the Netherlands and Poland did toleration go further. The explanation for this wider toleration in those two countries is complex, but in the Dutch case it is clearly connected to the early rise of capitalism, while in the Polish case it may have had its roots in a delicate religious balance.

In the eighteenth and nineteenth centuries the 'circle of toleration' is extended to include previously untolerated groups, and the justification of toleration shifts from religious to secular grounds. Here are a few secular arguments:

- *Scepticism*: it is impossible to prove the existence of God.
- *Progress*: humanity progresses if there is a competition of ideas (see John Stuart Mill's argument).
- *Autonomy*: how we should behave can be determined rationally through the exercise of human reason.

Ch. 2:
Freedom
pp. 42–43

Some contemporary theorists argue that these secular arguments are themselves intolerant and incompatible with a pluralistic society: scepticism is a rejection of religious belief, and autonomy, while not a rejection, cannot be endorsed by someone who believes revelation or natural law is the source for guidance on moral conduct. For this reason there has been a 'rediscovery' of modus vivendi toleration, and this is reflected to some extent in the multiculturalism debate. This rediscovery is also a reaction to the development of liberal thought in the following three centuries. In the rest of this chapter we consider that development, by focusing on three strands of theory: contractarianism, rights-based liberalism and utilitarianism.

Contractarianism

Thomas Hobbes's *Leviathan* (1651) was published against the background of the English Civil War, which was, in part, a manifestation of the wider religious struggles in Europe. *Leviathan* is one of the great books of political theory, and arguably the first significant work of modern political thought. The conclusion Hobbes draws – that it is rational to submit to a powerful sovereign – may not appear liberal, but the way he reaches that conclusion draws on ideas which have become a major part of liberal reflection on the state. The method he uses for justifying obligation to the state is contractarian: we are to imagine a situation in which there is no state – the state of nature – and ask ourselves whether it is better we remain in the state of nature or agree to submit to a sovereign (or state). It is certainly controversial to describe Hobbes as a liberal, but what we argue is that his thought has influenced a specific stream of liberal thought. However, it should be acknowledged that it has also influenced traditions of thought hostile to liberalism, as illustrated in the work of German thinker Carl Schmitt (1888-1985), who saw in the mythical, mortal God Leviathan a very personal, wilful power and a charismatic source of authority in contrast to the rationalism of liberal authority.

It is important to understand the historical context of Hobbes's work. To a large degree Hobbes is concerned to provide an argument against rebellion. In mid-seventeenth-century England it was radical reformers – sects such as the Levellers and the Diggers – who were among the most likely rebels. A large part of *Leviathan* is concerned with blocking off theological arguments for rebellion. There is a tendency for contemporary readers to ignore this part of the book, regarding it as anachronistic, and concentrate on the apparently more 'secular' parts. Given that it is still the case that political order is challenged not just by competing interests, but also competing moral conceptions (some of which have a theological basis), the concerns which motivated the work cannot be dismissed as irrelevant to the contemporary world.

Hobbes was the first of the classic contract theorists – later important contractarians are Locke, Rousseau and Kant. The contract tradition went into decline around the end of the eighteenth century. John Rawls is credited with reviving it in the second half of the twentieth century. There are important differences between these thinkers, but there is a common, three-part structure to a contract theory:

1. a description of a situation in which there is no state;
2. an outline of the procedure for either submitting to a state or agreeing to a certain set of coercively enforced political principles – this is the 'contract';
3. a description of what is chosen – the state, or political institutions.

Since our concern is with contractarianism rather than the details of specific political theories, we will employ a modern 'rational choice' treatment to explain the contract. Hobbes's *Leviathan* can be interpreted as an attempt to solve what is called the 'prisoner's dilemma'. The prisoner's dilemma is an imaginary 'game' intended to represent, in a very pure form, moral (and political) relationships. We imagine two people arrested for a crime and interrogated separately. If both remain silent each will be convicted of a relatively minor offence, and spend a year in prison. If both confess, each will receive five years for a more serious offence. If one confesses but the other remains silent, then the confessor will go free, whilst the other will receive a ten-year sentence. Clearly, the actions of one affect the outcome for the other, as can be seen from the payoff table:

Version 1		Second prisoner Remains silent	Confesses
First prisoner	Remains silent	1, 1	10, 0
	Confesses	0, 10	5, 5

If we assume that the prisoners are purely self-interested then each will attempt to achieve his first preference. The preference-ordering of each can be tabulated as follows:

	1st preference	2nd preference	3rd preference	4th preference
First prisoner	0, 10	1, 1	5, 5	10, 0
Second prisoner	10, 0	1, 1	5, 5	0, 10

It is not rational to remain silent whilst the other prisoner confesses, and so the likely outcome is that each will confess, with the consequence that each will satisfy only his third preference. What, however, makes the 'game' interesting is that each could do better by agreeing to remain silent. The prisoner's dilemma is a non-zero sum game: a gain for one prisoner does not result in an equivalent loss for the other. The explanation of how, through cooperation, each prisoner might move from his third to his second preference is a contemporary rendition of the reasoning behind Hobbes's contract theory. The third preference represents the non-cooperation characterising the state of nature, the agreement to remain silent is equivalent to the contract itself, and the satisfaction of the second preference equates to life under a state. There are *burdens* as well as *benefits* to submitting to a state – we are required to conform to laws which will in many different ways restrict our freedom, but we also gain the benefits of security, and with security comes increased prosperity, and a guarantee that we will enjoy a significant amount of personal freedom.

Some commentators argue that the rational strategy for each prisoner is to forgo his first preference in order to achieve his second preference. This is incorrect: for each prisoner, achieving his first preference should remain his goal. What he wants is an agreement with the other prisoner that each will remain silent, but then to break the agreement in the hope that the other prisoner will honour it. Individual rationality dictates he will aim to free-ride on the other's compliance; that is, gain the benefits of cooperation, which is the avoidance of four years (five less one) in prison, without paying the cost of cooperation, which is one year in prison. Of course, as rational actors each prisoner understands the motivations of the other, and so a 'voluntary' agreement is ineffective. What they need is a third-party enforcer of the agreement. The enforcer imposes sanctions on free-riders, such that there is an incentive to comply. If each can be *assured* of the enforcer's effectiveness then a move from each prisoner's third preference to his second preference can be achieved. In political terms, the enforcer is the state, an entity, that, in the words of Max Weber, successfully commands a monopoly on the use of coercion in a particular territory.

There are three difficulties with the Hobbesian solution to the prisoner's dilemma:

1. The existence of an enforcer, or state, does not fundamentally alter the motivations of those subject to it: each still seeks to satisfy his own interests. This engenders a fundamental instability in the political order: we are always looking over our shoulder at other people, convinced that given the opportunity they will break the law. Such law-breaking might, for example, take the form of evading payment of taxes necessary to maintain a police force.

2. The second objection to Hobbes can be broadened out into a critique of the aims of classical contract theory – as distinct from the aims of the contemporary contractarianism of Rawls. Hobbes, Locke, Rousseau and Kant were occupied above all with the question of an individual's obligation to obey the state and its laws. A law by its nature commands obedience, but what is termed 'political obligation' is concerned with the existence of moral reasons for obeying the law: by asking whether a person has a political obligation we put into question the legitimacy of law. From the preceding discussion it is not difficult to see how a contractarian might argue for political obligation. We are all better off under a state than in a state of nature and therefore we are under an obligation to obey the state. But what if the benefits of cooperation are unequally distributed? Consider another version of the prisoner's dilemma:

Version 2		Second prisoner Remains silent	Confesses
First prisoner	Remains silent	4, 1	10, 0
	Confesses	0, 10	6, 5

The preference ordering of each prisoner is identical to the first version. The difference lies in the respective payoffs from cooperation relative to non-cooperation: the first prisoner gains two years of freedom whereas the second prisoner gains four years. It might therefore be *rational* for each prisoner to submit to an enforced agreement, but it is not necessarily fair. Given the unfairness of the situation it is hard to argue that those who are disadvantaged relative to others have a *moral* obligation to obey the state. This brings us to the third objection to Hobbes.

3. In both versions there was a unique solution to the dilemma – but what if instead of one set of payoffs there were multiple sets? Let us imagine that the agreement is not about simply obeying or not obeying the state, but is concerned with the creation of a certain kind of state. We have to decide on the economic and political structure of society: should power be concentrated or dispersed? Should there be strong private property rights or, alternatively, collective ownership of economic resources? How much freedom should individuals have? Do we want an extensive welfare state or should individuals be required to buy health cover and education? Whatever is chosen, we are all better off under some kind of state than no state, but there is not a unique solution. The principles or institutions we choose will benefit people in different ways: if 'a' represents the state of nature, and 'b . . . z' a range of alternative political systems, then you might be better off under any of 'b . . . z' than under 'a', but your preferred system will not be shared by all other citizens. For twentieth-century contractarians the aim of the contract is to create a certain set of political institutions – or principles of justice – rather than simply contract into the state. For example, Rawls accepts the logic of the solution to the prisoner's dilemma, but that is merely the starting point for a theory of justice: it has to be both rational *and reasonable* to submit to the state.

The fundamental problem with Hobbes's argument is that he reduces the legitimacy of the state to self-interest. His starting point is a materialist conception of human nature: human beings are 'bodies in motion', continually desiring things, and never fully satisfied (Hobbes, 1991: 118–20). Because there is scarcity of desired objects, humans are brought into conflict with one another. Their greatest fear is death, and that fear is the key to understanding why the state of nature is a 'war of all against all' (Hobbes, 1991: 185–6). Although Hobbes outlines the 'laws of nature' that he claims exist in the state of nature, these are best interpreted as akin to scientific, rather than moral, laws. For example, we are required to seek peace, unless war is necessary for self-defence, but this can be understood as a prudential instruction rather than a moral requirement (Hobbes, 1991: 190).

A twentieth-century theorist, John Plamenatz, criticised Hobbes on grounds that if his description of the state of nature were accurate, then people would be too nasty to stick to any agreement, and if they stick to the agreement then the state of nature cannot be as Hobbes describes it (Plamenatz, 1991: 193–7). One of the insights of game theory, of which the prisoner's dilemma is an example, is to provide a solution to this apparent paradox: what we seek is an agreement, equivalent to the prisoners' agreement to remain silent, but what we fear is that other people will 'defect' from the agreement. It follows from this that prisoner's dilemma-type situations are 'assurance games'. In short, people are not nasty but fearful. Furthermore, the real challenge is not agreeing to create a state, but *maintaining* the state. Consequently the 'game' that models the problem is not a one-off prisoner's dilemma, but a repeated prisoner's dilemma. Using a real-world example: should you honour business contracts? If you acquire a reputation for breaking such contracts then people will not do business with you, so it pays to be trustworthy. Strictly speaking, this is not a prisoner's dilemma, for the incentive structure is changed; nonetheless, it supports Hobbes's argument without relaxing the derivation of political authority from self-interest.

Even if the need for a good reputation solves the first problem, it leaves unresolved the second and third problems. The second might simply be dismissed by Hobbes – after all, he makes no claim to the fairness of the state. All that is required is that each individual can ask themselves: am I better off under this state than in a state of nature? If the answer is 'yes' – and it almost certainly will be – then it is rational to submit to the state. The third problem is trickier. We said the context to Hobbes's political thought was the challenge to state authority generated by religious dissent. Given Hobbes's model of human nature, there seems no place for religious motivations, but if the Kingdom of God is not of this world, then contrary to what Hobbes claims, physical death is *not* the thing to be most feared. The worst thing is separation from God. Hobbes was certainly aware of the force of theologically grounded motivation, and argued that there should be a single state religion, with outward conformity, but no attempt to coerce a person's inner thoughts. What he did not reckon with was the challenge to the stability of the state – the agreement to submit – arising not from a clash of interests, but from differing moral judgements. When we contract into the state we do not simply give up our natural liberty to pursue our interests, we also give up the right to determine what is morally correct.

Hobbes and Liberalism

The case for treating Hobbes as a liberal rests on a number of characteristics of his thought:

(a) It implicitly entails a rejection of natural authority – the authority of the sovereign derives from a contract and not from inheritance or divine right.

(b) People are equal in the state of nature because, with stealth, the weakest can kill the strongest. Admittedly this is a claim about individuals' physical powers – and a questionable one at that – rather than a claim for moral equality.

(c) Later contract theorists fundamentally revised the nature of the contract, but the basic method remains, so Hobbes's argument has proved remarkably productive of liberal thought.

In the next section we turn to two other contract theorists – Locke and Kant – but we argue that their thought is sufficiently different to Hobbes's to warrant attributing a distinct stream of liberal argument to them.

Rights-based Liberalism

Locke

Most courses in the history of political thought yoke together Thomas Hobbes and John Locke, and compare and contrast their contract theories. A simplistic comparison would describe Locke's state of nature as a rather less unpleasant place to be than the Hobbesian equivalent, and that this affects their attitude to the contract, and to the rights individuals should enjoy under the state. For example, Locke thinks we have a right to rebel against the state, whereas Hobbes rejects such a right. These superficial differences conceal more significant ones, such that it is possible to say that Locke was not simply the next in line in the contract tradition, but articulated a distinct stream of liberal thought, one which emphasised moral rights. That tradition has had a huge impact not only on political thought in Locke's native England, but also, and perhaps especially, in the United States.

As we saw, Hobbes maintained that people were free and equal in the state of nature, and that there existed 'natural laws'. On the face of it, Locke offers a similar description of the state of nature, but his understanding of freedom, equality and natural law is quite different to that of Hobbes:

- Hobbes's liberty is simply the absence of restraint, whereas Locke's liberty takes the form of actionable rights.
- Hobbes understood equality in naturalistic rather than moral terms. For Locke, we are equal because no person has a natural right to subordinate another.
- Unlike Hobbes's laws of nature, Locke's laws have a theological basis – we have a natural duty to preserve ourselves, a duty owed to God, who created us.

Ch. 4:
Justice
pp. 89–91

For Locke, moral rights precede the contract to create a state, and the role of the state is to settle disputes over the interpretation of those rights, and ensure that violations of the rights are punished. The most important among the rights are rights to private property, which are grounded in rights in one's own body. Self-ownership is, however, derivative of God's right, as creator, in his creatures (Locke's theory of private property was discussed in relation to a contemporary reworking of it by Robert Nozick). Economic and social life is possible in the state of nature. People can enter contracts – that is, exercise their powers – and individuals have the right to enforce them. Furthermore, at an early stage in the economic development of society individuals are materially satisfied – they do not compete for scarce resources. Only later, with a rise in population, does the problem of scarcity arise (Locke 1988: 297–8).

What makes the state of nature 'inconvenient' is the absence of a body that can *authoritatively* determine when rights have been violated and *effectively* enforce a remedy (Locke, 1988: 329–30). Hobbes was obsessed with effectiveness, but because there was no pre-contractual law in Hobbes's state of nature there was nothing to adjudicate. Because individuals in Locke's state of nature have the capacity to recognise the moral law, and the state is created as a judge and an enforcer, it follows that should the state fail in these tasks individuals are justified in rebelling against it.

Locke and Liberalism

There is much that is anachronistic in Locke. In particular, his claim that native Americans do not possess property because they cannot recognise natural law, and thus America was 'unowned' (Locke, 1988: 293), is an embarrassment to contemporary defenders of Locke. Also, the Christian basis of his thought is problematic in modern, pluralistic societies, although his appeal to natural law does provide a route to a secularised notion of human rights. However, overall, the key contributions that Locke made to the liberal tradition are:

(a) The idea that there are what Robert Nozick calls 'side constraints', which limit what the state, or society in general, can do to human beings (Nozick, 1974: ix).

(b) Natural (or moral) rights provide a standpoint from which we can judge the state. Unlike Hobbes, the obligation to obey the state is not for Locke an 'all or nothing' matter. Although we give up a certain degree of moral judgement when we contract into the state, we do not 'hand over' all our autonomy.

(c) There is much more discussion of the institutions of liberal democracy in Locke than in Hobbes, and that discussion has been hugely influential. Locke is identified as a key influence on the formation of the American Constitution.

Kant

From a different intellectual tradition Kant defends the idea of 'side constraints', and thus moral rights. More difficult to understand than Locke, but arguably a much more sophisticated philosopher, his moral theory is a standard part of the moral philosophy syllabus, but his political theory is less commonly found in a course on the history of political thought. However, one very powerful reason for studying Kant is that in the twentieth century there has been a huge revival of interest among political philosophers in his work, and he has been an important influence on such major thinkers as John Rawls and Jürgen Habermas.

We will briefly set out Kant's moral theory, and then explain how it underwrites his political theory. In *Groundwork of the Metaphysics of Morals* (Kant, 1996: 37–108), Kant outlines a method for determining how we should behave – the categorical imperative. He offers a number of formulations, the differences intended to capture different aspects of moral relationships. Simplifying a great deal, what is morally right is what would be chosen if we were to view a situation from an autonomous standpoint, unaffected by emotional, and other, attachments. If we abstract from those attachments then we will necessarily see the world from a universal perspective; moral reasoning entails *universalising* a 'maxim' (a maxim is a claim that we intend to form the basis of a moral law). If we cannot universalise that maxim then it cannot become a moral law.

Kant provides a simple example: a shopkeeper knows he can get away with overcharging a customer, but feels moved to inform the customer that she has been overcharged. So the 'maxim' is: 'I should always be honest' (Kant 1996: 53). This maxim can form the basis of a moral law only if it can be universalised, meaning that anybody in the shopkeeper's situation can make the same judgement, and the shopkeeper in a different situation can apply that maxim. Universalisation entails abstraction from people and situations. Perhaps the customer is a friend, and friendship moves the shopkeeper to be honest, or alternatively, the customer is a child, and the shopkeeper feels bad about cheating a child, or maybe the shopkeeper 'just knows' it is wrong to overcharge. These cannot justify the maxim because they depend on the particular identities of the agents, or on particular emotions.

The categorical imperative is not a tool for making everyday judgements. This becomes clear when Kant, in one of the formulations, maintains that one should will that your maxim becomes a 'universal law of *nature*' (Kant, 1996: 73). This indicates that the task is not to make case-by-case judgements, but think 'holistically': we imagine a *society* governed by universal laws. Such a society Kant describes as a 'Kingdom of Ends', for if we universalise we must necessarily treat other human beings as ends and not means (Kant, 1996: 80). In contrast to Locke, these laws are not given to us by God, or through our senses, but are 'constructed' by human beings exercising powers of reason. Through construction of moral laws we lift ourselves above our animal natures and prove our autonomy. There is a crucial political point here: we can be coerced into *conforming* with what morality requires, but we cannot be coerced into acting *for the right reasons*. The shopkeeper can be motivated to be 'honest' by threat of punishment, but he would not be acting morally because he is not being moved by reason.

Some contemporary political theorists draw an anarchist conclusion from Kant's argument. Robert Paul Wolff argues that we can never reconcile moral autonomy and political authority (Wolff, 1970: 18–19), but in fact in his political writings Kant does defend the state. He even maintains that a civilised state is possible among a 'nation of devils . . . just so long as they get the constitution right' (Kant, 1996: 335). To understand the relationship between morality and politics we need to distinguish internal freedom and external freedom. The former – which can also be called autonomy – entails the ability to be motivated to act morally by the force of reason alone. The latter is the idea that the freedom of one person must coexist with the freedom of all others. This is expressed as a system of rights, coercively enforced by the state.

The state serves the end of morality by helping to realise the 'Kingdom of Ends'. The difficulty with this argument is that human agents must will the creation of that 'Kingdom', whereas in a political community – under the state – we are coerced into behaving in accordance with other people's rights. Attempting to resolve the conflict between autonomy and coercion has been central to the liberal project. One way of resolving it would be to posit two standpoints that a citizen can adopt: the standpoint of moral autonomy and the standpoint of a subject of law. As an autonomous agent you will the creation of a political community in which each person's rights are respected, but you also know enough about human nature to recognise that rights will have to be protected through coercion, such that you are at the same time willing the creation of a *coercive* political community. This would, of course, create a divide within human psychology between moral autonomy and political subjectivity.

Kant and Liberalism

The rights-based tradition of liberalism has sometimes been characterised as entailing the priority of the right over the good. These terms are attributed to Kant, but the precise definition was given by moral philosopher David Ross. He defined the right as 'that which is obligatory' and the good as 'that which is worth pursuing' (Ross, 1930: 3). There are many different forms of goodness: aesthetic evaluation, friendship, the pursuit of truth are but a few. Kant's political theory can be categorised as 'right based' because the purpose of the state is not to realise goodness but to ensure that people respect each other's rights. The 'right' – note the singular – is the name Kant gives to the coexistence of individual rights. A political consequence of the priority of the right over the good is that the state's functions are limited.

If the state is only justified insofar as it protects individual rights it cannot have purposes of its own which are independent of that function. Michael Oakeshott, whose work draws on liberal and conservative thought, makes a useful distinction between the state, or political community, as an *enterprise association* and as a *civil association*. In an enterprise association people have a shared project, and the state acts as an agent to realise that project. Such a project might be theological in character, but it could also be secular. For example, the attempt to create an 'equal society', where equality is an end in itself, would constitute an enterprise. Oakeshott argues that a political community is a civil association of individuals with disparate aims, and the state works to permit the continuation of that association: the association has no ends of its own.

Utilitarianism

Utilitarians hold that political institutions function to increase the overall level of welfare – or utility – of a society. At first sight this appears fundamentally opposed to rights-based liberalism, and indeed to contractarianism: utility maximisation implies that there is a thing called 'society' which has aims over and above those of individuals, or that the aims and interests of individuals are subsumed in 'society'. While there are tensions between utilitarianism and rights-based liberalism, and much of the debate within the liberal tradition is between these positions, there are shared historical roots, such that they are both clearly part of the liberal tradition. Furthermore, in the twentieth century revisions to utilitarian theory have had the consequence of closing the gap to some degree between utilitarianism and rights-based liberalism.

The claim that utilitarianism entails the maximisation of utility requires elaboration: what is utility? How do we maximise it? What does utilitarianism actually require of individuals? Different utilitarian thinkers have defined utility in different ways: Jeremy Bentham defined it as happiness, John Stuart Mill as pleasure, G.E. Moore as certain ideal states of mind. All of these definitions conceptualise utility as something 'mentalistic' – a feeling or state of mind. This raises an epistemological question: how do we know someone is happy, or feeling pleasure, or has the right state of mind? Contemporary utilitarians avoid the epistemological question by defining utility as preference satisfaction. This has the advantage that there are available real-world systems for ordering preferences: voting and markets. When we cast a vote or buy a pair of shoes we are expressing a preference.

To maximise utility we have to be able to measure it, and two options are available: either we add up instances of utility (cardinal measurement), or else we rank instances of utility (ordinal measurement). The definition of utility affects how we go about measuring it: mentalistic definitions lend themselves to cardinal measurement, while preference satisfaction fits best with ordinal measurement. In fact, it was the difficulty of measuring pleasure or happiness that led to a shift to defining utility as preference satisfaction.

We now come to the third – and most obviously political – question: if we are utilitarians, how should we behave? There are some standard criticisms of utilitarianism:

- What makes people happy, gives them pleasure, or what they prefer is completely open: if torturing another person gives you pleasure, then it must be counted into the 'maximand' (that which is to be maximised).
- We cannot respect the law if breaking it will increase utility.
- Utilitarians cannot respect individual rights – J.S. Mill's attempt to establish a 'sphere of non-interference' (rights) on the basis of 'human interests in the widest sense' (utility) is incoherent.
- One person could be made to suffer excruciating pain in order to give a million people each a minuscule amount of pleasure. A less extravagant criticism is that utilitarians cannot be concerned about the distribution of welfare, but merely its overall level.
- You are as much responsible for what you allow to happen as what you do in a more direct sense of doing. For example, given the choice between (a) killing 1 person and 'allowing' 19 to live, or (b) 'standing by' while all 20 are killed, utilitarianism requires you to kill that 1 person (Smart and Williams, 1973: 98–9).

These criticisms are dismissed by utilitarians as unrealistic. The way to avoid them, it is claimed, is to distinguish between direct and indirect utilitarianism. Direct utilitarianism – or 'act utilitarianism' – requires that you seek to maximise utility on every occasion. Indirect utilitarianism, which includes 'rule utilitarianism' and 'institutional utilitarianism', separates action and justification: what we should do is follow rules, such as respecting individual rights, and the consequence of doing so is that utility will be maximised. Institutional utilitarianism is compatible with contractarianism: in the contract situation we agree to a set of institutions, the operation of which will maximise utility.

Utilitarianism and Liberalism

There is no doubt that since the early nineteenth century, utilitarianism has developed in sophistication. However, our concern is with the relationship of utilitarianism to the other members of the 'liberal family'. What makes utilitarianism part of the family?

(a) As do Hobbes, Locke (despite his Christianity) and Kant, utilitarians reject 'natural authority'. Although it is possible to give utilitarianism a Christian cast, it is clear that it developed out of a secular, 'natural–scientific', world view. The calculability of pleasure or happiness fits neatly with the rise of science and the rejection of the idea that there are forces beyond human consciousness.

(b) Utilitarians still hold to the liberal 'presumption in favour of freedom' and the 'presumption of natural equality'. People are free to express their preferences, and coercion is only justified in order to bring about the greatest good, and people are equally 'generators' of utility – John Stuart Mill attributed this formula to the earlier utilitarian thinker Jeremy Bentham: 'each to count for one and nobody for more than one' (Mill 1991: 198–9).

(c) In concrete political terms, utilitarians have invariably been 'radical' in their attitudes to social problems. In many ways they represent the 'left-wing' liberal alternative to the libertarianism of Locke and Kant, although you need not be a utilitarian to be on the left of the political spectrum.

(d) Most important of all, utilitarianism grew in parallel with the development of democracy. The high point of utilitarian thought was the nineteenth century, although it continued to be the dominant philosophical method for justifying political principles until the 1960s when there was a revival in contractarianism. The decline of contract thinking around 1800 went hand in hand with scepticism about using the contract – actual or hypothetical – to explain political obligation in a *mass* society. Utilitarianism seemed to provide a much more convincing method of justification in democratic societies: the calculation of utility dovetails with the counting of votes, although it was only in the twentieth century, with the development of preference satisfaction as the definition of utility, that a more direct link between utilitarianism and democracy was established.

Conclusion: Prostitution Laws

We began this chapter with a discussion of anti-prostitution laws in Sweden, and especially the prohibition on the purchase of sexual services. This may have seemed a very odd case study to head a chapter on liberalism, but it is interesting in that it reveals tensions within liberal political thought, especially when the Swedish policy is compared to the Dutch one. A number of arguments have been advanced by the Swedish government for the law:

1. Prostitution is 'harmful not only to the individual prostituted woman or child, but also to society at large'.

2. Combating prostitution is central to Sweden's goal of achieving equality between men and women, at the national level as well as internationally. Prostitution is a gender-specific phenomenon: most prostitutes are female, and most buyers are male.

3. Women who suffer additional oppression, such as racism, are over-represented in the global prostitution industry. In societies where the status of women has improved, prostitution has fallen.

4. The fact that an exchange relationship operates – sex for money – does not justify the relationship, because there is an immense imbalance in the power relation of buyer to seller.

5. It is important to 'motivate persons in prostitution to attempt to exit without risking punishment' (note: the seller of sexual services is not prosecuted).

6. Because it is assumed that men who buy sex are acting from a natural, male drive, their 'underlying motives have seldom been studied or even questioned'.

7. By adopting these measures Sweden has 'given notice to the world' that it regards prostitution as a serious form of oppression of women.

8. Since the Act came into force there has been a 'dramatic drop' in the number of women in street prostitution, and the number of men who buy sexual services has also fallen.

9. Public support for the law is 'widespread and growing': an opinion poll in 1999 revealed 76 per cent supported the law, and 15 per cent opposed it. In 2001 the figure in favour was 81 per cent, with 14 per cent against (http://www.sweden.gov.se/content/1/c6/03/16/13/110ab985.pdf).

The first point to make is that critics of the law would argue for a distinction between public and private: it is possible to disapprove of prostitution but believe that consenting adults should have the right to make choices. This is a development of the argument for toleration, but here extended far beyond religious toleration. It may appear that the Swedish state has simply rejected toleration but, in fact, the language used to justify the law is an implicit acknowledgement that the limitation on the purchaser's freedom requires justification: 'in any other context, [prostitution] would be categorized as sexual abuse and rape' and 'the fact that these acts are committed in exchange for payment does not in any way diminish or mitigate the immense physical and mental damage inflicted on [prostitutes'] bodies and minds'. The power imbalance between prostitute and client is so great that the former cannot be deemed to be a consenting adult. Obviously one can disagree with this assessment, but the debate over the harm caused by prostitution, and whether prostitutes can really consent, is fought out on liberal terms.

Several of the arguments set out in the Swedish government's defence of the Sexual Services Act make reference to the good *consequences* of banning the sale of sexual services. It is often commented that Sweden has a particularly strong idea of the 'common good', and this has sometimes resulted in laws which seem to impinge on individual freedom. There are a number of reasons for this, one being the dominance of the centre-left Social Democrats in post-war Sweden. The general point is that utilitarian – or consequentialist – reasoning is clearly in evidence in the justification for the anti-prostitution law. The harm caused by prostitution is harm to 'society at large'; the law is part of a package aimed to promote gender equality; the operation of the law has resulted in a dramatic drop in prostitution. In addition, the high level of public support is taken as a justification for the law. Obviously, in a democracy you have to win support for laws, but quite often legislatures will pass laws that are unpopular, or decline to pass laws which would be popular. As we have argued in previous chapters liberalism and democracy should not be run together, for individual freedom can conflict with democracy, which in a mass society often takes the form of preference aggregation.

Finally, several arguments make reference to 'motivations': prostitutes should be 'motivated' to exit their way of life and male motives should be 'questioned'. In addition, Sweden had 'given notice to the world' that it regarded prostitution as a form of oppression, with the implication that it sought to change attitudes in other countries. The Swedish state is using its coercive power to motivate people and change attitudes, and thus to bring about a 'good' state of affairs. For a rights-based, Kantian, liberal this is an illegitimate extension of state power, and indeed a contradiction in terms, for you cannot coerce people into acting for the right reasons. It is important to distinguish the motivation argument from the harm argument. A defender of rights-based liberalism might accept that prostitutes cannot consent, and so buying their services is a form of harm and should be illegal, but motivating people – that is, changing their attitudes – even if it were successful, would be incompatible with moral autonomy.

In the Netherlands, by contrast, prostitution is accepted as a fact and the task is to manage it in order to avoid its worst consequence. Although toleration of prostitution may seem a long way from religious toleration the Dutch policy implicitly draws on a tradition that has deep roots in the Netherlands: modus vivendi liberalism. Although they have broken down, until relatively recently Dutch society was characterised by 'pillarisation' (*verzuiling*) whereby social institutions were vertically divided between Protestants, Catholics and 'social-democrats' (embracing the 'secular'). That meant that Catholics had their own political parties, schools, universities, newspapers, TV stations, and trade unions and this was, likewise, the case for the other two pillars. Whether this constituted a pure modus vivendi, or whether there were moral and political values underlying all pillars and guaranteeing social stability is a matter of debate. Nonetheless, in contrast to Sweden – with its powerful social democratic and egalitarian ethos – the Netherlands has always been more willing to *tolerate* moral, religious and political difference.

Summary

At the heart of liberalism is the belief that people are naturally free and equal. That does not mean that there are no limitations on freedom, or that people must be equal, or treated equally, in all respects. Rather, we are presumed to be free and equal, and departures from freedom and equality require justification. Viewed historically, liberalism developed out of the settlement of the Wars of Religion, with the emphasis on toleration of religious difference. Such toleration was gradually extended beyond the sphere of religion to other aspects of belief and lifestyle. Several strands of liberalism emerged after the seventeenth century, and we identified three: contractarianism, rights-based liberalism (and libertarianism) and utilitarianism. Although there are significant philosophical differences between them, they are all clearly part of the 'liberal family'. Much of the left–right debate in contemporary politics operates around different interpretations of liberalism. For example, both Rawls and Nozick can be described as liberal, but they come to quite different conclusions about the role of the state.

Questions

1. Is 'toleration' a coherent concept?
2. Can the justification for the state be reduced to 'mutual advantage' – that is, the combined effects of the pursuit of self-interest?
3. Can you believe in moral rights if you do not believe in God?
4. Can there be a utilitarian theory of rights?

References

Hobbes, T. (1991) *Leviathan* (ed. C.B. Macpherson) London: Penguin.

Kant, I. (1996) *Practical Philosophy* (ed. M. Gregor) Cambridge: Cambridge University Press.

Locke, J. (1988) *Two Treatises of Government* (ed. P. Laslett) Cambridge: Cambridge University Press.

McGrath, A. (1988) *Reformation Thought: An Introduction* Oxford: Blackwell.

Mill, J.S. (1991) *On Liberty and Other Essays* (ed. J. Gray) Oxford: Oxford University Press.

Nozick, R. (1974) *Anarchy, State, and Utopia* Oxford: Basil Blackwell.

Plamenatz, J. (1992) *Man and Society: Political and Social Theories from Machiavelli to Marx. Vol. 1, From the Middle Ages to Locke* London: Longman.

Ross, D.W. (1930) *The Right and the Good* Oxford: Oxford University Press.

Smart, J.J.C. and Williams, B. (1973) *Utilitarianism: For and Against* Cambridge: Cambridge University Press.

Wolff, R.P. (1970) *In Defense of Anarchism* New York: Harper & Row.

Further Reading

There are a couple of good, short, introductions dealing with liberalism as a whole: John Gray, *Liberalism* (Buckingham: Open University Press, 1995), and David Manning, *Liberalism* (London: Dent, 1976). Of the major thinkers discussed in this chapter, the Oxford University Press 'Past Masters' series provides very short, useful, overviews, written by major scholars in the field, with guidance on further reading: Richard Tuck, *Hobbes* (Oxford: OUP, 1989); John Dunn, *Locke* (Oxford: OUP, 1984); Roger Scruton, *Kant* (Oxford: OUP, 1982); John Dinwiddy, *Bentham* (Oxford: OUP, 1989). More generally on the social contract tradition (which does encompass Locke and Kant), the following are helpful: Michael Lessnoff, *Social Contract* (London: Macmillan, 1986); Jean Hampton, *Hobbes and the Social Contract Tradition* (Cambridge: CUP, 1986); Patrick Riley, *Will and Political Legitimacy: a Critical Exposition of Social Contract Theory in Hobbes, Locke, Rousseau, Kant, and Hegel* (Cambridge MA: Harvard University Press, 1982). On utilitarianism see: Geoffrey Scarre, *Utilitarianism* (London: Routledge, 1996); Anthony Quinton, *Utilitarian Ethics* (London: Duckworth, 1989); and for a very readable debate between a utilitarian and a critic of utilitarianism, see Williams (1973).

Weblinks

Stanford Encyclopedia of Philosophy entry on liberalism:
http://plato.stanford.edu/entries/liberalism/

On the Dutch and Swedish Prostitution Laws:
A series of links to discussion of the Swedish laws (some comparisons with the Netherlands): http://www.bayswan.org/swed/swed_index.html

Chapter 9

Conservatism

Introduction

Conservatism is an elusive ideology. Although there are conservative streams of thought in parties and movements calling themselves 'conservative', the main ideology of these movements is a combination of liberalism and nationalism, with the former particularly dominant. There are far fewer 'small c' than 'big c' conservatives. Yet despite its marginalisation, conservatism is a distinct ideology, and conservative thinkers present arguments of continuing relevance. Above all, conservatives challenge the idea that society can be planned in a rational way without regard to tradition and historical experience. This core idea leads them to support national institutions, but not radical nationalism; individual liberty against state power, but not the natural rights that many liberals defend; spontaneous order, but not anarchism; community, but not socialist collectivism.

Chapter Map

In this chapter we will:

- Outline the main elements of conservatism.

- Discuss the work of four key conservative thinkers: David Hume, Edmund Burke, Michael Oakeshott and Leo Strauss.

- Draw out the practical implications of conservative thought.

- Distinguish conservatism from the other traditional ideologies.

The Monarchy – an Anachronism?

The annual State Opening of the British Parliament by Queen Elizabeth II

Source: WireImage/Getty

The idea that the position of Head of State should be occupied by someone who achieved the office merely by an accident of birth seems incompatible with the concept of merit, which, in Western liberal democracies, applies to most other jobs. But in Belgium, Denmark, the Netherlands, Norway, Spain, Sweden, and the United Kingdom the Head of State is an hereditary figure – a monarch. Although the powers of these monarchs vary, none is purely 'symbolic' – he or she appoints Government ministers, signs off laws, makes speeches, receives foreign dignitaries and dispenses patronage. Such political influence seems to conflict with the spirit of democracy. Even viewed as a symbolic figure the monarchy is problematic. Tom Nairn in his book *The Enchanted Glass: Britain and its Monarchy* argues that the Queen is at the apex of a petrified class system and its existence is a sign of Britain's social and political immaturity (Nairn, 1988: 120–3).

- Given these criticisms is there a case for the institution of the monarchy?

Conservatism: an Elusive Ideology?

Anybody with a basic knowledge of party politics, but coming to political theory for the first time, may assume that 'conservatism' is simply the ideology of political parties calling themselves 'conservative', such as the Conservative Party in Britain, or the Conservatives in Canada (or one of its predecessor parties, the Progressive Conservatives). However, an analysis of the aims and policies of these parties would suggest that their ideological make-up is hybrid and changeable. Take the British Conservative Party, which was during the twentieth century the most electorally successful 'conservative' party in the world; its ideology shifted to such an extent that under Margaret Thatcher (British Prime Minister, 1979–90) it would be best described as 'national liberal'. The Thatcher government was economically liberal: it extended the use of market mechanisms in the domestic sphere, and pursued a pro-free trade policy in the international sphere, through, for example, the Single European Act (1986). It was 'national' in that emphasis was placed on the restoration of national pride after what was perceived to be a policy of 'managed decline' in the period 1945–79. Although parties carrying the name 'liberal' tend to have a stronger social dimension, maintaining that welfare provision is necessary to enable people to live autonomous lives, social liberalism and economic liberalism are members of the same ideological family. They are not conservative.

If the Thatcher government was not really conservative, then what is conservatism? Etymology can mislead, but it is useful to start with the word 'conservative'. The idea of 'conservation' or 'preservation' suggests that conservatives stand opposed to progress. This is why the name of one of the predecessor parties to the Canadian Conservative Party – the Progressive Conservatives – seems like an oxymoron. In fact, as with compound names of many political parties, it was the result of a merger of two parties, rather than the 'progressive' being an adjectival qualification of 'conservative'. Nonetheless, even if it had been a deliberate ideological label, it is not an oxymoron: conservatives can be progressive. What is distinctive about conservatism is its attitude to progress – progress must be careful, tentative, respectful of past practices, pragmatic, and go with the grain of human nature. Cynics might, however, define a conservative as a person who only accepts change after it has happened.

If conservatism has an enemy, it is 'rationalism' – an approach to political problems derived from the application of abstract concepts. Quite often conservative thinkers appear to reject abstract thought altogether, with the consequence that it is difficult to talk of a conservative political *theory*. However, it is still possible to identify features of conservative thought that are distinct and allow us to describe conservatism as a distinct ideology.

Basic Elements of Conservatism

As with all ideologies there are significant differences between different thinkers and streams of thought, but there are also some common elements, or themes, in conservatism. In this list of features we begin with the most 'philosophical' elements and gradually move to the more concrete, political ones:

1. *Rejection of 'rationalism'* Conservatives often use the metaphor of a ship at sea to explain their objections to what they call 'rationalism' (it should be noted

that rationalism is a pejorative term and those identified as rationalists by conservatives would not use this label to describe themselves). You are at sea, and your ship develops a fault, which if not dealt with will result in the ship sinking. The 'ship' is the state, or the set of political institutions that make up the state, while the 'sea' is society or culture in the widest sense. The 'fault' is a metaphor intended to illustrate the stresses and strains that political institutions frequently face. Rationalism would entail 'analysing' – or breaking down – the ship into its components in the hope of understanding the source of the fault and so rectifying it. The conservatives' point is not hard to discern: we cannot deconstruct the ship while at sea, but we must do something about the fault or we will drown.

2. *Experience matters* Continuing with the metaphor of the ship, our response to the fault must be based on past experience and, if necessary, a cautious process of trial and error. The 'conservatism' of conservatives rests not on an irrational veneration of the past but on a recognition of the limited nature of human reason, and for this reason conservatives can be progressive, and embrace change. What they fear are radical experiments: human beings cannot adequately predict the full consequences of their actions, and while some experiments may make the world a better place we cannot be sure that they will.

3. *Human nature* While there are some marked differences within conservative thought concerning human behaviour, capabilities and motivation, there is broad agreement that human beings are limited in their capacity to comprehend the society in which they live. This does not mean that humans are stupid, but rather that no individual mind can understand the complexity of social relations, and there is no 'super mind' which is capable of doing so. Here the conservative critique of socialism is most apparent: socialist planning presupposes a mind capable of making complex economic decisions. Socialism is doomed to failure because, first, it is inefficient, and, second (and perhaps more worryingly), it requires a concentration of power in the hands of the state. Conservatives tend to support the free market on the grounds that the distribution of goods depends on the decisions made by millions of individuals without the necessity for central control. This brings them close to the libertarian stream of liberalism but, importantly, conservative support for markets is not based on the individualist premise of moral rights to private property, but on a claim about the limits of human capabilities.

4. *Rejection of 'visionary politics'* Conservative thinker Edmund Burke famously observed that 'at the end of every vista, you see nothing but the gallows' (Burke, 1975: 344). He had in mind the visionary politics of the French Revolution (1789). Visionaries do not recognise the pluralism of everyday life – the fact that individuals have conflicting needs, desires and values. A vision implies a common project for society which overrides that pluralism. A later thinker, Michael Oakeshott, makes a distinction between society as a 'civic association' and an 'enterprise association': an enterprise implies a common purpose, whereas a civic association rests on certain rules of conduct that allow individuals to live together.

5. *Respect for institutions* An institution is a rule-governed activity. Conservatives maintain that institutions evolve, rather than being created at a determinate point in history. This may seem to misdescribe the history of many national

institutions; for example, the United States and modern France had 'founding moments', and the process of decolonisation in the period after 1945 resulted in the creation of many new states. However, conservatives argue, first, that the instability of many newly created states is evidence of the importance of evolution, and, second, where institutions appear to be successful it is because they have adapted over time. The US political system is a good example – contemporary US institutions are radically different to those created by the founding fathers. The fact that many Americans do not recognise this fact, and hold that their institutions are continuous, actually reinforces the conservatives' argument: a belief in continuity, alongside adaptation, is a 'necessary fiction'. Institutions suppress the asocial tendencies of human nature, and they provide a focus for allegiance.

6. *Suspicion of authority* This feature of conservatism may seem to contradict the last one; however, to say that conservatives are suspicious of authority does not entail its rejection. What conservatives are wary of is the accumulation of state power, which for reasons discussed above is incompatible with a recognition of the limits of individuals to grasp complex social relations. Although politicians calling themselves 'conservatives' are not shy about using state power to suppress movements they consider to be a threat to social order, more reflective conservatives will argue that institutions are not abstract entities, but have to be run by human beings, who are always in danger either of abusing their position or, even if well meaning, of putting into practice policies which have unintended bad consequences. From this position conservatives can make some interesting alliances – while rejecting statements of universal human rights detached from a social or legal system, they nonetheless stress 'our ancient liberties' and will join forces with civil liberties groups against, for example, measures intended to combat terrorism.

Civil Liberties and Counter-terrorism Legislation

The challenge that terrorism poses to civil liberties provides an interesting example of how conservatives and liberals can join forces on a public policy issue but from subtly different perspectives. In the wake of the attack on the World Trade Center on 11 September 2001, many Western countries have introduced new counter-terrorism laws; in Britain, most controversially, this entailed internment of non-nationals on the authority of the Home Secretary (Interior Minister). That judgement was subject to a judicial review, but in secret, without all the evidence being available to an internee's lawyer, and internment being ultimately decided by the 'balance of probabilities' that the person is a threat rather than the belief that it is 'beyond reasonable doubt' that they are a threat. The highest legal authority (the Law Lords) determined that the law was unfair because it applied only to non-nationals, and was a 'disproportionate' response to the threat; in response the government offered 'control orders', such as restrictions on movement, instead of incarceration, and extended this to nationals as well as non-nationals. Liberals – in the wide, non-party, sense of that term – argued that the anti-terrorist laws in both original and revised versions were a violation of human rights, where rights are entitlements individuals have irrespective of their nationality. Conservatives – again, in the wide sense of the term – also attacked the legislation, but focused much more on the *erosion* of 'ancient liberties', such as habeas corpus – liberties achieved over centuries and contained in documents, such as Magna Carta (1215) and the Bill of Rights (1688).

These points are intended to provide an overview of conservatism. To get a better idea of conservative thought, and to understand its strengths and its weaknesses, it is best to consider the work of particular thinkers. We focus on four: David Hume (1711–76), Edmund Burke (1729–97), Michael Oakeshott (1901–90), and Leo Strauss (1899–1973). Of the four Leo Strauss's work least manifests the above elements of thought. However, he is an important influence on what is called 'neo-conservatism' – a term much used in current political debates in the United States – and the discussion of Strauss will allow us to assess the degree to which neo-conservatism is really conservative.

David Hume

Eighteenth-century Scottish philosopher David Hume (1711–76) is often described as the first conservative political theorist; certainly he is the first major thinker to offer a *philosophical* defence of conservatism. For that reason it is necessary to explain how Hume derives his political theory from his epistemology (what we can know) and practical philosophy (how we should behave, or what motivates us to act in certain ways).

Although their relevance to politics may not, at first sight, be obvious, it is necessary to set out a number of Hume's philosophical claims:

1. Human understanding must be drawn from experience. All the materials of thinking – perceptions – are derived either from sensations or from reflection. Although 'reflection' will generate complex ideas, which we do not directly experience, all such ideas are combinations of simple sensations. If philosophers use a term, such as 'cause' or 'freedom', then we can test whether it has any meaning by breaking the idea down to its simple sensations, or 'impressions'.

2. Simple impressions must be connected together, or 'associated'. At any moment there is a great deal going on in a person's mind, but we cannot reason if the contents of one's mind are arbitrary: we need to connect, or associate, ideas. There are three principles of association: resemblance, contiguity and causation. The last is problematic because it takes us beyond experience: Johnny throws a brick through the window and so 'causes' the window to break, but all we *see* are Johnny and his body movements, the trajectory of the brick, and the breaking window.

3. We attribute causes to events on the basis of experience, and more specifically, habit. For example, we grasp the causal properties of gravity by observing falling objects. Beliefs are built on habits, but a belief is itself a sensation and not something external to experience. Although every occurrence is a simple, or unique, sensation, the observation of repetition creates an 'internal impression', or reflection.

In summary, we can say that what Hume rejects is the idea that 'reason' transcends, or goes beyond, what can be observed. To grasp the political significance of this rejection we need to consider Hume's moral philosophy. Morality is concerned with action, but not simply action, for a person's motives or 'reasons for action' are important in assessing whether an act is right or wrong, good or bad. In keeping with his emphasis on experience as the basis of knowledge, and applying it to action, Hume argues that any assessment of a person's actions, and that person's own assessment of what they should do, cannot be based on something which transcends experience. Indeed, reasoning about what should be done is itself severely limited: one can at best assess the most effective means to a given end, but the end itself is beyond assessment. If Jane wants to murder John, then reason can be used to determine the most effective means – shooting, poisoning, strangulation and so on – but it cannot be employed to assess the end itself, that is, whether Jane ought to kill John. Hume is not arguing that murder is acceptable, but rather that what stops Jane murdering John is *sentiment*: to twenty-first-century ears this word has slightly saccharine overtones, but in the eighteenth century it was an important philosophical concept. A sentiment is a pre-rational feeling towards somebody or something. Against Hobbes's theory, Hume does not believe that human beings are motivated purely by self-interest, but rather their sentiments are limited: they are concerned with their own interests, or those very close to them, such as family, but they are capable of sympathy, and so are moved to act in ways beneficial to other people.

Human beings' motives are mixed: although they are self-interested they are capable of limited sacrifices of their own self-interest for the benefit of others, and it is important that such beneficence is based on a simple sympathy rather than being concealed self-interest. In Hobbes's political theory, although each person was better off under a – any – state than under no state, the absence of genuine moral sentiments made people distrustful of one another, and rendered society unstable. As does Hobbes, Hume argues that we are all better off under a state, especially a state that guarantees the protection of private property, but for Hume the very success of such mutual advantage depends on a suspension of self-interest. This observation leads to Hume's famous rejection of the social contract and, by extension, his rejection of the liberal tradition.

The social contract is a fiction: no political society was ever created by a contract. More important than Hume's historical observation is his discussion of the implications for political legitimacy of holding the view that society was the result of a contract. Political authority, or legitimacy, arises from the habit of obedience to a power that initially is recognised as neither legitimate nor illegitimate, but as simply 'given' – in legal language, such power would be termed *de facto*, as distinct from *de jure* (Hume, 1963: 462). The implication of Hobbes's argument was that any monopolistic political power was preferable to none at all, such that this distinction is invalid: whatever gets us out of the state of nature is 'legitimate'. Hume, in part, endorses Hobbes's argument for state over anarchy, but because Hume ties legitimacy to sentiment, and sentiment only develops gradually, the state acquires legitimacy after the fact of its existence (Hume, 1963: 538). Crucially, the degree to which it is legitimate depends on how effective it is in protecting individuals' interests and engendering moral sentiments conducive to social order. While Hume rejects revolution as a leap into the unknown, the implication of his argument is that repressive, authoritarian states will have limited success in building their legitimacy.

Justice is a virtue operating in any society in which strangers come into contact with one another. The rules of justice are the product of artifice and contrivance, and are intended to protect private property. Crucially, the rules evolve over time as people become habituated to them. We recognise that they serve our interests, but our allegiance to them cannot be reduced to self-interest, for we respect them even when it might be in our interest to break them. There develops an 'intercourse of sentiments' – a 'conversation' between citizens out of which emerges a limited benevolence detached from narrow self-interest (Hume, 1978: 602). Many critics suspect that moral sentiments, or sympathy, are still egoistic, for what human beings care about is that they will be held in esteem by others, and, therefore, doing the right thing is pleasurable. Hume himself seems to suggest this: 'every quality of the mind, which is *useful* or *agreeable* to the *person himself* or to *others*, communicates a pleasure to the spectator, engages his esteem, and is admitted under the honourable denomination of virtue or merit' (Hume, 1978: 277). However, pleasure is compatible with sociability in a way that self-interest is not.

Edmund Burke

If Hume was the first great conservative thinker, then Edmund Burke (1729–97) must be the most famous. In part this is due to the fact that in the canon of *general* philosophers Hume is up there with Plato and Kant as one of the 'greats' but, because his contributions were primarily to the core areas of philosophy, Hume's political reflections are regarded as subsidiary. Burke, on the other hand, is not among the great general philosophers, and is regarded primarily as a political thinker (he did, nonetheless, make a notable contribution to aesthetics). Indeed, Burke was not only a political thinker, but that rarity among political philosophers – a politician.

As with Hume, the philosophical starting point for Burke's conservatism is his rejection of abstractions, such as the natural rights proclaimed by the French Revolutionaries in 1789. Abstractions become embodied in theories, and theories become dogma, and a dogmatic approach will not permit criticism. The political consequence of abstract thought, Burke argues, is terror. Against abstraction, theory and dogma, Burke defends habit, taste and prejudice. The concept of prejudice is the single most important concept in Burke's conservative political theory. Today, 'prejudice' is a pejorative term, so it is important to understand how Burke uses it. A prejudice is a pre-judgement, or a judgement made without recourse to theoretical abstractions; in contemporary philosophical language we might use the term 'intuition' rather than prejudice. For Burke, the wisdom of other people, including previous generations, is a resource that must be respected if we are to avoid disastrous social consequences. The main thrust of Burke's *Reflections on the Revolution in France* is to contrast a society – France – which has abandoned prejudice in favour of 'theory', with a society – Britain – which has remained close to its traditions, to which it is prejudiced. Burke, claiming to speak on behalf of his fellow countrymen, observes:

> that we have made no discoveries, and we think that no discoveries are to be made, in morality; not many in the great principles of government, nor in the ideas of liberty, which were understood long before we were born, altogether as well as they will be after the grave has heaped its mould upon our presumption, and the silent tomb shall have imposed its law on our pert loquacity (Burke, 1969: 84).

If Burke's view seems to us excessively deferential, it is worth considering a contemporary example of Burkean prejudice. Unless you have appropriate medical training, when you go into the operating theatre as a patient you permit people to do things to you that you do not fully understand, and to this extent you defer to the judgement of other people. But perhaps this example is a poor illustration of Burkean prejudice, because surgery is a technical skill, whereas we assume that any rational person can make a judgement, based on reason, regarding the organisation of society. Surgery is a specialism, politics is not. In the following section we discuss a more sophisticated version of this argument: Oakeshott's distinction between technical and practical knowledge.

To mid-twentieth-century conservatives, faced with what they termed 'totalitarian societies', Burke seemed ahead of his time, with the terror he predicted would follow the French Revolution being repeated in a more organised form in Stalin's Soviet Union and Hitler's Germany. However, it should be noted that Burke opposed the extension of democracy which would take place in the nineteenth century, and although there are, as John Stuart Mill observed, dangers in majoritarian democracy, the combination of civil liberties and participatory political structures – what later political scientists would term the 'civic culture' (Almond and Verba, 1963: 5–10) – has served as a bulwark against political authoritarianism. And, of course, while post-1789 French history has been complex, the Revolution did lay the groundwork for a strong liberal–democratic system.

Burke, like Hume, rejects the liberal idea that duties – or political obligations – are derived from a contract. Unlike Hume, he does not attempt to explain duty in any terms at all. To attempt an explanation of duty is futile, and liable to have deleterious political consequences. Furthermore, unlike liberals, Burke does not make a sharp distinction between state and society: the 'state' is the political organisation of society, and for that reason it emerges from society. Although Burke himself does not pursue this line, a consequence of this argument is that the state has, for many conservatives, a role in shaping human behaviour, even in what liberals term the private sphere. The legal moralism of James Fitzjames Stephen and Patrick Devlin has its roots in a Burkean view of the relationship between state and society. The irreducibility of duty to something else, and this organic state–society relationship give Burke's politics a religious cast. Although Burke was highly ecumenical in his religious beliefs – he admired Hinduism, and defended Irish Catholics – he does value religious belief and organisation, arguing that they are central to a prosperous, stable society.

Ch. 2:
Freedom
pp. 51–53

Burke's conservatism is often misunderstood. He is sometimes assumed to be a straightforward reactionary. Yet his interventions on policy towards the American colonies, India and Ireland, would suggest he was, in the context of his time, a progressive. In addition, he argued strongly for parliamentary control over the Crown. Finally, he was not opposed to all revolutions, maintaining that the Glorious Revolution of 1688 in England was an historic achievement (although he denied the Glorious Revolution was, in fact, a revolution at all, but rather a reassertion and restoration of 'ancient liberties'). He also defended the American Revolution. While Burke is sometimes wrongly painted as a reactionary, there is another danger, and that is using Burke's arguments out of their historical context. Burke's famous 'Speech to the Electors of Bristol' has been quoted in subsequent centuries by elected representatives who vote in ways contrary to the wishes of their electors (as measured by such things as opinion polls). On his election as the representative for the English city of Bristol Burke addressed his 5,000 electors:

> Parliament is not a congress of ambassadors from different and hostile interests; which interests each must maintain, as an agent and advocate, against other agents and advocates; but parliament is a deliberative assembly of one nation, with one interest, that of the whole; where, not local purposes, not local prejudices, ought to guide, but the general good, resulting from the general reason of the whole. You choose a member indeed; but when you have chosen him, he is not member of Bristol, but he is a member of parliament. If the local constituents should have an interest, or should form an hasty opinion, evidently opposite to the real good of the rest of the community, the member for that place ought to be as far, as any other, from any endeavour to give it effect (Burke, 1975: 158).

Burke's argument needs to be handled with care; he believes that parliament as an *institution* is what matters. Individuals do not have natural rights, the use of which transfers the individuals' authority on to the institution, but rather the institution has shaped individuals' rights, such as the right to vote. This also explains why Burke was prepared to submit himself to the electors of Bristol and yet at the same time ignore their wishes if they conflicted with the collective judgement of parliament (in fact, faced with defeat at the subsequent election, in 1780, Burke decided against submitting himself once again to the electors of Bristol). When Burke is quoted today it is without adequate understanding of his conservatism; while a (philosophical, ideological) liberal may defend the idea that constituents' wishes on occasion be set aside, the reasons for doing so, and the mode in which it is done will be quite different to that of a (philosophical, ideological) conservative. For a liberal the strongest grounds for a representative to reject the majority preference of their constituents would be to defend minority rights; but, equally, a liberal would maintain that the representative should explain, or justify, their position to the constituents.

Michael Oakeshott

Hume and Burke were, in approximate terms, contemporaries, writing as they were in the eighteenth century. We now, however, jump a century to consider the work of Michael Oakeshott (1901–90). For Anglophone political theorists, Oakeshott is generally regarded as the key conservative thinker of the twentieth century. However, his philosophical position underwent a significant shift in the 40 years between his first major work, *Experience and its Modes* (published in 1933), and his last major work, *On Human Conduct* (1975). Our focus will be on one highly influential 1947 essay 'Rationalism in Politics' (Oakeshott, 1962), with a few comments on the latter book.

The 'rationalism' to which Oakeshott refers characterises Western culture as a whole, and not simply one particular ideology or party. Oakeshott's critique is not, therefore, directed solely at socialism, but at modern 'conservatives' who, in fact, are liberal rationalists. A rationalist 'stands (he always stands) for independence of mind on all occasions, for thought free from obligation to any authority save the authority of reason' (Oakeshott, 1962: 1). Oakeshott goes on to provide a detailed list of attributes of the rationalist in a florid style of writing that will attract some readers but irritate those with a more analytical cast of mind. It is the analytical approach that, for Oakeshott, characterises rationalism.

The rationalist rejects (Burkean) prejudice, custom and habit, and believes in the 'open mind, the mind free from prejudice and its relic, habit' (Oakeshott, 1962: 3). The rationalist holds that it is possible to reason about political institutions, and the fact that something exists, and has existed for a long time, is no ground for respecting or retaining it. This lack of respect for the familiar engenders a political attitude of radical change rather than gradual reform. Conservatives, who respect the familiar, will seek to patch up existing institutions. The rationalist disrespect for institutions extends to the world of ideas; instead of a careful engagement with the complex intellectual traditions that have shaped Western societies, a rationalist engages in a simplification – an 'abridgement' – of those traditions in the form of an 'ideology' (Oakeshott, 1962: 7). The rationalist in politics is, in essence, an engineer, obsessed with the correct technique for solving the problem he perceives to be immediately at hand. Politics is a series of crises to be solved. Because he rejects appeal to tradition, and tradition is specific to a particular culture, the rationalist assumes that there are universal solutions to problems, and that political institutions cannot be peculiar to this or that culture. Under the umbrella term of rationalism Oakeshott places together what appear to be diverse political positions, theories, projects and ideologies: the early nineteenth-century utopian socialism of Robert Owen; the League of Nations and the United Nations; all statements of universal human rights; the right to national or racial self-determination; the Christian ecumenical movement; a meritocratic civil service. He even goes on to list 'votes for women' as a rationalist project (Oakeshott, 1962: 6–7). We have not reproduced the entire list – it is long – but it is worth noting that it is so hetero-geneous, and its items almost arbitrary, that one cannot help wondering whether Oakeshott himself is guilty of abridging traditions of thought by subsuming diverse phenomena under the pejorative label of rationalism. Aware of this charge, later on in the essay he maintains that rationalism, like an architectural style, 'emerges almost imperceptibly', and that it is a mistake to attempt to locate its origin (Oakeshott, 1962: 13).

In Part Two of his essay Oakeshott's argument becomes more interesting as he advances a theory of knowledge. He distinguishes two kinds of knowledge: technical and practical (Oakeshott, 1962: 7–8). Technical knowledge is formulated into rules that are deliberately learnt, remembered, and put into practice. Whether or not such knowledge has *in fact* been formulated, its chief characteristic is that it *could* be. An example of technical knowledge is driving a car, the rules of which are, in many countries, set out in books, such as, in Britain, *The Highway Code*. Another example is cooking, where the rules can be found in cookery books. Practical knowledge, on the other hand, is acquired only in use; it is not reflective, and cannot be formulated as rules. Most activities involve the use of both types of knowledge, so a good cook will draw on both technical and practical knowledge. If you want to be a cook technical knowledge will be insufficient, for what you need is practice. The acquisition of practical knowledge requires an apprenticeship, but the key feature of an apprenticeship is not subordination to a 'master', but continuous contact with the object of the practice: it is the food that is important, not the master chef. This argument gives Oakeshott's observations a libertarian, even an anarchist, cast.

Rationalists reject practical knowledge, and recognise only technical knowledge. Because the latter can be contained between the covers of a book it seems to guarantee certainty, whereas practical knowledge is diffuse. An ideology, which is a form of technical knowledge, can be expressed in a set of propositions, whereas a tradition of thought – which is a kind of practical knowledge – cannot be. The list of features of conservatism provided in the first section of this chapter might be an example of rationalism, as it appears to reduce conservatism to a set of propositions, or elements (we would, however, argue that these elements were open, and fluid, and were only intended to orient the thinker, rather than provide an exhaustive description). The certainty that the rationalist attributes to technical knowledge is, Oakeshott claims, an illusion, for technical knowledge is simply a reorganisation of existing knowledge, and only makes sense in the context of such pre-technical knowledge (Oakeshott, 1962: 12–13).

At the time of writing – 1947 – Britain, as with most other Western European democracies, was in the process of creating a relatively comprehensive welfare state, and developing more state interventionist economic policies, such as the nationalisation of key industries. The essay 'Rationalism in Politics' can be seen as part of a broader intellectual intervention. It is notable that a number of works that could be interpreted as critical of the extension of state planning, and state power, were published at this time, including Friedrich von Hayek's *Road to Serfdom* (1944) and Karl Popper's *The Open Society and its Enemies* (1945). However, both of these works were clearly in the liberal (or libertarian) 'rationalist' tradition. Oakeshott observes that Hayek's book, although critical of state planning, exemplifies rationalism, for it develops one rationalist doctrine – free market libertarianism – in order to counter another – namely, state socialism (Oakeshott, 1962: 21–2). What this shows is that one can only participate in contemporary – that is, 1940s – politics by advancing a doctrine. This argument is leant retrospective force by the fact that Hayek became one of the major influences on the free market, or neo-liberal, reaction to the welfare state in both Britain, under Margaret Thatcher, and in the United States, under President Ronald Reagan. As we suggested at the beginning of this chapter, the Thatcher Government (1979–90) was not really conservative, and despite the Republicans' use of the term conservative the Reagan Administration (1981–9) was likewise not, in Oakeshott's terms, conservative, but rationalist.

Oakeshott is quite rude about politicians:

> . . . book in hand (because, though a technique can be learned by rote, they have not always learned their lesson well), the politicians of Europe pore over the simmering banquet they are preparing for the future; but, like jumped-up kitchen-porters deputizing for an absent cook, their knowledge does not extend beyond the written word which they read mechanically – it generates ideas in their heads but no tastes in their mouths (Oakeshott, 1962: 22).

Rationalism is the politics of the 'inexperienced'. Oakeshott uses the term 'experience' in a philosophical sense, meaning contact with tradition – certainly, politicians who have held office are experienced in the everyday sense of the word, but it is experience in problem-solving rather than the recognition of the importance of tradition. Oakeshott argues that the history of Europe from the fifteenth century onwards has suffered from the incursion of three types of political inexperience: the new ruler, the new ruling class and the new political society. If a person does not belong to a family with a tradition of ruling then he requires a 'book' – a 'crib' – to tell him what to do. Machiavelli provided an early example, with *The Prince*. Later 'books' include Locke's *Second Treatise of Civil Government*, but in the history of rationalism nothing compares with the work of Marx and Engels, who wrote for a class 'less politically educated . . . than any other that has ever come to have the illusion of exercising political power' (Oakeshott, 1962: 26). This is a crude caricature of Marx and Engels, and indeed of their readership, although it does contain an element of truth: the recitation of doctrine can relieve people of the effort of thought.

Interesting in the light of Burke's support for American independence is Oakeshott's critique of the American political tradition. The newly independent United States had the advantage of a tradition of European thought to draw upon, but unfortunately the 'intellectual gifts' of Europe largely consisted of rationalist ideas. This, combined with the mentality of a 'pioneer people' creating political society from scratch, has given rise to a highly rationalist political system with, unsurprisingly, a powerful emphasis on legal documents, such as the Constitution. Somewhat ambivalently, Oakeshott suggests that this gave the United States an advantage; he does not develop this thought, but he might mean that the United States was eminently suited to the increasing rationalisation of domestic and world politics, and so on track to become a superpower.

Oakeshott's critique is radical; indeed it is difficult from a reading of 'Rationalism in Politics' to see what political order would reconcile technical and practical knowledge. The attack on the 'new class' of politicians is so comprehensive as to imply that even Burke was insufficiently conservative. Oakeshott's argument would suggest a rejection of democracy. Since any return to a non-rationalist political project would itself be rationalist – for that non-rationalist order would have to be set out in a programme – Oakeshott's argument appears purely negative, and its negativity creates a contradiction: is not rationalism itself a tradition? This is a standard problem with conservative thought: if what matters is what exists, and if what exists is an apparently rationalist political order, then on what grounds can a conservative criticise it? The restoration of the 'old order' is not, and cannot be, a conservative project. Oakeshott's distinction between technical and practical knowledge, and the idea of an increasing predominance of the former over the latter, are interesting ideas, but they are not necessarily conservative ones.

In his book *On Human Conduct* Oakeshott presents a more 'positive' conception of politics. In that book he makes an important distinction between a civil association and an enterprise association. An enterprise association exists for, and justifies its existence in terms of, a particular end, or relatively coherent set of ends (Oakeshott, 1975: 108–18). These ends may be abstract, such as the maximisation of utility, or more concrete, such as the desire to maintain a particular cultural community. The enterprise association may not have a fully comprehensive set of aims – it might grant that individuals pursue different projects – but it will have some common aims. The commonly expressed desire to 'make the world a better place' would imply an enterprise attitude, even if people disagree over the best means of achieving it. A civil association, on the other hand, is a situation of mutual freedom under the rule of law. It is more than a Hobbesian state, for it implies mutual respect, and as such is a moral conception, but it is less than an enterprise. The best way to think about a civil association is as a set of rules that command respect not simply because they serve each person's self-interest, but because they allow human beings to choose how to live their lives. Although Oakeshott appears reactionary with regard to democratic politics, his argument in *On Human Conduct* comes close to being a liberal one.

Leo Strauss and American Neo-conservatism

An émigré from Nazi Germany to the United States, Leo Strauss (1899–1973) is regarded as an important influence on what is called neo-conservatism. Given the prominence of neo-conservative ideas in contemporary US political debate this makes Strauss a controversial figure and, as his ideas have become popularised, also a misunderstood one.

To understand Strauss's conservatism it is necessary to start with his approach to the history of ideas and the interpretation of texts. As we will see Strauss's conservatism is very different to that of Hume, Burke and Oakeshott, and it reflects the culture of both his adopted home of the United States and the history of his country of origin, Germany. After a brief discussion of Strauss's work we consider its influence on contemporary neo-conservative thought in the United States.

Strauss sought to revive both the reading of texts in the history of political thought, and the natural right tradition. The relationship between *reading* and *natural right* may not, at first sight, be obvious, and even less their relationship to *conservatism*, but the three are closely entwined. Natural right stands opposed to cultural relativism. Modern thought, according to Strauss, is characterised by a rejection of objective validity in favour of relativism (Strauss, 1953: 9). The starting point for a defence of natural right is the claim that radical historicism – that is, the view that morality is the product of immediate historical circumstances – must hold at least one thing as given by nature, and that is experience. There are many definitions of nature, but Strauss identifies two relevant ones: nature as the beginning of all things and nature as the character of something. For human beings, recognition of the first must depend on authority. For example, in Judaism and Christianity, the book of Genesis provides an account of humankind's origins. A refusal to accept the authority of the Bible undermines the force of that account, and leads to disagreement about human origins. Recognition of the second – nature as the character of something – depends upon human experience. Hume exemplifies this approach: there must be a sensation in order to have confidence that a thing exists. Since moral ideas – right and wrong – cannot be observed, modern political thinkers deny their existence.

Natural right teaching, which can be traced back to the ancient Greeks, holds that the good life is that which perfects human nature – we become what, by nature, we should be ('nature' is here used in the second sense of 'character', rather than the first sense of 'origin'). The logic of natural right is that those possessing the greatest wisdom should rule, and their power should be in proportion to their possession of the virtue of wisdom (Strauss, 1953: 102). This is incompatible with the modern – that is, post-Hobbesian – emphasis on consent: the rulers rule by the consent of the ruled and not by appeal to the rulers' superior wisdom. Strauss argues that under modern conditions the conflict can be reconciled by the rulers drawing up a code – or constitution – to which the people consent, and to which they can pledge allegiance. It is not difficult to see where this argument is heading: the recognition of the United States Constitution as the expression of natural right, and that Constitution should not be interpreted simply as a framework through which conflicts are settled, but must be understood as embodying religious virtue. Commitment to a 'politics of virtue' requires the resistance of tyranny, and this has practical implications for foreign policy, which we discuss briefly at the end of this section.

Strauss links his defence of natural right with a particular interpretation of the history of political thought. Drawing on Judaic ideas, Strauss argues that when we read pre-modern – and some modern – political texts we must 'read between the lines' (Strauss, 1973: 490). Writing has two levels: a popular or edifying teaching directed to a contemporary audience (the exoteric), and a 'hidden' or secret teaching that is only revealed on careful reading (the esoteric). The great political thinkers had a storehouse of literary devices that allowed them to obscure the meanings of their texts. The reason why they had to do this is made clear in the title of Strauss's *Persecution and the Art of Writing*. Thought is the enemy of tyranny, but it can only fight tyranny in its own way, and on its own terms, and that is in a literary way. Esoteric writing survives tyranny and transmits its message between political thinkers, and to their intelligent readers, across the centuries. Quite clearly, a cultural relativist will reject this claim, and argue that the only audience capable of being moved by a writer is the contemporary, or near-contemporary, one.

Strauss died in 1973, but if you enter cyberspace and do a web search using the keywords 'Leo Strauss' you will encounter a heated debate over his influence. Like much Internet debate, the subtleties of thought tend to be lost. However, it is interesting to explore the connections between Strauss and neo-conservatism. Although the term 'neo-conservative' – or 'neo-con' – is more often used as a pejorative term by its opponents than by those identified as neo-conservative it still has validity. The prefix neo- is intended to identify the movement as a distinct stream within US conservatism. It indicates that adherents are new to conservatism, but also that traditional conservatism is the subject of critique, and must be infused with new policy positions.

Many, but not all, leading neo-conservatives began their political life supporting what, in American terms, is the left: state intervention in the economy, policies to overcome poverty and the civil rights movement. In demographic terms neo-conservatives are drawn disproportionately from the Jewish and the Catholic communities of mainland European origin. This is significant because traditional conservatism was perceived as dominated by the so-called WASPs (white Anglo-Saxon Protestants) and hostile to the waves of immigrants who came to the United States in the late nineteenth and early twentieth centuries. Those waves of immigrants were subjected to 'assimilationist' policies (the 'great melting pot') and neo-conservatives place great value on the idea of a common US culture against what they see as the separatist multiculturalist policies in operation since the 1960s. While many neo-conservatives strongly believe that the civil rights movement was justified in its aims, they oppose affirmative action policies. Furthermore, neo-conservatives are much more prepared to support state spending if it will enable people to become responsible citizens, but this is combined with an emphasis on rewarding hard work through reductions in taxation. This twin-track approach was manifested in several key domestic policies of the Bush administration: the 'No Child Left Behind Act', which involved increased intervention by the centre (federal government) in the education system in order to improve educational standards among deprived groups; large tax cuts for the well off; and, partial privatisation of the state pension system. There is a Straussian influence here: objective natural right presupposes common standards and a common culture on which is based a political community that promotes virtue. The discrimination against black (and other) Americans is morally wrong, but so is what neo-conservatives believe to be the separatism inherent in multiculturalism. Individual initiative should be rewarded because it reflects a perfectionist ideal: that is, we realise, or perfect, our nature through virtuous acts.

It is, however, in foreign policy that the influence of neo-conservatives is most keenly felt. As suggested above, Strauss argued that tyranny should be resisted, and that resistance must sometimes be in the face of widespread opposition. International institutions such as the United Nations simply reflect cultural relativism, such that a vote in the UN General Assembly or by the Security Council signifies nothing more than the balancing of interests, or cultural differences. A just nation must find the justification for its actions out of a reflection on natural right, and not through the support of international organisations, although it should attempt to persuade other nations to join it in a 'coalition of the willing'. What drove many thinkers and political activists from the Democratic Party to the Republicans was the perceived weakness of the left in confronting the Soviet Union in the 1970s – whereas the left sought containment of the USSR, the neo-conservatives argued for a roll-back of Soviet power. In policy terms, the left supported Strategic Arms Limitation Treaties (SALT), whereas the neo-conservatives argued for an aggressive arms war so as to force the Soviet Union to spend beyond its means. Significantly, this critique of perceived weakness extended to traditional conservatives such as President Richard Nixon (US President, 1969–74) who initiated the SALT talks and also famously engaged with (Communist) China. At the beginning of the twenty-first century neo-conservatives see fundamentalist Islam as the main source of tyranny and liken the refusal of many European countries to engage with this perceived threat as a political manifestation of a deeper cultural relativism and decadence.

Conclusion: the Monarchy

At the beginning of this chapter we asked you to consider whether there were any arguments for the monarchy. The strongest objections to the monarchy come from an egalitarian-liberal perspective: the institution is incompatible with moral equality and is fundamentally undemocratic. In this concluding discussion we present the conservative case for the monarchy. We will focus primarily on Britain. Although some of the arguments are generalisable it is central to the thought of Hume, Burke and Oakeshott that institutions emerge gradually from particular cultures, such that whilst the monarchy is 'appropriate' to Britain it may not be suitable for, say, France, Germany or the United States.

(a) *All political institutions – including the monarchy – should be viewed ironically.* Although the term 'irony' is used in everyday discourse to denote something coincidental such as a legislator being convicted under a law that he himself has passed, we follow Richard Rorty's definition of an 'ironist' as someone who realises that something – although not perhaps anything – can be made to look good or bad by being redescribed. Ironists are 'never quite able to take themselves seriously because [they are] always aware that the terms in which they describe themselves are subject to change' (Rorty, 1989: 73–4). Rorty was not a conservative, but 'ironic conservatism' is intellectually possible. An ironic conservative could simultaneously accept that there is something absurd about the hereditary principle but at the same time take seriously the monarchy. The irony lies in using the vocabulary of democracy to defend an undemocratic institution. The Queen herself, perhaps unintentionally, offered an ironic defence of the monarchy at a dinner held in her honour: responding to the toast of the (then) Prime Minister, Tony Blair, she said that whilst Blair may have a rough time he only has to face the voters once every four or five years, whereas she has to face them every day. Of course, this is ironic, because she has never faced the voters in an election but her claim was understood by the audience and not thought absurd. Irony succeeds because it involves the ability to switch between two vocabularies – hereditary privilege and democratic accountability – without reducing one vocabulary to the other. That such a statement could not have been made by Queen Elizabeth 1 (1533–1603), Queen Anne (1665–1714), or even Queen Victoria (1819–1901) suggests something important about conservatism: we can hold on to the 'form' of an institution, such as the hereditary monarchy, but its underlying justification can change significantly. That so many people can accept the monarchy 'because it works' without engaging in complex justifications implies also a sense of irony on the part of the public. That laconic irony – 'it works' – contrasts with the absence of irony displayed both by opponents of the monarchy, who are outraged by the hereditary principle, and the tiny minority who literally defend the principle.

(b) *There must be elites that exert cultural influence.* Many liberals (liberal in the philosophical sense) argue that political institutions must be defensible from the standpoint of each individual. What we call normativity – the force that moves people to behave in certain ways – has its source in the reasoning capacities of individuals. Implicit in the conservatism of Hume, Burke, and Oakeshott is a different model of normativity: it is the public culture of a society – and above all cultural elites – who exert influence. Rather than trying to justify institutions via the device of a social contract (Hobbes, Locke, Kant) or pre-political moral rights (Locke and Kant again), we should be concerned with the production and reproduction of cultural elites. We need a class society: we cannot accept that all ways of life are equally valuable. For a

Ch. 8:
Liberation
pp. 181–89

conservative the decline of deference in Britain over the last thirty or so years and the increasing soap opera behaviour of many members of the Royal Family is troubling. The response to the death of Diana, Princess of Wales, is an indication of the waning power of cultural elites to set an example to which the populace can aspire. The collapse in the distinction between public and private is a reflection of a wider cultural decline: that people who never knew Diana believed that they could 'mourn' in the same way as Diana's own family and that the Queen's concern for protocol was taken as a sign of coldness is an indication of the inability to make distinctions that are central to civilisation. The conservative defence of elitism is a reversal of Nairn's charge that the monarch symbolises a hierarchical society – conservatives agree, but argue that elites are necessary.

(c) *Political institutions must be capable of being visualised – we need a 'state aesthetics'.* It is argued that Britain (or the United Kingdom) lacks a codified constitution. Some interpret this to mean that it has no constitution, for there is no body of law above statute law, but most legal and political theorists maintain that there are laws, conventions and precedents that have a privileged status and taken together form the UK's constitution. A more interesting – or novel – perspective is offered (separately) by two German writers, Karl Heinz Bohrer and Hans-Dieter Gelfert. Gelfert argues that what holds the British political system together is the ability of its citizens to 'picture' it. More than the political systems of most other countries British politics has a visual aspect, most clearly demonstrated in the annual State Opening of Parliament, where each component of the political system follows a prescribed ritual. What holds the constitution together is not a single norm or set of articles contained in a written constitution, but a visual (aesthetic) ordering of the different powers (Commons, Lords, monarch), each in its place. Furthermore – and this is the aspect most relevant to the conservative defence of the monarchy – each ritual corresponds to an historical event, so that the *evolution* of the political system is also visualised (Gelfert, 2005: 94–5). Bohrer talks of a 'state aesthetics': the electoral system that almost always creates one-party majority governments, the rapid and highly visual transfer of power in which the new Prime Minister travels from meeting the Queen at Buckingham Palace to making their speech on the steps of 10 Downing Street, and the confrontational nature of the House of Commons (Bohrer, 1982: 236–40). Together these elements generate an aesthetic of power that lifts politics above the banal. The abolition of the monarchy would pull apart and dissolve that aesthetic.

(d) *Political wisdom must be transmitted across generations.* Oakeshott argues we need families trained to govern. Even if you think Oakeshott's argument unacceptable – or perhaps simply ridiculous – a more moderate conservative argument would be that in the face of a generally meritocratic political system there is an argument for a Head of State who carries accumulated institutional wisdom. Queen Elizabeth II became monarch in 1952 at the age of twenty-six. Her first Prime Minister was Winston Churchill. She is now on her eleventh Prime Minister. Most weeks she holds an 'audience' with the current Prime Minister. Nobody else is present and no Prime Minister, past or present, is likely to divulge the advice she has given. The Queen, it might be argued, has accumulated experience, and although she may have her interests – the preservation of the monarchy and its privileges – she is 'above party politics', such that she can act as a stabilising influence. Of course, it is precisely this secrecy – and secret influence – that troubles opponents of the monarchy.

(e) *The monarchy encompasses but transcends the 'people'.* England (then the United Kingdom) achieved statehood before the development of the concept of the 'people'. The result was that membership of the political community depended on the individual's relationship to the Crown rather than the belonging to a 'sovereign people'. That the British were 'subjects' rather than 'citizens' has been identified by many critics, such as Nairn, as a sign of democratic immaturity. There may be force to this observation, and the UK has since the 1940s, and especially since the 1980s, moved closer to the mainland European model of citizenship. However, an *unintended* benefit of the subject-model is that British citizenship is much more elastic and inclusive than the citizenships of other countries. You can even consider the monarchy a strange institution, but still identify with the Crown – the institution not the person – as a guarantor of rights, rather than the expression of a culture. It is significant that whilst there have been fierce debates about immigration there has never been a debate in Britain over multiple citizenship. As far as the British state is concerned you can carry a suitcase full of passports, just so long as you do not attempt to use the citizenship of another country to escape your obligations as a UK citizen.

What we have presented above is a conservative defence of the monarchy. We do not necessarily endorse these arguments, but we have sought to show that conservatism has a complexity and sophistication that it is often not properly appreciated. The monarchy is a good case study through which to illustrate that complexity, for on the face of it the hereditary principle seems indefensible, yet at the same time large numbers of people in the United Kingdom – probably a stable majority – support the monarchy. Are they immature, or suffering from false consciousness, or attracted merely to the soap-operatic aspects of the institution? Why does the popular defence of the monarchy so frequently extend no further than saying 'it works', or that all the alternatives are worse? A conservative has an explanation: we intuitively recognise the importance of the institution, such that we do not need to theorise its existence. Like so many other institutions it is simply there.

Summary

The neo-conservatism inspired by Strauss seems a long way removed from the conservatism of Hume, Burke and Oakeshott. Given the historical distance from present events of Hume and Burke it is difficult, and perhaps intellectually suspect, to speculate on how they would respond to events in the twenty-first century, but certainly Oakeshott, who is not so distanced, would have rejected the foreign policy adventures of neo-conservatives. However, Oakeshott's work was aimed at a deeper level than policy, or even institutional design, for he saw rationalism in all spheres of social life, and in all political movements. Apart from a common emphasis on the interpenetration of state and society, and consequently the recognition that politics is concerned with the development of virtue and not simply the resolution of conflicting interests, there is little that holds the four thinkers together (and Oakeshott, in his later work, rejects the idea that politics should promote virtue). The contemporary relevance of traditional conservatism is seen less as an active ideology – party political conservatives are not really conservatives – but as an important source of ideas critical of the dominant liberal ideology. The core of conservatism is its critique of rationalism.

Questions

1. If conservatives are sceptical about reason how can they criticise society?
2. What are the arguments for, and against, the monarchy, as it operates in the United Kingdom, the Netherlands, Spain and other countries? To what extent are arguments for the monarchy 'conservative'?
3. Under what circumstances should people attempt to overturn the existing political system?
4. 'Those who do not remember the past are condemned to repeat it' (George Santayana). Do you agree?

References

Almond, G. and Verba, S. (1963) *The Civic Culture: Political Attitudes and Democracy in Five Nations* Princeton, NJ: Princeton University Press.

Bohrer, K.H. (1982) *Ein Bißchen Lust am Untergang: englische Ansichten* Munich/Vienna: Suhrkamp.

Burke, E. (1969) *Reflections on the Revolution in France* (ed. Conor Cruise O'Brien), Harmondsworth: Penguin.

Burke, E. (1975) *On Government, Politics and Society* (ed. B.W. Hill) London: Fontana/The Harvester Press.

Gelfert, H.-D. (2005) *Typisch englisch: wie die Briten wurden, was sie sind* Munich: C.H. Beck.

Hume, D. (1963) *Essays, Moral, Political and Literary* Oxford: Oxford University Press.

Hume, D. (1978) *A Treatise of Human Nature* (ed. L.A. Selby-Bigge) Oxford: Clarendon Press.

Nairn, T. (1988) *The Enchanted Glass: Britain and its Monarchy* London: Radius.

Oakeshott, M. (1933) *Experience and its Modes* Cambridge: Cambridge University Press.

Oakeshott, M. (1962) *Rationalism in Politics and Other Essays* London: Methuen.

Oakeshott, M. (1975) *On Human Conduct* Oxford: Clarendon Press.

Rorty, R. (1989) *Contingency, Irony and Solidarity* Cambridge: Cambridge University Press.

Strauss, L. (1953) *Natural Right and History* Chicago, IL: University of Chicago Press.

Strauss, L. (1973) *Persecution and The Art of Writing* Westport, CT: Greenwood Press.

Further Reading

General introductions to conservative thought and practice include: Noel O'Sullivan, *Conservatism* (London: Dent, 1976); Ted Honderich, *Conservatism* (London: Penguin, 1991); Roger Scruton, *The Meaning of Conservatism* (Basingstoke: Palgrave, 2001). Both Scruton and Honderich are quite polemical – Scruton from a right-wing perspective sympathetic to conservatism, Honderich from a hostile left-wing perspective. John Kekes, *A Case for Conservatism* (Ithaca, NY and London: Cornell University Press, 1998), is not an introduction but is interesting if you want a more involved defence of conservatism. There are various anthologies of conservative thought, the most useful being Roger Scruton (ed.), *Conservative Texts: An Anthology* (Basingstoke: Macmillan, 1991), and Jerry Muller (ed.), *Conservatism: An Anthology of Social and Political Thought from David Hume to the Present* (Princeton, NJ: Princeton University Press, 1997). In these books you will find extracts from the most important conservative thinkers, including the four discussed in this chapter. Scruton has also edited a series of essays on conservative thinkers, although, as with the anthologies, the definition of 'conservative' is stretched quite wide: Roger Scruton (ed.), *Conservative Thinkers: Essays from the Salisbury Review* (London: Claridge, 1988). Finally, a discussion of Strauss's influence on US conservatism can be found in Shadia Drury, *Leo Strauss and the American Right* (Basingstoke: Macmillan, 1997).

Weblinks

Web searches using the key words 'conservative', 'conservatism' and even 'conservative thought' tend to throw up party political sites, or highly polemical sites. It is worth taking a look at these simply to get a flavour of how the term is used, and possibly abused, in cyberspace. However, for sites of greater relevance to this chapter we would recommend those dedicated to the conservative thinkers:

- David Hume: http://www.humesociety.org/;
  http://plato.stanford.edu/entries/hume/

- Edmund Burke: http://www.kirkcenter.org/burke/ebsa.html;
  http://plato.stanford.edu/entries/burke/

- Michael Oakeshott: http://www.michael-oakeshott-association.com/

- Leo Strauss: http://www.frontpagemag.com/Articles/ReadArticle.asp?ID=1233;
  http://www.straussian.net/

- Also useful is Roger Scruton's website: http://www.rogerscruton.com/ (as you will see from the Further Reading section Scruton is a prominent contemporary British conservative thinker).

Chapter 10

Socialism

Introduction

Is socialism dead? This provocative point was argued by many conservatives, and the former British Prime Minister, Mrs Thatcher in particular, after the collapse of the Communist Party states.

The difficulty in deciding whether socialism is dead is that socialism, like feminism, is bedevilled by the problem of variety. Socialism comes in many different shapes and forms. The recent Iraq War saw the British government, which would consider itself socialist, waging armed struggle along with the USA against a regime which would also call itself socialist. Do the diverse kinds of socialism have anything in common?

Can **socialism** be defined? Is it an impossible dream? Do more 'realistic' forms of socialism sacrifice their very socialism when they become more pragmatic? These are all questions we shall try to answer.

Chapter Map

- The problem of variety and a working definition of socialism.

- The problem of Utopia as one to which socialism is peculiarly prone. Three nineteenth-century socialists, regarded by Marxists as utopian, but who consider their own work scientific and realistic.

- Marxism as one of the variants of socialism: Marxism is a theory that tends to authoritarianism in practice.

- The distinct character of democratic socialism or social democracy and the impact made upon British labour by the 'revisionist' theory of Eduard Bernstein.

- The link between class and agency, freedom and determinism.

- The argument that socialists do not have to choose between being utopian or being realistic.

Tanks in the Streets of Prague

Young Czech girl lets her feelings be known as she shouts 'Ivan Go Home!' to Russian soldiers
participating in the suppression of the 'Prague Spring', 1968

Source: © Bettmann/CORBIS

Y ou are studying in Prague in 1968. In the spring there is much excitement because the leader of the Communist Party (CP) argues that Czech socialism is crying out for reform. Although you feel that the changes proposed are rather modest, you see them as steps in the right direction. Novotny had been replaced in January 1968 by Dubček as the party leader, who pledges to remove everything that 'strangles scientific and artistic creativeness'. Censorship is abolished and citizens given the right to criticise the government. With the Action Programme, passed in 1968, a much freer electoral system is proposed. There is no question, however, of opposition parties being permitted. The economy is to be more responsive to the market and the consumer, and workers' councils are to be established to assist in decentralisation.

However, you are understandably alarmed by the claims by the USSR in September that West Germany is planning to invade Czechoslovakia, and you are concerned that some communists regard the new proposals as dangerously 'revisionist'. In August of the same year, tanks roll into Prague from other countries in the Warsaw Pact (of which Czechoslovakia is a member) led by the USSR. Following the invasion, Dubček and the new president Svoboda are taken to Moscow and after 'free comradely discussion', they announce that Czechoslovakia will be abandoning its reform programme. In April 1969 Dubček is replaced as party secretary by a hardliner, Husak, the following year he is expelled from the party, and for the next 18 years works as a clerk in a lumber-yard in Slovakia.

Continued

The claim is made that Dubček intended to take his country out of the Warsaw Pact and reintroduce a capitalist society. Half a million members of the Czech Communist Party are expelled, and large numbers of writers, scientists, and artists lose their jobs. About 120,000 leave the country. The secret police become particularly active. It is estimated that only 2 per cent of the population support the invasion.

Confronted with a collision of this kind:

- Would you see one side as socialist and the other side as not?
- Or would you feel that two different kinds of socialism had come into opposition?

Are the members of the Warsaw Pact who invade Czechoslovakia:

- Betraying their commitment to socialism?
- Or is this the kind of action that flows from their commitment to Marxist principles?
- Is Dubček being naive to consider himself as a communist at all? Would the notion of change that he is proposing undermine not only Soviet control over Eastern Europe but lead to the development of market forces that would necessarily destroy socialism itself and lead to the introduction of capitalism?

The Problem of Variety

Tony Wright calls his book *Socialisms* (1996) in order to emphasise the plurality of approaches and doctrines that make up the socialist movement. The term is certainly elastic and covers a wide range of contradictory movements.

Some socialists are religious, others doggedly atheistic in character. Some advocate revolution, others reform. Nor are the alignments simple. Authoritarian socialisms may be atheistic (as in the communist tradition) but they need not be (think of Saddam Hussein's regime that claimed adherence to some kind of Islamic tradition). Some socialists like Tony Benn may be radical and admire the role of parliament, other socialists may stress the importance of parliament as a bulwark against radicalism. Others still invert this view and see parliamentary democracy as an obstacle to socialist advance.

The distinction between Marxism and social democracy is the major fault line among socialisms. Sometimes it is argued that the differences between Marxism and social democracy are so substantial that communism should be distinguished from socialism. Since Marxists referred to themselves as 'scientific socialists', we will reject this argument while stressing the differences between revolutionary and evolutionary varieties of socialism.

We will use the term social democracy interchangeably with democratic socialism. The history of socialist thought is thick with accusations of betrayal. Lenin believed that social democrats were traitors to socialism because they supported the First World War and opposed the Russian Revolution; socialists influenced by libertarian or anarchist ideas felt that Lenin and the Bolsheviks had betrayed the Soviet experiment by crushing the rebellion of Bolshevik sailors that took place in Kronstadt in 1921; Trotsky and his supporters felt that Stalin had reneged on the revolutionary traditions of Lenin by seeking to build socialism in one country; Mao and many Chinese communists believed that the Russians had surrendered to capitalism and the market after 1956.

These differences have deeply divided socialists. The British Labour Party repeatedly refused the request for affiliation from the Communist Party of Great Britain (CPGB) on the grounds that the latter supported dictatorship and not democracy, while communists have been deeply divided among themselves. This could come to armed conflict – as between the Soviet Union and the Peoples' Republic of China in the 1960s – or the intervention of Vietnam into Cambodia or Kampuchea in 1978. The Warsaw Pact's interventions into Hungary in 1956 or Czechoslovakia in 1968 (see the case study above) were intended to snuff out reform communists, and Western communists influenced by social democratic and liberal ideas called themselves 'Eurocommunists' so as to distance themselves from the Soviet system.

Social Democracy/Democratic Socialism	Marxism/Scientific Socialism
Moderate classes	Eliminate classes
Utilise the state	Go beyond the state
Parliament	Workers' Councils
Ethically desirable	Historically inevitable
Nation as a whole	Workers and their allies

Defining Socialism

It is interesting that Bernard Crick, in his book *In Defence of Politics*, which originally appeared in 1963 (Crick, 1992), saw conservatives, social democrats and liberals as exponents of politics – which Crick defined as an activity which seeks to conciliate and compromise. He contrasted them with nationalists, communists, and extremists of various kinds. Nevertheless despite their differences, we shall locate the common features of all socialists in terms of the following:

(a) *an optimistic view of human nature* – a view that human nature is either changeable or does not constitute a barrier to social regulation or ownership. The notion that humans are too selfish to cooperate and have common interests contradicts socialist doctrine.

(b) *a stress on cooperation* – all socialists hold that people can and should work together so that the market and capitalism need at the very least some adjustment in order to facilitate cooperation. Competition may be seen as an aid to, or wholly incompatible with, cooperation, but the latter is the guiding principle.

(c) *a positive view of freedom* – a notion that the question of freedom must be examined in a social context and therefore in the context of resources of a material kind. The right to read and write, for example, requires the provision of schooling if such a right is to be meaningful.

(d) *support for equality* – socialists define equality in dramatically different ways, but all, it seems to us, must subscribe to equality in some form or other. This, Crick argues, is 'the basic value in any imaginable or feasible socialist society' (1987: 88).

These characteristics explain why socialism, though a broad church, is not infinitely elastic. Dr Verwoerd, the architect of apartheid, was sometimes accused by his free-market critics of being a socialist, and the Nazi Party described itself as a 'national socialist' organisation. We want to argue that although socialism stretches from Pol Pot to Tony Blair, it cannot incorporate those who specifically and deliberately reject the notion of equality.

There is a further characteristic of socialism that is more contentious.

The Problem of Utopia

All socialists are vulnerable to the charge of utopianism – of trying to realise a society that is contrary to human experience and historical development. Socialists disagree as to whether utopianism is a good thing or a bad thing. In his famous book on the subject, *Utopia*, More created the notion of a good society (eutopia) that is nowhere (utopia = no place) (Geoghegan, 1987: 1). Karl Mannheim (an interwar German sociologist) in *Ideology and Utopia* (1936) defined Utopia as an idea that was 'situation transcending' or 'incongruent with reality': it 'breaks the bonds of the existing order' (1960: 173).

While some socialists have seen Utopia as a good thing, liberals and conservatives regard the notion of Utopia as negative – an irresponsible idealism that rides roughshod over the hard facts of reality that can at worst lead to nightmarish regimes of a highly oppressive and totalitarian kind. Heywood argues that all

Oscar Wilde commented:

A map of the world which does not include Utopia is not worth glancing at, for it leaves out the one country at which Humanity is always landing. And when Humanity lands there, it looks out and, seeing a better country, sets sail. Progress is the realisation of Utopias.

('The Soul of Man Under Socialism', *Complete Works of Oscar Wilde*, p. 1184, Glasgow: Harper Collins, 1996).

socialists are utopians since they develop 'better visions of a better society in which human beings can achieve genuine emancipation and fulfilment as members of a community' (1992: 96). He even extends this to Marxism where he describes communism as 'a utopian vision of a future society envisaged and described by Marx and Engels'. On the other hand, he acknowledges that the issue is controversial, since he also notes that Marx and Engels supported 'scientific socialism' and rejected what they called the 'utopian socialism' (Heywood, 1992: 115, 127).

Geoghegan declares himself 'in praise of utopianism' despite the fact that utopianism is characterised as a defence of an activity that is 'unrealistic', 'irrational', 'naive', 'self-indulgent', 'unscientific', 'escapist' and 'elitist'. He premises his praise on support for an 'ought' that is in opposition to an 'is' (1987: 1–2). But does this mean that socialism can never be realised? It is not clear from Geoghegan's argument whether socialist utopianism is an 'ought' permanently at war with an 'is', or whether the problem lies with the critics of utopianism who are guilty of a 'sad dualism': unreality, error and subjectivity on the one side; realism, truth and objectivity on the other (Geoghegan, 1987: 22). Can socialism overcome this dualism – so that it is both realist and utopian at the same time?

Bauman argues that we should view utopias positively – as a necessary condition of historical change (1976: 13) – but is it possible for a Utopia to avoid the charge that it is inherently unrealistic? Bauman insists that a Utopia 'sets the stage for a genuinely realistic politics'. It extends the meaning of realism to encompass the full range of possible options (1976: 13). Utopias make conscious the major divisions of interest within society: the future is portrayed as a set of competing projects (1976: 15). Bauman draws a distinction between perfection as a stable and immutable state, and perfectibility that paves the way for Utopia (1976: 19).

It is still unclear as to whether we can we ever have a society that is socialist. Bauman appears to argue that socialism is the counter-culture of capitalist society (1976: 36), and it cannot be empirical reality, a society in its own right.

Science and the 'Utopian Socialists'

Three socialists were singled out by Engels as being utopian. They were

- Henri Saint Simon (1760–1825)
- Charles Fourier (1773–1837)
- Robert Owen (1771–1858)

In fact, each of them considered their own work to be scientific and practical.

Saint Simon took the view that the French Revolution had neglected class structure in the name of human rights. He included industrialists and bankers in the 'producing' class, believing that workers and capitalists have a unity of interests, sustained by what Saint Simon believed would be a spread of wealth and ownership across society as a whole.

Is it right to call this argument 'utopian'? Saint Simon believed that the old order had unwittingly produced the basis for a new order, and indeed, he sounds like a Marxist steeped in Hegelian dialectics when he argues that 'everything is relative – that is the only absolute' (Geoghegan, 1987: 11). His celebrated argument that the state gives way to administration (so central to Marxist theory), was based upon a belief that the modern credit and banking system had already demonstrated its attachment to scientific principles, and that these could exert a discipline that would make the state redundant. Why did Engels call this system 'utopian' when it so manifestly stresses the importance of science and historical necessity? Saint Simon clearly does not fit into Engels' view that modern socialism is based upon the class antagonism between capitalist and wage worker (Marx and Engels, 1968: 399). But it does seem unfair to ascribe to Saint Simon (as Engels does to the utopians in general) the view that socialism is not an 'inevitable event' but a happy accident, when Saint Simon had laid so much emphasis on science and historical development.

Fourier, on the other hand, did consider the worker and capitalists to have conflicting interests. He was particularly concerned at the way in which the industrial revolution has stripped work of its pleasure. His solution was to establish 'phalanteres' – cooperative communities of some 1,600 people working in areas of around 5,000 acres in the countryside or small towns. Fourier was adamant that his was not a utopian socialism. He described utopias as 'dreams', schemes without an effective method that have 'led people to the very opposite of the state of well being they promised them' (Geoghegan, 1987: 17). He believed that his socialism was based on a scientific project for reconstruction. Indeed, so precise a science was socialism, that Fourier took the view that civilised society has 144 evils; humans have 12 basic passions; they do 12 different jobs; and need 9 meals to sustain them.

As for Robert Owen: he saw himself as a practical, hard-headed person of business, and he owned cotton mills in New Lanark in Scotland. He was struck as to how under rational socialist management, they could still be profitable, and he decided to advocate village cooperatives between 300 and 2,000 people working land between 600–1,800 acres. It is true that his schemes were dogged by failure. The community that he established at New Harmony in the USA collapsed after three years in 1827, and his labour bazaars at which goods were to be exchanged according to the amount of labour embodied in them, did not survive the economic crisis of 1834. His national trade union was called a 'grand national moral union for the productive classes', but his dictatorial leadership demonstrated the problem with his theory of character. Character was, as Geoghegan points out, externally determined, so that only an exceptional person (like Owen!) could initiate reform for a relatively passive population (Geoghegan, 1987: 14).

He had, however, a lasting effect on the British labour movement as a practical reformer, and the consumer cooperatives that he advocated still exist – the Co-op stores – on every high street in British cities today. Although Owen's notion of science stems from an uncritical reading of the Enlightenment, he certainly regarded himself as a person of scientific, secular and empirical values. Indeed, a youthful Engels was to describe Owen's views as 'the most practical and fully worked out' of all the socialists (Geoghegan, 1987: 23).

Introducing Marxism

The belief that socialism should be scientific and not utopian is highly contentious. There is a terminological point that we need to tackle right away. In the *Communist Manifesto* of 1848, Engels was to explain that the term 'communism' was preferred because it was seen as a working class movement from below. Socialism, he argued, was a respectable movement initiated from above (Marx and Engels, 1967: 62). Later Marxists called themselves socialists and social democrats. It was only after 1917 when Lenin and the Bolsheviks wanted to distance themselves from other socialists (who had supported the First World War and opposed the Russian Revolution) that the term 'communist' was resurrected.

Berki has argued that Marx transformed socialism from underdog to a 'fully grown part of the modern landscape' (1974: 56). Both Marx and Engels highly prized scholarship and learning. Marx was a philosopher, who devoted most of his life to studying political economy, and in 1863 published *Das Kapital*, or *Capital*, a work that Engels was to describe as the bible of the working class. Engels, for his part, read and wrote widely about natural science, anthropology, history, politics and economics, and both regarded science, not as the pursuit of facts rather than values, but simply as coherent and systematic thought.

Why did Engels in particular see Saint Simon, Fourier and Owen as utopians? In the *Communist Manifesto* Marx and Engels praised the 'utopians' for producing 'the most valuable materials for the enlightenment of the working class'. Measures like the abolition of the distinction between town and country; the disappearance of the family; the wages system; the private ownership of industry; the dying out of the state; and a positive relationship between the individual and society were suggested by the utopians and became part of Marx and Engels' own arguments. Nevertheless, the label is contentious, for Marx and Engels clearly regarded the utopians as painting 'fantastic pictures of a future society', a fantasy which reflected the historically undeveloped state of the working class itself (1967: 116).

Why then was Marxism seen as scientific? Marxism, Marx and Engels argued, is a scientific socialism, because it is

- *a theory of class conflict.* It holds that in class-divided societies there are incompatible social interests that lead to exploitation. This is why class is both an economic and a political reality, since between the classes there is war. In contrast, the utopians seek change through general principles of 'reason' and 'justice'.
- *a theory of revolution.* Such is the incompatibility of class interests, change can only come through revolution. Although the *Communist Manifesto* describes

revolution in violent terms, Marx's later position was that revolutions can be peaceful, even constitutional, but they will be violent if necessary. Because classes are political as well as economic entities, they seek to control the state in their own interest, so that the state has a class character. Utopians, by contrast, seek peaceful and sometimes piecemeal change, appealing to all classes in society for support, and invariably seeing the state as part of the solution rather than part of the problem.

- *a theory of history.* All societies are basically moulded by the conflict between the forces of production (which embrace science and technology) and the relations of production (the system of ownership). These two elements form a basis upon which arises a 'superstructure' that incorporates political institutions, educational systems, culture and ideas. In class-divided societies the conflict between the forces and relations of production creates the need for revolution, so that under capitalism, the social character of the forces of production comes into sharp and increasing conflict with the private relations of production. That is why revolution is inevitable. After this revolution, class divisions disappear, and with the disappearance of these divisions, the need for a state itself withers.

- *a theory of society.* Central to this theory of history is a theory of society which argues that people enter into relations of production 'independent of their will'. This means that although human activity is a conscious activity, the consequences of this activity are never the same as those intended. Capitalism is seen as a system that unwittingly creates the working class, educates them through factory production, goads them into struggle and ultimately drives them to revolution. By way of contrast, 'utopians' do not see capitalism as a contra-dictory system, a system that is self-destructive. They do not accept the particular role of the workers in providing leadership to a political movement for social emancipation, nor do they accept the need for a communist or socialist party to provide leadership for revolution. Socialism, as far as they see it, is merely 'desirable' and not inevitable.

The Authoritarian Consequences of 'Scientific Socialism'

In our view, there are a number of problems with the theory (and not merely the practice) of 'scientific socialism'. We would list them as:

(a) the argument of inevitability – the major problem;

(b) the theory of class war;

(c) a rejection of 'moralism',

(d) the question of leadership – a relatively minor problem.

It will be argued that together these problems explain why Communist Party (CP) states following the theory of 'scientific socialism' have proved vulnerable to popular (even proletarian) protest. We have seen how attempts to make Communist Party states more democratic were resisted by the Soviet leadership in 1968 and today only North Korea, Cuba, China and Vietnam remain as CP states. Former CPs changed their names – usually to include democracy in their title – and they invariably describe themselves as socialist rather than communist. What relationship exists between the hapless fate of these states, and the theory of scientific socialism? It is worth giving this question some thought.

The Inevitability Argument

In Part I of the *Communist Manifesto*, the victory of the proletariat is described as 'inevitable', as in the famous comment that 'what the bourgeoisie . . . produces, above all, is its own grave-diggers. Its fall and the victory of the proletariat are equally inevitable' (Marx and Engels, 1967: 94). This has become a central theme of Marxism in general, and Engels was to argue that revolutions are 'the necessary outcome of circumstances, quite independent of the will or guide of particular parties' (Hoffman, 1995: 135). Marxism is 'scientific' because it arises from the real movement of history that compels people to do things whether they like it or not. Revolution is (in some sense of the term) a 'natural' process, driven by the antagonistic conflict between the forces and relations of production at the heart of society. It is therefore unavoidable. There are a number of problems with the 'inevitability argument'.

What Happens when Revolutions are 'Bourgeois' in Character?

In the *Communist Manifesto* Marx and Engels declare that 'Communists every-where support every revolutionary movement against the existing order of things' (1967: 120). Contrary to the utopians who support socialism rather than capitalism, Marxists will support a 'bourgeois revolution' in countries where liberal constitutionalism has yet to prevail: in Germany, as the *Communist Manifesto* points out, communists will fight with the bourgeoisie where the latter are acting in a revolutionary way. This notion is of the utmost importance, for it explains the attraction of Marxism in colonial countries or autocratic regimes of a feudal or semi-feudal kind. But what has a liberal revolution to do with communism?

One of the most contentious aspects of the *Communist Manifesto* derives from the argument that once the old absolutist regime has fallen, 'the fight against the bourgeoisie itself may immediately begin'. The argument here focuses on Germany in 1848. Given the much more advanced conditions of European civilisation and 'a much more developed proletariat', 'the bourgeois revolution in Germany will be but the prelude to an immediately following proletarian revolution' (Marx and Engels, 1967: 120). This sentence was seen by the Bolsheviks as giving the October revolution its classical Marxist credentials, since Russia of 1917 was deemed analogous to Germany of 1848, because of the combination of material backwardness and heightened political consciousness. The destruction of Tsarism – the bourgeois revolution – could then be 'the prelude to an immediately following proletarian revolution'.

Hunt has argued at some length that this formulation – which nowhere else occurs in Marx's writing – was put in to appease the members of the Communist League who commissioned the *Manifesto*. They did not like the idea of a bourgeois revolution anyway, but a bourgeois revolution immediately followed by a proletarian one, was enough to sugar the pill. Hunt's argument is that this notion of permanent revolution – that a bourgeois revolution becomes relatively quickly a proletarian one – does not square with classical Marxism and the emphasis placed elsewhere in the *Communist Manifesto* on the gradual, step by step, education of the proletariat preparing them for revolution and power (Hunt, 1975: 180, 246). Whatever tactical considerations played their part in this fateful formulation, the argument is never actually repudiated by Marx and Engels, although they did later speak of the *Communist Manifesto* as an 'historical document which we have no longer any right to alter' (Marx and Engels, 1967: 54). Whether we find Hunt's argument convincing, the point is that the notion that one revolution can immediately follow another has had significant historical consequences, and has come to be seen as part and parcel of Marxist theory.

The implication is that relatively undeveloped countries can become socialist or communist without the lengthy period of preparation which capitalism unwittingly and normally allows the proletariat. Since this period is precisely the one in which workers become familiar with liberal ideas and institutions, it is not difficult to see that the omission or dramatic compression of such a period can only increase the need for the authoritarian leadership of a 'vanguard' party, and authoritarian political institutions themselves. Is it surprising then that the USSR, and later the People's Republic of China, followed a development in which the liberal tradition was suppressed, rather than made the basis for further political advance?

What Happens when Revolutions are 'Pre-mature'?

Engels told the German socialist Weydemeyer that 'we shall find ourselves compelled to make communist experiments and leaps which no-one knows better than ourselves to be untimely' (Hoffman, 1995: 135). But if revolution is deemed inevitable, then Marxists will 'find themselves' compelled to support 'experiments' and 'leaps' which are not only untimely, but can only be sustained by authoritarian institutions. A good example of this problem can be seen in relation to Marx and Engels' attitude towards the Paris Commune. Because of the heroism of the Communards, Marx extolled the virtues of the Commune. This he did in a book called *The Civil War in France*, which outlined a radical polity that became the basis of Lenin's blueprint in *The State and Revolution* written in 1918.

Ch. 11:
Anarchism
p. 228

Yet the Commune was in reality influenced by Blanquism (a rather elitist and coercive egalitarianism named after the French socialist Blanqui, 1805–81) and anarchist trends, and reflected what has been called 'an unsophisticated anti-bureaucratism' (Hoffman, 1995: 137) – an anti-bureaucratism that enshrined anti-liberal political practices. Despite his private reservations, Marx felt obliged publicly to support an 'experiment' that could only have succeeded if power had been concentrated in an unambiguously authoritarian manner.

Rosa Luxemburg, the Bolshevik Revolution and Stalinism

Marx's 'support' for the Paris Commune is not an isolated example. The Polish Marxist, Rosa Luxemburg, was to defend the Bolshevik Revolution in the same way and for the same reasons that Marx and Engels had praised the Paris Commune. The Bolsheviks, she argued, have acted with immense heroism: the Revolution was an act of proletarian courage, and she supported it. On the other hand, she was alarmed by the authoritarianism of Lenin and Trotsky and she was particularly critical when the two leaders dispersed the Constituent Assembly in 1918, when it was returned with a socialist, but not a Bolshevik majority. She thought that the revolution was bound to fail. In fact, the Russian Revolution succeeded by crushing its opponents, and Luxemburg, who was assassinated by German soldiers in 1919, never lived to see how a virtue was made of necessity first by Lenin and then by Stalin.

A whole generation of communists in liberal countries were prepared to support Stalin and Stalinism on the grounds that such rule was 'inevitable'. This position also created a grave dilemma for Stalin's critics like Trotsky who supported the Russian Revolution and had shown his own illiberal tendencies. Crick expresses quite a common view when he says that 'it would have made little difference had Trotsky, not Stalin succeeded Lenin' (1987: 62). Engels was to argue (in response to the anarchists) that 'revolution is the most authoritarian thing there is' (Tucker, 1978: 733). A theory that regards such an event as 'inevitable' will produce despotic political practices.

The Concept of Class War and the Problem of Morality

Let us look at the other factors that arguably demonstrate a link between Marxism as a scientific socialism and the authoritarianism that created the popular upheavals in 1989. Marxism embraces a polarising concept of class war, and this can only reinforce its authoritarian consequences. Such a concept has excluded or marginalised a whole series of struggles – for women's equality, gay rights, religious toleration, ecological sensitivity, etc. – which are clearly central to the goal of emancipation, but which don't fit in with the notion that the proletariat and only the proletariat, has a leading role to play. A disdain for moral argument encourages the view that rights don't matter since we must choose between proletarian morality and bourgeois morality.

Leadership is a problem for all political movements that seek to change society in the interests of the poor and the relatively inarticulate, since people from relatively comfortable backgrounds will tend to monopolise leadership skills. This problem is aggravated by a belief that utopian ideals are mere fantasies. A 'scientific' attitude ought to be tolerant and empirical, but in Marxism, the notion of leaders spearheading revolutionary processes that are deemed inevitable and historically necessary, must give a further twist to an authoritarian version of socialism whose state and political institutions are illiberal, and – despite Marxist theory on this point - refuse to 'wither away'.

The Paris Commune

The Paris Commune was created in 1871 after France was defeated by Prussia in the Franco-Prussian war. The French government tried to send in troops to prevent the Parisian National Guard's cannon from falling into the hands of the population. The soldiers refused to fire on the jeering crowd and turned their weapons on their officers.

In the free elections called by the Parisian National Guard, the citizens of Paris elected a council made up of a majority of Jacobins and Republicans and a minority of socialists (mostly Blanquists – explicitly authoritarian socialists – and followers of the anarchist Proudhon). This council proclaimed Paris autonomous and desired to recreate France as a confederation of communes (i.e. communities). Within the Commune, the elected council people were paid an average wage. In addition, they had to report back to the people who had elected them and were subject to recall by electors if they did not carry out their mandates.

The Paris Commune began the process of creating a new society, one organised from the bottom up. By May, 43 workplaces were cooperatively run and the Louvre Museum became a munitions factory run by a workers' council. A meeting of the Mechanics Union and the Association of Metal Workers argued that 'equality must not be an empty word' in the Commune. The Commune declared that the political unity of society was based on 'the voluntary association of all local initiatives, the free and spontaneous concourse of all individual energies for the common aim, the well-being, the liberty and the security of all'.

On 21 May government troops entered the city, and this was followed by seven days of bitter street fighting. Squads of soldiers and armed members of the 'bourgeoisie' roamed the streets, killing and maiming at will. Over 25,000 people were killed in the street fighting, many murdered after they had surrendered, and their bodies dumped in mass graves.

The Commune had lasted for 72 days, and Marx, as President of the International Working Men's Association – the First International – expressed solidarity and support for the action. Yet 10 years later, Marx declared that the Commune was the rising of a city under exceptional conditions; that its majority was by no means socialist, nor could it be, and that with a 'modicum of common sense', a compromise with the French Government at Versailles could have been reached (1975b: 318).

The Dilemma of Democratic Socialism

Until 1914 (as noted above), the term 'social democrat' was widely adopted. It was used both by the Bolsheviks and the British Labour Party. In 1914 a great schism occurred. Some socialists supported the First World War, and this divide was deepened when the Bolshevik Revolution took place in 1917. Although socialists generally welcomed the fall of Tsarism in February 1917, many including those who considered themselves Marxists saw the seizure of power by Lenin in October 1917 as the act of mad man, a *coup d'état* rather than a genuine revolution, a premature act which ignored the 'unripe' conditions in Russia.

From then on, the concept of a social democrat became a term of differentiation, with the emphasis now on democracy. Socialists who opposed the Russian Revolution and subsequent Leninist and Stalinist rule, invariably called themselves democratic socialists – a term we shall use interchangeably with social democrat.

Socialism, it was argued, is concerned with reforms, not revolution: it must develop through parliamentary democracy, not through workers' councils or soviets. It must express itself through electoral victory, not a seizure of power: nor should socialists tie themselves to the leadership of the working class. Socialism involves the whole nation – not simply a part of it – and socialism must be realistic, attained through piecemeal reforms and in a manner that works with, and respects, the liberal tradition. As the French socialist, Jean Jaures put it, 'the great majority of the nation can be won over to our side by propaganda and lawful action and led to socialism' (Berki, 1974: 91–2).

Social democracy sees itself as everything that Marxism is not: democratic, reformist, realistic, open-minded and concerned with the moral case for socialism. What is its dilemma? It is so anti-utopian that it is vulnerable to the charge that it is no different in essence from liberalism and even more flexible versions of conservatism. Is it a movement in its own right? Berki makes the point that just as in Aristotle aristocracy can turn into its degenerate form, oligarchy, so social democracy can turn into its degenerate form, which is electoralism (1974: 104), i.e. a concern to win elections without worrying about principles at all.

In other words, social democracy suffers from a serious identity problem. It is so pragmatic and flexible, so concerned with avoiding divisiveness and outraging, as Durbin puts it, 'the conservative sections of all classes' (Berki, 1974: 103), that it becomes a form of conservatism itself (or liberalism), and cannot be called socialism at all. Socialism, we have argued, is vulnerable to the charge of utopianism: but a forthright rebuttal of utopianism of any kind may mean that the transformative element in socialism is lost, and socialism degenerates.

Eduard Bernstein and the German Socialists

Eduard Bernstein is a significant figure to examine, for his critique of classical Marxism formed the theory and practice of what came to be called social democracy. He influenced a tradition that was resistant to theory. In his work, social democracy is not only contrasted explicitly and in detail to Marxism, but its own premises are lucidly displayed. Indeed, the book that has the English title of *Evolutionary Socialism* was actually called (if one translates the German directly) *The Premises of Socialism and the Task of Social Democracy.*

Bernstein joined the German Socialists in 1872. When the warring groups united, the party went from electoral success to electoral success. In 1876 it won 9 per cent of the votes cast (Gay, 1962: 38–9). Bismarck, the German Chancellor, used the attempt to assassinate the Emperor (not it should be said by socialists) to harass the party. Bernstein, who was in Switzerland at the time, became converted to Marxism.

Despite the problems caused by Bismarck's anti-socialist law (which only lapsed in 1890), the party polled 12 per cent of the vote in the elections of 1881 (Gay, 1962: 52). In 1884 the party sent 24 members to the Reichstag – the German parliament. Under renewed pressure from Bismarck, Bernstein was forced to leave Switzerland, and went to London. In 1890 the party secured nearly 20 per cent of the vote in the national elections and increased its number of MPs to 35. By 1903 the SPD had 81 seats in parliament (Gay, 1962: 230).

Bernstein, Revisionism and the British Tradition

Engels, who died in 1895, had already expressed his concern for Bernstein's enthusiasm for the Fabians – British socialists who explicitly rejected Marxism and named themselves after the Roman emperor Fabius, famed for his step-by-step approach to fighting war. Engels was to accuse the Fabians (whose society was established in London in 1874) of 'hushing up the class struggle' (Gay, 1962: 106). Bernstein was impressed by the tolerance and liberalism he found in London, so much so that Karl Kautsky, then the great champion of Marxist orthodoxy, was to declare Bernstein 'a representative of English socialism' (Gay, 1962: 80).

In 1899 Bernstein wrote his *Evolutionary Socialism* – described as the 'bible of revisionism'. Bernstein had been asked by Engels to be one of the executors of the Marxist papers, and Bernstein was reluctant to accept that he had – in the theological jargon which Marxists embrace – 'revised' Marxism. He argued that his critique was a way of further developing Marxism: he was not destroying Marxism, since, as he put it, 'It is Marx who carries the point against Marx' (1961: 27). But what he argued was certainly explosive, and a different kind of socialism emerged in his critique.

Bernstein's Argument

Bernstein took the view that:

- small and medium-sized enterprises were proving themselves viable. Hence members of the possessing classes were increasing, not diminishing (1961: xxv). Society was not becoming more simplified (as the *Manifesto* declared) but more graduated and differentiated (Bernstein, 1961:49). Moreover, the constantly rising national product was distributed, albeit unequally, over all segments of the population, so that the position of the worker was improving (1961: 207). In agriculture, the small and medium landholding was increasing, and the large and very large decreasing (1961: 71).
- He followed the Fabians by arguing that the theory of value or surplus value in Marxist theory was unnecessary. Depressions are becoming milder. Modern banking and the internationalisation of trade create adjustment and flexibility in capitalism – not breakdown.
- He saw Marx's emphasis on dialectics (the world consists of opposing forces) as a snare, uncritically taken over from Hegel. Why not assume that cooperation is just as important as struggle? Socialism must be based on the facts, and it is a fact that there is compromise and cooperation between the classes.
- Ethical factors, in his view, create much greater space for independent activity than was seen to be the case in classical Marxism (Bernstein, 1961: 15). The notion of inevitability – a fusion of what is and what ought to be – must be decisively rejected. 'No ism is a science' (Gay, 1962: 158). Socialism is about what is ethically desirable: science is about what is.

- Democracy, for Bernstein, is 'an absence of class government' – it avoids both the tyranny of the majority and the tyranny of the minority. Democracy is the high school of compromise and moderation (1961: 142–4). The notion of the 'dictatorship of the proletariat' has become redundant. Socialism seeks to make the proletarian into a citizen 'and to thus make citizenship universal' (1961: 146).

- Socialism, declared Bernstein, is 'the legitimate heir' to liberalism 'as a great historical movement' (1961: 149). There is no really liberal thought that does not also belong to socialism. Industrial courts and trades councils involve democratic self-government (1961: 152). Socialism is 'organising liberalism' and requires the constant increase of municipal freedom (1961: 159). He was devoted to liberal parliamentarism (1961: 299), and if this parliamentarism becomes excessive, the antidote is local self-government.

- The SPD must fight for all those reforms that increase the power of the workers and give the state a more democratic form (Gay, 1962: 225). Bernstein described the Sozialistische Partei Deutschands (SPD) as a 'democratic-Socialist reform party'. Hence the trade unions, far from being schools for socialism (in Marx's revolutionary sense), were concerned with practical and non-revolutionary improvements. Trade unions are, declared Bernstein, 'indispensable organs of democracy' (1961: 139–40).

- He linked the practicality of trade unions with the empirical orientation of the cooperative movement (1961: 204). The class struggle continues, but it is taking ever-milder forms. Cooperatives, particularly consumer co-ops, encourage democratic and egalitarian forms of management.

Bernstein exemplifies the dilemma of democratic socialism. How can the social-democratic party navigate between what Gay called the Scylla of impotence and the Charybdis of betrayal of its cause (Gay, 1962: 302)? How can it be 'realistic' and yet remain socialist?

The British Labour Party and the Fabians

The British Labour Party has never been a party of theory. Although its members (and some of its leaders!) may not even have heard of Bernstein, it is Bernsteinism that provides the underpinning for its practice.

We have already mentioned the importance of the Fabians. The Fabian Society became a kind of think-tank for the Labour Party. The Fabians were influenced by the same kind of theories that so appealed to Bernstein – empiricism, a philosophy that argues that our knowledge comes through the observation of 'facts' – and a belief in piecemeal reform through parliamentary democracy. Socialism was not a philosophy for life, but a highly focused doctrine that concerns itself with the organisation of industry and the distribution of wealth. Examine Fabian pamphlets today and what do you find? Specific proposals on organising the civil service, the health service, tax reforms, social security benefits, European Monetary Union, and the like. Beatrice Webb (1858–1943) who played a key role in the Fabian Society and in the formation of the Labour Party, took the view that the whole nation was sliding into social democracy.

The Labour Party, Constitutionalism and the Trade Unions

The Labour Representative Committee in 1900 was formed by trade unions. These unions felt that they needed a political voice and would cooperate with any party engaged in promoting legislation 'in the direct interest of labour' (Miliband, 1973: 19). The Liberal Party did not oppose the two Labour candidates who won their seats in 1900.

After the formation of the Labour Party in 1906, a Trade Disputes Act was passed which strengthened the right of unions to strike, while the Trade Union Act of 1913 allowed the trade unions to affiliate to the Labour Party. Ramsay MacDonald, the Party leader, made it clear that political weapons are to be found in the ballot box and the Act of Parliament – not in collective bargaining (Miliband, 1973: 35).

The party itself received a constitution in 1918 and the famous clause IV that spoke of common ownership of the means of production was (rather cynically) inserted by the Webbs to give the party some kind of ideological distance from the conservatives and the liberals. Sidney Webb would, Tony Blair commented in 1995, be astonished to find that the clause was still in existence some 70 years later (1995: 12). It was not intended, Blair argued, to be taken seriously.

The 1922 programme made it clear that Labour stood for neither Bolshevism nor Communism, but 'common sense and justice' (Miliband, 1973: 94). It is true that it suited the liberals and conservatives to present, in Churchill's words, Labour as 'the party of revolution' (Miliband, 1973: 99), but in fact Labour's politics were always of a liberal and constitutional nature. It is revealing that during the crisis of 1936 when MacDonald was expelled from the Labour Party for entering into a national government with the Conservatives, the Tory leader, Sir Herbert Samuel, argued that it would be in the general interest if unpalatable social measures to deal with the economic crisis could be imposed by a Labour Government (Miliband, 1973: 176). In the 1930s the Labour leadership was opposed to the Popular Front government in Spain (see the Chapter on Anarchism), and contributed significantly to the appeasement of the extreme right.

Although the right-wing publicist Evelyn Waugh saw the country under occupation after the Labour electoral victory of 1945, in fact Morrison made it clear that the socialisation of industry would only work 'on the merits of their specific cases. That is how the British mind works. It does not work in a vacuum or in abstract theories' (Miliband, 1973: 279). There is a clear link between Sidney Webb's statement to the Labour conference of 1923 that the founder of British socialism was not Karl Marx but Robert Owen – the doctrine underlying the Party is not that of class war but human brotherhood – and Harold Wilson's comment at the 1966 conference that no answers are to be found in Highgate cemetery (i.e. where Marx is buried) (Miliband, 1973: 98, 361).

Blair's Socialism

The position of Tony Blair, and this stance is also Gordon Brown's whatever their other differences, follows this tradition of pragmatism, moralism and constitutionalism. Indeed, Blair makes it clear that the elimination of the old Clause IV was to facilitate a return to Labour's ethical roots (Wright, 1996: x). We must retain, he argues, the values and principles underlying democratic socialism but apply them entirely afresh to the modern world (Blair, 1992: 3).

The values of democratic socialism are 'social justice, the equal worth of each citizen, equality of opportunity, community'. Socialism is, if you will, social-ism (Blair, 1994: 4). In the 50th anniversary lecture of the 1945 Labour victory, Blair describes socialism as 'the political heir of radical liberalism' (1995: 8). He sees the New Liberals as social democrats, and he defines socialism as a form of politics through which to fight poverty, prejudice and unemployment, and to create the conditions in which to build one nation – tolerant, fair, enterprising and inclusive. Socialists have to be both moralists and empiricists. They need, on the one hand, to be concerned with values, but at the same time they must address themselves to a world as it is and not as we would like it to be (Blair, 1995: 12–13).

International Social Democrats

These notions have been internationally endorsed. The German SPD has sternly repudiated communism, and in its Bad Godesberg Resolution of 1959 – described by Berki as 'one of the boldest, most impressive "liberal" party manifestoes ever written' – it argues for competition where possible, planning 'as far as it is necessary'. It follows what the Swedish social democrats have called a 'matter-of-fact conception of man' (Berki, 1974: 98–9).

These comments capture the dilemma. Berki suggests that in a way social democracy can be characterised as 'utopian socialism minus utopian expectations' since it does not believe that ideals like justice, goodwill, brotherliness and compassion could be 'unreservedly realised' (1974: 101). Is social democracy so pragmatic and flexible that it cannot be called socialism at all?

Socialism and the USA

Commentators have often wondered why socialism has never really taken root in the US. Factors that deserve emphasis are the following.

- Although the US certainly had a war of independence against the British, those who supported the British were generally driven out, and so the American republics had little class structure, certainly among free born men.
- A high degree of mobility meant that free men acquired private property so that a cultural ethos of individualism rather than collectivism prevailed.
- Even after the Civil War when class divisions became stark realities, emancipatory movements championed the rights of the small 'man' rather than an oppressed class, and trade unions often supported free enterprise in a way that Europeans found astonishing.
- Roosevelt's New Deal, although seen by its enemies as 'socialist' in character, embraced a social or new liberalism that never really challenged the capitalist nature of the economy.

British Labour and the 'Third Way'

The strategy of the 'third way' has been adopted by the social democratic parties of other European countries (like Sweden, Germany and possibly, France), as well as the British Labour Party, and points to a path between free market capitalism and traditional social democracy. It stresses the need for public/private partnerships and a notion of equality that stresses 'opportunity' rather than 'outcome'. Wealth creation rather than wealth distribution is also emphasised. The importance of technological development is highlighted, along with education and competition. A conference was organised in the British foreign secretary's house at Chequers in 1997 to discuss the 'third way' and the strategy also influenced the Democrats in the USA when Bill Clinton was President. Critics on the left have described the policies of the 'third way' as neo-liberalism with a social touch.

Can Marxism be Rescued?

The idea of communism as a 'scientific socialism' does, indeed, lead to authoritarianism, but this is not because communism aims to create a classless and stateless society. Rather it is because Marxist theory embraces elements that make it impossible for the state to wither away.

Of the problems that need to be tackled if Marxism is to made credible, the first is discussed below.

The Notion of Revolution

The concept of revolution as a dramatic element focused around a seizure of power is problematic. Marx uses the term revolution in different ways. He and Engels speak in the *Communist Manifesto* of the constant 'revolutionizing of production' under capitalism (1967: 83) and in that sense, revolutions are occurring all the time. But revolution is also used to denote a transformation of state and class power – an event in which the character of society as a whole changes.

It is true that Marx was to argue that such an event did not have to violent, and he even puts the view in 1882 that if in Britain 'the unavoidable evolution' turns into a revolution, that would not only be the fault of the ruling classes but also of the working class. Every peaceful concession has been wrung out through pressure, and the workers must wield their power and use their liberties, 'both of which they possess legally'. That suggests that each step forward is a kind of revolution in its own right, and that the notion of revolution as a dramatic event that inevitably changes the character of society, is redundant (Hoffman, 1975: 211).

This is not typical of Marx's view. The notion of revolution as a dramatic event linked to a seizure of power, was, it seems to us, inherited uncritically from the French Revolution of 1789. It creates a polarisation that makes the assertion of common interests and consensus more, not less, difficult. Engels is right: revolutions are authoritarian events, and they create a new state that clearly distinguishes between revolution and counter-revolution, and this leads to the kind of insecurity and division that generates despotism rather than democracy.

The Inevitability Problem and the Liberal Tradition

Clearly, the notion of revolution as inevitable creates the problem of supporting revolutions that generate authoritarian states, and the consequent abuse of human rights. A scathing attitude towards morality can only aggravate the problem, but it does not follow from this that all elements of Marxism are authoritarian in orientation. Here the attitude towards liberalism is crucial. Not only did Marx begin his political career as a liberal steeped in the ideals of the European Enlightenment, but when he becomes a communist, he seeks to go beyond rather than reject, liberal values.

The distinction between 'transcending' and 'rejecting' liberalism is crucial to our argument. To transcend liberalism is to build upon its values and institutions: it is to develop a theory and practice that extends freedom and equality more consistently and comprehensively than liberalism is able to do. Socialism as a **'post-liberalism'** seeks to turn liberal values into concrete realities so that those excluded by classical liberalism – the workers, the poor, women, dependants – become free and equal, as part of an historical process which has no grand culminating moment or climax. Socialism as a 'pre-liberalism', on the other hand, negates liberal values by introducing a system that imposes despotic controls upon the population at large (whatever its claim to speak in the name of the workers), and it is well described in the *Communist Manifesto* as a reactionary socialism because it hurls 'traditional anathemas' against liberalism and representative government (Marx and Engels, 1967: 111).

The problem with Marxism is that it is an amalgam of pre-liberalism and post-liberalism. It is post-liberal in so far as it stresses the need to build upon, rather than reject, capitalist achievements. But while (conventionally defined) revolutions make sense in situations in which legal rights to change society are blocked, in societies that have, or are attempting to build, liberal institutions, revolutions lead to elitism, despotism and a contempt for democracy. The notion of class war does not place enough emphasis on the need to create and consolidate common interests, to campaign in a way that isolates those who oppose progress.

Again there is a tension here in Marx's writings between his view that a classless society will eliminate alienation for all, and his argument that the bourgeoisie are the 'enemy' who must be overthrown. This leads to the privileging of the proletariat as the agent of revolution, and hostility to all who are not proletarians.

The Question of Class and Agency

Socialists are right when they see class as something that is negative; freedom for all, as Marxism argues, is only possible in a classless society. Class privileges some at the expense of others. In liberal societies it encourages an abstract approach to be taken to equality and power so that formal equality coexists with the most horrendous inequalities of power and material resources. Class is thus divisive, and it generates the kind of antagonisms that require force (and therefore the state) to tackle them.

For this reason, Marx is right to argue that if we want to dispense with the need for an institution claiming a monopoly of legitimate force, we must dispense with classes. In a well-known comment, Marx argues that in class-divided societies, social relations are not 'relations between individual and individual, but between worker and capitalist, between farmer and landlord, etc. Wipe out these relations and you annihilate all society' (Marx and Engels, 1975a: 77).

This comment is not concrete enough, for workers also have a gender and national identity etc., and this materially affects how they relate to others. It is not that the class identity is unimportant: it is rather that it fuses with other identities since these other identities are also a crucial part of the process that creates class. Brown argues that class has become invisible and inarticulate, rarely theorised or developed in the multiculturalist mantra, 'race, class, gender, sexuality' (1995: 61). The point is that we do not need to present these other identities as though they are separate from class.

In our view, class is only seen in 'other' forms. Thus we are told (*Independent*, 8 May 2003) that whereas four-and-a-half per cent of white British men (age 16–74) are unemployed, this figures rises to 9.1 per cent for men of Pakistani origin, 10.2 per cent of Bangladeshis and 10.4 per cent of Afro-Caribbean men. There are not simply two sets of figures here (black and Asian men and unemployment): rather it is that unemployment is integral to the discrimination from which black and Asian men suffer. Class only becomes visible through the position of women, gays, ethnic minorities, etc. The diversity of form in which classes express themselves is of the utmost importance, and it is the reason why no particular group should be privileged over any other in the struggle to achieve a classless and stateless society.

Socialists must, in other words, seek to mobilise all those who are excluded by contemporary institutions. This goes well beyond the concept of a 'proletariat', although those who are poor and have to subject themselves to the 'despotic' rules of employers are an obvious constituency in the struggle to govern one's own life. It is impossible to be free and equal if one is subject to aggressive pressures from employers and managers. Democratising the workplace to allow greater security, transparency and participation is critical, and all those who suffer from these problems are natural constituents in the struggle for socialism.

The point is that we cannot exclude the wealthy and the 'beneficiaries' of the market and state from the struggle for socialism, even though it would be foolish and naive to assume that the 'haves' will be enthusiastic proponents for a socialist future! Nevertheless, it has to be said that those who drive cars (however rich they are), are still vulnerable to the health problems associated with pollution. They suffer the nervous disorders linked to congestion and frustration on the roads. Inequalities and lack of social control, whether within or between societies, make everyone insecure, and result in a futile and wasteful use of resources. Wealthy people who try to 'buy' peaceful neighbourhoods, are seeking to escape from problems that will inevitably affect them too.

Take another issue. It is becoming increasingly clear to 'establishments' in advanced industrial countries that if nothing is done about the divisions within the international community then liberal traditions will be eroded, as refugees move around the globe. We will all suffer as a consequence. Some years ago the British government announced measures to place terrorist suspects under house arrest. Although the victims of crime in say contemporary South Africa are predominantly the poor who live in the shanty towns, this scourge does not simply affect those who are on the margins of society. Everyone can be the victim of crime. Socialism – making people conscious that they are living in society and that everything they do affects (and may harm) others – is, it could be argued, in everyone's interests. There is an interesting parallel here with measures taken to combat cholera in nineteenth-century British cities. The disease was no respecter of class or wealth: it was in everyone's interests that it was eradicated. What is the point of having wealth and power if your health is devastated?

Marxists might argue that with divisiveness in the world increasing through a kind of globalisation that increases inequality, the notion of a proletariat must be viewed internationally rather than simply nationally. However, the danger still remains that such a perspective will take a narrow view of class and underplay the problem of cementing common interests across the globe.

Socialism and Inevitability

Marx sometimes makes it seem that socialism will arrive come what may. He speaks of 'the natural laws of capitalist production' 'working with iron necessity towards inevitable results', and in a famous passage, he likens the birth of socialism to pregnancy (1970: 10). The development of socialism is as inevitable as the birth of a child. This argument is, however, only defensible as a conditional inevitability – not an absolute certainty independent of circumstances. In the *Communist Manifesto* Marx and Engels comment that class struggle might end 'in a revolutionary constitution of society at large' or 'the common ruin of the contending classes' (Marx and Engels, 1967: 79). Not only is it impossible to establish a timescale for socialism, but its inevitability is conditional upon, for example, humanity avoiding a nuclear conflagration which wipes out humans, or the destruction of the environment which makes production impossible. Nor can it be said that liberal societies might not turn to the right before they turn to the left.

What a conditional inevitability merely states is that if humanity survives, then sooner or later it will have to regulate its affairs in a socially conscious manner, and that, broadly speaking, is socialism. Only in this qualified and conditional sense can it be said that socialism is inevitable. Marxism can be rescued if it makes it clear that 'inevitability' is conditional, drops a notion of revolution as a concentrated political event, and with it, a polarised and narrow notion of class. Whether it would still be Marxism is a moot point.

The Problem of Utopianism

We have argued that a credible socialism must draw upon social democratic and Marxist ideas. The problem with 'pure' social democrats as well as 'pure' Marxists is that they can be said to either embrace a (liberal) empiricist framework or they simply turn such a framework inside out.

The Problem of Determinism and Free Will

Bauman has argued that utopianism is compatible with everything but determinism (1976: 37), and in his hostility to utopianism, Marx sometimes gives the impression that he does not believe in free will. When he speaks of his theory of history as one in which people enter into relations 'independent of their will', does this mean that people have no will? What it means, it seems to us, is that what people intend (i.e. humans are beings with purpose and thus will) is never quite the same as what actually happens.

Take the following assertion of Marx's. The capitalist and landlord are 'the personifications of economic categories, embodiments of particular class interests and class relations' so that his or her standpoint can 'less than any other' make the individual 'responsible for relations whose creature he socially remains, however much he may subjectively raise himself above them' (1970: 10). This comment seems to suggest that our will cannot transform circumstances, and therefore we cannot create new relations. Yet Marx's third thesis on Feuerbach had already stated (against mechanical materialism which saw people as passive and lacking in agency) that the changing of circumstances and human activity coincide as 'revolutionary practice' (again an identification of revolution with ongoing change, not a dramatic one-off event!) This, it seems to us, is the answer to the problem of determinism and inevitability. If we assume that determinism negates free will and that we need to make a choice between them, then clearly determinism is a problem for socialism. For how can we change society if we do not have the will to do so? What if we go beyond such a 'dualism' and argue merely that determinism means that free will always occurs in the context of relations? Why is this concept of determinism a problem?

Circumstances determine our capacities. Our capacity to change circumstances involves recognising these circumstances and making sure that we correctly appraise their reality. To successfully strengthen the struggle for socialism, we need to attend to movements within our existing society which demonstrate that we can regulate our lives in ways which increase our capacity to get the results we want – whether it is in terms of transport policy, cleaning up the environment, giving people greater security and control in the workplace.

Whether these reforms or 'revolutionising activities' are effective depends upon how carefully we have assessed the circumstances that determine the context and the event. This kind of determinism does not undermine free will: on the contrary, it makes it possible to harness free will in a sensible and rational manner. If Marx is suggesting that there was a 'dualism' between free will and determinism, he would simply be turning classical liberalism inside out and not going beyond it. Classical liberalism argues for a notion of freedom independent of circumstances and relationships, and socialists might find it tempting (since they are critical of liberalism) to take the view that since circumstances determine the way people are, therefore people have no freedom or willpower. But if this was the position of socialists like Robert Owen (Hoffman, 1975: 139), arguably it was not the position of Marx's 'new' materialism, even though he and Engels sometimes gave the impression that it was.

Bernstein is a case in point. On the one hand, he saw himself as a positivist who stuck rigorously to the facts. On the other hand, since he was living in a society which was clearly not socialist, socialism is, he tells us, a piece of the beyond – something which ought to be, but is not (Gay, 1962: 158, 163). Abstract 'realism' coexists with abstract utopianism. The role of ethics is not integrated into a concern with the facts, and Marck has pointed out that such a theory can pay too much attention to 'short-run developments', ruling out in a dogmatic fashion, dramatic and unanticipated actions, 'apparently contradicted by the happenings of the day' (Gay, 1962: 162).

Bernstein's position on economic concentration bears this out. As Gay comments, after 1924 German industry centralised and cartelised as never before (1962: 172). The trends that he analysed in 1899 were not irreversible. In the same way Bernstein assumed that a new middle class would be democratic and pro-socialist. Yet anyone who knows anything about German history after the First World War, comments Gay, 'will recognize the fallacious assumptions of Bernstein's theory'. Inflation and the world depression traumatised large groups within the German middle classes: they saw descent into the proletariat as a horrendous possibility (Gay, 1962: 215). Bernstein's analysis put into the context of Germany between the wars, turned out to be wishful thinking. Whether government through a representative parliament can work depends upon the social structure and political institutions of a country – it allows of no dogmatic answer (Gay, 1962: 236). Once we see that reality is in movement, then we can fuse Utopia and realism. Utopia derives from the transformation of existing realities: but this Utopia is not to be located outside existing realities, it is part of them. In arguing that socialism must be a 'utopian realism', we avoid the dualism between facts and values, Utopia and reality, a dualism that bedevils so many exponents of socialism, whether of the right or the left. Bernstein's argument that socialists should always avoid violence is right under some circumstances, but it could hardly apply when the Hitler leadership in Germany destroyed parliamentary institutions and embraced fascism.

As has been argued in the chapter on anarchism, we need a state as long as humanity cannot resolve its conflicts of interest in a peaceful manner. For Bernstein because the state exists, it is here to stay! The 'so-called coercive associations, the state and the communities, will retain their great tasks in any future I can see' (Gay, 1962: 246). But to identify the state with community, and regard its mechanisms for settling difference as only apparently 'coercive', shows how far 'pure' social democracy is still steeped in the abstract aspects of the liberal tradition.

Gay is surely right when he comments that Bernstein's optimism was not well founded: it took short-run prosperity and converted it into a law of capitalist development (1962: 299). If, as A.J. Taylor has said, Marx was a dogmatic optimist (Marx and Engels, 1967: 47), so was Bernstein. Socialism requires a conditional concept of inevitability and a dialectical determinism – one that takes full account of human agency – so that it is neither optimistic nor pessimistic but is a utopian realism.

Summary

Socialism is certainly a broad church, but underlying its numerous forms is a concern with cooperation and equality, a belief that human nature can change and that freedom requires an adequate provision of resources. Socialism is peculiarly prone to the problem of utopianism because it seeks to establish a society that differs from the world of the present.

The work of Saint Simon, Fourier and Robert Owen demonstrates that socialists who were labelled 'utopian' by their Marxist critics, did not regard themselves in this light. Marxism is a variant of socialism that leads to authoritarianism insofar as it emphasises an unconditional inevitability, has a particular notion of revolution, and is apparently disdainful of moral judgement. Social democracy or democratic socialism rejects utopianism but runs the risk of a dogmatic adherence to a doctrine of realism that can be at variance with the facts.

Marxism can only be rescued from the problem of authoritarianism if it rejects the notion of revolution as a single political event, and adopts a broader view of class and a conditional notion of inevitability. The problem of Utopia in socialism needs to be meaningfully addressed by constructing socialism as a utopian realism so that neither half of this construct is stressed at the expense of the other.

Questions

1. Are Marxist organisations necessarily authoritarian?
2. Can the notion of revolution play a part within a democratic socialism?
3. Is socialism inevitable?
4. Is parliament a barrier to, or a precondition for, a viable socialism?
5. Is socialism necessarily utopian?

References

Bauman, Z. (1976) *Socialism as Utopia* London: George Allen and Unwin.

Berki, R. (1974) *Socialism* London: Dent.

Bernstein, E. (1961) *Evolutionary Socialism* New York: Schocken.

Blair, T. (1992) 'Pride without Prejudice' *Fabian Review* 104(3), 3.

Blair, T. (1994) *Socialism* Fabian Pamphlet 565, London.

Blair, T. (1995) *Let Us Face the Future* Fabian Pamphlet 571, London.

Brown, W. (1995) *States of Injury* Princeton, NJ: Princeton University Press.

Crick, B. (1987) *Socialism* Milton Keynes: Open University Press.

Crick, B. (1992) *In Defence of Politics* Harmondsworth: Penguin.

Gay, P. (1962) *The Dilemma of Democratic Socialism* New York: Collier.

Geoghegan, V. (1987) *Utopianism and Marxism* London and New York: Methuen.

Heywood, A. (1992) *Political Ideologies* Basingstoke: Macmillan.

Hoffman, J. (1975) *Marxism and the Theory of Praxis* New York: International Publishers.

Hoffman, J. (1991) *Has Marxism a Future?* Discussion Papers in Politics: University of Leicester.

Hoffman, J. (1995) *Beyond the State* Cambridge: Polity.

Hunt, R. (1975) *The Political Ideas of Marx and Engels*, vol. 1, Basingstoke: Macmillan.

Independent (2003) 'Britain today: A nation still failing its ethnic minorities' 8 May.

Mannheim, K. (1960) *Ideology and Utopia* London: Routledge and Kegan Paul.

Marx, K. (1970) *Capital*, vol. 1 London: Lawrence and Wishart.

Marx, K. and Engels, F. (1967) *The Communist Manifesto* Harmondsworth: Penguin.

Marx, K. and Engels, F. (1968) *Selected Works* London: Lawrence and Wishart.

Marx, K. and Engels, F. (1975a) *Collected Works*, vol. 4 London: Lawrence and Wishart.

Marx, K. and Engels, F. (1975b) *Selected Correspondence* Moscow: Progress.
Miliband, R. (1973) *Parliamentary Socialism*, 2nd edn London: Merlin.
Tucker, R. (ed.) (1978) *The Marx-Engels Reader*, 2nd edn New York and London: W.W. Norton.
Wright, T. (1996) *Socialisms* London and New York: Routledge.

Further Reading

- Wright's *Socialisms* (referenced above) is a most valuable summary of different positions.

- Crick's *Socialism* (referenced above) is very useful with a chapter excerpting texts on British socialism.

- Miliband's *Parliamentary Socialism* (referenced above) is a classic critique on Labourism.

- Geohegan's *Utopianism and Marxism* (referenced above) is a useful defence of the utopian tradition.

- Gavin Kitching's *Rethinking Socialism* (London and New York: Methuen, 1983) offers a very challenging attempt to rework socialism during the Thatcher period.

- David McLellan edition of *Marxism: the Essential Writings* (Oxford University Press, 1988) including valuable excerpts from various Marxist traditions and a piece of Eduard Bernstein.

- Anthony Giddens has written *The Third Way and its Critcs* published by Polity Press in 2002.

Weblinks

Very useful on the history of socialism and the various personalities that predominate:
http://www.spartacus.schoolnet.co.uk

Allows one to look at original texts on different aspects of socialism:
http://www.inter-change-search.net/directory/Society/Politics/Socialism/

Easy to get information of the different 'varieties' of socialism:
http://www.the-wood.org/socialism/

Material on Marxism:
http://www.marxist.org.uk/htm_docs/princip2.htm

Full text of the *Communist Manifesto*:
http://www.socialistparty.org.uk/manifesto/m2frame.htm?manifesto.html

Chapter 11

Anarchism

Introduction

Much is made in the press about the frequent anti-capitalist protests happening in various cities throughout the world, and it is argued that anarchists are behind these demonstrations. The word 'anarchist' is often used as a term of abuse, and is sometimes misused – but what exactly does it mean? What does it stand for, and why have some argued that **anarchism** has enjoyed a resurgence in recent years? On the face of it, it seems an absurdly self-defeating philosophy, so why does it remain influential? Who does it attract and why?

To answer these questions, in this chapter we will try to establish what anarchism is, and how different varieties of anarchism advocate different strands of argument (→ Chapters on the State; Liberalism; Socialism).

Chapter Map

In this chapter we will explore:

- The overlap with other ideologies while grasping the distinctive character of anarchism.

- Philosophical anarchism and free market anarchism, while noting their difficulties.

- The views of anti-capitalist anarchists such as Proudhon, Bakunin and Kropotkin.

- An actual experience of anarchism, during the Spanish Civil War.

- The problem of violence, and what role it plays in the new social movements.

- The problem which organisation poses for anarchism.

- The difficulties that arise when the distinctions between the state and government and force and constraint are ignored.

Death in Genoa

Italian riot police out in force during the anti-globalisation protests against the meeting of the G8, Genoa, July 2001

On a sunny Italian morning, a group of young politics students landed in Genoa to protest against the G8 summit. Before travelling they had been leafleted by anarchist groups and emailed regarding the details of the demonstrations, where they should stay, where preliminary meetings were being held locally to them, and what they should do once in Italy. They met their rendezvous outside the airport and hitched a lift to the Carlini Stadium, just east of the city centre, where the other protestors were gathering.

Inside the stadium they first noticed a group of men and women dressed head to foot in white overalls. They were, a friend explained, the Italian Ya Basta group, also called 'tutti bianci' ('all white'). They were busy making shields out of perspex for themselves, as well as makeshift body armour using thick rubber. Some of them were wearing gas masks.

There is a definite uneasy atmosphere in the stadium – the Ya Basta group want only to stage an act of civil disobedience such as a peaceful march and protest – whereas the anarchists are aiming to dismantle the 'Red Zone' fence that separates the delegates from the protestors, and employ tactics of maximum disruption and visibility to the assembled world media. Although they tell the group that they support the demonstrations against capitalism in principle, they also remind everyone of their own specific demands they want made, maintaining that a revolution against capital must be linked to a revolution against the state and government.

Over the forthcoming days, the group attend many meetings, some lasting up to nine hours, during which various factions negotiate for larger allocations of space along the Red Zone fence. At last, once the details have been amicably agreed upon, they march to the fence.

Continued

Almost immediately the protestors are drenched by the Italian police with water cannons. When the increasingly angry crowd try to pull down the fence the police use tear gas against them. Terrified, the crowds disperse, but are tracked by helicopters, from which further gas canisters rain down. Many arrests are made, seemingly indiscriminately, and force is used. Violent confrontations break out between the police and certain groups of protestors. Rumours start that a protestor has been killed by the police. That night, as the bedraggled, frightened and angry protestors return to the stadium, the rumour is confirmed.

One thing evident from the case above is that a lot of organisation is necessary if protestors are to protest effectively. Imagine you are a member of an anarchist committee whose job it is to contact the 250 people planning on travelling from Britain to Genoa, placing information on the Internet, consulting on leaflets, arranging accommodation, etc. How does this level of organisation compare to your initial conception of what it is to be an anarchist?

Imagine you are one of the anarchists returning to the stadium the night of the violence. Do you think your 'own specific demands' have been met by the day's protesting? Why?

At the G8 summit, force was answered with force. Imagine you were the Genoan Police Chief responsible for ensuring public order. How would you have tried to counter and control the anarchists?

The Relationship with Socialism

In her *Using Political Ideas* (1997) Barbara Goodwin has a separate chapter on anarchism and argues that the anarchist is 'not merely a socialist who happens to dislike the state'. She concedes, however, that there is much overlap and that many anarchists have analysed **capitalism** in a way that resembles that of socialists (1997: 122).

R.N. Berki, however, in his influential book *Socialism*, treats anarchism as a current within socialism and notes, for example, that it was Proudhon, a key anarchist as we shall see later in this chapter, who first called his doctrine 'scientific socialism' (1974: 12), and that Proudhon's significance for socialism is enormous (1974: 84). Berki makes many acute observations about anarchism in the context of his chapter on the evolution of socialism. In a section on socialist thought at the turn of the century he describes Michel Bakunin as a precursor to both Russian socialism and anarcho-syndicalism, about which more will be said later (1974: 83–8).

Andrew Vincent, like Goodwin, has a separate chapter on anarchism, and makes the point that the doctrine overlaps with both liberalism and socialism (1995: 114). But whatever the overlap between some kinds of anarchism and socialism, there is also an anarchism that is explicitly non-socialist, and in some of its forms even anti-socialist. It will be useful to say something about these first, since they are dramatically different from 'socialist' forms of anarchism.

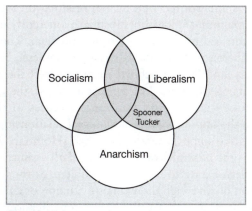

Figure 11.1

Philosophical Anarchists

We will take the view that although anarchism is a very old theory, it only emerged in systematic form in the eighteenth century as part of the Enlightenment. We will begin with what is widely agreed to be the first comprehensive account of anarchist principles, William Godwin's classic *Enquiry Concerning Political Justice* (1793).

Godwin was really a liberal, even though he abandoned the classical liberal view of natural rights and a state of nature. He argues that humans are social beings, are moulded by their environment and are imbued with a capacity to reason. True happiness, as far as Godwin was concerned, lies with the development of individuality. All individuals have a right to private judgement. Everything understood by organisation is 'in some degree evil' and he argued that communal institutions, even theatre and musical performances, could be seen as an invasion of our individuality. Society should be regarded as a 'luxury', rather than a 'necessity' and can never be more than the sum of its parts (Vincent, 1995: 125). Compulsory restraint violates a privately determined pursuit of happiness, and it is said that Godwin ends where Hobbes begins. While Godwin sees the state as vicious, evil and tyrannical, the premises of his theory are militantly individualistic. If this atomistic and abstract view of the individual leads to radical insecurity and arbitrariness in Hobbes, in Godwin it generates the 'unspeakably beautiful vision of a world' in which individuals freely exercise their private judgement (Hoffman, 1995: 114).

Godwin was opposed to property, the **market** and acquisitiveness in general, but he was no socialist. His opposition to the state extends to social relationships, and all individuals retain a sphere of private judgement that shuts society out. He may have hoped that small face-to-face communities would replace the state (with temporary coordinating bodies being transitionally necessary to resolve disputes and repel invaders), but he has been rightly called a 'philosophical anarchist' since his main preoccupation is with principles rather than practice.

Max Stirner is often bracketed with Godwin as a philosophical anarchist, but unlike Godwin, Stirner does not see individuals as benevolent and rational. He enthusiastically embraces the argument that consciousness (which is always 'alienated') is the source of our oppression. In Stirner's case, concepts like humanism, communism and liberalism are inherently oppressive because they are necessarily imposed upon the sovereign individual. The state of nature adhered to by classical liberals was essentially social in character, but individuals constitute the highest reality, and Stirner exhorts them to desert their natural condition. People have no rights of any kind. As a conscious egoist, the individual, in Stirner's view, is beyond good and evil and the oppressiveness of the state is no different in essence from the oppressiveness of all social relationships, indeed of ideologies. All subject the ego to some 'generality or other' (Hoffman, 1995: 115).

Stirner sees the natural world as a war of all against all, but unlike Hobbes who posits a powerful state to tackle this problem, Stirner advocates the formation of an association of sovereign individuals – a union of conscious egoists – who would spontaneously and voluntarily come together out of mutual interest. All 'teleological' categories – goals, purposes, and ends – are oppressive even if they are imposed by individuals upon themselves. This means that even a system of direct democracy is unacceptable. His union of egoists would enable individuals to accomplish more than they could on their own, and though Stirner's world is one without rights and morality, the union would create security and put an end to poverty. Marx and Engels in their lengthy critique of Stirner's *The Ego and His Own* point out that Stirner employs a concept of the unique individual which in practice, morally obliges other individuals, so that he is in the hapless position of attacking authority from moral premises which are not supposed to exist (Hoffman, 1995: 115).

In a more recent exposition of philosophical anarchism, Wolff argues that all adults are responsible beings who have a capacity for choice and a potential for autonomy that they lose if they obey the dictates of another. A person's primary obligation is to be autonomous. However, unlike Stirner and Godwin, Wolff accepts the case for a direct democracy, and he argues that people are bound by the decisions they have taken. The advantage of such a system is that the authority to which each citizen submits, 'is not of himself simply, but that of the entire community taken collectively'. Not only does this sound rather authoritarian, but Wolff argues that each person encounters 'his better self in the form of the state, for its dictates are simply the laws which he has, after due deliberation willed to be enacted' (cited by Dahl, 1989: 348). As an anarchist, he treats direct democracy as a form of the state.

All philosophical anarchists have the problem of moving from the individual to some kind of collective organisation which, on the one hand, is deemed necessary to realise anarchism, but which, on the other, contradicts anarchist principles. We will see if the free-market anarchists are better able to tackle this problem.

Free-market Anarchists

Nineteenth-century Americans like Spooner and Tucker argued for an anarchism that was an extension of liberalism: if individuals are free and equal, why should they accept the compulsion of the state? Locke's state of nature was seen as a world in which individuals are not subject to external discipline: why shouldn't things stay that way? But whereas nineteenth-century free-market anarchists were concerned about the structural inequalities that the market might generate – and they took the view that everyone should be an entrepreneur – more recent free-market anarchists have accepted capitalism, arguing that exploitation and **coercion** are simply the product of the state. Substantial inequalities are inevitable in a free society.

Free-market anarchists like Murray Rothbard take the view that state welfare is as pernicious as state warfare. Any attempt to regulate production prevents consumers from purchasing commodities that *they* wish to buy, while goods that everybody wants, like sanitation, roads, street lighting, are best provided by private enterprise. Disadvantaged groups, like the elderly, the unemployed and the disabled (for example) should be catered for by charity since state provision is invariably wasteful and open to abuse (Hoffman, 1995: 117).

It is not only the 'positive' functions of the state that ought to be 'privatised'. As far as modern day free-market anarchists are concerned, the market should take over the state's 'negative' role as well. Rothbard contends that people could insure themselves against bodily assault in the same way that they currently insure their possessions against theft. Aggrieved parties could then seek compensation and redress for injury through private tribunals, with the free market ensuring that arbitrators or judges with the best record in settling disputes would be hired.

But how would these judgments be enforced? Recalitrants who refused to abide by tribunal decisions would be subject to boycott and ostracism, and in more serious cases, guards and police could be hired to defend injured parties and enforce judgments. People who refused to comply with judgments could be placed in private prisons, and aggrieved individuals might decide (with the help of friends and relatives) to retaliate in person. Rothbard describes the state as 'the great legalized and socially legitimated channel of all manner of social crime', and getting rid of the state would strengthen the 'good' in human nature and discourage the bad (Hoffman, 1995: 118). Humans remain possessive individualists by nature, and it is this assumption that leads the libertarian thinker, Robert Nozick, in his classic work *Anarchy, State, and Utopia* (1974) to make the case for the minimal state.

Nozick's argument is interesting because he seeks to construct his non-anarchist case on individualist anarchist principles. He argues that individuals have natural rights, and their goods and bodies are protected by private protective associations. However, unlike Rothbard and the free-market anarchists, he accepts that through competition, one of the protective associations will emerge as dominant, and when it protects all who live in its domain whether they pay privately or not, it then becomes a 'minimal state'.

Some form of government seems to be essential if the problem of externalities or spillovers, as they are called, are to be dealt with. Negative externalities arise when, for example, a factory pollutes the environment and the cost that results is much less to the individual than to society at large. Some kind of collective association is needed to bring the offending individual to book, and make them change their ways. The principle of the minimal state is also necessary to tackle positive externalities as in a situation in which some, but not all, households in a neighbourhood pay for the protection of a policing agency. However, the presence of a policing agency may have a deterrent effect from which *all* households benefit, and premium payers, indignant at the fact that they are paying for services from which 'free-riders' benefit, withdraw from the scheme which then collapses.

How does Nozick justify the services of a minimal state that apply to all? Who funds such a service? Nozick argues that a minimal state emerges in a way that violates no-one's rights in the process, but how is the dominant protection agency which becomes the minimal state to exist without violating the rights of its competitors? Nozick's argument is that these competitive agencies are compensated because the minimal state provides protective services free of charge. But what happens if the agencies do not accept the monopolistic role of the minimal state? People are being compensated whether they like it or not, so that it is difficult to see how the minimal state avoids compulsion.

Moreover, once this compulsion has been justified, this is a principle capable of infinite extension. After all, if the provision of protection is deemed too 'risky' for competing agencies, why could not one argue, say, that the provision of low-cost housing or accessible medical services are too 'risky' to be left to private agencies? The New Liberals of the late nineteenth century showed just how painlessly the notion of 'protection' can be broadened. Will people feel secure if they are destitute and have no job? Are contracts really respected if the rich invade the security of the poor? Once you have the state, a consistent free-market anarchist could argue, how do you stop it from expanding?

Pressures to conform can only really be successful when everyone is, broadly speaking, in the same boat and can change places. There has to be a sense of common interest – freedom *and equality* – and if we begin with an order in which possessive individualism has divided society, how do we move to a condition of equality without regulation and compulsion, and even – horror of horrors – a role for government? Indeed, Marshall argues that 'anarcho-capitalists' should not be called anarchists at all (1993: 565).

Exercise

You are walking down the street when someone attacks you. You are living in a stateless society of an anarchist kind, there are no public order offences since everything has been privatised. There is, however, a tribunal to which you can turn in order to sue the person who assaulted you, for compensation, and this you are determined to do.

A number of problems face you:

1. The person who attacked you obviously does not regard you as a fellow human being who deserves respect.

2. Will he attend the tribunal hearings and pay up if the ruling goes against him?

3. What kind of pressures can be brought to bear upon this person to ensure that he cooperates? The tribunal has officials and you know where this person lives, but they have no powers to compel the person to attend.

4. The individual does have friends and family. Can they be relied upon to pressurise him to attend?

Anti-Capitalist Anarchists: Proudhon, Bakunin and Kropotkin

Proudhon was certainly a socialist, although he objected to communism on the grounds that it subordinates the individual to collectivity (Marshall, 1993: 238). It is the unequal distribution of property that creates disorder, but the answer, as he saw it, was 'mutualism' – a system that avoided the vices of both private property and collective ownership, and was based upon exchange and credit. Exchange would occur through associations that calculated the necessary labour time involved in a product. People could start businesses by borrowing from a mutual credit bank, and this economic reorganisation would make the state redundant. In Proudhon's view, parliamentary democracy is futile and counter-productive – 'Universal suffrage is counter revolution' is one of his many celebrated dictums (Marshall, 1993: 244).

Proudhon aroused the wrath of Marx who wrote his *Poverty of Philosophy* against Proudhon's *Philosophy of Poverty*. Marx objected to Proudhon's opposition to political involvement and trade unionism, and regarded his principles of justice and equality as woefully unhistorical. Proudhon's rejection of liberal principles of government meant that he regarded all forms of the state as anathema. He was also strongly nationalistic, patriarchal and for a period supported the autocratic Emperor Napoleon III who suspended parliamentary politics. Proudhon popularised the view that anarchy stood for order – despite the frequent use of the word as a synonym for chaos – and he is widely regarded as the father of anarchism.

Influenced by Proudhon but strongly collectivist in orientation was the Russian anarchist, Bakunin. Bakunin declares with an anti-Hobbesian fervour that 'man is born into society, just as ant is born into an ant-hill and bee into its hive' (Marshall, 1993: 291). The analogy with nature is important for Bakunin, since he takes the view that sociability and the desire to revolt is *instinctive*. It is both universal, and stronger among some rather than others. Bakunin took the view that the instinct for revolt was particularly strong among the Latins and the Slavs, and particularly weak among Germanic peoples. He saw revolution as a violent process, and what Marshall calls his 'apocalyptic fantasies' (1993: 306) manifest themselves in his belief that to create is to destroy. This slogan reappears during the May events – the student rebellion – in 1968 in Paris, and Berki notes that Bakunin's ideas became very fashionable in the 1970s in Western libertarian socialist circles (1974: 84).

Bakunin clashed with Marx in the First International and he was expelled in 1872. Nevertheless, although he and the 'authoritarian' Marx disagreed over strategy, he greatly admired Marx's critique of capital, and he was opposed not simply to the repressive hierarchy of the state, but to the inequalities and exploitation identified with capitalism. He was, however, passionately opposed to Marx's notion of the workers becoming a ruling class and having to control a transitional state. The workers' state, he insisted, would be nothing but a barracks; a regime where working men and women are regimented. We will have 'despotic rule over the toiling masses by a new, numerically small aristocracy of genuine or sham scientists. The people . . . will be wholly regimented into one common herd of governed people. Emancipation indeed!' (Maximoff, 1953: 287). Not only was Bakunin sceptical about the 'authority' of science, but he regarded religion and the notion of God as inherently statist and authoritarian.

Yet Bakunin argued the case for a secret association in which a revolutionary general staff would serve as intermediaries 'between the revolutionary idea and the instincts of the people', and this presumably accounts for his temporary attraction to the notorious Nechaev, a nihilist, terrorist and a man of no scruples. Against one's will, declared Bakunin, one is obliged to use 'force, cunning and deception' (Marshall, 1993: 282–4). Bakunin was hugely influential. Not only did he make an enormous impact upon French labour, Italian revolutionaries and, as we shall see, the socialist movement in Spain, but his anti-capitalism attracted support among those who espoused what was called anarcho-syndicalism.

Bertrand Russell has referred to syndicalism as 'the anarchism of the market place' (Berki, 1974: 87) and it focuses on the role of industrial workers who are to organise themselves into revolutionary syndicates, making 'war on the bosses' and not bothering with politics (Marshall, 1993: 441). The general strike is seen as the best weapon for ushering in the new order. Syndicates should take on social functions as the germ of the stateless, socialist society. But not all anarchists agreed with syndicalism. Emma Goldman feared that syndicalism trampled upon the rights of the individual by accepting a principle of majority rule, while the Italian Malatesta saw syndicalism simply as one of many means to achieve anarchist ends (Marshall, 1993: 444).

The contrast between Kropotkin and Bakunin is striking indeed. Although they were both Russian and both influenced by Marx's critique of capitalism, Kropotkin had great respect for science and was an accomplished geographer. Kropotkin espoused the ideal of a federal and decentralised society with the land and factories owned by the producers. He was sympathetic to syndicalism and argued that the great gains in the past had been made by the force of popular revolution, not through 'an evolution created by an elite' (Marshall, 1993: 317).

The Argument so Far . . .

Godwin believed that individuals should be allowed to freely express private judgements.

Stirner thought that individuals were sovereign and form a voluntary and spontaneous union of like-minded beings.

Rothbard was a free marketeer who took the view that the market could replace the state.

Nozick argued that a state was needed, but a minimal state that would protect property and enforce contracts.

The following were not only against the state, but against capitalism as well . . .

Proudhon believed in 'mutualism' – a scheme that allowed individuals to exchange goods and secure credit without the need for political involvement or trade unions.

Bakunin argued that humans should work together collectively and they had a natural instinct for revolt and solidarity.

Kropotkin believed that a communist society was possible through mutual cooperation and revolution.

Anarchism must proceed with the method of the natural scientists. Mutual aid was far more important to the evolution of the species than mutual struggle. The species that cooperates the most, is most likely to survive. Humans are by nature social and moral, and the greatest individual development comes through practising the 'highest communist sociability'. The socialist notion of a 'people's state' – here he agreed with Bakunin – is 'as great a danger to liberty as any form of autocracy' (Marshall, 1993: 321–6). Whereas Bukunin saw distribution as linked to the performance of work, Kropotkin also stressed need: production and distribution are integrated in communal enterprises so as to meet the physical and cultural needs of all (Vincent, 1995: 133).

He was offered a cabinet position (which he turned down) in the Provisional Government of Kerensky after the overthrow of Tsarism in 1917, and was bitterly critical both of the Bolshevik revolution (he sent letters to Lenin in vain) and the tactics adopted after the revolution. Kropotkin called himself a communist anarchist; Bakunin preferred to see himself as a collectivist, while Proudhon regarded himself as a mutualist but all were critical of capitalism, and all saw anarchism as a solution to the kind of inequality generated by a capitalist society.

Republican Spain and the Anarchist Experience

The Spanish Republic has become a valuable historical laboratory for trying to understand anarchism because this is the only example in the twentieth century in which anarchism succeeded in constructing a new society, at least in particular regions and for a few years. As Thomas comments, 'the Spanish Anarchists are the only Anarchists in European history to have made any mark upon events' (1965: 279).

The liberal tradition was weak in Spain. During the nineteenth century the church and the army had intervened to prevent or paralyse a liberal constitution and this had strengthened the widespread scepticism towards conventional political processes. Anarchist strength centred in Barcelona in the north where it was reinforced by separatist sentiments among the Catalans (and took the form of anarcho-syndicalism), and it was also strong among the impoverished peasantry in the south. When a Spanish Communist Party was formed in 1921, the anarchists were four times more numerous than the socialists. In Spain the mass of workers and peasants had followed Bakunin when he broke with Marx. The Confederación Nacional del Trabajo (CNT) had over a million members at the time of the First World War, and in 1933 the anarchist weekly *Tierra y Libertad* declared grandly:

> Workers! Do not vote! The vote is a negation of your personality . . . All the politicians are enemies . . . we need neither state nor government . . . Do not be concerned whether the Right or the Left emerge triumphant from this farce . . . Parliament . . . is a filthy house of prostitution . . . Destroy the ballots! Destroy the ballot boxes . . . hack off the heads of the ballot supervisors as well of the candidates . . . (Thomas, 1965: 95).

One could well argue that revolutions do not have to be violent, but this was not how Spanish anarchists saw the issue. The Communists had, following the Seventh Comintern Congress, thrown their weight behind the idea of a Popular Front (an alliance of liberal and left-wing forces), and in 1936 the left won a substantial electoral victory on a programme of radical reform. Franco with the army mostly loyal to him, led a rebellion. The socialists (and communists) were strong in Madrid but the anarchists retained control of Barcelona where all large industries passed to the CNT, and expropriation was considered the rule. Large numbers of people belonging to the old order were killed, and churches were destroyed. In some places, money was replaced by coupons, while in Andalusia in the south, where the anarchists were also strong, each town acted on its own responsibility. By 1937 some three million people were living in rural collectives.

The anarchists adopted military methods of organisation, and Miller cites Borkenau's comment that in one of the villages of Aragon, the agrarian revolution

Orwell comments that

I had come to Spain with some notion of writing newspaper articles, but I had joined the militia almost immediately because at that time and in that atmosphere it seemed the only conceivable thing to do. The Anarchists were still in virtual control of Catalonia and the revolution was in full swing . . . it was the first time that I had ever been in a town where the working class was in the saddle. Practically every building of any size had been seized by the workers and was draped with red flags or the black and red flag of the Anarchists; every wall was scrawled with the hammer and sickle and with initials of the revolutionary parties; almost every church had been gutted and its images burnt . . . Every shop and café had an inscription saying it had been collectivised . . . Waiters and shop-walkers looked you in the face and treated you as an equal. Servile and ceremonial forms of speech had temporarily disappeared . . . There were no private motor cars, they had all been commandeered . . . And it was the aspect of the crowds that was the queerest thing of all. In outward appearance it was a town in which the wealthy classes had practically ceased to exist.

Orwell, 2001: 32.

was almost the automatic consequence of executions (1974: 106–7). In September 1936 the anarchists entered the Catalan government calling it the Revolutionary Defence Council so as to avoid giving the impression 'to their already alarmed extremist followers' that they had joined a real government (Thomas, 1965: 367). Marshall argues that in so doing, they had started down the slippery slide to parliamentary participation and this meant sacrificing the social revolution to the war against Franco (Marshall, 1993: 461).

As the crisis continued, the anarchists entered the government in Madrid, with the anarchist Garcia Oliver becoming Minister of Justice and the CNT recognising the republican state as 'an instrument of struggle' (Thomas, 1965: 404). The defence of this action by the CNT's daily paper is regarded by Marshall as 'an unparalleled bout of dissimulation' (Marshall, 1993: 465). Oliver, 'for all his devotion to Bakunin', proceeded to establish a new code of state laws and defended the need for iron discipline in the popular army (Thomas, 1965: 470; Marshall, 1993: 465). In late April 1937 a civil war between the anarchists and the communist-backed government broke out in Barcelona, and some 500 were killed. Anarchist influence ebbed away, and although the CNT continued to collaborate with the government, they no longer took even nominal responsibility for its actions (Thomas, 1965: 558).

On 18 March 1938 the CNT signed an agreement with the socialist Union General Trabajadores (UGT) to subject industry to central economic planning – collectivisation everywhere was giving way to state control (Thomas, 1965: 671). In Madrid, the anarchists backed attacks on the communists, putting the blame for the perilous military position on the Popular Front government (Thomas, 1965: 750). By the end of March, Franco's victory was secured.

Focus

The Spanish Civil War

What does the civil war reveal about anarchism as an ideology? Leaving aside its fierce opposition to Marxism that had already been evident in the nineteenth century, the civil war points to a paradox at the heart of anarchism. In order to be effective, the militias had to adopt more conventional methods of organisation and the anarchists had to agree to enter into governments, trying in the Catalan instance to disguise the character of this institution. This points to a wider predicament. Anarchism is only likely to flourish in deeply divided conditions. A revolutionary situation inevitably throws up counter-revolutionary forces so that anarchists are likely to find themselves in positions of power in civil war-type situations. Dramatic changes are called for, and how is it possible to carry these through without organisation and a state? It takes a state to get rid of a state – that in essence seems to be the lesson of the events in Spain.

This argument conflicts with Marshall's view that the defeat of the anarchist movement in Spain arose from the failure to carry through the social revolution. The latter was sacrificed for the war effort, and if this and the seizure of power by the communists had not taken place, the outcome would have been very different. The failure, he suggests, was not a failure of anarchist theory and tactics (Marshall, 1993: 467).

The Problem of Violence

The question of **violence** is linked to the question of transition – how gradual is the movement towards a stateless society to be? Can a dramatic transformation of society take place bit by bit?

Godwin believed that it would take considerable time before society became sufficiently enlightened to adopt anarchist institutions, and Marshall has suggested that different types of anarchist organisation could be taken to secure progression towards the anarchist goal. Thus Proudhon's mutualism (involving the regulation of different private producers) could give way to Bakunin's collectivism (where people are rewarded according to their work), which in turn might yield to the more egalitarian idea of Kropotkin's communism where each is rewarded according to their need (Hoffman, 1995: 124).

It is true that many anarchists have seen that violence involves an intolerable conflict between ends and means. The Russian anarchist and novelist, Leo Tolstoy (1828–1910) rejected all forms of violence, whether revolutionary or statist: is there any difference, he asked between killing a revolutionary and killing a policeman? 'The difference is between cat-shit and dog-shit . . . I don't like the smell of either' (cited in Marshall, 1993: 377). Gandhi, influenced by Tolstoy, also espoused a militant pacifism. Carter argues that there are elements within anarchism that are peculiarly receptive to violence. The belief that many anarchists held, that a golden age might be realised through one apocalyptic outburst, an all-embracing revolution, can only encourage what Bakunin called the 'poetry of destruction' (Carter, 1978: 337).

Part of this 'utopianism' is the shunning of political organisation in its conventional form, for it might be argued – as we saw with the anarchists in Spain – that it is worse to cast a ballot than fire a bullet. If constitutional procedures are identified with 'statist' liberalism, then the alternative may have to be despotism and violence. It is revealing that Robert Michels turned from anarchism to authoritarianism, arguing that because the German Social Democratic Party was too hierarchical, all organisation is oligarchical in character. One sympathetic commentator has argued ruefully that 'a streak of pathological violence' runs through anarchism (Hoffman, 1995: 126). We see how after the crushing of the Paris Commune in 1871, many anarchists resorted to a 'propaganda by deed' – dramatic action designed to shake the masses out of their passivity – and these propagandist deeds often degenerated into acts of terror. The agonised slogan of radical black youth in the South African townships in the 1980s – 'liberation before education' – echoes comments by Italian followers of Garibaldi and Proudhon in the 1870s. A belief that everything is right which is not 'legal' can easily lead to violence even if it is justified as a way of avenging wrongs against the people, inspiring fear in the enemy and highlighting the evil practices of the state (Miller, 1974: 98–9).

Ch. 10: Socialism p. 228

Marshall quotes a passage from the CNT constitution printed on the membership card which states that 'the adversary does not discuss: he acts' (1993: 457), and even Kropotkin, whose personal life is often described in saint-like terms, displays what Marshall calls 'an uncomfortable mixture of quietism and aggressive elements'. Indeed, at one point in his life, Kropotkin supports the arguments of the anarcho-syndicalist Sorel that violence is the revolutionary whirlwind that energises 'sluggish hearts' (Hoffman, 1995: 126).

The problem of abolishing the state and authority seems to us to inevitably lead to the resort to violence; the perpetuation of the state in a new form, and a legacy of division and mistrust. But how are people to free themselves when they are oppressed? Oppression arises when a person is deprived of material and social resources and lacks esteem: how is this emancipation to be secured without organisation? Marshall argues that anarchists only reject authoritarian organisation, but it could be argued that all organisation requires some hierarchy and leadership – the very political qualities that anarchists reject (Hoffman, 1995: 124).

Miller cites the sad reflections of Emma Goldman as she compares the weaknesses of Russian anarchists when set against the organisational strengths of the Bolsheviks. The work of the anarchists, she remarks, 'would have been of infinitely greater value had they been better organized' (Miller, 1974: 97–8), but she fails to ask herself whether these weaknesses were a product of anarchist theory itself. What are anarchists to do if the masses fail to rise in revolt? Two responses are possible. Either anarchists simply wait (as Godwin seems to argue) until the spirit of rational enlightenment takes root in the minds of the masses, or (as in Bakunin's case) the people need a helping hand. He advocates, as we have seen, an 'invisible dictatorship' which seems to flagrantly contradict anarchist ideals.

Certainly, it is difficult to see how anarchists can combine revolutionary effectiveness without resort to force, given the fact that politics in terms of organisation, representation, leadership and compromise are ruled out in terms of the theory adopted. This is a problem not only for left-wing anarchists, but it also afflicts anarcho-capitalists who see the market as a source of freedom, but have the problem (among others!) of tackling those who have vested interests in perpetuating concentrations of state power. Rothbard notes that anarchists have to contemplate 'the extremely difficult course of a revolution against a power with all the guns in its hands' (Hoffman, 1995: 124).

Despite Marshall's argument that the civil war in Spain demonstrated the strengths and not the weaknesses of anarchist theory, it is difficult not to see that event pointing to the fact that anarchists in practice can only operate in contradiction to their own theory. Those who see anarchism as having a built-in propensity to violence whatever the pacifist claims of some of its adherents, are right. The theory cannot be understood without seeing a contradiction between ends and means.

Anarchism and the New Social Movements

Anarchism continues to be influential, with adherents like Herbert Read stressing the relevance of anarchism to the struggle for peace, secularism, a respect for art and the democratising of education. Comfort argues the case for sexual freedom, while Paul Goodman before his death in 1972, influenced many who took part in the counter-culture movements of the 1960s and 1970s. The relevance of anarchism to green movements and a concern about the deterioration of the urban and rural environment has been memorably stressed in the work of Murray Bookchin. Nature, he argues, is a 'complex of life', charged with ethical meaning. Nature is essentially creative, directive, mutualistic and fecund (Marshall, 1993: 605–6). This confirms the sociability and decency of humans. Without anarchism, there will be ecological disaster.

Bookchin's work is particularly important, because many of his positions have been adopted in the new social movements by people who may be unfamiliar with anarchism and would not regard themselves as anarchists. The new social movements concern themselves with a wide array of causes – animal rights and ecology; peace and women's rights; road building and the private transport, to name just some of them. New social movements are characterised, in our view, by a general anti-authoritarianism which sees conventional politics as stifling and treacherous; by a concern with breaking down barriers between the personal and political; and adopting a style of campaigning that unites ends and means and links enjoyment to efficiency. All this suggests that particular anarchist ideas have made a huge impact, even if anarchism considered as a comprehensive philosophy and systematic movement has not.

Green parties, like that in Germany, have enjoyed some electoral success, and have built into their procedures a libertarian distrust of authoritarianism, and what are regarded as the dangers inherent in conventional political organisation. At the same time, they have not ignored parliament or the state, and they have treated anarchism less as a dogma, and more as a set of values some of which are more relevant and valid than others.

The philosophy of direct action – that laws and private property are not sacrosanct – stems from an anarchist suspicion of the state. When people in Britain refused to pay their poll tax in the 1980s or occupied military and nuclear bases, they were acting according to anarchist values – understood in the sense of particular attitudes that may be appropriate for particular situations. Writing to your MP is all very well – but much more immediate action may be called for! A commitment to social justice; a belief in the worthiness of human nature; adherence to equality; a dislike of repressive hierarchy; a concern with the destruction of the environment; anxiety about poverty in the so-called Third World – these and many other movements are inspired by parts of anarchism, though not by anarchist philosophy as a whole.

Classical anarchism is seen as being in the same boat as classical Marxism: rigid, dogmatic; old-fashioned; weak on issues of women, children's rights and the environment – too concerned with ideological rectitude and theoretical rigour. Anarchists often link their dislike for large organisations to a belief that the market is corrupting and capitalism unfair. Turner argues that the natural supporters of anarchist values are those who are excluded from consumerist society and who see politicians as an elite and incapable of engineering real change. He speaks of anarchism having a more receptive and permanent home among an underclass that might include 'disaffected youth, the long term unemployed and inner-city dwellers in perpetual poverty' (1993: 32). Anarchism and anarchist values are clearly the price which society pays for a conventional politics that fails to ameliorate inequality and ecological damage.

The Problem of Organisation and Relationships

It has been said that anarchism 'owes more to conventional liberalism than some of its adherents are willing to admit' (Hoffman, 1995: 113). It is not only philosophical and free-market anarchists who embody the problems of the liberal tradition, so too do the anti-capitalist anarchists. The problem is that even when liberalism is militantly opposed, liberal values are turned inside out – they are inverted, but never meaningfully transcended, or moved beyond.

Marshall captures the problem in a graphic way when he criticises Bookchin and Kropotkin for committing the naturalistic fallacy of deriving an 'is' from an 'ought'. 'There is', he argues, 'no logical connection to make us move from fact to value' (1993: 620). But this is a misuse of the notion of a naturalistic fallacy. The 'naturalistic fallacy' should, it seems to us, refer to an erroneous belief in the timelessness of nature and of human links with nature. It is however quite another thing to argue that we cannot move from facts to value. This is a positivist (or empiricist) dictum that arises because thinkers cannot see that facts themselves embody relationships. Indeed, it is the relational nature of facts that gives them their evaluative or normative content. Thus, the fact that there are many women lawyers but few women judges, tells us something about the **relationship** between men and women in our society, and therefore it would be erroneous to assume that such a fact has no ethical implications.

This argument suggests that Marshall, an enthusiastic anarchist, is still committed to a liberal methodology, and to a liberal opposition to understanding individuals in terms of the relationships that identify them. We see this position in anarchist attitudes to organisation. Marshall may insist that he does not reject organisation per se, but only authoritarian organisation. The fact remains, however, that he accepts a philosophical standpoint that makes it impossible to see organisation as deriving from the relational character of humans. Even anarchists like Kropotkin and Bookchin fail to go along with the full implications of seeing humans as relational beings. By arguing that anarchism is based upon 'a mechanistic explanation of all phenomena' (Marshall, 1993: 318), Kropotkin accepts a static view of humanity – to which (like Bakunin) he ascribes an 'instinct' for sociability. His notion of the natural sciences is positivist and he appears to argue that because humans have evolved from nature, they are simply the same as other natural beings. The specificity of human relationships is not understood.

While Bookchin does stress that humans have a 'second nature' – different from but linked to their biology and their 'first nature' – it is revealing that he calls his blending of anarchism and ecology an 'ecotopia'. He proclaims that 'our Science is Utopia' without seeing that (traditionally defined) utopias 'on their own' are static and ahistorical, and postulate some kind of final end of history (Marshall, 1993: 621). This emphasises the ideal at the expense of the facts and ignores the dynamic and fluid nature of the real world. This abstract approach makes it impossible to account for relationships and the need for organisation – not simply to achieve a Utopia – but as an ongoing expression of human relationships.

The Problem of Hierarchy

Anarchists in general use the term 'hierarchy' in a negative way, but hierarchy itself is part and parcel of human relationships.

Turner notes the work of A.S. Neil, who believed that education was possible without any hierarchy. Neil was the founder of the 'free school' movement, whose designs for education modelled at his Summerhill school conformed to anarchist prescriptions. There were to be no compulsory lessons; no authority of teachers over pupils; an emphasis upon self-development rather than 'instruction'; no testing of knowledge against prescribed targets; and no need to attend anything (Turner, 1993: 31).

p. 4

While Summerhill school may have avoided authoritarianism, did it really avoid hierarchy as such? It is certainly true that the use of force in relationships is counter-productive and is incompatible with the nature of relationships themselves. Hence *repressive* hierarchy is inherently undesirable. But it does not follow from this that hierarchy in itself is wrong or oppressive. On the contrary, it exists in all relationships. The term 'authority' can be taken to assume persuasion and consent, but an authoritative relationship is one based on hierarchy. Surely when one goes to a doctor, you accept their authority, not because you are unwilling to question their advice, but because *in this situation* there is a hierarchy born of the fact that the doctor has a specialist knowledge of health which you lack. This is not a static hierarchy – you may become more knowledgeable yourself – nor is it a comprehensive hierarchy. If you are a motor mechanic, the doctor may well come to you for help, and the hierarchy is reversed.

In our view, it is impossible to conceive of a relationship without hierarchy. Each party is different, and it is this difference that creates the hierarchical character of relationships. There is clearly a hierarchical relationship between parents and children. This does not mean that they are not equal, for equality, in our view, means sameness *and* difference. The hierarchy is fluid and interpenetrating: sometimes the parent teaches the child; on other occasions, the parent learns from him. It is difficult not to conclude that anarchist opposition to hierarchy arises from what is essentially a liberal view that equality can only mean sameness, and that freedom is a spontaneity born of the complete absence of restraint – an **abstraction** that derives from the classical liberal view of individuals who originate in a natural world without constraint or relationship.

The Question of Self-determination and Constraint

Anarchists argue for self-determination and this is valid objective to aim at, but it is misleading to imagine that self-determination, like autonomy or emancipation (to take just two related concepts), is a condition that we 'finally' reach, for like the notion of perfection, emancipation would turn into a nightmare if it ever 'arrived'. For what would happen to those deemed unemancipated? They would inevitably be 'forced to be free'.

What makes emancipatory concepts absolute as well as relative is the fact that our relationships with other humans, like our relationships with the wider world of nature, are continually changing. We are absolute in the sense that all humans are the same – they must relate to nature and to one another in order to survive – but we are also relative to one another. The way we relate depends upon the world we find ourselves in, and the world we construct, and this makes us different.

Not only are humans both absolute and relative in their rights, but we are agents whose freedom derives from the recognition and transformation of necessity. This is why we are both free and constrained at the same time, for this world of necessity constrains us. Marx and Mill use the term 'coercion' to embrace morality and circumstances, but we favour a narrower view of coercion: coercion involves the threat of credible force. The kind of pressures that arise from being in society are better conceived of as a constraint and these constraints arise out of relationships, and are part and parcel of the price we pay as social beings, who can only become conscious of our individuality through relationships with others.

It is crucial to make the distinction which anarchism fails to make, between force and constraint. Force disrupts relationships, because one party loses their subjectivity and becomes a mere 'thing'. Constraint on the other hand, while sometimes unpleasant, is unavoidable and a condition for freedom. It is not possible to be free without recognising and transforming the constraints that act upon us, and even the most spontaneous act can only succeed if it acknowledges and works to change a world of constraint. When Bakunin took part in the uprising in the French city of Lyon and proclaimed 'that the administrative and governmental machinery of the

Focus

Utopianism and Realism

Anarchists are right to see the state as problematic, but to look beyond the state, the state has to be presented in a way that is realistic. Why should we assume that if an idea is realistic, it cannot also be utopian? Utopianism and realism need to be creatively combined, but this is only possible if one makes distinctions of a kind that break with the liberal tradition.

Of course, it is wrong to force a person to act against their will, but it does not follow from this that force can simply be abolished. The use of force as a way of addressing conflicts of interest can only be dispensed with when people have sufficient in common that they can 'change places'. An opposition to force under all circumstances constitutes utopianism without realism, for we need to work to create the conditions under which force becomes redundant.

Moreover, realism requires us to face the fact that relationships constrain as well as empower. This constraint becomes severe when used deliberately as a punishment, and although we would accept that the less of these kind of constraints the better, it is unrealistic to imagine that people can relate to one another and to the wider world of nature, without some kind of constraint being employed and involved. Hence the attempt to eliminate force as a way of tackling conflicts is strengthened by the distinction between constraint and force. Society is inconceivable without constraint and hierarchy, and anarchists weaken their arguments against the state by refusing to accept this.

state' have been abolished (Marshall, 1993: 286), he learnt that it takes more than words to overthrow a despotic state, and unsurprisingly, the rising was speedily crushed. The point is that alliances must be formed; existing institutions utilised; the people must be prepared and feel that such an action is justified; and the forces of the opponent must be marginalised and neutralised – all the things which require organisation and the acknowledgement of constraints are crucial if a political action is to meet with hope of success.

Anarchism and the Distinction between State and Government

The distinction between force and constraint translates into the opposition between state and government, and by condemning both, anarchists again leave themselves open to the charge that they are being utopian without at the same time being realistic.

Ch. 1:
The State

The distinction between state and government is a crucial one to make. Anarchists tend to regard the two as synonyms. Godwin finds that government is opposed to society. It is static and oppressive – 'the only perennial causes of the vices of mankind' – and looks towards its 'true euthanasia' (Marshall, 1993: 206–7). Kropotkin makes a distinction between state and government, but considers both equally oppressive and both should be abolished. Representative government is no more than rule by the capitalists (Marshall, 1993: 325). It is not difficult to see that this negative view of government as well as the state, is linked to a failure to distinguish between force and constraint.

Godwin saw public opinion as oppressive and irresistible as whips and chains. Orwell is cited sympathetically as an anarchist who found Tolstoy's pacifism potentially coercive, while Gandhi's doctrine of non-violence has coercive overtones which Marshall sees as bullying and constituting a 'totalitarian danger' (Marshall, 1993: 650). It is one thing to warn (as J.S. Mill did) that public opinion can be intolerant and needlessly intrusive, but it is quite another to suggest that moral pressures are a kind of 'coercion' and as unacceptable as brute force. If the constraints imposed by Mill's natural penalties and the use of moral pressures are deemed authoritarian, then constitutionalism and the rule of law have to be rejected, even when these institutions operate in a purely governmental, as opposed to an oppressively statist, way (Hoffman, 1995: 127).

Government, it could be argued, is inherent in organisation and relationships. It involves the use of constraint in order to resolve conflicts that arise from the fact that each of us is different from the other. For this reason, conflict is inevitable and so is government, but just as a sharp distinction needs to be drawn between constraint and force, so a distinction needs to be made between state and government. To link the state and government as twin enemies of freedom is to ignore the fact that stateless societies have governments, and that even in state-centred societies, the role of government is positive and empowering. With the rise of new liberal and socialist administrations, significant programmes of social reform have been introduced; the power of the trade unions has been strengthened; the health and security of the most vulnerable sections of society has been improved; and a modest redistribution of income and resources has been introduced. But these reforms are vulnerable and can be reversed, and force employed in an increasingly divisive way by the state. Indeed, one radical theorist has protested that were the state to disappear overnight, 'there would be an orgy of unlimited repression and exploitation by capitalism', but this comment rests upon a confusion of state and government. It is crucial to see that many of the activities undertaken in the name of the state are not necessarily and intrinsically statist in character (Hoffman, 1995: 123).

Anarchist attacks on the 'welfare state' as bureaucratic and oppressive can only be legitimately described as *anti-statist* if they are able to show that the provision of welfare and security undermines self-development and is thus part and parcel of the state's exercise of force. If this cannot be shown, then the provision of welfare and security – to the extent that it is genuinely developmental – is governmental rather than statist in character. The existence of 'interference' and constraint is not in itself evidence of oppression since such attributes are inherent in all organisations and in relationships.

Carter is right to argue that administration in itself does not require the use of violence (1978: 324), although, of course, administrators may act in a high-handed and undemocratic fashion and thus contribute to the alienation which causes the use of force, both by the opponents of the state, and by the state itself. Nevertheless, we need to keep government and the state conceptually separate, since it is wrong and counter-productive to identify government with oppression, simply because it involves pressures and sanctions of a constraining kind. Without a distinction between state and government (→ chapter on the State), it is impossible to move beyond the state.

Summary

Anarchism is often analysed as part of socialism, but anarchism is so distinctive that it deserves treatment in its own right. Philosophical anarchists are concerned with the autonomy of the individual as a theoretical problem, while free-market anarchists argue the case for replacing the state with an unfettered market.

Anti-capitalist anarchists are critical of Marxism either because, like Proudhon, they dislike collectivist solutions to the problem of inequality, or because, in the case of anarchists like Bakunin and Kropotkin, they are unconvinced by the need for a dictatorship of the proletariat in the transformation of capitalism into communism. The Spanish Civil War constitutes a veritable historical laboratory in understanding anarchism since anarchists were extremely influential during this period and their clashes with other sections of the left, and the tactics they adopted, are extremely instructive.

Anarchism is unable to handle the problem of violence, but it has played a significant role in the formation of new social movements. Anarchism runs into particular difficulty in its treatment of the problem of hierarchy and organisation. It is weakened through its failure to distinguish between state and government, and force and constraint.

Questions

1. Should those who seek to replace the market with the state be called 'anarchists'?

2. Discuss the proposition that the new social movements like the movement for peace, environmentalism and women's rights embrace part of anarchism rather than anarchism as a whole.

3. What do anarchists understand by 'hierarchy' and does it interfere with the demands of political organisation?

4. What do you see as the lessons of the Spanish Civil War?

5. Is the notion of a stateless society a mere anarchist fantasy?

References

Berki, R. (1974) *Socialism* London: Dent.

Carter, A. (1978) 'Anarchism and Violence' in J. Pennock and J. Chapman (eds), *Anarchism* New York: New York University Press, 320–40.

Dahl, R. (1989) *Democracy and its Critics* New Haven, CT and London: Yale University Press.

Goodwin, B. (1997) *Using Political Ideas*, 4th edn Chichester, New York, Toronto: John Wiley and Sons.

Hoffman, J. (1995) *Beyond the State* Cambridge: Polity.

Marshall, P. (1993) *Demanding the Impossible* London: Fontana.

Maximoff, G. (ed.) (1953) *The Political Philosophy of Bakunin* New York: The Free Press.

Miller, D. (1974) *Anarchism* London: Dent.

Nozick, R. (1974) *Anarchy, State, and Utopia* Oxford: Basil Blackwell.

Orwell, G. (2001) *Orwell in Spain* (ed. P. Davison) Harmondsworth: Penguin.

Thomas, H. (1965) *The Spanish Civil War* Harmondsworth: Penguin.

Turner, R. (1993) 'Anarchism: What is it?' *Politics Review* 3(1), 28–32.

Vincent, A. (1995) *Modern Political Ideologies* Oxford: Blackwell.

Further Reading

- Marshall *Demanding the Impossible* (referenced above) is a detailed and highly readable account of anarchist doctrines and personalities.

- Turner's short piece on 'Anarchism: What is it?' (referenced above) is very clear and comprehensive and raises the question as to why anarchism still continues to make an impact.

- Orwell's *Homage to Catalonia* (referenced above) provides a vivid account of the way in which the anarchists operated in Spain, and the difficulties under which they worked.

- Carter's piece on 'Anarchism and Violence' (referenced above) is both thoughtful and rigorous, and raises important theoretical problems within anarchism.

- Dahl's Chapter 3 in his *Democracy and its Critics* (referenced above) contains an amusing and instructive dialogue between characters he calls 'Demo' and 'Anarch' which is both critical and fair.

- Shatz's edition of *The Essential Works of Anarchism* (London, New York and Toronto: Bantam Books, 1971), contains extracts from classical and more recent anarchists so that you can read the arguments 'in the original'.

- A useful exposition of anarcho-capitalism can be found in Stone, C. (1978) 'Some Reflections on Arbitrating our Way to Anarchy' in J. Pennock and J. Chapman (eds) *Anarchism* New York: New York University Press.

Weblinks

This is very comprehensive. Items A1 and 2 are particularly valuable so is A4 and some of A5.
http://www.anarchistfaq.org

Used selectively something of value here.
http://www.anarchism.ws/

For anyone who wants a more detailed analysis of anarchism in Spain.
http://www.struggle.ws/spaindx.html

Chapter 12

Nationalism

Introduction

Nationalism has been a powerful force in modern history. It arouses strong feelings – for some, nationalism is tantamount to racism, but for others nationalist sentiment creates solidarity and stability, which are preconditions for freedom. These two perspectives are informed by history: in its most extreme form nationalism was, it is claimed, at the root of the genocidal policies of Nazi Germany, and yet it has also been the basis of liberation movements in such regions as Eastern Europe, Africa and Asia. The challenge for political theorists is to explain how the 'nation' can be a source of value and an object of allegiance. This is indeed a challenge: most liberals (and many anarchists) hold that the *individual human being* is the ultimate source of value, and the individual has claims against collective entities, such as the nation; many socialists are collectivists, but for them it is *class*, or *humanity* as a whole, that is the proper object of concern.

Chapter Map

In this chapter we will:

- Outline the debate around the meaning and origins of the 'nation' and of 'nationalism'.

- Consider the distinction between civic nationalism and ethnic nationalism using citizenship law as a case study.

- Analyse the role of nationalism in the work of two nineteenth-century liberal thinkers (Mill and Herder), and in the work of Marx and Engels.

- Discuss contemporary liberal defences of nationalism.

Only a Game?

Italians celebrate their FIFA World Cup victory in Berlin, July 2006

Source: © Andres Kudacki/Corbis

To what extent football (soccer) reflects, encourages, or is largely irrelevant to nationalism is a matter of debate amongst academics. A couple of incidents in Britain during the 2006 World Cup suggest that football has a 'dark side': a 17-year-old boy walking across a park in London was knocked unconscious merely because he was wearing a Germany T-shirt, and a man in Scotland was dragged from his car and beaten up for wearing an England top. Of course, the link between football and patriotism need not be negative: Germany was praised across the world for hosting that very successful – and largely peaceful – World Cup. It might be argued that it brought nations closer together.

Marxist thinker Eric Hobsbawm has argued that football is an indicator for the state of the nation and nationalism in the age of globalisation. Football is a kind of 'seismograph': the tension between nationalism and globalisation reveals itself in the way that wealthy clubs would like to form European or international super-leagues, but know that football's marketability is rooted in local and national allegiances (Hobsbawm, 2008). Supporters are now used to the cosmopolitanism of 'their' teams, but a complete break with any local or national identity would be a step too far. The tension is also revealed in the way that clubs resent the time taken out by – and risks of injury entailed in – their players playing for national teams.

What do you think: does football reflect or, alternatively, generate nationalism? Should we take football seriously as an expression of nationalism? Is Hobsbawm right in his claim that football reveals the tensions between nationalism and globalisation?

Nations and Nationalism

In the period from around 1850 to the start of the First World War in 1914 there was a marked rise in popular nationalist consciousness across Europe, with the unification of Italy in 1861 and Germany in 1871, and the so-called 'scramble for Africa' pitting the European nations against one another on that continent, while a precarious balance of power was maintained within Europe. After its defeat in the First World War the Austro-Hungarian Empire fragmented into 'new' nations such as Czechoslovakia and Hungary. There was much discussion of the right to national self-determination. In the period after the Second World War there was less theoretical interest in nationalism, with ideological debate centred on the struggle between liberal capitalism and state socialism; this was despite the fact that it was a period of significant nation-building in Africa and Asia in the wake of decolonisation. Since the dramatic events in Eastern Europe in 1989 there has been an extraordinary resurgence of interest in nationalism; in large part this has been due to the recognition that powerful nationalist sentiments survived 40 years of state socialism in Eastern Europe. So while nationalism is a 'traditional ideology' it is very much one the study of which is in the ascendant.

In previous chapters we have cautioned against overreliance on dictionary definitions of concepts in political theory. While it can be useful to trace the etymology of words, everyday usage is too diverse and conflicting to provide guidance on the correct employment of concepts, the meanings of which are bound up with particular theories. The word 'nation' is a good example of the dangers of dictionary definitions. Dictionaries trace the word 'nation' to the Latin *natio*, and the Latin term was certainly used in the medieval period. For example, there is a debate about whether Scotland was really a nation before the Act of Union with England in 1707; one of the documents used in favour of the claim that Scotland was indeed a nation is the Declaration of Arbroath (1320), which was written in Latin and uses the term *natio*. The difficulty with this argument is that *natio* can be translated as 'place of birth' – note the English word 'natal' – and the 37 signatories when they make reference to themselves as a 'nation' may not necessarily have possessed the modern consciousness of nationhood (Davidson, 2000: 48–9). The point is that words do not, in themselves, settle arguments over the nature of nationalism. Meanings are embedded in theories. However, it is useful to set out a variety of *competing* definitions of 'nation' and of 'nationalism', and try to identify commonalities and divergences. We start with 'nation':

> The totality of people who are united by a common fate so that they possess a common (national) character. The common fate is . . . primarily a common history; the common national character involves almost necessarily a uniformity of language (Otto Bauer in Davis, 1967: 150).

> A nation is a community of sentiment that could adequately manifest itself in a state of its own: hence a nation is a community which normally tends to produce a state of its own (Max Weber in Hutchinson and Smith, 1994: 25).

> [A nation is] a named human population that shares myths and memories, a mass public culture, a designated homeland, economic unity and equal rights and duties for all members (Anthony Smith, 1991: 43).

[A nation] is an imagined political community – and imagined as both inherently limited and sovereign . . . all communities larger than primordial villages of face-to-face contact (and perhaps even these) are imagined. Communities are to be distinguished, not by their falsity/genuineness, but by the style in which they are imagined (Benedict Anderson, 1991: 6).

A nation is a group of people who feel themselves to be a community bound together by ties of history, culture and common ancestry. Nations have 'objective' characteristics that may include a territory, a language, a religion or common descent (though not all of these are always present), and 'subjective' characteristics, essentially a people's awareness of their nationality and affection for it (James Kellas, 1998: 3).

All five definitions begin with the idea of a 'collective': 'totality of people', 'community of sentiment', 'named human population', 'imagined political community', 'group of people . . . community' but disagreement exists on how this collective is held together. Bauer maintains the nation possesses a 'common character' or 'common fate', which necessarily entails a shared language. Weber argues that sentiment – or fellow feeling – holds the collective together, but that it also has a political project, namely the drive to create a state. Smith is more pluralistic in his understanding of what makes the collective cohere: myths, memories, mass public culture, homeland, economic unity, rights and duties. The last basis is, however, distinctly political: the nation has a legal dimension. Anderson maintains that we 'imagine' the nation: because we will never meet more than a tiny fraction of our fellow citizens the national community is imaginary, constructed above all through the medium of literature. Finally, Kellas draws attention to the objective *and* subjective dimensions of nationhood – nations require 'objective materials' such as territory or language, but there must also be a corresponding consciousness of belonging to a nation.

In fact, although Kellas makes it explicit, subjectivity – or consciousness – is implicit in the other four definitions: 'national character' (Bauer), 'community of sentiment' (Weber), '[sharing] myths and memories' (Smith), *imagined* political community' (Anderson). The idea of consciousness is central to understanding the political-philosophical significance of the nation: a 'nation' that existed outside the consciousness of its 'members' would be of little interest to political theorists: it is the act of valuing the nation, or more precisely that we *ought* to value the – or *our* – nation, or that it is *permissible* (even if not required) to be partial to our compatriots, that is the focus of our concern in this chapter. There has been an extensive debate amongst political scientists on the historical origins of the nation: is it pre-modern ('primordial') or a modern phenomenon? For political theorists this is of only subsidiary interest – if a group of people believe that their nation is primordial and that belief conditions their behaviour then whether that nation, or any nation, is in fact primordial is beside the point.

It is nationalism, rather than the nation that is of interest to political theorists, so what then of 'nationalism'? Again, we have competing understandings of nationalism:

It is a theory of political legitimacy, which requires that ethnic boundaries should not cut across political ones, and in particular, that ethnic boundaries within a given state . . . should not separate the power holders from the rest (Ernest Gellner, 1983: 1).

Nationalism is a doctrine invented in Europe at the beginning of the nineteenth century. It pretends to supply the criterion for the determination of the unit of population proper to enjoy a government exclusively of its own, for the legitimate exercise of power in the state and for the right organisation of a society of states. Briefly, the doctrine holds that humanity is naturally divided into nations, that nations are known by certain characteristics which can be ascertained, and that the only legitimate type of government is national self-government (Elie Kedourie, 1993: 9).

By nationalism I mean the sentiment of belonging to a community whose members identify with a set of symbols, beliefs and ways of life and have the will to decide upon their common political destiny (Montserrat Guibernau, 1996: 47).

Whereas the term 'nation' refers to some kind of entity, 'nationalism' would appear to be a body of doctrine, theory or beliefs about the nation, its historical significance and moral importance.

Political theorists, who tend to operate with *universalist* concepts such as human nature, freedom, equality and justice, have found it difficult to explain nationalism, which is, essentially, *particularist* – that is, it assumes that national boundaries are morally significant. At best, nationalism has been incorporated into other ideologies, such as liberalism or socialism, as a derivative concern. For example, liberals or socialists may argue that all human beings are equally worthy of moral concern, but the world is a better place if it is organised into nations – world government would be inefficient, or dangerous, because it would concentrate rather than disperse power. Most of this chapter focuses on liberalism, although with some comments on the Marxist view of the nation. As a way into the liberal debate over the ethical status of the nation we consider the distinction frequently made between 'civic' and 'ethnic' nationalism, using citizenship law as a case study.

Citizenship – 'Civic' and 'Ethnic' Nationalisms

Michael Ignatieff defines a civic nation as 'a community of equal, rights-bearing citizens, united in patriotic attachment to a shared set of political practices and values' (Ignatieff, 1993: 7). For a civic nationalist 'belonging' to a nation entails a rational choice rather than an inheritance. In contrast, an ethnic nationalist maintains 'that an individual's deepest attachments are inherited, not chosen' (Ignatieff, 1993: 7). The distinction between the two forms of nationalism has been attributed to Hans Kohn, who, in his discussion of nationalism in the nineteenth century, defined 'Western' nations, such as France, Britain and the United States as civic, and 'Eastern' nations, such as Germany and Russia, as ethnic. Civic nationalism appears to be an expression of, or at least compatible with, the liberal values of freedom (autonomy, choice) and equality (equality of individuals and equality of nations). But is this so? Indeed, is civic nationalism a coherent notion? To explore these questions we consider citizenship laws in four countries – Switzerland, Germany, Britain, and the United States. We are particularly interested in the distinction between two principles governing the acquisition of citizenship: *jus sanguinis* and *jus soli*.

Switzerland

Swiss citizenship law is based on three principles: (a) triple citizenship level; (b) *jus sanguinis*, or determination through the family line, as distinct from *jus soli*, or determination through place of birth; (c) prevention of statelessness. With regard to the first principle, every Swiss is a citizen of their commune of origin, their canton of origin, and of the Confederation. Children born to Swiss parents living abroad will lose their citizenship by the age of 22 unless they indicate to the authorities they wish to retain it, although 'reinstatement' is a possibility, especially in order to prevent statelessness.

The most controversial aspect of Swiss citizenship is the rejection of *jus soli*: it is possible to be a third-generation resident and still be denied citizenship. Naturalisation requires approval by a local citizenship committee; individual applications may be put to a local referendum in which voting information includes pictures of the applicants. One native-born 'foreigner', 23-year-old Fatma Karademir, whose parents are Turkish, applied for citizenship through her local village citizenship committee, but was rejected and told she had to live another 10 years in Switzerland before the committee could really judge her suitability for citizenship. She complains that longevity in the country counts for less than the answers she gives to the committee: 'They'll ask me if I can imagine marrying a Swiss boy . . . or if I like Swiss music, or who I'll support if Switzerland play Turkey at football – really stupid questions' ('Long Road to Swiss Citizenship', BBC website, 20 September 2004). In 2004 a proposal to ease the naturalisation process was defeated by 57 to 43 per cent in a national referendum; a separate proposal to grant the right to citizenship to grandchildren of immigrants was defeated by 52 to 48 per cent.

Germany

The traditional basis for acquiring German citizenship was through descent (*jus sanguinis*), meaning that you had to prove that one or more of your parents was German, with the possibility of restoration of citizenship to those stripped of it by the Nazi regime, or to their descendants. A law passed in 1953 extended the concept of membership of the nation (*Volkszugehörigkeit*) to all ethnic Germans in Eastern bloc countries. Thus the law was highly inclusive of anyone who could prove German descent. On the other hand, until the year 2000 millions of 'guest workers' were denied the right to citizenship because the law did not recognise the principle of acquisition of citizenship by place of birth (*jus soli*), except under certain circumstances and at the discretion of the state. The new law, which came into effect on 1 January 2000, allowed the children of non-German parents to acquire, by right, citizenship if one parent has had a minimum legal residence in Germany of eight years and has held an unlimited residence permit for at least three years. Under most circumstances, the child who acquires citizenship in this way must, before the age of 23, revoke any other nationality – in principle, Germany does not tolerate multiple citizenship. In addition, new citizens must demonstrate competence in the German language, and swear allegiance to the principles of the constitution.

Britain

In theory, loyalty to the British monarch, as expressed through the holding of a British passport, has been the primary determinant of 'nationality'; however, there are different categories of passport, not all of which grant *citizenship*. In the period from 1948 to 1981 Britain moved closer to other European countries in adopting a citizenship law, partly based on *jus sanguinis* and partly on *jus soli*. Compared to many countries, the proof of integration required as part of the naturalisation process is light: basic competence in English (or Welsh, or Scots Gaelic), being of 'good character', and swearing (or affirming) that you will 'be faithful and bear true allegiance to Her Majesty Queen Elizabeth the Second her Heirs and Successors according to Law'. Citizenship ceremonies were introduced in 2004, and since then new citizens have also been required to pledge loyalty to the country's rights, freedoms and democratic values. Multiple citizenship is permitted.

Ch. 6:
Citizenship
p. 121

United States

The United States sees itself as, historically, a 'country of immigration'. For that reason, the principle of *jus sanguinis* might be thought weak; however, as in most countries, a family connection does provide a person with a privileged access to citizenship. That said, historically, naturalisation has been an extremely important route to citizenship; perhaps unsurprisingly, the symbolic dimensions are very important. In addition to legal residency requirements, an applicant must be of 'good moral character', and there is a long list of criminal offences that preclude a person from citizenship. They must show attachment to the principles of the Constitution, be competent in the English language, demonstrate knowledge of US history and government (a pass of 6 out of 10 questions from a battery of 100 is required). Finally, the applicant must swear an oath of allegiance – this takes rather longer than the seven-second British oath.

Citizenship and Civic Nationalism

These brief outlines of the citizenship laws of different countries appear to lend plausibility to the idea that the principle of *jus sanguinis* implies an ethnic conception of the nation, while *jus soli* implies a civic conception, but this is an oversimplification. Consider, for example, Germany's citizenship laws. Germany was unified relatively late, and it is argued that national consciousness preceded the formal creation of Germany as a political entity, albeit Prussia had existed as a significant power since the late seventeenth century and, in addition, there emerged a federation of German states and principalities after Napoleon Bonaparte's defeat in 1815. Despite this gradual unification of Germany, only in 1871 was an approximate correspondence of national and political boundaries achieved, such that Germany was, prior to 1871, in effect a stateless nation. We have to say 'approximate' because the cultural boundaries of Germany, defined above all by the German language, did not correspond to the political boundaries even of post-1871 Germany. The consequence was that the newly unified Germany had serious difficulty in defining citizenship, and it was only in 1913 that the citizenship law was codified. The self-understanding of the German nation as primarily a cultural entity, which had been given political identity as a state, fundamentally affected that law. On the face of it, German nationalism would appear, therefore, to be ethnic rather than civic, and the overtly racist laws passed during the Nazi years appear retrospectively to reinforce this perception of German nationalism. Much of the discussion in the German and international media in the late 1990s of the German citizenship law reforms focused on what appeared to be archaic blood-line notions of citizenship. However, it is quite possible to interpret the 1913 German citizenship law as a response to modern conditions: a developing nation with indeterminate boundaries requires criteria for citizenship, and some idea of culture or ethnicity seemed the most appropriate. The available ingredients of nationhood meant that Germany had to rely on ethnic criteria in order to create a *modern* nation. This is not to say that there is no connection between the 1913 law and the citizenship laws promulgated by the Nazis in the 1930s, but simply that the use of apparently ethnic criteria does not preclude the possibility that Germany was – Nazi years apart – basically a civic nation. Conversely, those nations described by Kohn as civic are not free of ethnic criteria for citizenship.

The Debate over German (Re-)unification

The fall of the Berlin Wall in 1989 and the 1990 (re-)unification of East and West Germany generated an interesting debate between three German intellectuals: philosopher Jürgen Habermas, cultural critic Karl-Heinz Bohrer and novelist Günter Grass. Each presented a distinct position on the nature of the German nation, and more broadly on the role of nationalism in political life. Grass argued against unification mainly on the grounds that

> there can be no demand for a new version of a unified nation that in the course of barely 75 years, although under several managements, filled the history books, ours and theirs, with suffering, rubble, defeat, millions of dead, and the burden of crimes that can never be undone (Grass in James and Stone, 1992: 57–8).

The division must remain as a tangible symbol of those crimes. Bohrer, on the other hand, argues that the crimes to which Grass refers have their roots, in part, in the parochialism of the 'police states' which constituted the pre-1871 Germany; what Germany needs is a sense of nationhood. He accepts that the Holocaust is the 'great, unavoidable fact of our modern history', but a cultural regeneration of Germany – nationalism rather than parochialism – is the best guarantor of liberal democracy. Habermas, while accepting the legitimacy of unification – and it is unification rather than reunification, for the 'two Germanys' in no way correspond to the Germany of 1937 – argues for a form of civic nationalism, based on what he calls 'constitutional patriotism'. His argument revolves around a complex debate concerning the legal nature of the 1990 unification: in effect, it extended the West German 'constitution' (1949 *Grundgesetz* – Basic Law) to East Germany, rather than creating a new constitution (*Verfassung* – this word was not used in 1949 because it was always assumed that the division of East and West would be temporary). Had there been a new constitution, endorsed by a referendum, the German people would quite literally have 'constituted' themselves rather than seeing the unified nation as the product of 'pre-political imponderables like linguistic community, culture, or history' (Habermas in James and Stone, 1992: 97).

Note: This debate is reproduced in Harold James and Marla Stone (eds), *When the Wall Came Down: Reactions to German Unification*.

As with Germany, the development of British and US citizenship laws were a response to their specific geographic and historic conditions. As Samuel Huntington argues, the United States can be considered a settler society rather than an immigrant society, and those original settlers defined themselves as British and Protestant; while post-Independence America sought to distance its political institutions from any particular Christian denomination, a belief in God was implicit in being American, and the structures of the Protestant world-view were deeply embedded in the nation. The large numbers of non-Protestants who migrated to the United States in the period between the civil war (1861–5) and the First World War were 'assimilated' into the existing value system (Huntington, 2004: 95–8).

In the case of Britain, the very loose citizenship laws that operated until 1981 were a response to the specific historical conditions of British nation-building and transformation; in particular, the need to cement the relationship between England and Scotland, which was achieved to a significant degree through the building of an empire. The point is that 'being British' relied on ethnic criteria just as much as 'being German' did; what made British identity appear more civic was that loyalty to the nation was expressed through loyalty to a constitutional monarchy, rather than to the 'British people'.

All nationalisms have three characteristics: they imply a relationship of an individual to the collective that is in significant ways non-voluntary, they entail partiality and they involve exclusion. Even civic nationalism has these features. First, you may be free to leave your country but you never chose to be a citizen of your country. Second, as a citizen you stand in a special relationship to your country: nationalism implies you are *permitted* to be 'partial' to your compatriots (non-civic nationalism may entail a *requirement* to show partiality). Finally, although a civic nation may succeed in providing non-racial or non-ethnic criteria for citizenship all nations involve belonging, and belonging implies its opposite: not belonging, or exclusion. From the perspective of political theory a nationalist must defend these three features of nationalism: non-voluntariness, partiality, and exclusion. In the remainder of this chapter we explore a number of attempts to do this. We start with two important nineteenth-century liberal thinkers – Mill and Herder – move on to a nineteenth-century socialist perspective (Marx and Engels), and then explore contemporary liberal approaches to nationalism.

Liberalism and Nationalism: Mill and Herder

At first sight liberalism and nationalism appear odd bedfellows: for nationalists the most significant moral entity is the nation, whereas for liberals the most significant is the individual human being. Where there is a conflict between the claims of the individual and those of the nation, liberals and nationalists will diverge over which should take precedence. Furthermore, the priority given to the individual by liberals normally rests on features all human beings share, such that the logic of liberal individualism is moral *universalism* (individualism might also lead to egoism, but we will ignore that possibility here). In contrast, nationalists are *particularists*: although some nationalists will argue that there is a universal need to belong to a nation, nationalism entails regarding one's own nation as 'special'.

The difficulty with this apparent rejection of nationalism is that historically liberalism and nationalism have often been combined into a single political programme: the struggle for national self-determination has been expressed in the language of freedom, self-government and accountability. The question is whether the apparent affinity of liberalism and nationalism is simply a historical accident, or whether there is a deeper philosophical compatibility that is not captured by an oversimplistic derivation of universalism from individualism.

Jean-Jacques Rousseau may be interpreted as the first significant liberal thinker to make an explicit case for nationalism. His defence of nationalism was based on the importance of a 'people' possessing a general will, the recognition of which supposedly guarantees individual freedom; the general will is not reducible to the wills of individuals, or to a simple aggregation of wills (Rousseau, 1968: 247–9). Rousseau's theory is highly abstract, and seems unconnected to the political realities of his time, but it has been influential in the development of a popular nationalism based on democratic self-government. What provides the link between liberalism and nationalism in Rousseau's theory is the idea of democracy, such that a better understanding of the relationship between the individual and the nation is:

Nation ← → Sovereign People (democracy) ← → Individual

However, there are still difficulties involved in reconciling nationalism and liberalism. First, as we have argued, democracy and liberalism, while closely related, can conflict: democracy does imply that each person's interests should be given equal consideration, but to make decisions we have to rely on a voting system, such that some people's preferences will almost inevitably be overridden. To protect individual freedom, we need rights that cannot be removed by the majority. The threat from majorities exists whether or not there is strong nationalist sentiment, but it is deepened by the existence of such sentiment. Second, even if we can guarantee the rights of individuals within a democracy, a world divided into nation-states raises issues of international justice: there are strong and wealthy nations, and there are weak and poor nations. If individuals matter then they matter irrespective of their nationality.

While the nation *may* be a threat to liberty and to international justice, there are grounds for holding that a world of nation-states is more likely to guarantee liberty and justice than some other form of political organisation. Two quite different lines of argument suggest themselves; both are liberal but, in fact, correspond respectively to civic and ethnic forms of nationalism. The first – civic – argument is that the world is more stable and efficient if organised around nation-states, where each nation respects the territorial integrity of the others. As we suggested earlier, this argument attaches *instrumental* value to the nation: that is, the nation serves the purposes of individuals. The second – ethnic – argument maintains that individuals need culture as a means of self-expression, and the nation-state is the embodiment of culture. Such an argument assumes that nations have *intrinsic* value – valuing individual lives means respecting an individual's culture, the political expression of which is the nation-state. In terms of the history of political thought, John Stuart Mill was an important exponent of the first position, while Johann Gottfried von Herder defended the second.

John Stuart Mill

In his book *Considerations on Representative Government* (published 1859) Mill argues that 'free institutions are next to impossible in a country made up of different nationalities' (Mill, 1991: 428). A 'nation' Mill defines as a portion of humankind united 'among themselves' by common sympathies, which make them cooperate with each other more willingly than with those of other nations. These common sympathies may be based on 'race and descent', language, religion, shared memory and political antecedents. Mill states that the last of these is the most important, and yet his brief discussion of nationalism actually focuses much more on the need for a shared language than the existence of historic political institutions. Without a shared language a 'united public opinion' cannot exist; if, say, two major languages coexist, then public life is vertically divided, with each group reading different newspapers, books and pamphlets, and each looking to its own political class, which speaks to them in their own language.

The danger with a 'multinational' – meaning, a multilingual – state is that the army, as the security wing of the state, is held together by obedience to its officers, and not by a shared sympathy. Although Mill does not argue for a popular militia, he does imply that the army, and other security forces, must have popular legitimacy. Faced with popular discontent, an army made up of one particular ethnic–linguistic group will just as soon 'mow down' the members of another group, as they will 'foreigners' (Mill, 1991: 429). In a multinational state the objective of the government will be the maintenance of stability, and that will entail balancing competing linguistic groups, such that instead of developing fellow feeling differences will become institutionalised. Mill concedes that there are successful multinational states, the best example being Switzerland, and he also accepts that geographical 'intermingling' can be such that some states must be multinational. But he considers it preferable that 'peripheral' minorities be absorbed by larger nations: a Breton is better to share 'the advantages of French protection, and the dignity and prestige of French power, than to sulk on his own rocks, the half-savage relic of past times' (Mill, 1991: 431). Similarly, Wales and the Scottish Highlands are better absorbed into Britain. Today, these remarks seem anachronistic: the emphasis now is on respecting differences within the nation-state, and ensuring that 'threatened' languages such as Breton, Welsh and Scots Gaelic survive – note, for example, that the British naturalisation process requires competence in English *or* Welsh *or* Gaelic. However, the anti-ethnic basis of Mill's argument is significant: the 'admixture' and 'blending' of nationalities is to the benefit of humanity, because it softens the extremes between people (Mill, 1991: 432). In essence, Mill's nationalism is 'assimilationist' – nations are culturally hybrid, but the political project must be to create fellow feeling, because this guarantees the development and reinforcement of individual freedom.

Johann Gottfried von Herder

Herder is a major point of reference within the tradition that takes the nation to be a pre-modern ethnic community. For this reason it might be thought that he cannot also be a liberal. Yet, in fact, Herder has been influential among those liberals who see human beings as necessarily cultural beings. At the heart of culture is language, and Herder anticipates one of the dominant themes of twentieth-century philosophy in arguing that human self-consciousness is dependent on language: the very capacity to think presupposes language. Furthermore, language is necessarily collective, and while it is possible to identify universal features, languages are particular; a language is not simply a means by which we name things, but in writing, reading and speaking a particular language, such as English or German, we locate ourselves and others in a particular world of emotion and sentiment. (For a modern application of Herder's reflections, see Breuilly, 1993: 55–9.)

Herder is attempting to reconcile Enlightenment and Romanticist views of human nature. Under the influence of the former, Herder argues that to be free, autonomous agents we need language, but under the influence of the latter, he maintains that language summons up an emotional world. Herder also attempts to reconcile progress and tradition: the transmission of culture from one generation to another involves both the preservation of culture, or tradition, and the confrontation of the old with the new. This has implications for his understanding of nationalism: since newness is part of tradition, and can come from outside a culture as a 'foreign influence', nations should not be chauvinistic. However, while Herder distances himself from extreme nationalism, he also maintains that cultures cannot be manufactured out of nothing, and that each culture – or nation – has a distinct character which should be preserved.

While language is one of the most fundamental capacities of human beings, the roots of political organisation lie in the family, and this is what gives rise to his organic view of the nation: the nation is not an organism in the sense that there is a hierarchy of parts, as the metaphor of the human body would imply, but rather the nation develops from its most basic unit of organisation. Herder draws an egalitarian and non-authoritarian conclusion from this: elites cannot create nations, and they must not impose their wills on individuals, but rather individuals must be free to develop themselves. Like the growth of an oak tree from an acorn, national development must come from 'within'. The difficulty with Herder's argument is that the family inevitably has paternalistic, if not patriarchal, overtones, and derivation of the nation from the family is problematic, for citizenship involves relationships with people you have never met and will never meet. Ethnic nationalism embodies all the limitedness of the family without preserving its positive features as a small-scale, 'face-to-face' community, based, at its best, on ties of affection.

Socialism and Nationalism: Marx and Engels

Marx and Engels make various comments on nationalism in the *Communist Manifesto*: responding to the charge that communists want to abolish the nation-state Marx and Engels argue that the workers have no nation of their own, and that national divisions have become increasingly irrelevant as capitalism has developed – the capitalists have created a single world bound together by free trade. Marx and Engels were 'collectivists', but the historically significant 'collective' was the working class, as the most advanced, and first 'truly revolutionary', class. Although they avoid using the language of morality, believing that moral beliefs are the product of existing (capitalist) society, and the task is to create a new society, it is possible to discern a moral message in their work: the task is to create a classless society in which human beings recognise their common humanity. In his early work, Marx called this 'species consciousness'. So the historical task is to develop (proletarian) class consciousness, and the ultimate moral aim is to overcome human alienation. This appears to leave little room for nationalism.

Ch. 10:
Socialism
pp. 223–24

Marx and Engels do, however, argue that during the revolutionary phase the workers must 'make themselves into a nation': 'since the proletariat must first of all acquire supremacy, must rise to be *the* national class, must constitute itself the nation, it is, so far, itself national, though not in the bourgeois sense of the word' (Marx and Engels, 1967: 23). During what they call the 'dictatorship of the proletariat' it is necessary to take hold of the state and use it both to defeat counter-revolutionaries and to transform the relations of production. But this a temporary phase, and just as the aim is for the state 'to lose its political character', that is, its coercive character, so it is necessary that the nation lose what might be termed its 'particular' character – in the latter phases of the process the national revolutions will become international. Because Marx and Engels said very little about what a classless society – or world – would look like, it is unclear what place nationalist consciousness would have in such a society, or world. Cultural differences would not necessarily disappear, but they could not determine the distribution of resources. Nonetheless, even if the future of nationalism is unclear, nationalist consciousness does play a role in the revolutionary period, and broadly speaking Marx and Engels argued that if nationalist movements serve the class struggle, then they should be supported. More specifically, they maintained:

1. Nations must have a certain *minimum size* and large and powerful ones were to be encouraged – what Engels called the 'miserable remnants of former nations' should dissolve. A distinction is drawn between historic and non-historic nations, where 'history' is understood as actions and movements possessing class significance. The 'miserable remnants', examples of which include the Basques, Bretons and Gaels, have no historic significance. They argue that after a workers' revolution there will always be the danger of counter-revolution, led by 'conservative' elements in society, and that these 'rotting remnants' would be among them. Interestingly, Mill also maintains that these peoples are better absorbed into larger nations.

2. National self-determination was to be encouraged if it helped revolution. In the main Marx and Engels believed that national struggles should only be encouraged in the big nations of central and west Europe: France, Britain and Germany. Struggles on the 'edge of Europe' were not generally supported. Which means, for example, that they did not in 1848 support the Irish struggle against the British – they later changed their views, and the reasons for the shift in their position are briefly discussed below.

3. They opposed Russia, which they saw as the primary source of reaction in Europe, and so tactically supported the Habsburg (Austro-Hungarian) Empire – which meant opposing nationalist movements among, for example, the Czechs, Slovaks and Serbs (Mill supported these struggles). Basically, their attitude to the nationalisms of their time was determined by the role that they played in the historic class struggle.

4. Ireland: from an orthodox Marxist perspective Ireland in the nineteenth century appears backward – Engels describes it as the agricultural appendage of Britain, or more specifically England. It had not developed capitalism (except in a small north-eastern corner of the country) – which was a precondition of a workers' revolution. What is more, the Catholic Church was a source of 'false consciousness'. But Marx and Engels gradually shifted to the view that the liberation of Ireland was a condition for revolution in Britain: Britain (or England) was the nation most likely to experience revolution, but the Irish constituted a source of competition to British workers, which worsened the conditions of the latter, but without fuelling revolution, because British workers saw their struggle against Irish labour as nationalist (and religious) in character. Paradoxically, through granting Ireland independence British and Irish workers would develop class solidarity, and recognise that the bourgeoisie was their true enemy.

Liberalism and Nationalism: Individualism versus Communitarianism

Contemporary liberal debates over the status of the nation focus on a number of distinct questions:

1. What is the nature of the human person, or 'self' – is he or she in some sense independent of his or her 'community' (where one such community is the nation), or 'constituted' by that community?

2. Does the existence of the nation carry special moral duties to our fellow citizens? To what extent would such duties limit our freedom?

3. Does the existence of the nation give us a reason for favouring our compatriots over others? What would be the implications of such 'partiality' for the distribution of resources between nations?

Yael Tamir makes the point that liberals cannot ignore the nation: it forms the sociological basis of our political life. The world is organised around nations. Liberals may have problems *thinking* like nationalists but they certainly *act* like nationalists. Nations, Tamir suggests, provide contexts in which people live their lives. Following Benedict Anderson's definition, she views the nation as an 'imaginary community' (Tamir, 1993: 8). This implies an active capacity to identify: so, in answer to the first question, a person is (partially) constituted by their attachments, but in response to the second question the duties entailed in belonging to a nation are largely self-assumed. This has two practical consequences: individual choice must be valued, and the right to national self-determination is a right held by individuals and not by a collective. It is individual Kurds who (should) claim the right to nationhood rather than an entity called

Kurdistan. Kurdistan exists because it is imagined as a community by individuals identifying themselves as Kurds. There is, however, a problem of circularity: Kurds identify with Kurdistan because they believe Kurdistan exists, such that their believing Kurdistan exists does not bring Kurdistan into existence. In response, it could be argued that Kurds have to believe that Kurdistan exists independently of their beliefs even if, in fact, it only exists because lots of people style themselves 'Kurds' and identify with a particular land mass, language, customs and so on. On this argument all 'social entities' are necessary fictions.

Whether social entities exist independently of individual beliefs and actions is a problem for philosophers of social science (see, for example, Ruben, 1985), but our concern is primarily with the ethical question: what is the moral status of this social entity we call a nation? The question of the constructedness of the nation is relevant, in that a person might reasonably argue that it is individuals, who through their beliefs, construct the nation. This may lessen the claims that the nation has on the individual: if a Kurd can say that Kurdistan only exists because a group of individuals 'construct' that nation then it would appear to give moral primacy, or authority, to the individual over the collective. However, this argument may be less compelling than it appears at first sight, in that the nation may be constructed but the process of socialisation might be so strong that an individual cannot imagine themself as anything other than Kurdish, or English, or French, or whatever.

There is another problem with the claim that because the nation is constructed somehow the individual is free to belong or not to belong to it. The 'necessary fiction' of the nation implies that nationalism depends upon the myth of a really existing social entity. The word 'myth' is not an entirely pejorative term, for as Anderson argues there is a need for 'sacred stories' which purport to explain the 'origins' of the nation (see Anderson, 1991). Nationalism depends on forgetfulness: forgetting the factual, highly contingent formation of the nation. The problem for liberal political theorists is less one of the authoritarian implications of elevating the nation over the individual – although that is a concern – but much more the deception necessarily entailed in effectively constructing the nation. Liberals believe in transparency and nationalism is bound up with mythology.

At the heart of both these problems – the implicit authoritarianism and the mythology of nationalism – is the question of the nature of the self. If individual human beings are the source of authority then the claims of any collective are limited or constrained by our individual rights, and the idea that political institutions must be justified to each individual requires 'transparency'. In the 1980s there was a significant debate within Anglo-American political philosophy between 'individualists' and 'communitarians'. John Rawls was taken to be representative of liberal individualism: the derivation of political principles from the 'original position' was individualist in that each individual 'chose' the principles through their own powers of reason independently of any prior attachments, such as family, culture or religion. In his influential critique Michael Sandel argued that Rawls's model of the individual was flawed, because a person denied knowledge of their identity is in no position to value anything at all (Sandel, 1998: 179). How can you know what you want if you do not know what social ties or religious beliefs you have?

Ch. 4:
Justice
pp. 83–84

One of the problems with communitarianism is that taken to its logical conclusion there is no individual standpoint from which we can criticise 'our community', and values are entirely relative to 'my' community.* Given that we may belong to more than one community we need to be able to negotiate our conflicting loyalties: this is evident in the conflict that, historically, Catholics have felt between Church and nation, and which many Muslims feel between Islam as a universal community of believers and the nations to which they belong. There is another implication of communitarianism that was not pursued to the same degree within that debate, but which has been a topic of discussion within the broader justice debate: communitarianism implies that it is legitimate to show partiality towards members of 'our community', which in this case means the nation.

Thomas Nagel makes a distinction between agent-relative and agent-neutral reasons for action, and correspondingly between two attitudes we can adopt to our lives: partiality and impartiality (Nagel, 1991: 10–20). You can view your life as special to you or you can view your life as 'just one among many'. Emerging from these two standpoints are the two kinds of reasons (or motivations). A parent is acting partially – to be more precise, is acting from agent-relative reasons – when he shows a concern for his children which he does not bestow on other people's children. His justification is that they are *his* children, meaning that the identity of the children is of central importance. Their identity as *his* children explains his partiality towards them. Let us assume the parent is very wealthy, such that his partiality results in significant material benefits for his children. But let us also assume that he has egalitarian beliefs: he thinks that all children should get a 'fair deal', and that means that he as a rich person should pay high levels of tax in order to fund an extensive and effective education system. Insofar as he is motivated by concern for all children in accepting as legitimate high taxes he is acting from agent-neutral reasons: other parent's children are of equal value to his own. Nagel thinks that there is an almost ineliminable conflict between partiality and impartiality, but – and this is the interesting point – each presupposes the other (Nagel, 1991: 14). When a parent shows partiality to his children he is necessarily committed to the view that '(all) parents should show special concern for their children'. In reverse, impartiality implies partiality. This mutual implication of partiality and impartiality clarifies but does not resolve the tension between the two standpoints.

We have taken the parent–child relationship as one example, but Nagel argues that the tension manifests itself across the social and political field. Nationalists – of all types – must assume that membership of a nation implies the legitimacy of agent-relative reasons: you can show special concern for *your* compatriots. This implies a lesser concern for members of other nations, even if partiality entails impartiality, meaning that you have to accept 'multiple partialities': a French person's partiality towards other French people commits them to accepting that a Japanese person is 'entitled' to show partiality towards fellow Japanese. As suggested above this does not resolve the conflict: at most it might commit members of rich countries to avoiding exploiting poorer ones. It does not commit the rich nations to significant

---

*Sandel recognised this problem and a 1998 re-issue of his book maintained that what was important were objective 'ends', such as friendship or the pursuit of certain forms of excellence (Sandel, 1998: xi). Rather than being a communitarian Sandel appears to be a perfectionist.

redistribution of resources. It is significant that Britain spends 20 times more on funding its domestic health service than on overseas aid.

One response is to reject partiality altogether and argue for global impartiality. In other words, there is nothing special – that is, morally significant – about our compatriots. Within the justice debate this position is termed 'cosmopolitanism' and we explore it in more detail in Chapter 21 (Global Justice). Since the concern in this chapter is with nationalism we will focus on the opposing position: particularism, the 'particular' here being the nation.

David Miller, in his book *On Nationality*, offers what he terms a discriminating defence of nationalism. He suggests that it is possible to 'acknowledge the claims of national identity without succumbing to an unthinking nationalism which simply tells us to follow the feelings of our blood' (Miller, 1995: 183–4). He follows the communitarian argument that we are, in part, constituted by our social attachments – in this case our nation – and that this gives us reason to act partially towards our fellow nationals. The nation should not be confused with the state. The national community has five characteristics: (a) there is a shared belief that the members belong together by virtue of what they believe they hold in common; (b) the nation has a history, and the members of the nation are conscious of that history; (c) it is 'active in character'; (d) it is associated with a particular geographical space or 'homeland'; (e) it has a public culture (Miller, 1995: 27). Miller argues that national myths may be essential to reinforcing a sense of community and to the successful transmission of moral values across generations.

German President Gustav Heinemann (1899–1976: President 1969–74) once responded to the question whether he loved his country: 'I don't love my country; I love my wife.' He might have been joking but the implication was that you might love somebody with whom you have freely entered a relationship, or feel pride in one's own achievements, but you cannot love what you have not chosen or be proud of something you have not yourself done. Miller would accept that this is true but nonetheless you can, as a result of self-reflection, identify with your nation, such that membership of the nation becomes integral to your conception of a good life. Identification through self-reflection is analogous to free choice and personal achievement.

Miller makes a distinction between ethical universalism and ethical particularism. The first leads to cosmopolitanism, and that entails rejecting the nation as ethically significant, whilst the latter allows space for partiality towards one's compatriots. However, that partiality is not absolute: nation A may be morally required to intervene in the affairs of nation B to prevent human rights violations, so long as A's interests are not significantly damaged. Negatively, one nation should not intervene in the affairs of another without compelling reasons for doing so. Miller's argument may be viewed less as an outline of what nations require and permit of us, but more an attempt to establish a moral space in which we can pursue particularist aims. We discuss the implications for global distributive justice of this argument in Chapter 21, but close by observing that the tension between an instrumental and non-instrumental defence of the nation – reflected in the work of, respectively, Mill and Herder – is not resolved by Miller. If Miller is offering an updated version of Mill's very underdeveloped justification of the nation then it must be possible for us to recognise that nations are constructs and have no claims in themselves against us.

Conclusion: Football and Banal Nationalism

Michael Billig argues that the central thesis of his book *Banal Nationalism* is that 'there is a continual "flagging", or reminding of nationhood' (Billig, 1995: 8). Political leaders in France, the United States, or Britain do not define themselves as 'nationalist' – nationalism is a term applied to those on the 'fringe', whether fighting for independence from a larger nation or seeking to radicalise the consciousness of a nation through, for example, racism. But those leaders *are* nationalist, for they daily remind their citizens of the importance of nationhood through 'banal' – that is ordinary, everyday – acts. Political and cultural discourse is suffused with nationalist rhetoric: the word 'national' appears in official titles of state bodies, along with visual symbols; newspapers have national and international news; the promotion of tourism rests on a few identifiable 'signifiers'. Sport itself is organised around the nation-state. Right-wing British politician Norman Tebbit coined what became known as the 'Tebbit test': unless you support the England cricket team when it plays against such teams as India, Pakistan, Sri Lanka or the West Indies you cannot really be British (he conveniently ignored the fact that England was not Britain, and that, for example, Scotland has a cricket team).

As Billig says, 'the metonymic image of banal nationalism is not a flag which is being consciously waved with fervent passion; it is the flag hanging unnoticed on the public building' (Billig, 1995: 8). A metonymic image is one that locates a person in relation to something else, in this instance a collective entity – the nation.

While Billig's argument can be criticised it is a useful way of concluding our discussion on nationalism. Billig argues that nationalism is a powerful force, but most of the time we do not realise its force; only at times of crisis does it erupt. Political theorists, operating with universalist concepts, find nationalism a difficult phenomenon to understand, let alone use as a justification; they cannot, however, ignore it. The question is whether we should be so concerned about nationalism – does it matter which team a person supports so long as they obey the law? After all, millions of people do not support any cricket, football or rugby team, professing themselves utterly bored with sport. The most compelling argument for taking nationalism seriously is, as Mill observed, that it does provide connections between people that, at a time of crisis, may be essential for the maintenance of liberal-democratic institutions. Those ties may be sporting, or linguistic, or based on an appreciation of cities and landscape, and it is possible that we do not need to share all of them – we can be bored by sport – but we need some of them.

The conflict identified by Hobsbawm between the nationalist passions of football fans and the universalising logic of capital illustrates the problematic status of nationalist sentiments. The football business is instrumentalising particularist (local or national) sentiment: it wants to make money but it will only make money if such sentiment exists. A parallel between markets and politics can be made: political systems, at the domestic level, must be stable and capable of being reproduced across generations. Politicians tap into the – frequently banal – nationalism of everyday life in order to achieve stability and reproduction, but nationalist sentiments, if uncritical or radical, will undermine the international political system, as well as threaten the rights of minorities within the nation-state.

Just as football teams have to reconcile the conflicting demands of the particular (nationalist sentiment) and the universal (in this case, the universal language of money), so must politicians reconcile domestic and international demands. Political theorists have the task of trying to resolve these tensions at a theoretical level.

Summary

For political theorists nationalist sentiment is problematic because it seems to resist universalist concepts. While it is possible to talk about universal rights to national self-determination and assert that all nations are equal, both the reality of international politics and, perhaps more importantly, the concept of nationhood undermines that claim. Even the softest, most civic, nationalist will be forced to concede that their nation is special, for how else can they explain the value of nationhood? Of course, if we say, as liberals do, that the individual is the ultimate source of value and focus of concern, a similar objection can be raised: your individual life is especially valuable to *you*. However, because the nation-state entails a massive concentration of power the ethical particularism within nationalism is of special concern. On the other hand, a world of nation-states may offer the best way to realise values such as freedom, justice and equality, and a history of nationalism that focused on the extremism of Nazi Germany or the virulent nationalisms of some contemporary states – thinking here of the Balkans in the 1990s – may fail to do justice to nationalism as a liberationist ideology.

Questions

1. Is a multilingual nation inherently unstable?
2. Is the instrumental defence of nationalism coherent?
3. Are nationalism and socialism compatible?
4. What are the arguments in favour of the abolition of nations and the creation of a world government?
5. A Scottish nationalist, bemoaning the lack of majority support among Scots for independence, labelled Scots '90-minute nationalists'. Is it possible to be a strong supporter of a national football team but reject political nationalism?

References

Anderson, B. (1991) *Imagined Communities: Reflections on the Origin and Spread of Nationalism* London: Verso.

Billig, M. (1995) *Banal Nationalism* London: Sage.

Breuilly, J. (1993) *Nationalism and the State* Manchester: Manchester University Press.

Davidson, N. (2000) *The Origins of Scottish Nationhood* London: Pluto Press.

Davis, H. (1967) *Nationalism and Socialism: Marxist and Labor Theories of Nationalism to 1917* New York: Monthly Review Press.

Gellner, E. (1983) *Nations and Nationalism* Oxford: Basil Blackwell.

Guibernau, M. (1996) *Nationalisms: The Nation-State and Nationalism in the Twentieth Century* Cambridge: Polity Press.

Hobsbawm, E. (2008), *Globalisation, Democracy and Terrorism* London: Abacus Books.

Huntington, S. (2004) *Who Are We?: America's Great Debate* London: Free Press.

Hutchinson, J. and Smith, A. (eds) (1994) *Nationalism* Oxford: Oxford University Press.

Ignatieff, M. (1993) *Blood and Belonging: Journeys into the New Nationalism* London: BBC Books and Chatto & Windus.

James, H. and Stone, M. (eds) (1992) *When the Wall Came Down: Reactions to German Unification* New York and London: Routledge.

Kedourie, E. (1993) *Nationalism* Oxford and Cambridge, MA: Blackwell.

Kellas, J. (1998) *The Politics of Nationalism and Ethnicity* Basingstoke: Macmillan.

Marx, K. and Engels, F. (1967) *The Communist Manifesto* introduction and notes by A.J.P. Taylor, London: Penguin.

Mill, J.S. (1991) *On Liberty and Other Essays* (ed. J. Gray) Oxford: Oxford University Press.

Miller, D. (1995) *On Nationality* Oxford: Clarendon Press.

Nagel, T. (1991) *Equality and Partiality* Oxford and New York: Oxford University Press.

Rousseau J-J. (1968) *The Social Contract* translated and introduced by Maurice Cranston Harmondsworth: Penguin Books.

Ruben, D-H. (1985) *The Metaphysics of the Social World* London: Routledge and Kegan Paul.

Sandel, M. (1998) *Liberalism and the Limits of Justice*, 2nd edn Cambridge: Cambridge University Press.

Smith, A. (1991) *National Identity* London: Penguin.

Smith, A. (1998) *Nationalism and Modernism: A Critical Survey of Recent Theories of Nations and Nationalism* London: Routledge.

Tamir, Y. (1993) *Liberal Nationalism* Princeton, NJ: Princeton University Press.

Further Reading

There are several good introductions to the study of nationalism. From the above bibliography Kellas (1998), Smith (1991) and Smith (1998) are useful overviews; also by Anthony Smith: *Nationalism: Theory, Ideology, History* (Cambridge: Polity Press, 2001). Other books in the bibliography very much argue a line – the most influential are Anderson (1991), Gellner (1983), Hobsbawm (1992), and Kedourie (1993). General – and brief – introductions not listed in the bibliography include: Kenneth Minogue, *Nationalism* (London: Batsford, 1967) and Fred Haliday and Umut Özkirimli, *Theories of Nationalism: A Critical Introduction* (Basingstoke: Palgrave Macmillan, 2000). For a useful collection of essays: Umut Özkirimli, *Nationalism and its Future* (Basingstoke: Palgrave Macmillan, 2003). Books focusing on the ethical aspects of nationalism in addition to Tamir and Miller include Andrew Vincent, *Nationalism and Particularity* (Cambridge and New York: Cambridge University Press, 2002) and Margaret Moore (ed.), *National Self-Determination and Secession* (Oxford: Oxford University Press, 1998).

Weblinks

An article with an extensive bibliography:
http://plato.stanford.edu/entries/nationalism/

A very extensive list of (largely academic) links:
http://www.nationalismproject.org/

Another extensive list of links, although more of a mix of 'popular' and academic:
http://www.socresonline.org.uk/2/1/natlinks.html

A more history oriented site:
http://www.fordham.edu/halsall/mod/modsbook17.html

Chapter 13

Fascism

Introduction

The word 'fascist' is often used as a word of abuse. Fascists are seen as people who act in authoritarian ways and seek to impose their views and values on others, but **fascism** is more complicated than this. First because fascism needs to be more precisely defined, and second, the question arises as to whether it is a movement of the past, or can it be said that fascist movements still exist today? Everyone has heard of Hitler (1889–1945) but Hitler called his party the National Socialist German Workers' Party: can he still be called a fascist? Not many movements have come to power since 1945 that can unambiguously be called fascist – but can we describe movements in these terms when they don't necessarily declare themselves in favour of Hitler or the founder of Italian fascism, Mussolini?

This chapter will explore these issues, and those listed below, in order to tackle the questions: what is fascism; is it an ideology at all, and can a grasp of it help us in understanding certain political movements in today's world?

Chapter Map

- A definition of fascism is offered – a task that is clearly crucial if the question of whether it is a general movement or simply an Italian movement of the inter-war period is to be tackled.

- The development of fascism in Italy: this was the particular movement that gave the general movement its name.

- The relationship of Nazism to fascism – it will be argued that Hitler's National Socialism was an extreme form of fascism.

- The relationship of fascism to capitalism and class. This not only throws light on the relationship between fascism and socialism but is important if we are to explain the rise of fascism.

- The view taken by fascists towards liberal ideas and the European Enlightenment in order to gauge the depth of the rejection of 'reason', liberty and equality.

- The fascist view of the state.

- Fascism today, the form that it takes, and the conditions under which it is likely to become increasingly influential.

'Never Again'

Auschwitz-Birkenau
Source: © Michael St. Maur Sheil/CORBIS

You are conscious of considerable media coverage given of the 60th Anniversary of the destruction of the Nazi concentration camp at Auschwitz and of the existence of Holocaust Day, a day that commemorates the murder by the Nazis of millions of European Jews, the killing of travellers (Gipsies) and of political opponents. Interviews with victims bring tears to your eyes, and former concentration camp-attendants explain why they were able to kill inmates. You are horrified at the information you receive – the starvation, brutality, the killing and the sophisticated methods used for nefarious purposes – and you can only agree with the general theme of 'never again'. At the same time you have read about the genocide of the Tutsis in Rwanda in Africa, and the grisly ethnic cleansing in former Yugoslavia where whole communities were wiped out, women raped and men placed in concentration camps. The media is full of the following: Jewish cemeteries have been desecrated, black people killed by gangs and even by the police, Muslims are 'blamed' for terrorist atrocities like the destruction of the Twin Towers in 2001 because these actions were committed in the name of Islam and extreme right-wing movements like the British National Party or the Freedom Party in Austria are campaigning to have immigrants expelled from the countries in which they have settled. At the same time you read about left-wing regimes denounced as fascist when they violate the human rights of political opponents. Inevitably a number of questions suggest themselves.

1. Are we witnessing the re-emergence of fascism in our modern world?

2. When does a racist become a fascist? Are the two synonymous and if not, how do we differentiate them?

3. Can we call people who support nationalism, fascists?

4. Is opposition to immigration fascist in character?

Defining Fascism

**Ch. 10:
Socialism**

Fascism is sometimes used as a word of abuse – against movements or individuals who are intolerant or authoritarian. Fascism is certainly intolerant and authoritarian, but it is more than this. It is a movement that seeks to establish a dictatorship of the right (i.e. an ultra-conservative position that rejects liberalism and anything associated with the left). It targets communists, socialists, trade unionists, liberals through banning their parties and their members, so that these groups cannot exercise their political, legal or social rights. It is anti-liberal, regarding liberal values as a form of decadence and sees them as opening the floodgates to socialist, communist and egalitarian movements.

Defining fascism raises a problem. Fascism as a movement extols action and practice over ideas and theory. It uses ideas with considerable opportunism, mixing socialist ideas, avant-garde positions, anti-capitalist rhetoric, ecological argument, and pseudo-scientific ideas to do with race and ethnicity in a veritable pot pourri. Is it an ideology at all? Trevor Roper described fascist ideology as 'an ill-sorted hodge-podge of ideas', and Laski has argued that any attempt to find a 'philosophy of fascism' is a waste of time (Griffin, 1995: 1, 276). Kitchen contends that the 'extraordinary collection of half-baked and cranky ideas certainly did not form a coherent whole' (1976: 28). We shall argue however, that while fascism is peculiarly flexible as an ideology, there are particular features that characterise it, so that a general view of fascism can be created. Vincent argues that fascism 'often occupies a middle ground somewhere between rational political ideology on the one hand and opportunist adventurism on the other' (1995: 142).

The term derives from the *fasces* – the bundle of rods carried by the consuls of ancient Rome and the word *fascio* was used in Italy in the 1890s to indicate a political group or band, usually of revolutionary socialists (Heywood, 1992: 171). National defence groups organised after the Italian defeat at Caparetto in 1917 (→ Box), also called themselves *fasci* (Vincent, 1995: 141).

Fascism is, however, essentially a twentieth-century movement although it draws upon prejudices and stereotypes that are rooted in tradition. Italian fascism saw itself as resurrecting the glories of the Roman Empire and Rocco, an Italian fascist, saw Machiavelli as a founding father of fascist theory. Nazism (which we will argue is an extreme form of fascism) was seen by its ideologues as rooted in the history of the Nordic peoples, and the movement embodied anti-Semitic views that go back to the Middle Ages in which Jews, for example, were blamed for the death of Christ, compelled to be money-lenders, confined to ghettos and acquired a reputation for crooked commerce.

Fascism and Communism

Fascism appeals particularly to those who have some property but not very much, and are fearful that they might be plunged by market forces into the ranks of the working class. We would, however, agree with Griffin that there is nothing 'in principle' that precludes an employed or unemployed member of the working class, an aristocrat, city dweller or peasant, or a graduate 'from being susceptible to fascist myth' (1995: 7). Fascism is particularly hostile to communism, since it is

Battle of Caparetto

This battle involved some 600,000 Italian casualties and was the worst disaster in the history of the Italian armed forces. Ernest Hemingway based his *A Farewell to Arms* (1929) on the war between Austria and Italy between 1915 and 17, reading military histories and first-hand reports to flesh out the background. His novel centres around an American, Frederic, who speaks Italian, and fights for the Italians. He lived, we are told, 'in Udine' and saw that things were going 'very badly' (1985: 10).

Frederic tells the priest (whom he befriends): They (the Italian army) were 'beaten to start with. They were beaten when they [the military authorities] took them from their farms and put them in the army. That is why the peasant has wisdom, because he is defeated from the start. Put him in power and see how wise he is' (1985: 157).

In October 1917 Italy was occupied by Germany. Germany reached Udine on 28 October 1917 and the Italians lost about 600,000 men in a week. This is the lowest point in the war and Frederic deserts.

Ch. 12:
Nationalism

opposed to the cosmopolitan contentions of Marxist theory, and its belief in a classless and stateless society. It is a movement that dislikes universal identities of any kind, although of course fascists may call for unity with kindred spirits in other countries. Nevertheless, it is intensely nationalistic, and takes the view that the people must be saved from enemies whose way of life is alien and threatening. Differences are deemed divisive and menacing, and war extolled as a way of demonstrating virtue and strength. The idea that people are divided by class is rejected in favour of the unity of the nation or people, so that industry is to be organised in a way that expresses the common interest between business and labour. In practice, this did not happen, and Kitchen argues that the social strata that provided the mass basis for fascism, did not actually gain from its policies (Kitchen, 1976: 65).

Fascism and Religion

Fascists vary in their attitude towards the Church (extreme fascists may see religious organisations as a threat to the state) but they regard religion in a loose sense as being a useful way of instilling order and loyalty. Certainly, they use a religious style of language in invoking the need for sacrifice, redemption, and spiritual virtue and attacking materialism, consumerism and hedonism as decadent and unworthy. Although women can be fascists as well as men, fascism is a supremely patriarchal creed, by which we mean that women are seen as domestic creatures whose role in life is to service men, to have children, to be good mothers and wives, and to keep out of politics.

Fascism and Liberalism

Fascism is hostile to the liberal tradition, and its dislike of the notion of reason makes it difficult to pin it down (as we have commented above) as an ideology. It stresses action as opposed to words and yet propaganda and rationalisation are crucial to the movement. It regards the individual as subordinate to the collectivity in general, and the state in particular. Liberal freedoms are seen merely as entitlements that allow the enemies of the 'nation' or the 'people' to capture power. Fascist regimes are highly authoritarian, and use the state as the weapon of the dominant party to protect the nation, advance its interests and destroy its enemies. They are strongly opposed to the idea of democracy (although fascists may use democratic rhetoric to justify their rule or use parliamentary institutions to win access to power), and regard the notion of self-government (the idea that people can control their lives in rational way and without force) as a dangerous myth. As a movement based upon repressive hierarchy, fascism argues that all institutions should be controlled by 'reliable' leaders, and the leadership principle comes to a climax with the supreme leader, seen as the embodiment of the nation and the people. Fascist leaders may be civilians, but they are closely identified with the army and police, since these institutions are crucial to rooting out opponents. Fascist movements extend beyond the state, but the violence of these movements is condoned and encouraged by the state, and given tight control over the media, this violence is then justified in the light of fascist values.

Fascism and Conservatism

Fascists see themselves as revolutionary in that they are concerned to rejuvenate a tired and decadent society, and some fascists speak of creating a 'new man' in a new society. They are, therefore, anti-conservative as well as anti-liberal, although, as we shall see, they may form tactical alliances with other sections of the right where they can establish momentary common ground. Many regimes, loosely called fascist, are in fact conservative and reactionary systems – Franco's Spain, Petain's 'Vichy' France (a regime that collaborated with the Nazis who occupied the country), Japan under Tojo, etc. They may have fascist elements within them, but they are not really anti-conservative in character.

Fascism in Italy

Commentators generally agree that there was no fascism before the First World War and that it began in 1922–3 with the emergence of the Italian fascist party. The fascist movement was in power in Italy for 18 years (1925–43). Benito Mussolini, the leader of the Italian fascists, had campaigned for Italy's entry into the First World War. The parliamentary Fascio of National Defence was formed in 1917 and drew heavily upon veterans from the war to make up its extra-parliamentary forces. The movement took off when the left organised factory occupations in Milan during the 'red years' of 1919–20, and in November 1920, a fascist party was formed. In October 1922 Mussolini persuaded the king, Victor Emmanuel III, by means of a threatened putsch (dramatised by the March on Rome) to allow him to become Prime Minister of a coalition government.

The action squads, veteran soldiers from an elite battalion, were in theory absorbed into the Voluntary Militia of National Security, but dissatisfied elements in June 1924 killed the socialist deputy, Matteotti, who was a major parliamentary critic of Mussolini. Mussolini then suppressed all the other parliamentary parties and created a regime made up purely of fascists. Until 1929 Mussolini was concerned to consolidate the new system, and in the next decade he embarked upon the conquest of Abyssinia and formed an alliance with Hitler's Germany. Although Italy joined the Second World War on Hitler's side, in July 1943 Mussolini was ousted by the king and disaffected Fascist leaders and Italy sued for peace with the anti-German allies. Mussolini was 'rescued' by German troops and in a small town near Lake Garda, an Italian Social Republic was proclaimed and lasted from 1943 to 45.

Nationalism and War

Mussolini had argued strongly for intervention in the First World War, and war was treated by the fascists in Italy as a force for rejuvenation and life. War enabled the nation to constitute itself as a vital, living force, hence Maronetti (1876–1944), leader of the Futurist movement, spoke of the need for a nationalism that was 'ultra-violent, anti-traditionist and anti-clericalist', a nationalism based on 'the inexhaustible vitality of Italian blood' (Griffin, 1995: 26). The First World War was crucial to win the battle for civilisation and freedom. Maronetti believed that this war would enrich Italy with 'men of action', while Mussolini in 1914 broke with the 'cowards' who opposed the war, and declared in 1917 that those who fought in the trenches, were the 'aristocracy of tomorrow', 'the aristocracy in action' (Griffin, 1995: 26–8). The regime's slogans were 'believe, obey, fight'.

The war was regarded by Roberto Farinacci (1892–1945) as the creator of a new Italian nation, and in Mussolini's view, the First World War brought about a 'profound psychological transformation' among the peasants in the countryside, with veterans becoming leaders in the rural areas. In Hemingway's *Farewell to Arms*, Frederic says to the priest that the Italian army 'were beaten to start with' when they took the peasants from their farms 'and put them in the army. That is why the peasant has wisdom, because he is defeated from the start. Put him in power, and see how wise he is' (1985: 157). Clearly, Mussolini would not have agreed with Hemingway!

Physical exercise was to develop skills, according to the Italian leader, 'which may be necessary in a future war'. War was linked to nationalism. The nation, Mussolini declared shortly before the march on Rome, is a myth to which all must be subordinated, and Costamagna (1881–1965) insisted that from a cultural point of view, only the individual nation constitutes a *universum*, a concrete universal. The Italian nation, argued the National Association in 1920, embraces people of the future as well as the present, in a venture that is both domestic as well as international in character: the nation either perishes or dominates. War has, said Luigi Federzoni (1878–1967) of the same Association, 'regenerating properties' which 'have taken effect miraculously and mysteriously in the soul of the Italian people'. War is 'the sole hygiene of the world' (Griffin, 1995: 38; 41–2; 44–5; 71, 85).

Corporativism, Violence and the State

There is a strong economic imperative for fascism. D'Annunzio, a fervent nationalist and military leader who had occupied the Adriatic port of Fiume in September 1919, argued for a corporate structure that embraced employees and employers, public and private, within a state that expressed the common will of the people. Mussolini organised the whole country into 22 corporations. Lyttelton argues that these were held up as fascism's 'most imposing creation': in fact, they served no serious function except as a front for groups of leading industrialists to control raw material allocations and investment decisions (Griffin, 1995: 97).

The trade unions were seen as contributing loyal employees within this structure – strikes and lockouts were banned – and syndicalists like Sergio Panunzio (1886–1944) saw in revolutionary trade unionism or syndicalism, a force that would transcend its adolescent phrase by building up the state. A new national class was to be created – the essence of a civilisation that is neither bourgeois nor proletarian. Mussolini spoke of 'conscious class collaboration', and although the regime attacked both liberalism and socialism, the tiny Italian Social Republic declared that it aimed to abolish the whole internal capitalist system (Griffin, 1995: 47, 49, 64, 87). In practice, employers were regulated by the Italian state, but anti-capitalism was more rhetoric than reality.

Ch. 20: Political Violence p. 451

Maronetti spoke of 'violence, rehabilitated as a decisive argument', and when links were forged with Hitler's Germany, Mussolini declared that both Fascists and Nazis believe in violence 'as the dynamo of their history'. The work of the French anarcho-syndicalist Sorel was hugely influential because Sorel had extolled both the importance of myth and the need for violence (Griffin, 1995: 36, 45, 79).

Not surprisingly, the state was given a pivotal role, a spiritual and moral entity that, Mussolini declared, is the conscience of the nation. The state is the foundation of fascism: the state organises the nation and is concerned with the growth of empire. Giovanni Gentile (1875–1944) was the key intellectual of the regime, and drawing upon a version of Hegelian idealism, he pronounced the Fascist state to be an 'ethical state': it is the state of 'man himself'. The leader is revered with a capital 'L'. Mussolini ridiculed the 'demo-liberal' civilisation, while praising Hitler for creating 'a unitary, authoritarian, totalitarian state, i.e. a fascist one', although he acknowledges that Hitler operated in a different historical context. Oneness is asserted with a vengeance: in Mussolini's words, the 'order of the day is a single, categorical word which is imperative for all' (Griffin, 1995: 63, 70, 72–3, 79, 82).

Reason is rejected: as an anonymous fascist put it, 'blood is stronger than syllogisms'. (A syllogism is a logical statement in which a conclusion is drawn from two propositions e.g. all dogs are animals, all animals have four legs, and therefore, all dogs have four legs. A false syllogism!) Mussolini was likened to a Messiah who evangelised millions, and despite the anti-clericalism of some fascist supporters, a pact with the Vatican was signed. Irrationalism and mysticism expressed itself in racism. It is a myth to think that racism was only developed by the Italian fascists at the insistence of the Nazis. The invasion of Ethiopia was presented as the salvation of the Italian race, and even before the alliance with Hitler, Mussolini had spoken of the danger that the (so-called) 'coloured races' posed to the 'white race' with their fertility and rate of multiplication. Miccari (1898–1989), one of the key Fascist intellectuals, warned against the kind of modernity that is a racket manipulated by 'Jewish bankers, war-profiteers, pederasts, brothel keepers', and Volpe (1876–1971), official historian of fascism, argued that the voice of anti-Semitism was not entirely new in Italy (Griffin, 1995: 60, 80). It is true that a much more systematic racism developed as a result of Nazi pressure (many Jews had actually been recruited to the party and were now expelled), but we can certainly say that fascism built upon a racist culture that is integral to fascism.

Intellectual Roots

Although fascist intellectuals drew upon Machiavelli, Nietzsche and Hegel, there was an important tradition of elitism in Italian political thought that was more recent and more influential.

Mosca (1858–1941) had taught constitutional law at the University of Palemro between 1858 and 1888, and the Universities of Rome and Turin. In 1884 he published *Theory of Governments and Parliamentary Government*, but is best known for his *The Ruling Class*, that appeared in 1896. All societies, he argued, are governed by minorities whether these are military, hereditary, priestly or based on merit or wealth. He accepted that ownership of property could be a factor in accounting for elite rule, but he rejected the Marxist account that sought to privilege this particular factor. The ruling class or elite owes its superiority to organisational factors, he argued, and its skills alter according to circumstance. What he called the 'political formula' or the ideological mechanisms of rule varied, but whatever the form, all states are necessarily elitist in character, whether their legitimating myth is the divine right of kings, popular sovereignty or the dictatorship of the proletariat.

Democracy, in his view, is simply a more subtle form of manipulation, and the parties offered inducements for people to vote for them. The 'political class' need to be distinguished from other sections of the elite, like industrialists, but in 1923 Mosca introduced in his work the argument that elites could compete through rival political parties. People of lower socio-economic origin can be recruited in order to renew elites. Unlike other elitists, he was, however, fiercely critical of Mussolini, and his theory is best described as conservative rather than fascist.

Rather more hawkish was Pareto (1848–1923). Pareto had taken the chair in political economy at the University of Lausanne in 1894, publishing his *Cours d'économie politique* (1896, 1897). In 1900 he declared himself an anti-democrat, arguing that the political movements in Italy and France were simply seeking to replace one elite with another. While he approved of Marx's emphasis upon struggle, he rejected completely the notion that a classless society was possible. In 1906, Pareto published his *Manual of Political Economy*, where he presented pure economics in mathematical form.

As far as he was concerned, human action is mostly non-logical in character, and stems from non-rational sentiments and impulses: what Pareto called underlying 'residues'. In his most important political and sociological work, the *Mind and Society* which he wrote in 1916, he distinguishes between Class I residues, inventive, imaginative capacities, and Class II residues, conservative, persistent tendencies.

All government is government by an elite who use a combination of coercion and consent. Class I residues predominate when 'foxes' are in control – manipulative politicians who create consent – and Class II residues when violence is necessary. Each of these residues has its strengths and weaknesses, and the 'circulation of elites' can be explained as 'lions' – those who rule through brute force – replace 'foxes'. He saw in Mussolini a politician with a lion-like character who had displaced wily politicians.

Perhaps most important of all in analysing the intellectual roots of fascism was the work of Michels (1876–1936), a disillusioned German socialist who gained an academic position in Turin, and was greatly influenced by syndicalism. In 1911 he published *Political Parties*. Here he argues that all societies and all organisations are subject to 'an iron law of oligarchy' (i.e. a small group controlling the masses). Struck by what he saw as the contrast between the official statements of the German Social Democratic Party and the timidity of its political practice, he argued that oligarchy is present even in parties apparently committed to the norms of democracy. The fact that leaders are in practice autonomous from their followers derives from the constraints of organisation. Although he wrote a good deal about psychology, Michels argued that oligarchical tendencies are based upon organisational rather than psychological factors. The complexity of organisations can only be grasped by professional leaders who have communication skills, and who understand the rules of elections and other external pressures. This leadership is made all the more entrenched by what Michels regarded as the incompetence and emotional vulnerability of their mass membership.

In 1914 Michels wrote a study of Italian imperialism and published widely on politics and sociology. In 1930 he wrote the entry on 'Authority' for the *Encyclopaedia of the Social Sciences*. He admired fascism and argued that, as with Bolshevism, it was a reflection of the general tendency to oligarchy. Michels also wrote a good deal on nationalism, with his later writings becoming increasingly anti-democratic in tone (Beetham, 1977).

Fascism in Germany

Nazism is, in our view, a form of fascism. Despite historical and cultural differences, both Hitler and Mussolini saw striking similarities in each other's regimes, and the Nazis were greatly influenced by Mussolini's theory and tactics. It is true that Hitler's movement was more extreme than that of Mussolini's. Its racism was more aggressive, its hatred of democracy more intensive, and its expansionism more grandiose. However, as will become clear from the analysis of its features, it was a form of fascism, and there is no need to take the position that the differences between Hitler and Mussolini's regimes outweighed their similarities.

A Brief History

The collapse of the German war effort saw the creation of a republic: an uprising of the left had been smashed by a socialist government that cooperated with the army and the employers. As Griffin has shown in detail, there were German fascists whose version of nationalism, idealisation of war, anti-liberalism and anti-Semitism was at variance with the Nazi view (1995: 104–15). Hitler had made contact with the German Workers' Party (DAP or Deutsche Arbeiterpartei), a fanatical nationalist grouping. Since the clauses of the Versailles Treaty limited the Reichswehr (the German army) to 100,000, Hitler was demobilised in 1920. He became leader of the DAP which was then renamed the National Socialist German Workers' Party

(NSDAP). A putsch was attempted in 1923, and Hitler was given a short prison sentence by a sympathetic court. Nazis were regarded as isolated fanatics until 1930: yet in 1933 the movement had seized power. In 1928 the NSDAP won only 2.6 per cent of the popular vote. The Versailles Treaty which ended the First World War had punitive effects on Germany: all colonies were lost while it is calculated that the reparations bill equalled 1.5 times the total GNP of Germany in 1929. Although the economy had improved in the 1920s, the depression had catastrophic effects. Investment and industry collapsed, and unemployment was officially estimated at some 30 per cent: the real figure was nearer half.

The Social Democratic Party of Germany (SPD) had headed a coalition government until 1930: when this fell apart, the President ruled by decree for three years, real wages were halved, and Hitler had meanwhile stressed the need for a party capable of winning elections and conducting effective mass propaganda. In the elections in 1930, the Nazis came second to the SDP, and two years later, they received 37 per cent of the vote. Large employers began to support the Nazis and although many thought Hitler 'tactless' and his economic policies 'utopian', his militant anti-Bolshevism appealed to them, and they backed him for Chancellor. He was appointed to the position in 1933, and the Nazis received 3 posts in an 11-strong cabinet. Goebbels vowed that 1933 would strike the French revolutionary year of 1789 out of history.

By July 1934 Germany had become a one-party state, and the Nazis embarked on their task of building a Third Reich and New European Order. War broke out in 1939 and the defeat of the Nazis was secured in 1945.

Anti-Capitalism

Although virulently anti-Marxist, the Nazi movement was in the 1920s strongly anti-capitalist as well. The first programme of the party spoke of the need to share profits, nationalise the trusts, increase pensions and provide free education. Hitler referred to the need to make the working people national, while Strasser (1892–1934), killed in the purges of 1934, attacked capitalism and argued for the emancipation of the worker through 'participation in profits, property and management'. Gründel saw the creation of a new type of human being as constituting the end of the property-owning bourgeoisie (Griffin, 1995: 117, 123, 128) while Goebbels had said in 1928 that 'no honest thinking person today would want to deny the justification of the workers' movements'. Indeed, he had complained in 1926 that Hitler wanted to 'compensate the aristocrats' and not 'disturb private property. Horrendous! . . . we are Socialists. We don't want to have been so in vain!' There is evidence to suggest that those who supported the Nazis were less likely to be unemployed, but rather threatened with unemployment, i.e. the middle and lower middle classes rather than the industrial workers.

The body particularly concerned with advancing Nazi interests among trade unionists (the NSBO) became an increasing embarrassment to the Nazi leadership. The 'Night of the Long Knives' that saw the liquidation of the leadership of the SA (stormtroopers) was justified by Hitler on the grounds that a second revolution had to be avoided at all cost. Socialism continued in the party's title, but it was mere rhetoric. The Nazi economic programme was presented as a form of 'soldierly socialism', but the real target was Marxism and democracy. Marxism, it was said, always follows capitalism as its shadow'. Steding (1903–38) spoke contemptuously of 'the purely mercenary capitalism of the stock exchange' (Griffin, 1995: 141, 152). These policies often involved taking away certain freedoms from employers. For example, the introduction of some labour-saving machinery was banned and government permission had to be obtained before reducing their labour force. The government also tended to give work contracts to those companies that relied on manual labour rather than machines.

p. 296

The German economy remained capitalistic, although with extensive state control. The attack on the Jews was clearly linked to the virulent opposition to Marxism and internationalism, and although Germany had a potent anti-Semitic tradition to draw upon, it has been argued that before 1933, the Nazis placed relatively little emphasis upon anti-Semitism.

Hitler had attacked Jews in *Mein Kampf*, but he had toned down his anti-Semitism while gaining power because he was anxious not to alienate Jewish business leaders. Henry Ford had been compelled to stop publishing anti-Semitic attacks in the United States after the Jewish community organised a boycott of Ford cars in the late 1920s. In the same way, Lord Rothermere, owner of the *Daily Mail*, had been forced 'to toe the line' when Jewish businessmen had withdrawn advertising from the newspaper. Hitler began to leave out anti-Semitic comments from his speeches during elections, and during the 1933 General Election, Jewish businessmen even contributed money to his party.

However, after 1933 Jews were increasingly excluded from mainstream life, and the Nuremburg laws of 1935 stripped Jews of their citizenship and made inter-marriage illegal. During Crystal Night over 7,500 Jewish shops were destroyed and 400 synagogues were burnt down; 91 Jews were killed and an estimated 20,000 were sent to camps. The only people who were punished for the crimes committed on Crystal Night were members of the SA who had raped Jewish women (since they had broken the Nuremberg Laws in so doing). The numbers of Jews wishing to leave the country increased dramatically, and it has been calculated that between 1933 and 1939, approximately half the Jewish population of Germany (250,000) left the country. This included several Jewish scientists (like Albert Einstein) who were to play an important role in the fight against fascism during the war. Speer recalls that the Ministry of Education was not inclined to support nuclear research on the grounds that nuclear physics was seen as the product of the Jewish mind (1970: 228).

By the beginning of 1942 over 500,000 Jews in Poland and Russia had been killed by the SS, and at the Wannsee Conference in 1942, a final solution was proposed which led to the systematic termination of Jewry. It has been estimated that between 1942 and 1945 around 18 million were sent to extermination camps. Of these, it has been suggested that between 5 and 11 million were killed.

Statism, Women and Colonialism

The Nazis extolled the principle of oneness. The party was Germany, with a single will, faith, flag and leader. Although the Nazis opposed organised religion, a concordat was signed with the Pope (the Catholic Church could continue if it did not 'interfere' in politics) and Himmler (1900–45), head of the SS, told the SS that they must believe in God. The religion of the Jews is godless.

Goebbels spoke of 'forging the German nation into a single people'. Benn, who was a National Socialist, ceased to support the Nazis after the purges of 1934, had declared that Nazi rule manifested itself in the 'total state' – an institution that asserts the complete identity of power and spirit, individuality and the collective. 'It is monist, anti-dialectic, enduring, and authoritarian'. The strong state, argued Schmitt, transcends diversity: every atom of its existence is ruled and permeated by the principle of leadership (Griffin, 1995: 147, 134–5, 138–9).

p. 297

The Nazis, of course, espoused an explicit and militant patriarchy. Paula Siber, acting head of the German Association of Women, argued that 'to be a woman means to be a mother'. The woman belongs wherever care is required and she manages 75 per cent of the nation's income by running the home. Hitler disliked women who were interested in politics. By introducing measures that would encourage women to leave the labour market, the level of unemployment could be further lowered. Women in certain professions such as doctors and civil servants

Anti-Semitic Propaganda

It is worth noting that before 1933 Streicher's virulently anti-Semitic *Der Stürmer* was opposed by some Nazis and it was only after taking office that its circulation reached half a million. As is argued in the Comenius History Project, a survey of NSDAP members' and their reason for joining found that 60 per cent of respondents made no reference at all to anti-Semitism, while 4 per cent openly expressed disapproval of it.

Analysis of Nazi posters in the period from 1928 to 1932 has revealed the following:

Enemy groups targeted by NSDAP posters, 1928–1932

	Total no. of posters	Percentage
The 'system'	15	12.1
November-parties	25	20.1
SPD/Marxism	39	31.5
Centre Party/allies	10	8.1
KPD	6	4.8
Jews	6	4.8
Miscellaneous	23	18.6

The subjects chosen for front page headlines in the official daily, the *Volkische Beobachter* between the crucial July 1932 election and Hitler's installation in power, confirms the picture. Between 1932 and 33 anti-Semitism only featured in just over 3 per cent of the cases: the paper was much more concerned with the 'threat' of Bolshevism, Marxism and the trade unions, and the economic problems facing people (http://www.stevenson.ac.uk/comenius/articles/totalitarianism/uk_dg/naz_1h.htm).

By rejecting the authority of the individual and replacing it by the numbers of some momentary mob, the parliamentary principle of majority rule sins against the basic aristocratic principle of Nature . . .

The receptivity of the great masses is very limited, their intelligence small, but their power of forgetting is enormous. In consequence of these faults, all effective propaganda must be limited to a very few points and must harp on these in slogans . . .

Adolf Hitler, *Mein Kampf* (1925) London: Radius Books/Hutchinson, pp. 24, 165.

Women in Nazi Germany

Women were seen as inferior beings who must procreate for the good of the nation. They were to give up work in order to fulfil this biological purpose. During the election campaign of 1932, Hitler promised to take 800,000 women out of employment within four years. In August 1933 a law was passed that enabled married couples to obtain loans to set up homes and start families which meant that single men and childless couples were taxed more heavily. Married women doctors and civil servants were dismissed in 1934 and from June 1936 women could no longer act as judges or public prosecutors. Women were ineligible for jury service since Hitler believed that they were unable to 'think logically or reason objectively, since they are ruled only by emotion'.

However, during the war, it proved necessary to allow women to work in artillery factories and on farms. Medals were provided for women who had large families. The number of women in universities fell significantly. Girls were educated into becoming mothers – women were not to smoke or diet in case this affected their health as mothers.

In 1934 the *Ten Commandments* for the choice of a spouse were propagated:

1. Remember that you are a German.
2. If you are genetically healthy you should not remain unmarried.
3. Keep your body pure.
4. You should keep your mind and spirit pure.
5. As a German choose only a spouse of the same or Nordic blood.
6. In choosing a spouse ask about his ancestors.
7. Health is also a precondition for physical beauty.
8. Marry only for love.
9. Don't look for a playmate but for a companion for marriage.
10. You should want to have as many children as possible.

A common rhyme for women was:

Take hold of kettle, broom and pan,

Then you'll surely get a man!

Shop and office leave alone, Your true life work lies at home.

Information from http://www.historylearningsite.co.uk/Women_Nazi_Germany.htm
http:// www.germanculture.com.ua/library/weekly/aa080601b.htm
http://www.spartacus.schoolnet.co.uk/GERwomen.htm

were dismissed, while other married women were paid a lump sum of 1,000 marks to stay at home.

Hitler argued that the slogan 'emancipation of women' had been invented by Jewish intellectuals. The woman's world is her husband, her family, her children, and her home. The distinction between the two worlds was natural and necessary. 'The woman', he declared, 'has her own battlefield. With every child that she brings into the world, she fights her battle for the nation.'

A mystical belief in the state went hand in hand with a contempt for democracy and a belief in colonialism. The pursuit of colonies was defended as a source of raw materials and as an activity that was vital for Germany's living space. It was not, Ritter argued in 1937, 'an expression of imperialism' but a 'vital natural necessity' (Griffin, 1995: 137, 145).

Nazism and Fascism

A fiercely debated question relates to the relationship between Nazism and Italian fascism. Is there a general fascism of which Nazism is an example, or is the Nazism so unique and particular that it cannot be categorised in this way? As Griffin has pointed out (1995: 93), a number of scholars have argued that Nazism is *sui generis,* unique to the history of Germany. Allardyce, an American scholar, took the view that a generic fascism does not exist (Griffin, 1995: 302).

Similarities	Differences
Impact of the First World War	Attitude to organised religion
Hatred of liberalism and Marxism	Degree of anti-Semitism
Rejection of parliamentary democracy	Global aspirations
Belief in leadership principle	Use of socialism to describe party
Commitment to colonialism	
Admiration for the state	

Not only do we have the profound influence exercised over Hitler and the Nazis by the success of Mussolini in Italy, but the conditions that contributed to the rise of fascism in Italy exercised their influence in Germany as well. The table above shows that Kershaw is right to argue that the similarities between Nazism and other brands of fascism are 'profound' (cited by Griffin, 1995: 93).

Nazism is better understood by seeing it as a variant of fascism – of course, with its own particular features. The idea that racism was a German import into Mussolini's Italy is untrue, even though German fascism was much more extreme (and competent) than its Italian counterpart, and the genocidal policies towards the Jews was not part of the anti-Semitism of Italian fascism. Nevertheless, the case for considering Nazism as a form of fascism is overwhelming, and bears upon the important question of other forms of fascism that arose not only in the interwar years, but in the post-war period. Griffin's collection of documents is noteworthy for its inclusion of non-Nazi forms of German fascism. Spanish fascists like Primo De Rivera denied that they were imitating Hitler and Mussolini: he argued that 'by reproducing the achievements of the Italians or the Germans we will become more Spanish than we have ever been' (Griffin, 1995: 188).

Fascism and Capitalism

There can little doubt that fascists were anti-capitalist in their rhetoric. Radek, one of the communist leaders, was to describe fascism as the 'socialism of the petty bourgeois masses' (Kitchen, 1976: 2). Ramos (1905–36), a Spanish fascist, blamed the bourgeoisie and its 'agents, advocates and front men' for fragmentation, impotence, exhaustion and egoism. Rivera argued that fascism was neither capitalist nor communist: he advocated a national syndicalism that would pass surplus value, as he called it, 'to the producer as a member of his trade union'. La Rochelle, a French fascist, spoke of 'annihilating' liberalism and capitalism. A

Latvian fascist made it clear that 'we acknowledge private enterprise and private property' but are opposed to anarchy (Griffin, 1995: 186, 189, 203, 218).

Zetkin (see her biography on the website) influenced the Comintern in its argument that fascism 'by its origin and exponents' 'includes revolutionary tendencies which might turn against capitalism and its state' but in fact it is counter-revolutionary, supporting capitalism in a situation in which the old, allegedly non-political apparatus of the bourgeois state 'no longer guarantees the bourgeoisie adequate security' (Griffin, 1995: 261). The argument echoes Marx's comment in *The Eighteenth Brumaire of Louis Bonaparte* that when the parliamentary system seems to aid the socialists, then 'the bourgeoisie confesses that its own interest requires its deliverance from the peril of its own self-government' (Marx, 1973: 190). The merits of this argument are that it indicates the dangers which an explicitly illiberal regime poses to the bourgeoisie, and that in 'normal times', a liberal parliamentary system would be much more congenial to a bourgeois regime than an explicitly authoritarian one. It is only when there is the fear that a parliamentary system might help the enemies of capital to power in a situation of crisis and revolutionary threat, that 'deliverance' is sought. Miliband stresses that capitalists had to pay a high political price for a system that advantaged them: they had no real control over a dictatorship that arguably served their interests (1973: 85).

Miliband argues that the 'anti-bourgeois resonances' (1973: 80) are important if only to enable fascist movements to acquire a mass following, nor need we deny that supporters of these movements believed that an anti-capitalist revolution was underway. 'It is not only Jewish capitalists we will hang, but all capitalists!' declares a poster in the museum at the Dachau concentration camp. Miliband cites Mussolini in 1934 defending private property, and notes that big business under Hitler was given a key role in managing the economy. There was a dramatic increase in the power of capital over labour and an increase in profits. Miliband concedes that business under fascism had to submit to a greater degree of intervention and control than they would have liked, and put up with policies that they found disagreeable. Kitchen points out that industrialists disliked particular aspects of Nazi policy (the use of foreign slaves rather than women in the factories, for example, or the economic inefficiency involved in the mass murder of Jews), but he argues that in broad terms, the industrialists were satisfied with Nazi policy (Kitchen, 1976: 59).

As for fascism's supposedly revolutionary character: Miliband contends that the state not only does not significantly change in the composition of its personnel (except to purge it of 'traitors', liberals, etc.), but in Nazi Germany, for example, there were fewer people in the state from working class origin than before (Miliband, 1973: 82–4). This is why it is not satisfactory to describe fascism as 'a party of revolutionaries' (Linz, 1979: 18), since fascism sought not to transform society and the state, but to prevent it from being transformed. It is thus counter-revolutionary, rather than revolutionary in character. It is impossible to agree with Eugen Weber that fascism is not a counter-revolution, but merely a rival revolution (to communism) (Weber, 1979: 509).

The orthodox communist position – enshrined in the theses of the Comintern or Third International – was that fascism represented 'the most reactionary, most chauvinist, and most imperialist elements of finance capital' (Griffin, 1995: 262). It was only in the mid-1930s that communists dropped the notorious argument that social democrats were 'social fascists' and the enemy of the working class. 'Finance capital' in the orthodox definition cited above, refers to Lenin's argument in

Imperialism that bank capital has merged with industrial capital, but it seems less contentious to accept Miliband's point that fascism represented industrialists as well as bankers in a situation in which threat of left extremism made right extremism a necessary, if far from ideal, choice. George and Margaret Cole argued that fascism is state-controlled capitalism 'operated in the interests of the broad mass of property owners'. Horkheimer, a key figure in the neo-Marxist Frankfurt School, declared that 'whoever is not prepared to talk about capitalism should also remain silent about fascism' (Griffin, 1995: 267, 272).

Psychoanalysts argued that fascism is rooted in the human character – it is a form of personality structure, an authoritarian character, but this does not mean, as Adorno acknowledged, that such a structure can only be modified by psychological means (Griffin, 1995: 289), and it could well be argued that we still need to refer to capitalism and crisis to understand why fascism arises in certain societies and at certain historical periods, and not at others. Reich, who was expelled from the German Communist Party in the 1930s for his dissident views, had argued that fascism is the result of thousands of years of warping in the human structure: a number of later studies contended that fascism was an attempt to compensate for mothering and family life (Kitchen, 1976: 13, 23).

Fascism, Liberalism and the Enlightenment

'1789 [the year of the French Revolution, and the inauguration of the era of Liberty, Equality and Fraternity] is abolished' (Heywood, 1992: 174). This was how the Nazis proclaimed their victory in 1933. Although fascists specifically targeted Marxism, they saw Marxism as an ideology that built upon, and was thus rooted in, the assumptions of liberalism and the Enlightenment. Dunn quotes the words of Hitler: 'National Socialism is what Marxism could have been had it freed itself from the absurd, artificial link with the democratic system' (Dunn, 1979: 21).

The State of Nature, Equality and the Individual

Fascists not only deny that humans have ever lived outside of society, they interpret 'nature' in a repressively hierarchical manner. Although the idea that humans are self-contained atoms who are naturally separate and unrelated to one another constitutes a mystification of social reality, fascism attacked abstract individualism because of its universal and egalitarian claims. It dramatically threw the baby out with the bathwater.

Classical liberalism sees individuals as naturally free and equal. Fascism takes the view that nature is a force that embodies violence, instinct, and superiority: hence it rejects the whole notion of equality even as a formal attribute. Individuals are created by the community, and the community is interpreted in statist terms. It is true that Nazi ideologists gave a specifically racial and *völkisch* (peoples') dimension to the notion of community so that the community constituted a kind of soul. But all fascists see the community as 'natural', animated by some kind of life force – it is an emotional organism, not a rational construct – and it assigns superiority to the few and inferiority to the many.

The notion of humanity was attacked for two reasons: first because it ignored what was deemed to be racial superiority – of Aryans over Jews, whites over blacks, etc. – and second, because it implied that the mass of humans mattered. The progress and culture of humanity, declared Hitler, 'are not a product of the majority, but rests exclusively on the genius and energy of the personality' (Vincent, 1995: 157). The individual denotes not the ordinary and everyday human being, but the leader, the genius, the person who must be obeyed.

Nationalism

Liberalism has an ambivalent position towards nationalism because it has an ambivalent position towards the state. In the state of nature individuals are deemed cosmopolitan – they are outside both nation and state – but as they become conscious of the inconveniences of such a position, they not only form a state but acquire a national identity. Liberal nationalism, like the liberal state, seeks to reconcile universal freedom and equality with the necessary evil of particular institutions that divide the world. Liberal nationalists argue that all nations are equal, and the liberal state seeks to provide security for the free citizen. Just as fascism sees the community as somehow prior to the individual (an inversion of the liberal abstraction), so it sees the nation as the embodiment of superiority and domination.

Nationalism necessarily takes an explicitly xenophobic form, based on hatred. Hatred of foreigners, aliens, the weak, the vulnerable, the disabled, the needy, the female, and a characterisation of 'lesser' peoples and nations in terms of these 'despised' categories. Mussolini challenged those who saw Machiavelli as the founder of fascism, on the grounds that Machiavelli was insufficiently contemptuous of the masses – the herd, as Mussolini liked to call them – who gratefully accepted inequality and discipline (Vincent, 1995: 156).

Rationality

Liberalism and the Enlightenment see all individuals as rational, and thus capable of governing themselves. Fascism regards 'reason' as inherently abstract, and extols action as a force based upon instinct and feeling. You should 'think with your blood', and de Rivera of the Spanish Falange (a fascist movement that Franco tolerated and used) declared that the movement is not a way of thinking but 'a way of being' (Vincent, 1955: 155). It is the soul, not the mind, emotion and instinct, not reason and logic that ultimately count. Again fascism challenges, in a spirit of negative inversion, the abstractions of the Enlightenment. Reason is rejected – not made historical and concrete. Fascism dismisses not merely the weaknesses of liberalism (its chronic tendency to abstraction) but its conceptual strengths (its argument for the individual, universality, reason and self-government).

Colin Jordan who founded the White Defence League in 1958 and the National Socialist Movement in 1962, declared himself in revolt against liberalism, singling out for particular mention, its 'cash nexus', 'its excessive individualism', 'its view of man as a folkless, interchangeable unit of world population', its 'sickly humanitarianism' and its 'fraudulent contention' that the wishes of the masses are 'the all-important criteria' (Griffin, 1995: 325–6).

Fascism, Stalinism and the State

Fascism identifies the individual and the community with the state. Fascism inverts the classical liberal thesis, that humans dwell in a stateless order of nature, by arguing that humans derive their very nature and being from membership of the state. Although the Nazis liked to speak of the community in racial terms, they too held that the repressive hierarchies of the state are central to human identity.

Hence the explicit and dramatic statism of the fascist analysis. By arguing that humans are statist in essence, fascists reject the idea that freedom and force stand as mutually exclusive entities. On the contrary, force becomes something that ennobles and distinguishes humans, and since the exercise of force implies the existence of a repressive hierarchy, fascism rejects the notion of equality. The individual is a person who stands out from the mass, so that the leadership principle is woven into social analysis. Leaders are outstanding individuals who dictate to and mould the formless and ignorant masses.

It follows from this avowedly statist doctrine that the nation has enemies both from without and within who threaten its purity and cohesion. War and violent conflict are the only viable responses so that the crushing of the other is the way to affirm the self. Xenophobia and racism are built into the statism of fascist premises, and so is male chauvinism. The superior individual must be a 'he' since the notion of the female is identified with passivity and cowardice.

It is important not to see the state as itself a fascist institution, since states can be liberal and anti-authoritarian in character in which, through devices like the rule of law and parliamentary representation, state force is regulated and limited. On the other hand, it is also important to see the continuities as well as the discontinuities between fascism and the state. The use of force polarises, and can only be justified against those who are deemed 'enemies' of society. The nationalism that reaches its extreme form in fascism is inherent in the state, and it could be argued that there is a real tension between the state as an institution claiming a monopoly of legitimate force, and the notion of democracy as self-government.

Stalinism

Can one describe Stalinism – authoritarian communism – as a form of fascism? There are of course similarities. The concept of dictatorship is central to Stalinism and a particularly vicious and exclusionary form of class struggle is used to justify purges, mock-trials and authoritarian practices in general. There are also significant dissimilarities so that however tempting, it is, in our view, erroneous to see left and right authoritarianism, Stalinism and fascism as interchangeable.

In other words, the argument that became widespread during the Cold War, identifying communism and fascism as forms of **totalitarianism,** is superficial and misleading. Mommsen makes the point that this theory glosses over the structural features peculiar to the fascist party. The theory of democratic centralism may have operated to strengthen the leadership of Communist Parties but it was a theory of organisation alien to fascism (Mommsen, 1979: 153). Moreover, fascist and communist ideology are poles apart. Stalinism seeks to build a world that is ultimately stateless and classless in character – it draws upon a Marxist heritage to argue that under communism, people, all people, will be able to govern their own affairs.

This is not to deny the authoritarianism that existed (and still exists) in Communist Party states but it could be argued that the 'cult of the personality', the denial of democracy, the male chauvinism etc. in these societies stand in contradiction to the theories of communism. In fascism, on the other hand, these features are not in contradiction with the doctrine: they are explicitly enshrined in the theories and movements. This argument may not seem of much comfort to the inmate of a gulag who is worked to death in inhuman conditions, but it points to a qualitative difference between the statism of fascism and statism of Stalinism. Moreover, as

Stalin's Purges

Stalin was admired by Hitler, and the latter told Speer that if Germany won the Second World War, Stalin would remain in charge of Russia (1970: 306). The famine in the early 1930s that followed collectivisation in Russia killed between six and seven million people. The purges that began in the mid-1930s were directed against dissidents within the party and in society at large, and took millions of lives. About 35,000 military officers were shot or imprisoned. Robert Conquest has estimated that by 1938 there were seven million victims in the labour camps, where the survival rate could drop to some 2 or 3 per cent. The purges have been summarised as follows:

Arrests, 1937–8 – about 7 million

Executions – about 1 million

Died in camps – about 2 million

In prison, late 1938 – about 1 million

In camps, late 1938 – about 8 million

By the time Stalin died in 1953, the camps' population had increased to some 12 million.

Source: http://www.gendercide.org

Exercise

You are having a cup of coffee in a crowded coffee shop in your Students' Union when four young men sit at your table and begin talking. Because you are on your own, you cannot but hear their conversation. 'There are too many blacks around here', says A. 'I agree, they should all be sent back to their place of origin', comments B. 'But some of them were born here', interjects C. 'That's irrelevant', says D. 'Whether they were born here or not, they are not part of our race, and they just don't fit in.' 'Indeed', declares A, 'I have noticed that the lecturers make a fuss of them, as though they are more important than us whites.' 'Yeah', says B, 'what do you expect when most of the lecturers are communists and Jews? I think that the university should only employ decent-minded Christians – people with sensible views.' C protests. 'That would be undemocratic.' 'So what?', says D. 'Our democracy is a farce anyway – we need strong rule by someone we can look up to. This notion of majority rule is an idiotic liberal idea anyway.' 'In fact', comments A, 'there are blacks in my street and tonight a group of us is going to show them what we think of them with something hard and large through their windows.'

- A, B and D are clearly right-wing extremists. They are racists.

- Which would say is a fascist?

- Although you find their views deeply upsetting, would you call the police?

Kitchen points out, communism sought to radically change the means of production, whereas fascist regimes did not, and this throws further doubt on the proposition that similarities between fascism and communism outweigh the differences (Kitchen, 1976: 31).

Fascism Today

One of the objections that Kitchen makes to the German thinker Ernst Nolte's theory of fascism, is the view that fascism belongs only to the past. It does not exist today. This is not only a complacent view of fascism, it confuses a movement with its historical manifestations (Kitchen, 1976: 40–1). It is true that fascism arose in the interwar period, and that one of the problems of identifying post-war fascism is that the revulsion of most of the world against Nazism in particular, has meant that contemporary fascism generally avoids too close an identity with the models of the past. Fascists in Europe have had the problem in the post-war period of getting to grips with the defeat of Mussolini and Hitler in the Second World War. There have been a variety of responses.

The Unrepentant Apologists

Some have taken the view that Hitler and Mussolini were correct in their policies although they were defeated by the Allied forces. Jordan, who founded the White Defence League in 1958 and the National Socialist Movement in 1962, took the view that fascism (even in its extreme Hitlerian form) is as relevant as ever, and the West European Federation set up in 1963 espoused explicitly Nazi doctrine. The New European Order established in Switzerland supported similar views (Griffin, 1995: 326–8).

The Holocaust Deniers

Some fascists try to undercut the argument of their critics by denying that the Nazis had in fact brought about the Holocaust. The leader of the Belgian fascist movement during the Second World War, Degrelle, argued to the Pope in 1979 that Auschwitz could not have exterminated large numbers of Jews, travellers, etc. and that anyway, the terror bombing of the Allies and the gulags of Stalin put into perspective any human rights abuses the Nazis might have caused. The term 'final solution' did not mean extermination – this is another of the deniers' contentions – and that during the war, other nations had concentration camps too (Griffin, 1995: 330–7). Irving, an historian who has built his reputation on 'reassessing' the Holocaust, admits the terrible atrocities of the camps, but argues that these took place against the instructions of Hitler who merely wanted to have Jews transported to Madagascar, an island off the African coast (Griffin, 1995: 330–7). To deny the existence of the Holocaust is a criminal offence in Germany, although it could be argued that obnoxious contentions like these should be exposed through argument rather than crushed by law.

The Critical Fascists

Mosley, the leader of the British Union of Fascists, before the Second World War, argued that Hitler had overreached himself – tried to achieve too much – and this was the reason for his downfall. The concentration camps and the sacrifice of the youth tarnished an otherwise noble ideal. Mussolini had badly miscalculated when he entered the war, but the harshness of his *squadristi* can be excused by 'the incredible savagery and brutality of the reds'. Chesterton, the first chair of the National Front, admits that fascism failed disastrously, and the 'excesses' of Hitler in particular, discredited the cause (Griffin, 1995: 323–4).

Some like Ernest Niekisch (1889–1967) argued that the fascist revolution had been hijacked by demagogues (i.e. leaders who appeal to prejudices for support) like Hitler, who was a travesty of the spiritual elite really required (Griffin, 1995: 319).

Eurofascism

The European Social Movement, founded in 1951, sought to unite Europe against communism, with Evola, an Italian fascist, arguing that such a Europe must be an empire. Mosley, on the other hand, spoke of the need for Europe to become a nation, with a pan-European government using Africa as a resource base (Griffin, 1995: 333–5). A number of those associated with what can be called a 'New Right' (not to be confused with the neo-liberalism of free marketeers) speak of the need to regenerate Europe so that it stands apart from communism and capitalism which in its liberal form, eradicates identity and imposes a vulgar and soulless 'rule of quantity' upon life (Griffin, 1995: 351).

Nationalist Salvation

Some fascists have turned to nationalism, arguing that a national revolution is necessary as a 'cleansing fire of purification'. Ultra-nationalists have utilised punk rock, heavy metal music, and football hooliganism (Griffin, 1995: 360, 363). However, parties like the British National Front claim to stand for democracy and accuse their opponents of not being supporters of 'genuine democracy'. Nationalism is presented as a doctrine for the equality of nations. The National Front (NF) sees itself 'as a radical party seeking deep and fundamental changes in British society. Unlike many other radical parties, particularly those of the past, we do not seek to impose our views on the population.' The implication is that such a party distances itself from the explicit authoritarianism of interwar fascism (http://www.nfne.co.uk/nfsop.html).

In 1982 John Tyndall formed the British National Party (BNP), and although he speaks of the 'degenerative forces' poisoning national life linked to liberalism and internationalism, the party speaks of wishing to extend democracy (http://www. bnp.org.uk/mission.htm) and objects to the idea that it is fascist or authoritarian. It is difficult to avoid the conclusion that parties like the BNP and the NF are parties of the extreme right, rather than fascist in the way we have defined the term here. On the other hand, the BNP, for example, has links with and invites speakers from explicitly fascist groups, so that the 'democratic' appearances of such organisations should not be taken at face value. La Oeuvre France, founded in 1968, describes itself as 'a strictly nationalist movement' and treats the accusation of 'fascism' and Nazism' as slurs against French people 'of good stock' (Griffin, 1995: 371–2). Of course, ultra-nationalist movements will be sensitive to the idea that they are derivatives of other movements and hence likely to resist the label of fascism on that score as well.

However, groups on the far right that have sprung up in former Communist Party states, like Romania, may espouse more explicitly fascist positions. The New Right movement founded in 1993 in Romania speaks of the need for an 'ethnocratic' state which it explicitly contrasts to a democratic state. The National Democratic Party of Germany, eclipsed in the late 1980s by the Republican Party and the German Peoples' Union, espouses Germany as a *völkish* national entity, but calls for social justice and equality within Germany's borders. The Italian Social Movement that won 12.7 per cent of the vote with the National Alliance (in March 1994), seeks to reconstruct the Italian state and it regards Mussolini as the greatest statesman of the twentieth century (Griffin, 1995: 379, 382, 387).

Focus

South African Apartheid

There is no doubt that the South African National Party and its policies of apartheid were widely admired by the extreme right elsewhere, including explicit fascists. A Mosley supporter, Webster, spoke of the South African nationalists as following 'the same path as Hitler did, but they will not be as hasty as he was' (Bunting, 1969: 71). During the Second World War, the National Party (NP) communicated with Nazis over their campaign to withdraw South Africa from supporting the Allies. The NP had cordial links with the Ossewabrandwag (the Ox-wagon Sentinel) which had also connections with the Nazis and whose paramilitary wing sought to overthrow the government. Vorster, a future Prime Minister, declared in 1942 that his Christian nationalism 'was an ally of national socialism' (Bunting, 1969: 98).

When Germany and Italy were defeated, the National Party began to distance itself from anti-English and anti-Semitic policies, and concentrated on developing the doctrine of apartheid. All those serving sentences for wartime offences were released after the Nationalist electoral victory in 1948. The stripping of Africans and (so-called) coloureds of their political rights, the outlawing of sexual relations between the 'races', the Suppression of Communism Act (which banned the party and imposed house arrest on opponents of the regime), the reservation of skilled jobs for whites, the control imposed on the trade unions, all these and many more acts had been envisaged by the National Party during the war period (Bunting, 1969: 110).

Bunting's detailed account of what he calls the Nuremberg Laws of grand apartheid and the title of his book *The Rise of the South African Reich* raises the question as to whether apartheid South Africa can be considered a fascist regime. The regime certainly resorted to terror against its opponents, and was brutal, explicitly racist and authoritarian. On the other hand, it was a parliamentary system for whites, and allowed limited liberalism in its treatment of the press, judiciary and opposition parties, provided they were relatively conservative in character. It comes close to being a fascist regime, and certainly Griffin is right to regard Afrikaner nationalist organisations like the Afrikaner–Weerstandsbeweging (the Afrikaner Resistance Movement) that developed in post-apartheid period, as fascist in practice (Griffin, 1995: 376).

Nevertheless, we would say that although apartheid was extremely right wing, it was not technically fascist, despite its pre-war and wartime roots.

Summary

Although fascism is a chaotic and opportunist movement, it can and should be defined. There are a number of characteristics – anti-liberalism, ultra-nationalism, the extolling of violence, militant statism, mass support etc. – that distinguish this twentieth-century movement from other movements.

Fascism arose first in Italy. The development of fascism in Italy needs to be explained, since this was the particular movement that gave the general movement its name. Contrary to widely held views, Mussolini's regime was racist, although it is true that systematic anti-Semitism only developed after the alliance with Hitler.

Nazism is seen as a form of fascism, and not simply as a historically unique movement. It is an extreme kind of fascism, emphasising the racial character of nationalism in a more aggressive and systematic manner. Its anti-capitalism was ultimately rhetorical as the liquidation of the leaders of the Nazi 'left' in 1934 demonstrates. Although fascism acquired mass support through espousing a rhetorical anti-capitalism, once in power fascist movements consolidated their links with big business. It is true that fascist leaders directed businesses and implemented policies that were not always to the satisfaction of the business community, but it is also true that backing from large capitalist corporations was crucial for fascism's success.

Fascism rejects liberalism and the Enlightenment. Ideas of reason, equality and emancipation are contemptuously dismissed in a specifically negative manner. Although there are problems with the ideas of liberalism and the Enlightenment, fascism unceremoniously throws the baby out with the bathwater. Fascists see the state itself as central to human identity and vital to the idea of community. The violence that the state both exercises and seeks to regulate is extolled by fascists, and although the liberal state is significantly different from the fascist one, there are similarities as well as differences in all forms of the state. Likewise, all left-wing authoritarianism is also statist in character, it is not correct to describe Stalinism, say, as a form of fascism. There are similarities but these are outweighed by their differences.

Fascist movements exist today but there are a number of problems in identifying them. Fascism was discredited by the defeat of Nazi Germany and Fascist Italy in the last war, and of course by the atrocities committed by the Nazis in the concentration camps. Post-war movements of the extreme right often deny that they are fascist in character – they may even claim to espouse democracy, although these claims should be approached with caution. The other problem with identifying post-war fascism is that extreme nationalist movements (that are not German or Italian) feel that to express allegiance to fascism would compromise their own claims to 'authenticity' and national uniqueness.

Questions

1. Can fascism be defined, and if so, how?
2. Is fascism a purely Italian phenomenon?
3. Why does fascism reject liberalism and the Enlightenment?
4. 'Stalinism is a form of fascism'. Discuss.
5. Comment on the argument that fascism is a movement of the inter-war period.

References

Beetham, D. (1977) 'From Socialism to Fascism: the Relation between Theory and Practice in the Work of Robert Michels', *Political Studies* 25(3–24), 161–81.

Bunting, B. (1969) *The Rise of the South African Reich* Harmondsworth: Penguin.

Dunn, J. (1979) *Western Theory in the Face of the Future* Cambridge: Cambridge University Press.

Griffin, R. (1995) *Fascism* Oxford, New York: Oxford University Press.

Hemingway, E. (1985) *A Farewell to Arms* London: Heinemann Educational.

Heywood, A. (1992) *Political Ideologies* Basingstoke: Palgrave.

Kitchen, M. (1976) *Fascism* Basingstoke: Macmillan.

Linz, J. (1979) 'Some notes towards a Comparative Study of Fascism in Sociological Historical Perspective' in W. Laqueur (ed.), *Fascism: A Reader's Guide* Harmondsworth: Penguin, 13–78.

Lyttelton, A. (1979) 'Italian Fascism' in W. Laqueur (ed.), *Fascism: A Reader's Guide* Harmondsworth: Penguin, 81–114.

Marx, K. (1973) 'The Eighteenth Brumaire of Louis Napoleon' in D. Fernbach (ed.), *Surveys from Exile* Harmondsworth and London: Penguin and New Left Review, 143–249.

Miliband, R. (1973) *The State in Capitalist Society* London: Quartet.

Mommsen, H. (1979) 'National Socialism: Continuity and Change' in W. Laqueur (ed.), *Fascism: A Reader's Guide* Harmondsworth: Penguin, 151–92.

Speer, A. (1970) *Inside the Third Reich* London: Weidenfeld and Nicolson.

Vincent, A. (1995) *Modern Political Ideologies*, 2nd edn Oxford: Blackwell.

Weber, E. (1979) 'Revolution? Counter-Revolution? What Revolution' in W. Laqueur (ed.), *Fascism: A Reader's Guide* Harmondsworth: Penguin, 488–531.

Further Reading

- Griffin's reader in fascism (referenced above) is an invaluable source of material with acute introductions and prefaces. Griffin has recently published *Moderism and Fascism* (Basingstoke: Palgrave, 2007).

- Kitchen's *Fascism* is comprehensive and readable, concise and incisive.

- Fromm's *Fear of Freedom* (London: Routledge and Kegan Paul, 1942) is a classic interpretation of fascism that draws upon psychoanalysis for its explanation.

- For detailed analyses of fascism in the inter-war period, see *the Fascism Reader* ed. A. Kallis (London and New York: Routledge, 2003).

- Albert Speer's *Inside the Third Reich* (referenced above) is a fascinating read.

Weblinks

For information about the Holocaust:
http://www.thinkequal.com

For useful sites on fascism:
http://dictionary.reference.com/search?q=fascism

For further information and bibliography:
http://en.wikipedia.org/wiki/Fascism

Part 3   Contemporary Ideologies

What is a New Social Movement?

We have argued that an ideology is a belief system focused around the state. The classical ideologies discussed in Part 2 took the legitimacy of the state to be a central concern, and this is true even of anarchist theories: although most anarchists reject the claim to legitimacy made on behalf of the state one of their main objectives is to challenge the state, and in this sense anarchists are 'state-focused'. Despite talk of 'globalisation' and the 'hollowing out of the state', the state remains important in political theory, and the new ideologies discussed in this part of the book do not dismiss it. They do, however, challenge the *sharp* distinction between domestic and international politics. For example, multicultur-alists argue that cultures do not equate to nations, and therefore allegiance to the state does not, as the British politician Norman Tebbit claimed, require that British Asians support the English cricket team against Pakistan. Similarly, an important feature of feminism is the linking together of women's experience across the world. While a traditional ideology, such as socialism (or Marxism, as one variant of socialism), stressed that the workers 'know no nation', and therefore class solidarity should transcend the state, the focus of socialist (communist) political action was capture of the state. Feminists, on the other hand, while prepared to work through state structures to achieve legal change, identify power relations at both substate and suprastate levels: women can be oppressed through family structures as well as by global forces. Ecologism represents an even more radical challenge to the significance of the state as the central focus of political thought. Ecologists – as distinct from environmentalists – see 'nature' as an interconnected whole, protection of which requires both small-scale organisation and global action. Small-scale, quasi-anarchistic communities are required as a means of avoiding environmentally damaging transportation of goods, while global agreements are necessary to tackle problems that by their nature do not respect state boundaries. Fundamentalism may also represent a challenge to the state: Islamic fundamentalism regards the state as a corruption of Islam (US fundamen-talism and Zionism do, however, appear highly nationalistic, although some variants of Zionism conceive of the Jewish State as a religious, rather than a secular, entity, and thus as quite different to the traditional state).

The challenge to the distinction between national and international politics is not the only significant divider between classical and new ideologies. In trying to understand what is 'new' about the new ideologies three differences – or discontinuities – can be identified. The first we have already identified – the challenge to the significance of the state. The second may appear trite: the 'new ideologies' are recent in origin. This point can, however, be expressed in a more sophisticated way: the new ideologies have emerged as a response to fundamental changes in the social and economic structures of advanced industrial societies. The third difference relates to the intellectual relationship of the new ideologies to the traditional ones: the former engage *critically* with the latter.

Social and Economic Change

The four ideologies that we discuss in Part 3 emerged after the Second World War. While they have intellectual roots predating the war, and indeed the roots go back centuries – think of Mary Wollstonecraft – *consciousness* of each as a *relatively unified system of thought* has only developed in the last 40 or so years. While it is crude to date an ideology simply from its first usage in public debate, the employment of these labels – these isms – in everyday debate is of some significance and, roughly speaking, the terms 'feminism' and 'ecologism' (environmentalism, Green thought) became current in the 1960s, multiculturalism in the 1970s, and fundamentalism (which had been employed in debates within US Protestantism in the 1920s) began to achieve wider application in the 1970s and 1980s. Without reducing these new ideologies to social and economic changes we suggest that they are, in part, the product of certain new socio-economic structures.

We have seen in Parts 1 and 2 that the traditional ideologies themselves changed in response to the massive social and economic change of the nineteenth century: John Stuart Mill's defence of representative democracy is a response to the rise of 'mass society', as is his concern with the 'tyranny of the majority'. Mill's political world is very different to that of, say, John Locke. Similarly, Mill's near-contemporary Karl Marx contrasts his own socialism with that of earlier 'utopian' socialists, and conservatism, the ideology that above all others claims to be historical – in the sense of responding to the world as it is, rather than providing a model of an alternative world – has undergone considerable adaptation from the eighteenth-century thinkers Hume and Burke to twentieth-century thinker Oakeshott. Given the extent of social 'rationalisation' which Oakeshott so bemoans, his thought has an elegiac quality when compared with that of earlier conservative thinkers. Fascism is, of course, a response to specific social and economic conditions, most especially a perceived mismatch between the development of state and economic structures. By entitling the first two parts of this book 'Classical Ideas' and 'Classical Ideologies' we are not suggesting that they are dead: they are continually developing as ideologies, and indeed some thinkers have argued that we are all liberals now (Fukuyama, 1992). Rather than seeing the contrast between classical and new ideologies as a distinction between 'dead' and 'living' we understand new ideologies as distinct systems of thought that have emerged out of, and in response to, changing social and economic structures, and those changes have also affected the classical ideologies.

What then are these changes? One way of addressing this question is to consider what might be termed the 'crisis of Marxism'. The development of this 'crisis' can be understood in terms of historical events, of which the final and most spectacular was the overthrow of state socialism in Eastern Europe in 1989 followed by its collapse in the Soviet Union in 1991. In the period dubbed 'the short twentieth century' (Hobsbawm, 1995) – 1914–91 – there have been a series of key events that arguably presaged the final collapse of the socialist project: the Molotov–Ribbentrop Pact between the USSR and Nazi Germany in 1939, the Soviet invasions of Hungary (1956) and Czechoslovakia (1968), and the imposition of martial law in Poland in the early 1980s. In parallel to these concrete political events there has been a deeper intellectual crisis. The central problem for Marxists has been the failure of the working class to develop a truly 'revolutionary consciousness'. Far from rising up as one, the working class (or classes?) splintered. In, for example, Weimar Germany (1919–33) there was a major split between the communists and the social democrats, as well as between left and right, with a significant section of the working class attracted to the far right Nazi Party (or NASDP). Also, as critics of Marx point out, those countries such as Russia that underwent proletarian revolutions were not the ones 'marked down' for it because they lacked sufficient industrial development. The fragmentation of Marxism into different streams of thought (McLellan, 1979) was a response to the crisis, but so was the adoption of Marxist categories of thought by (essentially) non-Marxist theorists. These theorists use the language of collective agency, oppression and liberation, but they are no longer applied to the working class, and the strategy of liberation is much more 'particularistic' – whereas the root idea of Marxism was that the transition to a classless society ultimately resulted in the liberation of humankind, and not simply one oppressed socio-economic class; new social movements, be they feminist, multiculturalist or ecological, do not *necessarily* make such a claim. We say 'not necessarily' because there is still a hint that women's liberation is good for men, or that human beings are part of nature, and so ecological justice is also human justice. Fundamentalism – or, at least, Islamic fundamentalism – can also be understood as a response to the crisis of Marxism: many parts of the Arab-Islamic world embraced Marxist ideology in the 1960s as a form of development, or catch-up, ideology. The failure of state-led socialism opened a space for another ostensibly egalitarian ideology – Islamic fundamentalism.

We have suggested that the four new ideologies are, in part, a response to the failure of Marxism, but conversely at least two of them – feminism and ecologism – have emerged due to rising levels of economic well-being (of course the survival of capitalism, against Marx's predictions, is part of the explanation of the crisis of Marxism). This may seem a strange claim, given that both are concerned with oppression. However, that feminism and ecologism emerged in the 1960s is significant. If we consider gender relations, even prior to the 1960s there were social changes taking place that fundamentally affected the balance of power between men and women: the wartime mobilisation of women to work in factories and on the land is generally regarded as significant in breaking down the distinction between the private (home) and the public (work and the civic sphere). The development of household appliances and a general improvement in living conditions reduced to some extent the pressure on women as the chief source of domestic labour. By the 1960s the speed of change had picked up, with Western industrialised countries experiencing significant economic and social changes: a shift from manufacturing (blue-collar) jobs to service (white-collar) jobs; greater availability of contraception, especially the pill (oral contraception); increasing educational opportunities, and the narrowing of the gap between men and women in educational attainment. Certainly feminism does champion oppressed women, but the leadership of women's organisations, as well as academic feminist theorists, are drawn disproportionately from relatively privileged social groups. This is not in any way to denigrate feminism – our concern here is simply to identify the reasons why feminism emerged as a fully fledged ideology when it did.

Turning now to ecologism, the link between rising prosperity and ecological consciousness may seem much more tenuous. However, political scientist Ronald Inglehart identified the emergence in the 1970s of a generation born during, or just after the Second World War – sometimes called the generation of '68 (with '68 a reference to the student disturbances of 1968) – that espoused 'post-materialist values': questioning of authority, liberal attitudes to human relationships, rejection of job security, importance of 'self-realisation' and individuality (Inglehart, 1977). The preceding generation, which had directly experienced the inter-war depression, the Second World War and the hardships of the immediate post-war period, were much more inclined to hold materialist values. The word 'materialist' should not be read as 'selfish' – the war generation simply wanted an end to the deprivations of the war, and so were strongly committed to job security and rising prosperity. The post-war generation might be thought more selfish because they took for granted the opportunities provided by the welfare state and economic growth policies. Nonetheless, the post-war generation did, according to Inglehart, display a distinct set of values, and it is not difficult to see how these values might lead that generation to reject traditional political ideologies and movements in favour of an ecological consciousness.

The socio-economic conditions that gave rise to the development of multiculturalism are slightly different, but are still connected to rising levels of prosperity among certain key groups. The post-war period was characterised by increasing levels of economic migration from south Asia and the Mediterranean fringe to the countries of central and northern Europe. For example, the so-called 'economic miracle' (*Wirtschaftswunder*) in West Germany was made possible by 'guest labour' from (especially) Turkey, and large numbers of south Asians came to Britain in search of work. These groups – disproportionately made up of men – tended to seek protection in their own communities, especially as tensions rose in the late 1950s. However, by the 1960s there emerged organisations that campaigned against discrimination. It is, however, significant that 'race' rather than 'culture' was the central concept, with the emphasis on overcoming 'skin prejudice'; this was paralleled on a much larger scale in the United States, with the emergence of a powerful Civil Rights Movement (although, of course, the African-American community had a quite different history to European immigrant communities). It is only in the 1970s and 1980s that there emerges a shift from the language of race, and the idea of a *multiracial* society, to culture, and the notion of a *multicultural* society. Certainly, some of the advocates of multiculturalism were first-generation immigrants, but many were the children of first-generation immigrants who argued that the recognition of pluralism required an analysis of society centred on culture rather than race. Again, as with feminism, while the aim was to overcome disadvantage, the political and intellectual leadership of this movement was relatively advantaged.

Critique of Classical Ideologies

We have already suggested that the new ideologies emerged, in part, as a response to the failure of Marxism, and we have also argued that rising prosperity changed the expectations and outlook of certain groups – women, the post-war generation and 'ethnic' (cultural) minorities. The combination of a recognition of the crisis of Marxism and the underlying socio-economic conditions which have given rise to these new ideologies means that there is a need to reconsider liberalism. With the collapse of state socialism it may be argued that liberalism lacks any competitor. This is the claim Francis Fukuyama made in his 1992 book *The End of History*; his thesis is contentious but were we, for the sake of argument, to accept that liberalism is the last (effective) ideology, it is still possible to see three of the new ideologies – feminism, multiculturalism and ecologism – as critical responses to the liberal tradition (fundamentalism stands opposed to liberalism, but there are few societies that can be described as *effectively* organised around fundamentalist ideas). These three ideologies are engaged in a *critique* of liberalism. It is important to use that word carefully: to engage in a critique of liberalism does not entail rejecting it but, rather, drawing out its truth. In particular, the central ideas of freedom and equality are taken up from the liberal tradition and turned against it. It might also be argued that the new ideologies employ the fragments of competing classical ideologies – socialism, anarchism, and even conservatism and nationalism – and seek to revitalise them through integration into a new kind of liberal ideology. How this is achieved will become clearer in our discussion of the particular ideologies, but it is useful to identify a couple of examples of critical engagement with the classical ideologies.

First, feminists and multiculturalism in particular have sought to challenge the liberal claims to freedom and equality. The dual claim to freedom and equality is subjected to an analysis of how *informal* power relations operate in society, and how formal legal and political relations, despite the appearance of impartiality, actually serve to reinforce informal inequalities. Of course, this line of attack is not new: Marxists have argued that material inequality restricts the effectiveness of the economic freedoms guaranteed by the liberal–capitalist state, but Marx still operated with a universalist model of liberation, whereby the abolition of capitalist relations of production would ensure equal treatment. The model of a classless society – which, admittedly, Marx did not outline in any detail – did not adequately account for 'difference', that is, the apparently paradoxical idea that equal treatment of men and women, or of cultural groups, requires recognition of the differences between them. Ecologists are even more radical in their adoption of the ideals of freedom and equality, in that they extend the 'moral community' to include non-human animals and even plant life.

Second, drawing on socialism (in particular, Marxism), the new ideologies take up the idea of collective oppression and collective action. Just as Marx argued that there was a revolutionary process of 'consciousness raising' whereby workers achieve, first of all, workplace consciousness, and then trade union consciousness, followed by national, and international, class consciousness, so feminists, multiculturalists, ecologists and fundamentalists argue for a process whereby the oppressed – women, cultural minorities, non-humans, co-religionists – come to recognise their oppression and, crucially, the causes of that oppression. Obviously the ideologies – and different streams within each ideology – will define the causes of oppression in their own way. Our linking together of these four ideologies is not intended to suggest mutual sympathy between them: many feminists regard multiculturalism as, in the words, of Susan Okin, 'bad for women' (Okin *et al.*, 1999), and fundamentalists of all hues consider multiculturalism to be the political expression of the moral and cultural relativism that they are fighting. The affinities between the four ideologies relate to the historical conditions under which they have emerged, and the style in which they engage with the classical ideologies.

References

Fukuyama, F. (1992) *The End of History and the Last Man* London: Penguin.

Hobsbawm, E. (1995) *Age of Extremes: The Short Twentieth Century, 1914–1991* London: Abacus.

Inglehart, R. (1977) *The Silent Revolution: Changing Values and Political Styles among Western Publics* Princeton, NJ: Princeton University Press.

McLellan, D. (1979) *Marxism after Marx: An Introduction* London: Macmillan.

Okin, S. *et al.* (1999) *Is Multiculturalism Bad for Women?* Princeton, NJ: Princeton University Press.

Chapter 14

Feminism

Introduction

Feminism is an ideology has always been highly controversial. It asks such questions as: do women have too much or too little power? It is not only controversial as far as traditional defenders of the status quo are concerned. Some women feel that they are in favour of equality with men, but do not like the idea of feminism. It has been said that we live in a post-feminist age and some contend that the main goals of feminism have been realised, so that it is quite unnecessary for feminists to continue their argument against male domination.

Feminism, however, is also controversial in the sense that different feminists mean different things by the term. There are different varieties that seem to have little in common. Just as writers have spoken of socialisms, so feminism has also been presented in the plural in order to indicate the diversity involved. In this chapter we shall follow the example of many writers in trying to explain these different feminisms, and also try to suggest a way of extracting some kind of unity out of this formidable diversity.

Chapter Map

In this chapter we will explore:

- The immense variety of different kinds of feminism.

- Liberal feminism; its strengths and its weaknesses.

- Radical feminism critically, and its claim to be a 'true feminism'.

- The meaning of socialist feminism and its limitations.

- Black feminism.

- 'Philosophical feminisms' and postmodern feminism in particular.

Women's Work?

Source: © Serge Kozak/zefa/Corbis

A huge amount of attention has been devoted in the media to the changing roles of women. An example of this can be found in a 2003 cover story of *The Observer* magazine, in which women who had become corporate executives were questioned as to how they perceived both their position, and those of women in general, in society.

1. One interviewee, Sunita Gloster, is head of an advertising agency and argues that more and more women are facing reality head on; they are more confident and expected to be treated with respect and fairness if they take time off to have children. 'Success', she says, 'used to be defined by a traditional male standard – rising up the corporate ladder, with rewards of money and status. Now women define success by a more feminine standard: satisfaction, fulfilment, making a difference – and that can come in many forms.'

2. Sahar Hashemi, who co-founded a chain of companies and who runs her own consultancy, insists that women want equality with, and not superiority over, men, and that they should celebrate being women, 'not try to disguise it'. 'Its about being women in our own right and doing things on our own terms.'

3. Patricia Hewitt, as a member of the British cabinet, argues that things are getting better but too many women who work outside the home feel that it is impossible to have children. 'An unofficial "parent bar" is operating, and I think that's the biggest issue for working women.'

4. Caroline Plumb, who developed a graduate recruitment and research agency, notes that women need to be stronger on self-promotion, declaring that 'success for me is about having an interesting life, and being exposed to a wide range of experiences and people'.

Continued

5. Ronnie Cook, a New Yorker running her own design consultancy in the UK, compares the 'warrior spirit' of American women with the more laid-back approach she finds in London. In her view young men differ in their attitude towards women from older men, and definitely have 'some feminine in them'.

6. Dawn Airey is the managing director of a TV channel. 'In my experience, women are much more likely to attack things head on, and men hate confrontation. I don't know why, but women also work harder.'

7. Dr Laura Tyson, dean of the London Business School, finds that 'women are talented team players, and the need in business now is for individuals who can lead and inspire through influence rather than by dictating. Women are more consensual, and the old power hierarchies are crumbling.'

8. Helen Fernandes, the first ever female surgeon at Addenbrooke's Hospital, argues that 'medicine has changed and the old sexism is dying out, but perception and archetypes still put women off'.

Do the verbal testimonies of successful women detailed suggest to you that women should pursue careers outside the home? How possible do you think it is to combine outside work and parental responsibilities? Can men do more to help in the home, and is it fair to think of domestic work as basically a woman's responsibility?

Make a list of men you know, and see whether you agree with the point made by some of the respondents in the test case that younger men are more egalitarian than older men.

Now make a list of women you know, and ask yourself whether they seek:

- equality with men;
- superiority over men;
- a position of subordination to men.

One of the respondents in the article took the view that 'there are only superficial differences between the sexes'. Do you agree? List the *social* differences between men and women, and see whether they are the result of biological differences or differences in conditioning, or both.

Liberal Feminism

Liberal feminism would appear to be the earliest form of feminism. Feminism has a particular relationship to liberalism, and it has been said that all feminism is 'liberal at root' (Eisenstein, 1981: 4). We are assuming here not only that earlier treatments of women were anti-feminist in character, but that the ancient Greek philosopher, Plato, does not count as a feminist although his views on women were remarkably atypical at the time.

Plato argues in *The Republic* that women can be among the elite who rule philosophically in his ideal state. Whereas Aristotle had contended that 'the relation of male to female is naturally that of superior to inferior, of the ruling to the ruled' (Coole, 1988: 44–5), Plato adopted (at least in *The Republic*) a gender-free view of political capacities. On the other hand, what makes his feminist credentials suspect is his explicit elitism. Only a tiny number of women would have been eligible to become rulers, and those that did, would (it is said) have to act just like men.

The position of women in medieval theory is depicted in explicitly hierarchical terms with women being seen as more sinful than men, inferior to them, and not equipped to take part in political processes. Aquinas follows Aristotle in arguing that a wife 'is something belonging to her husband', although she is more distinct from him than a son from his father or a slave from his master (1953: 103). Had not the Bible made the inferiority of women clear?

Mary Wollstonecraft

What is remarkable about the liberal tradition is that it challenges the notion that repressive hierarchies are natural. It thus opens the way for the feminist argument that if all are free and equal individuals, why can't women be equal to men? It is true that Mary Astell had contended, as early as 1694, that women should be educated instead of being nursed in the vices for which they are then upbraided (Brody, 1992: 28). However, Mary Wollstonecraft is rightly regarded as the first major feminist, and in her famous *Vindication of the Rights of Women* (first published in 1792), she argues for women's economic independence and legal equality. At the time she wrote, a married woman could not own property in her own right, enter into any legal contract or have any claim over the rights of her children. History, philosophy and classical languages were considered too rigorous for women to learn; botany and biology were proscribed from their educational curriculum, and physical exercise thought unsuitable.

Wollstonecraft directs her argument to middle-class women – women in what she calls the 'natural state'. The middle-class woman is the woman who is neither dissipated by inherited wealth, nor brutalised by poverty. Wollstonecraft had taken from Richard Price the Enlightenment principle that all people are rational. The problem lay with the environment. Physical frailty derives from a cloistered upbringing, and this was thought to impact negatively upon intellectual ability. She tackles in particular Rousseau's traditionalist view that women are inferior, seeing this as a betrayal of the liberal assumptions of his political theory. What Rousseau thought charming, Wollstonecraft considered immoral and dangerous. It is inconsistent to value independence and autonomy in men but not in women, particularly as patriarchy, or male domination, degrades men as well – 'the blind lead the blind' (Brody, 1992: 104).

Women, Wollstonecraft argues, are placed on a pedestal but within a prison (Brody, 1992: 50–1). Women ought to be represented in government and have a 'civil existence in the State' (Wollstonecraft, 1992: 265, 267). They should not be excluded from civil and political employments (1992: 291). The enlightened woman must be an 'active citizen' 'intent to manage her family, educate her children and assist her neighbours' (1992: 259). Friendship rather than gentleness, docility and a spaniel-like affection 'should prevail between the sexes'. The emancipation of women is, in Wollstonecraft's view, part and parcel of the case against autocracy and arbitrariness in general: why contest the divine right of kings if one continues to subscribe to the divine right of husbands (1992: 118, 119)?

Wollstonecraft's position has a number of shortcomings that we will deal with later, but it is generally acknowledged that she tended to juxtapose reason to feeling, identifying feelings with animal appetites that men exploited. Moreover, she saw perfection as a realisable ideal, a position undoubtedly influenced by the intensely religious character of her argument. Wollstonecraft's position was complex – and she has been seen by some writers as 'ambivalent, contradictory and paradoxical' – reformer and revolutionary, rationalist and woman of feeling (Brody, 1992: 67, 70).

John Stuart Mill

John Stuart Mill (influenced by his partner Harriet Taylor) wrote *The Subjection of Women* in 1869. In it, he argues that women should enjoy equal rights with men – including the right to vote. Women, he contended, were still slaves in many respects, and to argue that they are inferior by 'nature' is to presume knowledge of nature: until equality has been established, how do we know what woman's nature is? It cannot be said that women are housewives and mothers by nature, although Mill does say – and this position is controversial among feminists today – that they are 'most suitable for this role', and he feels that female suffrage can only assist women in supervising domestic expenditure (Coole, 1988: 144; Bryson, 1992: 55–63). Mill, it is suggested, contributed to liberal feminism by extending his liberal principles to the position of women (Shanley and Pateman, 1991: 6), and like Wollstonecraft, he argued that the family must become a school for learning the values of freedom and independence.

Liberal Feminism in Britain and the USA

Throughout the nineteenth century, liberal feminism had developed often as an extension of other emancipatory movements. In the United States, figures like Elizabeth Cady Stanton (1815–1902) and her lifelong friend, Susan Anthony

(1820–1906) raised the issue of women's freedom and equality as a result of experience in anti-slavery movements. Both edited a feminist journal in the 1860s called *The Revolution*. A National Women's Suffrage Association was set up after the civil war and women's suffrage was attained in the USA as a result of the nineteenth amendment to the constitution in 1920. In Britain, Mill's classic work had been preceded by the campaign against the *Contagious Diseases Act* (1864) that gave the police draconian powers to arrest prostitutes and those considered prostitutes, and when limited suffrage for women was achieved after the First World War, the struggle for its further extension was consolidated in the National Union of Societies for Equal Citizenship.

Liberal feminism appeared to have its greatest triumph in Britain when all women became eligible to vote in 1928. In other countries this was attained later – in France after the Second World War, while in Switzerland, women only received the vote in 1970. In Britain the Sex Discrimination Act and the Equal Opportunities Commission were established in the late 1960s.

Liberal feminism identifies itself, in the words of Winifred Holtby, 'with the motto Equality First' (Humm, 1992: 43) and it extended its concerns with the publication of Betty Friedan's *The Feminine Mystique* (1963) which argued that middle-class American women suffered from depression and alienation as a result of giving up a career outside the home. They were incarcerated in a 'comfortable concentration camp' – Friedan's dramatic name for the home. She was instrumental in setting up the National Organization of Women in 1966 that not only campaigned for equal rights (including 'reproductive rights' – a right to abortion and birth control), but also assisted American women in re-entering the labour market, and supported the establishment of childcare facilities in workplaces.

Exercise

You meet a woman who describes herself as a feminist. 'All women should be equal and be free to choose their own lifestyle', she argues.

You feel uneasy. You note the following factors in your mind:

1. Her mother is an MP and her father a headmaster.

2. The women concerned went to a very good school and has had a university education.

3. She has a job outside the home that is well paid.

4. She has young children and can afford to put them all day in a nursery.

5. Because her and her partner are both employed and are on good salaries, they employ someone to clean their house twice a week.

How important are these 'other' factors? The feminist you have met argues that 'all' women should be equal to men, but how many other women are in her relatively privileged position?

Problems with Liberal Feminism

Liberal feminism has been criticised on a number of grounds.

Radical Feminist Critique

Radical feminists protest that liberal feminism is too superficial in its approach. All feminisms agree with the extension of liberal principles to women in terms of the vote and civil liberties, but radicals argue that the notion of equality is too abstract to be serviceable. The point about women is that they are different from men, and to argue for equality implies that they aspire to be like men. But why?

Men not only oppress women but they are responsible for war, violence, hierarchy and the exploitation of nature and their fellows. Is this the model to which women should aspire? Radicals argue that it is not equality which women should want, but liberation – and freedom for women means being separate and apart from men. It means celebrating their difference from men and their own distinctive sexuality. Liberal feminists not only regard sexuality as irrational and emotional, but they uncritically accept that feelings should be transcended and they adopt a notion of reason that reflects male experience.

Feminism is not an extension of another ideology. It is concerned with the interests of women, and a new set of words needs to be developed to reflect the separateness of women. Some radicals like Mary Daly adopt a different style of writing, so as to make it clear that feminism represents as total a break as possible with male-constructed society. Politics is not simply about the law and state, as liberals think. It is about human activity in general and the celebrated slogan – 'the personal is political' – captures the radical feminist argument that interpersonal relations are as political as voting in elections. Radicals encourage women to meet separately – to voice their problems without men – and to take personal experience much more seriously than the liberal tradition allows.

Radicals see themselves as sexual revolutionaries, and thus very different from liberal feminists who work within the system. We shall see later that radicals have very different views from liberals on questions like prostitution and pornography.

Socialist Feminist Critique

The socialist critique of liberal feminism argues that liberal feminists ignore or marginalise the position of working-class women and the problems they have with exploitation and poor conditions in the workplace. The question of gender needs to be linked to the question of class – and legal and political equality, though important, does not address the differential in real power that exists in capitalist society.

Marxist feminists in particular want to challenge the view of the state as a benevolent reformer, and to argue that the state is an expression of class domination. The freedom of women has to be linked to the emancipation of the working class in general, with a much greater concentration on the social and economic dimensions of gender discrimination. Why should the right to join the armed forces and the police be a positive development if the police are used to oppress people at home and the army to oppress peoples abroad? Liberal feminism neglects the question of production and reproduction that lies at the heart of human activity.

Other Critiques

The black feminist critique particularly takes issue with the tendency of liberal feminists to treat women in an abstract fashion, and to assume that women are not only middle class, but white as well. Many of the objections that liberal feminists raise to the hypocritical politeness of men hardly apply to women who are subject to racist abuse and treated in a derogatory fashion because they are black.

The feminisms looked at so far can be called 'ideological' feminisms, and they overlap with what can be labelled 'philosophical feminisms': feminist empiricism, standpoint feminism and postmodern feminism.

Feminist empiricists take the view that feminism should be treated as an objective science which concentrates on the *facts* relating to discrimination. Feminist empiricists feel that it is unnecessary and counterproductive to hitch feminism to an ideological position, and that the norms of liberalism involve a value commitment that narrows the appeal of feminist analysis.

Standpoint feminists take the view that the position of women gives rise to a different outlook, so that liberal feminists are wrong to argue simply for equality with men, and to concern themselves only with legal and political rights.

As for postmodern feminists, they consider the tradition of the Enlightenment and liberalism to be hopelessly abstract. Not only is liberalism oblivious to the importance of difference – both between women and men and within women themselves – but the notion of freedom and autonomy as universal values reflects a prejudice which is part of the modern as opposed to the postmodern tradition.

Socialist Feminism

Socialist feminism arose out of the belief that feminism is not simply a legal and political question – though socialists (by which we mean socialist feminists) do support the case for the legal and political emancipation of women. Socialists take the view that women's emancipation is also – and primarily – a *social* question so that the movement for women's freedom needs to be linked with the struggle to transform capitalism itself.

Early socialists like the Frenchman, Charles Fourier, saw the liberation of women as integral to redefining the labour process so that it becomes pleasurable and fulfilling, and he saw, as Marx did, the position of women as symptomatic of the level of civilisation of a given society. Marx tended to see women as the victims of market forces, and he argues in an early text that the prostitution of women is only a specific expression of the general prostitution of the labourer (Marx and Engels, 1975: 295). In the *Communist Manifesto*, for example, Marx takes the view that women under capitalism are mere instruments of production, but Marx showed little interest in the position of women and regarded the relation of men and women as 'natural' rather than moulded by class relationships.

Engels' Contribution

Engels was much more interested in women and in his celebrated work, *The Origin of the Family, Private Property and the State*, published in 1894, he argues that in early tribal societies men, women and children lived together as part of larger households in which production was for use rather than exchange. Decision-making involved both men and women and because paternity or the position of a particular man as father could not be established in group marriage, collective property descended through women (i.e. matrilineally). 'The world-historical defeat of female sex', as Engels graphically describes it, occurs when men begin to domesticate animals and breed herds. Women seek monogamous relations in marriage (one wife–one husband) and the family is privatised. In the later bourgeois family, the woman's formal right to consent to marriage is neutralised by her lack of economic independence, and in the working-class family, the husband represents the bourgeois and the wife the proletarian – what nineteenth-century socialists liked to call the 'slave of a slave'.

In Engels' view, male domination would only disappear with the socialisation of production. With women involved in paid employment outside the home, housework itself would become a public and collectivised activity (Sacks, 1974: 207).

Bebel and Later Socialists

August Bebel of the German Social Democratic Party wrote a much more influential book than that of Engels – *Woman Under Socialism* (1878) – which followed the argument that women could only be emancipated through a proletarian revolution which resulted in their economic independence and the collectivisation of housework and childcare. However, unlike Engels, he was also conscious of the problems that were peculiar to women. Capitalist employment resulted in women being paid less than men, and women suffered from the problem of having to do all or most of the housework. Bebel also noted that economic subordination was linked to non-economic forms of oppression like a double standard of sexual morality, and inconvenient forms of dress (Bryson, 1992: 121).

Clara Zetkin, a German socialist who was to be a founder member of the German Communist Party, argued that class must take primacy over gender interests. She refused to cooperate with other women in campaigns for improved education, employment prospects and legal status, on the grounds that proletarian and 'bourgeois' women had nothing in common. Lenin was to declare at the time of the Russian Revolution, that 'the proletariat cannot have complete liberty until it has won complete liberty for women' (Rowbotham, 1972: 163) but this did not prevent him from extracting a pledge from Zetkin that personal matters would not be raised in political discussions (Bryson, 1992: 125). It is true that the new Soviet government was the first in history to write women's emancipation into the law (in 1918), but the right to abortion was removed in 1936 and the family which radical Bolsheviks had sought to abolish was idealised under Stalin as a crucial part of the disciplinary mechanism of the state.

Alexandra Kollontai was commissar or minister of social welfare in the first Bolshevik government and she sought to encourage women to set up, with state help, nurseries, laundries and educational campaigns. She fell from power in 1921 and the Women's Department that she headed, was abolished in 1929. She is also interesting because she argued for a new kind of relationship between men and women – one that would be less exclusive and not monogamous (Bryson, 1992: 137–40).

Women in the Communist Party States

In terms of more recent developments in Communist Party states, the regime in Romania was particularly oppressive with Ceausescu stating in 1986, some 20 years after an anti-abortion law had been passed, that those 'who refuse to have children are deserters, escaping the law of natural continuity' (Funk and Mueller, 1993: 46). In the German Democratic Republic (East Germany) abortion was legal and used as the main means of birth control, while 90 per cent of women of working age were in paid employment, and 87 per cent had completed vocational training (Funk and Mueller, 1993: 139). Despite the authoritarian character of these Communist Party states, the position of women in post-communist societies has worsened as reproductive rights have been scaled down (although in Poland the attempt to pass an anti-abortion law was blocked in 1991). Women have left the workforce, are much less represented in legislatures and have suffered as state nurseries have been closed; the gender gap in pay has widened, and pornography and prostitution have increased dramatically (Hoffman, 2001: 141).

The Domestic Labour Debate

Of course, many socialists disagreed vehemently with the Communist Party states, even while they maintained a loyalty to Marxism. The domestic labour debate which took place in the pages of the British journal, *New Left Review*, sought to examine the position of women in the home and their relationship to the capitalist economy. Some argued that domestic labour produces value in the same way that other labour does, and therefore women who work at home should be paid. Despite controversy on this point, there was general agreement that the family is linked to capitalism, and that domestic labour and who does it is an important issue for feminists to tackle (Bryson, 1992: 241).

Even socialists who disagree with Marxism have accepted the need to ensure that women in the workforce are paid equally and should be able to combine domestic and professional duties. Women and men may receive the same pay for the same job, but where there are occupations in which women predominate (like nursing and primary school teaching), workers in these occupations receive relatively low pay. Women in Britain earn about 75 per cent of men's pay – whereas the average over Europe is 79 per cent (http://news.bbc.co.uk/1/hi/business/1962036.stm). Socialist feminists feel that the market and free enterprise do impact upon women's lives, and that improving pay, employment prospects and conditions of work, are crucial questions for feminism to consider.

Problems with Socialist Feminism

Liberal Feminist Critique

Liberal feminists like Betty Friedan and Naomi Wolf (who wrote *Fire with Fire* in 1993), feel that socialist feminists are divisive in not accepting that some women might go into, and make a success of, business. Their dynamism and entrepreneurial flair should be both rewarded and acknowledged, and to regard feminism as a class question is unhelpful and narrowing. All women will benefit from a free system of production, based on the market and capitalism.

Women are individuals who should be entitled to exercise choice, and the tendency by socialist feminists to see work outside the home as crucial for emancipation is not borne out by the many women who choose to stay at home and live fulfilled and happy lives. Liberal feminists are not opposed to reforms that facilitate working outside the home, but they are opposed to an ideological position that seems to privilege this.

Liberal feminists would (like many other feminists) point to the authoritarian character of Communist Party states as evidence, not only of the generally problematic character of socialism, but of the negative way in which it impacts upon women's lives.

Radical Feminist Critique

Radicals are sceptical that the problems facing women are simply to do with capitalism. It is true that some socialist feminists have argued that there is a dual system that oppresses women – capitalism *and* patriarchy. Capitalism may reward men as 'breadwinners' thereby creating a division of labour that disadvantages women, and writers like Ann Ferguson see patriarchy as semi-autonomous – sexual oppression exists alongside class oppression and is not 'reducible' to it (Bryson, 1992: 243–5). Radicals feel that this argument merely serves to deepen the theoretical crisis faced by socialist feminists, since there is no reason to believe that pornography, prostitution and male chauvinist attitudes are specifically linked to a particular mode of production.

Indeed, many radical feminists developed their position as a result of experience in socialist movements where they were expected to take menial and 'feminine' roles by socialist men. Attempts to introduce the concept of patriarchy alongside the analysis of capitalism fail to get to grips with the fact that the former is wholly independent of the latter, and that when Marx treats the relations between men and women as natural, this is symptomatic of an inadequate methodology that cannot be rectified by simply tacking a critique of sexism onto Marxism or socialism. Catherine MacKinnon, in a much-quoted comment, argues that 'sexuality is to feminism, what work is to Marxism' (Humm, 1992: 117). The logics of the two are quite different, and any attempt to 'synthesise' Marxism and feminism, or feminism with socialism more generally, is bound to fail.

Black Feminist and Philosophical Feminist Critique

Black feminists believe that socialist emphasis upon class is as abstract as liberal emphasis upon the individual. Socialist feminism does not take the question of ethnicity seriously: it suffers from the problem of abstract universalism that means that it unthinkingly privileges a particular group or culture.

Feminist empiricists see in socialism the problem of ideological bias, and although some standpoint feminists like Nancy Hartsock are sympathetic to Marxism, standpoint feminism in general is unhappy with any privileging of class. After all, women experience oppression as women, and Gilligan argues in *In a Different Voice* (1992) that because women are socialised differently from men, they grow up with quite different notions of morality and relationships. This occurs in both working class and bourgeois homes.

As for postmodern feminists, socialism has what they call an emancipatory 'metanarrative' – particularly strident in Marxism – that stems from the Enlightenment and expresses an absolutist prejudice. The belief in progress, equality and autonomy, though different from the views of liberal feminists, still reflects a belief in a 'philosophy of history' that is ultimately arbitrary and implausible.

Radical Feminism

Radical feminism, as indicated from its critiques of other positions, takes the view that feminism ought to deal with the position of women, independently of other ideological commitments. As MacKinnon argues, 'feminism is the first theory to emerge from those whose interests it affirms' (Humm, 1992: 119).

Radical feminists argue that women are oppressed because women are women, and men are men. Male domination permeates all aspects of society – from sport to literature, dress to philosophy, entertainment to sexual mores. As Mary Daly argues, 'we live in a profoundly anti-female society, a misogynistic "civilization" in which men collectively victimize women, attacking us as personifications of their own paranoid fears' (Humm, 1992: 168).

Ch. 1:
The State

This ubiquity of 'maleness' extends to the state itself. Weber's view of the state as an institution which claims a monopoly of legitimate force is too limited, in MacKinnon's view, since this monopoly 'describes the power of men over women in the home, in the bedroom, on the job, in the street, through social life' (1989: 169). Patriarchy is a comprehensive system of male power and it arises from men. Oppression, as the *Manifesto of the New York Redstockings* in 1969 declared, is total, 'affecting every facet of our lives' (Bryson, 1992: 183–4).

Moreover, the radicals argue that women's oppression is the oldest and most basic form of oppression, and whether it arises from socialists who expect women to make tea while men develop political strategy, or it is expressed through black men like Stokely Carmichael who see women as having only bodies and not minds, the same point holds: all men oppress women, and all receive psychological, sexual and material benefits from so doing. Germaine Greer argues that her proposition in

The Female Eunuch (1970) still holds 30 years later – men hate women at least some of the time. Indeed, she reckons that in the year 2000 'more men hate more women more bitterly than in 1970' (1999: 14). Greer gives as good as she believes that women get, and argues that 'to be male is to be a kind of idiot savant, full of queer obsessions about fetishistic activities and fantasy goals – a freak of nature, fragile, fantastic, bizarre' (1999: 327).

Why does the antagonism between men and women arise? Brownmiller appears to suggest that the root is biological, and she speaks of the 'anatomical fact that the male sex organ has been misused as a weapon of terror' (Humm, 1992: 73), but radical feminists are aware of the dangers of a naturalist argument that reduces male domination to biology. Although MacKinnon speaks highly of Robert Dahl and endorses his view of politics as a system of power, authority and control, she almost certainly would not endorse his once-expressed view that women's subordination arises from the superior physical strength of males (Hoffman, 2001: 97). The relation of man and women is a social product, she argues, and a 'naturalist' view fails to see these relationships as historical and transitory (MacKinnon 1989: 56). Nevertheless, radical feminists reject Marxist accounts that male domination arose historically from class divisions, and they argue that patriarchy has always been around. Although radicals disagree as to how and when patriarchy came about, they all agree that it exists and it has done so in every known society (Bryson, 1992: 188).

What can be done about it? Radical feminists developed in the late 1960s the idea of an all-women's 'consciousness-raising' group. Indeed, MacKinnon describes consciousness-raising as the 'feminist method' (Humm, 1992: 119) – a coming together by women to describe problems collectively so that the existence of oppression can be confirmed. The solution can only be separatism, for the consequence of the fact that the personal is political (and by political is meant the exercise of repressive power) is that men and women should live their lives as separately as possible. As Greer puts it rather wittily, 'both could do without each other if it were not for the pesky business of sexual reproduction' (1999: 68).

Indeed, one radical famously argued that the basis of women's oppression lies with childbearing, as well as child rearing, and the conception of love (Bryson, 1992: 204, 201). Others are doubtful that this 'pesky business' can be so easily avoided. But sexuality is seen as an expression of power so that the distinction between rape and sexual activity is not a meaningful one, and the reason why radical feminists are so passionately opposed to pornography and prostitution is that they see these institutions as fundamentally linked to a demeaning view and treatment of women. Whether men intend to oppress women is beside the point: patriarchy is a structural system of male oppression which operates, whether men are conscious of oppressing women or not.

Radical feminists have sometimes advocated lesbianism as a solution to the problem of oppressive encounters with men. Feminists in general would accept that lesbianism is a legitimate lifestyle choice, but radicals often go further and argue that it is a necessary way of preventing male domination. Rich advocates a broader notion of lesbianism so that it does not have to embrace genital activity, but denotes a rejection of a compulsory heterosexuality imposed to prevent women from being individuals in their own right (Humm, 1992: 176–7). Because patriarchy is seen as a comprehensive system of male domination, even the most intimate of relationships becomes a matter for political scrutiny.

MacKinnon sees the whole notion of the public/private divide as oppressive and nothing more than a dangerous myth. The public is the private, just as the personal is political. Women's interest lies in overthrowing the distinction itself (1989: 120–1). Radical feminism is revolutionary. It is averse to differentiating one kind of patriarchy from another, and it is opposed to the kind of reforms that do not tackle the problem at its root. Radical feminists tend to identify pornography with sexual violence, and they regard prostitution as an act of force (Hoffman, 2001: 193).

Women, in the view of radical feminists, do not want equality with men. They want liberation and liberation is only possible if patriarchy is overthrown.

Problems with Radical Feminism

Liberal Feminist Critique

Liberal feminists disagree with radical feminists on a range of grounds. The first is that they see the idea that there is a war between the sexes as unfruitful. Men can be sympathetic to feminism (as J.S. Mill famously was), and it is wrong to assume that men cannot become adherents to the feminist cause. The notion of separatism is pessimistic and self-defeating.

Nor are liberal feminists persuaded by the arguments for patriarchy. The notion that male domination enters into the very fibre of relationships ignores the importance of privacy and choice. Women are, or can be, agents, and the notion that the personal is political is a totalitarian credo that does not allow individuals to decide matters for themselves.

Some liberal feminists argue that prostitutes are sex-workers who choose a profession that others dislike, and the legalisation of prostitution would enable women who wish to pursue careers in this area to do so without hindrance and condemnation. Liberal feminists see the campaigns against pornography as oppressive and authoritarian. Not only do such campaigners find themselves working with extremely conservative pressure groups, but the attempt to ban pornography leads to censorship – the prevention of people acting in unconventional ways which, liberal feminists insist, do not harm others.

Their attitude, in the eyes of liberal feminists, towards the state and legal reform is generally negative and radical feminists suffer from an absolutist outlook that prevents them from seeing that gradual change, based upon rational discussion, is far more effective than utopian fantasies.

Socialist Feminist Critique

Socialist feminists have no difficulty in extending the notion of politics at least to workplaces and the family, but they see the idea of sisterhood as dangerously abstract. Socialist feminists want to stress that women belong to different classes and their interests vary according to their class position. Socialist feminists are not necessarily opposed to the notion of patriarchy, but they insist that it is much more complex than the radicals imagine.

In the first place, it is a system that arises historically, and even if Engels' account is not wholly plausible, he is correct to assume that patriarchy has not always existed, and that it is connected with private property and the state. Second, socialist feminists want to distinguish between different kinds of patriarchy. There is an important distinction to be made between the kind of explicit patriarchy that exists in medieval and slave-owning societies, and a liberal patriarchy in which male domination coexists with liberal notions of consent and freedom. In fact, it is the gulf between theory and practice that makes the socialist critique possible, for women in developed liberal societies enjoy formal rights that contrast with their lack of real power. This kind of analysis is only possible if patriarchy itself is placed in a very specific historical context.

Socialist feminists, like liberal feminists, see no problem in forming alliances with men, since men can be in favour of emancipation just as privileged women can be opposed to it. It is true that men benefit from patriarchy, but the socialist emphasis upon *relationships* mean that men have their own lives limited and warped as a result of patriarchal prejudices which regard women, for example, as the natural guardians of children.

Even though socialist feminists would not accept extreme left-wing strictures against feminism as being inherently bourgeois and a distraction from class struggle, they tend to see the concern of radical feminists with lifestyle and sexuality as the product of a middle-class outlook that ignores the problems faced by women workers.

Black Feminist and Philosophical Feminist Critique

Black feminists are sceptical about a supra-ethnic notion of sisterhood. All women are not the same and the notion that they are fundamentally oppressed by men, could only be advanced by those who have never suffered from racist stereotyping. Women themselves can be racists and oppress black women (as well as black men), and the experience of subject women under slavery and colonialism demonstrate very different patterns of family and economic life to those assumed by radical feminists.

Rape is a case in point. The view of a black man as a potential rapist has been a formidable racist stereotype (particularly in the southern states of the USA) and black women who report assaults to racist-minded police, have a very different experience from white women who have been raped. Audre Lorde puts the matter in a nutshell in her open letter to Mary Daly, when she comments: 'The oppression of women knows no ethnic nor racial boundaries, true, but that does not mean that it is identical within those differences' (Humm, 1992: 139). A feminism that ignores ethnic or racial differences is a feminism that unthinkingly privileges one group over others.

Feminist empiricists reject the notion that science and objectivity are somehow male activities. It is true that patriarchal prejudices can claim scientific warranty, but this is poor science. Science is not to blame for male domination but is a powerful weapon for exposing and combating it. Facts which point to discrimination and inequality are crucial to the arsenal of feminist argument, and make it much more difficult for unsympathetic men to dismiss feminism as a man-hating, irrational doctrine.

Standpoint feminists are, it seems to us, more likely to be influenced by radical feminists and they can only distance themselves from radical feminism where they defend an argument that a woman's standpoint depends upon the particular social experience she has.

Postmodern feminists hold to the fact that power is exercised at every level in society, and it would seem therefore that they should be sympathetic to the radical feminist argument that male domination extends to apparently private as well as public institutions. In reality, however, postmodern feminists are particularly hostile to radical feminism since, as we shall see, they regard the whole notion of a 'woman' as problematically universalist in character. Radical feminism, in their eyes, suffers from deep-rooted binary divides – between men and women, reason and emotion, etc. – which leads these feminists to invert patriarchal arguments by accepting that there is a fundamental sexual divide. Instead of demonising women, they demonise men, but the same absolutist logic is at work.

Focus

The Pornography Debate

Andrea Dworkin and Catherine MacKinnon, two radical feminists in the USA, campaigned against pornography on the grounds that it harmed the interests of women everywhere. They secured the passing of the 'MacKinnon-Dworkin' ordinances in Minneapolis and Indianapolis in 1983 and 1984. These would have made it possible for women who considered that they had been harmed to sue producers, distributors and retailers of pornography. The first ordinance was vetoed by the mayor and the second overruled by the federal courts.

These attempts were seen as a model for use elsewhere. Campaigners have sought to achieve restrictions on pornography in Britain, and in 1986 Clare Short sought to introduce the 'Page Three Bill' which would have banned 'naked or partially naked women in provocative pages in newspapers' and fined offending publishers. The attempt failed. The Campaign Against Pornography was launched in the House of Commons in 1988. These campaigns have been challenged by other feminists who argue that pornography is a symptom rather than a cause of women's oppression; a legal attack on pornography, they argue, allies feminists with right-wing fundamentalists who are opposed to any portrayal of explicit sexual material through art and the media. The US liberal feminist Nadine Strossen sees both obscenity laws and feminist proposals to restrict pornography by law as violations of free speech (Bryson, 1999: 174–7).

Black Feminism

Black feminists are acutely aware of the question of difference. Indeed, the very existence of a 'black feminism' is a protest against the idea that women are all the same. Beneath the supposedly universal notion is to be found women who are often white, university-educated and of middle-class background.

Black feminists argue that there is sufficient in common in Britain between Afro-Caribbean women, African women and Asian women to assert a common identity. Of course, each of these categories is itself extremely diverse, but black women are considered to have a common experience. In the case of Britain, they are all 'outsiders', regarded as 'invisible' by the dominant culture, and judged to be 'ethnic' and abnormal, as though the majority community is itself without an ethnic identity and embodies normality.

Black feminism is a protest against marginalisation and the belief in monolithic identities. It rejects the idea that black women have to choose whether they want to be humiliated as women by patriarchal black movements or disregarded as blacks by a feminist movement that really speaks for white women. When the Nation of Islam marched in the USA in 2002, many black women found it very painful to decide between their dislike of patriarchy (which the Nation of Islam explicitly represented) and their concern about racism.

It is true that many white women turned to feminism as a result of their experience in anti-slavery and civil rights movements, but they failed to see that oppression is never simply universal – it always takes differential and particular forms. The notion that there is an *analogy* between women and blacks (Gayle Rubin wrote an essay in 1970 entitled *Woman as Nigger*) assumes that somehow black women do not exist!

The specific existence of black feminism contributes significantly to feminist theory as a whole by stressing the importance of a concrete approach that takes account of people's real life situations and differences. By noting that some women are black in societies where whiteness is seen as the 'norm', one is more likely to observe that women may also be poor, disabled, illiterate etc. Black feminism alerts us to the dangers of privileging one identity over others.

The assumption that the family is problematic for women is invariably made without taking account of the particular features of the black family that, in the USA for example, is often headed by women who also have to work outside the home. Barrett and McIntosh have conceded that their own study of the family ignored the very different structures that exist in the families of Afro-Caribbean and Asian people in Britain (Bryson, 1992: 254). As for rape and sexuality, quite different assumptions are made of black women, and in Whelehan's view, black women suffer from poorer mental health than their white counterparts (Whelehan, 1995: 117).

Black feminists have argued that it is not just a question of disadvantages accumulating alongside one another – as independent entities – so that a black women may suffer from gender, ethnic and class attributes. It is a question of developing a theory of oppression in which these 'multiple oppressions' reinforce one another, and lie at the root of stereotyping. Indeed, it is remarkable how similar class, racial and gender stereotyping are. This warns us against absolutising one kind of oppression, and opens the way to multiple alliances – of some women with some men for specific purposes. As the African-American writer, bell hooks has argued, black feminism stresses the value of solidarity – which unites similarity and difference – over the oppressively homogenous notion of sisterhood (Bryson, 1999: 35).

Whelehan has noted that during the 1970s it was commonly felt by radical feminists that analysis of related issues needed to be shelved, so that full attention could be given to the question of women. As she comments, this kind of argument ignores the fact that women can also suffer oppression as a result of their class, racial, gender and sexual orientation (Whelehan, 1995: 111). Not only does black feminism provide a challenge to a theory of domination, it poses a challenge to political theory as a whole. It invites a reconceptualisation of the notion of power and freedom, since those who are the subjects of black feminism have no, in Bryson's words, 'institutionalised inferiors' (1999: 34). Given the fact that there are relatively few black feminist academics, black feminism also poses the challenge of mobilising the considerable knowledge which the community has but has not produced in what Whelehan calls 'high theoretical' form (1995: 120).

Problems with Black Feminism

Liberal, Socialist and Radical Feminist Critiques

Liberal feminists are concerned about what they see as the divisiveness of black feminism as a distinct variety of feminist argument. Black feminists are rightly opposed to racism but the answer to exclusion and marginalisation is to expand the notion of the individual so as to incorporate groups like blacks whose experience of repression has been very different.

Lynne Segal speaks for many socialist feminists who express concern at the fragmentation that has taken place within the women's movement, and she notes in particular the problem of the growth of 'Black feminist perspectives' (Whelehan, 1995: 121). What about the real class differences that exist within black communities – will they not be ignored if a feminism is created which highlights blackness as the defining criterion?

Radical feminists are concerned that the opposition to male domination is diffused by a concern with difference. Although MacKinnon does not address herself to black feminism as such, she is suspicious of the argument about difference. Inequality comes first, she insists; difference comes after: difference, she says, is the velvet glove on the iron fist of domination (1989: 219). In other words, difference can distract us from the force and repression inherent in patriarchy, and distinguishing between black and white women, can – radical feminists argue – play into the hands of men who are anxious to downgrade the plight of all women.

The Critique of Philosophical Feminisms

Feminist empiricists believe that anything that ideologises feminism is a mistake. The statistic that 80 per cent of the mortality rate of illegal abortions came from women of colour (slightly broader than 'black' women) in the years preceding its decriminalisation in the USA (Whelehan, 1995: 117) is a revealing fact, and the danger is that it will not be as widely known as it deserves to be, if it is presented by a feminism perceived to be separatist and extremist. Standpoint feminists would acknowledge that different experiences are important and need to be taken into account, but this should not be juxtaposed to the common experiences which all women have, and which mould their particular outlook.

Although postmodern feminists are sympathetic to the point about difference, they argue that 'blackness' represents another form of 'essentialism', i.e. the belief in an abstract 'essence'. Some black women might not only reveal class differences, as the socialists warn: what about hierarchies in the communities that lead black Americans to be suspicious of Asian-Americans? Differences like these are simply swept under the proverbial carpet if blackness becomes the criterion for a particular kind of feminism. Whatever black feminists may say in theory, in practice the notion of a black feminism inevitably privileges blackness over other differences, while the idea that race must be explored in relation to gender and class ignores the other differences – of sexual orientation, region, religion, etc. – which problematise the very existence of the notion of woman.

Philosophical Feminisms

Feminist Empiricism

Feminist empiricists take the view that sexist and 'andocentric' (or male chauvinist) biases can be eliminated from scholarship and statements if there is a strict adherence to existing norms of scientific inquiry. If projects are rigorously designed, hypotheses properly tested and data soundly interpreted, then sexist prejudices can be dealt with alongside all other prejudices – as thoroughly unscientific in character (Hoffman, 2001: 55).

The more female researchers there are in the profession, the better, since women are likely to be more sensitive to sexist prejudices than men. However, the question is not one of female science, but of sound science. The fact is that women are dramatically under-represented in the decision-making structures of the UN or in legislative bodies or in the world of business – indeed in the 'public' world in general, except perhaps in certain new social movements like the peace movement and in certain professions. These facts can only be established through sound statistical techniques, and they establish the existence of discrimination in ways that cannot be ignored.

Feminist empiricism ensures that feminism has come of age, entering into mainstream argument and debate.

Standpoint Feminism

Standpoint feminism arose initially as a feminist version of the Marxist argument that the proletariat had a superior view of society because it was the victim rather than the beneficiary of the market. Standpoint theorists argue that because women have been excluded from power – whether within societies or in international organisations – they see the world differently from men.

Standpoint theorists differ in explaining *why* women have an alternative outlook. Do women have a more respectful attitude towards nature than men, because they menstruate and can give birth to children, or is it because they are socialised differently, so that nature seems more precious to them than it does to many men? Peace activists may likewise differ in accounting for the fact that women in general are more likely to oppose war than men.

Whatever the emphasis placed upon nature or nurture, standpoint feminists generally believe that women are different to men. One of the reasons why standpoint feminists see women as more practically minded than men, is because they often have to undertake activity of a rather menial kind. Bryson refers to Marilyn French's novel *The Women's Room* (1978) (quoted by Hartsock) in which a woman has the job of washing a toilet and the floor and walls around it: an activity, says French, which brings women 'in touch with necessity' and this is why they 'are saner than men' (Bryson, 1999: 23). Indeed, Hartsock seeks to redefine power as a capacity and not as domination, arguing that women's experience stresses connection and relationship rather than individuality and competition (Hartsock, 1983: 253).

Postmodern Feminism

Some make a distinction between postmodern feminism and feminist postmodernism. The distinction, it seems to us, is not a helpful one and we use the two terms indistinguishably. Those who say they are postmodern feminists but not feminist postmodernists sometimes define postmodern feminism as 'postmodernism with a standpoint bent' (Hoffman, 2001: 63), and we would suggest that the question of a 'standpoint bent' is best understood by looking at the section preceding this one.

Ch. 1:
The State

Postmodernists seek to overcome the dualistic character of traditional theory. We should refuse to accept that we are either critical (and want to overturn everything) or conservative (and want to keep things as they are). We need to be both subjective and objective, valuing the individual *and* society. In this way we avoid making the kind of choices that postmodernists call 'binary' and absolutist. This leads postmodernists to stress the importance of difference and plurality, and this is why postmodern feminists or feminist postmodernists argue that the notion of feminism as the emancipation of women is doubly problematic. First, because emancipation sounds as though at some privileged point in time women will finally be free and autonomous, and second, because the very term 'woman' implies that what unites women is more important than what divides them.

This, postmodernists argue, violates the logic of both/and, since it privileges sameness over difference. Indeed, Kate Nash argues that because postmodernism (we use the term interchangeably with poststructuralism) commits us to arguing that woman 'is not a fixed category with specific characteristics', we have to be committed to the concept of woman as a 'fiction' in order to be a feminist at all (Hoffman, 2001: 78)!

Problems with the Philosophical Feminisms

Liberal Feminist Critique

Liberal feminists are sympathetic to feminist empiricism. Indeed, one writer has described feminist empiricism as the 'philosophical underpinning of liberal feminism' (Hoffman, 2001: 56), and naturally liberal feminists are attracted to the stress on rationality, science and evidence. On the other hand, liberal feminists argue that questions of freedom and autonomy, the rule of law and individual rights involve values, and feminist empiricists seem to be committed to a notion of science that excludes values, basing their hypotheses and findings simply on facts.

Standpoint feminists suffer from the same one-sidedness that afflicts radical feminism. By probing women's experience in general, it does not respect the division between the public and the private, and by arguing for the superiority of the female standpoint, it makes alliances with well-meaning men more difficult. Both factors make standpoint feminists liable to embrace an authoritarian style of politics.

As for postmodern feminism, liberal feminists feel that its aversion to absolutes and modernism leads to scepticism and renders problematic the whole concern with women's rights.

Socialist, Radical and Black Feminist Critiques

Socialist feminism challenges the feminist empiricist notion of science as value-free and not itself ideological. An emphasis upon relationships leads to the view that facts do not speak for themselves but imply evaluation, and therefore it is naive to imagine that a purely scientific (rather than explicitly ideological) presentation of feminism will be more persuasive.

As for standpoint feminism, socialists argue that an emphasis upon women's experience needs to take more specific account of the impact of class and capitalism, while postmodern feminism leads to a kind of academic conservatism that makes emancipatory politics impossible.

Radical feminists feel that the emphasis upon science is male-oriented and that feminist empiricists underestimate the extent to which male mores have penetrated the academy. Radicals are more sympathetic to standpoint feminism, particularly where the difference and even superiority of women is emphasised, while postmodernist feminism is seen as a betrayal of women's interests and a rejection of the need for feminism at all.

To black feminists, feminist empiricism seems elitist and very 'white' since most black women find it difficult to obtain academic positions. As for standpoint feminism, it speaks (like radical feminism) of women in abstract terms, and therefore unthinkingly adopts the position of white women. Postmodern feminism is seen as indulgent and sceptical, and for all its emphasis upon difference, ignores the problems which black women face, and which make the notion of emancipation a meaningful ideal. Deconstructing modernity seems a rather hollow enterprise when women who are black have yet to obtain modernist goals of equality and autonomy.

Feminism and Diversity

It could be argued that the emphasis upon different strands of feminism is itself counter-productive. If feminism is defined broadly as the emancipation of women, then it becomes possible to see each of the different feminisms making a positive contribution to the development of feminism overall, while betraying a certain one-sidedness which needs to be discarded. A recent work has spoken of the need to recover 'feminisms from the intolerance of other feminisms' (Zalewski, 2000: 142) and it seems to us that we do not need to choose between one feminism and many feminisms. Feminism can only be constructed as a viable and dynamic theory through multiple feminisms.

Thus liberal feminism stresses the importance of people as free and equal individuals but, as Steans argues, 'liberal feminism is not merely feminism added onto liberalism' (1998: 17), while socialist feminists rightly emphasise the importance of class and capitalism as social institutions that negatively impact upon women. Despite its weaknesses, radical feminism argues for a notion of patriarchy that extends into all areas of life and it invites attention to relationships as the location of conflict.

Black feminists warn us eloquently against the dangers of ethno-centrism. Women can be black as well as white, and analyses say of the family and sexuality that might apply to white women, will not necessarily apply to black women. As for the philosophical feminisms, feminist empiricists stress the importance of a sophisticated presentation of the facts, while standpoint feminists are concerned with the way in which women's experience impacts upon their behaviour and outlook. Postmodernist feminism helpfully warns against static and ahistorical views of women that ignore the differences between them.

There is no need to juxtapose separate feminisms from the development of a feminism which is sensitive to difference, sees the need for alliances with men, acknowledges the problems from which all women suffer (albeit in different ways), and seeks to make feminism as convincing and well researched as possible.

The Problem of Prostitution and Pornography

To many people (who would not necessarily call themselves feminists at all) prostitution is scandalous and unacceptable. Surely it is right that soliciting and brothels are illegal even if prostitution as such is not. Prostitution is an affront to freedom, marriage, and the dignity of women. To others, this is a moralistic position that ignores the reasons that women become prostitutes. Prostitute women need help and recognising them as sex workers who should work in safer conditions (and pay tax!), would be a just and humane way of tackling the issue.

Draw up a list of arguments for and against the decriminalisation of prostitution and say why *your* solution to the question would meet the interests of both prostitutes in particular and women in general.

Pornography also arouses strong feelings. Is it merely a portrait of sexuality to which the prudish and puritanical object, or does pornography harm the interests of women and should be 'cleansed' from society?

How would you define pornography? Of course it can hurt people (think of the exploitation in which children may be involved) but does it have to? Based on your definition of pornography, consider the pros and cons of banning pornography.

Summary

Liberal feminism seeks to give women the same political and legal rights that men enjoy so that women can be regarded as rational and autonomous individuals. Liberal feminists are accused by their critics of disregarding the negative impact that capitalism and the market make upon women's lives; of ignoring male oppression in the so-called private sphere; and of embracing an ideology that is abstract and absolutist in tone.

Socialist feminism argues that questions of gender must be considered alongside questions of class. Marxist feminism particularly emphasises the problem posed by capitalism to the interests of women. Liberal critics contend that women can legitimately display their equality through becoming executives in business, and argue that it is wrong to assume that all women should work outside the home. Other feminists feel that socialists ignore the general problems faced by women in all societies, while postmodernists feel that the socialist 'metanarrative' is as abstract as the liberal one.

Radical feminists pride themselves on concentrating exclusively on women's problems, and insist that male oppression manifests itself in interpersonal relations as well as in more conventionally political arenas. They are accused by their critics of an authoritarian disregard for the individual and a prejudice against men. The differences between women, whether racial or class-based, must be taken into account, and it is wrong to assume that a scientific view expresses masculinist values.

Black feminists take the view that ethnic outsiders must be explicitly considered, and generalised views of women are unacceptable. Their critics feel that black feminists focus one-sidedly upon what is one form of oppression among many, and that they are guilty of essentialising blackness.

The philosophical feminisms stress either the importance of rigorous scientific methods (the feminist empiricists); the need to understand the distinctive character of a woman's outlook (the standpoint feminists); or the importance of plurality and difference (the postmodern feminists). Their critics feel that empiricism is vulnerable to the argument that facts themselves imply values; that a woman's standpoint varies dramatically according to circumstance; and that an excessive emphasis upon difference casts doubt upon the whole feminist project.

These divisions can be resolved by a notion of feminism that seeks to incorporate the strengths of each of the feminisms and exclude their weaknesses.

Questions

1. Is feminism still relevant in today's world?
2. Which theory of feminism – the liberal, the socialist, the radical or the black – do you find the most persuasive?
3. Can men become feminists or is feminism an ideology that only relates to women?
4. Do the biological differences between men and women have any social significance?
5. Are some women more likely to favour emancipation than others?

References

Aquinas, St T. (1953) *The Political Ideas of St Thomas Aquinas* (ed. D. Bigongiari) New York: Hafner.

Bebel, A. (1904) *Women Under Socialism* New York: New York Labor Press.

Brody, M. (1992) 'Introduction' in M. Wollstonecraft, *A Vindication of the Rights of Women* London: Penguin, 1–73.

Bryson, V. (1992) *Feminist Political Theory* Basingstoke: Macmillan.

Bryson, V. (1999) *Feminist Debates* Basingstoke: Macmillan.

Coole, D. (1988) *Women in Political Theory* Hemel Hempstead: Harvester-Wheatsheaf.

Eisenstein, Z. (1981) *The Radical Future of Liberal Feminism* London: Longman.

Engels, F. (1972) *The Origin of the Family, Private Property and the State* London: Lawrence and Wishart.

French, M. (1978) *The Women's Room* New York: Jove.

Friedan, B. (1963) *The Feminine Mystique* Harmondsworth: Penguin.

Funk N. and Mueller, M. (eds) (1993) *Gender Politics and Post-Communism* New York and London: Routledge.

Gilligan, C. (1992) *In a Different Voice* London: Harvard University Press.

Greer, G. (1970) *The Female Eunuch* London: Paladin.

Greer, G. (1999) *The Whole Woman* London: Doubleday.

Hartsock, N. (1983) *Money, Sex and Power* New York and London: Longman.

Hoffman, J. (2001) *Gender and Sovereignty* Basingstoke: Palgrave.

Humm, M. (ed.) (1992) *Feminisms* New York and London: Harvester-Wheatsheaf.

MacKinnon, C. (1989) *Toward a Feminist Theory of the State* Cambridge, MA: Harvard University Press.

Marx, K. and Engels, F. (1975) *Collected Works*, vol. 3 London: Lawrence and Wishart.

Mill, J.S. (1970) *The Subjection of Women* Cambridge, MA and London: MIT Press.

Plato (1955) *The Republic* Harmondsworth: Penguin.

Rowbotham, S. (1972) *Women, Resistance and Revolution* London: Allen Lane/Penguin.

Rubin, G, (1970) 'Woman as Nigger' in L. Tanner (ed.), *Voices from Women's Liberation* New York: Mentor.

Sacks, K. (1974) 'Engels revisited: women, the organization of production and private property' in M. Rosaldo and L. Lamphere (eds), *Women, Culture and Society* Stanford, CA: Stanford University Press, 207–22.

Shanley, M. and Pateman, C. (1991) 'Introduction' in M. Shanley and C. Pateman (eds), *Feminist Interpretrations and Political Theory* Cambridge: Polity, 1–10.

Steans, J. (1998) *Gender and International Relations* Cambridge: Polity.

Whelehan, I. (1995) *Modern Feminist Thought* Edinburgh: Edinburgh University Press.

Wolf, N. (1993) *Fire with Fire* London: Chatto and Windus.

Wollstonecraft, M. (1992) *A Vindication of the Rights of Women* London: Penguin.

Zalewski, M. (2000) *Feminism after Postmodernism* London and New York: Routledge.

Further Reading

- Bryson's *Feminist Debates* (referenced above) is particularly useful. It is comprehensive and written accessibly. Chapters 1 and 2 contain a valuable introduction to the feminist landscape. Bryson has recently edited with Georgina Blakeley a volume entitled *The Impact of Feminism on Political Concepts and Debates* (Manchester: Manchester University Press, 2007).

- Nicholson's *Feminism/Postmodernism* (London and New York: Routledge, 1990) contain a series of essays (Nicholson is the editor) written at a time when postmodernism was beginning to make an impact. Yeatman and Hartsock's essays are especially useful.

- Greer's *The Whole Woman* (referenced above) is lively and gives the reader a very good flavour of feminism as it emerged in the 1960s and 1970s.

- Engels' *The Origin of the Family, Private Property and the State* (London: Lawrence and Wishart, 1972) has been much commented upon, but is worth reading in the original.

- Shanley and Pateman's *Feminist Interpretations and Political Theory* (referenced above) contains critiques on a wide range of classical political thinkers and more recent theorists. Accessible and full of insights.

- Funk and Mueller's *Gender Politics and Post-Communism* (referenced above) has articles on the position of women after the collapse of the Communist Party states. Some very useful material here.

Weblinks

Have a look at: http://news.bbc.co.uk/1/hi/business/1962036.stm for up to date material on women's pay in relation to men.

For a survey of different feminisms:
http://www-lib.usc.edu/~retter/lst2.html

Chapter 15

Multiculturalism

Introduction

Beliefs and values, language and family traditions, dress and diet, are central to an individual's sense of identity. Most people would say that these things should be respected, and liberal democracy has developed into an ideology that places great stress on respecting diversity of belief and lifestyle. A fully human existence entails the freedom to live according to your cultural traditions. But what if a particular cultural tradition is hostile to liberalism? What if, for example, it holds that girls should be educated to fulfil a subservient role, limited strictly to the private sphere of the family? What if it advocates discrimination, or even violence, against adherents of other religions, or homosexuals, or different ethnic groups? These are questions raised by multiculturalism, an ideology that has emerged since the 1960s, but which stands in a complex relationship to older ideologies.

Chapter Map

In this chapter we will:

- Disentangle various concepts that often get run together in debates over multiculturalism; in particular, we will distinguish between culture, race, ethnicity and religion.

- Set out a number of theories of multiculturalism.

- Consider whether multiculturalism is bad for women.

- Apply these theoretical perspectives to real-life case studies.

Religious Dress Ban: Equality or Oppression?

Demonstrations against a law that would make the wearing of Islamic veils illegal in French schools, December 2003

Source: © Jerome Sessini/In Visu/Corbis

In February 2004 the French National Assembly voted 494–36 in favour of banning 'conspicuous' religious symbols in schools. The ban came into effect in September 2004, at the beginning of the new school year. France has a long tradition of *laicitie* (secularity), which is intended to draw a strict line between the state and religion; some advocates of the ban argue that it is necessary to protect the French state – of which the public education system is a part – from the 'threat' of Islamic fundamentalism. Others offer a more subtle defence: the ban ensures that Muslim girls and young women receive equal treatment as French citizens. By preventing those women wearing a veil (*hijab*), or other Muslim dress, they are being protected from their families who are intent on denying them equality in educational provision. Against the charge that the ban discriminates against Muslims it is stressed that the law applies also to Jewish skullcaps, large Christian crosses and Sikh turbans.

This case draws attention to questions of identity and equality: does treating people equally mean treating them in the same way? Most French people – 70 per cent of whom supported the ban – are either committed or nominal Christians, or have no religious beliefs and adherence; for them there is no injunction to wear a particular form of dress. For Muslims, on the other hand, there are requirements, although there are different interpretations of those requirements. Apart from conspicuous crosses, the new law does not have any impact on Christians and non-believers, whereas clearly it does affect Muslims. On the other hand, it could be argued that Islam treats men and women unequally, and this is manifested in gender-differentiated dress codes; the French parliament is, therefore, striking a blow for gender equality.

• What do you think: was the French parliament justified in passing this law?

What is Multiculturalism?

The term multiculturalism has gained wide currency in both academic and popular debate, and its employment is not restricted to political theory or political science: there are multicultural perspectives not only in other social sciences, but also in the humanities, and even in the natural sciences. For this reason it is important to demarcate the debate in political theory, and this requires making some distinctions:

(a) *Multiculturalism as an attitude* Although it is more usual to describe a person as cosmopolitan than multicultural, the two can be taken as synonyms, which define either a positive and open attitude to different cultures or, at least, respect for people, where such respect means recognising their rights to make choices about how they live their lives.

(b) *Multiculturalism as a tool of public policy* If you conduct an online search of university library holdings using the word 'multiculturalism' most items will be concerned with education policy, followed by other areas of public policy such as health and social services. Multicultural education policy is concerned with school organisation and curriculum; health and social policy focuses particularly on social inclusion and identifying the special needs of particular cultural groups.

(c) *Multiculturalism as an aspect of institutional design* Whereas policy questions assume the existence of a particular set of political institutions, the question here is what kind of institutions we should have. Examples of institutional design that make explicit the concern with cultural diversity include the power-sharing Assembly and Executive created in Northern Ireland as a result of the 1998 Belfast Agreement, and the constitutional arrangements for Bosnia-Herzegovina which resulted from the 1995 Dayton Peace Accords.

(d) *Multiculturalism and moral justification* Institutions are important, but political theory is not concerned merely with what political institutions should exist, but with how they are justified. It is possible for institutions to be respected for bad reasons, so 'justificatory multiculturalism' is concerned with reasons that all reasonable people can accept. What constitutes reasonableness is, of course, central to the debate. For the most part we will be concerned with this dimension of multiculturalism.

Culture, Race, Ethnicity and Religion

Culture

A difficulty that characterises the multiculturalism debate is the failure to explain what is meant by culture. Will Kymlicka, for example, in the opening lines of his book *Multicultural Citizenship*, makes the following claim:

> Most countries are culturally diverse. According to recent estimates, the world's 184 independent states contain over 600 living language groups, and 5,000 ethnic groups. In very few countries can the citizens be said to share the same language, or belong to the same ethnonational group (Kymlicka, 1995: 1).

In a few short sentences it is implied that 'culture' equates to a language group, an ethnic group and an ethnonational group. Kymlicka goes on to define the kind of culture with which he is concerned as an 'intergenerational community, more or less institutionally complete, occupying a given state territory, sharing a distinct language and history' (Kymlicka, 1995: 18) and further suggests that a culture provides 'meaningful ways of life across the full range of human activities' (Kymlicka, 1995: 76). The problem is that there is a proliferation of concepts with which culture is equated but this simply shifts the strain of definition on to these other, equally problematic, concepts.

In popular discussion culture is frequently run together with race, ethnicity and religion; while there are important connections between these concepts they are not synonyms. The structure of a religion is quite different to the structure of, say, a linguistic community, and each generates distinct political claims. How we define culture has significant implications for our understanding of multiculturalism and the relationship of multiculturalism to other ideologies.

If we want to find a serious discussion of culture we have to turn to anthropologists, for whom arguably culture is the central, defining concept of their discipline. We can characterise the anthropologists' discussion of culture as an attempt to answer the question: given a shared biological nature and largely similar physical needs, why is there such cultural diversity? Responses have fallen into two categories: universalist and relativist. Universalists include Marxists, who argue that culture is to be explained by underlying material forces and most nineteenth-century liberals: Mill, for example, argued that human beings have innate rational capacities that can only be realised under particular cultural conditions (Mill, 1991: 231). Universalism need not take an evolutionary form: functionalists argue that very diverse cultural practices can be explained by underlying, universal needs (Malinowski, 1965: 67–74). Relativists, on the other hand, take culture to be fundamental and not derivative. Ruth Benedict maintained that a culture is an integrated pattern of intelligent, albeit often unconscious, behaviour. Pattern theory implies that there can be no cultural *diversity* within a society, for culture is integral, and it is perhaps not surprising that those political theorists, such as Tully (1995), who make explicit their anthropological commitments, appeal to an alternative and more recent form of cultural relativism, that advanced by, among others, Geertz (1993). Culture for Geertz is a complex of signs, whose meaning is dependent upon perspective, not in the sense that an 'outsider' cannot understand the signs, but rather that such understanding – *interpretation* – must make reference to the context of the participants. For Geertz one does not 'have' a culture in the sense that culture is predicated upon a subject, but rather culture is a shorthand for a 'multiplicity of complex conceptual structures, many of them superimposed upon or knotted into one another, which are at once strange, irregular, and inexplicit' (Geertz, 1993: 10).

Race and Ethnicity

Race and ethnicity are concerned with somatic, or phenotypical, differences between people: that is, how other people look or sound, or any other way in which they are *perceived* to be different. There is a considerable sociological literature on race and ethnicity, but very little intellectual exchange between sociologists of race and political theorists of multiculturalism. The terms race and ethnicity are used interchangeably. Ethnicity denotes a group of people bound by blood-ties, and has its etymological roots in the Greek word for 'nation' – *ethnos* (although some Biblical commentators translate it as Gentile). Although most sociologists reject the notion that racial differences have a biological basis – there is greater genetic variation *within* groups perceived to be the same than *between* such groups – they accept that the discourse of race affects human attitudes and behaviour. Because it has social effects, race is real.

Until relatively recently, race (or ethnicity) rather than culture was the dominant concept in debates about citizenship and immigration. This is reflected in law. British legislation intended to outlaw discrimination carried the title of Race Relations Act(s) – of which there were three: 1965, 1968, 1976. The 1976 Act, which superseded the previous ones, defined a 'racial group' as 'a group of persons defined by reference to colour, race, nationality or ethnic or national origins' (Macdonald, 1977: 49). There is no mention of culture, or indeed religion. A complex relationship exists between anti-racist politics and multiculturalism. Since a person can be defined as 'different' by a range of characteristics, including language (and accent), bodily characteristics, dress, religion and diet, where the salience of each varies from one situation to another, legislation designed to protect that person cannot easily slot discrimination into a single category, such as racial, or religious, or cultural, or ethnic. In this sense race and culture are inextricably linked. However, race is relatively fixed as against culture – even if we reject race as a biological category, a person's race is *perceived* as fixed. Culture, because it is concerned with beliefs and lifestyle, possesses a greater fluidity. The danger which some anti-racists see in multiculturalism is that, in the name of respecting difference and fighting discrimination, multiculturalists deny people autonomy – they assume that cultural traits are fundamental to that person's identity.

Religion

Ch. 8:
Liberalism
pp. 177–81

Much debate about cultural diversity is really about the relationship of religion and politics – that is, of the consequences of the existence of conflicting belief systems, including secular ones, within a political territory. As such, multiculturalism as an ideology may have its roots in the much older debate over religious toleration, discussed in Chapter 8. Later in this chapter we will challenge that claim, but there is no doubt that in popular debate the place of Muslims and the role of Islam in Western society has become linked to a critique of multiculturalism, and so it is important to make a few brief remarks about religion.

Religion is a highly complex phenomenon. Eric Sharpe identifies four 'modes' of religion, that is, ways in which human beings are religious: (a) the *existential* mode, in which the focus is on faith; (b) the *intellectual* mode, which gives priority to beliefs, in the sense of those statements to which a person gives conscious assent; (c) the *institutional* mode, at the centre of which are authoritative organisations that maintain and transmit doctrines; (d) the *ethical* mode, which stresses the behavioural relationships between members of a religious community, and those

Leaving Home

If you were to leave the society in which you were brought up and live in another, what aspects of behaviour, belief and lifestyle would you give up first, and which would you give up last, or not give up at all? How you approach this thought experiment may depend on a number of factors:

- the age at which you emigrate;
- the circumstances of your emigration – it may be relatively free, or forced on you by persecution, or economic circumstances;
- the differences between the community from which you emigrate and the community of immigration;
- your gender may be relevant.

You may, in fact, have experienced migration. In that case, you can draw on your experience.

outside it (Sharpe, 1983: 91–107). What differentiates religions and sects is the centrality of one mode relative to another.

When considering the relationship of religion and politics in contemporary society it is important to keep in mind the dominant mode of a particular religion or sect, as well as the particular content of its beliefs or practices. There is a popular image of Islam as a radical, proselytising religion, and yet there is a stream of Islam – Sufism – which is inward-looking, mystical, and so relatively unpolitical. Viewing religion in terms of modes allows us to see both divergences within a particular religion as well as commonalities across religions. Those commonalities can generate conflict – as when, for example, two opposed proselytising religions face one another – as well as facilitate reconciliation.

Multiculturalism and Islamic Radicalisation

Before discussing various theories of multiculturalism it is worth bringing together the different concepts – culture, race, religion – discussed above and applying them to an issue that has generated a huge amount of popular commentary and opinion: the threat of radical Islam, or, more precisely, the process of radicalisation of young Muslims in the West. By 'radicalisation' is meant the development of attitudes carrying the likelihood of motivating the radicalised person to carry out actions which will undermine the liberal-democratic order.

A study for the British government identified the following factors as relevant to explaining radicalisation: (a) the individual's perception of society's acceptance of them; (b) the individual's perception of equal opportunities; (c) the individual's sense of feeling part of society; (d) the extent to which the individual identifies with the dominant values of society (http://www.communities.gov.uk/documents/communities/pdf/452628.pdf). It has been noted that on many measures of integration the four perpetrators of the 7 July 2005 bombings in London were 'well-integrated': college educated, employed, married, cricket-loving. When Mohammed Bouyeri murdered film-maker Theo van Gogh he attached a poem entitled 'In bloed gedoopt' ('Drenched in Blood') to the knife he used; the poem, with its rhyming couplets, was written in a style Dutch families send to one another at Christmas, thus not only a demonstrating an excellent command of the Dutch language but a highly developed sense of irony. It is clear that radicalisation is a complex process.

The British study in reviewing the literature came to the conclusion that radicalisation often involved a search for identity at a moment of crisis:

> whilst defining oneself is part of the normal process of identity-formation amongst young people, for those who are at risk of radicalisation, this process creates a 'cognitive opening', a moment when previous explanations and belief systems are found to be inadequate in explaining an individual's experience (Choudhury, 2007: 6).

Underlying the identity crisis is a sense of exclusion, intensified by experiences of discrimination, racism and blocked mobility. Radicalised individuals often have a fragmented identity – they strongly identify with some aspects of Britain (or another Western society) but are alienated from others. Discrimination rather than poverty is a crucial factor, which is one of the reasons why organisations such as Al-Muhajiroun (now a banned organisation in Britain) recruited in universities.

As well as alienation from some aspects of British (or Western) society the radicalised individual is also alienated from his family. The parents' version of Islam 'seems distant and irrelevant', and the religious leadership at the local mosque is poor, with Imams often unable to speak English. In many ways, radical Islam is Western: it addresses the needs of Muslims who have been socialised in the West, as distinct from immigrants to the West. Some writers, such as Tariq Ramadan, have argued that in response to both the traditional, often rural and un-Western, Muslim leadership of the mosques, and to the radical Islam of groups such as Al-Muhajiroun there must develop a 'European Islam'. He argues for a separation of religion and politics, and of religion and culture, and for a reinterpretation of Islamic texts in the light of Western experience (Ramadan, 2005: 4–5).

Several points of relevance to multiculturalism emerge from this brief discussion of radicalisation. First, religious conflict in the twenty-first century is only partially continuous with the religious conflicts of the sixteenth and seventeenth centuries. This is because a genuinely new problem has emerged in the twentieth century: the problem of identity. We explore this further in the section on 'Multiculturalism and the Politics of Identity'. Second, there is a socio-economic dimension to cultural diversity and exclusion: multiculturalism is not just about beliefs but also about resources. However, unlike traditional debates about resource distribution, conflicts arise not only due to poverty or absolute inequality, but to relative and perceived inequalities: concerns over distribution meet newer concerns about identity and self-worth. Third, there is a complex relationship between religion, race (ethnicity) and culture. Some discrimination against Muslims is likely to be explained as a gut reaction to 'phenotypical difference', and for far right parties, such as the British National Party, cultural difference has become a coded form of racism. Putting aside race there are genuine, non-racially motivated questions about the relationship between culture and religion, and we explore these further in this chapter, especially in the context of women's rights.

Multiculturalism and the Politics of Identity

Charles Taylor argues that the sense of who we are is constructed in the eyes of others, so that to fail to be recognised by others is to be denied the basis of one's identity: 'non-recognition or misrecognition can inflict harm, can be a form of oppression, imprisoning someone in a false, distorted, and reduced mode of being' (Taylor, 1994: 25). The politics of recognition is a modern concept, developing out of the collapse of hierarchies in the eighteenth century. Hierarchies were the basis of honour, and honour was linked to distinction, and hence inequality; against honour we have dignity, which Taylor takes to be the basis of a liberal–democratic society. At the same time as we shift from honour to dignity, we also experience individualisation: morality is no longer to be understood in terms of mores but is a matter of individual conscience, either in the form of a moral sense or, following Kant, the capacity of an individual to will the moral law. However, after Kant we get what Taylor terms a 'displacement of the moral accent': the inner voice is no longer primarily concerned to tell us what to do – to connect us to an objective moral order – but has become an end in itself. It is the terminus of identity. We have to be true to our 'inner voice' if we are to be 'full human beings'. The conjunction of inwardness and authenticity – following that inner voice – creates a danger that we lose sight of the fact that one's identity is only possible through other people's recognition of us. Somehow we need to reconcile the inwardness of authenticity with the 'outwardness' of recognition. In the days of honour the two were unproblematic because 'general recognition was built into the socially derived identity by virtue of the very fact that it was based on social categories that everyone took for granted' (Taylor, 1994: 34). Inwardly derived, as distinct from externally imposed, identity does not enjoy this automatic recognition, but must win it, and that process may fail, such that 'what has come about with the modern age is not the need for recognition but the conditions in which the attempt to be recognized can fail' (Taylor, 1994: 35). Recognition is recognition of *difference*, but this is combined with a traditional liberal emphasis on equality:

> The politics of difference often redefines non-discrimination as requiring that we make these distinctions the basis of differential treatment. So members of aboriginal bands will get certain rights and powers not enjoyed by other Canadians . . . and certain minorities will get the right to exclude others in order to preserve their cultural integrity, and so on (Taylor, 1994: 39–40).

The conflict between 'traditional' liberalism and identity politics would be less severe were it not for the fact that 'the demand for equal recognition extends beyond an acknowledgement of the equal value of all humans potentially, and comes to include the equal value of what they have made of this potential in fact' (Taylor, 1994: 42–3).

What is interesting about this presentation of multiculturalism is that culture is conceptualised not as an imposition or constraint, but as something we *identify with*, and in the process it becomes our *identity*. Despite Taylor's criticisms of traditional liberalism, his historical reconstruction of the development of multiculturalism as one strain of the politics of recognition – another is feminism – owes a huge amount to a liberal conception of the human subject. Culture is not, for

Taylor, something set apart from human beings, but rather it is through culture that we acquire the recognition of other people, and so self-respect. Although there are different theories of multiculturalism they share what may be called a post-liberal emphasis: that is, they have absorbed liberal conceptions, but at the same time engage in a critique of them. A consequence is that multiculturalism *as an academic debate* cannot be understood as a return to early liberal debates about religious toleration, debates rooted in a quite different conception of human nature. It is striking that, with the exception of Rawls's contribution, religion is not in the foreground of the theories of multiculturalism discussed in the next section. The difficulty is that the *popular debate* – in, for example, the media – does tend to focus on religion, and especially the relationship of Islam to liberal–democratic values.

Theories of Multiculturalism

In this section we survey four theories of multiculturalism. In thinking through each of these theories you should ask yourself three questions: (a) How does the theory conceptualise human identity? That is, to what extent is a person's communal – cultural, religious or ethnic – attachments 'constitutive' of what that person is, or what the person values about him- or herself? (b) What are the implications of the theory for personal freedom? Does the theory imply a greater or lesser freedom than is the case with 'traditional' liberalism? (c) Likewise, what are the implications of the theory for equality?

Multiculturalism as Hybridity (Jeremy Waldron)

Waldron takes as his starting point the controversy surrounding Salman Rushdie's novel *The Satanic Verses*. That novel, published in 1988, offended many Muslims, and resulted in a *fatwa* being proclaimed the following year against the author by the Ayatollah Khomeini. Waldron quotes from an essay in which Rushdie describes *The Satanic Verses* as a 'migrant's-eye view of the world'. It is, Rushdie says, written from the experiences of 'uprooting, disjuncture and metamorphosis'. He goes on to say that 'the Satanic Verses celebrates hybridity, impurity, intermingling, the transformation that comes of new and unexpected combinations of human beings, cultures, ideas, politics, movies, songs' (Rushdie, cited in Waldron, 1995: 93). Rushdie argues that 'mongrelisation' is the way that 'newness enters the world'.

The concept of hybridity is at the heart of Waldron's understanding of multiculturalism, which, he argues, must be 'cosmopolitan'. Understood in this way, multiculturalism represents a challenge to both liberalism and communitarianism. Against liberalism it implies a less rigid conception of what it means to live an autonomous life: 'if there is liberal autonomy in Rushdie's vision, it is a choice running rampant, and pluralism internalized from relations *between* individuals to the chaotic coexistence of projects, pursuits, ideas, images, and snatches of culture *within* an individual' (Waldron, 1995: 94).

Communitarians, on the other hand, fail to define 'community': is it a neighbourhood or the whole world? For the purposes of his argument Waldron defines community as an 'ethnic community' – 'a particular people sharing a heritage of custom, ritual, and way of life that is in some real or imagined sense immemorial' (Waldron, 1995: 96). Although we may need culture in a wide sense, we do not need to exist in a single culture, such as an ethnic community. Indeed, he goes further and argues that the only authentic response to modernity is the recognition of cultural hybridity: 'from a cosmopolitan point of view, immersion in the tradition of a particular community in the modern world is like living in Disneyland and thinking that one's surroundings epitomize what it is for a culture really to exist' (Wadron, 1995: 101).

Waldron does recognise the counter-charge to cosmopolitanism: that living with fragments of culture generates incoherence. As Benedict argued, the meaning of a particular item of culture depends on the whole, for a culture is all of a piece. Waldron argues, however, that real communities are disparate and overlap and are nothing like the aboriginal hunting bands or the 'misty dawn in a Germanic village' (Waldron, 1995: 102). Respecting culture does not entail valuing an entire culture, as if a culture were a self-contained thing, but rather 'meaningful options' come from a variety of cultural sources, and 'cultural erosion' is the key to cultural evaluation: the failure of a culture to survive indicates that one culture – or cultural trait – is better than another. Waldron's argument can be read either as a critique of multiculturalism or a particular model of multiculturalism. It is a critique if by multiculturalism is meant a deliberate policy of maintaining, either through financial support or the restriction of individual freedom, a particular culture, where culture is understood as an organic whole. It is a model of multiculturalism insofar as it presents a model of political society in which cultural diversity is valued.

The Right to Cultural Membership (Will Kymlicka)

In his first book, *Liberalism, Community, and Culture* (1989), Kymlicka argued that Rawls's theory of justice could, with a few revisions, accommodate the value of community. In subsequent work he has sought to defend cultural diversity within a Rawlsian framework: he argues that as individuals we have (moral) rights to cultural membership. He maintains that culture provides a 'context of choice'. This is problematic, for it is unclear whether culture is instrumentally or intrinsically valuable: does value reside in what we choose or in the fact that we have chosen it? If the ends we choose are of instrumental value then it would not much matter with which culture you identified, although the more compatible with liberal values the better.

Ch. 4: Justice pp. 82–88

Although Kymlicka makes clear that it is the ends we choose which matter, rather than our capacity to choose, the idea of culture as a context of choice does suggest that oppressive and illiberal cultures are less valuable than those which permit freedom, and so human autonomy – the capacity to choose – must have some intrinsic value. Kymlicka avoids addressing this tension within his theory and instead appeals to empirical examples to show that culture need not be oppressive. He cites Quebec as a culture that has 'liberalised':

> Before the Quiet Revolution [1960–6], the Québécois generally shared a rural, Catholic, conservative, and patriarchal conception of the good. Today, after a

period of liberalization, most people have abandoned this traditional way of life, and Québécois society now exhibits all the diversity that any modern society contains . . . to be a Québécois today, therefore, simply means being a participant in the francophone society of Quebec (Kymlicka, 1995: 87).

In the absence of an adequate theorisation of culture it is not clear whether the example of Quebec can help us to see whether 'cultural membership' enhances or diminishes freedom. After all, the struggle within Quebec is fundamentally over language, and although the freedom of one linguistic community is threatened by the other, the capacity to use language, whether it is French or English, is fundamental to human autonomy. Other dimensions of culture, such as religion, may not contain the same freedom-enhancing potential. Quebec shows that a culture *can* be liberal, but it does not establish that a culture is *necessarily* liberal.

Kymlicka argues that individuals should have rights to cultural membership. Rights are central to a liberal polity, and for the purposes of this discussion we can define a right as an advantage held against another (or others). Kymlicka distinguishes between three different types of right: self-government rights, polyethnic rights, and special representation rights. Self-government rights usually entail the devolution of power to a political unit 'substantially controlled by the members of an ethnic minority' (Kymlicka, 1995: 30). Examples of polyethnic rights would be state funding of 'cultural institutions' and exemptions from certain policies, such as those relating to the slaughter of animals (Kymlicka, 1995: 31). Special representation rights are intended to ensure the fair representation of minority groups (Kymlicka, 1995: 32). Each of these types of rights, but especially the first two, can take the form of an 'internal restriction' or an 'external protection' (Kymlicka, 1995: 35–44). Kymlicka maintains that empirical evidence shows most campaigns for cultural recognition take the form of a demand for external protections from wider society, rather than restricting the freedom of the members of that culture, and so are compatible with liberalism (Kymlicka, 1995: 38–40). The basic problem is that rights are a specific cultural form, and the effects of rights on a culture depend on how one conceptualises culture. If cultures are integral patterns (Benedict; Kroeber) then rights may well upset those patterns. If, on the other hand, we conceive culture(s) as overlapping semiotic relationships (Geertz) then we have a different problem: rights imply a uniform legal system and yet a semiotic theory of culture suggests that interpretation may be relativistic.

Constitutional Diversity (James Tully)

Tully's work has the virtue of making explicit its anthropological and philosophical presuppositions: from anthropology he defends the semiotic theory of Geertz against what he calls the 'stages' – that is, evolutionary – theory of nineteenth-century 'imperialists', and from philosophy he draws on Ludwig Wittgenstein's later language theory.

Constitutional uniformity (or modern constitutionalism) is the object of Tully's attack, and modern political thinkers are (largely) its proponents. Modern constitutionalism stresses sovereignty, regularity and uniformity, and this contrasts with the implied rejection of sovereignty and the irregularity and pluralism of 'ancient constitutionalism'. Although there are notable exceptions, Tully maintains that the process of colonisation entailed the confrontation of these two forms of constitutionalism, and contemporary cultural conflicts in, for example, the Americas have their roots in the imposition of an alien constitutional form on Native Americans (Tully, 1995: 34). This imperial legacy is still with us, not simply in political practice, but also in political theory. Writers such as Rawls and Kymlicka, while arguing for cultural diversity, do so in the language of modern constitutionalism (Tully, 1995: 44).

Drawing on Geertz and Wittgenstein, Tully contrasts two models of intercultural communication (he prefers the term 'interculturalism' to multiculturalism). The first requires shared terms of reference – so, for example, we might disagree about what rights people have, but we implicitly assume that rights have certain features (Tully, 1995: 85). The second is based on 'family resemblances' between cultures: we find common ground not through an implicitly agreed, shared language, but by a piecemeal case-by-case agreement, based on affinities between our different cultural traditions (Tully, 1995: 120). This suggests that constitutional formation cannot be understood from an abstract standpoint, such as Rawls's original position. And Europeans have resources within their own culture(s) to engage in such case-by-case communication; English Common Law is an example of an ancient constitution, and Tully considers it significant that there were examples of interaction between Europeans and Native Americans based on recognition of the *affinities* between their legal systems.

Tully's argument, while interesting and provocative, has a number of weaknesses. First, there is a tension between his espousal of a semiotic theory of culture, which stresses looseness of cultural boundaries, and his talk of 12,000 'diverse cultures, governments and environmental practices' struggling for recognition (Tully, 1995: 3) (he provides no source for that figure) and '15,000 cultures who demand recognition' (Tully, 1995: 8) (again, no source). To count something you have to identify it, and identification implies 'hard boundaries'. Second, he says very little about how cultural conflicts can be mediated in the contemporary world, despite the underlying purpose of his work being to show the relevance of ancient constitutionalism. It is not clear what institutional forms would express cultural diversity, especially for geographically dispersed minorities. Third, and most important, he fails to address the charge that protection of culture can have detrimental consequences for individual freedom. He does maintain that culture is the basis of self-respect, such that to be denied recognition is a serious thing, but he offers only metaphorical observations to support the claim that interculturalism is not a threat to individual freedom (Tully, 1995: 189).

An Overlapping Consensus (John Rawls)

We have encountered Rawls's work in previous chapters. The focus there was on his first book, *A Theory of Justice* (1972). In a later book, *Political Liberalism* (first published 1993), Rawls engages in a critique of the earlier work, arguing that it did not fully account for the 'fact of reasonable pluralism'. The idea that principles of justice are generated from a moral standpoint occupied by autonomous moral agents is a form of comprehensive liberalism, and as such is controversial. Reasonable people can deny that human beings are autonomous, or that political values derive from such autonomy. As the title of his later book indicates, what he came to defend was a *political*, rather than a *comprehensive*, liberalism.

Rawls lists a number of features of human interaction that explain why reasonable people can disagree: evidence is conflicting and complex; different weights can be attached to different considerations; concepts are vague; there are conflicts between different moral considerations, such as duties to family and duties to strangers; no society can contain a full range of values. He then goes on to define a 'reasonable conception of the good':

1. It entails the exercise of theoretical reason.
2. It entails the exercise of practical reason.
3. 'While a reasonable comprehensive view is not necessarily fixed and unchanging, it normally belongs to, or draws upon, a tradition of thought and doctrine'. It is not subject to 'sudden and unexplained changes, it tends to evolve slowly in the light of what, from its point of view, it sees as good and sufficient conditions' (Rawls, 1993: 59).

From the idea of reasonable pluralism Rawls offers an explanation of how citizens, from a variety of different reasonable comprehensive conceptions of the good can come to respect liberal political institutions. We develop an 'overlapping consensus': it is for citizens as part of their liberty of conscience individually to work out how liberal values relate to their own comprehensive conceptions, where a 'comprehensive conception' could be a religious belief system. Each reasonable comprehensive doctrine endorses the political conception from its own standpoint. Individuals work towards liberal principles from mutually incompatible comprehensive perspectives, and respect for those principles is built on the overlap between them.

Rawls does not give concrete examples of how such an overlapping consensus can be achieved, so to illustrate his argument we provide an example of our own: how might Muslims embrace, from *within* their comprehensive conception of the good, liberal political principles? Some possible grounds are as follows:

• Islam has a long history of toleration of Jews and Christians, grounded in the belief that Islam is an aboriginal and natural form of monotheism, which incorporates the prophets of the Jews and the Christians.

• So long as secular law is not incompatible with holy law (*sharia*), then the former should be obeyed. There are arguments in Islam for obeying secular rulers.

• *Jihad* (exertion, struggle) has been misinterpreted: a believer is required to carry out *jihad* by 'his heart; his tongue; his hands; and by the sword'. *Jihad* can be an individual, spiritual struggle.

• 'Islam' is often defined as 'submission' or 'self-surrender'. Submission understood as self-imposed discipline is not incompatible with respect for human freedom – a person might *choose* to submit.

- For Muslims, behaviour is classified as: (a) required – includes prayer, alms-giving, fasting; (b) prohibited – theft, illicit sex, alcohol consumption; (c) recommended – charitable acts, additional prayers and fasts; (d) discouraged – might include unilateral declarations of divorce by men; (e) morally indifferent. From the perspective of respect for secular law, only (b) might raise difficulties – but much will depend on what penalties are imposed for prohibited acts.

- Requirements on women to cover themselves can be interpreted as symbolic – in the Arab–Islamic world there is huge variation in what is required of women. Men are also required to be 'modest'.

Each of these points can be contested, but it is at least plausible to argue that Muslims can be *politically* liberal. Other citizens – Christians, Jews, Hindus, atheists and so on – will, of course, produce different lists of reasons for endorsing liberal principles. The task is not to agree on a set of reasons – reasonable people will always disagree – but to converge on a set of institutions from diverse standpoints.

The Argument so Far

The four theories discussed above raise a number of important issues in political theory:

1. Is cultural diversity intrinsically valuable, or simply the result of tolerating other belief-systems and ways of life? A concrete illustration of the difference between these two positions can be seen in education policy: some schools with a culturally diverse catchment area seek to be inclusive by getting pupils to celebrate all the major religious festivals. Here diversity seems to be valued as an end. On the other hand, many religions seek to establish or preserve faith schools; insofar as the state supports such schools cultural diversity appears here as toleration.

2. Should rights be accorded to individuals or groups? If culture is valuable then treating it as an individual good may undermine its integrity. If the rights are held by groups rather than individuals then there are significant implications for individual freedom: a religious group might, for example, coerce its members into remaining adherents. Kymlicka argues strongly against such coercion, but Tully is much less clear about the 'rights' of groups – although he deliberately avoids using the language of rights.

3. The various theories raise questions about the nature of the human person, or self: who are we? What constitutes our nature? Does it make sense to talk of the individual (person, self) as something existing independently of their culture, or is the individual essentially constituted by that culture? Kymlicka stresses independence. Rawls, in the later work which we discussed above wants to avoid any controversial claims about the nature of the person. Waldron argues for cultural embeddedness but with 'fluidity', and Tully seems to reject an idea of an independent, 'pre-cultural', self.

4. What are the implications for equality of the various theories? Critics, such as Brian Barry, argue that multiculturalism is both a distraction from the pursuit of traditional egalitarian policies, and actually undermines equality (Barry, 2001: 24). Defenders of multiculturalism, on the other hand, argue for a 'difference-sensitive equality'. The relationship between gender and culture provides an excellent test case both for the implications for equality of multiculturalism, and for the other issues raised above – the source of value, the status of rights, and the nature of the self – and it is to that relationship that we now turn.

Multiculturalism and Feminism

Is multiculturalism bad for women? Many feminists think so, but before outlining their objections it is important to acknowledge the affinities between the two ideologies. First, both stress the importance of recognising difference, and criticise liberalism for advancing an empty, characterless conception of the human agent. Second, while both stress difference, there are many feminists and multiculturalists who argue against essentialism – women's experiences and cultural experiences are not homogeneous: difference should not be defined in binary terms as them and us. Experience is heterogeneous. Third, at a more practical political level, feminism and multiculturalism pose the two main challenges to class-based politics, and thus to the traditional or classical ideologies of liberalism and socialism.

Despite these parallels it is not difficult to come up with – sometimes quite shocking – examples of the oppression of women in the name of culture (or the protection of culture). We present some below. All are drawn from minority practices in Western societies, but it is important to distinguish how a multiculturalist might defend the practice: (a) as a 'permission', meaning that the practice should not be prohibited by law; (b) as prohibited but where in law a person might raise a cultural defence in mitigation; (c) where the practice should be illegal, and the cultural defence not apply, but where a person would not be prosecuted for procuring something abroad (see forced marriage and female circumcision):

- *Polygamy:* the right of the husband to have more than one wife is not mirrored by the right of women to have more than one husband. The wives of a husband are often seriously materially disadvantaged and many women regard the practice as humiliating. (Polygamy is illegal in most Western societies but a cultural defence may be applied.)
- *Forced marriage:* this practice contradicts a fundamental right to order your private life by choosing your own partner. It is also the case that the daughter is often very young – 12 or 13 – and the prospective husband much older – in his 20s or 30s.
- *Female circumcision* (also known as genital mutilation; clitoridectomy): this is practised in 25 countries and affects eight million women worldwide. It is illegal in every Western country, but women who send their daughters abroad for such an operation are often not prosecuted.
- *Male violence:* it is, of course, a criminal offence for a man to inflict violence on his wife or children. However, there have been cases in several Western countries where the sentence passed has been less severe because the man has used a cultural defence, especially where the behaviour of the wife or daughter has been perceived to bring dishonour onto the family.
- *Access to resources:* there are cases of immigrant women being discouraged from gaining access to the resources enjoyed by the majority culture. One justification for making the acquisition of English a requirement of British citizenship is that men can no longer prevent their wives from acquiring language skills.

- *Segregation justified on religious grounds:* religious groups – including the Christian churches – are exempt from certain kinds of anti-discrimination legislation. This exclusion is often extended to educational establishments, where girls are not educated in the same way as boys.
- *Dress:* as we suggested in the case study at the head of this chapter there has been a big debate about whether Muslim girls should be allowed to wear the *hijab* in French schools. Such a measure would seem benign, but some women argue that by not permitting it the state is providing girls with a degree of autonomy, and protection from their families.

The Feminist Case against Multiculturalism (Susan Okin)

Susan Okin argues that multiculturalism is bad for women. She begins her critique by defining her terms. Feminism is 'the belief that women should not be disadvantaged by their sex, that they should be recognized as having human dignity equal to that of men, and that they should have the opportunity to live as fulfilling and as freely chosen lives as men' (Okin, 1999: 10). Multiculturalism is, she suggests, harder to 'pin down', but:

[partly consists in] the claim, made in the context of basically liberal democracies, that minority cultures or ways of life are not sufficiently protected by the practice of ensuring the individual rights of their members, and as a consequence these should also be protected through special *group* rights or privileges (Okin, 1999: 10–11, her emphasis).

Okin argues that cultures are not monoliths, but contain internal differences, one of the most important of which is the difference of gender. The problem is that in liberal societies culture is treated as part of the private sphere. This requires correction, and once corrected we have to face up to two important connections between gender and culture. First, the sphere of personal, sexual and reproductive life functions as a central focus of most cultures. Cultural groups are often particularly concerned with family law issues – divorce, child custody, family property and inheritance. Such a focus has a differential impact on boys/men and girls/women. Second, most cultures – by which Okin actually means *religions* – have as one of their principal aims the male control of women (patriarchy):

Consider, for example, the founding myths of Greek and Roman antiquity, and of Judaism, Christianity, and Islam: they are rife with attempts to justify the control and subordination of women. These myths consist of a combination of denials of women's role in reproduction; appropriations by men of the power to reproduce themselves; characterizations of women as overly emotional, untrustworthy, evil, or sexually dangerous; and refusals to acknowledge mothers' rights over the dispositions of their children (Okin, 1999: 13).

Okin argues that whilst discrimination and gender-stereotyping exist in Western liberal democracies, the worst forms of discrimination have been removed – at least at the level of law. Women from minority cultures in Western societies should not be denied the rights enjoyed by the majority culture.

Responses to Okin

Okin's critique of multiculturalism generated a significant debate and responses to her essay are contained in the book *Is Multiculturalism Bad for Women?* (Okin's essay is the first in the book). Below we explore the most interesting of the responses to Okin from that book, but supplemented by Gita Sahgal's *Refusing Holy Orders*, and Bhiku Parekh's *Rethinking Multiculturalism*. We are not necessarily endorsing all (or any) of these counter-arguments; rather, our aim is to stimulate debate.

1. *Valid and invalid cultural defences.* If we are studying minority cultural practices, then it is important that we are sensitive to the context, and this can work both for and against Okin, although in both cases she can be criticised for being insensitive to context. As Katha Pollitt argues, if a man murders his wife because he believes she has been unfaithful, and then appeals to 'his culture' as mitigation, we can reasonably ask the question – is he telling the truth? Are men allowed to do this 'back home' (Pollitt, 1999: 28–9)? Even if they are, is shame the same concept when your culture is in the majority as against being in a minority? Furthermore, if we take Shari'ah as the legal basis for the cultural defence, the 'right' of the husband to kill his wife is based on a conception of law which is grounded in equivalence, such that even if a man is permitted to carry out a sentence, he must be authorised by a court. In addition, Shari'ah requires a high level of proof. In conclusion, the murder is not a cultural act because the background structure which would make it such an act is absent. Multiculturalists are not, contrary to what Okin claims, committed to defending the husband in this case.

2. *Source material.* Related to the last point, Okin culls her examples from criminal cases in the United States. As Homi Bhabha argues, this distorts the cultural context because 'cultural information' is being used for very specific ends (Bhabha, 1999: 81). Furthermore, the forum is alien to those cultural practices. Okin uses concepts, such as patriarchy, without respect for the context. Her treatment of religion can similarly be criticised. When discussing clitoridectomy she cites an interview in the *New York Times* as authoritative. Obviously, Okin is only one writer, but her style of argument *typifies* much discussion of multiculturalism by those critical of it: the use of inappropriate sources reveals a serious failure to engage with the context of behaviour.

3. *Is multiculturalism bad for women?* There are two approaches to the relationship between gender and culture. You could argue that culture is *especially bad* for women, and not just quantitatively but qualitatively – that is, culture is gendered – or you could maintain that culture is bad *for everyone*. The second argument might seem a bizarre defence of multiculturalism, but it could be used in order to move to a more sophisticated idea of the relationship between culture and gender. Take the example of circumcision. Boys are also circumcised: is male circumcision 'genital mutilation'? We need to consider the reasons for male circumcision: medical grounds in specific cases (everywhere), on general medical grounds (particularly in the USA), and on ritual/religious grounds. Female circumcision takes three forms (see Parekh, 2006: 275–6) of which two are not equivalent to male circumcision. What reasons are given for

these practices? Control of sexuality dominates reasoning, but then the great monotheistic religions have all been concerned with controlling sexuality, and not just of women, but also male sexuality. However, there is no doubt that – viewed from a liberal perspective of gender-blindness – women 'suffer' more than men. The question is whether it is valid to reduce culture to patriarchy.

4. *Western(ised) women*. Okin contrasts the imperfect, but basically sound, attitude to gender amongst the liberal mainstream with the deeply patriarchal attitude to women in most non-Western societies. However, it could be argued that this rests on – to use a hackneyed phrase – ethnocentrism. Women's advantages among the liberal majority are defined in terms of legal rights. These are important, but an emphasis on rights ignores the background culture of Western societies, which is based on commodification and exchange: is being a culturally sexualised object of the male gaze a liberating experience? The argument might be that at least Western(ised) women have a choice: they are free to dress how they like, marry whom they like, and choose to have children or not. Furthermore, violent husbands can be prosecuted without appeal to a cultural defence, or the victimised wife being cast out of her community. This may be true, but then it undermines part of Okin's critique of non-Western cultures, namely, that we should see them as the transmitters of patriarchal attitudes. If we are going to take a 'whole culture' view of non-Western cultures – that is, study their informal as well as their formal practices – then the same standards should apply to Western culture. Parekh observes that Muslim girls in France and Netherlands chose to wear the *hijab* in part to reassure their conservative parents that they would not be corrupted by the liberal culture of secular schools, and partly to indicate to both Muslim and non-Muslim boys that they are not available.

5. *Experience*. Okin makes some rather patronising remarks about older women. She argues – quite rightly – that cultural recognition gives power to certain people, usually older men, and that intercultural communication should involve asking women what they think, but she then says that it should be 'younger women' because 'older women often are co-opted into reinforcing gender inequality' (Okin, 1999: 24). This raises big questions about who has the right to speak, and whether an individual is always the best judge of their own interests. Okin seems to be following in the Marxist tradition of attributing false consciousness to women, but this contradicts one of the major components of the feminist movement: namely, to ask women what they want. Furthermore, feminists stress that white, Western, middle-class women should not assume that their voice is identical to that of, say, black, working-class, non-Western women.

6. *Religion*. Gita Sahgal has studied women's resistance to religious fundamentalism, and observed that some women went on to reject their religious upbringing, whilst others reaffirmed it, as illustrated by these three women:

> I used to be a very good religious wife, as was expected of me. I was deeply religious and had a shrine in my room at which I used to worship. When I decided after much praying, to leave my husband, I couldn't stand it anymore. I took the shrine outside and threw it away. I can no longer believe. I can't go to the temple anymore. My children go with their friends because they have fun, but I don't.

A Muslim woman will observe what is expected of her. She will pray five times a day and fast at Ramadan. But she will no longer be the slave of man.

I am proud to be a Muslim. I have become a Muslim to a much deeper extent since I left home. But now it is not imposed on me (Sahgal, 1992: 193).

The point is that these responses are unpredictable, but underlying Okin's critique is a reductionist view of religion. Because she has defined it as patriarchal – down to what she calls its 'founding myths' – she is incapable of recognising how women who define themselves as liberated might reaffirm their religion.

Despite these criticisms Okin is quite right to argue that minority cultures focus their self-defence very strongly on the private, domestic sphere. For example, the cultural defence that Islam prohibits the charging of interest on money is never used when somebody is in court for failure to pay off his credit card. The fact is that the domestic sphere is conservative in all societies, but what makes minority cultures appear especially conservative is that they are cut off from the wider structure of social institutions.

Conclusion: Head Scarves and Women's Rights

We have presented a number of theories of multiculturalism: considering how the insights from these theories – and the reactions to those theories – might be applied to the controversy of the *hijab* is an effective way of drawing out both the philosophical bases and political implications of multiculturalism. We organise our concluding reflections around a number of themes:

(a) *Agency and identity* We argued in the section on Multiculturalism and the Politics of Identity that multiculturalists draw on the liberal conception of the human agent as a free being capable of shaping his or her identity, but criticise liberals for offering an 'empty' or 'a-cultural' conception of human agency. To varying degrees, the thinkers discussed in the previous section offer what they claim is an improved model of human identity and human agency. The *hijab* represents the outward sign not only of Muslim identity, but a gendered Muslim identity. In wearing the *hijab* a woman distinguishes herself as a woman from other women. Whether or not this is a good thing we explored in the section on culture and gender.

(b) *Culture versus rationality* If culture is something we are born into and take for granted, then reason, which entails conscious evaluation and criticism, would appear hostile to culture. Again, insofar as liberalism stresses a rationalist approach to politics it is perceived as hostile to multiculturalism. Much of the work of multiculturalists is concerned with reconciling culture and reason. Although they offer very different conceptions of reason, for Tully, Rawls and Kymlicka the way we reason about just institutions is central to their defence of multiculturalism. Defenders of the French ban argue that the French state is giving young Muslim women the space in which they can make judgements about their religious identity and beliefs; such a defence presupposes that it is possible to stand back from your culture and evaluate it.

(c) *Freedom* Whereas liberals tend to discuss freedom in abstract terms, exemplified by charters of fundamental freedoms, multiculturalists contextualise freedom. Certainly many of the thinkers we have discussed defend the traditional liberal freedoms, but they also argue that liberalism can be intolerant, and it is most often intolerant when it claims to be defending freedom. For example, Muslim women 'forced' to wear the *hijab* may claim that Western, non-Muslim women are not free if they are continually the object of the male sexualised gaze. Of course this claim can be challenged, especially when Muslim women are indeed forced to wear the *hijab*, but the claim is at least provocative: freedom is enjoyed *in a cultural context*. You can be formally free but oppressed by social mores.

(d) *Difference and equality* Both feminists and multiculturalists have forced liberals to re-evaluate their idea of equality. For liberals, human beings are morally equal, and that moral equality translates into a certain political equality, and a rather limited material equality. Men and women, as well as different cultural groups, may be morally equal, but they are still different – how we translate that conjunction of equality in difference into political principles and political institutions is a major challenge. The French state has made a judgement in favour of secular equality, whereas defenders of the *hijab* argue for equality in difference.

Summary

Multiculturalism emerged in the 1960s as a distinct area of academic debate, and over the following decades the language of cultural diversity supplanted that of race and religion. Given the dominance of liberalism as an ideology, much discussion in the field of multiculturalism has revolved around the relationship between liberalism and multiculturalism, with the two standing in a complex relationship to one another. Multiculturalists reaffirm the values of freedom and equality but rearticulate these as equality in difference, and freedom in context. Although there are continuities with earlier debates over religious difference and toleration – debates that dominated political discourse in the seventeenth and eighteenth centuries – multiculturalism cannot be understood as simply a return to these earlier disputes, rather it is post-liberal, in the sense that it has absorbed the liberal emphasis on human self-expression, but challenges liberals to provide a more adequate understanding of self-expression, one that places much greater emphasis on cultural identity.

Questions

1. Does treating people equally mean treating them in the same way? Can you think of situations in which cultural difference may be a legitimate basis for difference in treatment?

2. Is it possible to pick and mix cultural traits?

3. Is separatism the only way to respect cultural difference?

4. Is multiculturalism bad for women?

References

Barry, B. (2001) *Culture and Equality: an Egalitarian Critique of Multiculturalism* Cambridge: Polity Press.

Bhabha, H. (1999) 'Liberalism's Sacred Cow', in S. Okin *et al. Is Multiculturalism Bad for Women?* Princeton, NJ: Princeton University Press.

Choudhury, T. (2007) *The Role of Muslim Identity Politics in Radicalisation* (a study in progress) London: Department for Communities and Local Government, available at: http://www.communities.gov.uk/documents/communities/pdf/452628.pdf.

Geertz, C. (1993) *The Interpretation of Cultures: Selected Essays* London: Fontana.

Kymlicka, W. (1989) *Liberalism, Community, and Culture* Oxford: Clarendon Press.

Kymlicka, W. (1995) *Multicultural Citizenship* Oxford: Clarendon Press.

Macdonald, L. (1977) *Race Relations: The New Law* London: Butterworth.

Malinowski, B. (1965) *A Scientific Theory of Culture, and Other Essays* Chapel Hill, NC: North Carolina University Press.

Mill, J.S. (1991) *On Liberty and other essays* (ed. J. Gray) Oxford: Oxford University Press.

Okin, S. (1999) *Is Multiculturalism Bad for Women?* J. Cohen, M. Howard and M. Nussbaum Princeton, NJ: Princeton University Press.

Parekh, B. (2006) *Rethinking Multiculturalism: Cultural Diversity and Political Theory*, 2nd edn Basingstoke: Palgrave Macmillan.

Pollitt, K. (1999) 'Whose Culture', in S. Okin *et al. Is Multiculturalism Bad for Women?* Princeton, NJ: Princeton University Press.

Ramadan, T. (2005) *Western Muslims and the Future of Islam* New York: Oxford University Press.

Rawls, J. (1972) *A Theory of Justice* Oxford: Clarendon Press.

Rawls, J. (1993) *Political Liberalism*, pbk edn New York: Columbia University Press.

Rushdie, S. (1988) *The Satanic Verses* London: Viking.

Sahgal, G. (1992) 'Secular Spaces: The Experience of Asian Women Organizing' in G. Sahgal and N. Yuval-Davis, *Refusing Holy Orders: Women and Fundamentalism in Britain* London: Virago Press, 169–97.

Sharpe, E. (1983) *Understanding Religion* London: Duckworth.

Taylor, C. (1994) 'The Politics of Recognition', in A. Gutmann (ed.), *Multiculturalism: Examining the Politics of Recognition* Princeton, NJ: Princeton University Press.

Tully, J. (1995) *Strange Multiplicity: Constitutionalism in an Age of Diversity* Cambridge: Cambridge University Press.

Waldron, J. (1995) 'Minority Cultures and the Cosmopolitan Alternative', in W. Kymlicka *The Rights of Minority Cultures* Oxford: Oxford University Press, 93–119.

Further Reading

A general book on the importance of culture in people's lives is Michael Carrithers, *Why Humans have Cultures: Explaining Anthropology and Social Diversity* (Oxford: Oxford University Press, 1992). Two fairly straightforward discussions of culture are provided by Geertz (1993) – read the first essay in the book – and Benedict (1935), Chapters 1–3. On religion, read Sharpe (1983). On the historical development of multiculturalism – or the 'politics of recognition' – read Taylor (1994). For various competing theories of multiculturalism you should read Waldron (1995); Tully (1995); Rawls (1993); Said (1991); see also

Jürgen Habermas, 'Struggles for Recognition in the Democratic Constitutional State', in A. Gutmann (ed.) *Multiculturalism: Examining the Politics of Recognition* (Princeton, NJ: Princeton University Press, 1995) and other essays in that volume.

Weblinks

Websites on multiculturalism – especially those originating from the United States – tend to be highly polemical. Nonetheless, they do provide a flavour of the passions aroused by the multiculturalism debate.

A right-wing libertarian website against multiculturalism is:
http://multiculturalism.aynrand.org/

Kenan Malik attacks multiculturalism from a Marxist perspective:
http://www.kenanmalik.com/essays/against_mc.html

UNESCO have an online journal, *International Journal on Multicultural Societies:*
http://www.unesco.org/most/jmshome.htm

A discussion of the Canadian Multiculturalism Act:
http://laws.justice.gc.ca/en/C-18.7/

Chapter 16

Ecologism

Introduction

Ecologism has only emerged as a fully fledged ideology since the 1960s. As with all recent ideologies it has intellectual roots stretching back centuries, but the construction of a relatively autonomous set of ideas and prescriptions for action is a very recent occurrence. Ecologism should be distinguished from environmentalism – for environmentalists, the desire to protect the environment is based primarily on concern about the consequences of environmental degradation on human beings, whereas for ecologists, something called 'ecology', or 'nature', is the source of value. It follows from this distinction that whereas environmentalism can be combined with other ideologies, ecologism is distinct. In terms of political practice, politicians from across the political spectrum have embraced the rhetoric, and sometimes the policies, of environmentalism.

Chapter Map

In this chapter we will:

- Distinguish ecologism from environmentalism.

- Outline the so-called 'ecological crisis'.

- Explain how environmentalism and ecologism might fit with other ideologies.

- Discuss the thought of two ecologists: Aldo Leopold and Arne Næss.

- Discuss the arguments of one – controversial – environmentalist: Garrett Hardin.

- Advance a critique of ecologism.

Nuclear Power? Yes Please!

Source: © Lloyd Cluff/CORBIS

In the 1980s plastered on cars and on lapel badges was the German slogan around a smiley 'sun' face: 'Atomkraft? Nein Danke' ('Nuclear Power? No Thanks'). Central to the German Green movement – and virtually all Green movements – is the rejection of nuclear power as expensive, dangerous, and inextricably linked to the nuclear weapons industry. It therefore came as a shock to many Green activists when one of its leading theorists, James Lovelock – the man who had coined the word 'Gaia' to describe the mutual dependence of all life forms – came out in favour of nuclear power. Lovelock argued that the threat from global warming is now so great that 'nuclear power is the only green solution' (*Independent*, 24 May 2004). The 'great Earth system' – Gaia – is, he says, 'trapped in a vicious circle of positive feedback': extra heat from any source is amplified and its effects are more than additive. This means that we have little time left to act. The Kyoto Protocol, which aimed to cut omissions, is simply a cosmetic attempt 'to hide the political embarrassment of global warming'. If we had 50 years to solve the problem then it might be possible to switch from fossil fuels to 'renewables' such as wind and tide power, but realistically those sources will only make a negligible contribution to the world's energy needs over the next 20 or so years. There is, Lovelock claims, only one immediately available source of energy which does not contribute to global warming and that is nuclear power. Opposition to nuclear power is based on an 'irrational fear fed by Hollywood-style fiction, the Green lobbies and the media'. These fears are, according to Lovelock, unjustified: 'we must stop worrying about minuscule risks from radiation and recognize that a third of us will die from cancer, mainly because we breathe air laden with "that all pervasive carcinogen, oxygen"'.

- Is Lovelock right? (for background information on nuclear power see Weblinks)

Ecologism or Environmentalism?

Of the four chapters on new ideologies in this book, this one has proved to be the most difficult for which to find an appropriate title. As we saw in Chapter 14, while there are feminisms the general label 'feminism' is broadly accepted by radical, socialist and liberal feminists. At least three possibilities suggest themselves for this chapter – ecologism, environmentalism and green (or Green) thought – and these differing possibilities carry distinct ideological implications. In the view of those who call themselves ecologists, environmentalism denotes an attitude compatible with almost all the competing ideologies. Environmentalists attach value to the 'environment' or 'nature' but only in relation to human consciousness and human concerns, and as such the environment is slotted in as a subordinate component of alternative ideologies, such as liberalism, socialism or feminism. Environmentalism is anthropocentric – that is, human-centred. Ecologists, on the other hand, assert that nature has intrinsic value, and that the task of ecologism is to engage in a critique of the anthropocentric world-view, which in socio-economic terms manifests itself as industrialism. Ecologism is eco-centred. This does not mean that ecologists do not embrace values and perspectives derived from other ideologies, but rather those perspectives are assessed from the standpoint of the eco-system, or earth, as an irreducible and interdependent system. Whereas environmentalists share a post-Enlightenment belief in the uniqueness of the human perspective on the world – that is, they place human beings above, or outside, nature – ecologists challenge that philosophical position, maintaining that human life only has value insofar as it is a 'knot' in the 'net' of life, a net which connects together not only non-human animals, but non-sentient entities, such as trees, rivers and mountains. Indeed it is the net rather than the knots that is of ultimate value.

Students of politics are most likely to have encountered the political face of the green movement rather than be aware of the underlying philosophical differences within environmentalism, and one of our aims in this chapter will be to connect the philosophical ideas to the political movements (we discuss the rise of the Green movement in the section on green politics). The links are less direct than some writers on environmentalism recognise. To illustrate this, consider the idea of an environmental crisis (discussed in the section of the same name). Many people maintain that industrialisation, urbanisation and population growth have either brought about, or threaten to bring about, irreversible changes to the natural environment such that the future of life on earth beyond more than one or two hundred years is in jeopardy. Some writers maintain that the difference between ecologism and environmentalism rests, in part, on attitudes to the seriousness of this crisis, with ecologists being very pessimistic, and environmentalists being more optimistic. There is some validity in this characterisation of the differing attitudes, in that ecologists maintain that the causes of the crisis are not simply scientific–technical; the roots of the crisis lie in human attitudes to nature – we see nature as a resource to be exploited for our benefit. However, a human-centred approach to the environment could also explain the crisis; without condemning human attitudes to nature it could be argued that environmental degradation is the collective consequence of rational individual behaviour. Microbiologist and environmental theorist Garrett Hardin argued that overpopulation will have catastrophic consequences, and that food aid to the developing world should be ended so that population levels can be allowed to fall 'naturally' (his argument is discussed later in this chapter). Hardin is often thought of as an ecologist, and his misanthropic argument is used against ecologism, but, in fact, Hardin reasons from straightforwardly human-centred premises: human beings will suffer from overpopulation.

Although ecologism (also called 'deep ecology') is the primary focus of this chapter, we will also discuss environmentalism. We will consider how environmentalism can be a strand in almost all the other ideologies discussed in this book, and why environmental concerns now play such a significant part in the politics not only of the West, but also the East. The reason is obvious: there is a consensus that humanity faces an environmental crisis, and that later in this century many other social and political problems – above all, war and famine – will have their root causes in the negative environmental changes brought about human beings. We begin by considering this environmental crisis.

Environmental Crisis

Most popular discussion of environmentalism – and ecologism – takes place within the context of a discussion of the so-called 'environmental crisis'. The first point to note is the singularity of the phrase: there is a crisis. This is controversial, for it may be that there is a series of distinct environmental problems. However, virtually all ecologists, and many environmentalists, argue that these problems are interconnected, and a coherent engagement with the environment must recognise this fact. Among the specific environmental problems are the following:

- *Global warming* This is acknowledged by most, but not all, scientists as the most serious environmental problem facing the planet – the minority who challenge the consensus do not question the evidence of global warming, but question its causes, arguing that warming is not primarily caused by human activity. However, the majority of scientists do believe that humans are largely responsible for global warming. The earth's temperature is maintained by the 'greenhouse effect' – a layer of gases in the atmosphere traps a small percentage of the sun's radiation – but the burning of fossil fuels increases the greenhouse effect, with the result that sea levels will rise due to the melting of the ice caps, with some fairly obvious consequences for low-lying land areas. At a certain point in the process of global warming life-forms will be threatened.

- *Resource depletion* Some resources, such as fish, are, with careful stewardship, naturally replenished; other resources, such as coal and gas, are not. Both types of resource are threatened by excessive demand and so overproduction (this raises the question of the 'tragedy of the commons', discussed in the section on Garrett Hardin).

- *Localised pollution* This may not cause a global crisis, but poor air in places such as Mexico City can have a debilitating effect on inhabitants.

- *Decline in species* Although the effects of species loss – or decline in biodiversity – are unclear, many ecologists would argue that the loss of species is bad in itself, regardless of its wider impact. The use of agricultural chemicals and the genetic modification of crops are identified by some environmentalists as the cause of the decline in biodiversity.

- *Nuclear war* This will not, of course, be a direct environmental problem unless nuclear weapons are actually used (although nuclear weapons testing has had environmental consequences). In the 1980s, when consciousness of the threat of nuclear war was much higher than it is today, scientists speculated that the use of intercontinental ballistic missiles could result in a 'nuclear winter': atmospheric pollution caused by dust, soot, smoke and ash would prevent the sun's rays from penetrating for a period of time long enough to eradicate most plant life and create a new ice age. Since the 1980s there has been a proliferation of states with nuclear weapons.

Students of political theory cannot be expected to be experts on the scientific causes of environmental problems, and the focus of this chapter is on the philosophical ideas behind, and ethical issues raised by, ecology, many of which can be understood without reference to the environmental crisis. However, the crisis does raise interesting questions about the relationship between science and politics. Ecologists are critical of scientific rationality, and yet employ scientific evidence to support their arguments. (We consider this apparent incoherence in our critique of ecologism.) Furthermore, while there is widespread distrust of scientists employed by multinational companies, and to a lesser extent by government agencies, scientists who speak on behalf of environmental groups enjoy a high level of trust.

Green Politics

Green political parties and movements emerged in the 1970s. In terms of political influence the most successful Green party is the German Green Party (Die Grünen/Bundnis 90). By 1982 they were represented in the parliaments of six of West Germany's regions (Länder), and they entered the Federal Parliament (Bundestag) in 1983, winning 5.6 per cent of the vote. In the following election their support rose to 8.3 per cent, and other parties began to adopt environmental policies. However, during the 1980s it became clear that there was a major schism between Realos (realists) and Fundis (fundamentalists); the former wanted power within the existing political system, while the latter challenged that system. Opposed to German unification in 1990, the Greens fell below the 5 per cent of the vote required for seats in the Bundestag (although their Eastern equivalent – Bundnis 90 – won 6 per cent of the Eastern vote, and thus seats). The internal dispute within the party was won by the Realos and the party – now in alliance with Bundnis 90 – grew in strength through the 1990s. Between 1998 and 2005 the Greens were in coalition with the Social Democrats at federal – national – level.

The German Greens, as with other European Green parties, draws its strength disproportionately from young, public sector middle-class workers. One explanation that is often advanced for the rise of the Green movement is the emergence of

Environmental Movements

The Green movement encompasses more than just Green political parties – conservation and environmental pressure groups are also important. Indeed, as membership of political parties declines, so the membership of pressure groups increases. Figures from Britain indicate the importance of such groups, as shown in Table 16.1.

Table 16.1

Membership (in thousands)	1971	1991	1997	2002
Royal Society for the Protection of Birds	278	2,152	2,489	3,000
World Wide Fund for Nature	12	227	241	320
Wildlife Trusts	64	233	310	413
Friends of the Earth	1	111	114	119

Source: http://www.statistics.gov.uk/StatBase/ssdataset.asp?vlnk=6230&Pos=3&ColRank=2&Rank=272

'post-materialist values': quality of life issues are more important than increasing income and enhanced career status. Such a view presupposes that a society has achieved a certain level of material comfort, and so the Green phenomenon may rest on a contradiction: the possibility of a Green politics depends on the generation of surplus goods and, therefore, the consumer society of which Greens are so critical.

Environmentalism and Other Ideologies

As we will suggest later in this chapter, ecologism is a distinct ideology, whereas environmentalism can be a strand in other ideologies, such as liberalism, conservatism, and socialism. Below we briefly outline possible links between the ideologies discussed in this book and environmentalism – what we are identifying are the affinities between environmentalism and the particular ideology in question. It should be stressed, however, that some of the affinities identified below also hold between *ecologism* and these other ideologies. This does not, however, undermine the claim that ecologism is distinct.

- *Liberalism.* Liberals tend to be universalists. They argue that human beings have rights independently of the culture to which they belong. Just as individuals have rights across space (culture, geography) so they have rights across time: future – that is, not-yet-existing – generations have moral claims. If we leave the world more degraded than we found it then we are violating their rights.

- *Conservatism.* At a simplistic level conservatives and environmentalists share a belief in conservation. Although conservatives focus on the preservation and transmission of cultural traditions, respect for the environment – the maintenance of a sense of place – is also important. At a deeper philosophical level conservatives share with many ecologists a scepticism towards rationality.

- *Socialism.* Environmentalists oppose the exploitation – in the pejorative sense of that word – of the natural world. Socialists oppose the exploitation of human beings. There is more than a metaphorical equivalence between socialist and environmentalist opposition to exploitation: the people most likely to suffer the consequences of environmental degradation are the poor, especially the poor in the developing world. This is often the result of a deliberate policy of 'dumping'.

- *Anarchism.* Anarchists share with some environmentalists a hostility towards authority, and some anarchists join forces with environmentalists in their opposition to what they see as the authoritarian character of globalisation. Anti-globalisation anarchists tend to stress the importance of self-sufficient communities of freely associating individuals, although this brings them closer to ecologism than environmentalism.

- *Nationalism.* Some of the concerns mentioned above – the loss of a sense of place due to globalisation – also inform nationalism, and provide a link between nationalism and environmentalism. More specifically, many nationalists are concerned with the effects on the nation of migration, which itself can be a product of both globalisation and the environmental crisis. Immigration is viewed as a threat to the cultural integrity of the nation-state.

- *Fascism.* Polemical opponents of environmentalism (and ecologism) sometimes talk of 'eco-fascists', and the links between Nazism and early twentieth-century green movements are highlighted. The idea of an organic and hierarchical order in nature is, it is claimed, mirrored in a social hierarchy. Sometimes, it is simply the perceived fanaticism of the Green movement, and its utopian desire for a clean world that motivates the charge of fascism.

- *Feminism.* The links between feminism and environmentalism (and ecologism) seem more metaphorical than real. The idea of Mother Earth implies the femininity of nature. Ideas of growth and nurturing also summon up notions of motherhood and of the mother–child relationship. In contrast, the rationalism which some environmentalists, and most ecologists, oppose is masculine. Of course, it is precisely such essentialism that many feminists oppose: the characterisation of women as nurturing and not rationalistic actually contributes to women's oppression.

- *Multiculturalism.* Multiculturalists value cultural diversity. Environmentalists and ecologists value natural diversity. As a multiculturalist might seek the preservation of a minority language, so an environmentalist seeks to preserve an endangered species. As with conservatives and nationalists the multicultural ideal of society is one where people have a 'sense of place' – where, for example, the high street (or main street) of one town is very different from another and there are not clone or identikit high streets.

- *Fundamentalism.* As with the charge of fascism it tends to be opponents of environmentalism and ecologism who draw a parallel with fundamentalism. If ecologism – rather than environmentalism – is viewed as a religion then it is not difficult to take the next step to describing it as fundamentalist. We will pursue the religious aspects of ecologism in our critique of ecologism.

It is clear that there are links and affinities between these various ideologies and both environmentalism and ecologism, but we want to argue that there is a distinctive core to ecologism which can be summed in the distinction between an anthropocentric ethic and an ecocentric ethic. We consider two important theorists of ecologism: Aldo Leopold and Arne Næss.

Aldo Leopold and the 'Land Ethic'

Aldo Leopold (1887–1948) is important as a precursor of ideological ecologism. The essence of his 'land ethic' was that 'land' was an interdependent system, and not a commodity; human beings were part of the 'land community' and not masters of it; for human beings to understand themselves they must grasp the 'whole' of which they are a 'part'; and 'a thing is right when it tends to preserve the integrity, stability, and beauty of the biotic community . . . it is wrong when it tends otherwise' (Leopold, 1987: 150). What Leopold called 'land' was what later ecologists would call the eco-system, biosphere, Gaia, 'earth' ('Spaceship Earth'), and by 'community' Leopold meant an interdependent whole, the members of which were not simply human beings, or even all sentient beings, but all the life forms.

Underlying the land ethic was a controversial philosophical claim: from observation of the empirical world human beings can derive reasons for action. This violates Hume's 'naturalistic fallacy' argument: claims about how people should behave cannot be generated from observational facts – the moral 'ought' cannot be derived from an observation of what 'is'. This is a recurrent problem with ecologism and we discuss it in more detail later. Another philosophical, or ethical, claim is that the history of morality is characterised by an expanding circle of concern, whereby we now consider the ownership of other human beings – slavery – wrong, but we have not yet expanded the circle of concern to include the land. The land ethic enlarges the boundaries of the community to include soils, waters, plants and animals. In fact Leopold links these two philosophical claims by arguing that morality has undergone an ecological evolution, suggesting that the moral ought emerges over time from a growing realisation of what is. Such evolution has its origins in:

> the tendency of interdependent individuals or groups to evolve modes of co-operation. The ecologist calls these symbioses. Politics and economics are advanced symbioses in which the original free-for-all competition has been replaced, in part, by co-operative mechanisms with an ethical content (Leopold, 1987: 143).

The extension of ethics to land is an 'evolutionary possibility and an ecological necessity'. Certainly, Leopold argues, individual thinkers have condemned the abuse of the land, but 'society' has yet to embrace the land ethic. The conservation movement is the embryo of such social affirmation. Leopold's land ethic was shaped by his experiences of state-led conservation of the 1930s and 1940s in the United States, and this led him to a salutary conclusion: respect for the land cannot be achieved if the state assumes sole moral responsibility for the environment. Rather, *individuals* must change their motivations, and this is a powerful and central claim of the ecological movement. Leopold noted that farmers were prepared to take ecologically friendly measures so long as those measures were consistent with their profit margins. He observes that the existence of obligations is taken for granted when what is at issue are better roads or schools but 'their existence is not taken for granted, nor as yet seriously discussed, in bettering the behaviour of the water that falls on the land, or in the preserving of the beauty or diversity of the farm landscape' (Leopold, 1987: 145).

A difficulty which Leopold observes in moving from dominion over the land, driven by the desire for profit, to stewardship of the land, is that many members of the land community have no economic value: 'of the 22,000 higher plants and animals native to Wisconsin, it is doubtful whether more than 5 per cent can be sold, fed, eaten, or otherwise put to economic use' (Leopold, 1987: 145). But such plants and animals have, Leopold claims, 'biotic rights'. This would seem to entail a rejection of a human-centred attitude to the environment, but it is unclear whether this is really the case, with Leopold suggesting that if a private landowner were ecologically minded he would be proud to be the custodian of an eco-system that adds 'diversity and beauty' to his farm and community (Leopold, 1987: 146). Furthermore, the assumed lack of profit in 'waste' areas has proved to be wrong, but only after the destruction of most of it.

To express the interdependence of nature Leopold uses the image of a pyramid, with a plant layer resting on the soil, an insect layer on the plants, a bird and rodent layer on the insects, and so on up through various animal groups to the apex layer, which consists of the larger carnivores. There exist lines of dependency between these layers, largely determined by the need for food and energy. Industrialisation has changed the pyramid in a number of ways. First, by reversing evolution: evolutionary change lengthened the food-chain through the emergence of more complex life forms; industrialisation shortens the chain by the elimination of both predators and of seemingly useless organisms. Second, by the exploitation, which puts geological, and other formations, to new uses, such as the generation of energy, and removes them from the 'natural chain'. Third, transportation disconnects the chain and introduces forms from one environment to a new, quite different, one, and with sometimes unintended consequences. Leopold summarises the idea of the pyramid as an energy circuit in three basic ideas:

1. Land is not merely soil.
2. Native plants and animals keep the energy circuit open; others may or may not.
3. Man-made changes are of a different order than evolutionary changes, and have effects more comprehensive than is intended or foreseen (Leopold, 1987: 148).

Leopold does not assert dogmatically that human-made changes necessarily threaten the continuation of life. He concedes that Europe has been transformed over the last two millennia, but that the 'new structure seems to function and to persist'; Europe, he concludes, has a 'resistant biota . . . its inner processes are tough, elastic, resistant to strain' (Leopold, 1987: 148). However, the correct perspective for an ecologist to adopt is global, and the earth as a whole, he maintains, is like a diseased body, where some parts seem to function well, but the whole is threatened with death. As with many ecologists, he identified population growth as a major cause of this 'disease':

> The combined evidence of history and ecology seems to support one deduction: the less violent the man-made changes, the greater the probability of successful readjustment in the pyramid. Violence, in turn, varies with human population density; a dense population requires a more violent conversion (Leopold, 1987: 149).

Conservationists fall into two groups, labelled by Leopold A and B: group A regards the land as soil and its function as a commodity, whereas group B regards the land as a biota, and its function as 'something broader', but 'how much broader is admittedly in a state of doubt and confusion' (Leopold, 1987: 149). While he may not have been aware of it, this distinction is an early statement of a divide which becomes clear after the 1960s – that between environmentalists and ecologists. Crucial to the coherence of ecologism is an explanation of that 'broader' function or value which troubled Leopold.

Arne Næss and 'Deep Ecology'

Ch. 15:
Multiculturalism
pp. 351–53

Arne Næss is credited with coining the contrasting phrases 'deep ecology' (more precisely: 'long-range deep ecology movement') and 'shallow ecology', with the spatial language intended to denote the depth of questioning of human values and reasons for action. To use John Rawls's language, deep ecology offers a comprehensive conception of the good for society and individuals, whereas shallow ecology offers a less-than-comprehensive, possibly merely political understanding of environmental values. Næss presents the idea of depth and comprehensiveness in the form of a table with four levels, with Level 1 being the most comprehensive, or 'deepest'.

Level 4	Actions	Individual behaviour
Level 3	Policies	Particular policies carried out by governmental and non-governmental agencies
Level 2	Platform principles	Packages of policies derived from an ideological standpoint or movement
Level 1	Ultimate values	Grounded in, for example, a comprehensive philosophical or religious position

Næss argues that we do not have to agree on ultimate values in order to engage in deep ecological action; there is a process of moving up and down the stages, such that action can be guided by a plurality of different sets of ultimate values. We will explore the coherence of this idea shortly, but the point to make here is that the criticism that deep ecology is intolerant because it fails to respect the pluralism which exists in a modern society is not necessarily valid. Næss's emphasis on the plurality of ultimate values was, in part, born out of his experience in creating cross-cultural peace and ecological activist movements. As Næss argues:

> ecologically responsible policies are concerned only in part with pollution and resource depletion. There are deeper concerns which touch upon principles of diversity, complexity, autonomy, decentralization, symbiosis, egalitarianism, and classlessness (Næss, 1973: 95).

What Næss sought to do was develop a set of 'platform principles' (Level 2) – in other words, a manifesto, albeit a non-dogmatic one – around which people with diverse ultimate values can unite. Below are eight principles formulated by Næss and his friend and fellow deep ecologist George Sessions while out on a hiking trip in Death Valley, California:

1. The well-being and flourishing of human and non-human life on Earth have value in themselves (synonyms: intrinsic value, inherent value). These values are independent of the usefulness of the non-human world for human purposes.
2. Richness and diversity of life forms contribute to the realisation of these values and are also values in themselves.
3. Humans have no right to reduce this richness and diversity except to satisfy vital human needs.
4. The flourishing of human life and cultures is compatible with a substantial decrease of human population. The flourishing of non-human life requires such a decrease.
5. Present human interference with the non-human world is excessive, and the situation is rapidly worsening.
6. Policies must therefore be changed. These policies affect basic economic, technological and ideological structures. The resulting state of affairs will be deeply different from the present.
7. The ideological change is mainly that of appreciating life quality (dwelling in situations of inherent value) rather than adhering to an increasingly higher standard of living. There will be a profound awareness of the difference between big and great.
8. Those who subscribe to the foregoing points have an obligation to directly or indirectly try to implement the necessary changes.

(Næss and Sessions cited in Devall and Sessions, 1985: 70)

Unlike Leopold, Næss was a trained philosopher, and so shows a greater awareness of the need for a credible philosophical basis for ecologism. Deep ecology requires an explanation of how particulars, such as individual animals, fit into the whole; Næss argues that part of the definition of an organism, such as a human being, is that it exists only in relation to something else. He uses the metaphor of the knot – a knot exists only as part of a net, and human beings are knots in the biospherical net (Næss, 1973: 95). Human beings are intrinsically valuable, but any statement of that value must make reference to the whole.

Næss accepts that any realistic form of social organisation requires some 'killing, exploitation, and suppression' (Næss, 1973: 95). However, in principle, we should be biospherical egalitarians, meaning we should have deep respect for all forms of life – to restrict that respect to human beings is to mis-recognise humans, for the value we attach to each other must depend on a full understanding of who we are – 'knots in the biospherical net'. Diversity enhances the potential for survival, and the chance of new modes of life; ecological diversity should translate into respect for cultural diversity. However, diversity must be of the right kind – diversity due to class hierarchy is incompatible with the symbiosis inherent in the biospherical net. This is important, because it is possible to read into nature hierarchy rather than equality; what Næss must, however, show is that mutual dependence really does imply equality. After all, there is a sense in which a master is dependent on his slave.

Deep ecologists, Næss argues, must fight pollution and resource depletion, and in this struggle they have found common cause with shallow ecologists, or environmentalists, but such an alliance can be dangerous because it distracts attention away from the comprehensive concerns ecologists should have. For example, if prices or taxes are increased in order to reduce pollution, then we need to know who will bear the cost – if it is the poor, then the egalitarianism implicit in the biospherical net is not being respected. Deep ecology favours 'soft' scientific research that limits disturbances to the environment, respects traditions, and is aware of our state of ignorance.

Autonomy and decentralisation are central to Næss's understanding of the forms of political organisation appropriate to deep ecology: 'the vulnerability of a form of life is roughly proportional to the weight of influences from afar, from outside the local region in which that form has obtained an ecological equilibrium' (Næss, 1973: 98). A self-sufficient community produces less pollution, and depletes fewer resources, than the existing interdependent world. Such a community is more democratic because the chain of decision-making is much shorter – if decisions are made through a chain of authorities, such as local, national and supra-national, then if those decisions are made by majority vote the chances of local interests being ignored increase with the addition of every link in the chain.

Garrett Hardin and the Ethics of the Lifeboat

Garrett Hardin was a highly influential environmentalist. Although his arguments were neither original, nor profound, there are good reasons for discussing his work. First, he was concerned with a major issue for environmentalists: population growth (a secondary, but related, issue that concerned him was immigration to the developed world from the developing world). Second, he is sometimes, and quite erroneously, labelled an ecologist, as distinct from an environmentalist, and his arguments are quoted in political debates against ecologists. Third, he challenged one of the fundamental human rights – the right to procreate – and, more generally, his work raises important questions about global justice, questions to which we return in Chapter 21.

Hardin's most famous essay was 'The Tragedy of the Commons', which was based on a presidential address delivered at a meeting of the Pacific Division of the

Ch. 8:
Liberalism
pp. 182–85

American Association for the Advancement of Science at Utah State University in June 1968. In the following 30 years it was reprinted in many collections, and Hardin himself revised it several times. The central problem is, by Hardin's own admission, not original; indeed, it is simply a statement of the prisoner's dilemma, which we discussed in Chapter 8. We are to imagine common lands on which herdsmen graze their cattle. So long as the numbers of herdsmen and cattle are low the commons will recover from the effects of grazing, new grass will grow, the cattle will be fed, and the herdsmen will make a living and so not starve. However, if the number of herdsmen and cattle grow – perhaps because population growth is no longer kept in check by war and disease – there will come a point at which the commons will not recover, and indeed deteriorate to the point where even the original low level of grazing would not be supported. As we saw in our analysis of the prisoner's dilemma, even if an individual herdsman recognises the consequences of his actions – that is, can see clearly the 'tragedy' before him – it is in his interests to continue grazing.

Hardin makes a point that appears to echo those of deep ecologists: the harm from an individual action cannot be 'pictured' – the effects may not be discernible for years, and effects are, in any case, cumulative. Such is the case with the tragedy of the commons. Morality must take into account the full effects of an action; in Hardin's words, it must be 'system sensitive'. Without questioning the validity of Hardin's argument, it is important to distinguish his 'system' from that of Leopold or Næss – the long-term effects which concern Hardin are the effects on *humanity*. Hardin's argument, while concerned with environmental degradation, is thoroughly anthropocentric.

Almost all moral and political theorists have accepted that actions have to be assessed against their full consequences, so Hardin's argument is directed much more at popular moral beliefs, rather than at previous thinkers – indeed, it is doubtful that he is aware of the heritage of the arguments he propounds. Hardin argues that a popular morality focused simply on the rights of individuals, without regard to the system, will have catastrophic consequences; in particular, he objects to the United Nations claim, as restated in the Declaration on Social Progress and Development (1969) (http://www.unhcr.ch/html/menu3/b/m_progre.htm) that 'parents have the exclusive right to determine freely and responsibly the number and spacing of their children' (Article 4):

> If each human family were dependent only on its own resources; if the children of improvident parents starved to death; if, thus, overbreeding brought its own 'punishment' to the germ line – then there would be no public interest in controlling the breeding of families. But our society is deeply committed to the welfare state, and hence is confronted with another aspect of the tragedy of the commons (Hardin, 1994: 334–5).

Hardin's comment makes reference to 'our society' – meaning the United States – and its commitment to the welfare state. The tragedy of the commons is, of course, a metaphor for the world's resources, and not every society has a welfare state. However, Hardin's audience is his own people, and the question of population growth is, for Hardin, closely linked to that of immigration. Since population growth is much higher in the developing world than in the developed world, migration from the former to the latter is a consequence of population growth. And Hardin has three fairly straightforward policy proposals: end the despoliation of the 'commons' insofar as this is within the power of the United States and other developed countries to do; stop food aid to the developing world; and severely restrict migration to the developed world.

We will say something about these proposals shortly, but we need to consider Hardin's underlying philosophical position. Hardin is not a philosopher, and so we have to engage in some speculation to capture his basic position, but it seems to amount to this: human beings are naturally selfish, or, at least, they are overwhelmingly concerned with their own survival. That some people are lucky to live in relatively wealthy societies and others in poor societies may be cause for a bad conscience, but it does not change the ethical situation. That most Americans are descended from people who 'stole' from Native Americans does not mean that they have an obligation to help the less fortunate:

> We are all the descendents of thieves, and the world's resources are inequitably distributed. But we must begin the journey to tomorrow from the point where we are today. We cannot remake the past. We cannot safely divide the wealth equitably among all peoples so long as people reproduce at different rates. To do so would guarantee that our grandchildren and everyone else's grandchildren, would have only a ruined world to inhabit (Hardin, 1974: 567).

Hardin employs the analogy of a lifeboat to illustrate his argument. Two-thirds of the world is desperately poor, while a third is relatively wealthy. Each of those wealthy nations can be likened to a lifeboat; in the ocean outside the lifeboat swim the poor of the world, who would like to clamber on board. If there are 50 people on a boat designed for 60, and 100 swimming in the water around the boat, what are we – where 'we' means those in the boat – to do? We could respond to the Christian call to be 'our brother's keeper' or the Marxist injunction to give to each 'according to his needs', but since all 100 are our brothers (and sisters) and all are equally in need, we have to choose: we could choose ten, which would leave us with no emergency capacity and would require us to explain why we did not admit the other 90, or we could take all 100, with the consequence that the boat will sink. Alternatively, each of the 50 could choose to sacrifice their life, but that altruistic act will not solve the global crisis.

The 'harsh ethics' of the lifeboat become harsher when population growth is taken into account. The people in the boat are doubling their numbers every 87 years; those swimming on the outside are doubling their numbers every 35 years. Hardin argues that it is misleading to talk about satisfying human needs, as if needs were minimal conditions, such as basic food and health care, which once met left a surplus to be distributed. Rather, because the satisfaction of needs has the effect of increasing the population, there is no end to the satisfaction of needs. The only ethical response is to refuse to satisfy the needs by restricting immigration – stopping people getting on the lifeboat – and not giving food aid to those 'outside the boat'. A consequence of this harsh policy would be that countries, once solely responsible for their own well-being, would learn to manage, albeit after a great deal of suffering.

The Argument so Far

From our discussion of Leopold and Næss, and drawing on other ecological writings, we can summarise the key components of ecologism as follows:

1. The belief that there is something which can be called 'ecology' or the 'biosphere'; this is an interconnected whole on which all life depends.

2. The natural world, which includes all forms of life, has intrinsic value, and should not be used as an instrument to satisfy human wants; there is much debate within the ecological movement about the nature of this value, and we discuss this below. However, there is an intuitive sense that ecologism requires being 'in touch' with nature.

3. The quality of human life will be enhanced once human beings recognise 1 and 2: ecologism is not concerned to devalue human beings, but rather to get us to think about who we really are.

4. The structure of the natural world should be mirrored in the social and political world; the interdependence – but diversity – of the former translates into a commitment to a more equal society, respectful of difference.

5. To achieve ecological and social justice requires not simply a change in the social, economic, and political organisation of society, but a fundamental change in human motivation.

6. Ecologism is a distinct ideology, which sees in both liberalism (capitalism) and socialism a common enemy: industrialism. Industrialism *by definition* cannot be compatible with an ecological consciousness. For ecologists the earth is a physical object, with natural physical limits; industrialism, which is committed to economic growth, cannot respect the integrity and finitude of the earth.

7. Ecologists seek a sustainable society – that is, one which is in tune with nature. In practical terms, this requires a reduction in consumption.

8. Although there is a division within deep ecology, a strong theme in ecological thought is distrust of technological fixes – that is, a belief that advances in technology will overcome environmental problems.

Critique of Ecologism

We have set out the central elements of ecologism. In this final section we explore some of its ethical and political weaknesses. Our aim is not to provide conclusive objections but to raise problems, with the intention of stimulating debate. For that reason we have posed a series of questions, which we then discuss.

Do Ecologists have a Plausible Account of why we should Value 'Nature'?

The central claim of ecologism is that there is value in the natural world that cannot be explained simply by reference to human wants, needs or consciousness: nature, or the environment, or the ecosystem has *intrinsic value*. The difficulty with this claim is that to say something has value is to make an evaluation, and such evaluation presupposes a capacity to evaluate, and only human beings possess such a capacity, therefore values are human-centred.

An ecologist might respond by asking us to imagine a beautiful valley that no human being has ever seen – would something be lost if that valley ceased to exist?

If we conclude that something would be lost, then does that not show that value is independent of human consciousness? The difficulty is that the question asks us to *imagine* such a valley; while it is possible that a valley exists which no human eyes have ever seen, we nonetheless have the *concept* of a valley, and criteria for evaluating its beauty. Perhaps, however, the ecologist is making a different claim: value does indeed depend on the human capacity to evaluate, but it does not follow that values are human-centred. Lovelock makes an interesting comment in his article on nuclear power that we discussed at the beginning of the chapter: 'as individual animals we are not so special, and in some ways are like a planetary disease, but through civilisation we redeem ourselves and become a precious asset for the Earth; not least because through our eyes the Earth has seen herself in all her glory' (*Independent*, 24 May 2004).

Life after People

Life after People is the name of a documentary produced by the History Channel. It imagines what life on earth would be like if people suddenly disappeared (it does not imagine a cataclysmic disaster killing everybody). Drawing on a wide range of experts and employing computer graphics it provides a timeline for the disappearance of evidence of human activity and the implications for non-human animal and plant life. It predicts that after:

~1 day: Fossil fuel plants would run down, turning off the lights and resulting in the flooding of subways.

~10 days: Food would rot and domestic animals would have to seek other sources of food.

~1 year: Plants would sprout all over cities. The Hoover Dam would cease generating power as mussels clog up its pipes. Radio and television signals travelling through outer space would deteriorate into undetectable background radiation.

~5 years: Urban areas would be completely covered in vines and trees.

~25 years: London and Amsterdam would flood.

~50 years: Steel structures, such as bridges, would be in danger of collapse.

~100 years: By this stage major steel bridges would have collapsed.

~200 years: Major landmark buildings, such as the Empire State Building and the Eiffel Tower would have collapsed.

~500 years: Concrete structures would break up.

~1,000 years: Today's cities would be virtually unrecognisable as the collapsed structures become mounds covered in vegetation.

~10,000 years: the Hoover Dam would collapse. Among the few recognisable structures left would be the Egyptian Pyramids and sections of the Great Wall of China.

Is this a depressing prospect? If you really believe that nature has intrinsic value and that nature is superior to culture you must welcome the above scenario. This is not to suggest that humanity can continue behaving as it has done for the past 150 years, but we do need a more sophisticated view of the relationship between nature and culture.

It may be that bonobos, for example, share 98 per cent of their DNA with human beings, but what a difference 2 per cent makes.

If by saying nature has 'intrinsic value' ecologists are arguing that it is not reducible to the emotions of individual human beings, then there are certain implications. First, while it does provide a ground for environmental respect and protection, it still places human beings in a privileged position – although we cannot disprove the possibility, we have no reason to believe that non-human animals, let alone non-animal members of the biotic community, are capable of such appreciation of the natural environment. Second, if the natural world has intrinsic value, then the possibility exists that the created world also possesses intrinsic value, and where there exists a conflict between the two worlds it is not clear which should have the greater claim to protection. This is our next question, or challenge, but before moving on consider the scenario 'Life after People' on the previous page.

Can Ecologists Respect the Created World – that is, Culture?

Throughout this chapter we have operated with the distinction between nature and society (or culture), or the natural world and the human world. This accords with the everyday sense that there is a distinction: imagine looking out of the window at a tree-lined street of apartment blocks. Human beings have constructed the apartments and planted the trees, but because the apartments function according to human design, whereas the trees, despite being planted in neat lines, develop according to processes understood, but not set in motion, by human beings, we reasonably enough say the trees are part of nature, and the apartments are part of the artificial, human world.

That distinction is valid, but difficulties arise for ecologists when they make further claims: (a) that the natural world forms an interconnected whole *set apart from* the human world, and on which the human world is dependent; (b) that the natural world has intrinsic value, whereas the human world does not. The interconnectedness–separateness thesis can be challenged in the following way: there is no part of the globe untouched by human activity, and therefore insofar as there are connections, these are between the two worlds. Of course, the ecological critique rests precisely on accepting as a fact that human beings have transformed the world, and for the worse! Their point is that we depend on the natural world, understood as a whole connected together through complex processes, such that the human world is secondary. This claim could be accepted by *environmentalists*: certainly, if we do not allow, say, fish stocks to be replenished because of over-fishing or marine pollution, there will be no fish in the supermarket, and no profits to be made from fish.

An *ecological* argument would require accepting not simply (a), but also (b): the natural world is separate and valuable in a way the human world is not. This is open to challenge. Venice is clearly one of the great human creations – a world heritage site – built on a lagoon, and requiring considerable human intervention in the natural environment. That city, or at least the part of it most people understand as Venice, is under threat of sinking due to the combined effects of subsidence and rising sea levels; in addition, the lagoon is polluted through heavy industrial activity in the region. That there are natural processes at work, which are in part the result of a global environmental crisis, can be accepted by *environmentalists*, but that Venice itself has less value than naturally occurring phenomena is surely open to challenge. That, however, is the conclusion that an ecologist must draw.

The priority given to the natural world by ecologists rests in part on a 'hierarchy of needs', with physical reproductive needs at the base, and other needs, or 'wants', of lesser importance. For example many ecologists regard food production as more important than tourism, and indeed many are hostile to tourism. Yet in an advanced capitalist system tourism satisfies the needs of those economically dependent on it.

Ecologists sometimes suggest that we can have the benefits of the modern human world even if we remove the material conditions – industrialism – for modernity. Kirkpatrick Sale argues for a self-sufficient community, which does not engage in significant trade with other communities; such a community would ensure 'a wide range of food, some choices in necessities and some sophistication in luxuries, [and] the population to sustain a university and large hospital and a symphony orchestra' (Sale in Dobson, 2000: 118). Setting aside economic considerations about whether a low-trade world could sustain a high level of medical care, the social world that gives rise to relatively cosmopolitan institutions such as universities or orchestras has been one in which there is interaction between communities and cultures. Perhaps the argument is that we should preserve the cultural achievements of a modern industrial society, but without the costs; if that were Sale's point, then it would amount to a much more generous compliment to an industrial society than most ecologists are prepared to pay.

Are Ecologists Hostile to Individualism (or Individual Human Rights)?

One way to overcome the binary distinctions between humans and nature, and between nature and culture which we have discussed above is to redefine the human 'self'. An ecologist could argue that it is meaningless to talk about *your* emotions or subjectivity, as distinct from that which is 'outside' you. If we collapse the difference between 'self' and 'other', where the other includes, for example, the mountain range, or the river, that you are looking at, then it is unnecessary to talk about intrinsic value. However, it is difficult to understand what this extended self would be like, and more significantly, the *political* effect of accepting that such a self exists would be to internalise all the conflicts which presently exist between selves, understood in the narrow, everyday sense of individual self-conscious beings. When a person feels a conflict between their interests and the interests of the 'community' (in Leopold's very wide sense of that term), then it could be argued that an ecologist could claim that the individual's 'true self' is in tune with nature, and that their 'individualised' self is only a part of nature. Consequently, the 'community' is justified in 'helping' that person to overcome their 'internal' conflicts.

Ecologists maintain that the language of rights – of individual entitlements held against other people – is part of a false, anthropocentric view of the world. Not only are rights – and especially rights to private property – destructive of nature, but they present a flawed model of human relations. People would be happier in more communal relations. It is interesting that many ecologists are sceptical about animal rights. Certainly among those most hostile to the notion that animals have rights are the anthropocentric theorists of the traditional ideologies, such as socialism or liberalism, but the extension of rights from human beings to non-human animals derives from an individualist world-view: the theory of animal rights does not challenge anthropocentrism. Ecologists, on the other hand, tend to have a robust attitude to animal life, accepting that all animals are locked into a cycle of life and death, and the whole – Gaia – is more important than the parts.

Ecologists must have an account of human motivation, for presumably something has to change in terms of the relationship between human beings and nature. There are three possibilities: (a) changes in technology that conserve resources, slow down depletion or allow for economic growth without serious environmental consequences; (b) changes in the way we organise society, providing incentives or sanctions so as to alter behaviour; (c) changes in human motivation, which alter behaviour without requiring external incentives or sanctions. Ecologists are sceptical about (a), and prefer that (b), social and political changes, follow from (c), changes in motivation. It is significant that Hardin rejects (a) and (c) but endorses (b), arguing that only coercive measures will avert a global disaster.

A thread that runs through ecologism is that human behaviour in an industrialised society is bad for the environment, but also bad for human beings. This suggests that there is a 'real' human nature, which is fundamentally good, but is distorted by human acquisitiveness, which is fed by, for example, advertising. Since the achievement of a sustainable society depends on a change in motivation, a great deal depends on the plausibility of this view of human nature. Furthermore, ecologists must show that it is impossible to create and maintain a sustainable society without a change in motivation: technology will not fix environmental problems, and coercion is unacceptable and will lead to authoritarian regimes. Ecologists must argue, either that the real human nature will emerge fairly quickly as we move towards sustainability, perhaps because the human benefits of such a society will soon be apparent, or that changing human beings will be a major task.

Are Ecologists Hostile to Reason and Rationality?

It was argued that ecologists have to make some concession to human-centredness: for nature to have intrinsic value there must exist beings capable of evaluation. Yet there is, arguably, a further concession to be made to anthropocentrism: the capacity to evaluate depends upon complex rational machinery that seeks to connect together different values, experiences and actions. Rationality depends on language and not simply a non-linguistic observation of nature. The idea of interconnectedness, which is a core doctrine of ecologists, is made possible by human reason; arguably, there is no interconnectedness in the world, except what the human mind connects together. This is not say that there is no physical world external to the mind, nor that its value depends on the subjective attitudes of individual human beings, but rather that the human mind, defined as a set of capacities shared by individual human beings, and made possible through language, is the means through which the world is viewed as interconnected.

More specifically, ecologists have an incoherent attitude to natural science. A major aspect of natural science is the acquisition of knowledge through repeatable experiments – experiments that must take place in a controlled environment.

Science necessarily abstracts from the 'particular', and seeks to acquire knowledge by finding something which is not unique to a particular thing – the individual rat in the laboratory is only of scientific interest insofar as its physiological or psychological behaviour is generalisable, meaning that its behaviour must not be peculiar to that particular rat. This observation is not about the ethics of vivisection, but rather about how we acquire knowledge of the world: natural science is advanced through distance from nature, and not by being in touch with nature. Yet at the centre of ecologism as a political movement is continual appeal to the scientific evidence of environmental degradation – evidence acquired through a fundamentally anti-ecological rationality.

In part, the ambivalent attitude to natural science has its roots in the ecologists' conflation of science and technology, and, relatedly, of human rationality in general with a particular variant of it: instrumental rationality. Science developed in the early modern period as the result of changes in humans' understanding of their place in the world – only once the material world is seen as lacking in intrinsic spiritual qualities is it possible to treat it in an experimental way (Kuhn, 1962: 111–35). Technology, on the other hand, dates back to the earliest human activity – it is simply the marshalling of natural processes to serve human ends. Of course, advances in scientific understanding have aided technological advance, and many ecologists will argue that neither science nor technology are in themselves to be rejected, but rather it is the degree of intervention in, and alteration of, natural processes which is at issue. The danger with ecologism is that it fails to distinguish between human enquiry – the drive to understand the world – and human wants, that is, the desire to use the natural world for human ends. Human-centredness is narrowly defined by ecologists as instrumental reason; nature is used as a means, or instrument, for human ends. But you do not need to be an ecologist in order to challenge instrumental reason; you can move completely within a human-centred view of the world and still raise *rational* objections to the idea that because we have the scientific knowledge to do something, such as clone human beings, then we should do it.

Is Ecologism Compatible with Human Equality?

As we have seen, ecologists tend not to respect the distinction between facts and values, or is and ought. Of course, we should not accept uncritically the claim that the distinction cannot be bridged, and elsewhere we have addressed this challenge, but here we are concerned with ecologists' arguments. The approach adopted by many ecologists is to draw *analogies* between the natural world and the social world. Andrew Dobson offers the following (Dobson, 2000: 22):

Nature		Society and politics
Diversity	→	Toleration, stability and democracy
Interdependence	→	Equality
Longevity	→	Tradition
Nature as 'female'	→	A particular conception of feminism

In effect, ecologists are asking us to look at nature, consider its intrinsic value, and draw conclusions about how we should behave to it, and to each other. The problem, which Dobson acknowledges, is that people can draw quite different conclusions from nature: interdependence can imply hierarchy rather than equality, and the supposed femininity of nature may imply 'natural roles' that restrict human autonomy. Dobson talks about the 'lessons from nature', but it is not simply that we disagree about the social implications of our observation of the natural world, but rather that there are no lessons – or, in more philosophical language, reasons for action – to be derived from such observation.

At a more practical political level there are concerns about the impact of Green policies on the poor – that is, the poor in developed countries and the poorest nations. The demand made by the developed world that developing countries severely curb their carbon emissions is regarded by the latter as hypocritical: Western Europe and North America have enjoyed the benefits of pollution as a result of their early industrialisation and are now denying the 'majority world' the possibility of economic growth. Within the industrialised West the imposition of 'green taxes' impacts disproportionately on the poor, because they have to commit a greater proportion of income to paying for energy. These problems are not insuperable but it is significant that Green parties across all the developed countries draw their support primarily from the better off.

Is Ecologism Compatible with Value Pluralism?

Critics argue that ecologism, unlike environmentalism, is not simply a political programme, but requires individuals to endorse religious or spiritual beliefs that they might reasonably reject. Despite Arne Næss's insistence that ecologists can come together from a variety of different religious and philosophical perspectives, the ecological critique of industrialism identifies human motivation as the source of acquisitive attitudes, demands very significant changes in the way society is organised, and holds out the prospect of a reconciliation between human beings and nature that extends beyond political ideas. Most orthodox monotheists – Jews, Christians, Muslims – would interpret ecological ideas as a form of pantheism (earth as God) or panantheism (earth as part of God), standing against the metaphysical separation of God as creator from his creation. Many atheists would treat ecologism with the same suspicion that they treat other religions.

Summary

Ecologism's distinctiveness can be found in its emphasis on the interconnectedness of life on earth, and the demand for a fundamental change in human relations to nature – where nature, of course, is part of humanity, and humanity part of nature. It offers a critique of both liberalism and socialism, and while recognising the important differences between those ideologies it finds commonalities: a commitment to economic growth that is incompatible with the finite nature of the earth. Humanity's ambitions exceed the resources of its home.

Questions

1. Are there major philosophical differences between environmentalists and ecologists?
2. Is ecologism compatible with democracy?
3. Is ecologism compatible with socialism?
4. Should an ecologist be concerned with animal rights?

References

Devall, B. and Sessions, G. (eds) (1985) *Deep Ecology* Salt Lake City, UT: Gibbs Smith.

Dobson, A. (2000) *Green Political Thought* London: Routledge.

Hardin, G. (1974) 'Living on a Lifeboat' *Bioscience* (24)10, 561–8.

Hardin, G. (1994) 'The Tragedy of The Commons' in C. Pierce and D. Ven de Veer, *People, Penguins and Plastic Trees: Basic Issues in Environmental Ethics* London: Wadsworth, 330–8.

Kuhn, T. (1962) *The Structure of Scientific Revolutions* Chicago, IL and London: University of Chicago Press.

Leopold, A. (1987) *A Sand Country Almanac, and Sketches Here and There* New York and Oxford: Oxford University Press.

Næss, A. (1973) 'The Shallow and the Deep, Long Range Ecology Movements' *Inquiry* 16, 95–100.

Further Reading

Dobson (2000) is the clearest introduction to Green political thought. Other useful discussions of ecological thought and practice include: John Barry, *Rethinking Green Politics: Nature, Virtue, and Progress* (London: Sage, 1999); Alan Carter, *A Radical Green Political Theory* (London and New York: Routledge, 1999); John Dryzek, *The Politics of the Earth: Environmental Discourses* (New York: Oxford University Press, 2005); Robyn Eckersley, *The Green State: Rethinking Democracy and Sovereignty* (Cambridge, MA and London: MIT Press, 2004); David Pepper, *Eco-socialism: From Deep Ecology to Social Justice* (London: Routledge, 1993). A good collection of the most important writings on ecologism is Andrew Dobson (ed.), *The Green Reader* (London: Deutsch, 1991). More philosophical are the following: John Benson, *Environmental Ethics: An Introduction with Readings* (London: Routledge, 2000); Robert Elliot (ed.), *Environmental Ethics* (Oxford: Oxford University Press, 1995); Robert Elliot and Arran Gare (eds), *Environmental Philosophy: A Collection of Readings* (Buckingham: Open University Press, 1983); Dale Jamieson (ed.), *A Companion to Environmental Philosophy* (Malden, MA and Oxford: Blackwell, 2003); Robin Attfield, *Environmental Philosophy: Principles and Prospects* (Aldershot: Avebury, 1994).

Weblinks

The following sites are 'theoretical' in orientation:

- A very extensive list of links:
  http://www.erraticimpact.com/~ecologic/

- A couple of websites (largely) hostile to ecologism and environmentalism: http://www.lomborg.com/ (Lomborg is author of *The Skeptical Environmentalist*, a book in which he questions the global warming thesis); http://www.environmentalism.com/

These sites are activist in nature:

- http://www.foe.co.uk/

- http://www.earthwatch.org/

- http://www.greenpeace.org/international/

On nuclear power:

- Environmentalists for Nuclear Energy (Lovelock is a member of this organisation, and the article discussed above can be found here): http://www.ecolo.org/

- World Nuclear Association (another pro-nuclear power body): http://www.world-nuclear.org/

- Union of Concerned Scientists (US organisation opposed to nuclear energy): http://www.ucsusa.org/clean_energy/nuclear_safety/index.cfm

- Swedish Anti-nuclear Movement: http://www.folkkampanjen.se/engfront.html

Chapter 17

Fundamentalism

Introduction

Politicians and the media speak more and more about the threat of 'fundamentalism' and how fundamentalism stands at odds with liberalism and democracy. But what is fundamentalism? How and why does it arise? Is it solely an Islamic phenomenon, or can other religions also have their fundamentalist proponents as well? We will argue that all ideologies can be expressed in a fundamentalist fashion. What is the relationship between fundamentalism and the contemporary world?

Chapter Map

- **Fundamentalism** as a relatively new concept and more than a label.

- Fundamentalism as an ideology that can be either secular or religious.

- Fundamentalism and 'fundamentals'. The contradictory relationship to modernity.

- The rejection of democracy and the propensity to violence.

- The relationship between Islam and fundamentalism.

- The link between fundamentalism and the Christian right in the USA.

- Fundamentalism in Israel.

- Huntington's 'clash of civilisations' and fundamentalism.

The Diversity of Fundamentalisms

A group of Christian fundamentalists display signs informing people that corrupt worldly governments will give way to God's kingdom, Ocean City, New Jersey, USA, 1987

You are poring over the newspaper one day and you note the bewildering array of references to fundamentalism. There are chilling quotations from Osama Bin Laden with his latest diatribe against Americans and Jews, and the resonance that this is having from young supporters in mosques who adhere to the tenets of Islamic fundamentalism. There is also a piece on the election campaign of the American president with emphasis on his concern to placate, and yet somehow distance himself from, Christian fundamentalists. Can he take a position on abortion or homosexuality that satisfies both Christian fundamentalists and more liberal-minded republicans? Meanwhile the Israeli president is under fire for seeking to move any settlers out of (a few) Palestinian areas, and there is speculation as to whether he is doing this in order to maintain the other settlements that the international community deems illegal. His critics within Israel are labelled 'Jewish fundamentalists'.

In the Business section of the paper there is a lively debate about globalisation with one of the contenders arguing that international economic policies are too often motivated by what she refers to as 'market fundamentalism'. The paper seems to assume that the term 'fundamentalist' is self-explanatory, although it is clear that very different movements are being given the same label. Most are religious, but not all, and each is strongly opposed to the other. Islamic fundamentalists are hostile to Christian fundamentalists and vice versa. Both are critical of Jewish fundamentalists, and all three are opposed to market fundamentalism.

- Is the concept of fundamentalism coherent? Consider whether the term applies to all religions, or to one religion in particular. Is it fair to consider Islam inherently fundamentalist in character, or can all religions express themselves in fundamentalist form?

- It is often noted that in Enver Hoxha's (communist) Albania, religion was actually banned while portraits of the 'leader' peered out from every tree! Can someone committed to atheism, like a Marxist, or a secularist, also be fundamentalist in character?

- Fundamentalists claim that they are seeking to restore the purity of their particular creed. Yet fundamentalism seems to be a reaction to change and modernity. Just what is the relationship between fundamentalism and contemporary life?

- We are continually being told that the world is becoming a global village. Does globalisation have something to do with the rise of fundamentalism?

Label or Concept?

Fundamentalism is a relatively recent idea (although an old phenomenon). It relates to the interpretation of a creed that is intolerant of argument and debate, so that those who oppose a particular variety of fundamentalism are deemed 'enemies' and 'traitors'. Giddens, a sociologist who writes extensively on fundamentalism, comments that the term has only come into currency quite recently. As late as 1950 there was no entry for the word in the *Oxford English Dictionary* (Giddens, 1994: 6). This gives us an important clue as to its meaning since although fundamentalists see themselves as looking to some kind of 'original' blueprint, the concept, as we will define it, is quite new and cannot be understood without analysing the pressures of the modern world.

Sidahmed and Ehteshami argue that fundamentalism is a label rather than a concept (1996: 14), and it is true that the term can be used in a dogmatic manner without thought being given as to what it might mean. It will be argued here that the term can be a concept (i.e. something with a proper theoretical basis) and, therefore, it is not merely a descriptive but an evaluative term. Fundamentalism tells us what a creed looks like in such a way that it is unattractive to those who are open-minded. Like all political concepts, fundamentalism is both descriptive and evaluative (→ Introduction), and the fact that the concept will be used negatively (as something to avoid), does not mean that we are not describing it as accurately as we can.

Fundamentalism (like liberalism and secularism) is a contested category (i.e. it arouses controversy) but this does not make it so ambiguous that coherent exposition is impossible. We are not simply using the concept as a term of abuse: we are trying to expound it in as fair a way as we can.

Fundamentalism and Religion

The term was first applied in a religious context at about the turn of the century. It is important to understand its origins. It referred to a defence of Protestant orthodoxy against the encroachments of modern thought. In the first decade of the twentieth century, a series of 12 volumes entitled *The Fundamentals* was produced in the USA, containing 90 articles written by Protestant theologians. Three million copies were printed and they were distributed free of charge. However, as the *New Oxford Dictionary* points out, although one of the meanings of fundamentalism does relate to a strict and literal interpretation of the Bible by Protestants, the term, says the dictionary, can also be linked to any religion or ideology, 'notably Islam'.

Certainly within religion, 'restorationist' movements in Christianity and Judaism show striking similarities to fundamentalist Islamic movements. Recent developments in Hinduism and Shinto also reveal commonalities with what is happening elsewhere (Kepel, 1994: 2–3). Moreover, fundamentalism can refer, not only to any religion, but to any ideology. For example, reference is often made to 'market fundamentalism'. Any ideology, no matter how potentially tolerant, can be presented in fundamentalist terms, and therefore we cannot agree with the argument that the term relates essentially to understanding religion.

It is true that one fundamentalism feeds off another, and the construction of globalisation in fundamentalist terms has provoked a defensive religious fundamentalism as a response. The idea that the world has to conform to a view of liberty and democracy that stems from the White House in the USA – a fundamentalist kind of liberalism – has encouraged groups to espouse, for example, an Islamic fundamentalism in opposition.

Giddens comments that fundamentalism protects a *principle* as much as a set of doctrines, and hence can arise in religions like Hinduism and Buddhism that had hitherto been ecumenical and tolerant. Fundamentalism, he adds, not only develops in religion but can arise in any domain of life subject to forces undermining traditional forms – whether this concerns the idea of nation, relations between people of different cultures, the structure of the family or relations between men and women. People feel threatened by these changes and look for ideas that attack the European Union, feminism, anti-racism, or whatever. This reaction need not (as our examples suggest) take a purely religious form. Secular ideologies may also be expressed in fundamentalist fashion. Think of the interpretation of French republicanism used to justify banning the headscarf among Muslim schoolgirls. Critics have described the anti-religous writer, Richard Dawkins, as not only a neo-Darwinist, but also as an atheist fundamentalist. The neo-conservatives in the USA could be described as fundamentalists even though they don't subscribe to Islam, and militantly atheist regimes like Stalin's Russia could be seen as treating Marxism in a fundamentalist fashion.

It is wrong, therefore, to assume that fundamentalism has to be religious in character, let alone Islamic, although veiled Muslim women and bearded Muslim men, book burners and suicide bombers have emerged, as Sayyid points out, as fundamentalist icons in the Hollywood films, like for example, *Not Without My Daughter* and *True Lies* (1997: 8).

Exercise

You live in a cosmopolitan city that has a large Muslim minority. One day you pass a stall handing out literature and you are surprised to see that freedom is regarded as a pernicious Western concept. When you suggest that the answer to the world's problems is 'more democracy', it is clear that those handing out literature vigorously disagree and argue that only a return to 'true Islam' can save the world.

- Is this an accurate picture of the Islamic tradition? You have Muslim neighbours who seem quite liberal minded.

- Strong opposition to Darwinism is expressed by Islamic fundamentalists. Where else have you heard opposition to Darwin's theory of evolution?

- Your friend who hears this debate says that all religion is wrong, and this is why she is a convinced secularist. Can secularism be as intolerant and judgemental as religious fundamentalism?

Fundamentals and Fundamentalism

Some writers suggest that fundamentalism merely involves a concern with the 'fundamentals' of a creed. This is far too broad a view of fundamentalism and it is also somewhat naive. It leads writers to describe as fundamentalist, mainstream groups who are pluralistic, democratic and inclusivist (Moussalli, 1998: 14).

A useful definition and observation is the following. Fundamentalism is a tendency that 'manifests itself, as a strategy or set of strategies, by which beleaguered believers attempt to preserve their distinct identity as a people or group'. This identity is felt to be at risk in the contemporary era, and these believers fortify it 'by a selective retrieval of doctrines, beliefs and practices from a sacred past'. These retrieved fundamentals are refined, modified and sanctioned in a spirit of shrewd pragmatism, as a bulwark against the encroachment of outsiders. The fundamentals are accompanied by 'unprecedented claims and doctrinal innovations'. These retrieved and updated fundamentals are meant to regain the same charismatic intensity today that (it is believed) was in evidence when the 'original' identity was forged from formative revelatory experiences long ago (Sidahmed and Ehteshami, 1996: 5).

Although fundamentalists hark back to a past that they seek to re-enact, this past is heavily doctored with mythology. The retrieval by fundamentalists (as pointed out above) is 'selective' and 'innovatory'. Tariq Ali comments that fundamentalist Islamists chart a route to the past that mercifully for the people of the seventh century, never existed (2002: 304). This is why it cannot be said that all Muslims are fundamentalists. The leaders of fundamentalist movements are not theologians, but social thinkers and political activists.

It is often assumed that fundamentalists are genuinely concerned with resurrecting the fundamentals of a religious system. Hiro speaks of Islamic fundamentalists as releasing Islam from scholastic cobwebs and ideas imbibed from the West (Hiro, 1988: 1–2), but this, in our view, is not so. Fundamentalists are not conservatives trying to recover old truths. They want to remould the world in the light of doctrines that are quite new. Take the view that the regime in Saudi Arabia has of the Islamic religion. It can certainly be described as extremely conservative, but it is not fundamentalist. On the contrary, the gap between the wealthy few and the majority of salaried Saudis has been exploited by fundamentalist forces. It would be more accurate to say that conservative governments like the regime in Saudi Arabia have provoked fundamentalism, rather than being fundamentalist itself. The fact that the royal family is pragmatic in its domestic and foreign policy and adopts a Western outlook and behaviour, instigates the growth of fundamentalist tendencies as a reaction to it (Nehme, 1998: 277, 284).

Of course, terminology differs. Roy makes a distinction between an Islamism that is willing to get involved in social and political action in revolutionary fashion and a 'neo-fundamentalism' that is concerned simply with religious teaching (1999: 36). What Roy calls Islamists, we call fundamentalists, and it is for this reason that we identify Islamic fundamentalism, for example, as a militant and anti-modernist movement that exploits Islam rather than seeking to defend its basic tenets. Muslims in general oppose violence and militancy: the Islamic University of Gaza may want people to return 'to our basics' (Jensen, 1998: 203), but it is not fundamentalist. Fundamentalists, as we define them, may claim a respect for fundamentals, but we should not overlook the cynicism, demagoguism (i.e. liberties taken with logic and reason) and 'selective retrieval' involved in their activity.

Modernity and Tradition

Ali describes religious fundamentalism as a product of modernity (Ali, 2002: ix), and yet, as will become evident later, it is hostile to modernity. This is true of all fundamentalism, whether religious or secular. As Kepel points out, Christian fundamentalists seek not to modernise Christianity but to Christianise modernity, just as Islamic fundamentalists seek, he says, to 'Islamize modernity' (Kepel, 1994: 66, 2).

Fundamentalism is best described (forgive the seeming paradox) as a modern movement opposed to modernity. Fundamentalism is a product of modernisation – urban and intellectual in character. Fundamentalists use modern methods of propagating their ideas and recruiting adherents: what they attack are the emancipatory traditions, the belief in freedom, equality and self-government, that have characterised modern ideas since the Enlightenment. It is important to emphasise here the tension between form and content. Armstrong argues that fundamentalisms are 'essentially modern movements' that could take root in no other time than our own. They have absorbed, she says, the pragmatic rationalism of modernity that enables them to create an ideology that provides a plan of action (Armstrong, 2001: viii, xiii).

How can fundamentalism be both traditionalist and anti-traditionalist, modern and anti-modern? It is traditionalist in the sense that fundamentalists claim (although, as it has been argued, such claims need to be taken with a healthy pinch of salt) to be resurrecting traditions. However, as Giddens notes, the point about traditions is that you don't have to justify them – they normally contain their own truth, a ritual truth, asserted as correct by the believer (1994: 6). Fundamentalism arises in the novel circumstances of global communication (Giddens, 1994: 48), where traditions are being challenged, and these traditions cannot, it seems, be effectively defended in the old way. Hence, the context is one of profound anti-traditionalism. We rather like Roy's description of Islamism (or what we call Islamic fundamentalism) as the *sharia* (the holy book dealing with law) plus electricity (Roy, 1999: 52), while Armstrong speaks of fundamentalist movements having a 'symbiotic relationship' with modernity (Armstrong, 2001: xiii).

The backdrop of fundamentalism is a globalised world in which cross-cultural communication has not only become possible but also obligatory. Fundamentalism accentuates the purity of a given set of doctrines, not simply because it wishes to set them off against other doctrines, but because it rejects the idea of debate and discussion with people who have different points of view. It is opposed to what Giddens calls a dialogic engagement of ideas in a public space (Giddens, 1994: 6). While fundamentalists reject the notion of a 'changing of places' essential to dialogue, the audience is nevertheless global. An imaginary tradition is championed in an aggressive, dogmatic and polarising way.

There is a curious love/hate relationship to the market. On the one hand, Osama Bin Laden T-shirts can be seen for sale in shops in Mozambique next to T-shirts with adverts for the drink 'Coca-Cola' emblazoned on them. Suya Mura is a traditional village in Japan that is publicised for its tourist potential (Giddens, 1994: 86–7). At the same time, fundamentalism Bin-Laden style rages against the wickedness and corruption of international capitalism. Modern technology, the Internet and the Wall Street stock exchange are utilised in order to advance fundamentalist opposition to modernity – i.e. to liberal values.

Not surprisingly, many of those who challenge modernity are themselves products par excellence of this modernity. They have been through a secular education often with a bias towards technical disciplines, and they handle sacred texts in a way that challenges the conservatism of rabbis, (Muslim) ulemas or priests (Kepel, 1994: 4). Armstrong makes the point that whereas Westerners tended to see the Ayatollah Khomeini – the first ruler of Islamic Iran – as a throwback to the Middle Ages, much of his message and ideology was modern. He described Islam as 'the religion of those who desire freedom and independence. It is the school of those who struggle against imperialism' (Armstrong, 2001: 250, 256; see also Sayyid, 1997: 90). A very modernist formulation! Gray notes that radical Islamist views resemble European anarchism far more than they do Islamic orthodoxy (2003: 24, 79).

Indeed, some writers even see a kind of postmodernism (see the Essay on Difference on the website) in fundamentalism. Brown speaks of it as a 'foundationalism without a grand narrative' (1995: 35). In other words, fundamentalism combines cosmopolitan relativism (Muslims are different) – hence there are no 'grand narratives' that many postmodernists say they dislike – with a dogmatic belief in rightness and wrongness – hence 'foundationalism'. Falk argues, for example, that politicised religion is a form of postmodern protest against the mechanisation, atomisation and alienation of the modern world (cited by Wolff, 1998: 50). We would see postmodernism as a critique of modernism that goes beyond it, rather than an anti-liberalism that rejects democracy, the Enlightenment and universal promise. It is, therefore, better to speak of fundamentalism as an anti-modernism, rather than a postmodernism.

It is the deficiencies of modernity that produce fundamentalism. It has been said that the question of fundamentalism cannot be dissociated from the process of nation- and state-building and its failures. A fundamentalist is someone who has become conscious of the acute inequalities within and between countries, but who is also convinced that the current strategies of development will not succeed in alleviating them. Fundamentalism has developed in a situation where the state failed to provide the newly urbanised citizens with structures to replace the old communal ones. The alienated individual projects their frustrations on a world scale, seeking to create a community of believers who share a similar *Weltanschauungen* (world outlook) (Zoubir, 1998: 127, 131–2).

It does not follow that because fundamentalism is a kind of modernist reaction against modernity, we defend modernity. On the contrary, it is (as noted above) the failures of modernity that have created such an extreme and negative reaction. We are certainly not implying that liberalism or modernity itself is a desirable and natural norm.

Fundamentalism, Democracy and Violence

The refusal of dialogue makes fundamentalism dangerous, for increasingly the use of violence is counter-productive and the only way of advancing humanity's interests is through argument and debate (see Chapter on the State, p. 11). By rejecting democracy, fundamentalism necessarily leads to violence.

(Abstract) ethics, not democracy, is the watchword, and the value expected in the political domain is not liberty, but justice (Roy, 1999: 10–11). Choueiri, in his analysis of Islamic fundamentalism, comments that democracy is seen as a violation of God's sovereignty – the desires and opinions of secular majorities represent an outright usurpation of God's laws. Choueiri notes that in fundamentalist eyes, humanity has reverted to an age of ignorance. Some movements support democracy simply as a means to a non-democratic end (1996: 20–1). As Ali Belhaj, star preacher for the Islamic Salvation Front in Algeria has put it, democracy is no more than a corruption or ignorance which robs God of his power and seeks to bestow this power upon his creatures (Kepel, 1994: 46).

Is it true that all forms of fundamentalism reject democracy? Kepel argues that the various movements of re-Christianisation cannot reject democracy as an alien graft on their own system: they have to speak the language of democracy and this 'democratic constraint' influences what these movements actually say (Kepel, 1994: 197). Yet Armstrong cites an American fundamentalist who praises the early puritans for opposing democracy, and she refers to American fundamentalists who see democracy as a modern heresy to be abolished, and look towards the reorganisation of society along biblical lines (Armstrong, 2001: 273, 361). Moreover, as will be seen in Wilcox's analysis of the religious right, fundamentalist Christianity can also be militantly exclusivist and extol violence. Naturally, different fundamentalist movements are affected by their particular environment (the degree of poverty, unemployment and authoritarianism), and this accounts for their differential severity and harshness.

Nevertheless, the link between fundamentalism and the dislike for democracy applies generally, and explains the propensity by fundamentalists for violence. Thus, the public and private violence of men against women – a gender fundamentalism – involves a refusal to communicate in situations in which patriarchal conditions are under challenge. There is no question of men imagining what it is like to be a woman, for differences are absolutised, and used to justify the domination over the 'other'. Likewise, with the violence of what Giddens calls exclusionary ethnic groups (1994: 48): fundamentalisms of various kinds can act to sharpen up pre-existing ethnic or cultural differences. Whenever fundamentalism takes hold, degenerate spirals of communication threaten where one antipathy feeds on another antipathy, hate is heaped upon hate (Giddens, 1994: 243, 245).

Violence, as we have argued elsewhere, involves a radical absence of common interest, so that the target of violence is seen as an enemy rather than a fellow human being. Active trust established through an acceptance of difference is the enemy of fundamentalism. By difference, Giddens means the opposite of what we have called 'division'. Dialogic democracy involves a recognition that everyone is different and this difference is a positive and unifying attribute (Giddens, 1994: 129). In a post-traditional age, he argues, nationalism stands close to aggressive fundamentalisms, embraced by neo-fascist groups as well as by other sorts of movements or collectivities (1994: 132). The point about fundamentalism, as it is conceptualised here, is that it is new so that, as Giddens points out, neo-fascism is not fascism in its original form – it is a species of fundamentalism steeped with the potential for violence (Giddens, 1994: 251).

What is Islamic Fundamentalism?

It is widely held that fundamentalism is a 'green threat' in the post-cold war world. The Islamic religion is seen as the new enemy to democracy, the US and the West – a cancer destroying 'Western' values, but to conflate the Islamic religion with fundamentalism is itself a fundamentalist distortion of reality, intended to project all conflicts as a war either by or against Islam, some kind of resurrection of the Crusades. It is a view held by the Christian right and extreme Zionists, and it involves a dramatic and unwarranted homogenising of Islam.

As Ali points out in his revealingly entitled *The Clash of Fundamentalisms*, the world of Islam has not been monolithic for thousands of years. The social and cultural differences between Senegalese, Chinese, Indonesian, Arab and South Asian Muslims are far greater than similarities they share with non-Muslim members of the same nationality (Ali, 2002: 274). Roy even argues that Islamism has 'social-democratized' itself (1999: xi). A comparison between Zoubir's analysis of Islamic fundamentalism in Algeria and Robinson's assessment of the Muslim Brotherhood in Jordan demonstrates not only the diversity within Islam, but the necessary features which make up an Islamic fundamentalism.

Following the successful liberation war with France, the state in Algeria, Zoubir points out, lost its legitimacy and its *raison d'être* in the eyes of a youthful and disenchanted population (1998: 132). Little was done to provide employment or housing for the young people who deserted the countryside for the shanty towns. The Algerian regime offered modernisation without secularisation, with a demagogic and equivocal position on religious and cultural issues. It was, and still is, corrupt and inefficient, and this has led to a identity crisis with disastrous consequences – an identity crisis which has been intensified by the defeat of Arab nationalism and the humiliations suffered by Arab regimes against Israel (Zoubir, 1998: 133). Many mosques were built in Algeria and were it not for their totalitarian conception, the fundamentalists could have provided the basis of a credible counter-hegemony programme along classic Gramscian lines. Whereas the Italian Marxist Gramsci urged the construction of a working class hegemony or intellectual and moral supremacy based upon socialist values, fundamentalists in Algeria have sought an illiberal and anti-democratic domination. Many of the individuals who followed Nasser or Marx in the 1960s, are fundamentalists today. Chaotic liberalisation of trade, and a cut in food subsidies and unemployment have all fed fundamentalism. Large segments of society have been marginalised, leading to widespread anger, despair, banditry and utter hatred towards the state and its clienteles (Zoubir, 1998: 139).

Robinson's study of Muslim brethren in Jordan and their party the Islamic Action Front (formed in 1992 when parties were legalised), is a study of Islamists who are not fundamentalists, since, as Robinson points out, these organisations express their opposition to secularism in democratically permissible ways (Robinson, 1998: 173). A leader of the Muslim Brethren says: 'we have never believed in violence or intellectual terrorism' (1998: 182), but as it becomes more working class in composition and Palestinian influence increases, the Islamic Action Front has become increasingly divided (Robinson, 1998: 189). If inequalities continue to grow and the crisis in Israel/Palestine worsens, then this Islamic movement may turn to fundamentalism, not because it is Islamic, but because it will react negatively to a failing modernity.

Algeria not only offers a classic case study of the conditions which give rise to (Islamic) fundamentalism, but it also provides a model of how not to deal with the problem. Zoubir notes that the FIS (Islamic Salvation Front) emerged as the most mobilised and best-structured party in the country – it was legalised in 1989 despite its avowed opposition to republican principles (Zoubir, 1998: 143–4). It looked certain to win the elections in 1992 when the army stepped in, cancelled the elections and banned the organisation. Since 1992, terrorism and banditry have plagued the country and successive governments have failed to regain a minimum level of trust and legitimacy (Zoubir, 1998: 154).

Ali argues that had the FIS been allowed to become the government, then divisions beneath the surface would have come to the fore. The army could then have warned that any attempt to tamper with rights guaranteed by the constitution would not be tolerated (Ali, 2002: 306). This would, at least, have put the argument squarely in favour of the concept of democracy that the FIS explicitly rejected. In fact, since the army's counter-productive action and the mutual escalation of terrorism it has engendered, faith in the FIS has also been eroded, as Zoubir points out, and the only concern by Algerians is for civil peace, physical and economic security (Zoubir, 1998: 157).

The comparison between the FIS in Algeria and the Islamic Action Front in Jordan is revealing. It not only shows that there is significant diversity between Islamic movements even in the Middle East, but reveals the kind of conditions which need to be present before a fundamentalist movement can take root. Islamic ideology differs considerably from country to country or movement to movement. It delineates a wide spectrum of thought, from the transparently ultra-conservative to a convolution of eclectic liberal ideas. It is thus inappropriate to categorise, as Bina puts it, all these movements as 'fundamentalist'. If applied indiscriminately the yardstick of fundamentalism runs counter to the very act of reconciliation of Islam with existing social formations that are, by necessity, transitory and historical (1994: 17–18). Adherence to Islam, as with other religious movements and movements in general, necessarily reflects the particular conditions in which fundamentalism takes root.

Nasser's Egypt had been a beacon of Arab progressivism. Nasser sought to destroy the Muslim brotherhood and his government tried to turn the clerical graduates of the Islamic University of Al Azhar into mere transmission belts for his ideology. Nasser treated the Muslim Brotherhood with 'unexampled brutality' and those leaders who had not been hanged, took refuge in oil sheikdoms in the Arabian Peninsular (Kepel, 1994: 18). In 1966, Sayyid Qutb, a member of the Brotherhood, was executed: his message, hugely influential, was that true Muslims should break with the existing world and build a real Islamic state (Kepel, 1994: 20). Armstrong quotes his comment that 'Humanity today is living in one large brothel! One only has to glance at its press, films, fashion shows, beauty contests,

Myths about Fundamentalism

- Fundamentalism is necessarily about religion.
- Fundamentalists seek to return to 'fundamentals'.
- Fundamentalists are hostile to all things modern.
- All Muslims are fundamentalists.

ballrooms, wine-bars, and broadcasting stations' (Armstrong, 2001: 240). After the traumatic military defeat by Israel in 1967, Islamic orthodoxy began to gain increasing numbers of adherents. The sharp increase in the price of oil that followed the Arab–Israeli war of 1973 accelerated the flight from the countryside.

Yet in Egypt, as elsewhere, it is possible to be an Islamist without being a fundamentalist. Abul Fotouh who is head of the Egyptian Medical Association and a leader of the Muslim Brotherhood, does not find the Western way of life at odds with Islam. 'At the end of the day', he comments, 'we have a set of common humanist values; justice, freedom, human rights and democracy' (*The Economist*, 2003: 6). However, Hammoud indicates that in Egypt, it is the particular circumstances rather than the particular religion that has given rise to a fundamentalist opposition. The economic situation has led to increased inequality, productivity has decreased and unemployment has rocketed (Hammoud, 1998: 306). Fundamentalists in Egypt, as elsewhere, have begun to offer social and relief services which the modern state has signally failed to provide. The use of repression and emergency against opponents has helped to create a revolutionary opposition, and devastated confidence in notions of dialogue and consensus that are crucial to a democratic culture (Zoubir, 1998: 329–31).

American Fundamentalism and the Religious Right

Anyone who thinks that fundamentalism is a purely Islamic phenomenon should pay some attention to the ideas and impact of Christianity in Italy (and France) or on the religious right in the USA. When American Christian fundamentalists Jerry Falwell and Pat Robertson, declared that the attack on 11 September was a judgement of God for the sins of secular humanists, they were expressing a viewpoint not far removed from that of the Muslim hijackers (Armstrong, 2001: viii). In Italy, an organisation called the 'People's Movement' provided a valuable back-up resource for the Christian Democrats, although it reserved the right to campaign against any Christian Democrat suspected of harbouring secularist sympathies. Its weekly journal stigmatised secularised Christians as 'Catho-communists' (Kepel, 1994: 72–3). In France, an estimated 200,000 people have been involved with a charismatic revival, with supporters making common cause with those Islamic fundamentalists outraged by the 'Islamic veil' affair where the state insisted that Muslim schoolgirls must dress in a secular fashion.

Fundamentalism (strictly defined) in the USA was rooted historically in the American south, and the depression of 1929 was seen 'as a sign of God's vindictive punishment on an apostate America as well as a sign of Christ's imminent return'

(Kepel, 1994: 107). A poll in 1969 revealed that there were some 1,300 evangelical Christian radio and television stations, with an audience of about 130 million. Between 1965 and 1983 enrolment in evangelical schools increased sixfold, and about 100,000 fundamentalist children were taught at home. The enemy were 'secular humanists' who, fundamentalists alleged, sought to reduce the world to slavery (Armstrong, 2001: 267, 269, 272).

In Kepel's view, Reagan was elected in 1980 largely because he captured the votes of most of the evangelical and fundamentalist (using the term somewhat narrowly) electors who followed the advice of politico-religious bodies like the Moral Majority. Just like the Islamic militants, the young American fundamentalists have had higher education (usually studying the applied sciences), and they have come from the large cities in the northern and southern states (Kepel, 1994: 8, 137).

Boston argues in his critique of Pat Robertson that Robertson's political unit, the Christian Coalition (launched in 1989) has a budget of $25 million with 1.7 million members and 1,600 local affiliates in all 50 states (Boston, 1996: 16). Robertson owns the Christian Broadcasting Network (CBN) and, in his view, only Christians and Jews are qualified to run government. Not surprisingly, he and his movement deny the separation of church and state. His support for Israel is premised on the assumption that he believes that Zionism in Israel will unwittingly contribute to the conversion of Jews to Christianity. In the 1980s he was a champion of South Africa's system of apartheid. The wealth of CBN can be seen from the fact that the CBN can clear between $75 and $97 million tax-free profit, and the political impact of his Christian Coalition is evident in Boston's contention that it holds the country's majority party, i.e., the Republicans, in a headlock (Boston, 1996: 132, 166, 183, 238).

Predictably, the Christian Coalition, like the Moral Majority before it, is also virulently anti-feminist in character (Wilcox, 1996: 9), and Coalition supporters follow the historic pattern of religious fundamentalists of keeping themselves apart from an impure world and (in their case) doctrinally impure Christians. Wilcox estimates that about 10–15 per cent of the public support the religious right and there may be as many as four million members of the Christian Right and possibly 200,000 activists in politics (Wilcox, 1996: 36, 71). The movement has always used the best technology available. In general, the Christian Right opposes any notion of compromise, and they tend to be intolerant of those they disagree with. They do not accept the civil liberties of liberals, although it is true that the more members of the religious right participate in conventional politics, the more reconciled to democracy they become (Wilcox, 1996: 107–8, 111). For many, imposing Christianity on non-believers increases the odds that the souls of these hapless infidels will spend eternity in heaven. Fringe elements (in an interesting counterpart to Muslims who believe in a punitive version of the *sharia*) favour Mosiac law that would involve stoning sinners (Wilcox, 1996: 125).

Some fundamentalists showed their contempt for US law by blockading abortion clinics, and in the words of Randall Terry, they saw themselves as working for a nation 'not floating in an uncertain sea of humanism, but a country whose unmoving bedrock is Higher laws' (Armstrong, 2001: 360). Like fundamentalism elsewhere, there is a reaction against modernism, which Christian fundamentalists fear will inevitably erode traditional values. As Wilcox points out, there is a small but significant trend to liberalism in the American public, and young Americans are far more liberal than the older cohorts they are replacing (Wilcox, 1996: 144). Falk has analysed the increasing convergence of religion and politics as a growing adherence to postmodernism (1988), but although postmodernism challenges the separations and dualisms of the liberal tradition, fundamentalism does not.

For this reason, liberation theology is not fundamentalist at all, but seeks to challenge religious conservatism in exciting and innovative ways. It stands in contrast to what Falk himself calls a few islands of fundamentalist success that disclose the religious revision of modernism in an oppressive direction (Falk, 1988: 380). It is not the rise of postmodern religion that is fundamentalist or cultist in character. It is rather movements that reject or merely negate modernism. The West, as Falk puts it graphically, has 'killed' God with its consumerist spirit (1988: 381) so that there has been a remarkable surge of fundamentalist religion in the last few decades (Falk, 1988: 385). This is why it is problematic to speak of American fundamentalism as exhibiting, in Armstrong's words, postmodern tendencies, although she is right to note that it has 'a hard-line totalitarian vision' of the future (Armstrong, 2001: 362).

Even in the 1980s, it was clear that the 'coming out' of US fundamentalists in the form of the 'moral majority' and evangelical Christianity, represented a determined assault on the modern lifestyle of 'secular' Christianity. The AIDS epidemic has been seen as a kind of objective confirmation of the fundamentalist critique of modernism and fundamentalists express their hostility to the preoccupation with means rather than ends associated with modernist solutions (Falk, 1988: 387). When Falk argues that a religion with postmodern strivings links emotion to reason and sees connections and relatedness as primary categories of knowledge (1988: 388), he demonstrates (however unwittingly) why the fundamentalism of the religious right in the USA cannot be seen in postmodernist terms. Indeed, what makes the religious right fundamentalist is the violence of its language and some of its practice (think of bombings against abortion clinics, for example), and the stark chasms it poses between the purists 'saved' and those whose lifestyle and values commits them to eternal damnation.

Jewish Fundamentalism and the Israeli State

A tiny minority of orthodox Jews in the 1920s began to see in Zionism – a belief that Israel represents a natural homeland for the Jews – a more holistic vision after the trauma and constrictions of exile, as Armstrong notes, and they were strongly opposed to secular Zionists. In the 1940s, they established their own schools (2001: 259). Rabbi Yehuda who led the Gahlet, an elite group within religious Zionist circles, declared that every Jew 'who comes to Eretz Israel [biblical Israel] constitutes . . . another stage in the process of redemption'. The war of 1967 in which Israel conquered the Golan Heights, the West Bank and the Gaza strip, was deemed proof that redemption was under way (Armstrong, 2001: 261, 263).

Kepel sees 1977 as a signpost year in which the dominant Zionist tradition was critically re-examined as Labour lost its first election in the history of Israel. Judaism was redefined in terms of observance and ritual (Kepel, 1994: 6). The war of 1973 ended in 'a psychological defeat for the Jewish state', and in the confusion and questioning of certainties there emerged the Gush Emunim (Bloc of the Faithful) that became the self-proclaimed herald for the re-Judaisation of Israel. Gush Emunim was formed by a bloc of hawkish secularists and religious Zionists.

It replaced the legal concept of the state of Israel with the biblical concept of the Land of Israel, and sought to plant more and more settlements in the occupied territories (Kepel, 1994: 140–1). The Zionist ideal needed to be renewed and fully realised. Israel was seen as a unique state that was not bound by international law (Armstrong, 2001: 280, 282).

After Rabbi Kook's death, Gush Emunin split: a few identified the Palestinians as Amalekites, a people so cruel that God had commanded the ancient Israelites to slay them without mercy (Armstrong, 2001: 346). Terrorism was resorted to: Gush Emunin extremists were suspected of murdering students at the Islamic University of Hebron and making attempts on the lives of Palestinian mayors, and the organisation encouraged other groups to embrace the cause of re-Judaisation as well. Ultra-orthodox groups began to recruit among university students and among Sephardic Jews who were often immigrants from the Arab countries in which groups like Gush Emunin had been quite unknown.

Religious parties represent such groups in parliament and they exercise real leverage on coalition governments. These groups argue for a sharp break between Jews and gentiles, with a demand for the strict observance of prohibitions and obligations. As with Protestant fundamentalists, devout Islamists or Catholic organisations like Communion and Liberation, secularism is seen as suffocating by 'reborn' Jews, with the Enlightenment blamed for plunging humanity into 'a hostile sea of doubt' and cutting it adrift from 'firm moorings in a theocentric universe' (Kepel, 1994: 140–3). Some, like the Russian émigré Herman Branover who went to Israel in 1972, found Zionism and Israeli society intolerably secular. Nevertheless, even secular Zionists were held to be the unwitting bearers of a messianic redemption (Kepel, 1994: 147, 155).

Stern religious observance is regarded by fundamentalists here, as elsewhere, as compatible with making use of the technology and apparel of the modern world. Gush received some support from the Israeli party Likud, but subsequently resorted to a terrorism that was officially denounced (Kepel, 1994: 161, 163). A plan to dynamite the mosques on the Temple Mount in Jerusalem was foiled by the Israeli secret service. Kepel finds striking similarities between these Jewish conspirators and the Islamic fundamentalist group which assassinated Sadat in 1981 – a process of re-Judaisation or re-Islamisation taken to extremes. Gush has a membership of some 50,000, most of them resident in the occupied territories (Kepel, 1994: 169–70). From the mid-1980s, the ultra-orthodox Jews (the haredim) became the most highly visible advocates of re-Judaisation, drawing support particularly from Sephardic Jews (Kepel, 1994: 178). The orthodox parties are able to wield substantial power. Although they receive only 15 per cent of the vote, they control several ministries and obtain large subsidies to strengthen their network of practising Jewish communities (Kepel, 1994: 180, 190). The Lubavitch believe that Israel should be cleansed of its Zionist accretions in order to become a 'Torahcracy' over the Land of Israel (i.e. Israel as projected in the Bible) (Kepel, 1994: 189). Hence, they should, in our view, be regarded as extreme Zionists rather than anti-Zionists.

The assassination of Rabin, like the assassination of Sadat, showed, as Armstrong points out, that two wars are being fought out in the Middle East. One is the war against Israel; the other is the war between the secularists and the religious (Armstrong, 2001: 353).

Four Facts about Fundamentalism

1. Fundamentalism is a concept rather than a label and it relates not simply to religion but to any ideology.

2. Although fundamentalism takes the form of a return to fundamentals, in fact fundamentalists are highly selective and innovative with regard to sacred texts.

3. Fundamentalism is a product of modernity and makes use of modern technology, although it also rails against modernist ideas.

4. Fundamentalism espouses the use of violence to settle conflicts of interest, and is profoundly anti-democratic.

Differentiating Religious Fundamentalisms

- *Islamic fundamentalism* is not the same as devotion to Islam. Fundamentalism arises in situations of severe social, political and economic dislocation, and as the portrait of the Egyptian Muslim Brotherhood reveals, Muslims can espouse liberal and democratic values.

- *American fundamentalism* expresses itself as a bigoted and intolerant Christianity. Its proponents have substantial resources, owning radio stations and targeting the Republican party. American fundamentalism is anti-feminist, anti-Semitic and anti-Islam and it rejects modernity. Hence it is anti-modernist rather than postmodernist in character.

- *Jewish fundamentalism* takes the form of a religious orthodoxy that opposes secular Zionism. It seeks an Israel that is not bound by international law and expands to its biblically ordained frontiers.

Focus

Fundamentalism and the State

Some fundamentalists see the nation-state as an alien Western invention and look towards some kind of revolutionary International to cleanse the world of its imperfections. Yet the emphasis on violence and polarisation show that whether or not fundamentalists consciously support the need for a state, their arguments are statist through and through. The view of opponents as enemies to be crushed by an organisation which monopolises truth and legitimacy, projects in extreme form attitudes which exist even in the liberal state. Hence the ease with which the US President after 9/11 began to invert the sentiments of Al Qaeda, declaring that 'those who are not with us, are against us'.

While we are not suggesting that the state per se is a fundamentalist organisation, there is a continuity between the extolling of violence against enemies by fundamentalists and the use of force by the state. The same cynical, instrumental and ambiguous attitude towards modernity is evident in both, so that although they are different, fundamentalism – particularly if it can be blamed on a rogue state – is grist to the mill of the state's own contradictory identity.

An institution which links conflict with violence and seeks to justify monopolistic practices must operate in terms of divisions and dualisms which under pressure, can easily become fundamentalist in character. The state, while not fundamentalist in itself, harbours fundamentalist leanings in its bureaucratic soul.

The 'Clash of Civilisations': a Fundamentalist Thesis?

The link between fundamentalism and the state is well exemplified by Huntington's contention that globalisation is leading to a clash of civilisations. He explicitly identifies his position with the realist theory of international relations (1996: 185), and argues that the tools of realism – a state-centric view of the world which remains basically changeless – leads to an understanding of (violent) conflict in terms of cultural and what he calls 'civilizational' difference.

While he concedes that minorities in other cultures may espouse Western values – by which Huntington means the values of what he calls democratic liberalism – dominant attitudes in non-Western cultures range from widespread scepticism to intense opposition to Western values (Huntington, 1996: 184). Although almost all non-western civilisations are resistant to pressure from the West – including Hindu, Orthodox, African and even Latin American countries – the greatest resistance to Western power has come from Islam and Asia (Huntington, 1996: 193).

Civilisations, Huntington argues, are the ultimate human tribes, and the clash of civilisations is tribal conflict on a global scale. Trust and friendship between the civilisations will be rare (1996: 206). He sees a deeply conflictual relation (Huntington takes it for granted that conflict is always violent), not simply between Islamic fundamentalists and Christianity but between Islam itself and Christianity. Conflict is a product of difference. In civilisational conflicts, unlike ideological ones, kin stand by their kin (1996: 209–10, 217). Thus, the Gulf War is interpreted as a war between civilisations (1996: 251), and religion, in Huntington's view, is the principal defining characteristic of civilisation, so that what he calls 'fault-line wars' are almost always between people of different religions (1996: 253). At the global level, the clash is between the West and the rest. At the micro or local level, it is between Islam and others (1996: 255). The longer a fault-line war continues, the more that kin countries are likely to become involved (1996: 272).

Huntington takes the view that it is futile and counter-productive for countries to integrate their peoples. A multicivilisational United States, he argues, will not be the United States: it will be the United Nations. We must reject the divisive siren calls of multiculturalism (1996: 306–7, 310). Cultural identities inevitably collide in an antagonistic manner. 'We know who we are only when we know who we are not and often only when we know whom we are against' (1996: 21). Here is realism with a cultural twist! Nation-states are and will remain the most important actors in world affairs, but their interests, associations and conflicts are increasingly shaped by cultural and civilisational factors. He has also argued that the USA is now threatened by immigrants from Latin America who are altering the national identity of traditional America.

The Clash of Civilizations, it could be argued, is itself a kind of fundamentalism: but not only does it not arise from, it is staunchly opposed to the Islamic tradition. Huntington believes that human history is the history of civilisations (1996: 40). Islamic civilisation in particular and non-Western culture in general, is on the ascendant, and it is wrong to assume that with 'modernisation', the world becomes more amenable to Western values. In fact, he argues, the world is becoming more modern and less Western (1996: 78). Of course, people are different, but for Huntington these differences can only lead to exclusion and antagonism. Thus, he

Criticisms of Fundamentalism

- Fundamentalism differs from the state, but it is important to note the continuities. Fundamentalism seeks to monopolise the truth and use violence against enemies. So does the state. Of course fundamentalism is much more extreme than, say, the liberal state, but it takes to an extreme what are statist tendencies.

- Huntington's 'clash of civilisations' thesis is an example of a kind of academic quasi-fundamentalism that absolutises differences, and sees violent conflict in terms of cultural and 'civilisational' values. Instead of seeking to distinguish between e.g. liberal and fundamentalist Islamic doctrines, he treats Islam as a homogeneous culture that is staunchly opposed to 'Western values'.

insists that religion posits a basic distinction between a superior in-group and a different and inferior out-group, and cultural questions (like the mosque at Ayodhya or the status of Jerusalem) tend to involve a yes-no, zero-sum choice. For self-definition and motivation, people need enemies (1996: 97, 130). Here is the core of a quasi-fundamentalism.

Of course, civilisational differences are real and important, but Huntington is wrong to see them as a necessary source of antagonism. Abou El Fadl has rightly stressed the mixed lineage of civilisations (2003: 82). It is true that many Muslims are not convinced when the US attempts to present its demonisation of political figures like the deposed Iraqi leader, Saddam Hussein, as something other than raw hostility to Islam per se. It should however be remembered that it was a US-led NATO that intervened in Kosovo to defend the human rights of people of Muslim faith against their Serbian (and Christian Orthodox) oppressors. This hardly fits the clash of civilisations thesis.

Huntington himself links what he calls 'Muslim assertiveness' to social mobilisation, population growth, and a flood of people from the countryside into the towns (1996: 102, 98). This is surely a social rather than a purely cultural explanation for antagonism. Moreover, only a realist schooled in state-centric analysis and rooted in American triumphalism, could ignore the adverse effect of the insensitivity and arrogance of US policy-makers upon others. It is not that the differences he speaks of are unimportant. Rather it is that he fossilises them, fails to see the contradiction between the 'culturalist' and sociological dimensions of his analysis and he ignores the tensions within the so-called Western tradition between neo-liberal and social democratic strategies and values. His work is a good example of the way in which an extreme statism (with its conservative and superficial assumptions) can lead in the direction of fundamentalism. Divisions are taken for granted, so that it could be argued that there is a danger that the fundamentalism of the 'other side' is merely inverted rather than transcended.

Summary

Fundamentalism is sometimes seen as a mere label. In our view, it is more than this. It is a concept despite the fact that it is a relatively new idea. Although fundamentalism is often identified with religions, any ideology, no matter how secular, can take a fundamentalist form. Fundamentalism is not about the 'fundamentals' of a creed. Fundamentalists exploit the creeds they espouse in order to make them dogmatic, militant and violent in character.

Fundamentalists have an ambivalent attitude towards modernity. On the one hand they oppose it: on the other they not only make use of it, but fundamentalism can only be understood as part of the modern world. Fundamentalism sees deep divisions between the 'pure' and the 'contaminated'. It rejects dialogue and debate, and regards violence as the only way of tackling conflict.

It is wrong to assume that Islam is necessarily (or has a particular tendency to be) fundamentalist in character. Where Islamists turn to fundamentalism, this is not because of their religion, but because of the particular circumstances in which they find themselves. Fundamentalism can take a Christian form. If we look at the Christian right in the USA, we see that not only are they wealthy, but they are politically influential and reject democratic values. In Israel Jewish fundamentalism has a love/hate relationship with Zionism. On the one hand, Jewish fundamentalists are concerned at the way in which some Zionists treat religion purely as a national identity rather than a sacred creed. On the other hand, they see the state of Israel as a first step towards building an Israel of biblical proportions.

The 'realism' of Huntington can be viewed as a kind of academic quasi-fundamentalism as a result of the author's contention that differences between civilisations necessarily lead to violence and antagonism.

Questions

1. Is fundamentalism simply about religion?
2. Is fundamentalism inherent in Islam?
3. Is the media treatment of fundamentalism fair?
4. Is fundamentalism a modern phenomenon?
5. How should democrats handle fundamentalists?

References

Abou El Fadl, K. (2003) '9/11 and the Muslim Transformation' in M. Dudziak (ed.), *September 11 in History* Durham, NC and London: Duke University Press, 69–111.

Ali, T. (2002) *The Clash of Fundamentalisms* London: Verso.

Armstrong, K. (2001) *The Battle for God* New York: Ballantine Books.

Bina, C. (1994) 'Towards a New World Order: US Hegemony, Client-States and Islamic Alternative' in H. Mutalib and H. Taj ul-Islam, *Islam, Muslims and the Modern State* Basingstoke: Macmillan, 3–30.

Boston, R. (1996) *The Most Dangerous Man in America* New York: Prometheus Books.

Brown, W. (1995) *States of Injury* Princeton, NJ: Princeton University Press.

Choueiri, Y. (1996) 'The Political Discourse of Contemporary Islamist Movements' in A. Sidahmed and A. Ehteshami (eds), *Islamic Fundamentalism* Boulder, CO: Westview Press, 19–33.

Economist, The (2003) 'In the Name of God', 13 September.

Falk, R. (1988) 'Religion and Politics: Verging on the Postmodern' *Alternatives* XIII, 379–94.

Giddens, A. (1994) *Beyond Left and Right* Cambridge: Polity Press.

Gray, J. (2003) *Al Qaeda and What It Means to be Modern* London: Faber and Faber.

Hammoud, M. (1998) 'Causes for Fundamentalist Popularity in Egypt' in A. Moussalli (ed.), *Islamic Fundamentalism* Reading: Ithaca, 303–36.

Hiro, D. (1988) *Islamic Fundamentalism* London: Palladin.

Huntington, S. (1996), *The Clash of Civilizations* New York: Simon and Schuster.

Jensen, M. (1998) 'Islamism and Civil Society in the Gaza Strip' in A. Moussalli (ed.), *Islamic Fundamentalism* Reading: Ithaca, 197–219.

Kepel, G. (1994) *The Revenge of God* Cambridge: Polity.

Moussalli, A. (1998) 'Introduction to Islamic Fundamentalism: Realities, Ideologies and International Politics' in A. Moussalli (ed.), *Islamic Fundamentalism* Reading: Ithaca, 3–39.

Nehme, M. (1998) 'The Islamic-Capitalist State of Saudi-Arabia: The Surfacing of Fundamentalism' in A. Moussalli (ed.), *Islamic Fundamentalism* Reading: Ithaca, 275–302.

Robinson, G. (1998) 'Islamists under Liberalization in Jordan' in A. Moussalli (ed.), *Islamic Fundamentalism* Reading: Ithaca, 169–96.

Roy, O. (1999) *The Failure of Political Islam* London and New York: I.B. Tauris.

Sayyid, B. (1997) *A Fundamental Fear* London: Zed Books.

Sidahmed, A. and Ehteshami, A. (1996) 'Introduction' in A. Sidahmed and A. Ehteshami (eds), *Islamic Fundamentalism* Boulder, CO: Westview Press, 1–15.

Wilcox, C. (1996) *Onward Christian Soldiers* Boulder, CO: Westview Press.

Wolff, K. (1998) 'New New Orientalism: Political Islam and Social Movement Theory' in A. Moussalli (ed.), *Islamic Fundamentalism* Reading: Ithaca, 41–73.

Zoubir, Y. (1998) 'State, Civil Society and the Question of Radical Fundamentalism in Algeria' in A. Moussalli (ed.), *Islamic Fundamentalism* Reading: Ithaca, 123–67.

Further Reading

- Giddens's *Beyond Left and Right* (referenced above) contains a very useful chapter on fundamentalism.

- Kepel's *The Revenge of God* (referenced above) contains invaluable material about religious fundamentalism.

- Moussalli's edited volume *Islamic Fundamentalism* (referenced above) is very useful and comprehensive.

- Wilcox's *Onward Christian Soldiers* (referenced above) provides a survey of the religious right in the USA.

- Huntington's *The Clash of Civilizations* (referenced above) is a real, if contentious, classic.

- *Fundamentalism: A Very Short Introduction* (Oxford: Oxford University Press, 2007) is worth looking at.

Weblinks

Quite good on the link between religion and fundamentalism:
http://www.vexen.co.uk/religion/fundamentalism.html

For the question of the market and fundamentalism, see
http://www.opendemocracy.net/debates/article-2-95-1248.jsp

For a piece on fundamentalism as a concept, see
http://www.shellier.co.uk/fundamentalism.htm

Part 4 Contemporary Ideas

What do we mean by a New Idea?

In the last part of this book we discuss four concepts: human rights, civil disobedience, political violence, and global justice. What distinguishes these four concepts from those discussed in Part 1 – state, freedom, equality, justice, democracy, citizenship, and punishment – is their relatively recent emergence within political theory. Of course, the 'classical' ideas themselves have undergone change and much of our discussion in Part 1 focused on contemporary debates, but those debates revolved around 'problems' that emerged in the *earlier* phases of modernity. For example, the problem of state legitimacy and political obligation, the justification of property rights, arguments over the nature of the human agent, conflicts between freedom and equality, and the debate about the nature of political authority and collective decision-making.

The term problem is used here in a precise, philosophical sense as a puzzle that requires a solution, rather than as in everyday usage, which roughly defines a problem as a fault, weakness or contradiction. An analogy from the world of music will illustrate what we mean: one of the 'great revolutions' in Western music took place in the first decade of the twentieth century. Although anticipated by nineteenth-century composers, Arnold Schoenberg (1874–1951) is normally credited with the first atonal composition (that is, a work not composed in a key). Schoenberg did not set out to be a musical revolutionary, but rather he sought to save the tonal system; it was recognition that developments within tonality (such as chromaticism) had generated irreparable incoherences which led him to take those developments to their conclusion. In this sense Schoenberg had inherited musical problems – or puzzles – from his predecessors, such as Beethoven, Wagner and Mahler. To some extent political theory can be understood as an attempt to address problems inherited from preceding theorists, and the treatment by contemporary thinkers of classical concepts, or problems, is analogous to Schoenberg's engagement with tonality. The analogy should not be taken too far: music is a relatively self-contained art form, whereas political theory, by its nature, is an engagement with the empirical world, a world it cannot control but that it must interpret.

Political theory can best be thought of as involving two tracks: there is a body of theory, parallel to musical forms, that later theorists engage with and which newcomers to the discipline may find strange and distant from the everyday world of politics, but there is also necessarily an engagement with that world of politics. We would argue that the two tracks are related, for changes in society will eventually work their way through to theoretical reflection, and this process is clear in the emergence of the new ideologies discussed in Part 3. However, theorists must also maintain some distance from the world of politics, for otherwise they will be unable to distinguish the merely transitory and parochial from the significant. Without necessarily endorsing his wider philosophy, two observations from Friedrich Hegel are apt here: 'philosophy is time reflected in thought' and the 'the Owl of Minerva begins its flight at dusk'. Political thought must respect the particularity of history but in a way which does not reduce that particularity simply to a series of discrete events, and the Owl of Minerva – that is, understanding – may not emerge, or 'take flight', until we have achieved a necessary perspective on those events.

Engagement with traditional problems of political theory, combined with social and political changes external to the discipline of political theory, but to which political theorists must respond, can generate new problems. It is these new problems that justify separating out the classical and the new ideas.

Although the concepts discussed in Part 4 bear affinities with traditional concepts, they do, nonetheless, constitute a break with tradition. Consider human rights: early modern natural law theory appears at first sight the progenitor of human rights discourse. The idea that human beings have a moral status as children of God, or are implanted by God with a moral sense, does not seem entirely alien to the contemporary understanding of human rights as standards of behaviour owed to people simply by virtue of their humanity and thus transcending cultural particularity. But the shift from a theological to a secular justification renders the similarity between natural law theory and contemporary human rights theory superficial: human rights are grounded in the idea that the individual human being is a 'self-originating source of valid claims' against others, rather than being part of a natural, or cosmic, order. The problem to which human rights are supposedly the answer is quite different to the problem to which natural law was a response: human rights function as a standard for international politics, whereas natural law was intended as a means of rejuvenating Christianity in the context of ecclesiastical corruption.

Civil disobedience and the theorisation of political violence can also be understood as responses to new problems. Indeed the two concepts dovetail together. Henry Thoreau is widely credited with writing the first work on civil disobedience (in 1849), but it is only after the Second World War that civil disobedience becomes a significant issue in political theory. We argue that although civil disobedience, that is, peaceful but illegal action, is possible in non-liberal societies – Gandhi's campaign against British rule in India being an example – it raises a special problem for a liberal society. Again, we use the word problem in a precise sense, meaning a puzzle that demands a solution. The *puzzle* is this: we have special obligations to obey laws passed through the use of a democratic procedure, but that procedure can generate unjust laws which we have an obligation to disobey. This problem does not exist for a non-democratic society because there is no obligation to obey its laws, even if the laws themselves are 'just'. It follows that in a world where there are no liberal democratic societies civil disobedience will not be a prominent political issue (which is not to say that civil disobedience is not possible in such a world: repressive governments may be met with non-violent resistance). Until the twentieth century there were few, if any, fully liberal democratic societies – the denial of the vote to women ensured this was the case.

Early modern theorists could think only in terms of rebellion or revolution, not civil disobedience.

The concept of political violence, which encompasses the older debate over just war but alongside non-state violence in the form of terrorism, is related to civil disobedience, in that in part it is problematic when directed at liberal democratic societies. The differentiation of terrorism as one form of violence among other distinct forms is a consequence of the development of the liberal democratic value of peace: whereas pre-modern societies gloried in violence – think of the esteem attached to chivalry – modern liberal societies stress the importance of peace and order. When liberal democracies use military force they claim to operate within rules of war. Terrorism is characterised as the absence of rules, hence the use of the word 'terror'. We argue that the rather clichéd distinction expressed in the statement that 'one person's terrorist is another person's freedom-fighter' is not a useful one, and that the use of terror must be contextualised: against liberal democracies, where there exists a real possibility of political change, terror cannot be justified. In non-liberal societies, or where liberal societies are engaged in proxy wars, it is more difficult to draw a line between the justified and the unjustified employment of terrorist tactics. The point we make here is that the study of terrorism – both empirically in what is called 'terrorology' and ethically in political theory – is a relatively recent phenomenon, emerging under social and political conditions in which the classification of acceptable and unacceptable uses of violence has changed fundamentally.

Chapter 18

Human Rights

Introduction

A human right is an entitlement to treatment that a person enjoys simply by virtue of being a human being. Human rights are universal, meaning that possession of such rights is not contingent on belonging to a particular state or culture. Although the concept can be traced back to the eighteenth-century Enlightenment – the 'rights of man' – it is only in the twentieth century that a human right became a major concept in political discourse. The widespread ratification by states of the Universal Declaration of Human Rights, which was created in 1948, three years after the end of the Second World War, has changed world politics; although individuals are frequently denied their human rights, even by states purporting to respect them, the fact of the existence of human rights has shifted international politics from being based simply on nation-states' interest to one based on the recognition that individuals have claims against their own state. Human rights are open to the criticism that they are the product of a particular time and place – post-eighteenth-century Europe, or the West – and their 'imposition' is a form of imperialism. They can also be criticised for elevating individualism above collectivism, and 'negative' rights (to be left alone) above 'positive' rights (to a particular level of resources).

Chapter Map

In this chapter we will:

- Consider the modern discourse of human rights by reference to the Nuremberg trials.

- Study human rights documents, and their philosophical implications.

- Outline the universalism versus relativism debate.

- Assess five attempts to defend a set of universal human rights.

Free to Believe?

Missionary with Turkana Tribe, Kenya, 1986

Source: © Daniel Lainé/CORBIS

Article 18 of the Universal Declaration of Human Rights states that

everyone has the right to freedom of thought, conscience and religion; this right includes freedom to change his religion or belief, and freedom, either alone or in community with others and in public or private, to manifest his religion or belief in teaching, practice, worship and observance.

The development of conceptions of religious toleration was crucial to the development of liberalism and religious freedom, and along with certain prohibitions, on, for example, slavery and torture, are taken to be among the most fundamental human rights. Despite this, even in Europe – arguably, the 'homeland' of human rights – the right is restricted: some European countries do not, for example, permit the building of mosques with minarets, and opposition is not based on planning grounds, but on hostility to a visible Islamic presence.

African scholar Makau Mutua, in a critique of human rights (Mutua, 2002), argues that the right to practise one's religion is sometimes in tension with the right to proselytise, and as the former is based on the more fundamental value of self-determination, it should take priority. This means it is legitimate to restrict the 'missionary, messianic' religions of Christianity and Islam from, in effect, continuing their colonialist projects. Religions do not compete on a level playing field, and the human rights regime 'not only forcibly imposes on African religions the obligation to compete – a task for which as non-proselytising, non-competitive creeds they are not historically fashioned – but also protects the evangelizing religions in their march towards universalization' (Mutua, 2002: 94).

- Should religion be accorded the full protection of Article 18?

Human Rights after Nuremberg

A 'human right' can be defined as an entitlement to treatment a person has simply by virtue of being 'human', and as such human rights must be applicable irrespective of time and place. If we were to say that a person's rights are conditional on their being a citizen of a particular state, or belonging to a particular culture, then the rights would not rest simply on the fact of being a human being, and they would not be universal. This raises a difficulty for human rights discourse. The language of human rights is a modern phenomenon, traceable to the eighteenth-century Enlightenment, but only embodied in legal documents in the twentieth century. This suggests that human rights are culturally specific – that is, the product of a particular time (modern period) and a particular place (the West). For critics of human rights the problem of cultural relativism is thought to be fatal – the alleged universalism of human rights simply masks a form of cultural imperialism.

There is no doubt that while human rights are claimed to be universal the widespread use of the concept is a relatively recent phenomenon. It is only with the formulation and signing of the Universal Declaration of Human Rights (hereafter referred to as the UDHR) (1948) that respect for human rights has become a significant consideration in domestic and international politics (that does not mean that human rights are, in fact, respected). Alongside the philosophical discourse and political rhetoric there has also developed a body of international human rights law and a set of international legal institutions, such as the International Criminal Court (ICC) in The Hague (Netherlands). So there is a history to human rights. In the course of this chapter we will discuss whether the historicity of human rights undermines the claim made for their universality.

The UDHR was 'adopted and proclaimed' by the General Assembly of the newly formed United Nations on 10 December 1948. It was developed against the background of the Nuremberg War Crimes Trials, which followed the defeat of Nazi Germany in May 1945. There were two sets of trials: those of the 'major war criminals', before the International Military Tribunal (1945–6), and those of the 'lesser war criminals' before the US Nuremberg Military Tribunals (1946–9). The Nuremberg process was criticised by some commentators as a series of show trials based on 'victor's justice'; after all, among the indictments were acts that had undoubtedly been carried out by the victorious Allies, such as the terror raids that destroyed many German cities. However, Nuremberg is significant for the study of human rights, in part because of its flaws, and, in part, because it introduced novel concepts. The legally significant features of the Nuremberg process were as follows:

- The indictment, or charges made against the defendants, were created *ex post facto* and were not related to the laws of Germany. The indictment contained four counts (types of charge): (a) conspiracy to wage an aggressive war; (b) planning, preparation and waging of an aggressive war; (c) war crimes that included, for example, the mistreatment of prisoners of war; (d) crimes against humanity.
- The compulsion defence – 'I was only obeying orders' – was removed.
- The *tu quoque* defence was removed – *ad hominem tu quoque* means 'at the person, you too' and effectively amounts to the defendant saying 'you committed the same crimes, so you have no authority to judge me'.

- The indictment made reference to violations of 'international conventions', but there is no citation of those conventions, with the implication that it was a loose term meaning the 'general standards of criminal law in civilised societies'.

Although the motivation among the leadership of the Allied powers to create the Nuremburg process was largely political, there was a moral consciousness at work, a consciousness that became stronger in later decades. Consequently, Nuremberg posed a problem: on the one hand there was a sense of what can be termed the 'objective wrongness' of what the Nazi regime had done that manifested itself as revulsion at the acts of those on trial. On the other hand, the trials seemed to depend on the creation of post hoc, or retroactive, laws. Retroactive laws violate the principle that there can be no crime without an antecedent law: if you do something that is legal at the time of doing it, then you should not later be prosecuted for that act. If retroactive laws are created then power is arbitrary (other troubling aspects of Nuremberg included the rejection of both the *tu quoque* and compulsion defences). There has been considerable debate among legal and political theorists about the retroactivity problem; some theorists argue that German law was suspended at a point during the 1930s, and therefore the laws of Weimar Germany (1918–33) should form part of the basis of the indictment. Other theorists appeal to conventions, such as the prohibition on murder, which all right-thinking human beings, and all properly functioning legal systems, recognise as valid.

The point about Nuremberg is that German law of the Nazi period could not form the basis of the judgment, and so other laws or conventions, not rooted in a particular legal system, had to be used. Nuremberg is not simply an interesting historical problem, because it has relevance for contemporary debates about human rights: if there are human rights as defined at the beginning of this section, then they are universal, and the universality extends across national boundaries and across times. The Nuremberg problem will not disappear when the last alleged Nazi war criminal has died, for it is fundamentally a philosophical problem: how can there be human rights if there are no laws embodying those rights? But if human rights only exist where there are laws stating those rights, then how can they be universal? The post-Nuremberg codification of human rights in the UDHR and the Genocide Convention (1948) helps to solve a legal problem, but not the political-philosophical one. To explain, the UDHR was (eventually) signed by the governments of most states, and through the force of treaty law human rights have been given legal validity. Had there been such a declaration in the 1920s to which Germany had signed up, and that was not rescinded by the Hitler regime, then there would have been a clearer legal basis for Nuremberg (there was such a basis for the third count of war crimes: the Geneva Conventions of 1864, 1906 and 1929). However, this does not solve the philosophical problem: if a nation refuses to sign up to any human rights conventions does that mean it is not obliged to respect human rights?

This question – and the distinction between legal and philosophical problems – reveals an ambiguity at the heart of human rights discourse. When we use the term 'human rights' are we referring to a set of legal rights, or to moral rights, or, perhaps, to some form of political rhetoric that is based on neither legal nor moral grounds? If human rights equate to certain legal rights enjoyed by individuals through international law, then disputes about human rights will take place in a legal framework, by reference to legal documents and judgments. If, however, human rights are moral rights, then disputes are settled by reference to moral concepts and moral arguments. Put simply, as legal rights human rights are individual entitlements backed up by the force of law; as moral rights, they are individual entitlements supported by the force of argument. As tools of international politics, human rights are intended to secure certain outcomes: a state widely recognised as violating human rights may find itself shunned by other states and, consequently, its interests damaged. Many advocates of human rights rely on a mixture of treaty law and 'shame' to advance their cause. However, the political uses of human rights can generate cynicism. One of the justifications given for the bombing of Serbia in 1999 was that it was an 'exceptional measure to prevent an overwhelming humanitarian catastrophe', namely the mass deportation and killing of Kosovars. Yet the same description could be applied to the situation since 1995 in the province of Chechnya, where Russia has suppressed a breakaway movement, and engaged in a serious violation of human rights. The reasons for action in Kosovo and inaction in Chechnya is, in small part, logistical, but mainly the recognition of realpolitik: Russia has nuclear weapons.

The best approach for further study of the morality, legality, and politics of human rights is a consideration of human rights documents, and in the next section we focus on two: the UDHR, and the European Convention on Human Rights (ECHR). However, before discussing these documents some comments on the pre-twentieth-century origins of human rights are required. Certainly, the idea that humans have rights by virtue of their humanity can be traced back to the eighteenth century 'rights of man' and these rights are grounded in the Enlightenment conception of the human being as a rational agent. Although many Enlightenment thinkers were reluctant to extend such rights to non-European peoples, and in some cases to women, it could be argued that the logic of rational agency implies that prima facie all human beings have rights. But there are attempts to trace the origins of human rights much further back in time and, furthermore, demonstrate that they have both Western and non-Western sources. Religious documents, such as the Vedas, the Bible (Hebrew and Christian), and the Qur'an, it is argued, either make explicit or at least imply standards of treatment and duties and obligations that are recognisably universal. These attempts to show that human rights have plural sources of justification are really motivated by a contemporary concern to dispel the impression that human rights are a Western, imperialistic imposition on non-Western cultures. Such a discourse may, in fact, serve a useful functioning in generating respect for human rights, but there is also mythology at work here: a proselytising religion, such as Christianity or Islam, is implicitly universal, but it does not follow that the rights it accords are based on humanity. Rather, a person is equal as a Christian or a Muslim, and insofar as Christianity respects non-Christians or Islam non-Muslims that respect is grounded in a view of the 'other' as a potential convert.

A pluralistic argument for human rights – one that stresses the importance of history – may be summed up in a metaphor. Full international respect for human rights is a historical achievement akin to reaching the top of a mountain. The history of human rights can then be characterised as the ascent of the mountain: distinct religions and cultures tackle the climb from different sides of the mountain, such that they cannot see one another or recognise that they are engaged in a common pursuit. Only once they have reached the mountain top will they be able to acknowledge their shared history. This is an attractive metaphor, the force of which depends on ignoring the reasons advanced by different religious and philosophical systems for respecting 'universal' human rights.

Human Rights Conventions

Literature on human rights tends to fall into two groups, with limited cross-over between them: human rights law and philosophical discussions of human rights. While respecting the difference between these approaches it is useful for students of political theory to establish the connections between them, because legality and morality are both important in debates about the relationship between the state and citizen. To this end we will look at two human rights documents: the Universal Declaration of Human Rights (UDHR), and the European Convention on Human Rights (ECHR). There are important differences between these two documents, and the aim of our study is to draw out the philosophical and political implications of each document.

Universal Declaration of Human Rights (1948)

The UDHR consists of a Preamble and 30 articles. The Preamble asserts that the 'inherent dignity and of the equal and inalienable rights of all members of the human family is the foundation of freedom, justice and peace in the world'. Without specifying the events it acknowledges the 'barbarous acts which have outraged the conscience of mankind', and asserts that human rights must be protected through law.

The 30 articles are reproduced in summary form below. We have grouped them together for purposes of discussion; they are not, in fact, grouped in this way in the UDHR.

Article(s)	
1–2	Human beings should be treated equally, irrespective of personal characteristics or citizenship.
3	Right to life, liberty and security of person.
4–5	Prohibition on slavery, and on torture.
6–11	Equality before the law: equal protection by the state; right to an effective remedy for violation of one's rights; prohibition on arbitrary arrest and detention; right to a fair trial; presumption of innocence until guilt is proven; prohibition on retroactive laws.
12	Prohibition on arbitrary interference in private life.
13–14	Freedom of movement, including emigration; right to asylum in another country.
15	Right to nationality; prohibition on deprivation of nationality.
16	Right to marry; prohibition on forced marriage.
17	Right to own property; prohibition on arbitrary seizure of property.
18–20	Freedom of thought, conscience and religion; freedom of opinion and expression; right to peaceful assembly; prohibition on compulsion to belong to an association.
21	Right to political participation; equal access to public service; 'the will of the people shall be the basis of the authority of the government'.
22–26	Right to social security; right to work, and the free choice of employment; equal pay for equal work; right to 'just and favourable remuneration'; right to join a trade union; right to rest and leisure; right to an 'adequate' standard of living; 'motherhood and childhood are entitled to special care and assistance'; equal protection of children; right to education; right of parents to determine the kind of education their children receive.
27	Right freely to participate in the cultural life of the community.
28	'Everyone is entitled to a social and international order in which the rights and freedoms set forth in this Declaration can be fully realised'.
29	Everyone has duties to his or her community; the exercise of the above rights can only be limited in order to meet the 'just requirements of morality, public order and the general welfare in a democratic society'.
30	Nothing in the Declaration should imply that any state, group or person can engage in actions destructive of any of the rights and freedoms set out in it.

Several important points can be drawn from this document:

1. Although reference is made to the importance of legal protection, the document provides for no legal mechanisms, such as courts, to enforce human rights, and the linguistic style of the document lacks the precision a good legal document should possess.

2. Many of the rights themselves can be grouped: (a) rights that essentially amount to being left alone; (b) rights to participate in the political structure of the country, and to enjoy the protection of its laws; (c) rights to associate with people of your own choosing; (d) social rights, such as employment protection and a minimum level of resources. The first three groups clearly reflect the ethos of a liberal democratic society, whereas the last was a concession to the realities of power politics in the post-war period, where the Soviet Union was keen to stake out a distinct moral position, one that stressed social goods.

3. The rights are limited by Articles 29 and 30, which talk of the duties of individuals – the reference to the 'requirements of morality' leaves open the possibility that the rights could be interpreted in significantly different ways in different cultures.

European Convention on Human Rights (1950)

The European Convention on Human Rights – officially the Convention for the Protection of Human Rights and Fundamental Freedoms – was adopted in 1950 by the Council of Europe, an international organisation that began with 10 member states and now has 46 (http://www.coe.int). The Preamble to the ECHR makes explicit its relationship to the UDHR by stating as its aim the 'collective enforcement of certain rights stated in the Universal Declaration'. There are, however, several important features that distinguish the ECHR from the UDHR. These differences flow from the fact that the ECHR is intended as a legal document, whereas the UDHR is a general statement of aspiration:

1. Many of the articles of the ECHR are double-headed, meaning that the first part sets out the rights, but the second states a limitation on the right. For example, Article 10 is concerned with freedom of expression, but this is then limited by various considerations, including 'national security', 'public safety', 'protection of health and morals' and the 'protection of reputation'.

2. Section I of the document sets out the rights and freedoms of individuals, but Section II – which is about half the document – is concerned with the powers of the European Court of Human Rights, which was established by the Convention. Part III – Miscellaneous Provisions – deals with various issues relating to the obligations of the contracting states.

3. The ECHR has been amended – through protocols – many times since its creation; in most cases this has entailed strengthening, or extending, the rights contained in it. For example, Protocol 6 (1983) restricted the use of the death penalty to times of war or national emergency; Protocol 13 (2002) prohibits the death penalty in all circumstances (not all Council members have ratified Protocols 6 and 13 see http://www.worldpolicy.org/globalrights/dp/maps-dp-echr.html).

4. Although there is, unsurprisingly, a strong overlap between the rights contained in both documents, the ECHR omits the 'social rights' (Articles 22–26) of the UDHR. Given that the 10 founding members of the Council were all Western European, this is to be expected (Eastern states joined only after the collapse of state socialism in 1989 – Russia, for example, joined in 1996).

Why the UDHR and the ECHR are Significant

The Declaration and the Convention are important in what they reveal about the nature and justification of human rights, and in the rest of this chapter we will pursue these further:

1. Human rights privilege certain values over others: there can be no doubt that human rights are individualist, in the sense that the integrity of the individual – their body and mind – and the choices they make, are the object of protection. Certainly Articles 22–26 of the Declaration stress the social conditions for action, and they raise important questions that we consider in Chapter 21, but the 'core' human rights are individualist. This raises the question of whether human rights are compatible with cultures that place stress on individualism. Would it matter if they were not compatible? We pursue these questions later in this chapter.

2. The differences between the two documents are interesting and important and raise the issue of what happens to the concept of a human right when we try to apply it in a concrete legal-political situation: must a human right be a legal right? Even if a human right need not be a legal right might it not be that the only human right worth having is one that can be enforced in law? This raises the Nuremberg question: can we have rights that are not recognised in any legal document?

3. Rights will conflict – rights can conflict with one another, and they can conflict with certain duties. A system of rights must, therefore, be compossible, that is, the rights must be mutually possible. Furthermore, rights must be 'actionable', meaning that the fulfilment of the right cannot require impossible actions. To use a slightly silly example, if you have 100 people, and 50 oranges, then you cannot give each person a right to an orange, or, at least, a whole orange. The ECHR strives for compossibility and actionability.

Rights – Some Conceptual Issues

We have approached the concept of human rights by looking at actual documents rather than justifications for human rights. The rest of this chapter will be devoted to the question of justification, but as a preliminary it is important to make some conceptual distinctions regarding rights – that is, rights in general, rather than specifically human rights.* We focus on three aspects of the concept of rights: types of rights; the nature of the right-holder; conflicts between rights.

*A more comprehensive discussion of rights can be found in the website essay 'Rights'.

- *Types of rights:* a generic definition of a right is an 'entitlement', but legal theorist Wesley Hohfeld argued that there are, in fact, four distinct types of right – claims, privileges (or liberties), powers, and immunities (Hohfeld, 1923: 12). A right is a relationship: correlating to a claim is a duty; to a privilege a 'no-claim'; to a power a liability; and to an immunity a disability. So if you have a claim someone else (one person or a group) has a duty. Drawing on Hohfeld we can make two points: (a) rights carry 'costs' for others; (b) what is called a right in the UDHR or ECHR is often a bundle of Hohfeldian rights with an internally complex structure – for example, the 'right to marry' involves exercising *powers* and through those powers generating *claims*, and insofar as the right to marry is constitutionally protected the state is disabled from interfering, meaning you have an *immunity* against the state.

- *The nature of the right-holder:* can very young children – conceptually – have rights? Can non-human animals have rights? Those who reject children's rights or animal rights argue that only a being capable of exercising choice (more technically: exercising a power) can have rights. It does not follow that there are no duties towards children and animals, but simply that those duties do not 'correlate' to rights. Such a theory of rights is called the will theory (it is also known as the choice theory). Theorists who argue that children and animals can – conceptually – have rights argue that to have a right is to be the *beneficiary* of the performance of a duty. A child need not be capable of exercising a right in order to have rights. Benefit theory (or interest theory; recipience theory) takes a much wider viewer of who can have rights, although with the consequence of weakening the distinctiveness of rights. This argument is important not so much in justifying human rights as in explaining what can count as a human right.

- *Conflicts between rights.* We have suggested that a scheme of rights must be compossible and that the ECHR, as a legal document, pays much more attention to this than the UDHR. It is important to make a distinction between the *violation* of a right and the *overriding* of a right. Violation is simply the arbitrary setting aside of a right. If a right is overridden then this entails providing reasons for setting that right aside. Such a reason will make appeal to weights between different considerations, such as individual freedom as against collective security. Importantly, human rights need not be absolute: it is a mistake to confuse universality with absoluteness. A human right is a consideration that must always be taken into account irrespective of cultural differences, but it does not follow that a particular human right cannot be overridden. Perhaps some human rights are absolute, but absoluteness is not a necessary feature of a human right.

Relativism versus Universalism

So far we have talked about the concept of a right and about the historical origins of human rights documents and mechanisms of enforcement. What we have not discussed is the justification of human rights. We assume that the *fact* of law does not necessarily *justify* a law. Once we accept this we are forced to confront the cultural relativism thesis, which can be stated thus:

> Values have to be understood as part of a complex whole; that complex whole is 'culture'. When discussing the universal applicability of 'human rights' we must take into account the impact that they will have on particular cultures. For some cultures those rights express central values, for others they may, with some revision, be compatible with that culture, but for others they may be wholly inappropriate and damaging.

Cultural relativism does not necessarily entail the rejection of morality: the UDHR may be valid for certain cultures. What cultural relativists challenge is the claim to *universal* application. This raises the question as to whether a relativist can endorse some form of human rights. One possibility is to distinguish 'state' and 'culture': the Council of Europe is composed of more than 45 states, but it could be argued that there is a single European culture, which has its roots in Christianity (medieval Europe was often referred to as Christendom). Similarly the Islamic world is composed of many states bound together by Islamic culture (it might also be argued that the Arab world, as part of the wider Islamic world, is a distinct culture). If we endorse the distinction between state and culture then it might be possible to talk of trans-national standards of treatment. Those standards would allow a distinction to be made between two ways of rejecting human rights: (a) *violation* of culturally accepted human rights by a particular regime; (b) *legitimate rejection* of human rights on cultural grounds. For example, it could be debated whether Saudi Arabian penal policy, such as public beheadings and the amputation of hands, is grounded in Islamic teaching and Arab custom, or whether it simply serves the interests of the Saudi state to have such apparently draconian forms of punishment.

This argument, while plausible, is difficult for a defender of human rights to embrace. As we suggested in the first section of this chapter, human rights are rights that individuals have by virtue of their humanity. The cultural argument makes rights, or any other standard of treatment, contingent on a person's culture. While there may be a role for culture in the justification, formulation and implementation of human rights, the radical culturalism that forms the basis of the cultural relativism thesis is incompatible with a defence of human rights. We need then to consider arguments against cultural relativism or, put another way, arguments for universalism. We set out five theories.

Intuition and Consensus (Donnelly)

Jack Donnelly, in his book *Universal Human Rights in Theory and Practice*, defends what he terms weak cultural relativism, which entails strong universalism. Weak cultural relativism assumes that human rights are universally applicable but allows that 'the relativity of human nature, communities and rules checks potential excesses of universalism'. Strong cultural relativism holds that culture is the principal source of the validity of a right or rule, and 'at its furthest extreme, strong cultural relativism accepts a few basic rights with virtually universal application but allows such a wide range of variation that two entirely justifiable sets of rights might overlap only slightly' (Donnelly, 2003: 90).

The looseness of the language of the UDHR Donnelly regards as a strength. The UDHR is a general statement of orienting value, and it is at this level – and only at this level – that a moral consensus exists. For example, Articles 3–12 'are so clearly connected to basic requirements of human dignity, and are stated in sufficiently general terms, that virtually every morally defensible contemporary form of social organization must recognize them' (Donnelly, 2003: 94). Below we discuss the 'rational entailment' argument, of which there are several versions, but the central idea is that certain standards of treatment can be derived from the conditions which humans require for action, and as such a society cannot deny those standards without also denying the preconditions for its own existence. Donnelly's statement has the appearance of such an argument, but in fact he then goes on to appeal to human intuition. By 'intuition' is meant a strong sense of, or belief in, the rightness or wrongness of something, but without the ability to give a complete explanation of that sense or belief. Donnelly identifies the intuition that people should be treated in a certain way irrespective of their culture by means of a question:

> In twenty years of working with issues of cultural relativism, I have developed a simple test that I pose to sceptical audiences. What rights in the Universal Declaration, I ask, does your society or culture reject? Rarely has a single full right (other than the right to private property) been rejected (Donnelly: 94).

He recalls a visit to Iran in 2001, where he posed the above question to three different audiences. In all three cases discussion moved quickly on to the issue of freedom of religion, and in particular to atheism, and to apostasy by Muslims, which the UDHR permits, but Iran prohibits. Donnelly observed that the discussion was not about freedom of religion, but rather about Western versus Islamic interpretations of that right (we discuss freedom of religion in the final section of this chapter).

Particular human rights are like essentially contested concepts in which there are differing interpretations but strong overlap between them. So long as outliers are few, we can talk about a consensus around human rights. Such outliers would be cultures that do not accept a particular human right. The fact that increasing numbers of states are prepared to sign up to the UDHR, and to later, and more specific, United Nations conventions Donnelly takes to be evidence of a dynamic consensus in favour of human rights. He also observes that when Western states criticise non-Western states for apparently barbaric practices that criticism is sometimes accompanied by a serious lack of self-awareness; in 1994 18-year-old American Michael Fay was convicted by a Singaporean court of vandalising hundreds of thousands of dollars worth of property. He was sentenced to three months in jail, required to pay a fine and, most controversially, was condemned to six strokes of the cane (the cane would leave permanent scars). There was widespread condemnation in the United States. Donnelly tersely observes that President Clinton, while condemning the sentence 'failed to find it even notable that in his own country people are being fried in the electric chair' (Donnelly, 2003: 99).

To sum up, Donnelly's observations are interesting, but two points are problematic. First, an intuition in favour of human rights at best indicates that there may be something underlying those rights which is, in some sense, universal, but if this is so then it should be possible to move beyond intuition and provide reasons for respecting human rights. Second, the fact that *states* have signed up to human rights conventions does not entail *cultural* agreement: human rights must be recognised as valid by large parts of the populations of states, and not simply by the leadership. In many states the governing elites are disconnected from their peoples, and although states may be considered the main actors with regard to human rights, respect for such rights does depend on popular recognition.

Contractualism (Rawls)

The fact that increasing numbers of states are prepared to sign up to human rights conventions does not in itself amount to an argument for the universality of human rights, but it may provide an element in an argument. In Chapters 4 and 8 we discussed the idea of the social contract, which has been a device used by liberal political theorists to justify state power. Our discussion focused on the 'domestic' use of the contract: political theorists such as Hobbes, Locke, Rousseau and Rawls were concerned with the relationship of the individual to the state. This contrasts with an 'international contract', which is a contract not between individual human beings but between states. We also made a distinction between a quasi-historical contract, whereby we could imagine that people could have agreed to create a state, and the hypothetical contract in which the contractors are idealised and the contract is a thought experiment rather than an imagined historical event.

Interestingly enough, whereas defenders of the historical contract do not claim that there was actually an agreement to enter the state – they claim simply that it was imaginable – international legal institutions can plausibly be described as the product of an agreement between the member states of the international community: agreements to create international institutions. Of course, there is not a single 'moment' of agreement, for the ratification of a convention can take place over decades. Furthermore, there has never been an international agreement to create a single state; such an agreement would constitute the dissolution of all existing states. The closest the international community has come to the creation of a single, multinational global power has been the formation of the United Nations with the commitment by member states to provide military personnel to enforce international law.

The problem of enforcement may be thought a serious deficiency of international law, and one that can only be remedied through the creation of a single state. However, there is a considerable body of international law, such as commercial law, which states respect without recourse to a global enforcement agency. As Locke argued, enforcement, while important, is not the main deficiency evident in the state of nature, for a more significant deficiency is the absence of a body capable of interpreting, and indeed determining, the law. Even if all states subscribed to the UDHR, its wording is so general as to require a third-party judgement on its meaning. In practice, the United Nations effectively contracts out the interpretation of human rights to bodies such as the European Court of Human Rights. The general point to make is that a hypothetical international contract differs from a domestic one in that its object is not the creation of a world state that will enforce human rights, but rather it is a device for creating a charter of human rights and associated multinational institutions. States will not then be able to violate human rights on grounds of disagreement about their interpretation, and will have incentives – such as the desire for reputation – to respect them.

John Rawls offers a philosophical defence of this international contractualism in his book *The Law of Peoples* (1999). The underlying aim of that book is to outline the just foreign policy of a liberal society: when is intervention in the affairs of another state justified? What duties do liberal societies have to non-liberal ones? Although that aim is quite narrow, in the course of the book Rawls does present an argument intended to show that non-liberal, non-Western societies can respect human rights. Although he does not use these terms with great precision Rawls makes a distinction between four types of society or 'people': (a) *Liberal societies*, such as those which (largely) respect human rights conventions, and the conventions of war; (b) *Decent non-liberal societies*, of which there can be several variants, but the one type Rawls discusses possesses a 'decent consultation hierarchy' (hereafter referred to as 'decent societies'); (c) *Outlaw states* – states that violate the law of peoples, by, for example, waging aggressive wars or engaging in serious violations of human rights; (d) *Burdened societies*, where poor socio-economic conditions make respect for international law difficult.

Rawls applies the idea of the original position and the veil of ignorance developed in his theory of domestic justice to international law, but there are some significant differences between how these devices are used in Rawls's theory of (domestic) justice, and in his theory of international justice. Liberal societies agree among themselves on a 'law of peoples', and then decent societies endorse those same principles (Rawls argues that liberal democratic societies, by their nature, will tend to respect the human rights of their own peoples and the sovereignty of other peoples). The law of peoples consists of eight principles: mutual recognition of each people's independence; honouring of agreements; legal equality of peoples; duty of non-intervention (except in the case of dealing with outlaw states and grave violations of human rights); right to self-defence; respect for human rights; respect for the rules of war; duty to assist peoples living under conditions that prevent them from becoming just (liberal) or decent societies. The law requires of liberal societies that they do not seek to change the fundamental character of a decent society.

To understand how a decent society could endorse the law of peoples, and consequently why a liberal society should tolerate a decent society, we need to know the characteristics of the latter. Rawls argues that a decent society is peaceful in that it pursues its interests through trade and diplomacy. The domestic laws of such a society are guided by a 'common good conception of justice', meaning that while it may not grant the freedoms to individuals enjoyed in a liberal society, in a fundamental sense all citizens are treated equally. There should exist a 'decent consultation hierarchy', which permits the possibility of dissent (the Arab–Islamic concept of *Shura* would be one example of a consultation hierarchy). Importantly, the common good conception of justice entails respect for human rights, including the right to life, liberty (freedom from slavery and forced labour), personal property and equality before the law. Although a decent society may not permit apostasy and proselytisation, it must accord a degree of religious freedom to minorities, and because that right is limited it must also allow citizens the possibility of emigration. The fundamental philosophical point Rawls makes about human rights is that they should not depend on a particular conception of the human agent as autonomous, but rather 'human rights set a necessary . . . standard for the decency of domestic political and social institutions' (Rawls, 1999: 80).

Human rights fulfil three roles: (a) they are a necessary condition of a regime's legitimacy; (b) they determine the limits of sovereignty – the law of people prohibits intervention in the affairs of another state except when that state is violating human rights; (c) they set a limit on the pluralism among peoples. Even if Rawls is correct in arguing that a decent society can respect human rights, are there any grounds for believing that they will do so for reasons other than state interest? Do they respect human rights for the 'right reasons', or because such respect is useful to establishing a reputation in international politics? A similar argument could be applied to the international behaviour of liberal states, but the difference between liberal and non-liberal societies is that human rights are deeply embedded in the culture of the former. Even if the leaders of liberal societies are cynical in their use of human rights rhetoric in international politics – intervening in Kosovo but not Chechnya – they may well (largely) respect human rights in their domestic political systems.

Rational Entailment (Habermas)

The rational entailment argument identifies certain conditions for the existence of social order and from those conditions maintains that there are certain standards of treatment which all societies should respect. The argument can take two forms – empirical and logical. The empirical version observes actual societies and claims that the long-term survival of a society depends on the recognition of human rights. This version has only limited plausibility – many societies function without respect for human rights; it is somewhat more plausible to maintain that human rights-respecting societies are more successful than human rights-violating ones, where success is measured by economic growth and political stability. The logical version does not deny that social life is possible without human rights, but rather that a human rights-violating society cannot justify its own political and legal organisation without falling into contradiction. In Chapter 3 we discussed the citizenship laws of Nazi Germany which effectively stripped Jews of their citizenship. Legal theorist Lon Fuller argued that Nazi law could not respect certain principles internal to law, such as the prohibition on non-retroactivity. Fuller is not suggesting that Nazi Germany did not 'function', but rather that it could not justify its laws; implicit in Fuller's argument is a belief in human rights, to which he is offering a logical entailment defence. Of course, a regime can simply choose not to justify its actions – although that is extremely rare – but refusal to engage in the justification process does not undermine the logical entailment argument.

Ch. 3:
Equality
pp. 65–66

Jürgen Habermas offers the best contemporary statement of logical entailment. Before we get to his defence of human rights against cultural relativism, it is necessary to set out briefly Habermas's rather complex theory of social change.

If we define 'culture' as the 'taken-for-granted horizon of expectations', then under conditions of modernity culture is threatened by rationalisation in the form of money (or the market) and bureaucratic power – relations between human beings become consciously instrumental, rather than implicit and taken for granted. There is a diminution of trust. Many theorists, especially in the German philosophical tradition in which Habermas has been formed, are pessimistic about the consequences of modernity. However, Habermas argues that the emphasis on instrumentalisation – or what he calls 'systemic rationality' – ignores the positive achievements of modernity, expressed in 'communicative rationality' (Habermas, 1984: 8–22). The growth in consciousness of human rights is one of the achievements of communicative rationality.

What does Habermas mean by 'communicative action'? People engage in speech-acts: person A *promises* to meet person B on Thursday, *requests* B stop smoking, *confesses* to find B's actions distasteful, *predicts* it will rain. Implicit in each speech act is an offer or claim. In the first two cases A is making a claim to normative rightness, in the third case a claim to sincerity, and in the final case a claim to truth. B can contest all three such 'validity claims' (Habermas, 1984: 319–28). The success of each speech act depends upon both parties orienting themselves to principles of reason that are not reducible to individual intentions: in addressing B person A treats B as an end in themselves. The validity claims are implicit in all human action, that is, they are universal. This seems a promising basis for defending universal human rights against the challenge of cultural relativism. However, the validity claims are abstract from everyday life, and so to redeem them requires appeal to a stock of culturally specific values. That means the content of human rights is dependent on culture.

One way to address this problem of cultural dependence is to maintain that politics is a dialogue, in which people bring to bear their different cultural perspectives, such that what emerges from the dialogue is something pluralistic yet coherent. For example, Muslims may be criticised by Western feminists for projecting a patriarchal conception of gender relations. By engaging in dialogue Muslims may reform their view of women's rights, but Westerners might also be obliged to recognise the deficiencies in their own understanding of family relations, by, for example, acknowledging the costs entailed in the commodification of sex in a liberal society.

Habermas argues that there is a tradition in Anglophone legal and political theory of conceiving of the state as grounded in the protection of individual private rights – rights derived from the market contract model. Hobbes is the *locus classicus* of this conception of individual–state relations. If we operate with such a theory then it is inevitable that individual rights will be a threat to cultural reproduction; in effect, increasing reliance on rights would be another example of the systemic rationality eroding the lifeworld. We are then left with a choice: either we assert the primacy of individual rights at the expense of cultural interaction, or we maintain the authority of the collective over the individual. Private rights entail the assertion of personal autonomy, but they ignore the other half of the concept of autonomy – public autonomy:

> from a normative point of view, the integrity of the individual legal person cannot be guaranteed without protecting the intersubjectively shared experiences

and life contexts in which the person has been socialized and has formed his or her identity. The identity of the individual is interwoven with collective identities and can be stabilized only in a cultural network that cannot be appropriated as private property any more than the mother tongue itself can be (Habermas, 1994: 129).

The implication of Habermas's argument is that universal human rights are, contrary to Rawls's theory, grounded in human autonomy, but that human autonomy itself has a collective dimension which must take into account cultural interpretations of human rights. Legality is central to the realisation of human rights, and Habermas's theory of law bears some resemblance to Fuller's: law is not reducible to the assertion of will – people are not simply subjects of law – but the formation of law is a discursive process. The legal realisation of human rights will inevitably involve local interpretation – for example, Muslim societies will interpret human rights differently to Western societies – but human beings are bound together through discourse, and discourse presupposes a conception of the human agent as autonomous.

Natural Rights (Finnis)

We touched on Finnis' work in our discussion of legal moralism in Chapter 2. Finnis is a leading contemporary interpreter and defender of the Aristotelian-Thomist tradition of natural law. Although he devotes only one chapter (of 13) of his book *Natural Law and Natural Rights* explicitly to human rights, he argues that 'right' is central to his entire argument, and it is important to understand the relationship between the singular 'right' and the plural 'rights'. The plural results from 'reporting and asserting the requirements or other implications of a relationship of justice *from the point of view of the person(s) who benefit(s) from* that relationship' (Finnis, 1980: 205, his emphasis). Surveying the development of the concept of right from its classical antecedent *jus*, Finnis notes that for Thomas Aquinas (1225–74) *jus* meant 'the fair' or 'fairness'. Relationships of justice – who is owed what – are secondary. By 1610 the Spanish Jesuit writer Francisco Suarez has reversed the priority and defines *jus* in terms of a moral power which each person possesses, and this way of thinking about justice is developed a short time later by Hugo Grotius: *jus* is essentially something a person has – it is a power (Finnis, 1980: 206–7). What we see is the development of rights from right. For Finnis, this takes a damaging turn in the work of Hobbes, who argues that a person has rights in the state of nature – that is, a situation in which there is no state, or political authority: since nobody is compelled to do anything each is free. The state for Hobbes is the rational outcome of the exercise of these 'natural rights'. But since nobody has any duties in the state of nature – for example, nobody is under a duty not to kill you – then we could, Finnis suggests, just as well say that there are no rights outside the state.

While Finnis accepts the post-Thomist pluralisation of rights he argues that the Hobbesian tradition loses sight of the connection between right and rights. The justification of human rights depends upon understanding that connection. The limitations on the rights contained in the UDHR and the ECHR are significant: they demonstrate that rights derive their validity from an underlying structure of 'right'. Were the only limitation on your rights the rights of others then Finnis' observation would not be particularly interesting, but others' rights do not constitute the only limits: there is also reference to morality, public morality, public health, and public order. These considerations cannot be reduced to the effects on *identifiable* individuals, but are 'diffuse common benefits in which all participate in indistinguishable and unassignable shares' (Finnis, 1980: 216). A scheme of human rights, such as the UDHR or the ECHR is:

> Simply a way of sketching the *outlines of the common good*, the various aspects of individual well-being in community. What the reference to rights contributes to this sketch is simply a pointed expression of what is implicit in the term '*common* good', namely that *each* and everyone's well-being, in each of its basic aspects, must be considered and favoured at *all* times by those responsible for co-ordinating the common life (Finnis, 1980: 214, his emphases).

It may be true that there is a necessary connection between right and rights, and that others' rights are not the only limitation on rights, but we need to establish in what sense rights are *natural*, and thus *universal*. Finnis maintains that there are goods which all cultures value: (a) life (including self-preservation and procreation); (b) knowledge (considered valuable in itself); (c) play (activities enjoyed for their own sake, lacking any point beyond their own performance); (d) aesthetic experience (appreciation of beauty); (e) sociability (including friendship, which is a non-instrumental relationship); (e) practical reasonableness; (f) religion (even if one rejects religious claims, to ask questions about the origin and purpose of life is essential to a 'full life') (Finnis, 1980: 83–4). Human rights are grounded in the protection of these goods: it is not difficult to see how particular articles of the UDHR function to enable their pursuit.

There are several problems with Finnis' argument. First, even if we can identify cross-cultural activities, such as the pursuit of knowledge or play, it does not follow that what we have characterised as 'common' to different cultures amount to 'goods' which can be pursued. Does the scientific knowledge of Western societies correspond to the voodoo knowledge of some African societies? Does the Netherlands fail to uphold respect for life because – under strict conditions – it permits a doctor to assist a person to die? Second, Finnis – like Habermas – wants to argue that we can derive these goods from reason, but unlike Habermas he generates a substantive list of goods which we 'ought' to pursue and protect. Furthermore, although Habermas can be criticised, at least his theory was grounded in the formal aspects of communication. Finnis, on the other hand, continually appeals to the intuitions of his reader; he has nothing else in his intellectual armoury. Third, the value of a particular activity is not as straightforward as Finnis suggests. For example the pursuit of knowledge may be motivated not by a search for truth but a desire for entertainment, and people often have sex for pleasure rather than, procreation. Overall, even if Finnis is right to argue that there are goods that transcend cultures, his argument lacks the binding quality necessary to generate a set of actionable, universal human rights.

Cruelty and Solidarity (Shklar and Rorty)

What motivated the UDHR and what moves people most strongly to protest against regimes that violate human rights is revulsion at cruel practices, such as torture. The difficulty with at least three of the other four theories – Donnelly's theory may be the exception – is that they abstract too much. We do not reason our way to human rights from an abstract standpoint of 'duty', but from imaginative identification with the victims of abuse. As Judith Shklar argues we 'put cruelty first'. That slightly odd formulation – it might imply valuing cruelty – is intended to convey a sceptical, negative basis for human rights, and to stress that considerations of cruelty take priority in the articulation of our sense of justice and injustice.

Cruelty Shklar defines cruelty as the 'willful inflicting of physical pain on a weaker being in order to cause anguish and fear'. By putting cruelty first, 'with nothing above it, and with nothing to excuse or forgive acts of cruelty' one 'closes off any appeal to any order other than that of actuality' (Shklar, 1984: 8). In understanding human rights as the political expression of our revulsion towards cruelty we avoid appeal to human essences, or reason, or a positive set of virtues, all of which carry the danger of ethnocentrism. Richard Rorty developed this idea in his book *Contingency, Irony and Solidarity* (Rorty, 1989). By 'contingency' Rorty means opposition to any idea of human essence, or nature, or any other ideas that supposedly provide the 'foundations' for law, morality, and politics. In rejecting philosophical universalism Rorty recognizes the danger that anything will be 'justifiable', or, more accurately, since no beliefs or values have a privileged status there is nothing that can be said against torture or genocide. To address this charge it is necessary to consider the other two concepts that appear in the title of Rorty's book: irony and solidarity.

Irony is the capacity to recognise that one's own values may not be ultimate – that it is always possible to describe the world in another way. To be ironic is to continue to hold on to one's beliefs and values *and at the same time* acknowledge the force of other conversations. Although we cannot provide any philosophical grounding for respect or tolerance the ironist will tend to recognise the rights of others. The ironist does not reason from an abstract standpoint but is capable of emotional identification; such identification might come through, for example, an appreciation of literature. Picking up on Shklar's idea of the 'actuality' the ironist will have special sensitivity to cruelty. Recognising the limitations of one's own beliefs, and sensitivity to cruelty, provide hope for an expanding circle of *solidarity*.

Rorty observes that if you were a Jew in Nazi-occupied Europe your chances of survival were greater if you lived in Denmark or Italy than if you lived in Belgium (Rorty, 1989: 189). He explains the difference in the following terms:

> Did [Danes and Italians] say, about their Jewish neighbors, that they deserved to be saved because they were fellow human beings? Perhaps sometimes they did, but surely they would usually, if queried, have used more parochial terms to explain why they were taking risks to protect a given Jew – for example, that this particular Jew was a fellow Milanese, or a fellow Jutlander, or a fellow member of the same union or profession, or a fellow bocce player, or a fellow parent of small children. Then consider those Belgians: Surely there were some

people whom they *would* have taken risks to protect in similar circumstances, people whom they *did* identify with, under some description or other. But Jews rarely fell under those descriptions (Rorty, 1989: 190–1, his emphases).

Rorty's interpretation of the motivations of the rescuers' has been challenged. Norman Geras argues, first, that there were prosaic reasons why a greater proportion of the Jewish population was murdered in some countries than in others – sometimes, it came down to the availability of escape routes, such as from Denmark to Sweden in what has become termed the 'Danish rescue', the availability of pre-war records of religious affiliation, and the actual form of administrative occupation, which varied considerably from one country to another (Geras, 1995: 10–11). Second, and more importantly, Rorty quotes no testimonies of rescuers or their friends and family. After working his way through a large number of such testimonies Geras found only one case in which a rescuer expressed his reasons for rescuing Jews as that they were fellow citizens (in this case, fellow Dane). Almost all used the language of 'common humanity' – in other words, the kind of universalism which Rorty rejects (Geras, 1995: 36).

Geras argues for a universalism based on the recognition of a common human nature, but it is not clear why Rorty rejects the *feeling* for humanity as the basis for human rights. Certainly, Rorty rejects any categorically binding conception of human reason, such as that advanced by Habermas, but it is consistent with Rorty's anti-foundationalism to be moved by another's suffering – to feel revulsion at cruelty towards that person – without any appeal to a shared membership of a parochial group. Perhaps what worries Rorty is that the recognition of humanity will take the form of a 'cold' Kantian duty, which we then *apply* to human beings.

Conclusion: Article 18

At the beginning of the chapter we posed the question of whether Article 18 of the UDHR was compatible with respect for cultural diversity. If it is not then it is quite possible to respond by saying 'so much the worse for culture', but this would be an inadequate response: human rights must be justified and not simply asserted, and so a defence of human rights must explain how such rights are universal.

In his book *Multicultural Citizenship* (1995) Will Kymlicka discusses the right to religious freedom, and identifies three elements to this right: (a) freedom to pursue one's (existing) faith (practice); (b) freedom to seek new adherents to that faith (proselytisation); (c) freedom to renounce one's faith (apostasy) (Kymlicka, 1995: 155–65). He also makes a distinction between internal restrictions and external protections, arguing for the latter against the former: a religious group must be protected from external pressure but not at the price of suppressing the freedom of its adherents to leave. It follows from this that the right to religious freedom must contain all three elements. Traditionally, in – for example – Muslim countries only the first element is respected, although it should be said that, historically, Muslims have shown much greater tolerance of religious minorities, such as Jews and Christians, than has been the case in Christian Europe with regard to its religious minorities.

Those who argue that human rights are individualistic will not be convinced by Kymlicka's understanding of the right to religious freedom as a right held primarily by the individual. Religion is a collective activity and can only be sustained as a collective activity, but the individual right to freedom of religion implies that as individuals we stand back from a religious community and assess its value for us. It might be, of course, that after reflection we affirm 'our' religious belief, but this implies that only cultures compatible with reflection and revision of belief are capable of recognising the human right to religious freedom.

Of the five defences provided Rawls comes closest to rejecting Article 18 on grounds that a society can be 'decent' without being 'liberal', and a decent society would respect the right to practise one's religion without necessarily permitting proselytisation. Donnelly is less clear, but suggests that there must be some latitude in the interpretation of religious freedom. Presumably, a less than clear affirmation of the good of religion and of knowledge would for Finnis be incompatible with natural right. And Habermas would maintain that freedom of belief and association is a precondition for discourse. Finally, Rorty's ironist would not impose any belief-system – including his or her own – as final, and would insist on religious freedom.

Summary

The fundamental philosophical debate around human rights is concerned with their alleged parochialism: that is, their origins in a particular culture. That something has a history does not, in itself, invalidate its claim to universality, but there is a particular problem about human rights even in those cultures from which they emerged: critics argue that human rights place a great moral weight on individual autonomy to the detriment of other values, such as welfare and community. For defenders of human rights, the increasing spread of human rights discourse indicates a welcome development in humanitarian moral consciousness; for opponents, human rights go hand in hand with the growing power of Western liberalism.

Questions

1. Why should states respect human rights?
2. If it can be shown that human rights discourse emerges from a Western tradition does this undermine the claim that they are universal?
3. Is the exercise of human rights compatible with respect for the environment?
4. Is the 'right to welfare' coherent?

References

Convention for the Protection of Human Rights and Fundamental Freedoms (European Convention on Human Rights): http://www.echr.coe.int/Convention/webConvenENG.pdf.

Donnelly, J. (2003) *Universal Human Rights in Theory and Practice* Ithaca, NY: Cornell University Press.

Finnis, J. (1980) *Natural Law and Natural Rights* Oxford: Clarendon Press.

Geras, N. (1995) *Solidarity in the Conversation of Humankind: the Ungroundable Liberalism of Richard Rorty* London and New York: Verso.

Habermas, J. (1984) *The Theory of Communicative Action*, Vol. 1: *Reason and Rationalization of Society* London: Heinemann.

Habermas, J. (1994) 'Struggles for Recognition in the Democratic Constitutional State', in A. Gutmann (ed.), *Multiculturalism: Examining the Politics of Recognition* Princeton, NJ: Princeton University Press, 107–48.

Hohfeld, W. (1923) *Fundamental Legal Conceptions as Applied in Judicial Reasoning* New Haven, CN: Yale University Press.

Kymlicka, W. (1995) *Multicultural Citizenship: A Liberal Theory of Minority Rights* Oxford: Clarendon Press.

Mutua, M. (2002) *Human Rights: a Political and Cultural Critique* Philadelphia, PA: University of Pennsylvania Press.

Rawls, J. (1999) *The Law of Peoples* Cambridge, MA and London: Harvard University Press.

Rorty, R. (1989) *Contingency, Irony, and Solidarity* Cambridge: Cambridge University Press.

Shklar, J. (1984) *Ordinary Vices* Cambridge MA: Harvard University Press.

UDHR (1948) *Universal Declaration of Human Rights,* available at: http://un.org/Overview/rights.html.

Further Reading

It is important to be clear about the nature of *rights* before venturing into a discussion of *human* rights – a good introduction is Peter Jones, *Rights* (Basingstoke: Macmillan, 1994). General discussions of human rights include: Maurice Cranston, *What are Human Rights?* (New York: Taplinger, 1973) and Ellen Frankel Paul *et al.* (eds), *Human Rights* (Oxford: Oxford University Press, 1984). More intellectually demanding are: Alan Gewirth, *Human Rights: Essays on Justification and Applications* (Chicago, IL: University of Chicago Press, 1982); R. J. Vincent, *Human Rights and International Relations* (Cambridge: Cambridge University Press, 1986). On the issue of cultural relativism read Simon Caney and Peter Jones (eds), *Human Rights and Global Diversity* (London: Frank Cass, 2001); Jane Cowan *et al.* (eds), *Culture and Rights: Anthropological Perspectives* (Cambridge: Cambridge University Press, 2001), and from the above references Donnelly (2003), Habermas (1994) and Rawls (1999).

Weblinks

There are many excellent human rights resources on the web:

From a more legal perspective:
http://library.kent.ac.uk/library/lawlinks/human.htm

The other sites are a mix of theory, law and advocacy:
Human Rights Resource Center: http://www.hrusa.org/
Human Rights Education Associates: http://www.hrea.org/
Human and Constitutional Rights: http://www.hrcr.org/
Amnesty International: http://www.amnesty.org/
Human Rights Watch: http://www.hrw.org/

Chapter 19

Civil Disobedience

Introduction

Civil disobedience is the non-violent breaking of a law on moral grounds. While there were theorists of civil disobedience in the nineteenth and early twentieth centuries, and the theory may be applicable to non-democratic societies, this chapter focuses on the post-war discussion of civil disobedience in a liberal democratic society. Although few people may ever engage in civil disobedience in their lifetimes it is not a peripheral concept, for the justification of civil disobedience touches on the moral basis of majoritarian democracy. Whereas in the pre-modern and early modern periods political theory was concerned with the right to rebel, the fundamental question raised by civil disobedience to a modern audience is this: how is it possible to have a general respect for the rule of law and yet break specific laws?

Chapter Map

In this chapter we will:

- Distinguish civil disobedience from legal protest, revolution, and 'mere criminality'.

- Discuss whether we have a special obligation to obey democratically agreed laws.

- Analyse one of the most influential philosophical discussions of civil disobedience – that advanced by John Rawls.

- Apply the theoretical discussion of civil disobedience to a case study: the Civil Rights Movement in the United States.

- Discuss Martin Luther King's justification of civil disobedience.

Protest and Survive?

Police officers arrest a group of women protesting against nuclear weapons at the Greenham Common Air Base in England, November 1983

Source: © Bettmann/CORBIS

In 1981 a group of women set off on a march from Cardiff (Wales) to Greenham Common, a British–American airbase located about 60 miles (100 kilometres) west of London, where Cruise Missiles (guided missiles with nuclear warheads) were to be sited. Once there, they established the 'Greenham Common Women's Peace Camp', and for the next two years attempted to disrupt construction work – which included the building of missile silos – at the base. Despite their efforts the missiles arrived in November 1983. However, the Peace Camp remained for the rest of the decade, and indeed some women continued there until 2000. There were frequent arrests, resulting in fines and, in a few cases, imprisonment. The local council made repeated attempts to evict the protestors. The 1987 Intermediate-range Nuclear Forces (INF) Treaty signed by the United States and the USSR resulted in the removal of the missiles from Greenham Common. By 1991 all the missiles had gone; in 1992 the US Air Force left, soon followed by their British counterparts. The women who remained after 1992 claimed they were now making a symbolic protest against all nuclear weapons. At the heart of the anti-nuclear protests – which took place across Western Europe in the early 1980s – was a belief that if they did not engage in peaceful law-breaking (civil disobedience) then humanity was doomed: the slogan of the British organisation, the Campaign for Nuclear Disarmament (CND) was 'protest and survive', an ironic comment on the title of a 1960s British government guide for citizens on how to survive a nuclear attack: 'Protect and Survive'.

- Were the Greenham common protestors justified in breaking the law?

Civil Disobedience and Law-breaking

In this chapter we are concerned with justifications for civil disobedience, and naturally it makes sense to start with a definition of 'civil disobedience'. However, as we shall see, definition and justification are closely related, so that a particular definition implies a certain understanding of the role civil disobedience plays in the political system. What we offer here is an initial definition, which will require further clarification: civil disobedience is morally justified law-breaking, *normally* intended to change a particular law or policy. Civil disobedience has then these components: (a) it involves breaking the law – it is not simply legal protest; (b) there are moral reasons justifying the action; (c) the aim is to change a law or policy; it is not intended to bring down an entire political system – civil disobedience is not revolution.

Of all the concepts discussed in this book, civil disobedience is among a relatively small group where theory and practice are closely related, and indeed where some of the most important theorists of the concept have been its practitioners. American Henry David Thoreau (1817–62) is credited with offering the earliest theory of civil disobedience. Thoreau was imprisoned for refusing to pay a tax that was intended to fund what he regarded as an unjust war by the United States against Mexico. In his essay 'Civil Disobedience' (1849), Thoreau argued that an individual had a moral duty to break an unjust law – you should, he suggests, 'let your life be a counter-friction to stop the machine' (Thoreau, 1991: 36). In other words, civil disobedience was intended to obstruct the implementation of immoral policies. Thoreau's argument was highly influential. Mahatma Gandhi (1869–1948) read 'Civil Disobedience' while in prison, and developed both its theory and practice in his struggle against British rule in India. But the theories of Thoreau and Gandhi are problematic because although they were directed at a political situation – war and occupation – they were motivated by a sense of personal integrity rather than an appeal to the sense of justice of their respective publics. A more promising *political* justification for civil disobedience was advanced by Martin Luther King.

As with Gandhi it was also from a prison cell that in 1963 King wrote what became known as the 'Letter from Birmingham City Jail' (King, 1991), a plea to fellow church leaders to accept the legitimacy of non-violent law-breaking in pursuit of equal rights for US citizens. Although inspired by Thoreau and Gandhi, King offers a two-level justification of civil disobedience: one level couched in theological terms and directed at church leaders, the other level expressed in secular language and aimed at his fellow citizens. Later in this chapter we will look in detail at King's letter.

Law-breaking

Criminals break laws, and so do people who engage in civil disobedience. How then do we distinguish the civilly disobedient from the merely criminal? In part, the distinction will rest on *how* the law is broken, in part on *why* it is broken.

Reasons for breaking the law fall into four categories, although the fourth is a subcategory of the third:

1. *Individual self-interest*: a law is not in the individual's interests.
2. *Group interest*: a law is not in the interests of a particular group.
3. *Morality*: a law is morally wrong.
4. *Justice*: a law is unjust.

All defenders of civil disobedience would reject the first category as justifying law-breaking – to break the law simply because it does not suit your interests is to engage in a criminal act. The second category is more complex. Marx argued that it was in the interests of a particular group, the working class, to overthrow the capitalist system and that as a result a classless society would be created. It follows that it is in the long-term interests of *all* human beings that the working class should succeed. But Marx advocated the complete transformation of society – that is, *revolution* – and not merely the removal of certain laws, for him there could be no appeal to morality, for morality is the product of existing, capitalist, society.

Civil disobedience, as distinct from revolution, must appeal to moral ideas accessible to those who support the existing laws. The willingness of the civilly disobedient to accept the penalties for their law-breaking assumes that the 'oppressors' can be moved by their actions. Consequently, most theories of civil disobedience rest on the third and fourth categories. However, as we will see, there is an important distinction between breaking a law because you judge it immoral, and breaking it because you believe it is unjust.

Although self-interest is not a justification for civil disobedience, self-interest might well be a motivating factor. For example, the segregation laws operative in the southern states of the United States before the 1960s damaged the interests of *individual* blacks and blacks as a *group*. This does not invalidate the claims of people such as Martin Luther King that he and other blacks were morally justified in breaking the law.

It is important to recognise how recent is the development of the concept of civil disobedience. Certainly, political philosophers prior to the twentieth century had much to say about rebellion, but the possibility that rebellion could be anything other than the overthrow of the political system was not seriously considered.

Civil Disobedience and Political Obligation

Ch. 8:
Liberalism
pp. 182–85

Although there is debate among political theorists about the kinds of moral reasons that can justify civil disobedience, there is general agreement that civil disobedience implies political obligation. Laws are broken by people who have a respect for the law. There are different arguments for political obligation, but the prisoner's dilemma is useful as a way of organising our thoughts about obligation and disobedience (see Chapter 8). The resolution of the dilemma entails an agreement to cooperate, where such cooperation will be enforced by the state. That resolution is threatened by free-riders, who seek to enjoy the benefits gained from cooperation while evading the costs. The image of the free-rider is of a person who breaks the law out of self-interest. However, there are morally motivated free-riders: submission to the state involves not only giving up self-interest but also a degree of moral judgement. It is this which underlies the claim that civil disobedience is only justified if it appeals to certain kinds of moral reasons – reasons shared by (most) fellow citizens.

Civil Disobedience and Democracy

Democracy and Obedience

Civil disobedience plays a special role in democracy, because it not only indicates the moral limits of majority rule, but also forces us to reflect on the justifications *for* majority rule. For that reason it is important to consider the relationship between civil disobedience and democracy. While many people living in a liberal democracy consider violating the laws of a non-democratic regime to be not only permissible but praiseworthy, they consider it wrong to break democratically agreed laws. Sometimes the objection to civil disobedience in a democracy is revised when people reflect on particular cases, but there remains a core conviction that democracy is special. Peter Singer provides a philosophical defence of this view in his book *Democracy and Disobedience* (1973). Singer uses a very artificial example to illustrate his argument; however, its artificiality helps to bring out the main lines of the argument.

Oxford University is a collegiate university, with most living and teaching centred around the individual colleges. Singer asks us to imagine that each college is equivalent to a state, and the colleges taken together represent the world system of states. The undergraduates in a college form what Singer calls the Association. Students cannot opt out of membership of the Association. A student could transfer to another college at the university, but she would be obliged to join *its* Association. Of course, they could leave the university, but we are to imagine that the whole world is Oxford University, so that short of death there is no possibility of leaving. The Association of each college has been in existence for as long as anybody can remember – if there was ever a point at which it was set up, the records have been lost. The Association charges a subscription from each student, and we can take this to be equivalent to taxation. At this point we come to alternative ways of making decisions on how much to charge and what the money is spent on:

- *The Leader* Some time ago one student who is now the Leader decided that decision-making was inefficient, and the decisions arrived at were stupid. He would now make the decisions, albeit guided by the interests of the other students. If anyone objected they would have to fight it out with the Leader's friends, who were the best fighters in the Association.

- *Democracy* Decisions are taken by a majority vote of all members of the Association. At the meetings all members are free to speak, subject to some essential procedural requirements, such as an agreed time limit on speeches. Meetings are conducted fairly, and the votes are calculated correctly. (There is a third model – the 'Senior Member' – but its introduction would unnecessarily complicate the present discussion.)

We assume that under each model decisions have been made without too much dissension – of course, some students will have found themselves on the losing side, but they have accepted whatever decisions have been made. However, an issue arises that causes serious dissension. The Association uses some of the subscription money to buy newspapers that are for general use in the common room, and must not be taken away. One day, it is decided that the common room should take a new paper, *The News*. One member of the Association – the Dissenter – objects to this newspaper, arguing that it is racist, and that other members of the Association, less attuned to the paper's bigotry, will be influenced by it to the detriment of the few black students in the college. Consider now the two models:

- *The Leader* The Dissenter asks the Leader to reconsider his decision, but the Leader is unmoved. The Dissenter 'takes things into his own hands' by getting up early each morning and removing the paper before the others have had a chance to read it.
- *Democracy* It had been agreed by majority vote, and after lengthy debate, that the common room would take *The News*. The Dissenter found himself in a minority. At the next and later meetings he attempts to get the decision reversed, but it becomes clear that a majority wants to take the paper. On realising this, the Dissenter behaves in the same way as under the other model: he removes the paper.

With regard to the Dissenter the initial question that Singer poses is not whether he has moral reasons for removing *The News*, but whether under the Democracy model there are special reasons for not removing it, reasons which do not exist under the Leader model. Participation, Singer suggests, is the key difference between democratic and non-democratic systems:

> the Dissenter, by voluntarily participating in the vote on the question of whether *The News* should be ordered, understanding that the purpose of the election is to enable the group to reach a decision on this issue, has behaved in such a way as to lead people reasonably to believe that he was accepting the democratic process as a suitable means of settling the issue (Singer, 1973: 50).

Democratic decision-making is a 'fair compromise' between people who have conflicting moral views.

Fair Compromise

Singer distinguishes between 'absolute fairness' and a 'fair compromise'. Fair compromise is fairness *given certain conditions*. To illustrate the distinction between absolute fairness and fair compromise he gives a couple of examples (the second involves a certain amount of gender-stereotyping, but it is Singer's example and not ours!):

- Two people claim a sum of money, and a judge is appointed to adjudicate between them. Although she can be sure only one has a legitimate claim, she cannot establish which one has the claim, and so divides the money up 50/50. This is a fair compromise. An example of an unfair compromise would be to flip a coin.
- A husband and wife argue over who should do night-time baby duties. The husband says he works all day and so should have an unbroken night of sleep,

whereas the wife claims she attends to the baby all day, and so should have a break at night. A fair compromise would be to alternate duties. An unfair compromise would be for the wife to do weekday nights, and the husband weekends.

The point about a fair compromise is that a person can still feel that the decision – to split the money, or to alternate baby duties – is unfair in an absolute sense, but that under the circumstances it is fair. As Singer argues with regard to the Dissenter: 'to disobey when there already is a fair compromise in operation is necessarily to deprive others of the say they have under such a compromise. To do this is to leave the others with no remedy but the use of force' (Singer, 1973: 36).

Singer argues that while we cannot consent – either explicitly or tacitly – to the procedure itself, we can consent by our actions to the decisions made under it. Singer borrows a concept from law to express the moral bindingness of participation: estoppel. He quotes an English judge – Lord Birkenhead:

> Where A has by his words or conduct justified B in believing that a certain state of affairs exists, and B has acted upon such belief to his prejudice, A is not permitted to affirm against B that a different state of facts existed at the same time (Singer, 1973: 51).

An everyday, non-legal example would be the British convention of buying a round of drinks in a pub (bar): if four people go to the pub and the first person buys four pints of beer, and then the second person does so, and then the third person likewise, the fourth, who has accepted three pints, can reasonably be expected to buy a round. He has not consented to the rule or convention of buying a round, but his acceptance of the three pints has affected the behaviour of his three friends.

Singer anticipates the objection that the Dissenter can avoid being bound through estoppel simply by not participating in the democratic process. He argues that the notion of a fair compromise generates not only an obligation to accept the decision of the majority, but also to participate in the process: it is not reasonable to sit it out. If you sit it out and then find the decision made is unacceptable you cannot have grounds for refusing to accept the decision, because you were unreasonable in prejudging the decision. People who do not vote can have no complaint against the decisions made by those who do.

Problems with Democracy

Singer's defence of obedience to a democratically agreed law is an 'all things being equal' defence. He does not argue that we should *always* obey such law. Although he does not discuss situations in which civil disobedience is justified, some of the more obvious ones are dealt with below:

(a) In a representative democracy – Singer's example was of a direct one – the elected representatives will not necessarily mirror the social, ethnic and gender composition of the electorate. The fact that elected assemblies often do not mirror their electorates is not in itself a justification for disobedience. However, if it can be shown that a particular group – for example working-class women – has not had its interests communicated then Singer's participation argument is invalidated.

(b) Most voting systems do not take into account the intensity of a person's preferences. A minority may feel *very strongly* about an issue, but they are outvoted by an *apathetic* majority. Civil disobedience can be a means by which not only are views communicated but the *intensity* of those views are made apparent.

(c) Some people find themselves in a permanent minority. This is exacerbated if electoral politics is based on one dominant social characteristic. For example, in Northern Ireland voting is largely along religious lines. In the period 1922–73 there existed a devolved parliament in Northern Ireland with the Protestant Unionists always in the majority and Catholics entirely excluded from power.

(d) Some people are denied the vote. The largest group is children. Their interests are affected by legislation over which they have no control. Civilly disobedient actions undertaken by children are rare but, arguably, groups of adults representing the interests of children could be justified in engaging in civil disobedience on their behalf.

(e) It could be argued that animals have interests and that these are clearly affected by the democratic process. Although it would be absurd to give cats and dogs the right to vote, there might be a duty of care on human beings, and that duty must be articulated. Some notable examples of civil disobedience have been based on concern for animal welfare; in Britain, there has been a long-running campaign against the use of animals in what are seen by some as unnecessary experiments.

(f) The decisions made today will affect future generations. The justification given for some acts of civil disobedience against the building of roads and airports is that fossil fuel emissions exacerbate global warming, which will have catastrophic consequences for future generations.

The implication of the above points is that democracy can on occasion break down, but that it can also be 'fixed'. The more radical challenge lies in the rejection of majority decision-making: a person may believe that a law is simply wrong, and no amount of institutional reform can create a situation in which the majority 'makes it right'. For example, defenders of animal experimentation for medical purposes will maintain that they have given due weight to non-human animals as beings worthy of moral respect, but that human beings have greater moral claims. Opponents of such experiments will disagree, and maintain that actions such as breaking into laboratories and releasing animals is justified on moral grounds. It is very difficult to find common ground between these two positions.

We live in a pluralistic society in which there is not only conflict between different individual and group interests, but also between different moral conceptions. The stability and legitimacy of the political system requires some agreement on moral principles. There need not be agreement on all moral issues – after all, liberalism has its roots in the recognition of pluralism – but there must be some agreement. In the next section we reconsider the arguments of Rawls, who does provide an account of that shared morality, but also justifies civil disobedience.

Rawls: Civil Disobedience and Conscientious Refusal

Rawls's discussion of civil disobedience has been highly influential among writers on civil disobedience; his account is unusual in locating the defence of civil disobedience in a wider political theory. For Rawls the issues raised by civil disobedience go to the heart of the moral basis of democracy.

The Context

We discussed Rawls's work in Chapter 4: as the title of his most important work – *A Theory of Justice* (1972) – implies, Rawls sets out a conception of a just society. Most of *A Theory of Justice* is concerned with what Rawls calls ideal theory; that is, he assumes for the purposes of his argument that people comply strictly with the principles to which they have agreed. He departs from this assumption in one relatively short section of the book – the discussion of civil disobedience. It is only in a society where there is partial, rather than strict, compliance with the principles of justice that civil disobedience has a role. This is because civil disobedience is an appeal to the majority – to its 'sense of justice'. The majority is being asked to respect principles that it implicitly accepts. In a (fully) just society there would be no need for civil disobedience and in an unjust society there is no sense of justice to which you can appeal.

The Obligation to Obey the Law

Rawls begins his discussion with an apparently paradoxical claim: we have a duty to obey unjust laws, but we are also morally entitled, and possibly have a duty, to disobey unjust laws. To understand this we need to consider the structure of Rawls's theory. The principles of justice are chosen from a position in which people are morally equal – the original position; but the chosen principles are fairly general in nature – they do not take the form of constitutional rights, or concrete laws, and *laws* are the object of civil disobedience.

There are several stages between the agreement to principles of justice and the creation of laws, and what happens between these stages is crucial to our understanding of Rawls's argument for civil disobedience. Rawls sets out a four-stage sequence for the production of law: (a) the first stage is the original position, in which people are denied knowledge of their identities and their society, and from which are generated the two principles of justice, which, roughly speaking, consist of a set of equal liberties and a social minimum (see Chapter 4); (b) a constitutional convention at which people know their societies but not their individual identities, and from which must be chosen a constitution for the particular society in question; (c) a legislative stage at which specific laws are created, but constrained by the constitution (Rawls argues that legislators do not know their identities – a more realistic model would be one in which they do, but feel the force of the principles of justice as embodied in the constitution); (d) the fourth – judicial – stage entails the application of rules, or laws, to particular cases by judges and administrators, and the following of rules by citizens. The possibility of injustice arises at this fourth stage (and, in the more realistic model at the third – legislative – stage) and therefore also scope for civil disobedience.

With this sequence of stages now in place we can return to the paradox of conflicting obligations. First, how can we have an obligation to obey unjust laws? At the first stage – the original position – we know that principles of justice must be embodied in a constitution, and constitutions provide the framework for law-making. We also know that people are in conflict with one another, and so laws will never be passed unanimously – there will always be winners and losers. What is required is a decision-making rule that is acceptable to all. It is highly unlikely that anything other than majoritarianism would be chosen in the constitutional convention. The danger is that the majority will sometimes pass unjust laws – laws which, for example, deny equal rights to minority groups. Therefore, we have a conflict:

- The principle of majority rule is effectively endorsed from stage one, which is a standpoint of moral equality, and therefore of justice.
- Majority rule will sometimes generate unjust laws.

If an individual felt entitled and, perhaps, obliged to break every law they deemed unjust, then majoritarian democracy would collapse, and in the process so would the possibility of a just society. The question, or challenge – 'what if everyone did that?' – can always reasonably be asked of someone engaged in civil disobedience.

Rawls argues that the original position argument only works if we assume that we have a moral duty to create and uphold just institutions – this is a 'natural duty' in the sense that it precedes the choice of particular principles of justice. This means we 'enter' the original position not knowing what principles we will choose, *but committed to respecting whatever principles are chosen*. We do not choose principles but then refuse to live by them.

The natural duty to create and uphold just institutions amounts to respecting the real difficulties of operationalising principles, and so not disobeying every law you think is unjust. On the other hand upholding justice also means resisting injustice. What civil disobedience then involves is making a judgement not between just and unjust laws but between *different types of unjust laws*. One suggestion Rawls makes for determining the point at which civil disobedience is justified is the degree to which a particular group bears the burden of injustice. If a group finds itself habitually, rather than occasionally, the victim of injustice then there are grounds for civil disobedience. The black community in the southern states of the United States up until the civil rights legislation of the 1960s is an obvious example.

The Nature and Role of Civil Disobedience

Given the fact that in a just society decisions will be made by majority vote – subject to many checks and balances – the possibility of civil disobedience arises for Rawls only in a democratic society:

> At what point does the duty to comply with laws enacted by a legislative majority (or with executive acts supported by such a majority) cease to be

binding in view of the right to defend one's liberties and the duty to oppose injustice? This involves the nature and limits of majority rule. For this reason the problem of civil disobedience is a crucial test for any theory of the moral basis of democracy (Rawls, 1972: 363).

The leading idea behind Rawls's theory of civil disobedience is that in breaking the law *the civilly disobedient are addressing, or appealing to, the sense of justice of the majority*. All the other points that Rawls makes, including the important distinction he makes between civil disobedience and conscientious refusal, lead back to this idea. Rawls sets out a number of conditions on civil disobedience:

1. *Injustice must be clear* What is unjust is determined by the principles of justice. Of the two, breaches of the first principle – equal liberty – are likely to be much clearer than denial of the second – guarantee of a social minimum (the difference principle). For example, to deny a class of adults the right to vote on grounds of their ethnic or religious identity, or their gender, would be clear infraction of the first principle. It is not only a clear injustice, but its remedy – granting the equal right to vote – is easy to grasp. On the other hand, significant economic inequality is much less *obviously* unjust, and the solution to the claimed injustice is not apparent.

2. *It involves breaking the law, rather than simply testing it* Some laws are broken in order to force a judicial judgment, but this does not constitute civil disobedience. As we will see this might rule out classifying significant aspects of the struggle against segregation in the southern states as civil disobedience.

3. *It need not involve breaking the law, which is the object of civil disobedience* Laws are broken in the process of engaging in civil disobedience, but they need not be the direct object of the civilly disobedient action. For example, in order to protest against an unjust war, you might sit down in the middle of the road, thus violating traffic laws, but it is not the traffic laws that are the target of the action (you will probably accept that it makes sense to have laws which prohibit people sitting down in the road!).

4. *It must be a public act* Civil disobedience is a communicative act – the majority is being given 'fair notice' that a law is unjust. The communicative act consists not simply in the transmission of information – that could be achieved through covert action – but in getting the majority to understand that the civilly disobedient are making an appeal. Indeed, there is a distinction between communicating something to the majority, and *appealing* to it.

5. *It must be non-violent and not constitute a threat* The reasoning behind this is similar to that behind (4) – the civilly disobedient want the majority to change the law for the right reason, namely because it is unjust and not because they fear the consequences of maintaining the law. Rawls could be criticised for naivety: one group may be genuinely non-violent and non-threatening, but their actions could be unintentionally threatening insofar as they make the majority aware of the existence of other, less peaceful, groups. The shadow of Malcolm X and the Nation of Islam was always behind that of Martin Luther King. Furthermore, it is not obvious that *non-violent* obstruction undermines the appeal to a sense of justice, and most campaigns have involved the deliberate *inconveniencing* of the majority.

6. *The civilly disobedient accept the penalties for law-breaking* Once again, the reasoning behind this point is that the civilly disobedient are appealing to, rather than threatening, the majority. Willingness to accept the penalties for law-breaking – that is, not resisting arrest – demonstrates sincerity. Such behaviour may embarrass the majority, who must ask themselves whether they really want to punish, often in a draconian fashion, clearly peace-loving people.

7. *Even if laws are seriously unjust, civil disobedience must not threaten the stability of the political system* The thinking behind this requirement is that a situation might arise where there are a number of groups justifiably engaged in civil disobedience, but the conjoint effects of their actions threaten the stability of the political system. In such a situation groups must show restraint. Although it is rather unrealistic, Rawls suggests that civilly disobedient groups might come to an agreement whereby groups take it in turns engaging in civil disobedience. One might wonder whether a political system that provokes so much civil disobedience is even partially just, but he may have in mind the United States in the 1960s, when there were civil rights actions *and* anti-Vietnam War actions.

8. *Civil disobedience takes place within fidelity to law* This underwrites the entire project of civil disobedience. The civilly disobedient do not seek to bring down the existing system, but rather they seek to strengthen it by removing injustice, such that the system will win the loyalty of all citizens. In this sense the civilly disobedient demonstrate fidelity – or faithfulness – to the law.

We round off our outline of Rawls's theory with a discussion of his distinction between civil disobedience and conscientious refusal.

Conscientious Refusal

A distinction can be made between disobedience on general moral grounds, and disobedience on the narrower – but still moral – ground of injustice. Rawls's aim in *A Theory of Justice* was to articulate a morality – a 'theory of justice' – appropriate to the political sphere. That political morality leaves open many other areas of morality. Conscientious refusal may be grounded in that political morality, but it need not be; it may be based on 'religious or other principles at variance with the constitutional order' (Rawls, 1972: 369). The clearest modern example of conscientious refusal is objection to military service, either for general pacifist reasons or because of opposition to a particular war. Rawls argues that such objections cannot be *automatically* accepted, for justice requires on occasion that people be prepared to defend – by force of arms – the political system. However, he concedes that the spirit of pacifism accords with the values underlying a just society – it is rare for nearly just societies to go to war against one another (this is the so-called democratic peace argument). He also argues that an unjust war – a war that violates the laws of peoples – can quite properly be the object of civil disobedience.

Conscientious refusal cannot be an appeal to the sense of justice of the majority. The danger with conscientious refusal is that it undermines the political order by substituting individual moral judgement for the collective judgement of society. An example would be the refusal to pay taxes that go towards the development and maintenance of nuclear weapons. It is possible that most people are 'nuclear pacifists' – while they might believe that a just war with conventional weapons is possible, the use of nuclear warheads represents a hugely disproportionate response to the aggression of another country. But, among nuclear pacifists, a majority might judge that the *threat* to use – rather than actual use of – nuclear weapons is better than submission to a foreign power. Of course, a nuclear power has to convince the putative enemy country that it really will use the weapons, and so there is an element of subterfuge, as well as risk, behind deterrence theory which seems at odds with the transparency one expects of a just society. Nonetheless, there can be reasonable moral disagreement, such that the will of the majority should prevail.

Another important distinction between civil disobedience and conscientious refusal is that the latter may entail a greater 'introversion' than the former: a significant strand in conscientious refusal is the striving for moral integrity, that is, a feeling that *regardless of the consequences* you cannot support a law or policy. Insofar as conscientious refusal is a form of 'moral purity' it is in tension with civil disobedience, which looks outwards towards the majority, and appeals to it to change. The idea of moral purity is central to Gandhi's *satyagraha*, which means an 'insistence on truth'. Because *satyagraha* is the moral basis of civil disobedience it is often – erroneously – translated as civil disobedience. One final point: conscientious refusal is not incompatible with civil disobedience because an individual might be *motivated* by their non-political moral beliefs, but still attempt to communicate in the language of justice to the majority.

Criticisms of Rawls

A number of criticisms can be raised to Rawls's theory, although one theme runs through several of the criticisms – its narrowness:

1. *Inconveniencing.* Civil disobedience may be intended simply to make a law unworkable. The tactic of one wave of people sitting down at segregated lunch counters, being arrested and then replaced by a second wave had the result of filling the jails until the process of justice ground to a halt. The majority may calculate that it is not in their interests to continue to support unjust laws. Certainly, this tactic entails no appeal to the moral sense of the majority and Rawls may be concerned that motivating the majority through appeal to self-interest – in effect, telling the majority that their lives are going to be made uncomfortable – is a weak basis for long-term political stability. It is an empirical question whether it works.

2. *Piecewise just society.* Andrew Sabl argues that instead of 'nearly just' societies it would be more accurate to talk of 'piecewise just societies': 'people can have a sense of justice and still, through prejudice or moral blindness, have a radically deficient conception of justice or of what justice entails in the particular circumstances' (Sabl, 2001: 316). This allows for the possibility that the communicative act entailed in civil disobedience will in Rawlsian terms fail, but that the inconveniencing of the majority will over time connect with a sense of justice, such that the children and grandchildren of the (say) Ku Klux Klansmen will come to recognise the injustice of the segregation that was abolished a generation ago.

3. *Civil courage.* That civil disobedience is only possible in a 'nearly just' society, with the implication that only rebellion is possible in an unjust society, fails to account for the possibility of 'civil courage' in extreme circumstances. In the latter years of the Third Reich there was, famously, an attempt by senior German officers to kill Hitler. This was the 20 July Plot (1944) – clearly an act intended to bring about regime change from within. There were also other actions which are best described as demonstrating 'civil courage': the 'White Rose' movement of Sophie Scholl, her brother Hans Scholl, and Christoph Probst (1943), and the Rosenstraβe Protest (1943). Given the extreme risks that the protestors ran – the Scholls and Probst were executed – and the unlikelihood of changing state policies these actions were brave but not political. In fact, the Rosenstraβe Protest, which was carried out by the non-Jewish wives of Jewish men about to be deported to the extermination camps, succeeded. It may be difficult to incorporate such acts of civil courage into a political theory but we should try.

4. *Rawls's conditions.* If civil disobedience can be intended to disable the state from carrying out its policies then some of Rawls's conditions on civilly disobedient acts become redundant. It is no longer essential – although it may be desirable – that an action be public. Certainly, publicity may be important in achieving one's objective and covert action may blur the distinction between civil disobedience and mere criminality. Likewise, the willingness to accept the punishment is desirable – for the same reasons – but, again, would not be essential, and Rawls's distinction between civil disobedience and conscientious refusal breaks down. Rawls is right to argue that at some point it must be possible to recognise the injustice of a law, where 'justice' denotes a specifically political conception, but a person engaged in civil disobedience need not be motivated by a sense of justice, distinct from a non-political but moral motivation.

Martin Luther King and the Civil Rights Movement

The aim of this final section is to apply the theoretical discussion of the previous section to a case study of civil disobedience: Martin Luther King and the Civil Rights Movement in the United States in the 1950s and 1960s. There are several reasons why we have chosen this: (a) it is the most famous example of civil disobedience and the one that influenced Rawls (*A Theory of Justice*, published in 1972, was written during the period of the Civil Rights Movement); (b) it is now 40 years since the main objectives of the movement were achieved, so we can assess its impact – from a Rawlsian perspective this is important, because if civil disobedience is an appeal to the majority to remove injustice *and so strengthen the political system*, then we need to see whether this was a result of the movement.

Historical Background to the Civil Rights Movement

The Civil Rights Movement has its roots in the struggle for emancipation from slavery in the nineteenth century. There were sporadic slave revolts before 1860, but it was during the civil war of 1861–5 that the struggle for emancipation become a central focus of American life. During the civil war, the Northern and

Western states of America had remained within the Union, while the 11 Southern states formed the Confederacy (the 11 were: Alabama, Arkansas, Florida, Georgia, Louisiana, Mississippi, North Carolina, South Carolina, Tennessee, Texas, Virginia). After President Abraham Lincoln issued the Emancipation Proclamation (1862), slavery became the main issue dividing 'North' (Union) and 'South' (Confederacy), but it is important to stress the constitutional struggle behind the issue of slavery, because this underlay the political debate in the 1950s and 1960s.

The 10th Amendment (the 10th article of the Bill of Rights) guarantees states' rights: 'the powers not delegated to the United States by the Constitution, nor prohibited by it to the States, are reserved to the States respectively, or to the people'. The 'states' rights' argument tended to be used by whichever bloc was in the minority: in the earlier nineteenth century the (minority) anti-slave states of New England asserted states' rights to prohibit the holding of slaves against the majority slave states. When the balance tipped in favour of anti-slavery, the now-minority slave states asserted their rights to maintain a social institution – slavery – which they held to be central to their life and culture.

The Union defeated the Confederacy and in 1866 Congress passed the Civil Rights Act (which followed the 13th Amendment to the Constitution, abolishing slavery), which declared that all persons born in the United States were citizens and so entitled to 'full and equal benefit of the laws'. However, white Southerners, while forced to accept the abolition of slavery, used state power – through the Democratic Party – to deny newly emancipated blacks their voting rights, educational opportunities and other benefits 'of the laws'. The so-called 'Reconstruction' (1865–77) was a failure. So by the beginning of the twentieth century most blacks in the South had lost the right to vote, and there was widespread *legally enforced* segregation of education, transport and other services. In the first half of the twentieth century American blacks were divided over the correct tactics to adopt against discrimination: Booker T. Washington (1856–1915) advocated abandoning politics in favour of economic advancement; W.E.B. Du Bois (1868–1963) founded the National Association for the Advancement of Colored People (NAACP), which demanded full equality in accordance with the US Constitution; after the First World War Marcus Garvey (1887–1940) advocated separation from white society, and even emigration to Africa.

The Civil Rights Movement

After the Second World War – ostensibly a war against racism in which many thousands of black servicemen had fought – the pressure for change increased. We will focus on particular events and tactics, rather than provide a narrative; several of the books (Further Reading) and websites (Weblinks) provide useful timelines.

Discrimination was so widespread – deeply institutionalised – in the South that it is difficult to pinpoint particular laws that were the object of civil disobedience. However, among the more blatantly discriminatory laws were: the denial of the right to vote (through a wide range of mechanisms); segregated schooling; segregated services, such as seats on buses and places at lunch counters; denial of entry to many facilities, such as libraries, cinemas and swimming pools; denial of places at colleges and universities; illegitimate restrictions on the right to protest;

failure on the part of the police to protect blacks against violence from white racists such as the Ku Klux Klan.

Not all the actions of the civil rights activists would fall under the category of civil disobedience. In fact, three strands can be discerned: (a) legal protests and actions, such as the Montgomery bus boycott (although, in fact, such actions soon became 'illegal' as legal devices were deployed against the participants); (b) actions through the courts, using or testing federal law against state law; (c) acts of peaceful law-breaking – that is, civil disobedience – such as refusing to obey police orders to disperse, and sitting at segregated lunch counters, where the proprietors could appeal to state law to enforce segregation. It is extremely important to understand how the Civil Rights Movement took place within a context of constitutional conflict, which mirrored the federal versus states conflict of the nineteenth century. Repeatedly, the federal level attempts to force desegregation on the South. Here are some key examples (federal level in bold):

- 1954: *Brown* v. *Board of Education of Topeka*: **Supreme Court** determines that segregation in public schools is unconstitutional.
- 1957: Nine black students are blocked from entering the formerly all-white Central High School, Little Rock, Arkansas. **Federal troops** sent in to protect the nine.
- 1961: James Meredith becomes first black student to enrol at the University of Mississippi; violence erupts and **President Kennedy** sends in 5,000 **federal troops**.
- 1963: 24th Amendment to the **Constitution** abolishes the poll tax, which had been used to prevent blacks registering to vote.
- 1964: **Congress** passes the Civil Rights Act – the most radical civil rights legislation since the 1866 Civil Rights Act.
- 1965: **Congress** passes the Voting Rights Act.
- 1965: **President Johnson** issues Executive Order 11246, enforcing affirmative action.
- 1967: *Loving* v. *Virginia*: **Supreme Court** rules that the prohibition on interracial marriage is unconstitutional.
- 1968: **Congress** passes another Civil Rights Act, this time outlawing discrimination in the sale, rental and financing of housing.

The laws that were the object of civil disobedience were state laws rather than federal laws; in general, the federal level was on the side of the Civil Rights Movement. We now consider some specific actions undertaken by civil rights activists: bus boycotts and freedom rides; sit-ins at lunch counters and other segregated spaces; marches, particularly on electoral registration offices.

Bus Boycotts

In romanticised accounts of the Civil Rights Movement the refusal of Rosa Parks to give up her seat for a white passenger is often taken as the starting point of the Civil Rights Movement. On 1 December 1955 Parks got on a bus in Montgomery (Alabama), and sat in the fifth row with three other blacks in the 'coloureds' section of the bus. After a few stops the front four rows filled up, and a white man was left standing; custom dictated that there could not be 'mixed' rows, so all four would be required to move; three of them complied but Parks refused. She was subsequently arrested. Significantly – from the perspective of civil disobedience – the charge was unclear: when a black lawyer tried to find out, the police told him it was 'none of your damn business'. (Legal theorist Lon Fuller argued that valid law must have certain characteristics, among which is clarity.)

Ch. 3:
Equality
pp. 65–66

It should be said that Parks's action was not entirely spontaneous; the Civil Rights Movement had been looking for a suitable 'victim' to publicise the issue of bus segregation and provoke a widespread boycott, and her action was not really the start of the Movement. There had been previous attempts to bring about a boycott. The boycott was effective, but the authorities then sought legal devices to end it: they required cab drivers to charge a minimum 45 cents per journey (black drivers had been charging 10 cents – the price of a bus ticket; the pro-boycott organisation, the Montgomery Improvement Association, the MIA, headed by King, then instituted a 'private taxi' scheme); a very old law prohibiting boycotts was used, and King was arrested; liability insurance on the private taxis was not granted. Eventually a *federal* court decided that such segregation was unconstitutional, and this was confirmed by the Supreme Court.

Freedom Rides

In 1947 the Congress of Racial Equality (CORE) set out to test the Supreme Court's 1946 ruling that segregation on interstate transportation was unconstitutional by sitting in 'whites only' seating. The so-called 'journey of reconciliation' met heavy resistance and was not a success. In 1961 the same strategy was adopted, but this time other court rulings had reinforced the claim for desegregation, and the campaign was better organised: white civil rights activists would sit in 'blacks only' seats and also use blacks only facilities at rest stops, and black civil rights activists would do the reverse on the same buses and at the same stops. They met a great deal of resistance, including mob violence and mass arrests. Ultimately they succeeded in getting the Interstate Commerce Commission to outlaw segregation. From the perspective of Rawls's criteria for civil disobedience, the freedom rides are a grey area: the *political* aim of the action was to shame President Kennedy, who was perceived at the 1960 election to be sympathetic to civil rights, but who on taking office in January 1961 was much cooler about tackling the Southern states. The *legal* aim was to test the Supreme Court's 1946 ruling. It is a matter for debate whether *testing* a law constitutes civil disobedience.

Sit-ins

The strategy here was very similar to the freedom rides: groups of black students would challenge segregation by sitting at 'whites only' lunch counters and wait until they were served; once served they moved to the next shop. There was also an element of boycott: the Woolworth's chain had segregated counters in the South, but mixed counters in the North – there was a boycott of New York shops designed to force the company to desegregate its entire chain. At first, the sit-ins met with little resistance – the students were not served, but neither were they harassed – but a white reaction did build up, with white youths attacking the activists, and the police then arresting the (peaceful) activists. A common tactic of the activists was for one group to be ready to take the place of the arrested group, with the consequence that the jails would soon fill up and the machinery of justice grind to a halt. Again, from our perspective this is interesting: Rawls says that civil disobedience must not only be non-violent – and the sit-ins certainly were non-violent – but also non-coercive. Arguably, incapacitating the justice system is coercive. Also, relatedly, and again contra Rawls, the reason why many actions, including the bus boycotts, worked was not because the majority became aware of injustice, but because their interests were damaged – pressure came from bus companies and stores to desegregate.

Electoral Registration Campaigns

The biggest flashpoint was over voter registration. In principle, blacks could vote, but the Southern states found numerous ways to make it difficult for them to register as voters: there were few registration offices in black areas; opening hours were highly restricted; potential voters were intimidated with the connivance of the authorities – photographs were taken and employers informed; there was often a tax (poll tax) for registration; there were literacy qualifications (although many blacks were better educated than the officials).

The most famous, or infamous, set of events took place in 1965 at Selma (Alabama). In 1963 just 1 per cent of blacks in Selma were registered to vote. After winning the Nobel Peace Prize (December 1964) King decided that Selma should be the focus of a campaign. After various marches, arrests, and considerable violence on the part of the authorities, events came to a head on 7 March 1965 with a march across Edmund Pettus Bridge in Selma (Pettus was a Confederate General) where protestors were met by police and state troopers, who ordered them to disperse. They then attacked the protestors; pictures of their actions were transmitted across the world. What followed was complex, involving decisions such as whether to accept legal injunctions on marches, but eventually the Voting Rights Act (1965) was passed, with the number of registered black voters rising from 23 per cent in 1964 to 61 per cent in 1969. Although it is clear that the Civil Rights Movement affected the general political debate, it is a matter of debate whether *individual* campaigns, such as that at Selma, were causally responsible for *particular* pieces of legislation, such as the Voting Rights Act. We now turn to King's justification of his actions.

Martin Luther King, 'Letter from Birmingham City Jail' (1963)

King's Letter was addressed to fellow – mainly Southern white – clergymen, some of whom had criticised King's campaign of civil disobedience. Given that Rawls argues civil disobedience is an appeal to the majority, it is important to recognise the *two* audiences King addresses: the clergy are the explicit addressees, but the majority of US citizens are the implicit addressees. Although he does not separate them out we can discern both Christian and secular arguments in the Letter; of course, the great majority of Americans define themselves as Christian, but King communicates awareness that Christian arguments are not sufficient to justify civil disobedience. In setting out King's argument, we follow his narrative of events. Obviously his account should not be treated uncritically, but since our prime concern is with how he justified his actions from his perspective, the veracity of the historical details can be left to historians.

King sets out 'four basic steps' in a campaign of civil disobedience (King, 1991: 69):

1. the collection of facts to determine whether injustice is 'alive';
2. negotiation;
3. self-purification;
4. direct action.

The action that resulted in King's imprisonment – and the occasion for the Letter – were illegal demonstrations in Birmingham, Alabama. These were directed against the 'whites only' and 'no coloreds' signs in shops, the segregated restaurants, and the deliberate negligence of the police in investigating 18 bombings of black homes and churches over the previous six years. With regard to the first step, there was little doubt that Birmingham had one of the worst records on civil rights in the South.

The next step was to negotiate before engaging in civil disobedience. There were attempts to get the shopkeepers to remove their signs. Promises were made but not honoured. A mayoral election in March 1963 between the reactionary Bull Connor and moderate – but still segregationist – Albert Boutwell resulted in the latter's victory, but because the three-man commission that had run Birmingham, and included Connor, refused to stand down, there was no movement on removal of discrimination. Negotiation had failed. The next step was 'self-purification'. This must be distinguished from what we identified as the introversion that sometimes characterises conscientious refusal. The aim of self-purification is to ascertain whether the protestors will be able to endure violence without reacting violently. To this end, workshops on non-violent protest were held.

Finally, we come to the act of civil disobedience. King argues that one of the aims of civil disobedience is to 'create such a crisis and establish such creative tension that a community which has constantly refused to negotiate is forced to confront the issue' (King, 1991: 71). The new Mayor Boutwell might be persuaded that resistance to desegregation was futile. It could be argued – and King was aware of this – that the effectiveness of civil disobedience rests on the existence of a violent alternative to it. Those engaged in civil disobedience need not intend to communicate this message for this message to be communicated through their actions. In 1963 the widely perceived 'alternative' to Martin Luther King was Malcolm X's Muslim movement. Indeed King cites this movement in his Letter, arguing that if civil rights activists are dismissed as 'rabble rousers' and 'outside agitators' then millions of blacks 'out of frustration and despair, will seek solace and security in black nationalist ideologies, a development that will lead inevitably to a frightening racial nightmare' (King, 1991: 77).

Responding to the question of how it is possible to obey some laws but disobey others, King argues that there are just laws and unjust laws:

an unjust law is a human law that is not rooted in eternal and natural law. Any law that uplifts human personality is just. Any law that degrades human personality is unjust. All segregation statutes are unjust because segregation distorts the soul and damages the personality. It gives the segregator a false sense of superiority, and the segregated a false sense of inferiority (King, 1991: 73).

In expanding on this distinction King cites the Christian 'church fathers' Augustine (354–430) and Aquinas (1225–74), Jewish philosopher Martin Buber (1878–1965), and Protestant theologian Paul Tillich (1886–1965). It may appear that King is appealing to a particular moral conception, drawn from Judaism and Christianity, rather than a *political* morality. Three points should be made. First, so long as the underlying appeal extends beyond your own particular conception of what is ultimately valuable, which for King is rooted in Christian teaching, then enlisting Christian (and Jewish) thinkers – Augustine, Aquinas, Buber, Tillich – is legitimate. In effect, King is saying 'I am a Christian, but you do not have to be a Christian to recognise the injustice I describe.' Insofar as we interpret King's argument for civil disobedience to be based on his Christian beliefs it might be thought he is engaged in what Rawls terms conscientious refusal, but conscientious refusal is not incompatible with civil disobedience – a person, such as King, can be motivated by a secular political morality *and* a Christian morality. What would be problematic is to appeal only to a non-political morality.

Second, the Letter was written to Christian clergy, so the Christian references are unsurprising. Third, King goes on to restate the argument in secular language:

> An unjust law is a code that a majority inflicts on a minority that is not binding on itself. This is difference made legal. On the other hand a just law is a code that a majority compels a minority to follow that it is willing to follow itself. This is sameness made legal (King, 1991: 74).

He gives a couple of examples, the first of which is problematic. Because the state of Alabama had denied blacks the right to vote they could not be bound by its laws. The danger with this argument is that even if blacks had voted, being in a minority they might have been subject to discriminatory laws. A rather better example is the denial of police permits to demonstrate: King accepts that there should be controls on demonstrations, but objects to the misuse of permits to deny civil rights activists the possibility of peaceful protest, while opponents of civil rights can protest unhindered. (We could also add that peaceful protestors were arrested, while their white attackers were let free; that prisoners were often released into the hands of the Ku Klux Klan; and that the right to choose who to serve in a shop or restaurant was asserted as a right when whites wanted to discriminate, but choosing to boycott buses was deemed illegal.)

King argues that a sign of the good faith of the civil rights activists is that they break the law openly and are willing to accept the penalties for law-breaking. These are, of course, on Rawls's list of conditions for civil disobedience. Finally, as if to underline the stabilising power of civil disobedience, King concludes his Letter with the following statement:

> One day the South will know that when the disinherited children of God sat down at lunch counters they were in reality standing up for the best in the American dream and the most sacred values in our Judeo-Christian heritage, and thusly, carrying our whole nation back to those great wells of democracy which were dug deep by the founding fathers in the formulation of the Constitution and the Declaration of Independence (King, 1991: 84).

What makes the Civil Rights Movement an important example of civil disobedience is that in philosophical terms it took place in the space between the constitution and lower-level law. This may also, however, raise some definitional difficulties. The most visible aspect of the civil rights struggle was the clash between supporters and opponents of equal rights in the streets, on the buses and at the lunch counters. But behind that struggle was another: a struggle between federal law and constitutional judgements on the one side, and the Southern states on the other. It is notable that when defenders of segregation organised themselves politically – at elections – they adopted the banner of States' Rights: the rights of the states against the president, Congress, and Supreme Court. Civil disobedience was made possible by: (a) the existence of a (basically) just constitution, and (b) the refusal at a lower level of law-making to respect the constitution. It could be argued that what the civil rights activists were doing was appealing, not to the majority of fellow Americans, but to the judiciary; in effect, they were forcing test cases for the legitimacy of state law. On the other hand, it might be maintained that it was through elected representatives in Congress – representatives of 'the majority' – that the great strides forward in civil rights were made.

The failure of the Civil Rights Movement to change Southerners' attitudes is revealed in the Congressional voting figures for the Civil Rights Act (1964). In the Senate, the Democrats divided 46–21 in favour (69 per cent in favour) and the Republicans were 27–6 in favour (82 per cent). All Southern Democratic Senators voted against. In the House of Representatives, the Democrats divided 152–96 in favour (61 per cent) and the Republicans 138–34 in favour (80 per cent). Of the Southern Democratic Congressman 92 out of 103 (89 per cent) voted against.

Summary

Civil disobedience may seem a marginal political issue, given that most citizens do not engage in it. However, the arguments for and against civil disobedience go to the heart of the moral basis of democracy and, in particular, the only viable form of democracy in a modern society: representative majoritarian democracy. While Rawls's theory of civil disobedience does not really hold up when it is tested against historical reality it provides a very useful framework within which to assess both the grounds, and the limits, of majoritarian democracy. More generally, the development of the concept of civil disobedience grew out of, but also represents a critique of, early liberal theories of political obligation; civil disobedience implies that human beings should retain a degree of moral autonomy *vis-à-vis* the state.

Questions

1. Does the fact that a law was passed through a democratic process give us a special reason for obeying it?
2. Can a person who engages in civil disobedience give a coherent answer to the accusation that 'if everybody did that, there would be a collapse in social order'?
3. Is there a valid distinction between civil disobedience and conscientious refusal?
4. Was the US Civil Rights Movement really an example of civil disobedience?

References

King, M.L. (1991) 'Letter from Birmingham City Jail' in H.A. Bedau (ed.), *Civil Disobedience in Focus* London: Routledge, 68–84.

Rawls, J. (1972) *A Theory of Justice* Oxford: Oxford University Press.

Sabl, A (2001), 'Looking Forward to Justice: Rawlsian Civil Disobedience and its Non-Rawlsian Lessons' *The Journal of Political Philosophy* 9(3), 307–30.

Singer, P. (1973) *Democracy and Disobedience* Oxford: Clarendon Press.

Thoreau, D. (1991) 'Civil Disobedience' in H.A. Bedau (ed.), *Civil Disobedience in Focus* London: Routledge, 28–48.

Further Reading

There is not an extensive literature on civil disobedience (although civil disobedience is often implicitly discussed in the context of political obligation). Nonetheless, the following are useful: H.A. Bedau (1991) contains 'classic' texts on civil disobedience. Another edited collection by Bedau is: H.A. Bedau, *Civil Disobedience: Theory and Practice* (New York: Pegasus, 1969). Two further studies are Chaim Gans, *Philosophical Anarchism and Political Disobedience* (Cambridge: Cambridge University Press, 1992) and Leslie Macfarlane, *Political Disobedience* (London: Macmillan, 1971). For some books on the Civil Rights Movement see: Adam Fairclough, *To Redeem the Soul of America: the Southern Christian Leadership Conference and Martin Luther King, Jr.* (Athens, Geo. and London: University of Georgia Press, 1987); David Garrows, *Protest at Selma: Martin Luther King, Jr., and the Voting Rights Act of 1965* (New Haven, CN and London: Yale University Press, 1978): John Salmond, *My Mind Set on Freedom: A History of the Civil Rights Movement, 1954–68* (Chicago, IL: Ivan R. Dee, 1997).

Weblinks

Most websites on civil disobedience are activist-oriented, but these can be interesting because they provide guidance on carrying out civilly disobedient acts – it is useful to compare this advice with Rawls's checklist:

- ACT-UP (gay rights organisation): http://www.actupny.org/documents/CDdocuments/CDindex.html

- Peace campaigners: http://www.activism.net/peace/nvcdh/

- Animal rights campaigners: http://www.animal-law.org/library/pamphlet.htm

- Fathers4Justice (a British-based group campaigning for fathers' access to their children): http://www.fathers-4-justice.org/

Chapter 20

Political Violence

Introduction

Since 11 September 2001, when the World Trade Centre and part of the Pentagon were demolished through terrorist attacks, the question of political violence has been widely debated in the media and elsewhere.

Just what is political violence? Can a practitioner of political violence be coherently distinguished from a guerrilla or freedom fighter? An analysis of political violence is particularly important, given the fact that authoritarian regimes may find it convenient to label all manifestations of violent opposition as 'terrorist' in nature. Why does political violence arise, and above all, what we can do about it? It is important that we try to understand it not as a way of condoning it but because we will never be able to eradicate this violence unless we understand it – its sources, its *raison d'être*, and its apparent justifications.

Chapter Map

- The liberal tradition and political violence. The traditional view of the state as an institution that does not itself use political violence.

- Salmi's distinction between four types of violence, and a critique of Salmi's position. The distinction between political violence and terrorism proper.

- Marx, Lenin and Mao's view of political violence. The problem of a general theory of political violence.

- The roots of political violence.

- The link between political violence and the state. The problem of US policy towards political violence.

9/11 and its legacy

Remains of the Twin Towers at Ground Zero, September 11, 2001

Source: © Paul Colangelo/CORBIS

Everyone can remember where they were when September 11 happened. There was saturation media coverage, and it was clearly the worst terrorist outrage anyone could recall since the Second World War. There was a sense of total unreality as a second plane collided with the tower of the World Trade Centre not long after the first plane had struck. Thousands of people were already at their desks in both towers, while some 80 chefs, waiters and kitchen porters were working in a restaurant on the 106th floor. Many who worked for firms located in the crash zone were killed instantly. Those on the floors above the collisions were already doomed, their escape routes cut off by fire. And then the news about the Pentagon. Overall, the estimated death tolls reached 3,030 with 2,337 injuries. Al-Qaeda was blamed for the atrocities, and there was a sense at the time that this was an event that was truly historic. Everything that has happened since then, the war on Afghanistan and Iraq, the passing of anti-terrorist legislation, the establishment of the internment camp at Guantamano Bay, has confirmed that this was an event with enormous repercussions. It has brought the question of political violence into everyone's consciousness.

Politicians and ordinary people alike condemned the atrocity. But why did it happen?

- Is the very attempt to understand the events of 9/11 an act of thoughtless condonation, or is understanding crucial to an effective way of responding to the action?

The act was denounced as 'evil'.

- Is this a useful category for characterising such outrages, or is the notion of evil unable to get to grips with the reasons why such an event happened?

What did the action achieve? Clearly it obtained massive publicity:

- But did it make it easier or more difficult to implement policies that would tackle the causes of the problem?
- What was in the minds of those who planned the event? Were they hoping for an intemperate response that would recruit supporters for their cause, or did they believe that this kind of action would bring about the kind of reforms that would address the problem of Palestine/Israel, global inequality, American hegemony, etc.?
- Is there a danger that by fully reporting such incidents, that 'the oxygen of publicity' (as Thatcher used to say) is given to the practitioners of political violence?

Liberalism and the Question of Violence

We normally define political violence as the use of political violence against individuals or the functionaries of the state. We need to be clear when the use of such violence is regarded as 'terrorist' and when it is not.

Definitions of political violence necessarily contain reference to acts of violence, and what makes political violence a negative term is that violence itself is seen as negative. Indeed, it is defined in one recent volume as 'a type of political depravity which unfortunately has become commonplace' (Harmon, 2000: 2). The generalised opposition to violence comes out of the liberal tradition.

In *Leviathan* written by Thomas Hobbes (1588–1679) (see the biography on the website) there is an emphasis upon avoiding war and establishing a commonwealth based on consent. No covenant can be valid which exposes a person to 'Death, Wounds, and Imprisonment' (1968: 169). Here is the view that force or violence negates freedom, and although Hobbes allows freedom to be consistent with fear and necessity, it cannot be reconciled with force. Indeed, so concerned is Hobbes with the problem of force and the individual's natural right to avoid it, that (unlike Locke) he takes the view that an individual is not bound to fight for the state (Hoffman, 1998: 46).

Locke (1632–1704) (see the biography on the website) likewise argues that only when someone is not under the 'ties of common law of reason', can 'force and violence' be deployed (1924: 125). It is true that Locke justifies slavery as a state of war continued between a lawful conqueror and captive (1924: 128), so that even if force can be lawful (a point to which we will return), the liberal tradition sees a conflict between violence and freedom, violence and rights.

The notion of political violence only becomes possible when violence is seen in negative terms. Whereas pre-modern thought regarded violence as a sign of human empowerment – hence the positive evaluation of the warrior – liberalism argues for a world in which market exchanges are defined as activity that has banished violence. Thus the praise for political violence, which is offered by Sheikh Azzam, reputedly the teacher of the Saudi terrorist, Osama Bin Laden, cannot be squared with the liberal tradition. The notion that political violence is some sort of an obligation in the Muslim religion is not only a dubious reading of Islam: it implies a legitimacy for violence which the liberal tradition cannot accept, at least as the criterion of a free person.

It is true that Hobbes refers to the force of the state as 'terror' (1968: 227), but the use of the term is atypical. It is much more common to refer to the use of force by the state, and violence used by the enemies of a state who resort to what is seen as illegitimate violence.

The State and Political Violence

The liberal tradition often distinguishes between force and violence – and thus force and political violence. State political violence refers to states that sponsor political violence, not the state per se as an organisation that uses violence.

Laqueur, who has written numerous works on the question of political violence, argues that Iran has sponsored the Hizbullah group in the Lebanon, and it has extended support to Shi'ite groups in Afghanistan and Palestinian groups like the Islamic Jihad. Iraq under Saddam Hussein, he argues, has been much more cautious in its support for terrorist groups (we shall later distinguish political violence and terror) but it did provide some shelter to the remnants of the Abu Nidal group and the People's Liberation Front for Palestine (Laqueur, 2003: 223–5).

Although we think that there is a strong case for using force and violence as synonyms, Johnston distinguishes sharply between the two on the ground that violence is force that violates some moral or legal norm, so that we can differentiate between, say, police force and criminal violence. He argues that it is important to combine confrontation and conciliation, reason and force in combating violence, and he identifies terrorists as criminals (Johnston, 1993: 16–17). It is true that criminals do not necessarily see themselves as acting politically, whereas terrorists do.

The argument is that because the force of the state is authorised and limited to specific purposes, it cannot be considered 'violent', and therefore the notion of political violence has to be restricted to those who oppose the state. Miller comments that 'it is a well-entrenched feature of our language that to describe an action as an act of violence is to condemn it forcefully' (1984: 403). Wilkinson contends that it is 'sheer obfuscation' to imagine that one can theorise about political violence in a value-free way (1979: 101).

In Miller's view, the force/violence distinction only applies when laws are general; when they are enacted in advance of behaviour they seek to control; when they do not discriminate between persons on irrelevant grounds; and the penalties are standardised and applied impartially (1984: 404). Violence is unpredictable and irregular. It is for this reason that the political theorist Pettit argues that only when force is used in an arbitrary way is freedom is compromised (1997: 302). A non-arbitrary use of force, i.e. the working of a liberal state, governed by a constitution, does not make you unfree so that Pettit's argument is that the force of a constitutional state does not lead to domination, and therefore should not be regarded as violence.

An Assessment of Salmi

Salmi, a development economist from Morocco, has written an important work entitled *Violence and Democratic Society*. In it he defines violence as an act that threatens a person's physical or psychological integrity (1993: 16), and he distinguishes between four categories of violence.

- *direct violence* involves deliberate attacks that inflict harm (kidnappings, homicide, rape, torture). This would certainly embrace political violence. Salmi distinguishes between direct and
- *indirect violence* when, he argues, violence is inflicted unintentionally as in cases of *violence by omission* when, say, inaction contributes to starvation or genocide (as in Roosevelt's failure to intervene in 1942 against Hitler's final

solution) (1993: 18). This indirect violence may also take the form of what Salmi calls 'mediated' (1993: 19) violence which occurs when individuals or institutions produce goods or trade in weapons of war which (again unintentionally) damage the health and environment of others. Salmi's third category relates to what he calls

- *repressive violence* (1993: 20) when people are derived of their political, civil, social or economic rights, while
- *alienating violence* (1993: 21) – his fourth category – embraces the kind of oppression (ethnic and male chauvinism, racism, hostile acts of homophobia, opposition to Aids' sufferers etc.) which undermines a person's emotional, cultural and intellectual development. What are we to make of these categories, and their link to the question of political violence?

It seems to us problematic to characterise direct violence as merely one form of violence among others. For this is the violence that deserves our immediate attention since it prevents people from (even in a formal sense) governing their lives. Salmi estimates that between 1820 and 1970 (after the Napoleonic wars through to the Vietnam conflict) some 68 million people died as a consequence of 'direct' violence, and this is the form of violence that, as the public rightly perceives, is the pressing problem (Salmi, 1993: 47). Whereas inaction (as in Salmi's second category) may be categorised as an evil, it cannot be said to constitute violence per se, although it may certainly be the *cause* of violence.

Again, what Salmi calls repressive and alienating violence may lead to direct violence, but until it does, it cannot be called violence (and thus political violence) as such, although like the so-called indirect violence of unemployment, it certainly harms people and should be condemned. Violence, as we see it, should be restricted to the infliction of deliberate physical harm: a case could certainly be made for incorporating abuse as violence where it leads to physical pain of the kind expressed through depression, etc. But violence becomes too broad a category if it is *linked* to any kind of pressure that affects someone's 'integrity' if by that is meant their capacity to act in a particular way.

For the same reason we would resist the argument of Bourdieu, a radical French social theorist, that violence can be symbolic or 'structural' (1998: 40, 98). Clearly, verbal and other forms of non-physical aggression are linked to violence, but we would prefer to distinguish between the causes of violence and violence itself. We will later challenge the notion that the liberal state only uses force and not violence, but we take the view that violence is best defined as the intentional infliction of physical harm.

Distinguishing Between Political Violence and Terrorism

It is our view that when political violence is used in conditions in which no other form of protest is permissible, then it would be wrong to call it terrorism. Miller argues that 'violence may be permissible in dictatorships and other repressive regimes when it is used to defend human rights, provoke liberal reforms, and achieve other desirable objectives' (1984: 406). Such violence should not be called terrorism, and the Thatcher government was wrong to describe the African National Congress (ANC) which resorted (among other tactics) to violence against the apartheid regime, as terrorist in character. The US government saw the ANC as one of the most notorious terrorist groups at the time. The point is that the ANC only resorted to violence as a response to the actions of a regime that banned the organisation and imprisoned its leaders.

Brian Bunting, a South African who has written widely on the anti-apartheid struggle, has documented in detail the laws passed in the period of 'grand apartheid' under Dr Verwoerd that, among other things, prevented peaceful protest. He cites the comment of Umkhonto we Sizwe (the ANC aligned Spear of the Nation) on its birth in 1961 where it talked about carrying on the struggle for freedom and democracy 'by new methods' which 'are necessary to complement the actions of the established national liberation organizations' (1969: 216). The ANC was no more terrorist than the partisans and liberation movements that fought against the Nazis during the Second World War. We would therefore disagree with the inclusion of the ANC in Harmon's glossary of terrorist groups (Harmon, 2000: 281). The violence employed by the ANC was regrettable, and it is worth noting that grisly 'neck-lacing' of those seen as regime collaborators (when individuals had old car tyres placed around their neck and these were then set ablaze with petrol) was a practice that the ANC never officially supported. The ANC is better described as a democratic rather than a terrorist movement. Chomsky (2003: 61) (→ biography on the website) speaks of the French partisans using 'terror' against the Vichy regime, but although he intends by this example to expose what he considers to be the hypocrisy of the USA, violence against illiberal systems should not be described in these terms.

This is not to say that the use of political violence in conditions in which it cannot be labelled terrorist, is not problematic. We should be careful not to idealise political violence. Movements that resort to violence inevitably commit human rights abuses as well, and anyone who thinks that liberation movements are purely and simply a 'good' thing, ought to see how, in contemporary Zimbabwe for example, the use of political violence can leave a legacy of authoritarianism and brutalisation. Reports from human rights groups have noted that in the first half of January 2004, there were 4 deaths, 68 cases of torture and 22 kidnappings, with much of the violence carried out by youths from the ruling ZANU-PF party (http://news.bbc.co.uk/1/hi/world/africa/1780206.stm).

In a moving work, *The Soft Vengeance of a Freedom Fighter* (1991), Sachs, a leading supporter of the ANC, a human rights lawyer and now a judge in South Africa, recalls the anguish he felt when he heard reports that Umkhonto we Sizwe were to target white civilians in the struggle to liberate South Africa. Having lost the sight of one eye and his right arm as the result of a car bomb in Maputo in Mozambique in 1988 (the work of agents of the South African security forces), Sachs feared that a free South Africa might come to consist largely of one-eyed and one-armed people like himself. He was hugely relieved to hear reports that his organisation was not planning to escalate violence in a way that would plunge South Africa 'in an endless Northern Ireland or Lebanon type situation, where action becomes everything and politics gets left behind' (Hoffman, 1994: 22). His anxiety testifies eloquently to the fact that violence remains a dangerous process even when it is (justifiably) used against illiberal states, and cannot be called terrorist in character. (See the Chapter on Anarchism.)

The Just War

Proponents of war have always presented their case in moralistic terms. Just war theory has been developed by Catholic theologians. They argue that pacifism is not appropriate in situations where one party to a violent conflict acts in a manner that is significantly worse than the other. This means that the belligerent state resorts to violence in a way that is clearly and unambiguously disproportionate. The notion goes back to ancient Roman theorists like Cicero and was reinforced by Augustine and Aquinas.

Before a just war can take place, there must be a massive invasion of human rights, and the resort to political violence must be recognised by political authorities. It is impossible to wage a just war if the objectives are linked to a narrow self-interest and self-aggrandisement. There must be a reasonable chance of success, and moreover, the counter-force must be directed against the functionaries of the hostile state, and not against the civilian population. This force must itself be proportionate to the objectives advanced, otherwise those who resort to counter-political violence become indistinguishable from the belligerent state itself.

Ending a just war is as important as starting it. Surrender must be accepted when it is offered, and punitive measures through war crimes tribunals etc. must be directed towards those directly responsible for the wrong-doing. Although supporters of the Iraq War have sometimes sought to defend it as a just war, opponents have argued that misinformation, the killing of civilians, the concern for oil, and the failure to secure international authorisation are some of the reasons why it cannot be described as a just war.

Political Violence, Ambiguity and the Liberal State

If political violence can be justified when a state is explicitly authoritarian and denies its opponents any channel of legal change (as in apartheid South Africa), it becomes terrorism when employed against a liberal state. The liberal state, as we have already suggested, is distinctive in its opposition to force or violence as a method of settling conflicts of interest. This is why under pressure, the liberal state has conceded rights to wider and wider sections of the community, and it promotes in the main a culture of self-reliance and universal freedoms. The opponents of the party in power are entitled to use, as Wilkinson (an academic expert on political violence) points out, the normal channels of democratic argument, opposition and lobbying through political parties, pressure groups, the media and peaceful protest (Wilkinson, 1979: 40).

Given the fact that the liberal state uses as its legitimating norm the notion that its laws are authorised, the use of violence against the liberal state is certain to be counter-productive. Groups like the June 2nd movement and the Baader-Meinhof group grew out of the West German student movement of the 1960s, and were hostile to the liberal state, believing that it merely represented big business. The bombings that they embarked upon succeeded only in provoking the state to tighter security policies with substantial public support. As Harmon points out, the motivating philosophy in the case of violence against liberal societies is often one of anarchism, and violent outrages do not advance, but set back, the cause of democracy. The movement against the Vietnam War (1965–73) created, in addition to a legitimate and sensible protest movement, small numbers of practitioners of political violence (whom we can legitimately call terrorists) like the Weathermen, who attacked the officials and property of the state (Harmon, 2000: 6).

Ch. 11:
Anarchism

Terrible ironies accompany the use of violence in liberal states. Take, for example, attacks by animal rights activists on the directors of companies believed to be involved with testing on animals. These movements justify the most appalling suffering of humans (who are also a kind of animal as well), and actions like these are invariably used by the media to diminish public sympathy for the animal rights cause. Is the destruction of property rather than individuals to be seen as terrorist (and not simply politically violent) in nature?

There are two problems here. The first is that the use of violence against property can easily (if unintentionally) harm individuals who are protecting such property, and the illegal nature of the act can have adverse political consequences. We would describe violence against property as a 'soft' political violence since in most circumstances peaceful forms of protest can create a change in opinion and would be more productive. But breaking the law per se does not count as political violence, and in the movement in Britain against the Poll Tax in the late 1980s, widespread public support was created for acts of defiance. The Poll Tax or Community Charge was calculated according to the number of people inhabiting a house, rather than the value of the property itself. In general, it could be argued that violence against property is likely to be counter-productive and set the struggle for democracy back. The cause is invariably overshadowed by the damage caused, and so the content of the protest is lost.

The use of violence in liberal societies is always inclined to be ideologically ambiguous. Laqueur argues with some justification that groups of the extreme 'left' often merge with, and become indistinguishable from, groups of the far right. Anti-Semitism may characterise practitioners of political violence who claim emancipation as their objective, and Laqueur poses the question: 'Is Osama bin-Laden a man of the left or right? The question is, of course, absurd' (2003: 8). But why? It is true that the extreme left can merge with the extreme right – but the distinction between left and right is still useful. Anti-liberalism can easily be left wing in character, but it depends upon whether this infringement of liberal values is resorted to as an attempt to emancipate humanity or privilege a particular group. The kind of Islamic fundamentalism that Al-Qaeda espouses is right wing, not simply because it is authoritarian, but because it opposes (even in the future) democracy, female emancipation, toleration, etc. It is impossible to be a left-wing anti-Semite although one can certainly be critical of the state of Israel and therefore be an anti-Zionist. Anti-Semitism is a particularistic creed (i.e. it does not espouse the freedom of all humans) and can therefore be legitimately characterised as a right-wing doctrine. Ideological ambiguity arises when logically incompatible elements are mixed together and whether something is of the extreme right or the extreme left depends upon the overall judgement we make of the mix.

Is Colonel Qaddafi, the current leader of Libya, a man of the left and right? He is a mixture but his nationalist chauvinism would tend to make him more right- than left-wing, although we would accept that authoritarian methods can be presented in the name of emancipation. As Harmon notes, his work extolling the virtues of a third way between capitalism and communism was, in the early 1990s, eagerly distributed by the British National Front (2000: 10). The point about political violence is that the use of violence by the left in conditions of liberal democracy can easily become linked to political violence of the right, as in the 'critical support' which some Trotskyite groups gave to the Iranian leader, Ayatollah Khomeini and the reactionary Taliban.

What are more difficult to categorise are movements like the IRA that (unlike the Red Brigades of Italy) enjoy a real base of popular support. Why? O'Day warns against the danger of forcing Irish political violence into a strait jacket (1979: 122). In Northern Ireland, the whole nature of the state has been problematic in liberal terms, and it is difficult, if not impossible, to envisage a minority becoming a majority, because of the nationalist divide. A liberal society can only operate to isolate extremists and advocates of violence if it offers meaningful political rights and the prospect of constitutional change. If this does not occur, then we have a classic 'tyranny of the majority' scenario that promotes illiberal values and institutions, as Northern Ireland dramatically demonstrated particularly before 1972 when the police force was partisan and unionists won seats in local elections through manipulating the electoral boundaries. Writing in 1979, O'Day can still speak of the 'deep-seated Catholic grievances' of the nationalist minority in the north (1979: 129). The fact that the Provisional IRA has called a cease-fire with the Good Friday Agreement of 1998, and its political wing has become more preoccupied with simply propagating republican values, suggests that its political violence was complicated by the popular support it enjoyed and the fact that it did not operate in a conventional liberal state.

O'Day comments that popular support 'may be passive, but it is, nonetheless, real and important' (1979: 124). The 1921 Treaty that partitioned Ireland was seen by republicans as a cynical exercise by the British that created, in the place of the historic nine-county Ulster, a six-county statelet with a contrived Protestant majority. O'Day speaks of the IRA as having 'enduring appeal'. In O'Day's judgement, much of the Irish activity is 'less properly described as terrorism than a particularly unpleasant form of violence springing directly from the grievances of an oppressed minority or the frustration of the young and unemployed' (1979: 126–27, 132).

Marx on the Problem of Political Violence

We have characterised Marxism (see Chapter on Socialism) as a mixture of post-liberal and anti-liberal views, views that build on liberalism and views that are authoritarian in character. The question of what counts as violence is all-important here, since if capitalism itself is seen as a form of violence, then Marxists would appear to condone counter-violence even in a liberal society, and this, in our argument, would make Marxism sympathetic to political violence.

Some argue that for Marx, death caused by indifference and neglect 'are as much a part of human violence as the violent acts of revolutionaries' (Harris, 1973–4: 192). Now there is no doubt that Marxist violence can be readily justified in conditions where workers either do not have a vote, or the franchise is fraudulent, but Harris's argument is questionable. For Marx does not regard the exploitation of labour by capital as violent, and in *Capital* he argues it is 'dull compulsion' of the relations of production that subjects labour to capital. It is not normally violence or force. *The Communist Manifesto* argues that when workers destroyed imported goods, smashed machinery and set factories ablaze, they failed to understand that it is the relations of production that need to be changed, not the instruments of production (Marx and Engels, 1967: 89). Random acts of violence are unhelpful and misguided.

It is true that Marx and Engels in the *Address of the Central Authority to the [Communist] League* speak of the fact that the communists 'must compel the democrats to carry out their present terrorist phrases' encouraging popular revenge against hated individuals or public buildings (1978: 202), but this was said in the throes of violent revolution against an autocratic system and cannot be taken as an endorsement of violence against a liberal state. What makes Marx sceptical about political violence in general is that it rests upon a belief in an abstract will, not in the maturation of material conditions. This is why he comments in *On the Jewish Question* that the belief that private property can be abolished through the guillotine as in the reign of terror by the Jacobins, is naive and counter-productive (Marx and Engels, 1975: 156). (The Jacobins were radicals who resorted to political violence and terror in the later phases of the French Revolution of 1789.)

The problem of violence arises in Marxism from the belief in the inevitability of revolution (→ Chapter on Socialism). Revolution invariably involves violence and if such violence is directed against a liberal society, it counts as political violence. Moreover, the idea that the use of violence is purely tactical and arouses no problem of morality, ignores the difficulty which violence creates in a liberal society.

The Leninist and Maoist Position on Political Violence

In countries like Tsarist Russia (1696–1917), the use of violence against particular individuals was deemed counter-productive by the Bolsheviks. Indeed, it was labelled political violence, even terrorism, both by its propagators and critics. What made such violence harmful was that it did not advance the cause of anti-Tsarism. Thus the killing of Tsar Alexander II who had come to power in 1881 created, as Laqueur points out, a backlash and was used to justify more severe policies on behalf of the regime. In the same way, the upsurge of democratic forces that compelled the Tsarist government to introduce a new constitution lost its impact when, as a result of 'terrorist' attacks in 1906, these concessions were withdrawn.

The problem here is that the attacks on particular figures are premised upon a flawed analysis of the political process. Many of the terrorists and champions of political violence, past and present (see Chapter on Anarchism), have been motivated by an anarchist philosophy which extols abstract willpower, and has little regard for broadening and deepening a popular movement opposed to a repressive regime. Marx and Engels condemned the Fenians – the Irish Republican Brotherhood – in London, not because the two revolutionaries did not sympathise with the cause of Irish freedom, but because they felt that blowing up people in London would not strengthen this cause. Even under repressive regimes, where political violence can be justified, terrorist-type violence, the killing of individuals and worse, civilian bystanders, can be counter-productive and lead to political marginalisation.

What is however problematic, is Lenin's view (for a biography of Lenin → website) that violence is normally necessary, and raises no ethical dilemmas. To describe the Bolsheviks as the 'Jacobins of contemporary Social Democracy' and to cite with approval Marx's comment that 'French political violence' involved a settling of accounts with absolutism and feudalism in a 'plebian manner' (Hoffman, 1984: 56) implies that violence is acceptable in, it seems, almost any context. For Lenin, it is an integral part of politics (→ Chapter on State, p. 11). To define a dictatorship – even the dictatorship of the proletariat – as authority untrammelled by laws and based directly on force (Lenin, 1962: 246), is to condone the use of violence by the post-liberal state, and it would seem, even against the liberal state. Such violence would, in the analysis adopted here, be regarded as terrorism.

It is surely revealing that Sorel, the French anarcho-syndicalist, at the end of his *Reflections on Violence*, has a hymn of praise to Lenin as a 'true Muscovite' because of his propensity to use violence (1961: 281). Sorel's own rather mystical deification of violence places him closer to the fascists (1961: 23), but it is instructive that he was an admirer of Lenin. Rosa Luxemburg (see the biography on the website) was to express her anxiety over the dictatorial methods and 'rule by terror' which Lenin and Trotsky adopted after the October revolution.

Mao Zedong's notion of guerrilla war draws upon classical Chinese writings and stresses the need to attack an enemy (that is numerically superior) at its weakest points (Schram, 1967: 156). What is new in Mao's formulation is the emphasis upon the need politically to win the confidence of the poor peasantry – a strategy that appears to contradict the notorious Maoist formulation that political power stems from the barrel of a gun. Mao's execution of 'enemies' becomes problematic in terms of the analysis here, when force was unleashed during his political opponents particularly during the Cultural Revolution. It is only after the establishment of state power that he can be regarded as not only a practitioner of political violence but a terrorist rather than a freedom fighter.

What we have called the anti-liberal elements within Marxism – in particular the notion of class war and revolution – create support for a political violence which can become terrorist in character. It is true that Marxism does not support the view (which Frantz Fanon, an Algerian revolutionary, endorsed), that violence is somehow an ennobling and 'cleansing' process. Fanon argues that violence 'frees the native from his inferiority complex and from his despair and inaction; it makes him fearless and restores his self-respect' (1967: 74). This kind of view sees the politically violent man or woman as a person without normal relationships: they are wedded to the Struggle or Revolution, not to family and friends. This view is inherent, it could be argued, in violence, and therefore on the surface of things, would seem opposed to Marxism's methodology (Marxism speaks of individuals entering into relations with one another). Nevertheless, Marxism does contain aspects that facilitate the use of violence, and thus terrorsim, in liberal and socialist societies.

A General Theory of Political Violence?

Laqueur argues that there will perhaps never be an authoritative guide to political violence because there is not one political violence, but a variety of political violences (he equates political violence with terrorism): what is true for one does not necessarily apply to the others (2003: 8).

Laqueur is certainly right to stress that political violence takes many different forms. In the nineteenth century political violence was linked to struggles for national independence and social justice, and sought to avoid civilian casualties. In the twentieth century, this has changed, and the most disturbing feature of what has been called the 'new political violence' is the way in which no distinction is made between functionaries of a particular regime and ordinary civilians. The IRA tried to give warnings for its attacks; so does ETA (the Basque Euskadi Ta Azkatasuna) – Al-Qaeda does not. A clear distinction, therefore, needs to be made between 'traditional' political violence that regarded civilian deaths as 'regrettable', and the political violence of groups like Al-Qaeda that specifically targets ordinary people.

While distinctions need to be noted, it has to be said that variety is common to all movements and 'isms'. Movements like socialism and concepts like democracy are also extremely variegated – political violence is no different. Laqueur insists that political violence 'more perhaps than most concepts', has generated widely divergent interpretations (2003: 232), but there seems to be no reason why this should be so. Of course, it is complicated by the fact that the term has now (mostly) acquired a distinctively pejorative tone but concepts like democracy have acquired, as we have pointed out, a distinctively positive connotation.

While the search for a 'general theory' needs to be sensitive to difference and variety, it is possible to argue that case for a definition of political violence while stressing the complexity and heterogeneous nature of the phenomenon. When Laqueur takes the view that 'the search for a scientific, all-comprehensive definition is a futile enterprise' (2003: 238), his problem arises because he assumes that such a definition must be beyond controversy and counter-argument. An impossible demand! He in fact goes on to provide a working definition – 'the systematic use of murder, injury, and destruction, or the threat of such acts for political ends'. The use of violence to challenge and remove an authoritarian or explicitly anti-liberal regime cannot be called terrorism.

Laqueur also argues that what makes a general theory impossible is the fact that there is not 'one overall explanation' of the roots of political violence (2003: 22), but this argument rests upon a false juxtaposition between the general and the particular: certainly a theory of political violence is complex and there are many factors involved. But this is true of all theory. It is a reflection of a complex world, infinite in its particularity. The general can only express itself through the particular, and when we come to present our own 'general theory', it is clear that multiple factors are necessarily involved.

It has been argued that, on the one hand, we should 'perhaps' think of political violences rather than political violence, thus freeing ourselves from the tyranny of the search for an all-embracing and universally acceptable definition. On the other hand, the term 'political violence' is still used in the singular (Gearson, 2002: 22).

The Roots of Political Violence

There is certainly no simple explanation for political violence, but finding its roots can only help to provide some guidance to this complex phenomenon. Political violence is not necessarily to be found in the harshest regimes since highly efficient dictatorships can make political violence extremely difficult, whereas it is a sad fact of life that regimes which are either democratic or partly democratic have become much more vulnerable to violent attack. Regimes which appeared democratic at the outset of such an attack may cease to be so – like the Uruguayan crushing of the Tupamaros – after the threat has been dealt with (Friedlander, 1979: 235).

Laqueur argues that while poverty is a factor, it should not be exaggerated: very poor countries may see civil unrest and even civil war, but not political violence. The followers of political violence might be poor, whereas the leaderships are wealthy and middle class: political violence 'rarely occurs in the poorest and richest countries, especially if these happen to be small societies in which there is little anonymity; between these extremes, political violence can occur almost anywhere'. He cites Kofi Annan, former Secretary General of the UN, to the effect that the poor suffer enough: why add to their misery by branding them potential practitioners of political violence (Laqueur, 2003: 16, 18)? Alongside poverty must be added national and ethnic conflict, although this kind of conflict has not been evident in some countries in which political violence has occurred. It is useful to distinguish between the 'symptoms' and 'causes' of political violence (von Hippel, 2002: 25). No strategy can be successful which simply addresses itself to the symptoms, and ignores the reasons as to why political violence arises. Just as it is difficult to define political violence, it is also difficult to locate the roots of such violence, but what can be said is that political violence arises because people cannot 'change places'. This is not because people are different, since we are all different from one another – in terms of our age, occupation, gender, outlook, etc. There are a multiplicity of factors involved in an inability to change places: significant disparities in wealth; religious intolerance; bitterness and despair; and the prevalence of a 'blame' culture which helps to convert differences into divisions. When these divisions are not understood, and no realistic strategy exists for overcoming them, we can have political violence.

The problem with the Laqueur analysis is that it sees political violence as insoluble. 'It stands to reason', he argues, 'that if all mankind were to live in small countries, preferably in small cities, and if all human beings were well off, there would be less violence', be it crime or political violence. 'But there is no reason to assume that violence would disappear altogether' (2003: 15). Laqueur seeks to argue that political violence per se is ineradicable. It is clear that no factor, on its own, will do the trick. Removing the problem posed by the state of Israel, eliminating world poverty, tackling repressive and injustice, reducing the frustration which inequality engenders, addressing a culture that glorifies war would clearly help to reduce political violence. But it would be foolish, indeed, to imagine that any particular factor, or even taking them together, would eliminate political violence. The way in which, for example, former colonies had their boundaries drawn – dividing linguistic and ethnic groups in arbitrary fashion – has stored up appalling problems that will take decades to resolve. Yet why should we assume that political violence will always exist?

To argue, as Laqueur does, that 'there are no known cures for fanaticism and paranoia' (2003: 10), is to suggest that psychological problems lie outside of social relationships and cause political violence. We know, for example, that depression and mental illness can arise from problematic family relationships and these are often linked to aggressive, authoritarian and patriarchal attitudes. Psychological problems have their roots in social relationships. To suggest that political violence will always be with us because it is a complex phenomenon, is to generalise from the contemporary world in a way that creates fatalism and despair. The point is that in a world in which poverty, national and ethnic injustices, patriarchal policies and practices were being tackled, people would be better able to 'change places' than they can at the moment. A reduction in political violence implies logically that political violence can be eliminated, since there is no evidence that it is part of human nature to murder, maim and destroy for political reasons.

Von Hippel is more positive than Laqueur. She notes that strong authoritarian states – like Egypt, Algeria and Saudi Arabia – may also provide conditions for political violence, just as the collapse of states, like the Sudan and Somalia, may provide a breeding ground. She concedes that 'sharpening the focus on root causes' can lead to 'politically awkward situations and policy choices'. Nevertheless, these need to be addressed if 'the counterterrorist campaign is to succeed' (2002: 38). It is difficult to eradicate political violence, but the problem is not in principle insoluble.

The Problem of Violence and the State

We have already cited Hobbes's comment that the state uses terror to maintain order. Friedlander argued in 1979 that perhaps it is time to use violence against those who resort to it (1979: 232). It seems to us that built into Weber's definition of the state is an emphasis on the use of violence to settle conflicts of interest, and therefore it can only be plain prejudice to assume that the state cannot or does not use violence against its enemies. Von Hippel concedes that 'no state has a complete monopoly on organized violence' (2002: 30) and as we have pointed out in the Chapter on the State (see p. 11), states claim a monopoly which they cannot and do not have.

There is a good deal of confusion in this area. On the one hand, one writer seems to think it necessary to separate political violence from the monopolistic use of violence claimed by states, and sees political violence as the work of subnational groups or non-state entities. On the other hand, he says that during the 1930s political violence became 'a state monopoly', 'reminding observers that enforcement political violence has been much more destructive than agitational political violence' (Gearson, 2002: 11, 15). The reference to 'enforcement political violence' surely implies that states can and do exercise violence, even terror.

Laqueur sees the argument that states use force as a 'red herring', although he concedes that the political violence exercised by states has caused far more victims than the political violence exercised by small groups. He gives the example of Nazi Germany and Stalinist Russia (2003: 237), and, it is important to note, even liberal states use force against those who are deemed to break the law. This force can be characterised as political violence. The political violence of the liberal state is usually implicit since attempts are made to regulate and limit the use of force by state functionaries. This political violence becomes explicit when states (like the current Israeli state) espouse policies of assassination against their opponents. It is true that there is a difference between the political violence of small groups and the political violence of the state (2003: 237), but the fact remains that while the use of force can under certain circumstances be justified, it can never be legitimate. We may have to use violence against those who will not respond to mere social and moral pressures, in order to create a breathing space in which constructive policies cementing common interests can be employed. In other words, we need to pay careful attention to the context in which political violence is used. The leader of the Palestinian group, Hamas, has stated recently that he regretted the death of women and children in suicide bombings, and declared that if the international community supplied his organisation with F-16s and helicopter gunships, they would attack the military forces of Israel with those instead.

States, in general, claim a monopoly of legitimate force so that the use of force to tackle conflicts of interest has to be authorised, and in liberal states, this means (as noted above) that force is legally regulated and formally limited. Two further things can be said about the violence of the state. The first is that it is often a response to violence from within the community, and a stateless society is only desirable if social order is secured through (what have been called elsewhere) governmental sanctions. Where government is relatively weak, then a state is important since it seeks, however partially, to secure a monopoly of force. Second, where it is impossible to arbitrate and negotiate around conflicts of interest, the violence of the state is justifiable, although, as argued elsewhere, this must be on the grounds that the use of violence is the only way to provide a breathing space to enable policies to be implemented which will cement common interests. Present violence can only be vindicated if it diminishes future violence.

Ch. 1:
The State

Nevertheless, the point is that states use violence against violence, and this is a risky and undesirable business. It may be provisionally justified in the sense that under the circumstances, there is no other way to create a framework for policies to create common interests, but the elimination of political violence must address the question of the state: otherwise we normalise and naturalise violence. The belief that the state is permanent may lead to the argument that political violence is here to stay. If states use violence against individuals, why should this not be described as political violence?

George Shultz, Secretary of State under Reagan (President of the USA, 1980–89), argued that political violence had to be dealt by force – not by mediation and negotiations which were seen as a sign of weakness (Chomsky, 2003: 48). We have made the point in the chapter on the state that violence is becoming easier and easier to inflict. It is also worth noting that the nature of war itself in changing: as Freedman points out, we have moved over the past century from a situation in which '90 per cent of the casualties of war were combatants to one where 90 per cent are civilians' (2002: 48). The use of violence is becoming more and more costly in character, while becoming easier and easier to inflict.

The Force/Violence Distinction and the Analysis of Political Violence

In characterising the force of the state as violence, we are not denying the differences which exist between formal and informal political violence. Indeed, a general definition of political violence presupposes, as argued above, the acknowledgement of serious and significant differences. But simply because two forms of a movement or institution are different, this does not mean that they do not also have something in common.

The argument by Johnston that states use force, whereas criminals and terrorists use violence (1993: 16–17) is unpersuasive, since with the best will in the world, it is impossible to limit force. Force by its nature always goes to extremes. State functionaries are not saints: their job – this is particularly true in the case of members of the armed forces – may be to injure and even kill, and it would be naive to think that this is possible in a way which is always proportionate and regulated. The same objection holds for Petit's argument that it is only when force is used in an arbitrary way, freedom is compromised. He equates the law with the force of the state (1997: 302), but why can't we have laws based upon social sanctions, so that offenders are punished but not in a statist manner (see Chapter on the State)? Of course, this is only possible when people can identify with one another, but these are the kind of sanctions which are used in everyday life in thousands of institutions which enforce rules and regulations against those who breach them. Petit's argument is that the use of force only makes you unfree when this force is arbitrary.

But how can force be non-arbitrary? The use of force even when it is regulated and supposedly limited, has an irreducibly arbitrary element since you cannot treat a person as a thing (which is what force involves) without an element of arbitrariness. How do you know the way in which the person upon whom the force is inflicted will respond? The perpetrator of force must be ready to act suddenly and unpredictably, so that the notion of arbitrary force is a 'pleonasm' i.e. force cannot be other than arbitrary. Petit acknowledges the problem when he concedes that criminal law processes often terrorise the innocent as well as the guilty and in practice, if not ideally, fines and prison sentences can be exposed as domination (1997: 154). It is true that non-arbitrary force is an 'ideal', but it is the kind of ideal which the state can only undermine as an institution claiming a monopoly of force.

Pettit argues that many people, responsive to ordinary norms, may not be so responsive if they knew that there was no great sanction attendant on breaking the norms (1997: 154). This, it could be argued, is wrong. Force, while transitionally necessary in a world where negotiation cannot work, weakens norms, creates resentment, and undermines rather than consolidates responsiveness to norms. Pettit takes the view that arbitrary interference involves a high level of uncertainty – there is no predicting when it will strike (1997: 85). This is surely a problem inherent in force itself.

To argue that the goal of the state is the promotion of freedom as non-domination (1997: ix), can only be naive, given the fact that the state as an institution involves arbitrariness and thus domination. Pettit contends that if the welfare and the world-view of the public are taken into account, then the act of law or state is not arbitrary (1977: 57). It is certainly true that a 'democratic' state is less arbitrary than an explicitly authoritarian one, but what makes the state inherently arbitrary is its use of force.

In the same way, the political theorist Dagger (1997: 94) does not recognise that forcing a person to be free is not simply a Rousseauian paradox: it is inherent within the state itself. Dagger, like Pettit, sees dangers in the criminal law but argues that while civic virtue is a positive good, punishment may be a necessary evil (1997: 79). The point is that the state is here to stay. This surely is the nub of the problem. Whether liberalism is accepted (as it is by Dagger) or rejected (by Pettit in favour of republicanism, a view that individuals should participate in politics), political violence can never be eliminated if we continue to rely upon an institution claiming a monopoly of legitimate force.

Chomsky has spoken of the unmentionable but far more extreme political violence of the powerful against the weak (2003: 7), but such an analysis is only possible when we see the state as an institutional expression of political violence itself. It is true that if powerful states would stop participating in political violence abroad, that would reduce the amount of political violence in the world by an enormous quantity (Chomsky, 2003: 20). Taking the official US government's definition of political violence – the use of violence to achieve political, religious or other ends through intimidation – are we not entitled to ask as to whether Israel's invasion of the Lebanon was not a 'textbook example' of political violence thus defined (Chomsky, 2003: 52)?

The Significance of September 11th

Nothing that has been argued so far suggests that force should not be used when innocent civilians are cruelly and heartlessly destroyed as happened on September 11th. The point is that using political violence against political violence is dangerous and can easily be counter-productive, for remember that according to our critique, the state itself is a violent institution that uses violence against violence. This is always a risky business.

Chomsky argues that the current leader of the 'War against Terror' is the only state in the world that has been condemned by the World Court for international political violence (2003: 50). Friedlander describes political violence as war and 'combating it is also war' (1979: 237), but might this kind of posture lead to the kind of laws that alienate not only civil libertarians, but citizens generally? Political violence has been defined in the PATRIOT Act passed in October 2001 in the USA in such a way that it could incorporate simple acts of civil disobedience.

Howard Zinn in his *Terrorism and War* contends that US foreign policy has promoted and provoked political violence. He cites a Defense Science Board that acknowledges the link between US involvement in international situations and the increase in violent attacks (2002: 9). His argument is that if you look at the death and indiscriminate bombing which has occurred, then it is impossible to avoid the conclusion that, for example, US is using violence against, even 'terrorizing Afghanistan' (2002: 11). He argues that 'we have to broaden our definition of political violence, or else we will denounce one political violence and accept another' (2002: 16). We must allow for the extension of the concept of political violence to the state itself. He insists that to understand political violence is not to justify it, and that to identify political violence simply with the fanaticism of individuals is superficial.

Zinn warns that there is a reservoir of possible practitioners of political violence among all those people in the world who have suffered as a result of US foreign policy (2002: 17). Not only can a policy of political violence against political violence be counter-productive, but it can also heighten inequalities at home and abroad. The infant mortality rate in the US is one of the worst in the world and now it is likely to increase (Zinn, 2002: 19). The sum of $350 billion is spent on being a military superpower; yet $101 billion could save eight million lives in the poorer countries of the world (2002: 18). War ravages civil liberties: even in 1979, it was argued that part of the cost of protecting the public against violence is the reduction of individual rights in a free society (Friedlander, 1979: 234). But the American public sees anyone who looks Middle Eastern, Arab or Muslim as potentially violent. War undermines the pursuit of truth, and encourages domestic imitators. McVeigh, who was a veteran of the Gulf War, described the children he killed in the Oklahoma bombing as 'collateral damage', while the factory bombed in the Sudan on the orders of President Clinton, produced not nerve gas but pharmaceuticals (Zinn, 2002: 21).

Zinn finds that since September 11th an atmosphere has been created in the USA in which it becomes difficult to be critical of American foreign policy (2002: 62). It has been said that the US now has a national strategy that trumpets freedom in the abstract but subordinates it to counter political violence in practice (Daalder, Lindsay and Steinberg, 2002: 411). It is difficult to see how the political violence of the weak can be defeated by the political violence of the strong. Kurth speaks of 'a dialectical and symbiotic connection, perhaps an escalating and vicious cycle' between Islamic political violence and American empire (2002: 404). Imaginative policies are needed which seek to address the roots causes of political violence, the poverty, insecurity, lack of self-esteem, injustice, inequality, etc. underlying the frustration and anger which expresses itself in violent form. Inverting political violence cannot eliminate it. As Daalder, Lindsay and Steinberg put it pithily, 'unless the United States closes the gap between its words and its deeds, it risks fuelling the very threats that imperil its security' (2002: 411).

Political Violence and 9/11

James Hamill, in a recent analysis of the Iraq War, comments that an animosity has been consolidated that may contain within it the seeds of a future political violence (2003a: 326). The ideological right, he argues, had long held the view that overwhelming force should be deployed regardless of international legal norms, and September 11th legitimised these ideas. They were expressed in a document in September 2002 outlining national strategy, and although attempts to establish a link between Iraq and Bin Laden's Al-Qaeda were 'unsuccessful', the policy of dismantling weapons of mass destruction via regime change was pressed (2003a: 328). Iraq provided the old-fashioned inter-state conflict that made the 'war against political violence' more concrete and tangible. This strategy document is seen as embodying a 'Bush doctrine' of comparable importance to the 'Truman doctrine' of 1947 that sought 'containment' of the Soviet Union (Kurth, 2002: 404).

Dr Hans Blix, head of the UN Monitoring Commission, has attacked the US and Britain for planning the war well in advance and contended that they were fabricating evidence against Iraq to legitimise the campaign (2003a: 330). Hamill provides a detailed argument to show that the armed action was in defiance of the UN Charter, and describes the action as 'a war in search of a pretext' (2003b: 9). Hamill's fear is that the launching of an illegal war will foster a climate in which more young people throughout the Arab world will become receptive to the crude anti-Western rhetoric of violent groups (2003b: 100). It will increase rather than diminish the impact of Bin-Laden style extremism, and encourage states to accelerate their own programmes to develop nuclear capability (2003b: 11–13).

Summary

The liberal tradition is the first to see violence in the political process as a phenomenon to be condemned. The predominant view is that it is wrong to see the state itself as a violent organisation. States may sponsor political violence, but political violence is best identified as the use of violence against the state.

Salmi has distinguished between four types of violence. Only his notion of direct violence involves physical force. The other concepts – indirect violence, repressive violence and alienating violence – use the notion of violence too broadly and fail to make the distinction between violence and the causes of violence. The distinction between political violence and terrorism is also a crucial one. When people are denied political and legal rights, they may resort to political violence. This violence may be problematic (even counter-productive) but it should not be described as terrorism. Terrorism only arises when political violence is directed against liberal states. Those opposing liberalism might be of the left or the right, or take a position that is ideologically ambiguous.

Marx generally identifies capitalist exploitation as 'coercive' (constraining would be a better term) rather than violent in character, and regards violence as justifiable where states deny political rights. Lenin, on the other hand, appears to justify violence even against liberal states. Despite argument to the contrary, political violence can be defined in general terms even though (like all phenomena) it is certainly a variegated and heterogeneous phenomenon. It is only possible to eradicate political violence if we can analyse its roots, although they may be extremely varied and multiple in character.

States, it could be argued, use terror to tackle conflicts of interest, so that the problem of political violence is connected to the problem of the state. Without recognising this, counter-violent measures (as US policy demonstrates) can make a bad situation even worse.

Questions

1. Is it possible to distinguish between a practitioner of political violence and a freedom fighter?
2. What role does the liberal tradition play in defining political violence?
3. Should we speak of political violences rather than political violence?
4. Is it correct to regard the state itself as a violent institution?
5. Do you agree with the argument that the recent war on Iraq has exacerbated rather than reduced the problem of political violence?

References

Bourdieu, P. (1998) *Acts of Resistance* Cambridge: Polity.

Bunting, B. (1969) *The Rise of the South African Reich*, revised edn Harmondsworth: Penguin.

Chomsky, N. (2003) *Power and Terror* New York: Seven Stories Press.

Daalder, I., Lindsay, J. and Steinberg, J. (2002) 'Hard Choices: National Security and the War on Terrorism' *Current History* 101 (659), 409–13.

Dagger, R. (1997) *Civic Virtue* Oxford: Oxford University Press.

Fanon, F. (1967) *The Wretched of the Earth* Harmondsworth: Penguin.

Freedman, L. (2002) 'The Coming War on Terrorism' in L. Freedman (ed.), *Superterrorism: Policy Responses* Malden, MA; Oxford: Blackwell, 40–56.

Friedlander, R. (1979) 'Coping with Terrorism: What is to be Done?' in Y. Alexander *et al.* (eds), *Terrorism: Theory and Practice* Boulder, CO: Westview, 231–45.

Gearson, J. (2002) 'The Nature of Modern Terrorism' in L. Freedman (ed.), *Superterrorism: Policy Responses* Malden, MA, Oxford: Blackwell, 7–24.

Hamill, J. (2003a) 'The United States, Iraq and International Relations', *Contemporary Review* 282, 326–33.

Hamill, J. (2003b) 'The United States, Iraq and International Relations', *Contemporary Review* 283, 7–15.

Harmon, C. (2000) *Terrorism Today* London: Frank Cass.

Harris, J. (1973–74) 'The Marxist Conception of Violence', *Philosophy and Public Affairs* 3, 192–220.

Hobbes, T. (1968) *The Leviathan* Harmondsworth: Penguin.

Hoffman, J. (1984) *The Gramscian Challenge* Oxford: Basil Blackwell.

Hoffman, J. (1998) *Sovereignty* Buckingham: Open University Press.

Johnston, S. (1993) *Realising the Public World Order* Leicester: Centre for the Study of Public Order, University of Leicester.

Kurth, J. (2002) 'Confronting the Unipolar Moment: The American Empire and Islamic Terrorism', *Current History* 101(659), 414–20.

Laqueur, W. (2003) *No End to War* New York and London: Continuum.

Lenin, V. (1962) *Collected Works*, vol. 10 London: Lawrence and Wishart.

Locke, J. (1924) *Two Treatises of Civil Government* London: Dent.

Marx, K. and Engels, F. (1967) *The Communist Manifesto* Harmondsworth: Penguin.

Marx, K. and Engels, F. (1975) *Collected Works* vol. 3 London: Lawrence and Wishart.

Marx, K. and Engels, F. (1978) *Collected Works* vol. 10 London: Lawrence and Wishart.

Miller, D. (1984) 'The Use and Abuse of Political Violence' *Political Studies* 37(3), 401–19.

O'Day, A. (1979) 'Northern Ireland, Terrorism and the British State', in Y. Alexander *et al.* (eds), *Terrorism: Theory and Practice* Boulder, CO: Westview, 121–35.

Pettit, P. (1997) *Republicanism* Oxford: Oxford University Press.

Sachs, A. (1991) *The Soft Vengeance of a Freedom Fighter* London: Paladin.

Salmi, J. (1993) *Violence and Democratic Society* London: Zed.

Schram, S. (1967) *Mao Tse-Tung* Harmondsworth: Penguin.

Sorel, G. (1961) *Reflections on Violence* New York: Collier.

Von Hippel, K. (2002) 'The Roots of Terrorism: Probing the Myths' in L. Freedman (ed.), *Superterrorism: Policy Responses* Malden, MA, Oxford: Blackwell, 25–39.

Wilkinson, P. (1979) 'Terrorist Movements' in Y. Alexander *et al.* (eds), *Terorism: Theory and Practice* Boulder, CO: Westview, 99–117.

Zinn, H. (2002) *Terrorism and War* New York: Seven Stories Press.

Further Reading

- Laqueur's *No End to War* (referenced above) is comprehensive and authoritative. Laqueur has written a huge amount on political violence, and this is his most recent volume.

- Miller's 'The Use and Abuse of Political Violence' (referenced above) contains some very useful insights into the question.

- Von Hippel's 'The Roots of Terrorism: Probing the Myths' (referenced above) offers a perspective that is both interesting and challenging.

- Hoffman's (1988) 'Is Political Violence Ever Justified?', *Social Studies Review*, 4(2), 61–2 is a brief and contentious polemic on the problem.

- Salmi's *Violence and Democratic Society* (referenced above) contains a challenging analysis as to what violence is and how we might identify it.

- Wilkinson's *Terrorism and the Liberal State* (referenced above) provides a very good overview from one of the country's leading academic authorities on the subject.

- Terry Eagleton's *Holy Terror* (Oxford: Oxford University Press, 2005) is a very stimulating read.

Weblinks

For the problem as it is seen in Britain:
http://www.homeoffice.gov.uk/terrorism/

For a detailed source that enables you to visit numerous sites:
http://uk.dir.yahoo.com/society_and_culture/crime/types_of_crime/terrorism/

For a useful survey of political violence by Halliday, see:
http://www.opendemocracy.net/debates/article-2-103-1865.jsp

For a useful guide to different sources and organisations
http://www.psr.keele.ac.uk/sseal/terror.htm

For a critique of US reactions to 9/11, see:
http://www.guardian.co.uk/comment/story/0%2C3604%2C1036571%2C00.html

Chapter 21

Global Justice

Introduction

The term 'global justice' encompasses debates over human rights, the justification of military intervention, and the international distribution of resources. In this chapter we focus on the last of these: the just, or fair, allocation of resources between nations, and between individuals across national boundaries. Among political theorists arguments over global justice emerged from, and took issue with, claims made in debates over 'domestic justice', which we discussed in Chapter 4. Three positions on global justice have been developed: 'cosmopolitans' maintain that it is incoherent to restrict justice to the sphere of the nation-state. Particularists (or partialists) argue that it is legitimate to show special concern for one's compatriots and the claims of justice can justifiably be restricted. Defenders of the third position – the 'political conception' – also argue for differential treatment of the domestic and global spheres, but they do so by stressing the complexity of morality and the importance of the political.

Chapter Map

In this chapter we will:

- Introduce some of the main issues in the global justice debate through a discussion of the problem of famine.

- Set out and critically discuss the three main positions in the global justice debate:

cosmopolitanism, particularism, and the political conception.

- Discuss justice over time – that is, justice between generations.

Famine – whose Responsibility?

Emergency supplies for famine-ridden Somalia are unloaded from an aeroplane, early 1990s

Source: © Chris Rainier/CORBIS

Famine provides the clearest and most compelling illustration of global inequality. That the wealthy enjoy luxury goods while others starve to death is, at least for most people, a demonstration of human immorality. But what responsibilities do the rich nations (or states) bear for famine? Garrett Hardin, in outlining his 'lifeboat ethics' (see Chapter 16), argues that the poor in developing countries bear responsibility for having too many children. Giving aid simply exacerbates the situation. Others argue that famine is the consequence of economic forces set in train by the industrialised, capitalist countries, such that 'we' – the wealthy – have caused famine and so have a responsibility not simply to relieve it when it happens, but to ensure that it never in fact happens.

Understanding the causes of famine is a useful way into exploring issues of global justice and we discuss those causes – and the rich countries' moral responsibilities – in the first section of this chapter. Before reading that section consider these questions:

- What is famine?
- What causes famine?
- If famine is not caused by the world economic system – we are not saying it is not, but simply posing a hypothetical – then do the rich countries have any moral obligation to relieve it?
- Should the relief of famine be the responsibility of individuals (through charity) or the state (through taxation)?
- How compelling is the claim that giving money is a waste of time because it will not go to the needy but be pocketed by corrupt governments?

The debate over global justice within political theory is a relatively recent development. It has been stimulated in large part by arguments over 'domestic' justice, which we outlined in Chapter 4. Although the global justice debate encompasses discussion of human rights and just war we will be concerned in this chapter with the question of international wealth distribution.

Famine

Singer on Famine

How individuals and states respond – or should respond – to famine throws into sharp relief central issues in the global justice debate. Peter Singer, in an influential article (Singer, 1972), argues that if you are passing a pond and see a drowning child then so long as you are not in danger of sacrificing something morally equivalent to that child's life you have an obligation to wade in and save the child. There may be a cost to you – perhaps you will ruin your expensive suit – but that cost has to be weighed against the loss of a life, and in the balance it is clear what you should do. The failure to make a significant financial contribution to relieve famine on the other side of the world is in all important respects no different to the refusal to jump in and save the drowning child.

Singer's argument is, on the face of it, very simple and he seeks to build it on two assumptions that any reasonable person would accept: (a) 'suffering and death from lack of food, shelter, and medical care are bad'; (b) 'if it is in our power to prevent something bad from happening, without thereby sacrificing anything of comparable moral importance, we ought, morally, to do it' (Singer, 1972: 231). Proximity to suffering is irrelevant – the child starving 7,000 kilometres away is no less important than the child drowning 50 metres from you. The potential number of rescuers is of no moral significance – that potentially millions could help the starving child but only you could save the drowning child may alter *how* you assist but not that you *should* assist. Imagine that you are among a group of onlookers seeing the child drowning: that others could help but are not helping in no degree reduces your responsibility to save the child. That there are millions of potential donors capable of relieving a famine does not reduce your obligation to donate to famine relief.

There are, of course, coordination problems in the case of famine, that – assuming you are the only potentially rescuer – do not exist in the pond example. The cost of saving the drowning child can be calculated as the loss of your $1,000 suit, while the costs of relieving famine are less clear. If we are all willing to give whatever is required to end the famine but lack communication we may end up giving too much. However, the existence of a mass media solves this problem. And prisoner's dilemma type situations do not arise here, because we are assuming that we have a moral obligation to help, such that even if nobody else gave any money you should still donate. The only sense in which the non-donors are 'free-riding' on your donation is that they are relying on *you* to fulfil *their* obligations to the starving.

Sen on Famine

To explore the problems with Singer's argument I will contrast it with another discussion of famine, advanced by Amartya Sen. Sen's work is not a response to Singer and the two explorations of famine are different rather than mutually incompatible: Singer is advancing an argument in moral philosophy about our duties as individuals, whereas Sen is offering an economic and political analysis of the causes of famine. Nonetheless, Sen's emphasis on the 'political' is important in allowing us to see that what may be required of us as *individuals* does not necessarily correspond to what is required of us as *citizens*, such that the cases of the starving child and the drowning child are not analogous. This is not to argue that we should not help people who are starving, but, rather, that the derivation of politics from morality is simplistic.

Sen distinguishes famines from endemic hunger, defining the former as a 'sudden eruption of severe deprivation for a considerable section of the population' (Sen, 1999: 160). He makes a number of empirical claims, the most striking of which are: (a) there is no connection between starvation and lowered food production, and (b) famines do not occur in democratic countries. Even when there is enough food in a country to feed everyone there can be starvation, because it is the *capacity* to buy food rather than its *availability* that is the key determinant of adequate nutrition. In a competitive democracy, with a free press and media, pressure is placed on the government to put in place measures to deal with the immediate food needs of the population and institute longer-term economic measures to restore the purchasing power of the affected group. Non-democratic regimes lack both the information flows and political incentives to respond properly to food crises (Sen, 1999: 180–1).

Famine cannot be understood, Sen maintains, out of the context of the entire social, economic, and political structure of a country. Food is not distributed through charity or a system of automatic sharing, but rather the ability to acquire food must be earned. What matters is not food production but 'entitlement', meaning the ownership and command of commodities (Sen, 1999: 162). Entitlement is determined by endowment, production possibilities, and exchange conditions. Most people's endowment is limited to their labour power, meaning that they are dependent on others for employment; should employment possibilities disappear then they are vulnerable to a complete loss of entitlement. Those employment possibilities are largely determined by production possibilities, such as the development of technology, and exchange conditions, meaning the price of goods relative to wages. Exchange conditions can change significantly, leading potentially to famine. In the 1943 Bengal famine, in which between two and three million people died, the exchange rate between food and other types of goods changed radically; for example, as people forwent having haircuts the rate of exchange between haircutting and staple foods fell in some districts by between 70 and 80 per cent (Sen, 1999: 164).

Crucially, there is not always a direct causal relationship between food availability and famine. The Bangladesh famine of 1974 occurred in a year of higher food production than any other year between 1971 and 1976 (Sen, 1999: 165), and where there is a link between food production and famine some sections of the population are unaffected, with food moving from poorer to richer areas. A boom in one area can lead to prohibitively high food prices in another: the 1943 Bengal famine was caused, in part, by a 'war boom' in urban Bengal. In summary, famine can only be explained within the context of the total economic structure of a society. The ethical significance of this will be discussed after we have considered the importance of the *political* structure of a society to causing or preventing famine.

Famine prevention is dependent to a significant extent on entitlement protection. After all, in the absence of social security payments some people in rich, Western nations would starve. The willingness of the wealthy in the West to contribute through redistributive taxation to help their poor compatriots may depend on a mixture of self-interest – fear of social unrest – and genuine compassion, but whatever the motivation there must be a background sense of obligation. The Irish famine of the 1840s provides a useful illustration of what happens when that sense is absent. For Irish nationalists the famine became symbolic of British attitudes to Ireland. The fact that food was shipped out of Ireland has led to the accusation that the famine was not only an act of omission – a failure to assist – but tantamount to act of commission: there was a deliberate policy of starvation, which, in effect, was genocide. Sen argues that there is nothing mysterious about food exports during time of famine: market forces determine that food goes to places where people can afford it. Preventing market interaction is not, Sen suggests, the answer; rather, intervention to enable people to acquire the ability to buy food is the correct response, and here politics and mutual sympathy are important. The British response to the Irish famine – just like their response to the Bengal famine a hundred years later – was not marked by a genocidal mentality, but was characterised by an absence of sympathy which, had it existed, would have led to pressure on the British state to put in place remedial and preventative measures. That British rule in India was not democratic and that Ireland did not enjoy the status of Scotland within the United Kingdom was significant, but what was especially significant in the Irish case – especially given that Ireland was not technically a colony – was cultural alienation (Sen, 1999: 173).

Ethical and Political Implications

Sen's analysis of the causes of famine may not appear inconsistent with Singer's: Singer would accept that while we have a moral duty to relieve famine how we fulfil that duty is a technical matter. Sen, on the other hand, is concerned with empirical, rather than moral, questions (although implicit in his discussion are moral claims, which he makes explicit in other writings). We would, however, make three points:

1. Once we recognise that there is a political dimension to famine then Singer's simple analogy between the drowning child and the starving child breaks down. The duty to rescue the child is straightforwardly a moral one: we do not wait to find out the child's nationality. There may be a moral duty to help a starving child, but in this case there is also a political dimension that alters the moral duty. Starvation is, almost by definition, suffering caused by the absence of food, and as such analogous to drowning, whereas famine is the absence of the means of acquiring food. This point cannot be dismissed simply as one about means – that is, saving the starving child is just a lot more complex than saving the drowning child – rather, the fact that the world is organised into nation-states means that there are other people who have a greater duty to save the starving child. This is a qualitative difference, and not just a quantitative one of proximity.

2. Singer suggests that communication enables us to recognise the needs of starving people; we cannot hide behind a 'lack of knowledge'. The needs of the starving child are just as obvious as those of the drowning child. In Sen's analysis the

causes of famine are complex. Certainly there are situations in which people are clearly starving and direct food aid is required; the cost of the aid is quantifiable and the media can report how much has been raised through private donation and state aid. However, preventing famine requires more complicated coordination, which even states and non-governmental organisations (NGOs) may find difficult to achieve. This is not simply a secondary point about how we fulfil our moral duties, but a fundamental one about morality: because complex situations require coordination we have to hand over responsibility to the state.

3. Faced with a world of suffering it is unclear what is required of us: it may be reasonable to ask someone to sacrifice his $1,000 suit in order to save a drowning child, but is it reasonable to hand over all your goods in excess of your basic needs in order to feed the starving of the world? One response is to say that so long as each person – through tax-generated development aid – gives (say) 1 per cent of their income the duty to help the starving is fulfilled. It would be easy to be cynical: people are just looking for excuses not to give up their luxuries for the sake of the starving. But a moral theory can be too demanding. To say that we ought to do something implies that we are able to do so – 'ought implies can' – and that means not only can we calculate what is required of us, but the demands made on us are not excessive.

There is an important respect in which Sen's analysis does support a moral duty to prevent famine and that is the recognition of the role that economic forces – supply and demand – play in causing famine. If the world is a single interdependent economic system, albeit with some capacity on the part of individual nations to manage their internal socio-economic relations, then we are all responsible for the conditions which lead to famine. As we will see, the interaction argument is an important one in the global justice debate.

In summary, the debate over famine opens up a number of issues: what the relationship between morality and politics should be, and what the demand for global redistribution presupposes about the nature of human agency – the complexity of the causes of, and solutions to, famine may mean that how we behave in our everyday lives does not translate directly or straightforwardly into duties to redistribute goods across national communities. It is these issues that are at the heart of arguments about global justice.

Cosmopolitanism

Interest among political philosophers in global justice is a relatively recent development and has been strongly influenced by work on 'domestic' justice, inspired above all by Rawls's *A Theory of Justice*, which we discussed in Chapter 4. Although there are internal differences we can identify three distinct positions: cosmopolitanism, particularism, and the 'political conception'. Defenders of cosmopolitanism have forced the pace in this debate, but the other two positions are not merely reactions to cosmopolitanism, but represent self-subsistent perspectives on global distribution. We start with cosmopolitanism, focusing on the work of Charles Beitz and Thomas Pogge.

Both Beitz and Pogge are strongly influenced by Rawls but criticise his refusal to extend his theory of domestic justice to the international sphere. However, as Beitz acknowledges, Rawls's position on global redistribution has its roots in his assumptions about the 'circumstances of justice', meaning the circumstances under which it makes sense to talk about justice and injustice. A starting point for Rawls is the idea that justice is about the fair distribution of the benefits and burdens of social cooperation (Beitz, 1999: 131). This description introduces elements of a social ideal into what should be a mere description of a social condition. Slaves in ancient Greece were part of society but neither willingly cooperated nor (arguably) benefited from the 'polis': 'it would be better to say that the requirements of justice apply to institutions and practices (whether or not they are genuinely cooperative) in which social activity produces relative or absolute benefits or burdens that would not exist if the social activity did not take place' (Beitz, 1999: 131). The international economy is not a cooperative scheme in Rawls's narrow sense but it is one in Beitz's wide sense of 'cooperation'. This has radical implications: Rawls's two principles of justice cannot be restricted to the nation-state but must – in some form – be implemented globally.

Although Beitz later weakened the requirement for cooperation from actual cooperation to the capacity for cooperation, he accepts that the absence of cooperation weakens the duty to redistribute wealth between states. In an imaginary world of self-contained ('autarkic') states redistribution would be limited to providing states lacking natural resources with the ability to acquire the conditions to acquire just political institutions and satisfy its citizens' basic needs (the idea that resource-rich countries pay a dividend tax is developed by Pogge and is discussed below). Where countries are not autarkic and thus potentially cooperative a stronger principle of distribution is required: Rawls's 'difference principle', whereby the poorest class must be made as well off as possible, should be extended globally.

Thomas Pogge digs further down into what he sees to be the incoherence of Rawls's non-extension of domestic justice to the world. The moral universalism implicit in Rawls's theory should, he argues, commit us to the position that all persons should be subject to the same system of fundamental moral principles and thus to the same assignment of the benefits and burdens arising from the application of those principles. Of course, at a less fundamental level people may be treated differently, but that differential treatment must be justified by reference to the fundamental principles. Equality is the default position. Inequalities that cannot be justified within a particular nation-state should not in principle be justified between nation-states. The task for critics of cosmopolitanism is to find principled reasons for treating the cases differently. To explore the possibility that such principles might be established he imagines a country called Sub-subbrazil (Pogge, 2002: 100). As its name suggests it is modelled on Brazil which, by various measures, such as the Gini Index, is one of the most unequal in the world, and thus can be used as a domestic counterpart to the global inequality that exists between the rich West (or north) and the poor south. Subbrazil might not be objectionable if the economic order was accepted by the majority, so we have to imagine that peaceful change from below is not possible and it is therefore not meaningful to talk of majority support for the existing economic system: Sub-subbrazil is just such a country.

Global Resources Dividend

One of Pogge's practical proposals for global redistribution of wealth is a Global Resources Dividend (GRD). Just as left libertarians reject the idea that individuals have full (or very strong) ownership rights over external resources, so Pogge rejects the notion that states have such rights (Pogge, 2002: 202–3). Countries that benefit from natural resources – such as oil and gas – should pay a dividend on income derived from the exploitation of those resources: he suggests as a target around 1 per cent of global income. The proposal raises a couple of issues and problems:

- What is a resource? Geographical position could itself be a benefit – Britain's position as an island played no small part in its early capitalist development. How do you disaggregate such a 'natural' benefit from beneficial political decisions?
- Should a country pay up simply because it benefits from resources – that is, even if it does not burden other countries? Pogge thinks that in practice the rich countries prop up resource-rich authoritarian countries, such as Saudi Arabia, such that resources are connected to global interdependence (Pogge, 2002: 202).

A Rawlsian would regard Sub-subbrazil as unjust, but then they should also regard the world economic system as unjust, because it is, in effect, Sub-subbrazil. So how can he set the minimal criteria for justice in the domestic sphere so much higher than in the global sphere? Put more simply, how can people in the West (north) consider severe poverty in their own country as unjust but not consider it morally acceptable that such poverty should exist in the south? Pogge considers a number of possible responses: (a) we can surrender the discrepancy between domestic and global standards of justice by either weakening the minimal criteria for domestic justice or raising them for international justice; (b) defend the discrepancy; (c) insist on the discrepancy but reject the universalist demand to justify it (Pogge, 2002: 101). Even if you disagree with Pogge's cosmopolitan position this is a useful way of setting out the terms of the debate. Advocates of strategies (a) and (b) operate within a universalist moral theory, whilst defenders of (c) reject universalism.

Pogge is less radical than Beitz in that he argues that we have only a negative duty to eradicate world poverty and not a positive one. Were there no global economy there may be a moral duty to assist those in need but it would not be equivalent to the duties owed to those with whom we interact. It is because the rich have contributed to a world economy that has generated not only poverty, but also bad government, that there is a strong duty to redistribute wealth (Pogge, 2002: 197–99). In effect, continuing to cause suffering is a violation of a negative duty owed to one another not to cause suffering.

Particularism

The two alternatives to cosmopolitanism are particularism (also known as partialism) and the 'political conception'. Following Pogge's framing of the debate over Sub-subbrazil both positions insist on, or defend, the discrepancy between domestic and global justice, but they differ in how they go about justifying it.

The political conception adopts strategy (b) – that is, it accepts the need for a universalist defence of the discrepancy. Particularism maintains the discrepancy but rejects the need for a universalist justification of it.

Alasdair MacIntyre offers a radically particularist defence of patriotism, and, by extension, rejects global justice. The defence is 'radical' in that he eschews appeal to universalism with regard to justice in general: universalism is false at the domestic level as well as in the global sphere. Patriotism should not, MacIntyre maintains, be defended by appeal to ideals: American politicians who claim that the United States deserves our – or Americans' – allegiance because it champions freedom are defending the ideal of freedom and not the USA as a nation (MacIntyre, 1995: 210). MacIntyre undercuts the cosmopolitans' strategy of forcing liberals to face up to the universalism implicit in their claims. Pogge argues that liberals are committed to moral universalism, such that their failure to extend justice globally is a moral blind spot. MacIntyre simply rejects universalism: patriotism is a 'kind of loyalty to a particular nation which only those possessing that particular nationality can exhibit' (MacIntyre, 1995: 210). Two nations may have achieved the same things – for example, economic prosperity – but those achievements are valued not just as achievements, but as the achievements of this particular nation. Patriotism belongs to a class of loyalty-exhibiting virtues, along with marital fidelity, love of one's family, and friendship.

MacIntyre contrasts these virtues with the derivation of value – valuing one's nation, family, friends and so on – from an impartial, or impersonal, standpoint. The latter would require that partiality towards one's nation, or one's compatriots, be justified universally. This might be done by arguing that patriotism is indeed a virtue but one which commits us to enabling citizens of other nations to value *their* nations. This generates a conflict between partiality and impartiality:

> What your community requires as the material prerequisites for your survival as a distinctive community . . . may be exclusive use of the same or some of the same natural resources as my community requires for its survival and growth into a distinctive nation. When such a conflict arises, the standpoint of impersonal morality requires an allocation of goods such that each individual person counts for one and no more than one, while the patriotic standpoint requires that I strive to further the interests of my community and you strive to further the interests of your community (MacIntyre, 1995: 213).

The impersonal standpoint – which translates politically into cosmopolitanism – has, MacIntyre argues, five features: (a) morality is composed of rules to which any rational person would assent; (b) the rules are neutral between rival interests; (c) the rules are neutral between rival beliefs; (d) the basic moral unit is the individual human being and individuals count equally; (e) the standpoint of the moral agent is the same for all and is independent of any social particularity. According to this view *where* and *from whom* you learn the principles of morality are as irrelevant as where and from whom you learn the principles of mathematics (MacIntyre, 1995: 214–15). For MacIntyre this is mistaken. Justice is concerned with the distribution of goods but those 'goods' are enjoyed in particular social settings: 'what I enjoy is the good of *this* particular social life inhabited by me and I enjoy *it* as what *it* is' (MacIntyre, 1995: 217, his emphases). That such goods could be enjoyed in other national communities does not diminish the fact that they are enjoyed *here*. It follows – and this is a big claim – that '*I* find *my* justification for allegiance to these rules of morality in *my* particular community; deprived of the life of that community, *I* would have no reason to be moral' (MacIntyre, 1995: 217, his emphases). He makes a further, but actually quite different point, about the relationship between morality and community. Being moral is not easy, for too often our self-interested desires conflict with what we know we ought to do, so 'it is important to morality that *I* can only be a moral agent because *we* are moral agents . . . I need those around me to reinforce my moral strengths and assist in remedying my moral weaknesses' (MacIntyre, 1995: 217, his emphases). MacIntyre summarises his defence of patriotism, and thus partiality to compatriots in this way:

> *If* . . . it is the case that I can only apprehend the rules of morality in the version in which they are incarnated in some specific community; and *if* . . . it is the case that the justification of morality must be in terms of particular goods enjoyed within the life of particular communities; and *if* . . . it is the case that I am characteristically brought into being and maintained as a moral agent only through particular kinds of moral sustenance afforded by my community, *then* it is clear that deprived of this community, I am unlikely to flourish as a moral agent (MacIntyre, 1995: 218, his emphases).

He goes on to argue that this dependence on community places limits on rational criticism of it (MacIntyre, 1995: 220). MacIntyre's argument is confused. First, he conflates the dependence on a community with dependence on a particular community – the excessive use of italics to emphasise pronouns (I, we) and indexicals (this, it, here) is really a way of driving a point home in the absence of an argument. Certainly, morality depends on socialisation, but liberals are right to argue that moral consciousness points beyond 'this' community. A person who values their own community will be capable of recognising that others will value their communities. Where MacIntyre is correct is in arguing that such recognition cannot lead to pure impartial treatment: a parent who recognises the rights of other parents cannot commit themself to impartiality between their children and other children without thereby contradicting the universal 'good' of parenthood. Partiality is intrinsic to parenthood. MacIntyre is also right to emphasise the social dimension of 'goods', but his objection to the impersonal treatment of goods is overstated: some goods are tied up with a particular community – it is not easy to export political stability or non-corrupt administration – but others are less marked by particular cultures: material aid being an example of an 'exportable' good.

Ch. 12:
Nationalism
p. 280

A less radical, and for that reason, more credible defence of particularism is provided by David Miller, whose work we discussed briefly in Chapter 12. In a manner seemingly similar to MacIntyre he distinguishes two positions, which he terms ethical universalism and ethical particularism. Universalists can accept 'agent-relative' considerations only so long as they do not conflict with universalism at a basic level. So a universalist would endorse as a basic principle 'relieve the needy', but maintain that this is best achieved if each of us takes care of the needy in our immediate environment (Miller, 1995: 51). The justification of this restriction is that we know better how to address the needs of those close to us, as against those further away. This is not, however, a defence of distance per se: for a universalist distance is a morally arbitrary fact. Another way in which a universalist can generate particularist duties is through contract: each person is assigned rights (more precisely, powers) to enter contracts of various kinds and the exercise of these rights (or powers) generates relationships which are necessarily partial. For a universalist the existence of a system of rights must itself be justified as valuable for all.

Miller argues that universalism relies upon an implausible picture of moral agency: it draws a sharp line between moral agency and personal identity, and between moral agency and personal motivation (Miller, 1995: 57). Applying these concerns to nationality and global justice Miller rejects two ways in which partiality might be justified from a universalist standpoint. The first models the nation-state on a club – just like we choose to join and benefit from a tennis club, and thus acquire obligations to the club, so we join, or could join, a state. Even if we reject contractualism as implausible it could still be argued that obligations arise from enjoyment of the benefits of cooperation. The problem is that this might justify an individual's obligation to the state, but it does not justify the world system of states, with its relatively strong obligations to compatriots and weak obligations to foreigners. Furthermore, contractualism does not capture the sense of 'belonging' that characterises national allegiance – we might develop allegiance to the tennis club but it is unlikely to be a major part of our identities because we were not socialised as members of the club.

An alternative argument is from specialisation: although we all have an obligation to save a life, if our own is not threatened, it is better that we leave the saving of life to those best qualified. So at the beach we leave it to the lifeguard to save a drowning person. However, the analogy with partiality towards compatriots does not work: 'why does it make sense to assign responsibility for the rights and welfare of Swedes to other Swedes and the rights and welfare of Somalians to other Somalians, if we are looking at the question from a global perspective? What is the equivalent here to the selection and training of the lifeguard?' (Miller, 1995: 63). As with the previous argument, this defence of the nation does not account for our emotional attachment to the nation.

Miller argues that differential treatment depends on recognising the importance of particularist claims at a basic level. Of two students asking for academic advice, given restraints on his time, Miller would favour the student from his own (Oxford) college. This seems reasonable, but only because entry to an Oxford college is the result of a contract and because the good which is being distributed – advice – is very closely bound up with the nature of the institution. Miller's extension of the example is less defensible: if two students need to be driven to the hospital for urgent treatment and only one can be taken Miller would again favour the student from his college. Even in the absence of any other differentiating features between the students it does not seem a relevant difference that one student belongs to his college and the other does not, and the hospital example is closer to the case of global aid than the academic advice one.

In fact, the hospital example does not serve Miller's case for particularism well. Part of what motivates particularistic attachments is the presence of reciprocity, such that 'outsiders' – members of other colleges, or citizens of other nations – are not isolated individuals, but members of other national communities (Miller, 1995: 73). We do not relate to outsiders simply as human beings, but as citizens of other countries. In the advice example the distribution of the good – advice – is conditioned by the fact that the student from the other college will be privileged in their dealings with tutors' from their college. An analogous situation does not arise with the drive to the hospital: here Miller is faced with a 'human being' rather than a 'college student'.

Unlike MacIntyre, Miller does not claim that moral agency is only possible within the particular community in which you are born. Indeed, living in a community relieves the individual of the pressure of excessive demands for impartiality. He does, however, develop the idea that the goods which are up for distribution have to be conceptualised in context, and furthermore, the criteria for distribution must also be understood contextually. Attitudes to money, work, honours, status, and political power are determined by our culture and thus the values we attach to these things are culturally determined. The criteria for a just distribution of the goods also vary: all societies have some notion of 'merit' but what in fact is meritorious differs between them (Miller, 2000: 169). How we measure deprivation can depend on intersubjective considerations: lacking a television or access to the Internet might be a deprivation for children in a society where these things are valued.

Miller acknowledges that there are millions of people in the world who are disadvantaged relative to others in an across-the-board sense – they score lower on every measure that corresponds to a significant good: money, housing, education, health care, political rights (Miller, 2000: 173). But given conflicting interpretations of the 'goods' which are to be distributed and of the criteria for distribution the task of developing a global, transcultural conception of justice would likely result in a very basic set of basic goods and correspondingly a relatively weak principle of global distribution. Miller sums up what he thinks are the demands of global justice under three heads: (a) the obligation to respect basic human rights; (b) the obligation to refrain from exploiting vulnerable communities and individuals; (c) the obligation to provide all political communities with the opportunity to achieve self-determination and social justice (Miller, 2000: 177).

What cosmopolitanism and particularism share is a collapsing of the distinction between the level of individual morality and politics. Although Miller comes closest to recognising that distinction with his emphasis on reciprocity both positions seek to derive political principles – principles of justice – from claims about the nature of the individual. Of course, they come to different conclusions about the nature of those principles, but nonetheless there is a conceptual similarity between them. The political conception of justice is based on an explicit distinction between justice and other virtues, or between justice as applied at the domestic level as against the international level. In the next section we discuss the work of two defenders of the political conception: John Rawls and Thomas Nagel.

Political Conception

Rawls argues that relatively well-ordered societies have a duty to bring burdened societies, along with outlaw societies, into the society of peoples (Rawls 1999: 106). A 'well-ordered' society is one which is stable and respects both basic human rights and the sovereign status of other nations. Such a society need not be liberal (see Chapter 18). It does not follow from what Rawls terms the 'law of peoples' that existing well-ordered societies must transfer resources to burdened societies in order to achieve the goal of bringing them into the society of peoples. Part of the reasoning is that transfers are indeterminate – we do not know at what point transfers must cease. This seems an odd point – surely, so long as we know our transfers are having some effect we should make them? A second, and more substantial, argument against transfers is that a society with few resources can be well-ordered if 'its political traditions, law, and property and class structure with their underlying religious and moral beliefs and culture are such as to sustain a liberal or decent society' (Rawls 1999: 106). Rawls goes on to make a subtly different point: the culture of a society is a very significant determinant of the wealth of that society. These are indeed distinct points. The first establishes the limits of a well-ordered society's duties to a burdened society – transfers are aimed at creating a well-ordered society and not directly at benefiting the individual members of that society. The second is an observation – grounded in Sen's work – on the causes of poverty. On this second point Rawls makes various elaborations: a society's population policy is extremely important; failure in food distribution rather than food decline is the cause of most famines, and the unemployed in *prosperous societies* would starve without domestic income transfers (Rawls 1999: 9, 109–10).

Rawls rejects the extension of the difference principle to international relations, arguing that the target of distribution is the achievement of a society's political autonomy and consequent upon that its joining the society of peoples. This argument fits with his rejection of the extension of domestic liberal justice to the international sphere: peoples are represented in the society of peoples, not individual human beings. A practical result of Rawls's position is that while he has a relatively egalitarian theory of domestic justice he has a relatively inegalitarian theory of international justice. One might admire Rawls's hard-headedness: it is extremely difficult to motivate citizens in prosperous societies to accept income transfers to poor societies, and that reluctance is not based solely on a lack of confidence in recipient governments to ensure the money benefits the worst-off in those burdened societies. Although Rawls does not make this point, a further argument for an inegalitarian theory of global justice is that in the absence of global economic institutions it is very difficult to determine when duties correlated to 'socio-economic rights' have been fulfilled. This contrasts with so-called 'negative' human rights, such as the right to practise one's religion or marry a partner of your choice. However, there are more fundamental objections to global egalitarianism at the heart of Rawls's theory of international relations, and to grasp these requires distinguishing three levels of justice: local, domestic, and global.

An illustration of local justice is the distribution of resources within a family; other examples include the rules governing voluntary associations, such as clubs or churches. Domestic justice, which is the primary concern of Rawls's *A Theory of Justice,* is concerned with the distribution of resources at the level of the nation-state. Domestic justice will affect local justice: the state will not tell families how to distribute housework and childrearing duties, but it must ensure that women get fair equality of opportunity. Likewise, domestic justice will *indirectly* affect the third level of justice: the global. For Rawls the primary ethical relationship holds between the individual and the state. Ethical issues in international relations – military intervention, global distributive justice, human rights – are only of indirect concern for individuals. It is interesting that Rawls's stated reason for writing *The Law of Peoples* is to establish whether or not liberal democracies should tolerate non-liberal societies, and, by extension, whether individual citizens of a liberal democracy have an obligation to support military intervention by their state in the affairs of another state.

The assumption that principles of justice are operative in a self-contained, closed society should not be understood as an endorsement of the *nation* as intrinsically valuable. The principles of justice will necessarily be coercively enforced, and that presupposes the existence of a *state* which we are obliged to obey, but the state is a juridical and not a cultural concept. This distinguishes his position from the patriotism of Alasdair MacIntyre and even from the more moderate ethical particularism of David Miller. That 'peoples' rather than individuals are the primary ethical entities in international politics does not contradict Rawls's 'individualism'. Rawls's aim in *The Law of Peoples* is to show that a liberal society can tolerate a non-liberal one:

> To tolerate means not only to refrain from exercising political sanctions – military, economic, or diplomatic – to make a people change its ways. To tolerate also means to recognize these non-liberal societies as equal participating members in good standing of the Society of Peoples, with certain rights and obligations, including the duty of civility requiring that they offer other peoples public reasons appropriate to the Society of Peoples for their actions (Rawls 1999: 59).

Many liberal political theorists – Nagel, whose work we discuss below, is among them – would reject this second idea of toleration. Certainly the stability of the international order may require refraining from what is commonly referred to as 'regime change', but we have no reason to tolerate non-liberal societies at that deeper level of 'civility'. Since a non-liberal people does not treat its citizens as free and equal then it cannot *itself* be treated as an equal among the community of peoples.

Rawls is not, however, advocating a MacIntyrian communitarianism. His refusal to extend the individualism of domestic justice to international politics can be explained by his rejection of a teleological view of the world, and of history. The 'society of peoples' does not serve an end, such as the gradual adoption of liberal values, even though the adoption of a law of peoples might have such a consequence. The 'universalism' of moral agents in the domestic sphere – modelled by the domestic original position – is of a different kind to the 'universalism' of the global sphere, as modelled by the global original position. That peoples rather than individuals are represented in the latter does not mean that 'peoples' have a primary, or ultimate, moral status.

Nagel rejects Rawls's toleration of non-liberal peoples but does endorse the political conception of (global) justice. Although there may be good, practical reasons for not intervening in the affairs of another sovereign state there are not principled reasons: 'it is more plausible to say that liberal states are not obliged either to tolerate nonliberal states or try to transform them, because the duties of justice are essentially duties to our fellow citizens' (Nagel, 2005: 135).

Nagel argues that sovereignty is the missing link in discussions of global justice. Justice, he suggests, applies only to a form of organisation that claims political legitimacy and the right to impose decisions by force, and not to voluntary associations (Nagel, 2005: 140). Both cosmopolitans and particularists fail to recognise this, and Rawls does not make it sufficiently clear. Sovereignty puts the 'political' into justice. As an empirical observation unjust and illegitimate regimes have for the most part been the necessary precursors of progress towards democracy and legitimacy because they created the centralised power that became the object of contest (Nagel, 2005: 146). In itself this argument is not persuasive against cosmopolitanism, but if we follow Hobbes and argue that even an unjust state fulfils a coordination role then we have made the first step towards separating the domestic and global spheres. The state answers the need for a solution to the prisoner's dilemma, such that an extra level of morality – a specifically political morality – is generated.

To illustrate this we briefly digress from Nagel's discussion to an argument for political obligation advanced by Richard Hare. Hare asks us to imagine that we are part of a 100-strong group that finds itself stranded on a desert island with no prospect of being picked up (Hare, 1989: 11). In short, we are stuck there and so have to make some decisions about how we are going to organise ourselves. Hare argues that we have a pre-political duty to wash and delouse ourselves to prevent the spread of typhus. That duty is most effectively exercised by creating hygiene laws which must necessarily be coercively enforced, and so requires the creation of a state. If we then survey the reasons why we obey the law they break down, first, into prudential (that is, self-interested) reasons: (a) you do not want to catch typhus, and (b) you do not want to be punished for disobeying the law. Second, there are moral reasons unrelated to the existence of law and the state: (c) you will harm others if you do not delouse, and (d) if you get typhus you will be a burden to others. Third, there are moral reasons that are related to the existence of law and the state: (e) the existence of a law *significantly* increases – relative to (c) – the harm you cause to others by not delousing; (f) you impose costs on the law enforcement agencies by disobeying the law; (g) you will encourage others to break laws; (h) you are taking advantage of those who obey the law (Hare, 1989: 11). Crucially, the third group of reasons depend for their force on the second group – we create law to solve a moral problem and to augment pre-political moral duties. It should also be noted that Hare's argument is universalist: the second class of reasons hold irrespective of nationality.

Hare is concerned with the problem of political obligation rather than global duties, but his argument usefully illustrates how the political duties can be moral and yet distinct from 'general' moral duties. Much of Nagel's work has been concerned with elaborating two standpoints: the partial and the impartial. We briefly discussed this distinction in Chapter 12. The chief point made there was that the two standpoints are mutually entangled: a parent who cares for their child is committed to the recognition that other parents stand in a special relationship to their children. The weakness of MacIntyre's particularism lay in his failure to recognise that partiality points beyond itself to impartiality, and a fully socialised moral agent recognises this. Of course, it is also the case that the standpoints conflict – recognising the claims of other parents does not resolve the conflict between the distribution of resources between children. The exercise of partiality will benefit some children more than others, and, likewise, partiality towards compatriots will disadvantage some individuals relative to others – for example, Swedes in relation to Somalis.

In his book *Equality and Partiality* (Nagel, 1991) Nagel is pessimistic about resolving this problem, but his argument about sovereignty does suggest a way forward. He advocates dualism against monism: in this context a dualist is someone who argues that morality has more than one level while the monist maintains that there is but one level (dualism is not in fact the best term because there may be more than two levels) (Nagel, 1991: 122). Political institutions, Nagel argues, create 'contingent, selective moral relations, but there are also non-contingent, universal relations in which we stand to everyone, and political justice is surrounded by this larger moral context' (Nagel, 1991: 131). Those universal relations are equivalent to the duties owed by parents to all other parents (and their children) and take the form of respect for the 'most basic human rights against violence, enslavement, and coercion, and of the most basic humanitarian duties of rescue from immediate danger' (Nagel, 1991: 131).

Nagel advances an interesting response to the charge that national boundaries are morally arbitrary. Cosmopolitans pick up on a point made by Rawls in *A Theory of Justice* in which he argues that a person's native endowments – intelligence, physical strength, good character – are from a moral standpoint arbitrary and should not determine the distribution of natural resources. If a person's natural abilities and resources should not affect distribution between citizens of a state then why should it be thought legitimate for a state to benefit from its natural resources? Indeed, given the role that natural abilities play in a person's sense of their identity it seems more legitimate for individuals to benefit from the exploitation of those abilities than for nations to be advantaged. Having huge gas reserves may have done wonders for Russian self-confidence but possession of those reserves is not essential to Russian identity. Nagel argues that Rawls's objection to arbitrary inequalities only has force because of the societal context: 'what is objectionable is that we should be fellow participants in a collective enterprise of coercively imposed legal and political institutions that generate such arbitrary inequalities' (Nagel, 1991: 128).

Justice between Generations

Ch. 16:
Ecologism
pp. 373–75

We have discussed the distribution of resources between peoples across national boundaries, but there is another dimension to global justice: distribution between generations over time. In everyday political debate this is most often raised in the context of resource depletion and population growth. In Chapter 16 we discussed Garret Hardin's 'lifeboat ethics': Hardin argued that the world's population was increasing at a rate which threatened the possibility of anything approaching a decent life for future generations. His concerns dovetailed with arguments over international aid: the human right to procreate and liberal migration policies were to blame for dangerous population growth. Sen also discusses population growth but argues that the key to slowing growth is to empower women, and once again this shows that politics matters: we need to grant people political rights and ensure the spread of democracy if we are to tackle economic problems (Sen, 1999: 211–13).

Political solutions precede economic ones. Parallel to this political debate there is a philosophical, or ethical, one and to illustrate the ethical problems raised by intergenerational justice we will – one last time – discuss Rawls's contribution to it.

Alongside his two principles of (domestic) justice Rawls adds a 'just savings principle' (Rawls, 1972: 284–93; Rawls, 2001: 159–61). This principle distributes benefits and burdens of cooperation between generations, but it is important to distinguish contemporaneous and non-contemporaneous generations. The first can be easily addressed by the two principles of justice: since agents in the original position are choosing principles which are to determine their prospects over an entire lifetime, conflicts between the different age groups do not raise special philosophical problems, although more detailed social policies will have to address demographic changes, such as the 'ageing' structure of Western societies, where there is a worsening ratio of working age to retired people. Justice between non-contemporaneous generations does, however, raise a major philosophical challenge: if we say it is better to exist rather than not to exist then we have a duty to bring a particular person into existence, but doing so may severely reduce per capita resources such that we cannot assure *that person* the minimum level of resources necessary to live a decent life. And we cannot employ a veil of ignorance that denies individuals knowledge of whether or not they will exist, for the one thing of which agents in the original position cannot be denied knowledge is the fact of their existence.

Rawls argues that our duty to future generations consists in reproducing the minimal conditions for a well-ordered society and we are not required to maximise the position of the worst-off class *of all time*, only the contemporary worst-off class. The just savings principle requires that each generation set aside resources for future ones. It will involve positive measures such as investing in technology, as well as negative policies such as not depleting finite natural resources. The similarity of Rawls's treatment of justice between peoples and between generations is significant: the object of both the law of peoples and of the just savings principle is to create and sustain the conditions for a well-ordered society. That is our duty to other peoples and our duty to future generations.

What makes intergenerational justice between non-contemporaneous generations such a radical challenge to Rawls's theory is that what we do today will affect not only the life prospects of future people, but whether they exist at all. There is a consensus that population growth is a threat to the quality of life of future generations, and we have a duty to see to it that such growth is checked. But to whom is that duty owed? Imagine we have a fixed level of resources, and in World 1 there are 5 billion people, whilst in World 2 there are 20 billion people. Average (per capita) resources will be higher in World 1 and its inhabitants are, therefore, better off than the inhabitants of World 2. If these are the only two worlds, is it the case that World 1 is the best of all possible worlds? It is not immediately obvious that it is, for one consequence of living in World 1 is that a large number of people would not be brought into existence. It is possible that none of World 1's people would have existed if a consequence of population control is that people defer having children. Of course, uncontrolled population growth could result in some, or all, of the inhabitants of World 1 not being brought into existence if in World 2 all children are born to, say, women under the age of 20, whereas in World 1 all children are born to women over the age of 20, but our concern is with World 2.

Agents in Rawls's original position are denied knowledge of their identities, but as Derek Parfit argues, the one thing of which they cannot be denied knowledge is the fact of their existence (Parfit, 1984: 392). This creates motivational difficulties: we can be impartial between existing people but not between existing and possible people. Although in his later work Rawls retains the just savings principle, he revised its derivation. He retains the idea that the principles in the original position are chosen in the present (Rawls, 2001: 160), but there is a shift in the motivational connection between generations. In *A Theory of Justice* he stipulated the generation choosing the principles of justice care for at least two subsequent generations. Rawls now acknowledges this is inconsistent with the motivational assumption of mutual disinterest (Rawls 2001: 160n). The agreement is, therefore, between all generations, and 'we say the parties are to agree to a just savings principle subject to the condition that they must want all previous generations to have followed it' (Rawls, 2001: 160). Since no generation knows its place among the generations this implies all later generations, including the present one, are to follow it.

There is, however, a tension in Rawls's derivation of this principle, which Parfit quite rightly picks up on, but does not state correctly. Rather than saying persons must exist in the original position, there is a duality: in entering the original position you confirm your *moral* existence, but because you do not know your generation then you cannot be sure you *actually* exist. Since the actions of one generation determine the size of a future population one of the questions which you as an agent in the original position must confront is whether you should exist. If the level of resources in the 20-billion population of World 2 falls below a certain 'social minimum' then conceivably we, as agents behind a veil of ignorance, could will that *some of us* should not exist, but it is arbitrary who does exist.

This may seem a rather precious philosophical problem but it is useful in separating out different moral and political theories. Rawls's problem only arises if we interpret him as a Kantian: moral and political principles are generated, or legitimated, from the pre-political standpoint of a rational agent. A more political reading of Rawls would leave questions of procreation to individuals (local justice) or states (global justice), so long as they did not violate human rights. A state might, for example, choose to disadvantage parents who have large families. Other moral theories solve the problem by rejecting Kantian individualism. Utilitarians, for example, are only concerned with the overall level of well-being either in total (classical utilitarianism) or per capita (average utilitarianism) – utilitarians are no respecters of persons and so the strange situation of having a moral duty to a person not to bring him or her into existence does not arise. Ecologists – distinct from environmentalists – see the earth as the ultimate object of moral concern, and not individual human beings, and so they would not conceive of intergenerational justice as the performance of duties correlating to the rights of future individuals.

Summary

We have explored three positions on global justice. The first position – cosmopolitanism – argues for an extension of the universalism of domestic justice to the global sphere. The discrepancy between domestic and global justice is, cosmopolitans argue, morally and intellectually unsustainable. The second position – particularism – maintains the discrepancy is justifiable because universalism is, at a basic level, false. The third position – the 'political conception' – recognises the force of universalist arguments but claims that morality has different levels and the fact that in a nation-state we are subject to coercive authority generates special duties in the domestic sphere that have no global equivalents.

Questions

1. Are national boundaries morally arbitrary?
2. In a world of self-subsistent – autarkic – states, would the rich have any obligations to the poor?
3. Should a state have full rights to benefit from natural resources located in its territory?
4. Does coercion make a difference to our moral duties?

References

Beitz, C. (1999) *Political Theory and International Relations* Princeton, NJ: Princeton University Press.

Hare R. (1989) *Essays on Political Morality* Oxford: Clarendon Press.

MacIntyre, A. (1995) 'Is Patriotism a Virtue?', in R. Beiner (ed.), *Theorizing Citizenship* Albany: State University of New York Press.

Miller, D. (1995) *On Nationality* Oxford: Clarendon Press.

Miller, D. (2000) *Citizenship and National Identity* Cambridge: Polity Press.

Nagel, T. (1991) *Equality and Partiality* Oxford and New York: Oxford University Press.

Nagel, T. (2005) 'The Problem of Global Justice' *Philosophy and Public Affairs* 33(2), 113–47.

Parfit, D. (1984) *Reasons and Persons* Oxford: Clarendon Press.

Pogge, T. (2002) *World Poverty and Human Rights: Cosmopolitan Responsibilities and Reforms* Cambridge: Polity Press.

Rawls, J. (1972) *A Theory of Justice* Oxford: Oxford University Press.

Rawls, J. (1999) *The Law of Peoples* Cambridge, MA: Harvard University Press.

Rawls, J. (2001) *Justice as Fairness: a Restatement, Cambridge*, MA: Belknap, Harvard University Press.

Sen, A. (1999) *Development as Freedom* Oxford: Oxford University Press.

Singer, P. (1972) 'Famine, Affluence, and Morality' *Philosophy and Public Affairs* 1(3), 229–43.

Further Reading

In addition to the works cited in the chapter – all of which are important contributions to the debate – the following books, chapters and articles are useful. Works on immigration by Joseph Carens, include, among others, 'Aliens and Citizens: The Case for Open Borders', in

W. Kymlicka (ed.), *The Rights of Minority Cultures* (Oxford: Oxford University Press, 1995); 'Immigration and the Welfare State', in A. Guttman (ed.), *Democracy and the Welfare State* (Princeton, NJ: Princeton University Press, 1988). Also on immigration: W. Schwarz, *Justice in Immigration* (Cambridge: Cambridge University Press, 1995). On the question of patriotism, in addition to MacIntyre's essay, see other contributions in R. Beiner (ed), *Theorizing Citizenship* (Albany, NY: State University of New York Press, 1995), and J. Cohen (ed.), *For Love of Country: Debating the Limits of Patriotism* (Boston, MA: Beacon, 1996). For more detailed work on famine and its causes read J. Drèze and A. Sen, *Hunger and Public Action* (Oxford: Clarendon Press, 1989). Two recent and important defences of cosmopolitanism are D. Mollendorf, *Cosmopolitan Justice* (New York: Westview Press, 2002) and S. Caney, *Justice beyond Borders: A Global Political Theory* (Oxford: Oxford University Press, 2005). Also influential has been H. Shue, *Basic Rights: Subsistence, Affluence, and U.S. Foreign Policy* 2nd edn (Princeton, NJ: Princeton University Press, 1996).

Weblinks

Most global justice websites are campaigns rather than academic in nature. A couple of relatively useful ones are:
http://www.globaljusticecenter.org/papers2005.htm
http://www.globalpolicy.org/globaliz/websites.htm

Conclusion

One of the questions that interests students of politics is the relationship between studying politics as an academic discipline and the practice of politics in the world outside. We thought that it might be useful to tackle this question by way of concluding this volume.

Academic Political Theory and Politics

What makes concepts political is that they respond to conflicts that arise in the world of practice. Academic political theory should address itself to the kind of issues that politicians themselves raise, and which are part and parcel of public debate.

We have already noted, in the discussion about ideologies, the problem of trying to treat politics in a purely neutral manner as though it was a study of mere behaviour or an analysis of words. But it does not follow from a critique of what came to be called 'apolitical politics' that academic political theory has no differences from the kind of political theory which appears in party manifestos and in the speeches of politicians.

The fact that academic political theory has something in common with the theory of the publicist and propagandist does not mean that it does not also have something which is different from everyday discourse. Academic political theorists write for individuals who are either academically trained or who are anxious to educate themselves in a systematic and coherent way. Academic political theory is not primarily geared towards convincing an audience of the ideological correctness of its position. Its task is to stimulate rather than persuade, so that rhetoric is curtailed in favour of logic, and sober evidence is offered in place of extravagant emotion. It is not the task of the academic political theorist to exhort people to undertake a particular course of action at a particular time and particular place. Although thinking about a problem is crucial to solving it, this is not the same as actually organising people to implement a solution.

Academic political theory can and should seek to raise the tone of public political debate. Good causes can be strengthened by good arguments, while party positions and publicist writing provide challenging points of reference to make academic political theory more relevant and useful. There is nothing wrong in

Thatcher making use of Hayek's work on the free market, even if (in our judgement) both were mistaken! Academic political theory differs from the theory of the public political world, but it is still *political* in character because, despite these differences, it has common features.

We hope that the mix of classical and new political ideas and ideologies has shown the relevance of theory to political practice, and that when you read the newspaper, see a TV programme or follow the arguments of a text, you will be better placed to make up your own mind as to the wider significance of the positions reported or championed.

Glossary

Abstraction   A conceptual and practical process that mystifies and conceals underlying social relationships.

Affirmative action   The apparent departure from equal treatment in order to help disadvantaged groups. Affirmative action is also known as reverse discrimination or positive discrimination.

Anarchism   A theory that seeks to abolish the state, but adopts statist tools of analysis and hence enjoys no success.

Atomistic   An approach that treats individuals and entities in purely discrete terms and ignores the relationships between them.

Authority   An exercise of power in which the moral status of the person exercising the power comes to the fore and is seen as legitimate.

Behaviouralism   An argument that sees human and natural activity as similar, and hence asks that the study of politics be presented as a 'natural science'.

Capitalism   A system of production that divides society into those who can hire the services of others, and those who are compelled to work for an employer.

Caste society   A society in which wealth and other goods are distributed according to some notion of natural inequality.

Citizen   A person able to govern their own life. Citizenship is an emancipatory situation towards which we move, but can never actually reach.

Civic nationalism   The view that nations can be held together by civic ties, such as willingness to participate in legal and political institutions. The alternative view is ethnic nationalism.

Civil disobedience   Law-breaking on moral grounds.

Class   An identity that divides people based upon economic, social, regional, religious, gender, ethnic and other differences.

Coercion   A concept and practice that is close to, but not the same as, force. Coercion involves a threat to use force where this force is credible.

Communitarianism A theory that stresses that all people belong to communities and can only identify themselves in relations with others.

Consent Uncoerced acceptance of something, such as state authority.

Conflict A clash of interests that can be tackled through violence, but only resolved through non-statist pressures. Conflicts of the latter kind are inevitable and arise from the fact that we are all different from one another.

Conservatism An ideology which is sceptical about reason: because human beings have limited rational capacities they must rely on tradition to guide them.

Constraint A natural or social pressure that ensures we do something that we had not intended to do.

Contestability A concept that points to the fact that an idea is controversial, or can be challenged.

Contractarianism A stream of liberal thought that imagines the state to be the product of a decision between individuals to agree to submit to it. Contractarianism implies individuals consent to the state.

Culture The often taken-for-granted web of social relations which encompasses many domains of experience, shapes a person's character, and may provide him or her with a set of values by which to live.

Deep ecology A form of ecologism, stressing both the interdependence of nature, and the need for fundamental human change; it is contrasted with 'shallow ecology', which is essentially environmentalism.

Democracy A society in which people govern themselves.

Difference Identifications that separate people and inevitably cause conflict to arise.

Division Differences that undermine common interests and necessitate the use of force.

Dualism A gulf between two entities, conceptual or real, that is impossible to cross. It points to a divide rather than a difference.

Ecologism An ideology centred around 'ecology', stressing the interdependence of all forms of life.

Egalitarianism A type of political theory which makes equality a fundamental concept.

Emancipation The capacity of people to act freely, and thus govern their own lives.

Environmentalism A movement which highlights the importance of preserving the earth's natural resources and guaranteeing a fair share of those resources for future generations. Unlike ecologism it can be combined with many different ideologies.

Equality   Treating 'like cases alike'; different types of equality depend on how we define what is meant by 'like cases' (see legal equality and equality of opportunity).

Equality of opportunity   The equalisation of the opportunity to acquire certain things, or, at least, guaranteeing that each person has a specified chance of acquiring those things.

Essentialism   An attitude that stresses the importance of one determining attribute and ignores all others.

Ethnic nationalism   The view that nations are held together by ethnic ties (*see* ethnicity). The competing view is civic nationalism.

Ethnicity   The identification of a culture with tangible, visual symbols and signs such as dress, food, or religious observance.

Fascism   A movement or political and social system that rejects parliamentary democracy, bans other political parties and movements, is hostile to the ideas of the Enlightenment and liberalism, and is particularly opposed to socialism and Marxism.

Feminism   A theory that works for the emancipation of women.

Force   A pressure that undermines the agency of individuals by physically harming them.

Freedom (or liberty)   The absence of constraint, or, alternatively, the existence of choice.

Free-riding   Gaining the benefits of cooperation without paying the price. This problem is central to the resolution of the prisoner's dilemma.

Fundamentalism   A belief in an ideology that is dogmatic, allows no debate, and holds to the absolute truth of the doctrine espoused.

Genocide   The attempt to destroy an entire ethnic or racial group; genocide can take place without mass murder – mass sterilisation is a form of genocide.

Global Justice   Theories of global justice are concerned with what obligations nation-states have to one another and obligations citizens of different nation-states have to one another.

Globalisation   A linkage between peoples of the globe that enables them to understand and empathise with one another.

Goodness (or goods, the good)   That which is worth pursuing – 'goods' need not be moral goods: a sharp knife is 'good' for killing people. The 'good' (singular) denotes a view of the world, such as a religion. (*See also* **rightness**).

Government   The resolution of conflicts of interest. It can occur at every level in society; it is inherent in social relationships, and needs to be contrasted with the state.

Green movement   The organised political expression of either ecologism or environmentalism.

Harm   Damage to somebody or something; normally, damage to a person's fundamental interests.

Hierarchy   An asymmetrical linkage that is inherent in relationships. It is normally assumed to be repressive, but it need not be.

Human rights   Entitlements to treatment which it is claimed individuals have simply by virtue of being human.

Humanitarian intervention   Military intervention in order to prevent the serious violation of human rights.

Identity   The sense of belonging to something or of sharing an attribute, such as religious belief, gender or ethnicity, with other people.

Ideology   A set of beliefs that are tied to either defending, placing demands upon or bringing about a state.

Individual   A person who is separate from others but who finds their identity through relating to these others.

Intuition   The sense that something is right and wrong, despite the inability to articulate reasons for that view. Much political theory entails appeal to intuitions.

Justice   Distributive justice is concerned with the fair distribution of the 'benefits' and 'burdens' of cooperation (retributive justice is a quite separate concept – it is the idea that a punishment should 'fit' a crime).

Law   A norm passed by a specific procedure and recognised as binding. A law does not necessarily need force as a sanction.

Legal equality   Each person has the right to a fair trial, and sanctions, such as imprisonment, are similar for all people.

Legal moralism   The view that the law should be used to enforce moral beliefs or practices – opponents of legal moralism do not reject morality, but argue that non-harmful acts should not be illegal.

Legitimacy   Power that has been authorised through an appeal to a wider constituency.

Liberalism   An ideology that takes freedom (or liberty) to be a fundamental value; it also regards individuals as naturally equal, although natural equality is, for many liberals, compatible with significant material inequality.

Libertarianism   A form of liberalism which takes private property rights to be of fundamental importance.

Liberty   *See* **freedom**.

Linguistic analysis   A view that theoretically challenging problems are problems arising from the use of language.

Market   A mechanism that enables exchanges to occur, but in a way which conceals the real power that people possess.

Marxism   A theory whose potential for emancipation is undermined by notions of class war, revolution and dictatorship.

Meritocracy   A society in which wealth, and other goods, are distributed according to innate ability.

Modernity   A term that denotes the onset of the liberal period so that modernism is used as a synonym for liberalism.

Momentum concept   A concept that has a potential for freedom and equality, but whose progress is infinite, and therefore can never be realised.

Monopoly   A process or agent that dominates a collectivity demanding an ultimate loyalty from its subjects.

Morality   A system of beliefs that emphasises the rightness or wrongness of an activity or process.

Multiculturalism   The existence of a number of cultures in a single political system; alternatively, an ideology which recognises that fact as important or values such diversity.

Nation   A collective, normally territorial, entity which commands allegiance. Some theorists argue that nations are the product of modernity, others claim they are 'primordial' or perennial.

Nationalism   An ideology that takes the nation to be of fundamental value.

Natural   A process that is developmental. What is natural is therefore susceptible to historical change.

Naturalism   A doctrine which treats the natural in a static and ahistorical way. It assumes that what exists at the present can never change.

Neoconservatism   An American stream of conservatism that stresses natural rights and the importance of resisting what it sees as tyranny.

Order   A stability in the possession of things; security against violence and a trust in others that promises will be kept.

Paternalism   Intervention to restrict a person's freedom on the grounds that it is in his or her interests.

Patriarchal   A static concept and practice that enshrines male domination. Patriarchy need not be pursued by biological men.

Perennialism   A body of theory concerned to explain the rise of the nation. Perennialists claim that nations predate modernity, although nationalism – consciousness of nationhood – is modern.

Political obligation   The moral obligation to obey the state. Many political theorists, especially anarchists, question whether political obligation is possible.

Political violence   The use of violence sometimes in situations in which people have reasonable avenues of peaceful protest.

Politics   A public process that involves resolving conflicts of interest. Politics is undermined by force, and is inherent at every level in all societies.

Post-liberalism   A theory that accepts liberalism but goes beyond it, by extending liberal values to all individuals and thus challenging the need for a state.

Postmodernism   A theory that goes beyond modernism and therefore challenges the dualisms and one-sidedness expressed in the modernist tradition.

Power   The capacity to exert pressure on a person or group so that they do something they otherwise would not have done.

Prejudice   Used in a specific sense by conservatives to mean judging the right action by appealing to habit and experience rather than to rational analysis.

Pre-modern   A theory and practice that has yet to obtain the institutions and to support the values of liberalism (or modernism).

Private   The sphere of life in which conflict is imperceptible or embryonic.

Private property   The division of material goods according to which individuals have an entitlement to a certain good, and can exclude other people from its use.

Public   The sphere of life in which conflict is manifest and has to be resolved.

Punishment   The infliction of hard treatment by the state as the result of breaking the law.

Race   A concept used to categorise people according to how they look (phenotypical similarity).

Radicalism   An approach that seeks to examine the roots of a phenomenon, disparaging rival approaches as superficial in character.

Reconstruction   The reworking of concepts so that an alternative to the status quo is charted.

Relational   An approach that stresses that individuals and collectivities only find their identity in relationships with one another.

Relationship   A linkage that is vitiated by force but whose mutuality is necessarily hierarchical in character and sustained by coercion and constraint.

Relativism   The rejection of **universalism**: moral norms are dependent on a cultural context.

Religion   An organised system of belief and practice centred around an idea of 'holiness' – that is, something outside historical experience.

Revolution   A fundamental transformation of something: revolutions can be social, economic, intellectual and political.

Rightness   That which is obligatory: for example, you should keep your promises. A person can do the right thing for bad reasons, so rightness must be distinguished from goodness.

Rights   Entitlements in law or simply as part of morality that do not involve harming oneself or others.

Slavery   A term that embraces people who are unfree and are the property of others. Although chattel slavery – the explicit and legal ownership of people – has largely died out in the contemporary world, the term can be applied analogously to people who have to work for or are wholly dependent on others.

Socialism   An ideology that asserts society is of equal importance to the individual, and it can therefore be regulated publicly in the interests of the individual.

Society   A group of people who relate to one another for specific purposes. Societies exist at all levels.

Sovereignty   The ability to govern one's own life: sovereignty is an absolute concept that can only express itself in particular historical circumstances.

State   An institution that claims a monopoly of legitimate force for a particular territory. This claim makes it contradictory and paradoxical.

State sovereignty   The claim by supporters of the state that the state has ultimate and final legitimate force over a particular society.

Static concept   One that is divisive in character and cannot, therefore, be reconstructed.

Statism   An approach that creates or accepts divisions and thus the need for force to tackle them.

Terrorism   The use of political violence in situations in which people have reasonable avenues of peaceful protest.

Totalitarianism   A movement or system that aspires to control every aspect of society in an authoritarian manner. It therefore rejects liberalism and democracy.

Toleration   The willingness to allow other people to behave in ways of which we disapprove. The first major historical form of political toleration was religious toleration.

Universalism   The belief that there are moral codes or values binding on all people, irrespective of culture. The alternative position is cultural or ethical **relativism**.

Utilitarianism   A stream of liberal thought that maintains political institutions should maximise the overall level of utility in society. Utilitarians disagree about the definition of 'utility', but possibilities include pleasure, happiness and preference-satisfaction.

Victimhood A belief, usually from victims, that their plight is caused by themselves or others who must be blamed and punished as a substitute for actively seeking the roots of their problem.

Violence A synonym for force.

Will A capacity to exercise choice as an agent.

Index

Page references in *italics* denotes glossary entry